AF573938

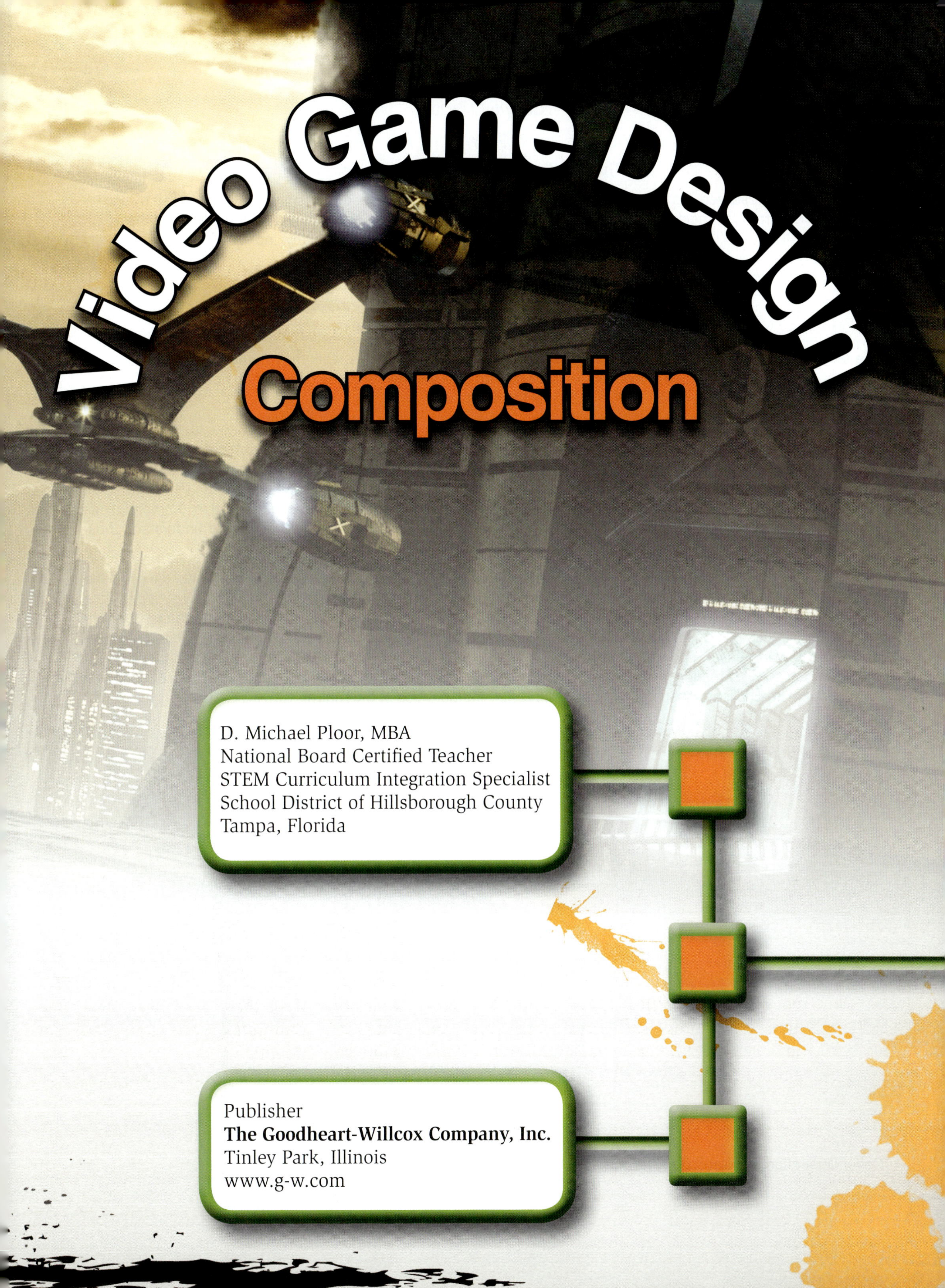

Video Game Design Composition

D. Michael Ploor, MBA
National Board Certified Teacher
STEM Curriculum Integration Specialist
School District of Hillsborough County
Tampa, Florida

Publisher
The Goodheart-Willcox Company, Inc.
Tinley Park, Illinois
www.g-w.com

Manufactured in the United States of America.

ISBN 978-1-60525-769-3

1 2 3 4 5 6 7 8 9 – 14 – 18 17 16 15 14 13

Cover illustration: Bertrand Benoit/Shutterstock.com

Introduction

Video Game Design Composition provides students a comprehensive volume of background knowledge and hands-on learning in every critical component of video game design. Video game design is a very diverse field that can benefit from the unique skills and experiences every individual has achieved. Each student can find where his or her technology, creativity, and leadership skills fit best within a design team. Students will benefit from the diversity of lessons presented.

Students will participate in a simulation of a real video game design team, seeing each project from origination to fruition. This provides a valuable lesson in team building that can be applied to any aspect of the technology and engineering industries in real-life careers.

Video Game Design Composition presents content in 13 chapters, with each chapter acting as a building block that supports the next skill learned. This allows students to learn the objectives of each lesson, practice the corresponding skills, and lay the foundation on which to acquire the next skill set.

Students will learn to design characters with personality and feeling. The characters are brought to life through design elements that match physical abilities and story elements. Within the story, characters will interact to build climax and resolution. Students will interweave story elements and player interactions to create a dynamic action to tell the story. Design is further refined to add strategy, puzzle, and immersion elements. Everything comes together with student-created quality game art, animations, and sound effects. Finally, students will develop skills in programming game interactions, physics, and real-world simulations.

Students will develop soft skills needed for success in any area of personal interaction and team building. These skills will develop seamlessly alongside of high-end technology hard skills. All lessons are scaffolded to provide a gradual progression and strengthening of skills. Each component escalates from beginner levels to mastery in stages. In the end, students will be technologically proficient and will demonstrate learning by constructing an original game build.

Studying *Video Game Design Composition* will expand student understanding of the role technology plays in modern society and the future of high-quality jobs. Applying the key lessons, skills, and content of this curriculum will provide great insight into a growing technological society and provide a solid foundation demanded for success in the future world of technology.

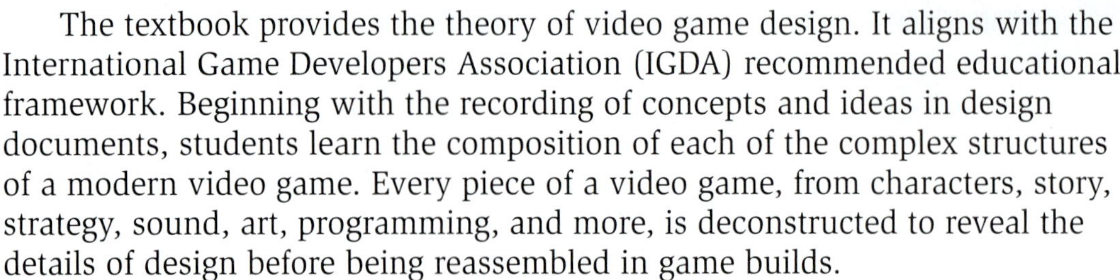

The textbook provides the theory of video game design. It aligns with the International Game Developers Association (IGDA) recommended educational framework. Beginning with the recording of concepts and ideas in design documents, students learn the composition of each of the complex structures of a modern video game. Every piece of a video game, from characters, story, strategy, sound, art, programming, and more, is deconstructed to reveal the details of design before being reassembled in game builds.

STEM

Science, technology, engineering, and mathematics (STEM) is the foundation on which our 21st century society builds and maintains economic growth. This curriculum integrates the *rigor* and *relevance* of STEM into fun and exciting classroom lessons. Taking rigor from each of the core areas of study and placing it in the context of video game design allows students to recognize the relevance of study. Students will gain experience in the skills needed for most of the new jobs projected over the next two decades.

Through application and integration of all core areas of language arts, science, mathematics, and social sciences, students become engaged in learning through doing. Application and synthesis levels of learning are maintained for a truly unique student experience. Through this meaningful engagement in learning, students become better in all core subject areas and the foundations of technology as presented in this text.

About the Author

D. Michael Ploor is the author of three textbooks on the subject of video game design: *Introduction to Video Game Design, Video Game Design Foundations,* and *Video Game Design Composition.* He is a National Board Certified Teacher in Career and Technical Education and holds an MBA degree from the University of South Florida. He maintains professional teaching credentials in Business Education (6–12) and Education Media Specialist (K–12). He is currently employed by the School District of Hillsborough County in Tampa, Florida, where he has been teaching video game design at the high school and middle school levels since 2001.

Mr. Ploor developed STEM curriculum while serving as the lead teacher in the Career Academy of Computer Game Design at Middleton Magnet STEM High School. Mr. Ploor has applied his skills as a STEM Curriculum Integration Specialist in designing innovative curriculum and by collaborating to construct the state standards for video game design in several states. He has also been instrumental in authoring competitive events for Career and Technical Student Organizations such as the Future Business Leaders of America (FBLA) and Phi Beta Lambda (PBL). He continues to work closely with many game design studios, producers, and software developers to align educational objectives to workplace-ready skills. In addition to publishing textbooks and lessons, Mr. Ploor provides professional development as a frequent presenter at regional and national conferences to promote STEM education and video game design curriculum for the high school and middle school levels.

Brief Contents

Expanded Table of Contents

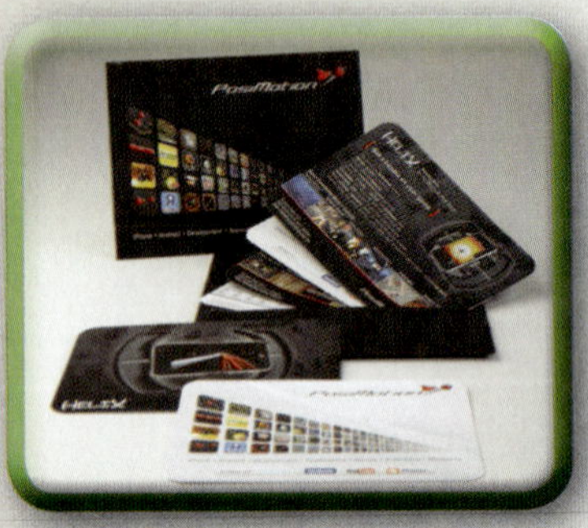

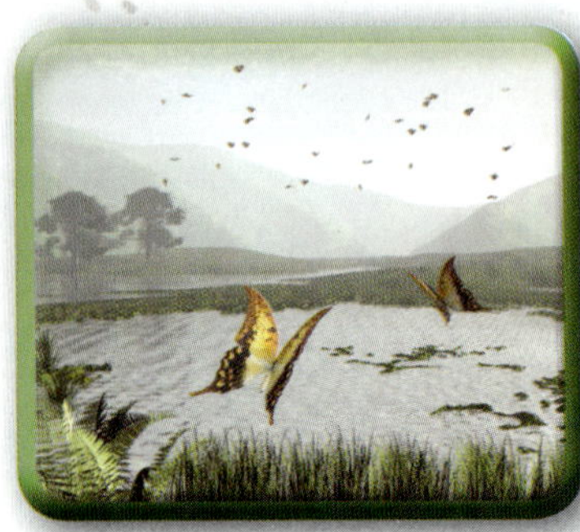

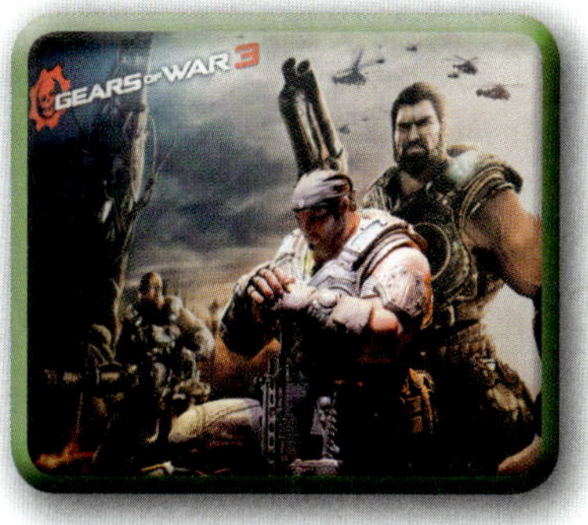
GEARS OF WAR 3

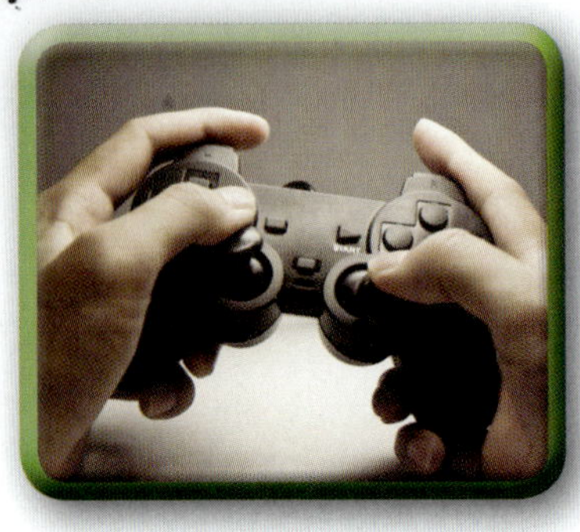

Chapter 4

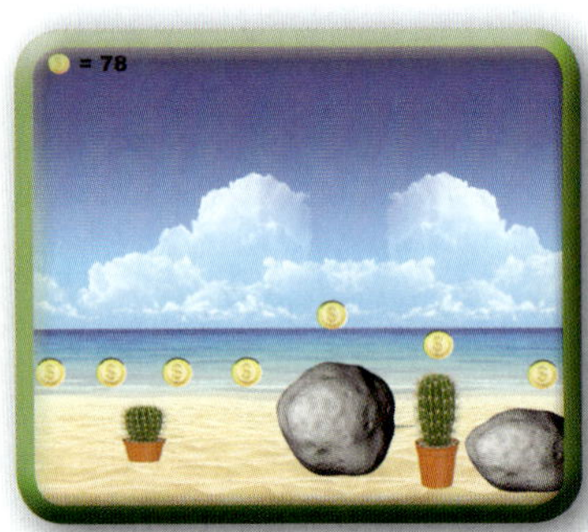

Chapter 5

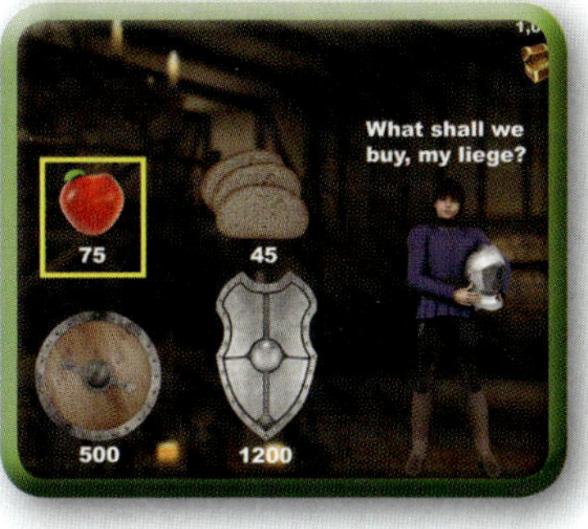

What shall we buy, my liege?
75
45
500
1200

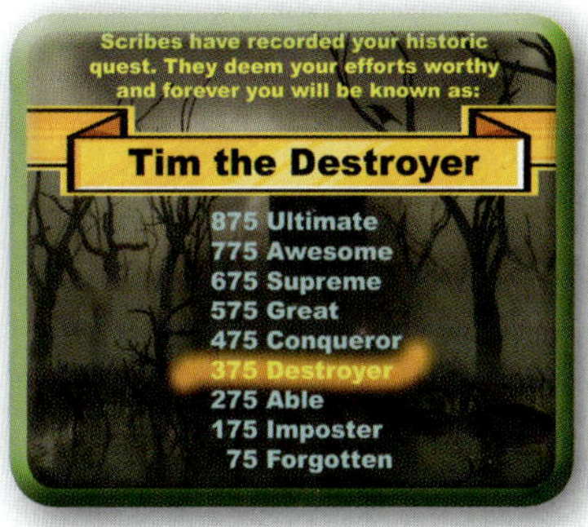

Scribes have recorded your historic quest. They deem your efforts worthy and forever you will be known as:
Tim the Destroyer
875 Ultimate
775 Awesome
675 Supreme
575 Great
475 Conqueror
375 Destroyer
275 Able
175 Imposter
75 Forgotten

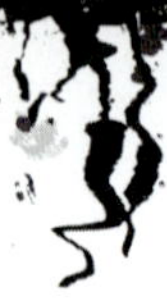

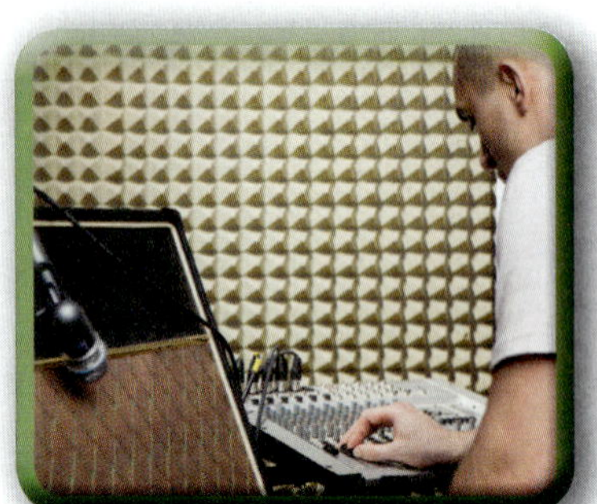

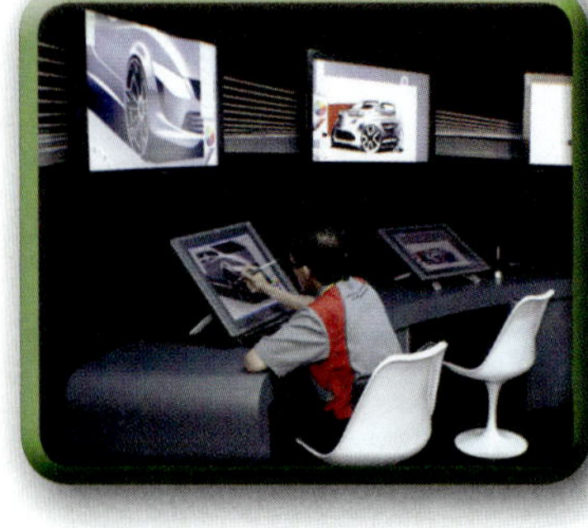

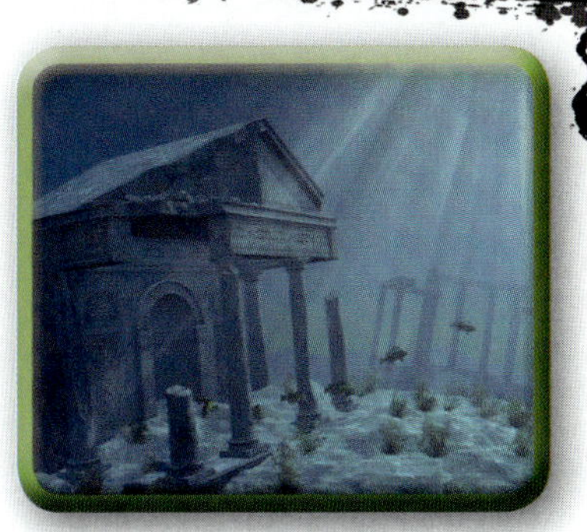

Chapter 10

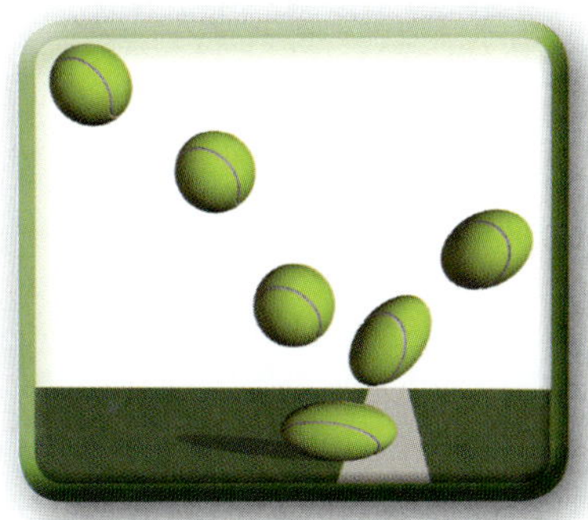

Chapter 11

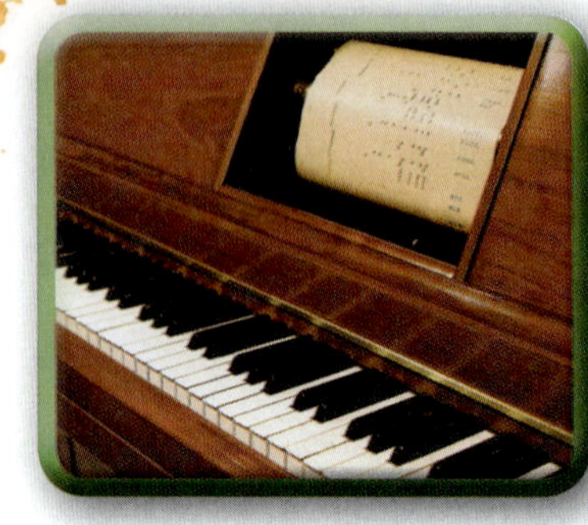

Chapter 12

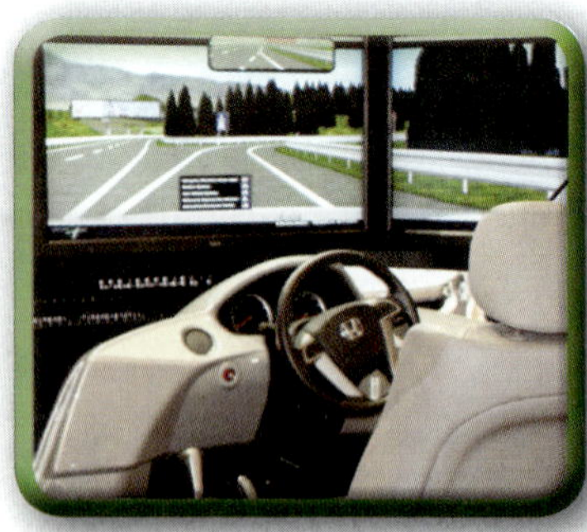

Chapter 13

Content Connected

Formative Assessment

Review Your Knowledge

These questions provide an opportunity to measure your knowledge of the content presented in the chapter. Included are vocabulary questions.

Apply Your STEM Knowledge

This section challenges you to apply the knowledge you have gained in the chapter and previous chapters to cross-curricular activities.

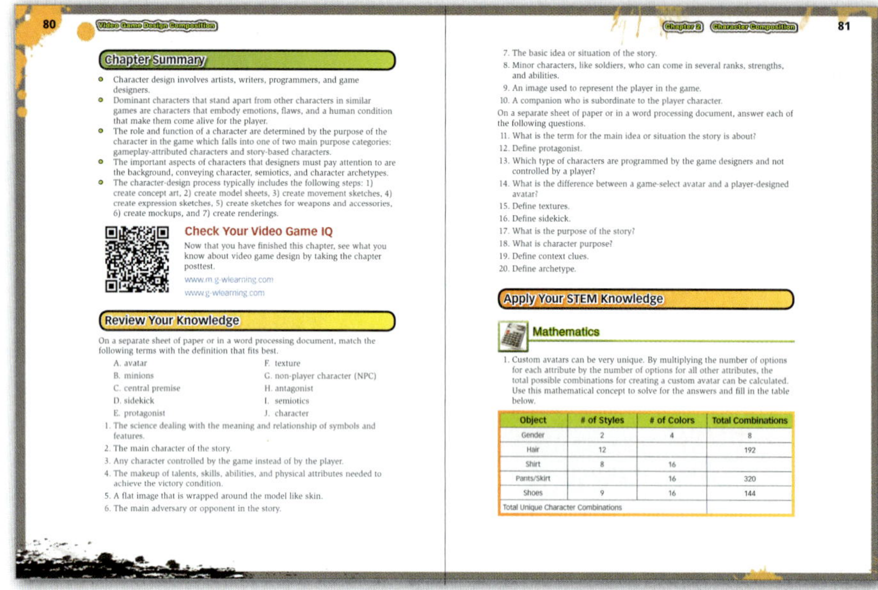

80 Video Game Design Composition

Chapter Summary

- Character design involves artists, writers, programmers, and game designers.
- Dominant characters that stand apart from other characters in similar games are characters that embody emotions, flaws, and a human condition that make them come alive for the player.
- The role and function of a character are determined by the purpose of the character in the game which falls into one of two main purpose categories: gameplay-attributed characters and story-based characters.
- The important aspects of characters that designers must pay attention to are the background, conveying character, semiotics, and character archetypes.
- The character-design process typically includes the following steps: 1) create concept art, 2) create model sheets, 3) create movement sketches, 4) create expression sketches, 5) create sketches for weapons and accessories, 6) create mockups, and 7) create renderings.

Check Your Video Game IQ

Now that you have finished this chapter, see what you know about video game design by taking the chapter posttest.

www.m.g-wlearning.com

www.g-wlearning.com

Review Your Knowledge

On a separate sheet of paper or in a word processing document, match the following terms with the definition that fits best.

A. avatar
B. minions
C. central premise
D. sidekick
E. protagonist
F. texture
G. non-player character (NPC)
H. antagonist
I. semiotics
J. character

1. The science dealing with the meaning and relationship of symbols and features.
2. The main character of the story.
3. Any character controlled by the game instead of by the player.
4. The makeup of talents, skills, abilities, and physical attributes needed to achieve the victory condition.
5. A flat image that is wrapped around the model like skin.
6. The main adversary or opponent in the story.

Chapter 3 Character Composition 81

7. The basic idea or situation of the story.
8. Minor characters, like soldiers, who can come in several ranks, strengths, and abilities.
9. An image used to represent the player in the game.
10. A companion who is subordinate to the player character.

On a separate sheet of paper or in a word processing document, answer each of the following questions.

11. What is the term for the main idea or situation the story is about?
12. Define protagonist.
13. Which type of characters are programmed by the game designers and not controlled by a player?
14. What is the difference between a game-select avatar and a player-designed avatar?
15. Define textures.
16. Define sidekick.
17. What is the purpose of the story?
18. What is character purpose?
19. Define context clues.
20. Define archetype.

Apply Your STEM Knowledge

Mathematics

1. Custom avatars can be very unique. By multiplying the number of options for each attribute by the number of options for all other attributes, the total possible combinations for creating a custom avatar can be calculated. Use this mathematical concept to solve for the answers and fill in the table below.

Object	# of Styles	# of Colors	Total Combinations
Gender	2	4	8
Hair	12		192
Shirt	8	16	
Pants/Skirt		16	320
Shoes	9	16	144
Total Unique Character Combinations			

End-of-Chapter Activities

Working in Teams

These activities require you to work collaboratively with a team to apply skills and knowledge in the content presented in the chapter.

Gamer Portfolio

An important part of searching for a job in the video game design field is having a portfolio of your work to show to employers or for college admissions. The Gamer Portfolio feature guides you through starting to build a portfolio.

College and Career Readiness

These activities provide real-world literacy skills in the areas of reading, writing, speaking, listening, and career and technical education to help prepare you for life beyond high school.

Event Prep

The Event Prep features provide guidance for preparing for Career and Technical Student Organization (CTSO) competitions.

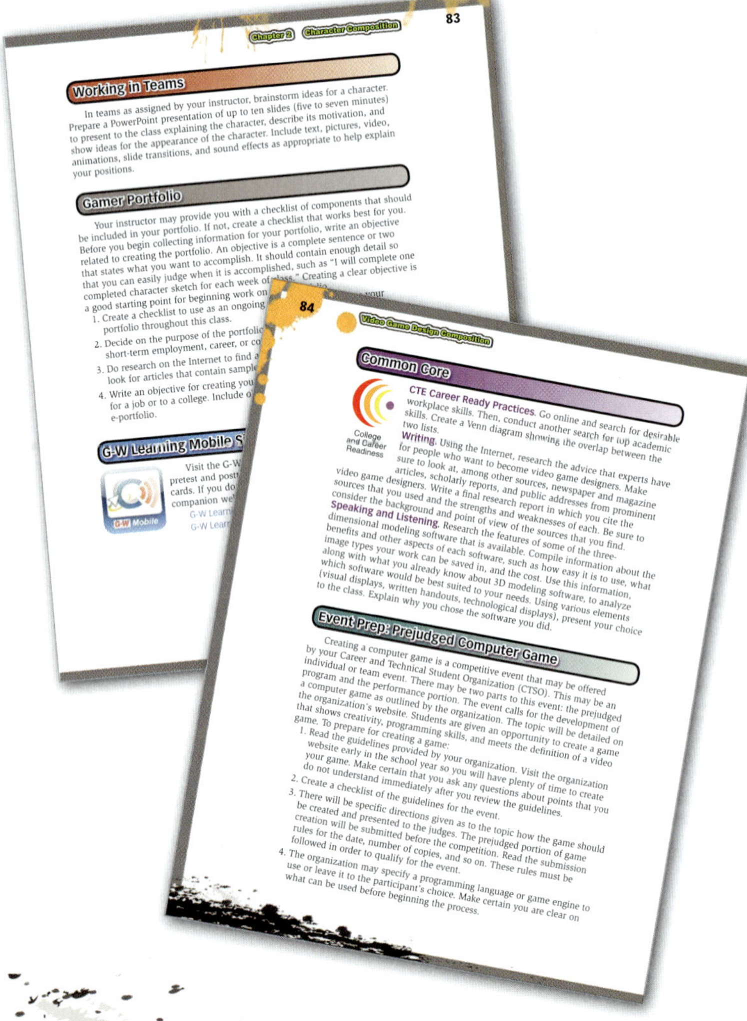

Chapter 3 Character Composition 83

Working in Teams

In teams as assigned by your instructor, brainstorm ideas for a character. Prepare a PowerPoint presentation of up to ten slides (five to seven minutes) to present to the class explaining the character, describe its motivation, and show ideas for the appearance of the character. Include text, pictures, video, animations, slide transitions, and sound effects as appropriate to help explain your positions.

Gamer Portfolio

Your instructor may provide you with a checklist of components that should be included in your portfolio. If not, create a checklist that works best for you. Before you begin collecting information for your portfolio, write an objective related to creating the portfolio. An objective is a complete sentence or two that states what you want to accomplish. It should contain enough detail so that you can easily judge when it is accomplished, such as "I will complete one completed character sketch for each week of class." Creating a clear objective is a good starting point for beginning work on your portfolio.

1. Create a checklist to use as an ongoing portfolio throughout this class.
2. Decide on the purpose of the portfolio short-term employment, career, or co
3. Do research on the Internet to find a look for articles that contain sample
4. Write an objective for creating you for a job or to a college. Include o e-portfolio.

G-W Learning Mobile S

Visit the G-W pretest and post cards. If you do companion we

84 Video Game Design Composition

Common Core

College and Career Readiness

CTE Career Ready Practices. Go online and search for desirable workplace skills. Then, conduct another search for top academic skills. Create a Venn diagram showing the overlap between the two lists.

Writing. Using the Internet, research the advice that experts have for people who want to become video game designers. Make sure to look at, among other sources, newspaper and magazine articles, scholarly reports, and public addresses from prominent video game designers. Write a final research report in which you cite the sources that you used and the strengths and weaknesses of each. Be sure to consider the background and point of view of the sources that you find.

Speaking and Listening. Research the features of some of the three-dimensional modeling software that is available. Compile information about the benefits and other aspects of each software, such as how easy it is to use, what image types your work can be saved in, and the cost. Use this information, along with what you already know about 3D modeling software, to analyze which software would be best suited to your needs. Using various elements (visual displays, written handouts, technological displays), present your choice to the class. Explain why you chose the software you did.

Event Prep: Prejudged Computer Game

Creating a computer game is a competitive event that may be offered by your Career and Technical Student Organization (CTSO). This may be an individual or team event. There may be two parts to this event: the prejudged program and the performance portion. The event calls for the development of a computer game as outlined by the organization. The topic will be detailed on the organization's website. Students are given an opportunity to create a game that shows creativity, programming skills, and meets the definition of a video game. To prepare for creating a game:

1. Read the guidelines provided by your organization. Visit the organization website early in the school year so you will have plenty of time to create your game. Make certain that you ask any questions about points that you do not understand immediately after you review the guidelines.
2. Create a checklist of the guidelines for the event.
3. There will be specific directions given as to the topic how the game should be created and presented to the judges. The prejudged portion of game creation will be submitted before the competition. Read the submission rules for the date, number of copies, and so on. These rules must be followed in order to qualify for the event.
4. The organization may specify a programming language or game engine to use or leave it to the participant's choice. Make certain you are clear on what can be used before beginning the process.

Content Connected

Reading Prep

A Reading Prep feature opens each chapter to engage you in the content to be presented in the chapter. These features are called out by the College and Career Readiness icon.

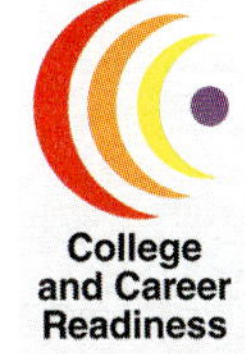

College and Career Readiness

Reading Prep. Before reading, observe the objectives for this chapter. As you read, focus on how the chapter is structured. Summarize the structure of the chapter. Does this structure make points clear, convincing, and engaging?

Green Gamer

The Green Gamer features share tips on how a gamer or video game design studio can engage in best practices for the environment.

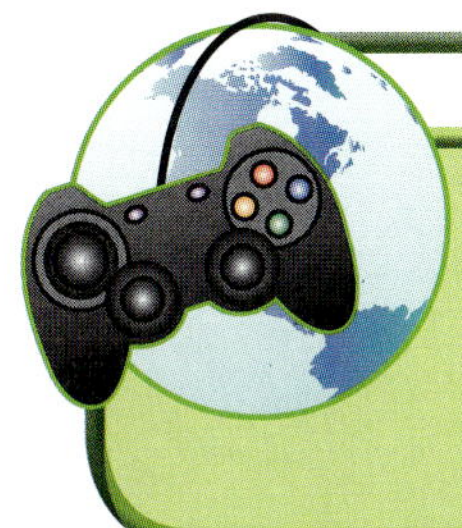

Green Gamer

Presentations typically consist of slideshows, website demonstrations, and handouts of important points for the audience. However, not everybody in the audience will take handouts with them. The unused handouts represent a waste of paper, ink, and energy. Instead of handouts, post information on YouTube, Facebook, or other website.

Ethical Gamer

The Ethical Gamer features provide information related to ethic issues facing gamers and video game design studios.

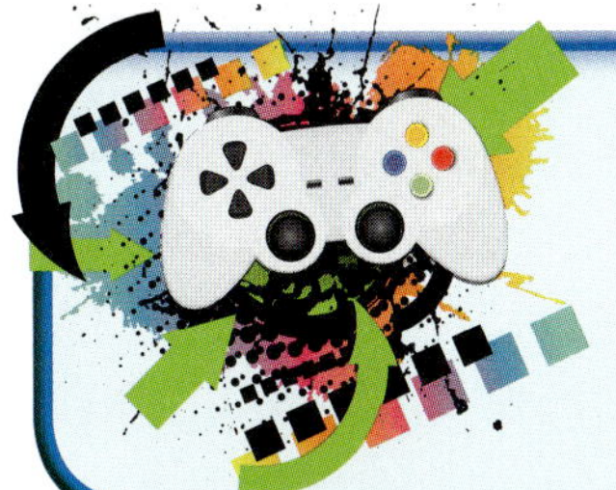

Ethical Gamer

It is unethical to present information as your own when it is not and doing so can be illegal. Do not use free artwork from the Internet and call it your own. In addition to being unethical and possibly illegal, doing so may be a reason for dismissal from your job.

Cheat Code

Cheat Codes provide vocabulary definitions for terms not defined in the context of the reading materials.

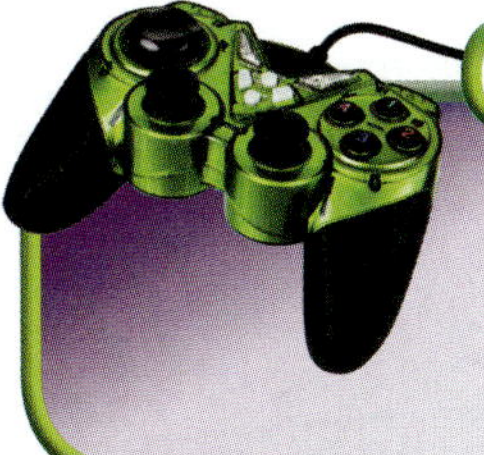

CHEAT CODE: CLOCK SPEED

The clock speed or clock rate is the speed at which the computer central processing unit (CPU) processes instructions. The higher the clock speed, the faster the computer.

Level Up!

The Level Up! features provide an opportunity to think about the material just presented and to engage in an activity at the point of learning.

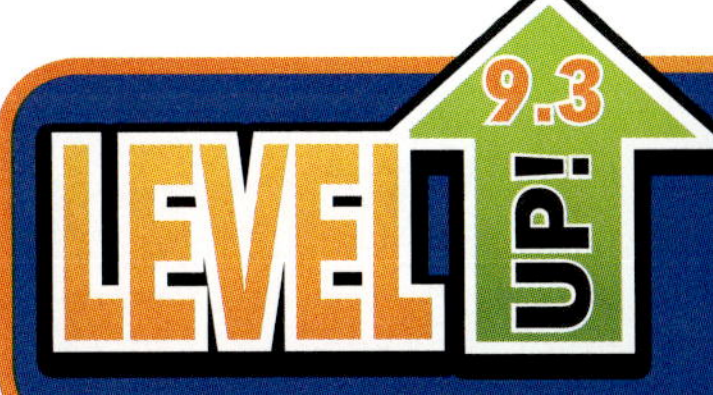

While playing your favorite game, see if you can identify how the designers used movement, emphasis, harmony, variety, balance, contrast, proportion, pattern, and unity in the graphics of the game.

Software Design Guide

The available software design guide (SDG) provides the hands-on application of the theory presented in the textbook. The SDG should be considered an integral part of the curriculum. It is where you take the theory learned in the textbook and use that knowledge to build video games. Working in simulated design teams, you will experience all aspects of video game design, from the planning stages, through the design and programming, and concluding with a capstone project.

Each chapter in the SDG is correlated to the textbook chapter. There are several activities for each chapter. Many of the activities are scripted game builds. These types of activities conclude with review questions. The last chapter in the SDG is a capstone project that requires you to apply all of the knowledge you acquired in the textbook and SDG.

Learning objectives for each chapter.

Daily bellwork to start each class period.

Learning objective for lesson. Provides an overview of the situation for the lesson. Step-by-step instructions for the game build in the lesson.

Anticipation guide for each chapter tracks learning progress from before the lesson to after completion of the lesson.

Technology Applied

Technology is an important part of your world. So, it should be part of your everyday learning. In this text and the available software design guide, you will find the following.

- A pretest and posttest are provided for each textbook chapter for self assessment. These can be accessed by scanning the QR code to visit the mobile site or you can visit the companion website to take the test.
- Data files needed for the game builds in the software design guide are provided on the companion website.
- Samples of the completed game builds in the software design guide are provided on the companion website.

G-W Learning Companion Website

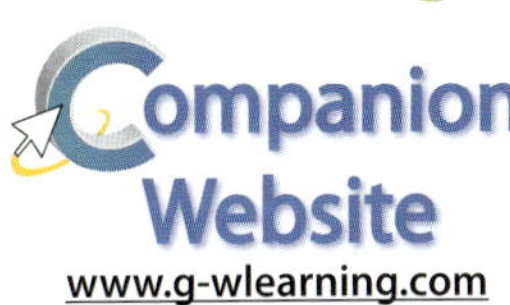

The G-W Learning companion website for *Video Game Design Composition* is a study reference that contains matching vocabulary games, e-flash cards, and interactive quizzes. Also included are data files for the game builds in the software design guide, as well as sample game builds.

G-W Learning companion website:
www.g-wlearning.com

G-W Learning Mobile Site

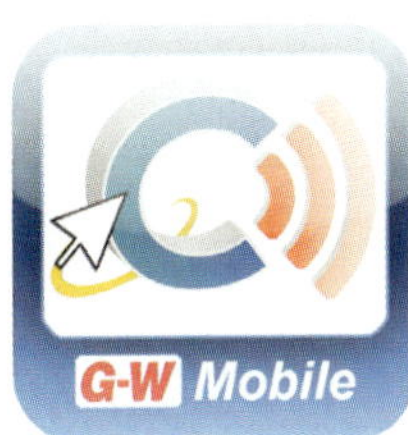

The G-W Learning mobile site* is a study reference to use when you are on the go. The mobile site is easy to read, easy to use, and fine-tuned for quick access.

For *Video Game Design Composition,* the G-W Learning mobile site contains chapter pretests and posttests and e-flash card vocabulary practices. If you do not have a smartphone, these same features can be accessed using an Internet browser to visit the G-W Learning companion website.

G-W Learning mobile website:
www.m.g-wlearning.com

Scan now!

Goodheart-Willcox QR Codes

This Goodheart-Willcox product contains QR codes*, or quick response codes. These codes can be scanned with a smartphone bar code reader to access information or online features. For more information on using QR codes and a recommended QR reader, visit the G-W Learning companion website at www.g-wlearning.com.

Scan now!

*An Internet connection is required to access the QR code destinations. Data-transfer rates may apply. Check with your Internet service provider for information on your data-transfer rates.

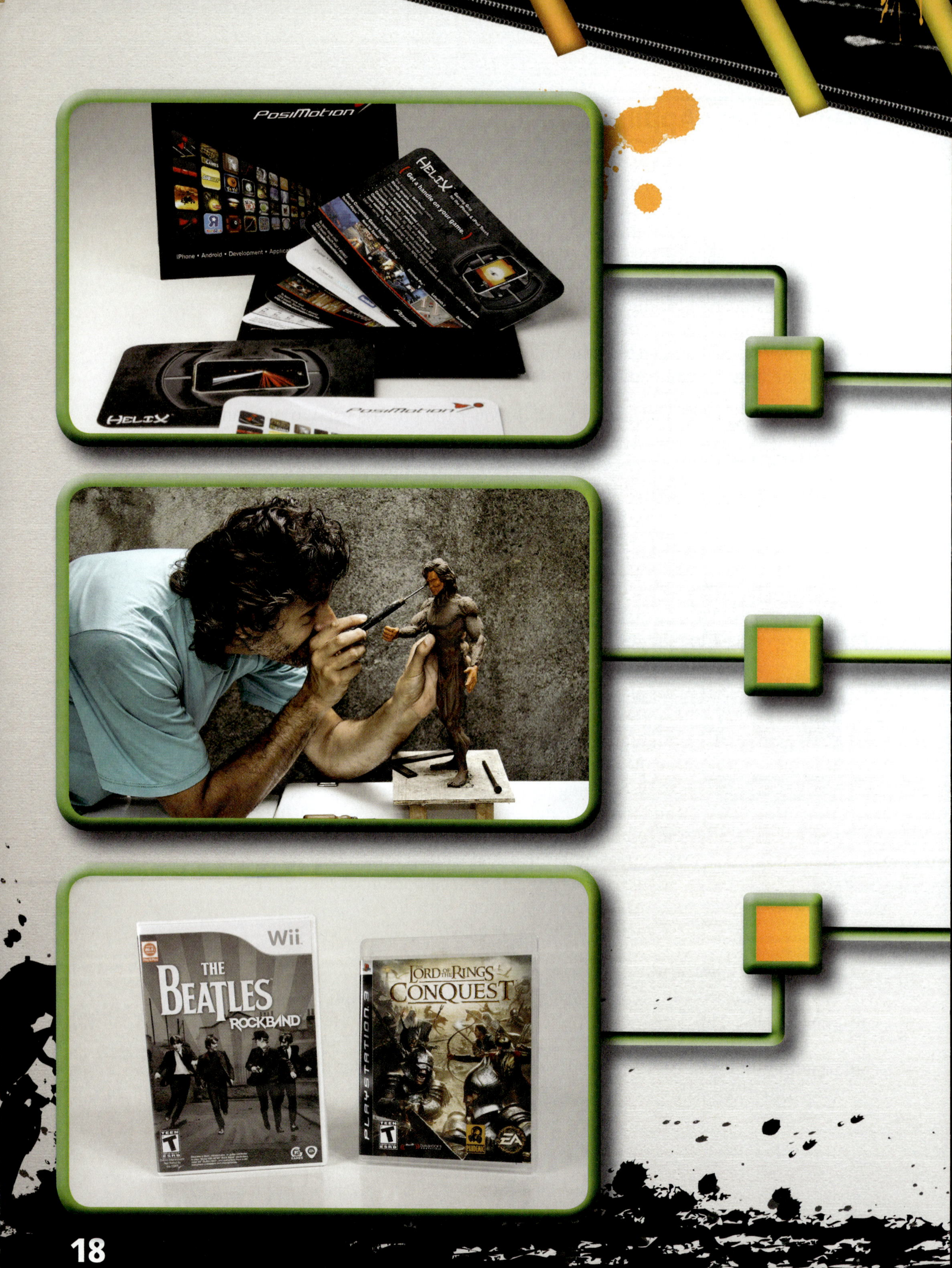
PosiMotion
HELIX
Get a handle on your game.
iPhone • Android • Development • Applica
Wii
THE BEATLES ROCKBAND
THE LORD OF THE RINGS CONQUEST
PLAYSTATION 3
TEEN
EA

Chapter 1
Design Composition

In this chapter, you will discover the process used to plan and create a video game for retail distribution. This process can be scaled down to plan a web-based game or handheld app. Following an organized process of design will help meet deadlines and keep the project on budget. So, get ready to power up the gamer that lives inside you and upload the information found on these pages.

Check Your Video Game IQ

Before you begin this chapter, see what you already know about video game design by taking the chapter pretest.

www.m.g-wlearning.com

www.g-wlearning.com

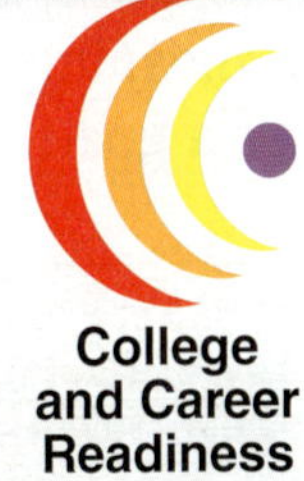

College and Career Readiness

Reading Prep. Review the table of contents for this text. Trace the development of the content that is being presented from simple to complex ideas.

Objectives

After completing this chapter, you will be able to:

- Detail the components of a game and differentiate between a game and a toy.
- List the roles and responsibilities of the specialists within a video game design team.
- Explain what is meant by the scope, or life cycle, of a video game.
- Outline the five Ps that guide the development of most video games.
- Define piracy and explain how it impacts the video game industry.
- Describe the four major types of business ownership.

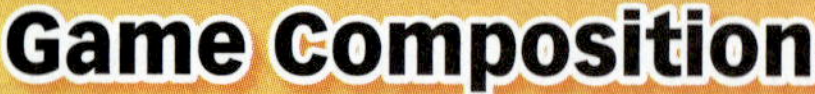

Game Composition

So you have downloaded a great new game app. But is it really a game? Not every app is a game. A game is a specific type of activity. As shown in **Figure 1-1**, a *game* has three parts: game environment, rules, and a victory condition. An activity must have all three components to be called a game. If there are no rules, for example, the environment is a toy, not a game.

Game Environment

The ***game environment*** is an area specifically designed to enable gameplay. A soccer field is a game environment. The area has been specifically designed to enable playing the game of soccer. The ground is flattened, trees are removed, boundary lines are painted, and goals are erected. A board game like *Monopoly* provides another great example of a game environment. The board is the environment that enables gameplay. The important part of the game environment is that it is designed to make play happen.

Video games have a special game environment. The game environment for a video game is a virtual world. It does not exist in the physical world like a soccer field or board game. The game environment for a video game can be a piece of land, a wooden square, a future outer space world, or one of many other possibilities. Whatever the game environment in a video game looks like, it is projected onto a video screen. The screen is what makes a video game a *video* game.

Rules

Within a game environment setup, the next requirement for a game is a set of rules. *Rules* state how a game is to be played, what is allowed, and what is not allowed. Rules give the game environment meaning and purpose. For example, the white lines on a soccer field have no meaning without rules. The game rules state that if the ball crosses an exterior white line, the ball is out of bounds and must reenter the game environment with a throw in, corner kick, or goal kick. Without rules, kicking the soccer ball into the net has no real meaning. Rules give special meaning to this action so the ball in the net scores a goal!

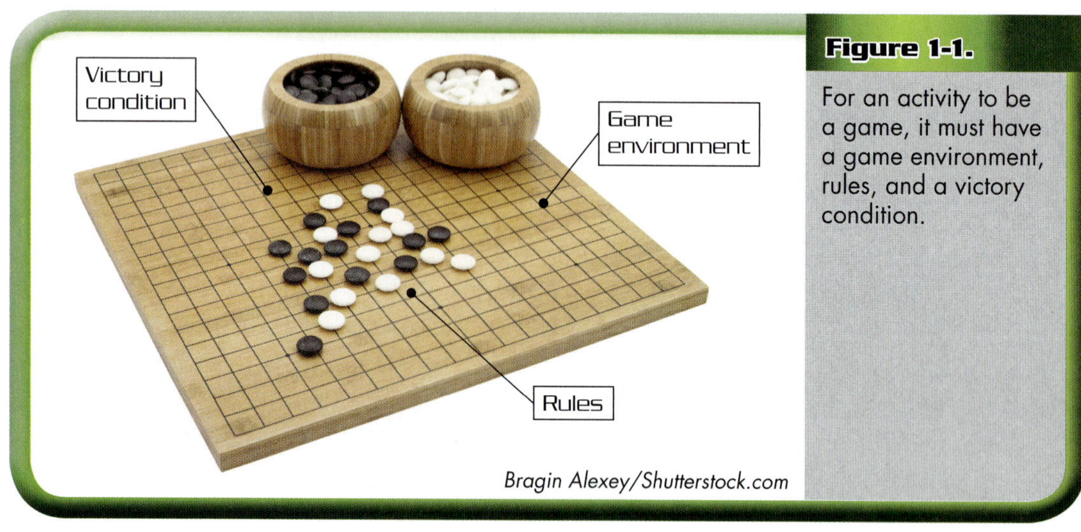

Figure 1-1. For an activity to be a game, it must have a game environment, rules, and a victory condition.

Together, the rules and game environment create a magic circle. The term ***magic circle*** refers to how the rules and game environment create structured play. It was coined by historian Johan Huizinga nearly 100 years ago, long before video games were invented. Inside the magic circle, an ordinary action, like touching a soccer ball with your hands, has special meaning. It is like someone blew a big bubble around the game environment, and inside this bubble things have different meaning and significance than they do outside the bubble. In the magic circle, people pretend. When playing soccer, you pretend that touching the ball with your hands is a foul. You pretend that the ball in the net is important. The magic circle allows pretend things to become more important than outside the magic circle. If you touch a soccer ball with your hands at the store, a guy in a striped shirt does not wave a yellow card in your face. That happens only inside the magic circle while the soccer game is being played.

Victory Condition

The final component of a game is the victory condition. A ***victory condition*** is what it takes to win the game. There is no standard victory condition. Different games allow for many different outcomes. In soccer, the team with the most points at the end of the game time is the winner. In checkers, the victory condition is eliminating of all your opponent's pieces from the game board. In a video game, the victory condition may be defeating the big boss, collecting the most points before running out of health or lives, or one of many other possibilities.

Toys

Toys do not have all three components—game environment, rules, and victory condition—and are, therefore, not games. Some toys are puzzles. For example, a jigsaw puzzle has a game environment (table you build it on) and a victory condition (all pieces in the correct order), as shown in **Figure 1-2.**

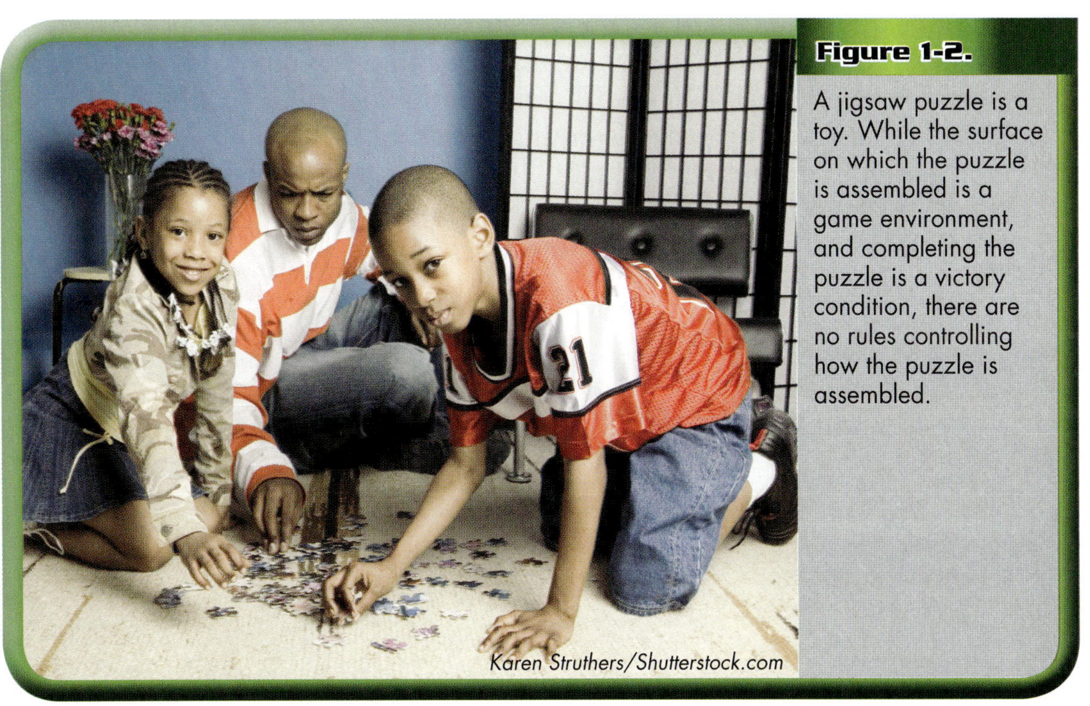

Karen Struthers/Shutterstock.com

Figure 1-2. A jigsaw puzzle is a toy. While the surface on which the puzzle is assembled is a game environment, and completing the puzzle is a victory condition, there are no rules controlling how the puzzle is assembled.

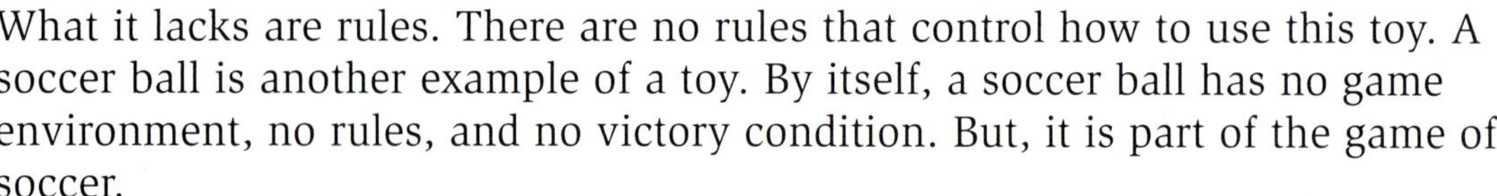

What it lacks are rules. There are no rules that control how to use this toy. A soccer ball is another example of a toy. By itself, a soccer ball has no game environment, no rules, and no victory condition. But, it is part of the game of soccer.

Some video "games" are really toys. Many simulation video games, such as *Nintendogs* or *DigiPets,* are not really games. These interactive toys have rules and a game environment that includes a video screen. They create a magic circle, but they do not have a victory condition. Therefore, they are not video games.

Video Game Classification

Video games come in many different varieties. To help organize games, compare gameplay. ***Gameplay*** is what the player does and how he or she interacts with the game while playing it. Games with similar gameplay have similar rules and core mechanics. ***Core mechanics*** is the computer programming used to enforce the rules. Games are grouped by similar gameplay into categories called genres. *Genre* is a major category of video game gameplay. Genres are further broken down into themes. *Themes* are subcategories of gameplay within a genre. **Figure 1-3** lists major genres and themes of video games.

- action: focuses on the player moving to build skill and increase game difficulty
- board/card/quiz: adapted from existing board games, card games, or quiz-show games
- educational: purposely built to train or educate the player
- fighting: uses character animations to perform a physical hand-to-hand battle
- music/party: uses songs and rhythm as the main feature
- puzzle: requires solving a spatial puzzle
- role playing: focuses on fantasy role playing whereby the player's avatar performs quests and battles to build skill points and increase power levels
- shooter: main feature is launching an object toward characters or objects
- simulation: seeks to emulate real-world situations and activities
- sports: derived from physical sporting games
- strategy: requires thought and planning to beat the opponent, either another player or a computer-controlled opponent
- toy: lacks interactivity, rules, or objectives

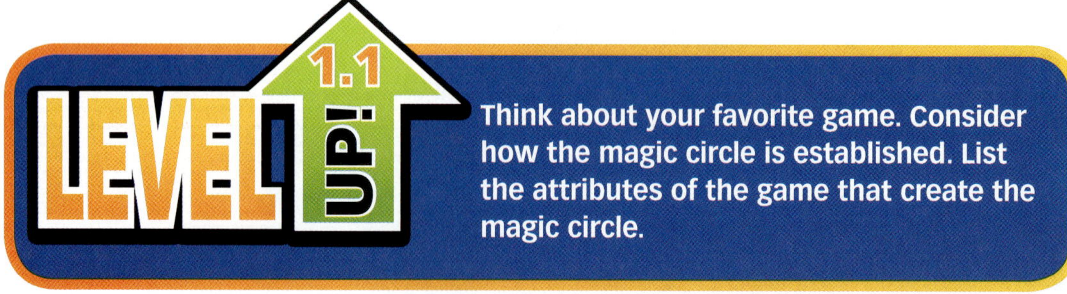

Think about your favorite game. Consider how the magic circle is established. List the attributes of the game that create the magic circle.

Video Game Genres and Themes

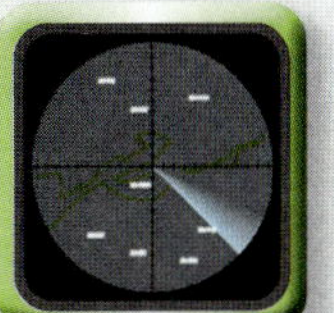

Action
Adventure
Bat and Ball
Crime
Flight
Horror
Platform
Tactical

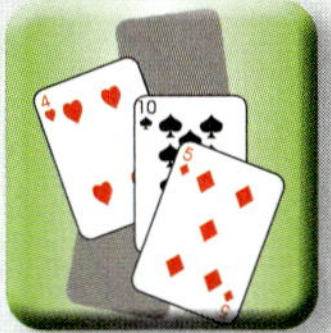

Board Games, Card Games, and Game (Quiz) Show

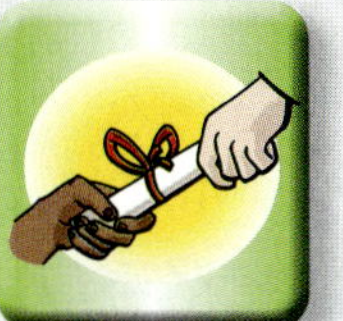

Educational/ Edutainment

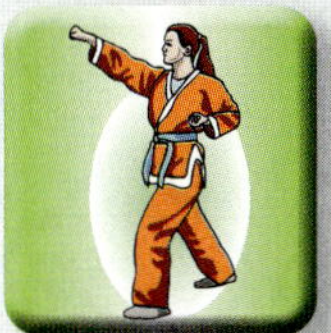

Fighting
Martial arts
Other

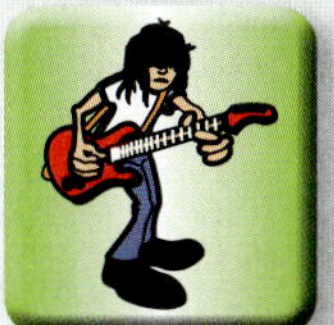

Music and Party
Dance
Music
Party
Singing

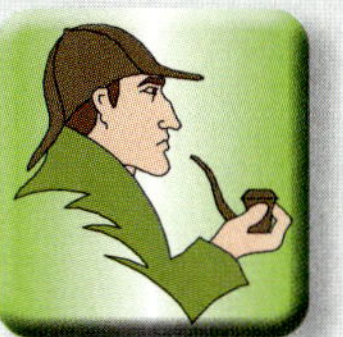

Puzzle
Guessing game
Logic puzzle
Mechanical puzzle
Transport puzzle
Word puzzle

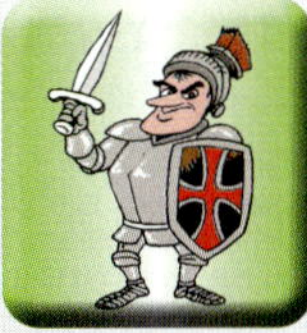

Role Playing (RPG)
Single/ multiplayer
Massive multiplayer

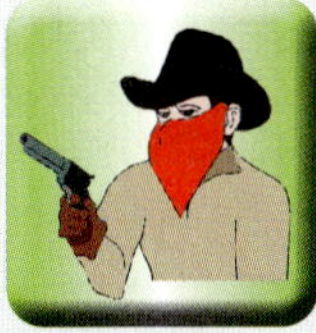

Shooter
First person
Side scrolling (shoot 'em)
Third person

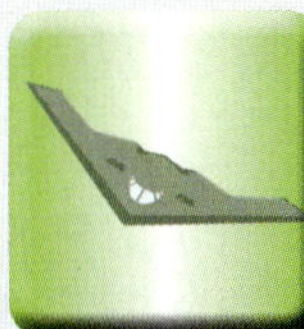

Simulation
A-life
Flight
Sim
Tycoon

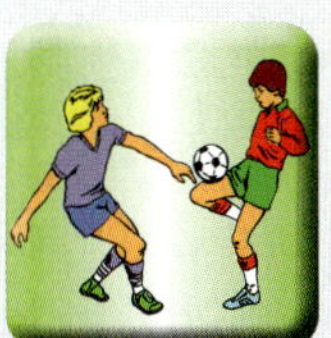

Sports
Baseball
Basketball
Bowling
Fishing
Football
Golf
Hockey
Hunting
Racing
Skateboarding
Snowboarding
Soccer
Tennis
Wrestling

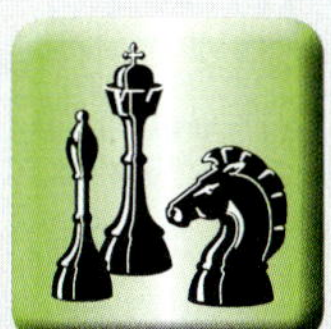

Strategy
Turn based

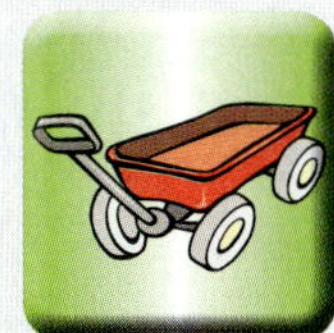

Toys
AI pets
Screen savers

Figure 1-3. These are some typical genres and themes for video games.

Goodheart-Willcox Publisher

Video Game Design Team

A ***design team*** is a group of very creative people who bring the idea of a video game into a playable version. The generic term *game designer* is used for almost everyone who works on a design team. In reality, each member of the design team is a specialist. Specialists have unique skills to complete a small set of tasks very well. Game design teams consist of specialists who have the right skills for a project.

The table in **Figure 1-4** can be used for a general description of major specialist roles on a design team. The actual title of a position may vary from game studio to game studio. However, the skills and responsibilities are generally those outlined in the figure.

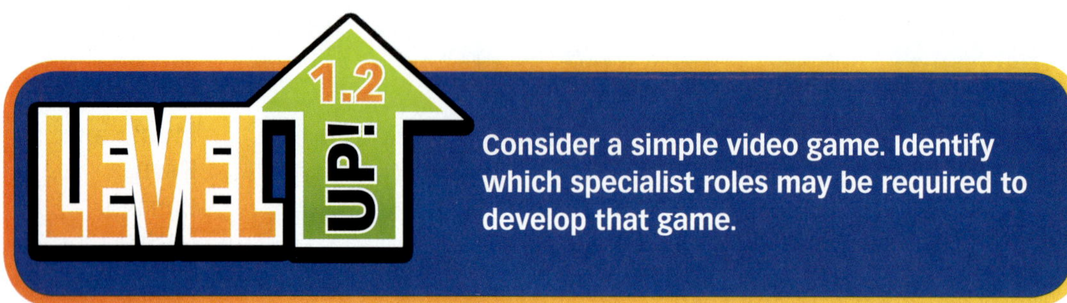

Consider a simple video game. Identify which specialist roles may be required to develop that game.

Role	Description
Producer	Internal producer works within the design studio; external producer works for an outside publisher or another design studio. Supervises game construction to make sure the game is done on time and on budget. Also the point of communication between the publisher and the design studio.
Creative Director	Sets the vision and direction of the design teams. Oversees many game projects at the same time. Checks the progress of each game in design to make sure it fits the concept and will have the quality needed.
Project Manager	Sometimes called the lead designer. In charge of a single game and responsible for assembling a team of specialists to get the job done right. Sets the schedule for the design timeline and gets budgets approved. Communicates with the team members to oversee that each is completing the tasks on time. Communicates with creative director on budget, time, and quality issues. Reports on progress of development.
Lead	Assigns tasks and makes sure everything aligns to the design documents of the game. In charge of a section of the design team. Lead artist is in charge of a team of artists. Lead programmer is in charge of a team of programmers.
Artist	Creates the visual components of the game, either 2D or 3D artistic elements. Subcategories of artist include 2D texture artists, environmental artists, and animators.
Programmer	Uses computer languages to create game engines, physics engines, and programs to make the game work and react to the input from the player.
Engineer	Usually a sound engineer or user interface engineer. Sound engineers create, edit, and mix sounds needed for the game, such as background music, voices of the characters, and sounds related to player movement. User interface engineers design custom controls for the player to input information into the computer and get output feedback from the computer.
Game Writer	Creates the plot, character personalities, backstory, and dialogue for the game. Develops the game manual.

Figure 1-4. These are typical titles for members of a video game design team and descriptions of their roles.

Goodheart-Willcox Publisher

Video Game Scope

Just like everything in nature, a video game has a life cycle. The life cycle begins with an idea for a video game and ends when the game is no longer being supported. The length of the life cycle depends on how complex the game is to create and program and how well the game sells.

Creating a game can be a huge production that takes years from concept to release date. A large-scale-production game, such as *Halo, Call of Duty,* or *Skyrim,* may have a budget over $100 million. These games may also have 50, 100, 300, or more employees working on the project. Making a large-scale-production game is a lot like making a Hollywood blockbuster film with regard to the size and scope of the project.

So, you have an outstanding game idea and want to turn it into a **triple-A game** so you and your friends can play together on a game console. But, you do not have $100 million to create the game. Fear not! You do not need to have millions to build a video game. Video game publishers fund most major video games. A ***video game publisher*** oversees the entire process of bringing the video game to the retail market. The publisher manufactures, markets, and supports each video game, or *title,* in its library. To finance your game, you need to pitch your idea for a video game to one of these publishers to see if they will take on your game project. Electronic Arts, Ubisoft, Capcom, and Activision are examples of video game publishers.

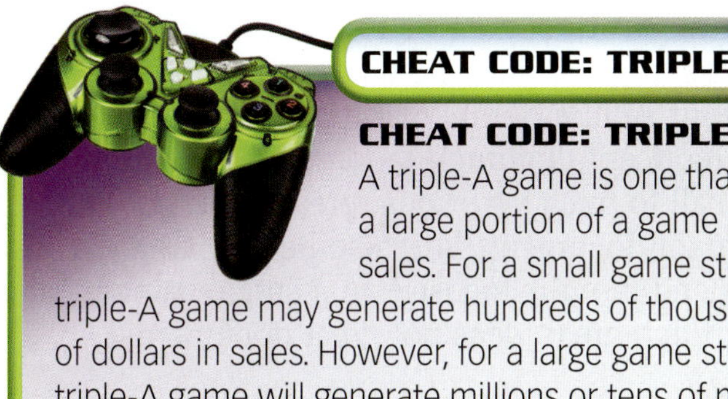

CHEAT CODE: TRIPLE-A GAME

CHEAT CODE: TRIPLE-A GAME

A triple-A game is one that generates a large portion of a game studio's sales. For a small game studio, a triple-A game may generate hundreds of thousands of dollars in sales. However, for a large game studio, a triple-A game will generate millions or tens of millions of dollars in sales.

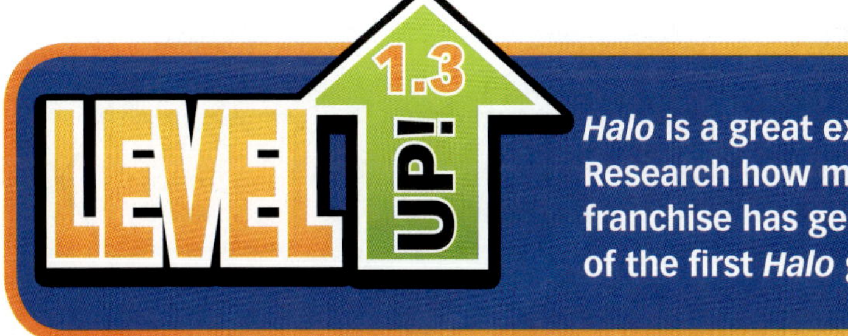

Halo **is a great example of a triple-A game. Research how much money the *Halo* franchise has generated since the release of the first *Halo* game.**

Project Composition

You pick up the phone and start calling video game publishers pitching your idea for a video game. Certainly they would want to hear about your super cool game idea. But, you quickly find out that nobody will speak with you about your idea. Most video game publishers require a formal sales presentation for game ideas so they can evaluate if the idea is worthy of the money needed to turn it into a game.

You will have to do a little preparation. You will not be getting rich today for that great idea you had yesterday. Getting an idea made into a video game takes time, planning, and preparation. Things move slowly just to get the process started. As shown in **Figure 1-5,** most video games are developed following the ***five Ps*** of video game publishing.

- pitch
- preproduction
- production
- post production
- patch and return distribution

Pitch

You need to package your great idea so the video game publisher will look at it. This starts with a pitch document. A ***pitch document*** is used to sell the game idea to the video game publisher or the decision makers at the game studio. The objective of this document is to quickly sell your game idea. Producers see hundreds of pitch documents a year. You need to get their attention quickly and get your selling points communicated well. There are two pitch documents: high-concept document and game-treatment document.

While you wait for the call to pitch your idea, prepare the presentation and refine your game-treatment document. But, also be prepared that you may never get the call. Do not spend months focused on a single game idea and preparing documents for it. Pitch great ideas not great documents!

High-Concept Document

The ***high-concept document*** is a one-page overview of the basic idea for your game. It is a résumé for your idea. Here is where those language arts

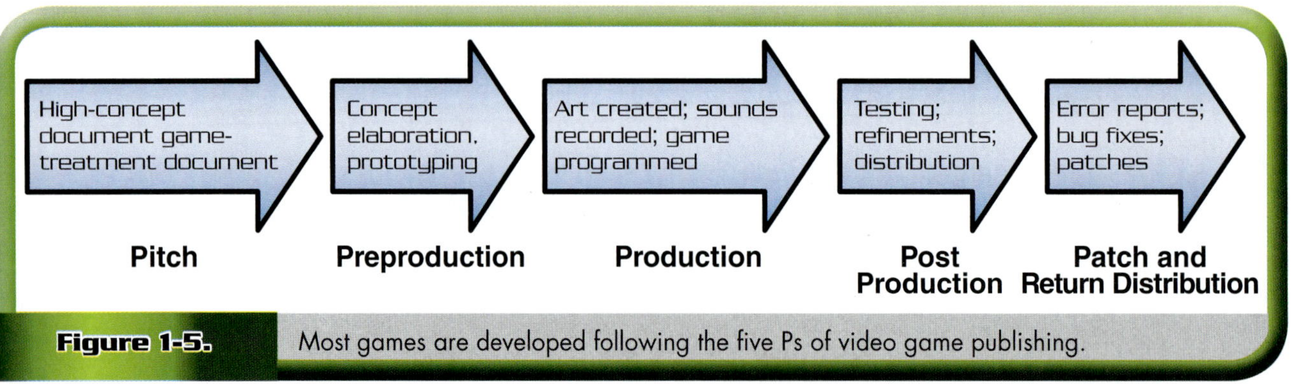

Figure 1-5. Most games are developed following the five Ps of video game publishing.

Goodheart-Willcox Publisher

skills you have been working on for years come into play. The high-concept document has the same introduction-body-conclusion model you have already learned. Beyond this, there is no standard format for a high-concept document, but it must include a few essential facts. The answers to the ***five essential questions*** form the foundation of the concept for the game.

- What is the game going to be about (genre type, basic idea)?
- Who is going to play this game (audience, age, target market, desired ESRB rating)?
- Who is the player, or protagonist, going to be in this game (player role, character types)?
- What will the player do in the game (victory condition, obstacles, opponents)?
- What will the world look like in the game (settings, levels, backgrounds, perspectives)?

You may only get one chance to sell the publisher on your idea. You need to have a great pitch document. Have others read your document and help edit and refine it. The publisher is really busy and might only agree to give you 30 seconds to catch his or her attention with your idea. Be concise and efficient with your wording. **Figure 1-6** shows a sample high-concept document for a game named *Elephant Fever.*

Introduction Section. The introduction section is the beginning of the pitch document. It provides an overview of the game concept. The introduction needs to quickly grab the reader's attention so he or she will keep reading. The introduction should be energetic and answer the first two essential questions. Remember, you are always *selling* in this document and never just *describing.* Keep these rules in mind.

- Always use active voice to get the reader excited about your amazing game idea.
- Always begin the introduction with the title of your game; for example, "*Elephant Fever* cleverly combines the excitement of a racing game with the tumbling fun of crashing elephants."
- Organize the document to be read quickly.
- Take your time; read, write, and refine.
- Sell the *hook.*

The hook is what makes your game special or different. Just like in fishing, if publishers swallow the hook, you can reel them in. In marketing, the hook is called the *unique selling proposition (USP),* sometimes called the unique selling point. A USP is what makes your game different or unique from other games.

Body Section. The introduction made the reader want more information. The body section is the meat of the high-concept document. It is where you give some tantalizing details that help explain your game. In the body section, you answer the last three essential questions.

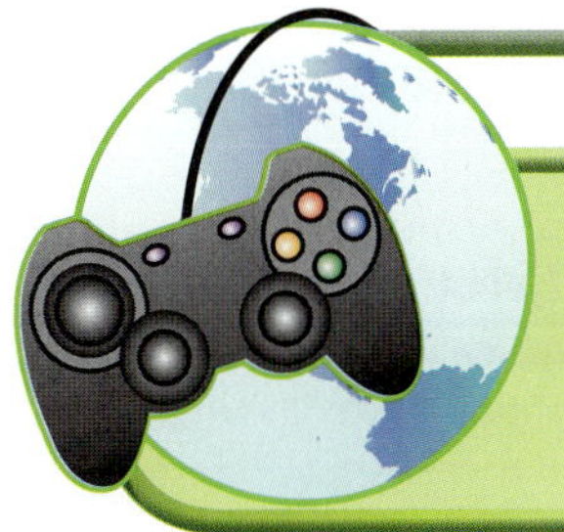

Green Gamer

If printed, the documents needed for game design may be many pages. Think about saving paper by keeping these documents electronically instead of in physical form. This can save paper, which also saves money.

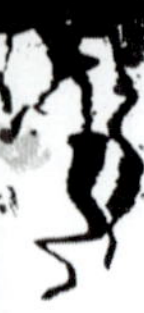

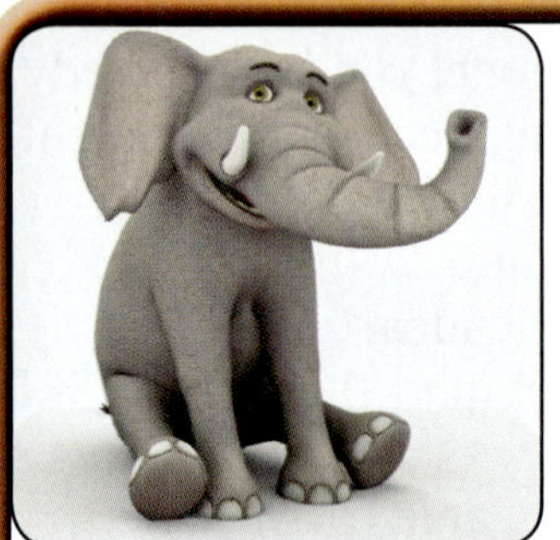

Elephant Fever

Elephant Fever cleverly combines the excitement of a racing game with the tumbling fun of crashing elephants. Choose your elephant and upgrade it with racing shoes, rocket boosters, and more. Jump on its back, grab the trunk, and steer your elephant to victory! The Wii remote gives kids under 12 control of the joystick-like elephant trunk in a *Mario Kart*–style environment. Elephants are a ton of fun and kids enjoy funny expressions on crashing elephants that rampage through the course. Pull back! No brakes! Luckily elephants come equipped with parachute-like ears for rapid stopping. I can hear the kids screaming for more. Mom is on her way to buy this game tonight. *Elephant Fever* will dominate the motion-based and handheld markets by combining innovative gameplay with wacky cartoon-land graphics.

Elephant Fever uses unique gameplay in a kid-friendly world of elephant racing. Capitalizing on the user-friendly features and interactive controls of the Wii system, this game will have kids jumping for joy! Tilt forward for speed, backward for brakes, left and right for steering. Tap the [B] button to engage booster rockets or fire peanuts.

Elephant Fever uses technology borrowed from other in-house racing games. Together with cartoonish graphics, this will keep production costs low while delivering high quality to the target market. Quickly adapt any racing engine to create the gameplay and simply map controls to the Wii remote. Artists will have little difficulty working with a pastel palette of solid lines and fills. The game world can use mostly flat graphic to create the 2.5D game world. Borrowed technology and simple graphics make a stable and profitable game.

The success of *Elephant Fever* is not limited to the Wii. This game appeals to the casual gamer of the iPhone, iPad, and Android markets. The Wii controls can be remapped to the accelerometers in a smartphone or tablet device. Truly insane gameplay will result when mapped to Kinect controls. A free demo has them hooked as they upgrade for more exciting levels, including motorboat- and airplane-like configurations for the elephants. Secondary revenue from paid elephant upgrades ensures profitability.

Elephant Fever is ideal for immediate production. The market awaits the newest sensation for Kinect, Wii, and iPhone. Low cost achieved from borrowed technology and porting to multiple platforms assures quick profits. My skills in managing a design team will doubly ensure success. My impressive portfolio of online and app development bring the perfect balance of talent and hard work to this project. Experience the rampage! Feel the stampede!

Figure 1-6. This is a high-concept document for the game *Elephant Fever*.

Goodheart-Willcox Publisher; image ©DM7/Shutterstock.com

You will also need to keep baiting the hook. Remember, you must always sell your idea. This document may not be read by a designer. It might be read by an investor. Bait the hook with points that will show the publisher how to reel in some money with your game.

Conclusion Section. The conclusion section is where you make a final pitch and sell yourself. This is the summary of everything you presented. Quickly summarize your idea for a game and why it will be successful. Include yourself as a valuable part of the team.

Game-Treatment Document

After you have sent the high-concept document off to a publisher, it is time to wait by the phone for a callback. However, when that call comes, you will need to have an expanded version of the pitch document to show the decision makers. The ***game-treatment document*** explains the vision of the game in greater detail than the high-concept document.

A complete set of the original pitch documents (game-treatment document) for the Irrational Games' *BioShock* is available on the web. Search for *BioShock pitch document.* This game-treatment document is about 15 pages long. Look at it to see how one game studio created a winning game-treatment document.

A brochure or presentation-folder format will give a polished feel to the game-treatment document and provide a quality example of your work. More importantly, the game-treatment document gives you the space to really sell your game. Common items included are:

- game introduction;
- genre and target market;
- platform;
- game description and plot overview;
- concept art or sketches;
- USP;
- legal issues; and
- reasons why your team is the best one to design the game.

A game-treatment document should be designed as a leave-behind document. A *leave-behind document* is something that stays with the publisher after you have made your presentation as a reminder of your proposal. **Figure 1-7** shows a leave-behind document from a game studio.

Game Introduction. Summarize the gameplay and technology of the game. This should be a quick brief explanation of the game. Summarize the game in just a few sentences.

Genre and Target Market. State the genre for the game. This tells the publisher what other games have similar gameplay to the proposed game. The *target market* is who the game is intended to appeal to most.

Platform. Stating the **platform** will help direct the designers to exploit unique characteristics of

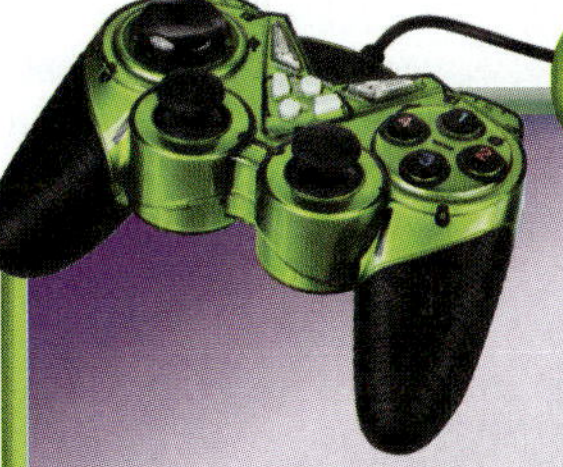

CHEAT CODE: PLATFORM

The platform refers to the device on which the game will be played. The platform may be Xbox, PlayStation, Wii, smartphone, PC, Mac, or other device. Often a game is available in versions for many different platforms. However, in some cases, a game may only be available for one platform.

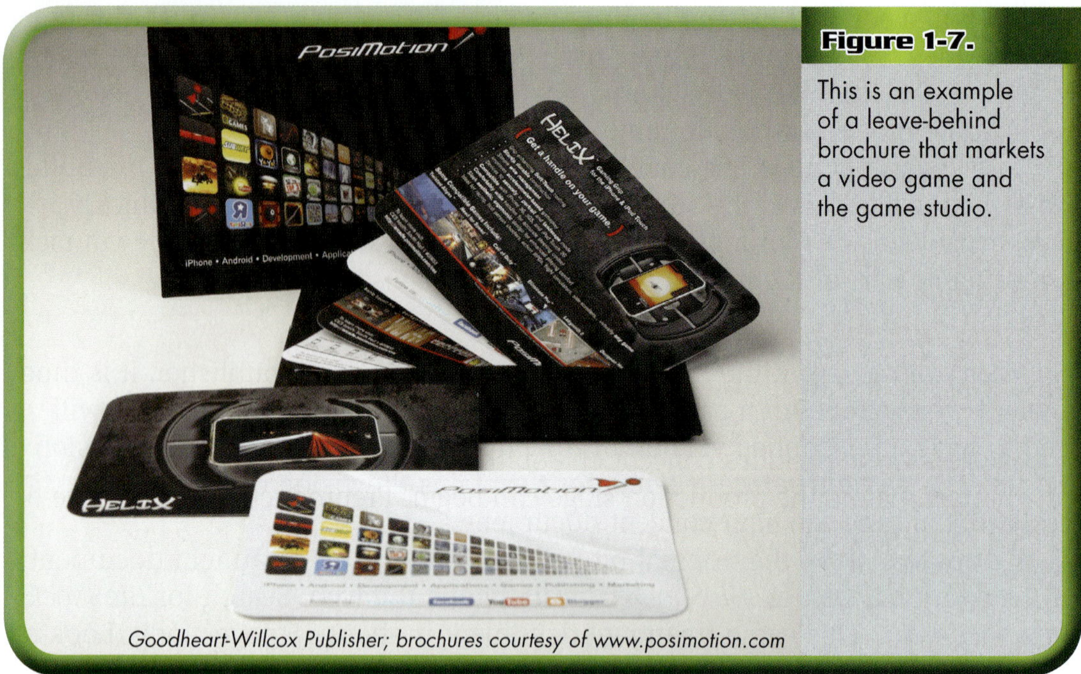

Figure 1-7. This is an example of a leave-behind brochure that markets a video game and the game studio.

Goodheart-Willcox Publisher; brochures courtesy of www.posimotion.com

the device. For example, the motion controller of the Wii game console can be used to provide a USP for the game.

Game Description and Plot Overview. Provide a detailed description of what the player will do in the game. This is presented as if the designer is speaking directly to the players and telling them what obstacles, options, and features they should be using in the game.

Concept Art or Sketches. Include a few sketches or drawings to show what you imagine the main characters will look like. Show any special character traits, features, or weapons that make this character different from characters in other games. Hand drawn sketches will do just fine. No need to get the character completed as a full 3D rendering.

USP. List the important differences your game has over other similar games. Be as detailed as needed to summarize the features. Fully explain why each is a unique feature or how it is significantly different from other games.

Legal Issues. This is an important area! Producers look this section over very carefully. If you use a character from a movie or TV show, you must state that here! You need to get permission from the author or artist if you are using a story or character that you did not personally create. If an item is public domain or has a commercial-use license, this must also be included. The publisher will find out if you have used **copyrighted** material without permission! Do not wait for the legal team to tell you that you are being sued for copyright infringement.

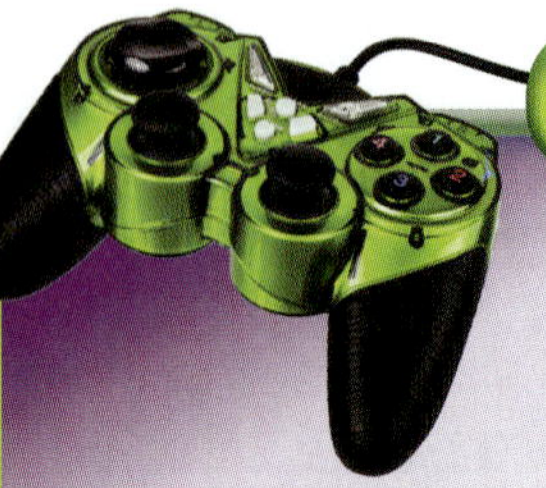

CHEAT CODE: COPYRIGHT

Copyright is an indication of legal ownership of creative works. As soon as a creative work is in tangible form, it is automatically copyrighted and owned by the author. For example, as soon as words are saved in a document file, music is recorded and saved, or artwork drawn on paper or saved to a file, the creation is copyrighted. Ideas cannot be copyrighted.

Choose Me! Describe the skills your team has that make it the best choice for this game design. Maybe the team has access to a content expert, includes a famous game designer, has a track record of creating successful games, or possesses other skill that make the team uniquely qualified to create the proposed game. This should be stated.

Preproduction

Alright! You got the call, made the pitch to a publisher, and the publisher has agreed to accept your game *Elephant Fever.* Now, the game moves into the creation stages of the design process. The three stages of creation are preproduction, production, and post production. The production and post-production stages are discussed later.

Preproduction includes concept elaboration and prototyping. These tasks must happen before the production stage can begin. Preproduction is the stage of development where all concept and design decisions are made. The game is not being programmed and completed at this stage. The purpose of the preproduction stage is to create the design documents needed for the production stage.

Design documents contain all of the decisions used to make the game. Design documents can be very detailed and hundreds of pages long. Everything that has to be done to make the finished game must be included in the design documents. If something is not in the design documents, it will not be in the game. Engineers, artists, and programmers will refer to the design documents to make sure the work they are doing fits the concept of the game. When a complete set of design documents is finalized, the preproduction stage is over, as shown in **Figure 1-8.**

The creation stages of game development are done by a video game developer. A *developer* is a game-design studio that is responsible for creating all of the art, sounds, programming, and design elements of the video game. Many publishers own developers, such as the EA Sports Tiburon studio owned by Electronic Arts. The game concept is passed from the publisher to developer to begin the preproduction phase.

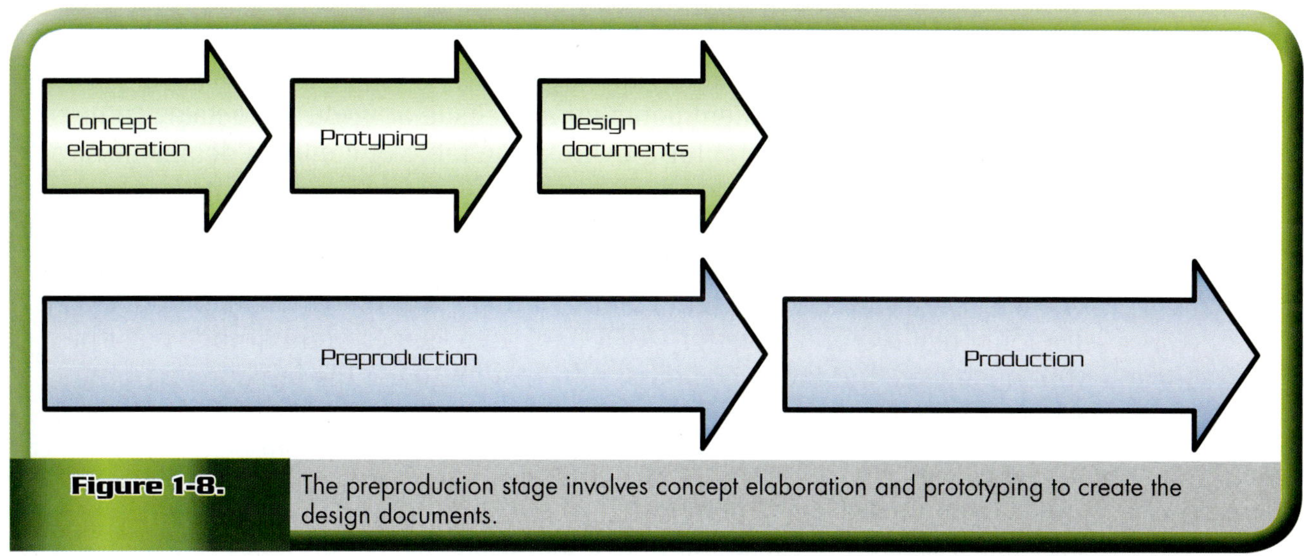

Figure 1-8. The preproduction stage involves concept elaboration and prototyping to create the design documents.

Goodheart-Willcox Publisher

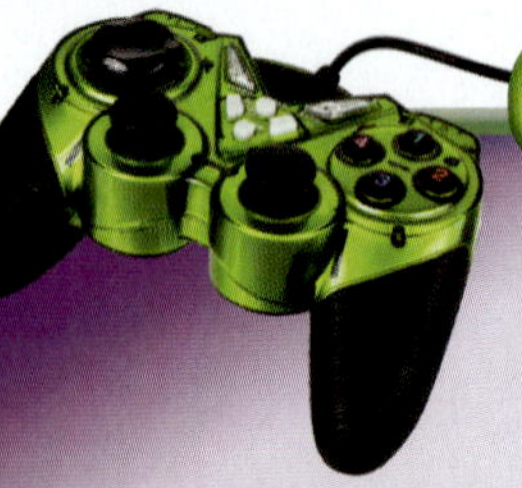

CHEAT CODE: GAME DESIGNER

A game designer works for the developer. The main tasks for a designer are to create the structure of the game and dream up great interactions within the game. Designers weave together all of the story threads, player interaction threads, character development threads, and many other threads to create the fabric of the game.

Concept Elaboration

Preproduction begins with concept elaboration. In concept elaboration, the idea from the pitch is refined and expanded to include all of the information about the game build. The basic idea from the original concept will need to have far more detail added to create a viable game. A team of **game designers** and subject matter experts work on the concept to elaborate, or expand, the idea to determine all of the elements needed for a game to work properly.

Subject matter experts contribute knowledge specific to any real-world elements represented in the game. Your great idea for a game may involve a realistic representation of World War II combat. A subject matter expert will have detailed knowledge of World War II battles and weapons to help guide the design team in creating realistic troop movements and tactics. This person would also know the types of weapons used in World War II, ammo, specifications, and limitations of each weapon so the game can be programmed as realistically as possible.

All of the concept elaboration information is recorded in design documents with more detailed information than the pitch documents. The resulting collection of design documents is called the ***governing game design document (GGDD).*** The GGDD will likely be 150–400 pages in length and take 400–1,000 hours to construct, depending on the scope of the game project.

The GGDD is used as a reference for everybody working on the project. Only the details that are needed to do the job correctly need to be included in the GGDD. Include as much information as needed on each topic and always allow for changes that will occur. This document is a work of communication. Do not make a large document filled with fluff. Everybody should be able to use the table of contents to quickly locate the needed information.

Figure 1-9 shows a partial template for a GGDD. The full template can be downloaded from the student companion website at www.g-wlearning.com. There is no standard format for a GGDD. The table of contents details most of the common major components. The order of the table of contents is also not standardized. If you search the Internet, you may find examples of GGDDs that are quite different. A game like *Bejeweled* has a very different GGDD than *Call of Duty.* They are very different games with very different game components. The only real requirements for GGDDs for your games are that they must be well organized and include enough information to get the job done properly.

Prototyping

As the design documents make it into final form, a small group of artists and programmers will be assigned to create a prototype. A ***prototype*** is a very basic version of the game to test that the concept can be constructed.

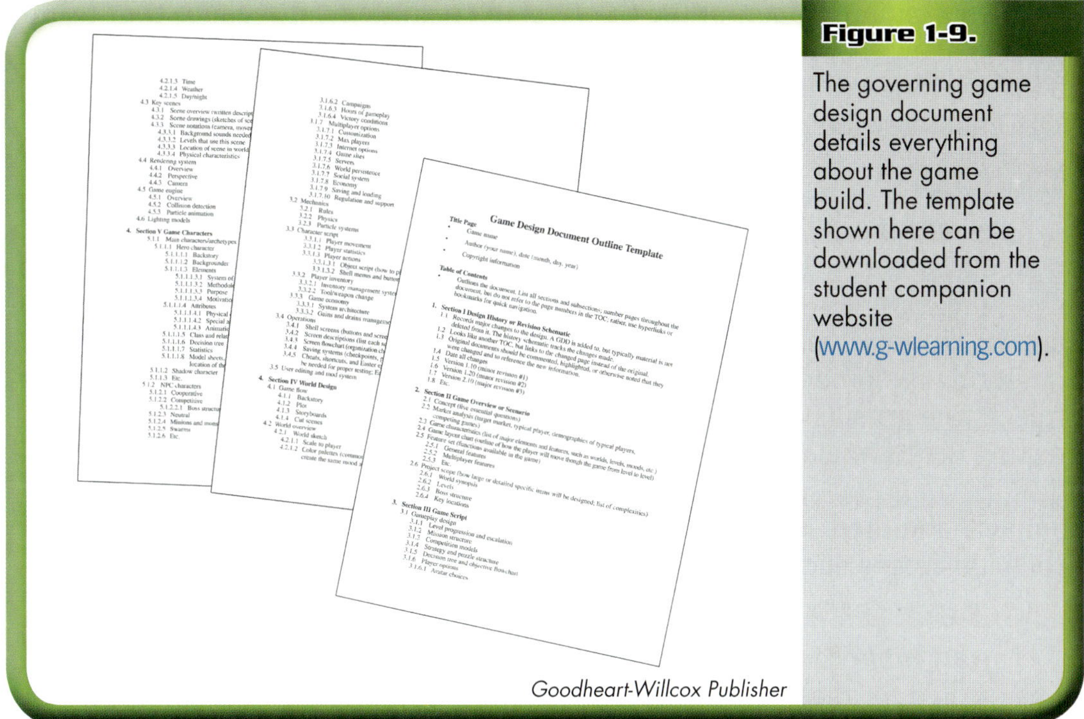

Goodheart-Willcox Publisher

Figure 1-9.

The governing game design document details everything about the game build. The template shown here can be downloaded from the student companion website (www.g-wlearning.com).

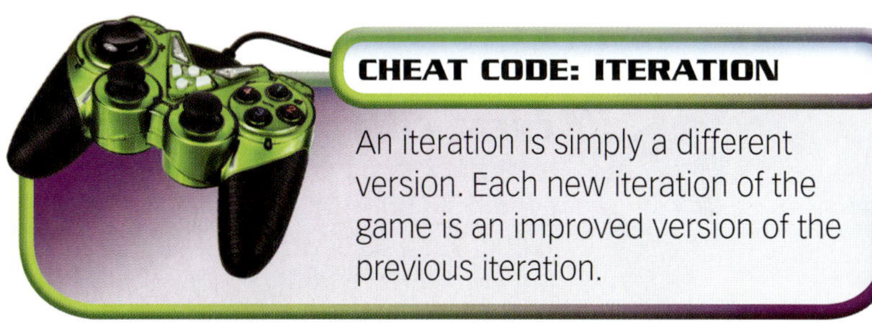

CHEAT CODE: ITERATION

An iteration is simply a different version. Each new iteration of the game is an improved version of the previous iteration.

The prototype is also known as the first **iteration** of the game build. The main function of the prototype is to be a proof of concept. The ***proof of concept*** shows that the concept can work. It tests all of the functions of the gameplay that are unique and different and is evidence that these ideas can be constructed. The prototype may be constructed with simple software, basic graphics, and little or no sound. Often, very little of the prototype is used in the actual finished game, it is just a proof of concept test build.

The prototype and the design documents are used to sell the game to the publisher and get approval to begin the production stage. In most cases, the game concept will only get provisional approval. ***Provisional approval*** means approval has been given to start the project, but only to a point before additional approval must be obtained to finish the project. It provides a small budget and short time frame to make it through the preproduction stage. The producer will monitor the team's progress and work ethics in addition to the game design skills.

Soft skills are personal qualities and behaviors, such as punctuality, teamwork, and attitude. These are just as important as hard skills. *Hard skills* are the technical abilities a person possesses. If the producer feels that your team does not have the soft and hard skills to get the job done, the project may be canceled or reassigned to a different design team. If your team does not meet deadlines, fights amongst itself, has bad attitudes, or exhibits other problems, your team will likely not get past the provisional approval.

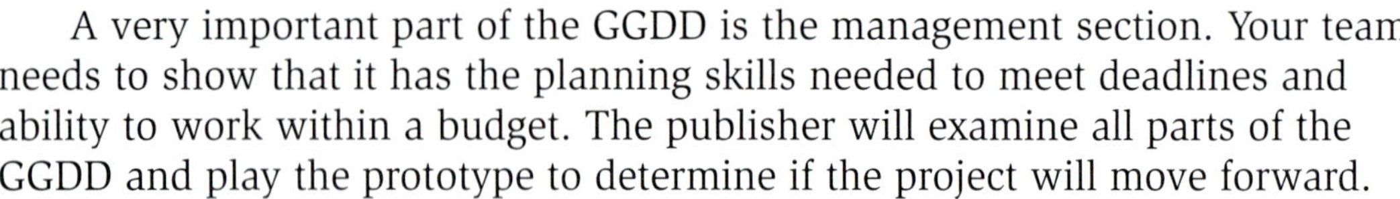

A very important part of the GGDD is the management section. Your team needs to show that it has the planning skills needed to meet deadlines and ability to work within a budget. The publisher will examine all parts of the GGDD and play the prototype to determine if the project will move forward.

Production

Congratulations! Your project has been approved! Your team can start working on production of the game build. ***Production*** is the stage where specialists such as artists, programmers, sound engineers, and other team members build all of the parts for the game and put them together to create a fully functioning game.

During the production stage, each of the specialists works on part of the project. The artists begin creating the art bible and the programmers begin creating the technical bible. These bibles are extremely detailed binders filled with drawings and specifications. When the production process is mostly complete and there is a version of the game that plays from start to finish, the production stage ends and the post-production stage begins.

Art Bible

The ***art bible*** contains a drawing or mock-up for every **asset** that needs to be created for the game. A mock-up is a physical three-dimensional model of a character, building, weapon, or other game asset. An artist might sculpt a character in clay to better see it from all angles, as shown in **Figure 1-10.** A weapon may be made out of cardboard or plastic so the artists can see how it will work and move. These mock-ups help the game artists see how to apply weight and balance to art assets. Photographs and sketches of these mock-ups are included in the art bible.

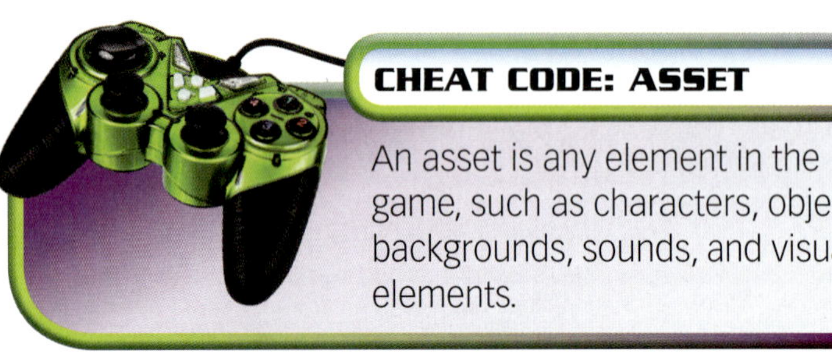

CHEAT CODE: ASSET

An asset is any element in the game, such as characters, objects, backgrounds, sounds, and visual elements.

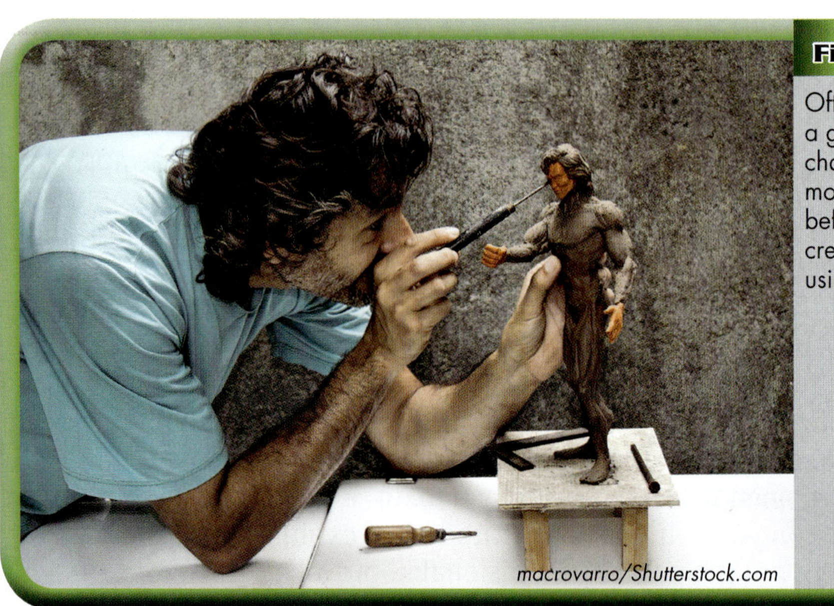

macrovarro/Shutterstock.com

Figure 1-10.

Often, assets for a game, such as characters, are modeled in clay before they are created electronically using a computer.

Artists are assigned the task of creating assets. Many times, the design company will use job-tracking sheets for each asset that needs to be created. A job-tracking sheet lists the name of the asset, its specifications, and the location where the completed asset will be stored. When the artist is assigned the task of creating the asset, he or she is given the job-tracking sheet. The artist then creates the art asset, uploads the file to the correct server location, signs the job-tracking sheet, and turns it in to the lead artist. The lead artist inspects the asset and either approves it or sends it back to the artist for revisions. This process is repeated until the entire art library is completed. For more about art construction, see the art chapter in this textbook.

Technical Bible

The ***technical bible*** is a binder filled with all of the programming structure for the game. The technical bible shows a flowchart of programming processes and network diagrams. These allow the individual programmers to know what they are required to do. A team of programmers will work on parts of the overall programming code and create subroutines for each interaction.

A ***subroutine*** is a group of code within the main game program that controls a segment of the overall program function. For example, a programmer might write a subroutine called **JUMP**. This subroutine controls the movement and physics of a jump movement by the character. The physics are simulated in the game environment. The **JUMP** subroutine alters the gravity setting and sets the strength of the upward movement to simulate a jump in the game. The subroutine that controls the user interface will call the **JUMP** subroutine when the player presses the correct button. The *user interface* is the system of controls and feedback that allows the player (user) to interact with the game. The statement that calls the **JUMP** subroutine might look like this:

IF the player presses the [↑] button, **THEN** the character will jump.

In this example, the [↑] button is the input for the user interface. The **JUMP** subroutine is executed when the player presses the [↑] button.

To create a complete game, there are many layers of programming that need to be coded. The assignments and specifications for all of these layers are included in the technical bible. For more about game programming, see the programming chapter in this textbook.

Engineered Game Assets

Engineers also create game assets. Engineers create the sounds and controllers for the game. If the game needs a custom controller, like the guitar controller used in *Guitar Hero,* then an engineer needs to create this device. Additionally, sound engineers create the many sounds used in the game. Everything from the noise a door makes as it is opened to the words spoken by a character need to be created, edited, and stored, as shown in **Figure 1-11.**

Level Design

Level designers assemble all of the assets and programming into a complete game level. Each part must work perfectly with all the other parts. Additionally, all the controls, menus, and GUI buttons have to work. ***Graphical user interface (GUI)*** refers to the buttons, icons, and other graphics that are needed

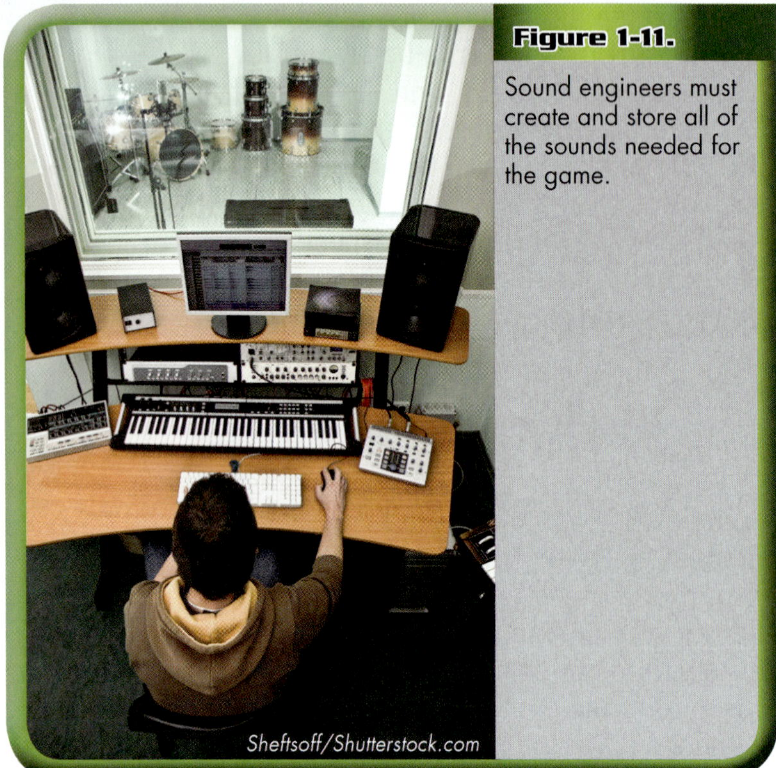

Figure 1-11.
Sound engineers must create and store all of the sounds needed for the game.

to work the game interface. This may be as simple as a **Continue** button after a cut scene or short movie segment. All of the parts of each level need to be in the right place and properly interact with other game elements. The level designer makes sure everything fits together correctly.

First Playable Level

The first **milestone** of the production stage is called the first playable level. The ***first playable level*** is the first iteration of the game's first level that can be played and tested. Unlike the prototype, the first playable level will be used in the actual game. With more refinement, each iteration of this level will get better and better until it is finished and ready to become part of the game.

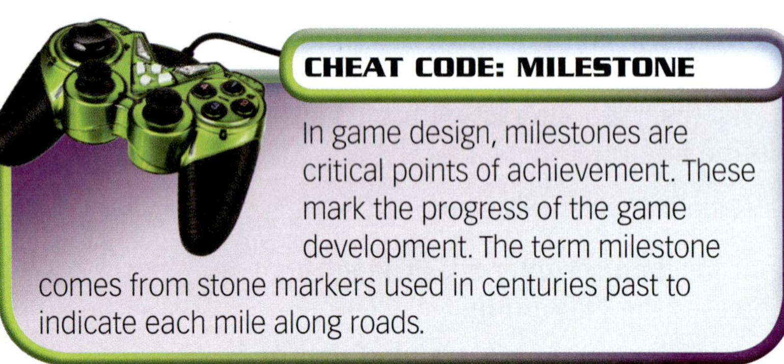

CHEAT CODE: MILESTONE

In game design, milestones are critical points of achievement. These mark the progress of the game development. The term milestone comes from stone markers used in centuries past to indicate each mile along roads.

Design Team Meetings, Game Revisions, and Project Management

During the production stage, the design team has many meetings to discuss progress and issues with the game project. Often, minor changes are made to the game based on these issues. Sometimes, however, major changes to the game are needed. All changes are recorded in the GGDD on the design history or revision schematic.

Minor issues might be changing a character design or the layout of the start page. When these revisions are made, the game typically is issued a revision number, such as version 1.10. This notation shows that the game is still in its first major version (1.xx), but it has been revised once (x.10).

A major change might include altering the structure of the opponent, using different network architecture, or switching to different game-engine software. Major changes result in a new version, which is indicated with a new version number. After the first major change, the version number becomes version 2.00. A minor revision to version 2.00 results in updating the version number to version 2.10. Each change is updated in the GGDD so the team understands how to modify any elements of the game.

The budget and deadlines will also be an important part of many design team meetings. Production schedules are very tight. A team member may be waiting on a character before he or she can begin the animation set. This waiting holds up the entire process. Detailed production schedules are shown graphically using a Gantt chart or other task organization document.

In a ***Gantt chart,*** the project is broken down into tasks and subtasks, a length of time is assigned to each task, and tasks that must be performed before other tasks are identified. **Figure 1-12** shows a sample Gantt chart in one type of project-management software. Many types of project-management software are available to help organize large projects. A software package like Microsoft Project can be used to create many organization and Gantt charts to schedule work and track progress. Microsoft Excel or Access can also be used to create a Gantt chart. As a project gets larger, more specialized project management software will be required to keep up with the project. Weekly meetings can provide the information to help update these charts.

The ***critical path method (CPM)*** is often built into a Gantt chart or **PERT** diagram. When managing a project using CPM, all tasks are first prioritized. The next step is to find dependencies for each task. A dependent task requires the completion of other tasks before this one can begin. If you think about building a house, the roof has dependency on the walls, and the walls have dependency on the foundation. The CPM would identify these

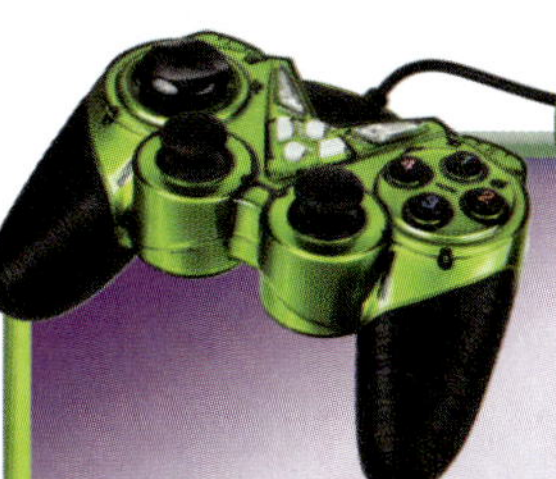

CHEAT CODE: PERT

In a project evaluation and review technique (PERT) diagram, the milestones for the project and the estimated completion time for each milestone are mapped. Each milestone can branch to other milestones in the series from beginning to end. Parallel branches indicate milestones that are not dependent. All parallel branches converge by the end of the diagram as all the milestones are assembled in the final stage of the project.

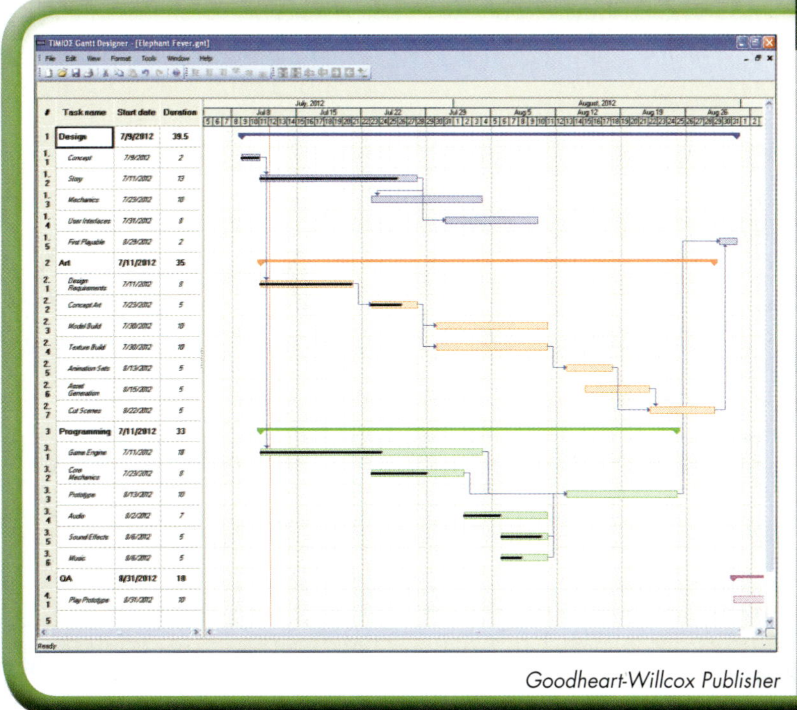

Goodheart-Willcox Publisher

Figure 1-12.

Using a Gantt chart is a good way to keep track of which tasks need to be completed before others and the progress of each task.

dependencies. Tasks are then scheduled in the most efficient progression. The tasks are then analyzed to find how the project can be fast tracked.

To ***fast track*** a project, analyze tasks to find which can be done in parallel, or at the same time. For example, a project can be fast tracked by completing the art at the same time as the sound is being done. Since these tasks are not dependent on each other, they can be done in parallel. This is shown in the Gantt chart in **Figure 1-12.**

Post Production

Post production is what happens immediately after the production stage is complete. ***Post production*** includes testing, tuning, and distribution, as shown in **Figure 1-13.** When most of the game is assembled it is called the *alpha version.* This is usually the milestone in the design process where the post-production stage begins. An alpha version should have all of the level starting screens, gameplay level, user interface, and end screens completed. The only real changes needed to the alpha should be error fixes.

Testing

Game testers known as the *quality-assurance (QA) team* go into full swing with the release of the alpha version to testing. As the game levels are completed, they need to be tested. Functionality testing and playability testing are done continuously to find and report all the errors in the game. The QA team must make sure that everything works! The production team works hard to fix errors as they are reported.

Game testers start the functionality testing of components for each level. ***Functionality testing*** is the process of evaluating if everything works the way it should. Functionality testing is often automated with computers. Computers are programmed to play the games and track errors. This allows the human game testers to focus on playability testing. ***Playability testing*** checks to see if the level difficulty is appropriate for a human player, makes sure the story flows, and verifies that objectives can be achieved.

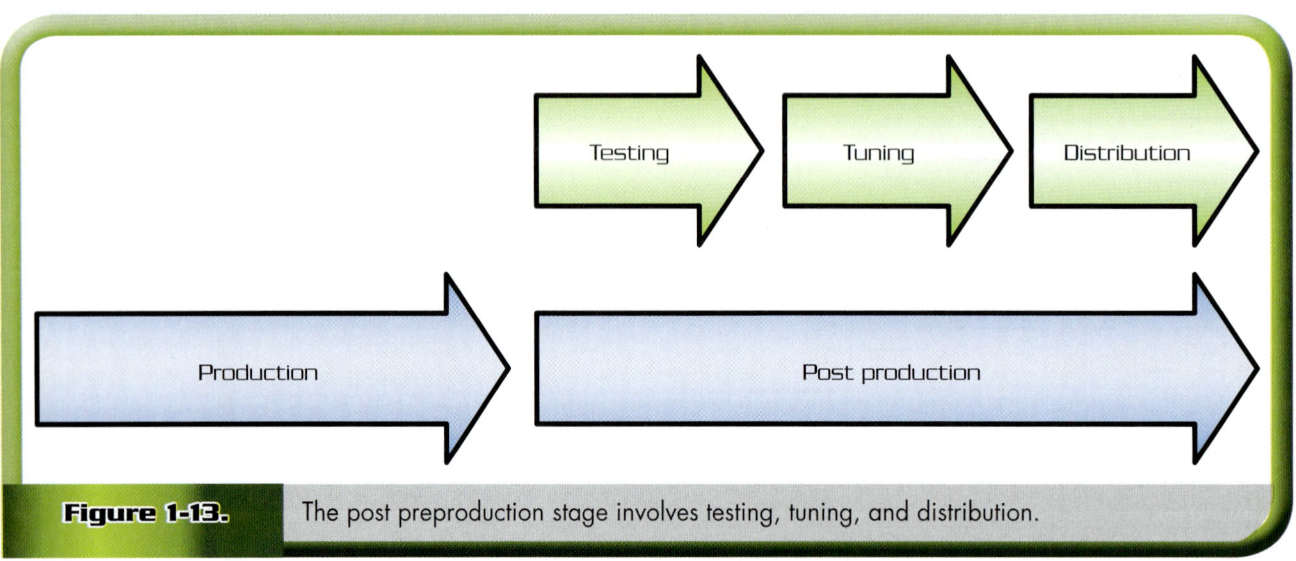

Figure 1-13. The post preproduction stage involves testing, tuning, and distribution.

Goodheart-Willcox Publisher

When an error is found, a bug report is created. A ***bug report*** is a document that lists the error, the location in the game, how the error occurs, and how important the error is. The bug report is sent back to the design team who will prioritize the errors. The most important bugs are fixed first. Sometimes, the least important bugs are not fixed. The importance level of an error is called the *bug type* or *bug level,* as shown in **Figure 1-14.**

It would be great if every bug could be fixed, but the team typically runs out of time and money. The budget is a major reason why games ship with errors. The design team needs to spend its money wisely to get the most done with the time and money available. A project goes ***over budget*** when more money is spent than was allowed for the project. Remember, time is money. When a production team of 100 people takes one week longer to build the game than was estimated, then the project will cost much more than planned. Imagine that each person makes $1,000 per week. A one-week delay will cost $100,000 ($1,000 per person × 100 people = $100,000).

Bug Type	Meaning	Examples
A	**Major problem!** The game cannot be released with this bug.	• Game is not fun to play. • Virus in game. • Game crashes. • Game features do not work properly. • Level is too difficult to complete. • Spelling errors. • Legal errors.
B	**Big problem!** The game can be released with this bug, but it will receive bad reviews for the error.	• Gameplay can typically be maintained. • Some features missing. • Graphic errors to backgrounds or other nonessential areas. • Incomplete menu or menu has options that are never available. • Levels are too easy to complete.
C	**Common problem.** This should be fixed if time permits, but release of the game will not be delayed by this bug. The easy fixes get done, while the difficult fixes are not done.	• Gameplay is uninterrupted by the error. • A minor problem that may be noted as a glitch by critics. • A problem that is not likely to be experienced by most players. • An error that is hard to duplicate.
D	**Suggested feature.** This bug will likely not be fixed prior to releasing the game unless there is remaining time.	• Gameplay is uninterrupted, but could be enhanced. • Adding a feature might make the gameplay better. • New technology could be applied. • Two buttons might be hard to press at the same time to activate a weapon.

Figure 1-14. Bugs are classified by level, or how important they are to fix.

Goodheart-Willcox Publisher

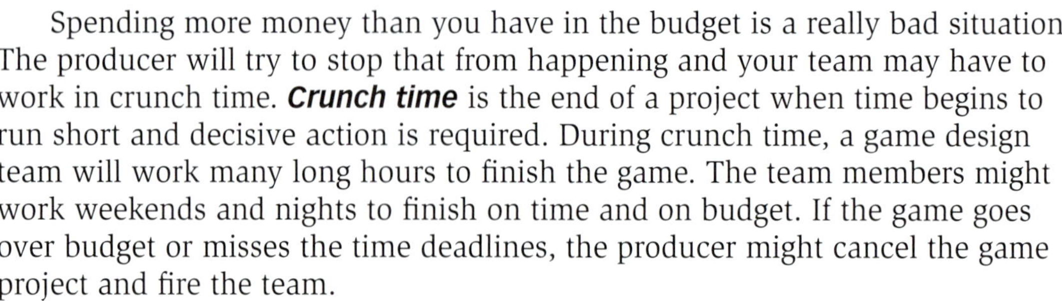

Spending more money than you have in the budget is a really bad situation. The producer will try to stop that from happening and your team may have to work in crunch time. ***Crunch time*** is the end of a project when time begins to run short and decisive action is required. During crunch time, a game design team will work many long hours to finish the game. The team members might work weekends and nights to finish on time and on budget. If the game goes over budget or misses the time deadlines, the producer might cancel the game project and fire the team.

Tuning

While the testing work is moving forward, another group of designers are working on tuning. *Tuning* is where the game is polished to perfection. The idea is not to add more features to the game, but to make all of the parts work perfectly together. Having a game with no bugs, no glitches, and no pointless activity will lead down the path to perfection.

A major part of tuning is actually removing parts of the game. The game must flow and keep with the story. If a section of gameplay does not add to the story or excitement, this will be identified during tuning and that part of the game will be taken out. It is better to have a really nice finished game than lots of frustrating dead ends.

When the alpha version has gone through testing and tuning, it enters the beta versions. A *beta version* is a more polished iteration of the alpha version. Beta versions are usually very close to the actual game that will be released to the public. Beta testing is done by a large number of different types of users.

Beta versions are released to loyal customers and players, called *beta testers,* as trial versions before the game is available to the general public. The idea is that actual players do not always follow the same path in playing the game as the designers. They do things very differently, and they find different problems. The design team evaluates the bugs reported by beta testers, ranks the bugs, and determines which ones to fix and the solutions.

Many game studios offer people like you the opportunity to beta test a game or level. Go to the website for various game studios and look for information on their beta testing program. You can apply to become a beta tester and just might get selected.

Another important decision for the publisher when the game is in the tuning stage is related to porting. ***Porting*** is converting a game from one platform to another. For example, a game may be programmed for the PlayStation 3 platform and then ported to the iPad platform. With two platforms available, the publisher has more potential customers who can purchase the game. Porting is a very efficient way to get your game in front of more potential buyers.

When all testing and tuning are complete, the game is finalized as ***ready to market (RTM).*** The RTM version is provided to the publisher as a gold master. The *gold master* is the disc containing the perfected final game that is used as the original from which all other copies will be made. The game in the package at a store or downloaded from the player's network is a copy of the original gold master disc. The publisher will create a game case, game manual, box, and other materials to package the game disc. When all of the packaging is complete and assembled with the duplicated discs, the games are ready to send to customers, as shown in **Figure 1-15.**

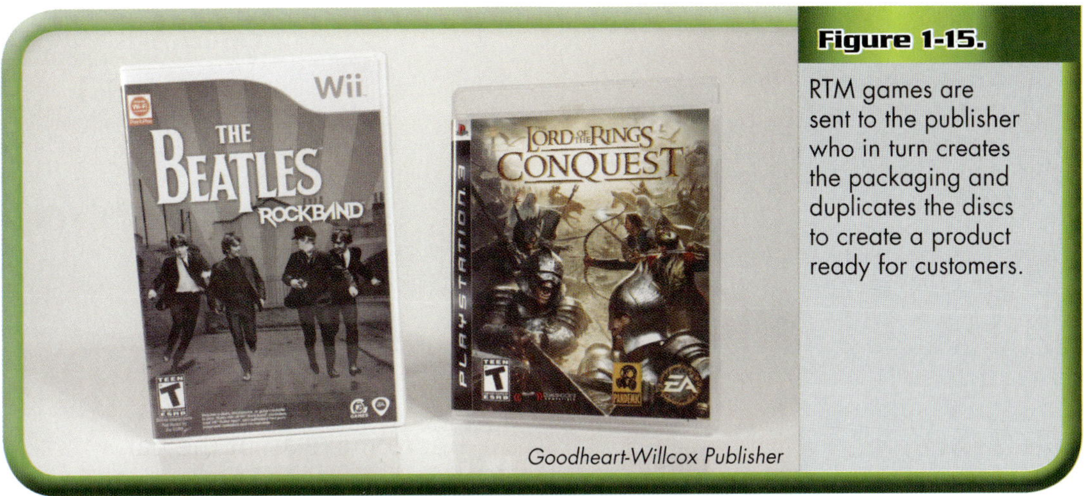

Goodheart-Willcox Publisher

Figure 1-15.
RTM games are sent to the publisher who in turn creates the packaging and duplicates the discs to create a product ready for customers.

Distribution

Distribution is how a game is sent to the customer. Today, a game can be released on a disc, online, as an app, or as a coin-operated cabinet. These are called *channels.* Often, games are released in more than one distribution channel. The publisher decides how the game will be sold to the public and which channels of distribution will be used. A *channel of distribution* is a chain of stops the product makes from the publisher to the final user. This is often a very complex supply chain that links all of the people needed to transport, buy, and resell the game before it gets in the customer's hands.

The most direct channel of distribution is direct marketing. In *direct marketing,* the publisher sells the game to the user. This is typically done through the publisher's website. A player can download the game or order a disc shipped directly from the publisher.

The next-most direct channel is reseller marketing. In *reseller marketing,* the publisher allows someone else to sell you the game. This is often done on an app market. A reseller such as iTunes will list many games for sale direct from the publisher. It is just a big store where you pull the product from the reseller. This works really well for online games and handheld device games. A game studio can act as its own publisher if it makes games for iPhone, iPad, Android, and other handheld devices. The apps can be sold directly from app stores that are linked to the handheld device. When someone buys and downloads the app, the game studio is paid a portion of the selling price. The reseller takes a percentage of the sale to cover its costs and make a profit.

The least direct distribution channel is retail marketing, **Figure 1-16.** In *retail marketing,* a boxed game is shipped from a manufacturing point and travels through several other points before reaching the customer. It is delivered by the publisher to the manufacturer. The manufacturer duplicates the discs and packages them in game boxes. The boxed games are put in larger boxes for shipping to a wholesale warehouse. A wholesale warehouse stores the large boxes of games before delivering them to retail stores. A customer visits the retail store and purchases the game from the store shelf. Along the way, each company in the supply chain takes a small percentage of the selling price to cover its overhead and make a profit.

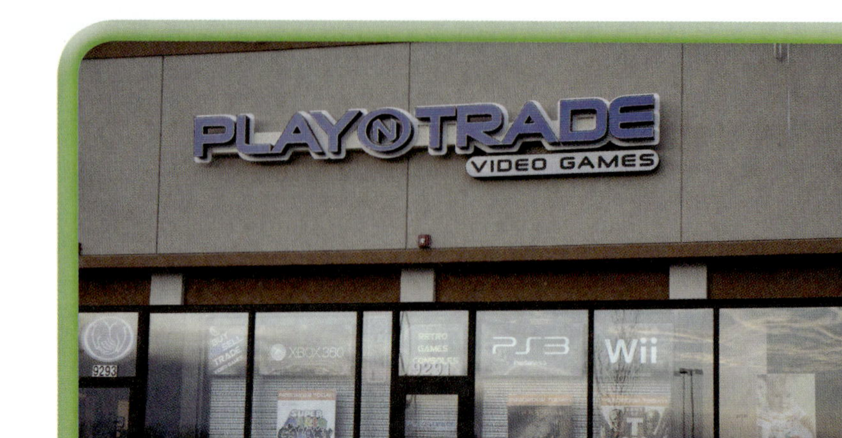

Goodheart-Willcox Publisher

Figure 1-16.

In retail distribution, a game makes many stops before reaching the retail store where the customer purchases it.

Patches and Return Distribution

When a customer purchases a game and it does not work, the game has to be fixed or refunded. If the problem is related to manufacturing the disc, the customer can take the game back for a replacement, if the seller accepts returns. If the problem is in the game itself, the publisher would rather fix the game than give the customer his or her money back.

When customers report problems with the game, the publisher creates error reports. These reports are then sent to the game studio where the bugs are prioritized. The bugs are fixed in order of priority. After bugs have been fixed, a game patch is issued. A ***patch*** is a software installation program that fixes known bugs or damaged programming. The game studio gives the patch to the publisher so it can be distributed to customers.

In many cases, the publisher will try to put a positive spin on patches that fix bugs. Instead of saying the game has bugs that need to be fixed, the publisher will tell the customers that the game needs an upgrade. You have probably had many games that as soon as you launch the game told you there was an upgraded version for you to install. You were happy to get an upgrade, right? An upgrade sounds so much better than a patch that fixes errors. When the game is upgraded, the customer is often downloading a patch that fixes errors. The customer gets to play the newest version of the game without ever knowing about the errors that were fixed.

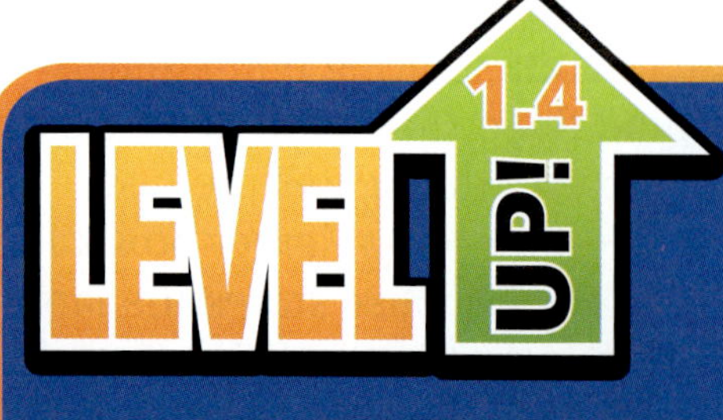

Think about the differences between distribution of downloadable games and games on disc. What are some major benefits to the publisher for distributing downloadable content? Why do customers like downloadable content? How does a customer benefit from buying the packaged disc version instead of a downloaded version?

Piracy

The entire video game design process is threatened by piracy. ***Piracy*** is the illegal copying or distribution of copyrighted material such as a video game. It is a form of theft. The person who sells or gives away a copy of the game takes money out of the supply chain. The publishers do not get paid. The designers do not get paid. Only the criminal gets paid.

Video game publishers and design studios often spend millions of dollars to make a video game. If the companies that make games do not receive money for their work, they will stop creating new games. Keep this in mind before you try to **jailbreak** your smartphone, download a serial number crack or keygen, or buy a pirated copy of a video game.

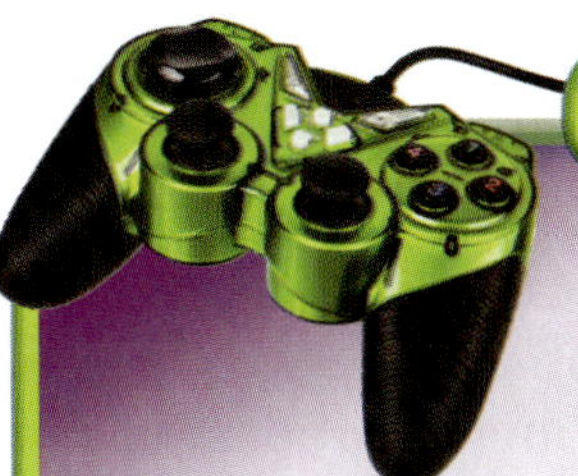

CHEAT CODE: JAILBREAK

To jailbreak a smartphone means altering the phone's operating system to allow greater control over the device. Generally, the term is used in relation to removing the restrictions on an iPhone, iPad, or iPod to allow apps to be purchased from somewhere other than the official Apple App Store.

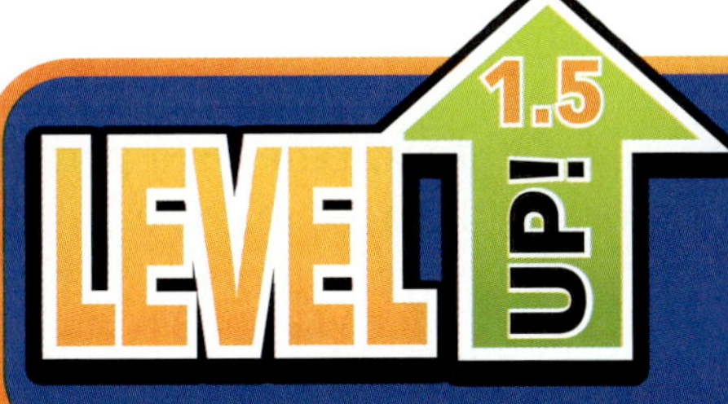

Research the topic of video game piracy. How much is it estimated that piracy cost the video game industry last year?

Types of Business Ownership

Businesses that create games are organized just like all other types of businesses. Additionally, there are several types of business ownership. The type of ownership will vary from one video game company to another. For example, a large video game publisher may have one type of ownership, but a small independent studio may have another type. There are four major types of business ownership: corporation, partnership, limited-liability company, and sole proprietorship.

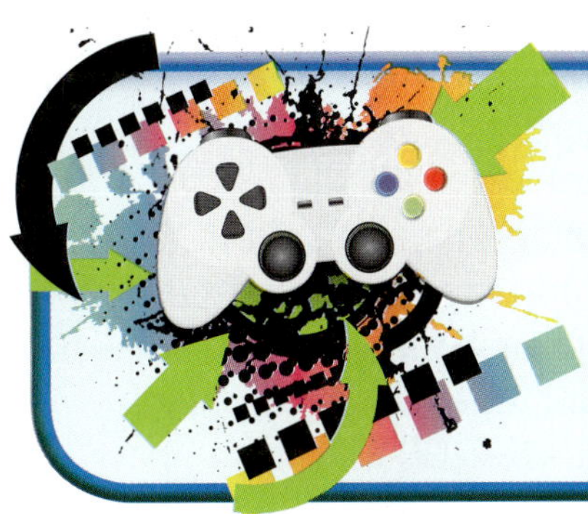

Ethical Gamer

Piracy of software is not only unethical, it is a crime. Downloading copyrighted games from file-sharing sites is piracy. Downloading cracks and keygens to unlock copy-protection measures is also piracy.

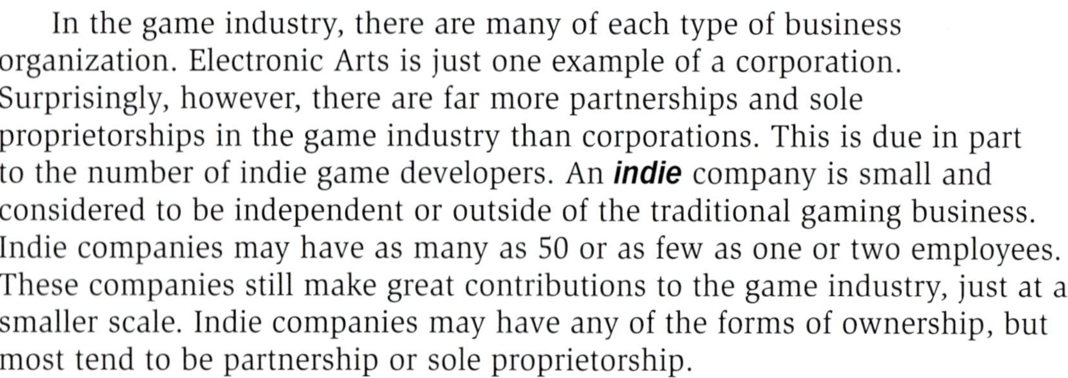

In the game industry, there are many of each type of business organization. Electronic Arts is just one example of a corporation. Surprisingly, however, there are far more partnerships and sole proprietorships in the game industry than corporations. This is due in part to the number of indie game developers. An ***indie*** company is small and considered to be independent or outside of the traditional gaming business. Indie companies may have as many as 50 or as few as one or two employees. These companies still make great contributions to the game industry, just at a smaller scale. Indie companies may have any of the forms of ownership, but most tend to be partnership or sole proprietorship.

Corporation

A *corporation* is a legal entity that limits the personal liabilities of its owners while being able to engage in activities such as entering into contracts, making money, and buying property. Liability is the responsibility for repayment of debt and financial judgments against an entity, such as a person or company. A corporation must file articles of incorporation in a state, which is not necessarily the state where the corporation is physically located. The *articles of incorporation* is a charter that is a legal document outlining how the business will be organized and managed.

The structure of a corporation is highly regulated by local, state, and federal entities. One of the most regulated parts of a corporation is ownership. Corporations are owned by stockholders. A *stockholder* is a person or company who has purchased stock in the corporation. There may be thousands of stockholders for a single corporation. You or your parents may already own stock.

CASE STUDY

Mobile Apps

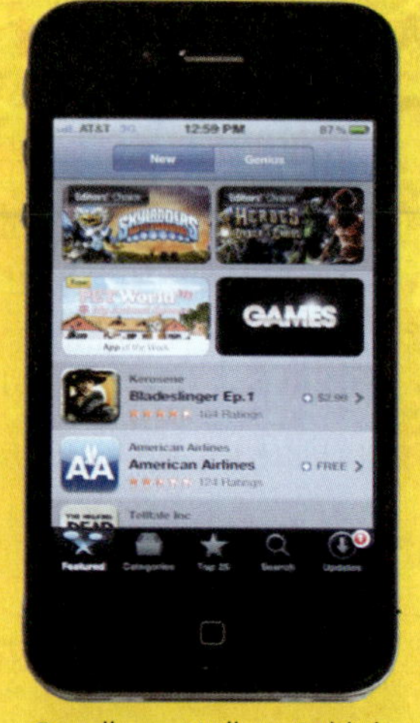

Goodheart-Willcox Publisher

A huge opportunity for indie companies is in mobile app development. A mobile app is a very small program that runs on a mobile device such as smartphone or tablet. Most mobile apps are limited in size so they can be stored on the small mobile device. Many are less than 20 megabytes to meet downloading and data restrictions. This is great news for small companies. A couple of designers working on weekends and evenings can produce a great app. Additionally, apps are very easy to sell. You do not need to get publishers and producers. The mobile app can be sold in a mobile app marketplace like iTunes. The indie company simply submits its app to the mobile app store for review. If there are no problems, the app may get approved and be listed at the app store for sale. Users can begin downloading the game as soon as it is posted.

Stock is a legal document for ownership of a portion of a corporation. In most cases, a corporation will issue thousands of ownership shares of stock. Larger companies like Apple or Microsoft will issue millions of shares. The percentage of ownership depends on how many shares you own versus how many shares are outstanding. For example, if you own 100 shares of stock and there are 10,000 shares outstanding; you own 1 percent of the corporation (10,000 ÷ 100 = 0.01 or 1 percent).

Investors buy stock in the hope that the corporation will make money and the value of the stock will increase. An investor may receive a stock dividend from the stock they own. A *stock dividend* is an amount of money paid to the owners of the company stock as their portion of the profits made by the company. Some companies distribute much of their profits in dividends, while other companies pay little or no money in dividends.

If the company does not pay dividends, then to make money the investor must rely on the price of the stock to increase. If you buy a stock for $10.00 per share and the company does well, the price may increase to $15.00 per share. If you could sell your stock at $15.00, you make a 50 percent profit on your investment.

$15.00 sale price – $10.00 purchase price = $5.00 profit
$5.00 profit ÷ $10.00 investment = 0.50 or 50 percent profit

You could also hold your stock and hope the stock price goes higher so you can sell it for more money later. Be careful, stock prices go up and down. If you sell stock for less than you paid for it, you have lost money. You can also lose money if the company goes out of business and the stock becomes worthless.

Partnership

A *partnership* is an agreement between two or more people to open a business together. It is a simpler business organization than a corporation, but all liability is assumed by the partners. While not legally required, a partnership should have a partnership agreement that details the ownership rights and organization of the company. There is far less governmental regulation over partnership agreements than corporations.

An equal partnership is one in which all parties own an equal share of the company. However, in many cases, one partner owns a higher percentage of the company than the other partner or partners. For example three people may be partners in a company with one person owning 50 percent and the other two owning 25 percent each.

A *limited partnership* is one in which at least one of the partners is just an investor and does not participate in the running of the company. For example, a limited partner might purchase 20 percent of the company, but cannot be involved in the day-to-day running of the business. The limited partner is a silent partner. If the silent partner becomes involved in the operations of the business, the ownership type becomes a general partnership as described above. A limited partner has limited liability and can only lose the amount invested.

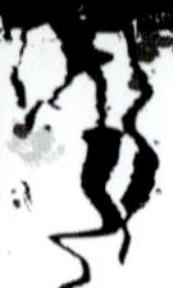

Limited-Liability Ownership

A limited partnership must carry the designation of LLP or LLC. *Limited liability company (LLC)* and *limited liability partnership (LLP)* are hybrids of a corporation and a partnership. Each takes portions of the partnership and corporation ownership types. An LLC or LLP limits the personal liability for its owners, similar to a corporation. However, an LLC or LLP has fewer regulations than a corporation, but more than a partnership. An LLC or LLP form of ownership is often attractive to small businesses. However, some states do not allow these forms of ownership.

Sole Proprietorship

A *sole proprietorship* is established when a single person opens a business. There is no legal separation between the business and the owner. All liability is assumed by the sole proprietor. However, there is very little government regulation of a sole proprietorship. A sole proprietorship is the simplest form of business ownership. You could go into business for yourself tomorrow as a sole proprietorship.

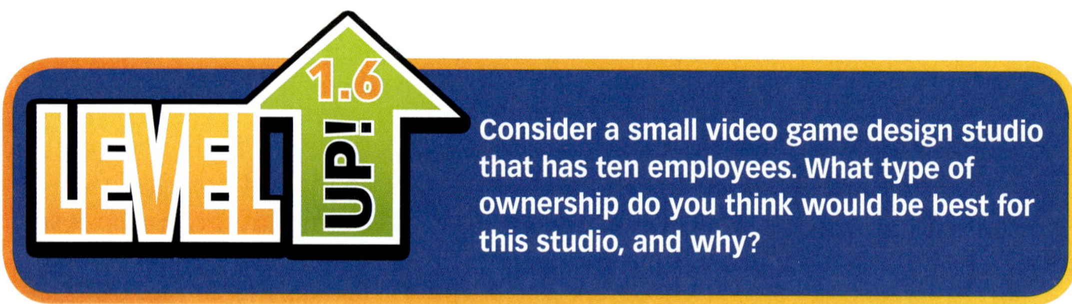

Consider a small video game design studio that has ten employees. What type of ownership do you think would be best for this studio, and why?

Chapter Summary

- A game has three components: game environment, rules, and a victory condition; if any one of these is missing, it is a toy, not a game.
- A video game design team consists of specialists such as: producer, creative director, project manager, lead, artist, programmer, engineer, and game writer.
- The life cycle, or scope, of a video game begins with an idea for a game and ends when the game is no longer being supported.
- The five Ps that guide the development of most video games are: pitch, preproduction, production, post production, and patches.
- Piracy is the illegal copying or distribution of copyrighted material, which leads to video game designers losing money.
- The four major types of business ownership are: corporations, partnerships, limited-liability ownerships, and sole proprietorships.

Check Your Video Game IQ

Now that you have finished this chapter, see what you know about video game design by taking the chapter posttest.

www.m.g-wlearning.com

www.g-wlearning.com

Review Your Knowledge

On a separate sheet of paper or in a word processing document, match the following terms with the definition that fits best.

A. first playable level	F. game-treatment document
B. game environment	G. video game publisher
C. pitch document	H. game designer
D. playability testing	I. magic circle
E. core mechanics	J. prototype

1. The person for whom the main task is to create the structure of the game and interactions within the game.
2. The way in which the rules and game environment create structured play.
3. Document that explains the vision of the game in great detail.
4. A very basic version of the game to test that the concept can be constructed.
5. The computer programming used to enforce the rules.
6. A check to see if the level difficulty is appropriate for a human player, make sure the story flows, and verify that objectives can be achieved.
7. An area specifically designed to enable gameplay.
8. The first iteration of the game's first level that can be played and tested.
9. Overseer of the entire process of bringing the video game to the retail market.
10. Document used to sell the game idea to the video game publisher.

On a separate sheet of paper or in a word processing document, answer each of the following questions.

11. What components are required to create a game?
12. What is a triple-A game?
13. What is a high-concept document?
14. What main duties are performed in preproduction.
15. What is a prototype game?
16. What is a mock-up?
17. Describe how the version numbering system works?
18. What is the difference between a level A bug and a level D bug?
19. Describe what occurs in the beta stage of post-production.
20. How does piracy cause game developers to go out of business?

Apply Your STEM Knowledge

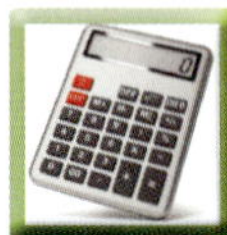

Mathematics

1. A game project employs 40 employees at an average rate of $240 per employee per day. Use this information to solve for answers below.
   A. What is the total employee expense for one day?
   B. Assuming a work day is only eight hours, what is the average hourly rate for an average employee?
   C. If the project does not meet the deadline by six days, calculating just employee expense, how far over budget is the project?
   D. If the game is direct marketed and sells for $40, how many games would need to be sold to cover the over-budget employee expense?
   E. How much would the company spend in average employee expenses if the game takes 120 days to create?
   F. If piracy reduces the amount of total sales by 20 percent, how much money was lost due to piracy of a $40 game that sold 150,000 units?

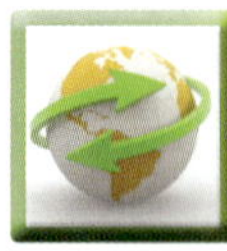

Social Studies

2. PERT and fast tracking require tasks to be performed in parallel to reduce the time it takes to complete a project. Parallel tasking, however, is not always a good thing. Research distracted driving behaviors and create a list of 12 common multitasking activities, like texting, that automobile drivers do while driving. Organize this list from most dangerous to least dangerous. Write a paragraph to explain your opinion of why drivers attempt parallel tasking while driving.

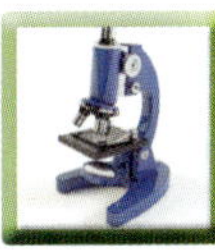

Science

3. The iterative process of game design means that several improved versions are constructed before making a final version. Research the scientific theory of human evolution through natural selection. Create a Microsoft PowerPoint presentation that describes how this theory uses different iterations of the human form. Alternatively, describe the interative process of the iPhone generations.

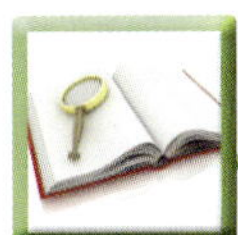

Language Arts

4. Use the Internet to research the most recent facts about video games from the Entertainment Software Association (www.theesa.com). Create a two minute PowerPoint and oral presentation to summarize the most interesting industry facts and statistics for the current year.

Language Arts

5. Prepare a PowerPoint presentation of up to ten slides (five to seven minutes) describing your findings or responses to each of the Level Up! activities in this chapter. Include text, pictures, video, animations, slide transitions, and sound effects as appropriate to help explain your positions.

Working in Teams

Form into teams as assigned by your instructor. Brainstorm ideas for a video game design. Prepare a presentation for the class describing the team's idea. Identify which team members will serve which roles on the video game design team. Each team member should explain his or her role on the video game design team to the class.

Gamer Portfolio

A portfolio is a selection of materials that you collect and organize to show your qualifications, skills, and talents. When you apply for a job, community service, or college, you will need a portfolio to showcase your qualifications for the opportunity for which you are applying.

There are two types of portfolios that are commonly used: print portfolio and electronic portfolio (e-portfolio). An e-portfolio is also known as a digital portfolio.

1. Use the Internet to search for *print portfolio* and *e-portfolio*. Summarize each type and create an overview of how to create each one.
2. You will be creating a portfolio in this class. Which portfolio type would you prefer to create? Write several paragraphs describing the type of portfolio you would prefer and why.

G-W Learning Mobile Site

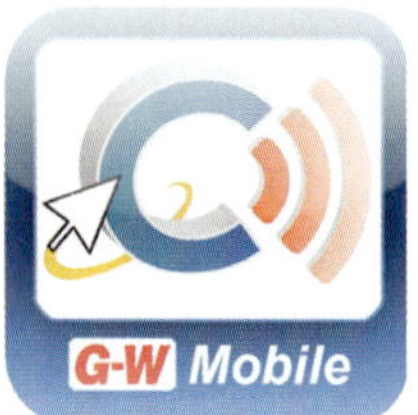

Visit the G-W Learning mobile site to complete the chapter pretest and posttest and to practice vocabulary using e-flash cards. If you do not have a smartphone, visit the G-W Learning companion website to access these features.

G-W Learning mobile site: www.m.g-wlearning.com

G-W Learning companion website: www.g-wlearning.com

Common Core

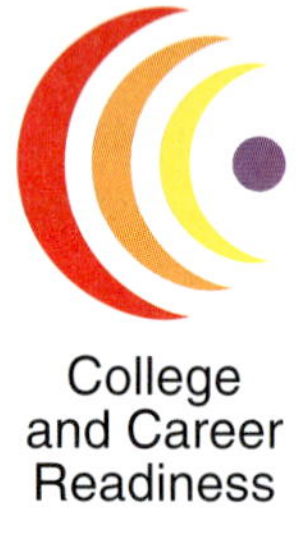

College and Career Readiness

CTE Career Ready Practices. For every action, there is a reaction whether it is immediately seen or not. There are positive and negative consequences for different actions and inactions. Make a list of five things that you have done for which there were either positive or negative consequences. Put a plus sign (+) beside the positive outcomes and a minus (–) sign beside the negative outcomes. What could you have done differently that would have changed each outcome?

Reading. Read a magazine, newspaper, or online article about the impact of technology on video games in the last decade. Determine the central ideas of the article and review the conclusions made by the author. Provide an accurate summary of your reading, making sure to incorporate the who, what, when, and how of the changes brought by technology.

Writing. Conduct a short research project to answer the question, "How do copyrights protect video game designers?" Write your report using information from multiple sources.

Event Prep: Student Organizations

Professional student organizations are a valuable asset to any educational program. These organizations support student learning and application of skills learned to be applied in real-world situations. Also, participation in career and technology education student organizations can promote lifelong responsibility for community service and professional development. There are a variety of organizations from which to select, depending on the goals of your educational programs. To prepare for any competitive event:

1. Contact the organization before the next competition. This gives you time to review and decide which competitive events are correct for you or your team.
2. Read all the guidelines closely. These rules and regulations must be strictly adhered to or disqualification can occur.
3. Competitive events may be written, oral, or a combination of both.

4. Communication plays a role in all the competitive events, so read which communication skills are covered for the event you select. Research and preparation are important keys to successful competition.
5. Go to the website of your organization for specific information for the events. Visit the site often as information changes quickly.
6. Select one or two events that are of interest to you. Print the information for the events and discuss your interest with your instructor.

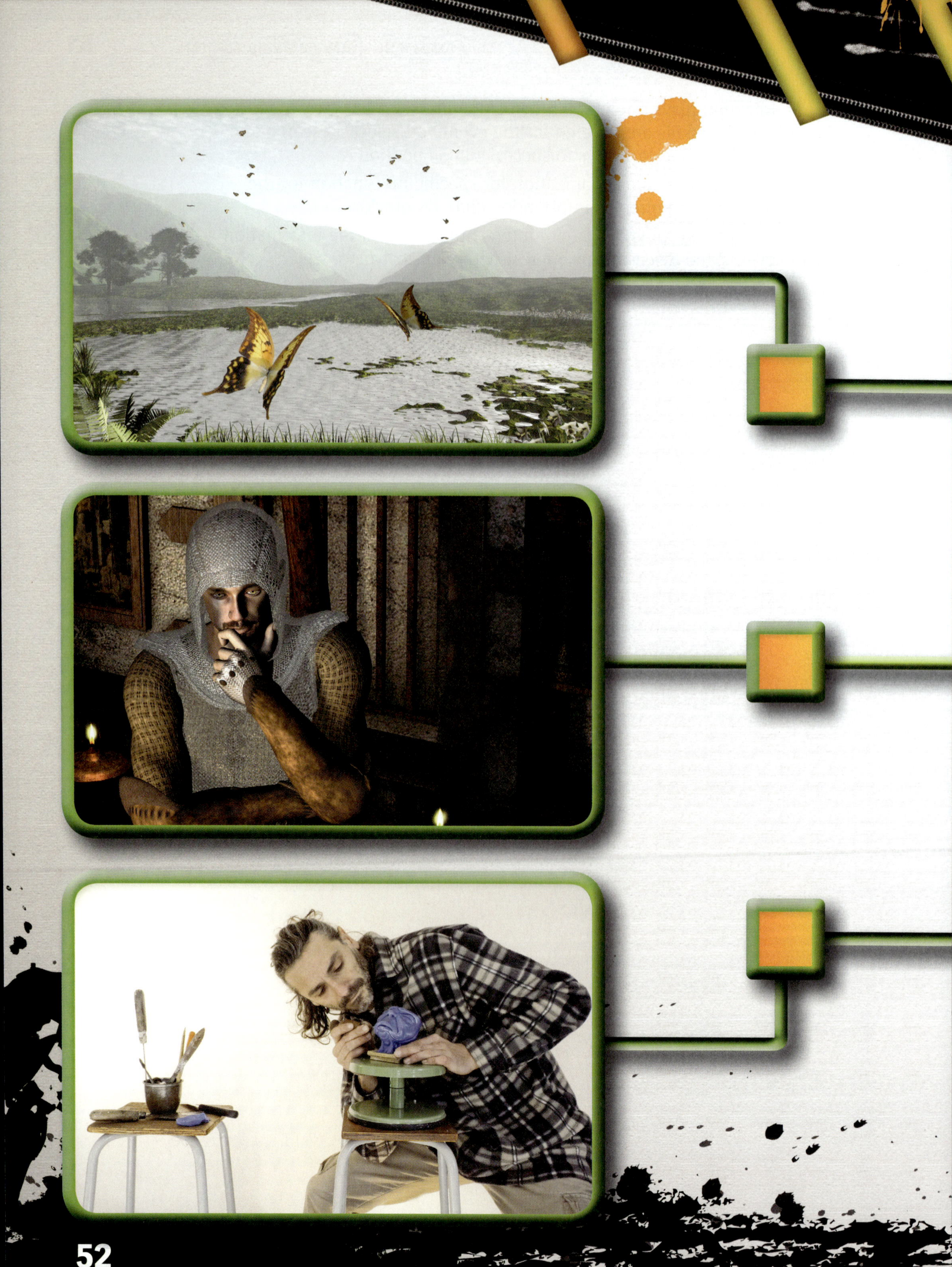

Chapter 2
Character Composition

In this chapter, you will learn how a character is developed and then interpreted into the final artistic design and movement for the game. It takes many parts to assemble a memorable character. With an interactive art form such as a video game, a character can be defined by how it looks, acts, and speaks. A great character will fit the story and be believable. It can be an important asset in the success of a game.

Check Your Video Game IQ

Before you begin this chapter, see what you already know about video game design by taking the chapter pretest.

www.m.g-wlearning.com

www.g-wlearning.com

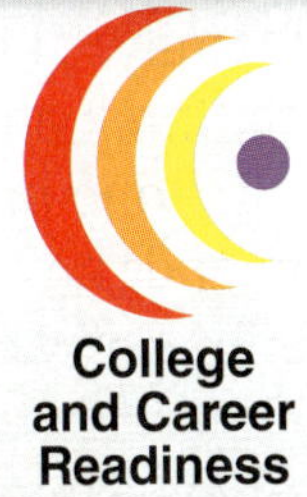

Reading Prep. Before reading, observe the objectives for this chapter. Keep these in mind as you read, and focus on the structure of the author's writing—was the information presented in a way that was clear and engaging?

Objectives

After completing this chapter, you will be able to:

- Provide an overview of character design for video games.
- Analyze what it takes to develop dominant characters and make them stand apart from other characters in similar games.
- Explore the role and function of a character and the ways in which these are determined by the purpose of the character in the game.
- Detail the important aspects of designing characters.
- Outline the character-design process.

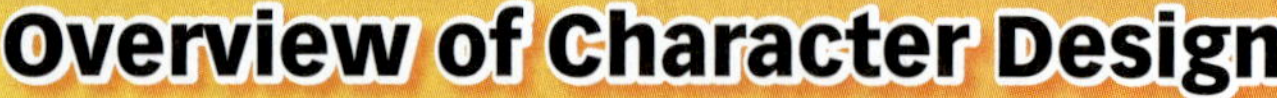

Overview of Character Design

One of the most monumental tasks in creating a video game is character design. This area encompasses every specialty in the design process. Artists conceive physical elements, writers craft emotional elements and dialogue, programmers create abilities, and game designers imagine conflicts and resolutions that shape these character attributes. When all of the parts of a character come together, a wonderful new being is created that will act and react to different story elements within the game.

The simple fact is that stories are about characters and what they do. Take the standard fairy tale opening line, "Once upon a time…". This statement immediately leads to, "there lived a (insert character), who (does something)".

In a practical example, the blanks can be filled in with the story of Shrek: "Once upon a time, there lived an Ogre who wanted people out of his swamp." When this character and what motivates him are clear, the conflict needed for the rest of the story can be created. The storytellers created a conflict by having other creatures invade Shrek's swamp. The rest of the story is about everything that happens to Shrek in his attempt to get his swamp back to the peaceful place he loved.

The story of Shrek forms around the **central premise** of how Shrek will act and react as each conflict presents itself and how that motivates him to internal change. In the story, Shrek is motivated to no longer live alone and allows Donkey and Fiona to live in his swamp as part of his family. The real conflict is with Shrek and his desire to be left alone in his swamp. In the end, he changes inside and no longer wants to be alone. His internal conflict (isolation) and his external conflict (swamp inhabitants) are both resolved through character development. By developing a full understanding of a main character, the rest of the story and supporting characters will emerge.

Great characters can launch a dynasty of games to tell their stories, as shown in **Figure 2-1.** Creating a fictional entity that has endearing qualities takes both creativity and skill. Once

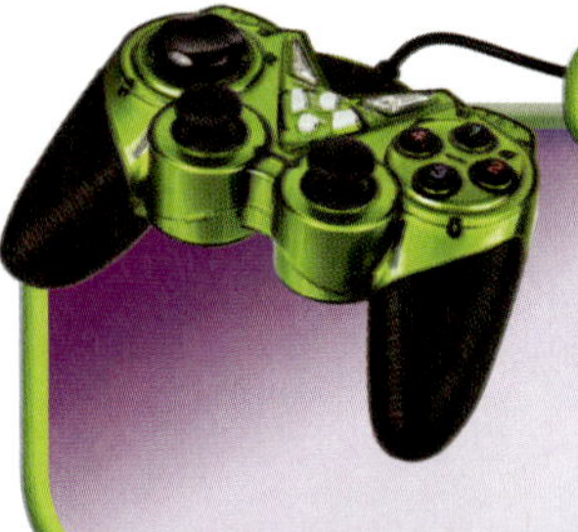

CHEAT CODE: CENTRAL PREMISE

The central premise is the basic idea or situation of the story. The central premise is what makes people want to understand the story and read it or play the game.

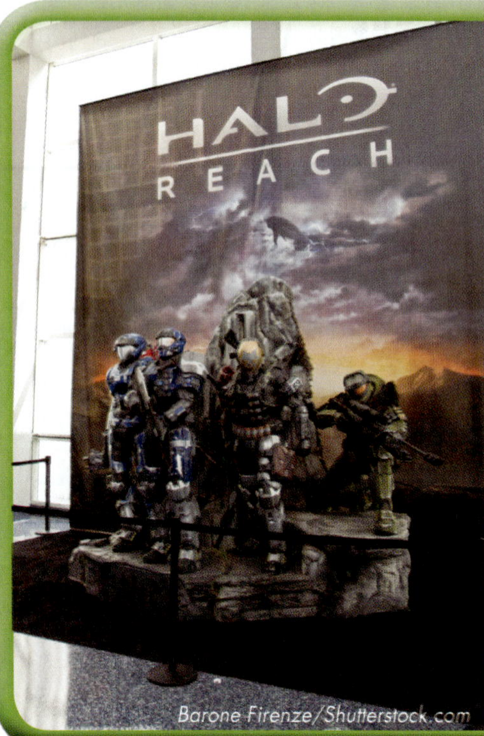

Figure 2-1.

The *Halo* franchise is, in large part, based on the character Master Chief. If *Halo* did not have this great character, would it have become the dynasty that it has?

a character is fully developed, the designers can place it in different situations and play out scenarios on how this character will react.

Mapping the thinking and emotional responses of a character lead to discovery of how the story will progress. As the character presses forward to resolve the main conflict, how does he or she deal with choices and consequences? Will the character have to make a choice that violates a core moral value? Will the character need to understand changes to his or her environment and alter the chosen course of action? What gameplay will allow the player to best understand the character? These questions and their answers await the great game designers of the future.

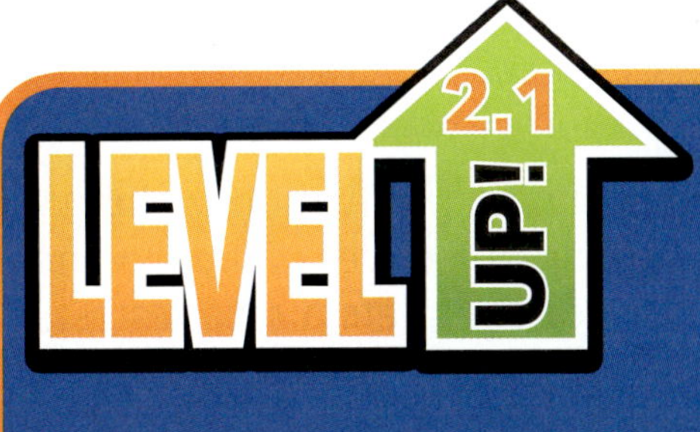

Begin thinking about a character that you would like to create for a game. What physical characteristics will the character have? What types of emotions will the character have? Write down your ideas. As you progress through this class, continue developing the character.

Developing Character

The two most identifiable and memorable features of a *great* game are gameplay and character. New and innovative ways of presenting action and story have changed gameplay. As these innovations entered the market, game studios quickly attached characters to the gameplay to help define the genre and brand the game.

Characters often become as memorable as the game itself. One of the most famous game characters is Mario. Nintendo has created an entire franchise of games around this very popular character. Mario was initially synonymous with the action-genre and platform-theme games. After defining this genre and theme, serving as the lead character, Mario's role expanded beyond platform games. Mario eventually became the centerpiece for many game genres and themes. Today, the character Master Chief defines the *Halo* series of games. Likewise, Altair is immediately identified with the *Assassin's Creed* games, as shown in **Figure 2-2.**

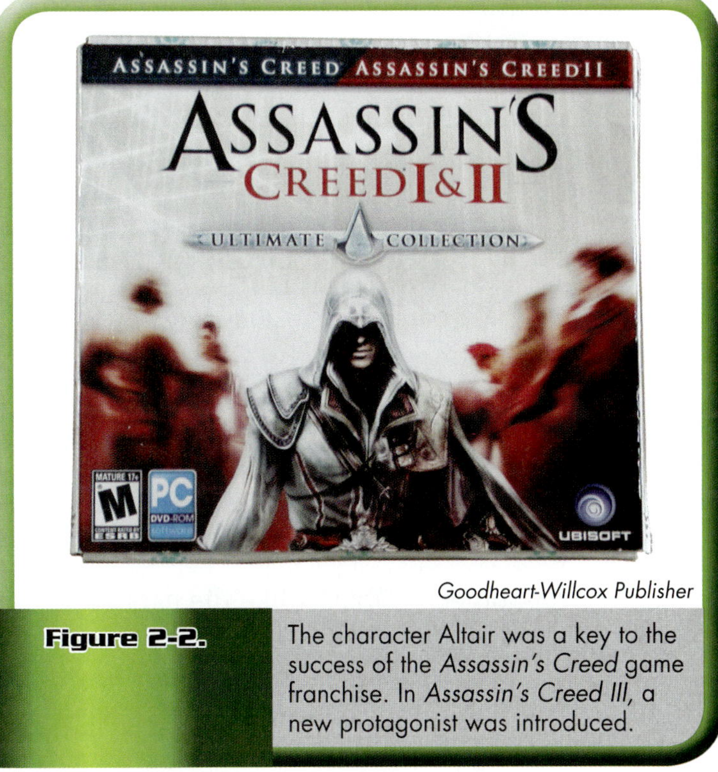

Goodheart-Willcox Publisher

Figure 2-2. The character Altair was a key to the success of the *Assassin's Creed* game franchise. In *Assassin's Creed III*, a new protagonist was introduced.

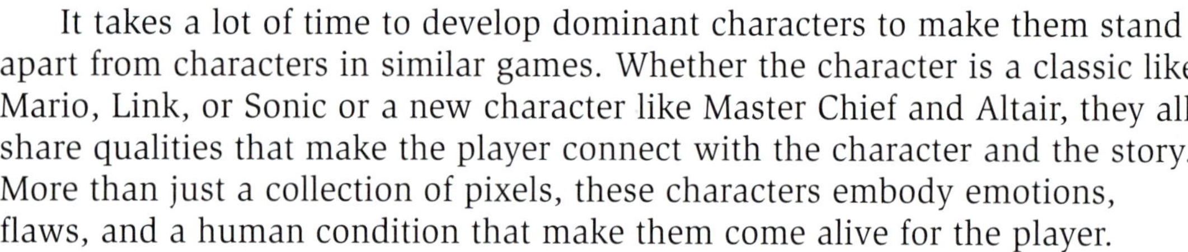

It takes a lot of time to develop dominant characters to make them stand apart from characters in similar games. Whether the character is a classic like Mario, Link, or Sonic or a new character like Master Chief and Altair, they all share qualities that make the player connect with the character and the story. More than just a collection of pixels, these characters embody emotions, flaws, and a human condition that make them come alive for the player.

Great characters do not just happen by accident. There is a process by which a character is developed and the designer forms the attributes of the character. Many of the character-development strategies used to create novels, movies, and plays can be applied to video games to create well-developed characters with depth.

Character Defined

A ***character*** is a motivated participant in the game. Motivation is the reason why the character seeks to achieve the game objectives. Whether the objective is to save the kingdom from the dragon or complete a race fastest, the character must be defined to have the ability to achieve the objective. The process of creating a great character begins by reverse engineering its ***character***—the makeup of talents, skills, abilities, and physical attributes needed to achieve the victory condition. Do not confuse *a* game character with *its* character. A character is a virtual presence in the game. A character's character is its makeup.

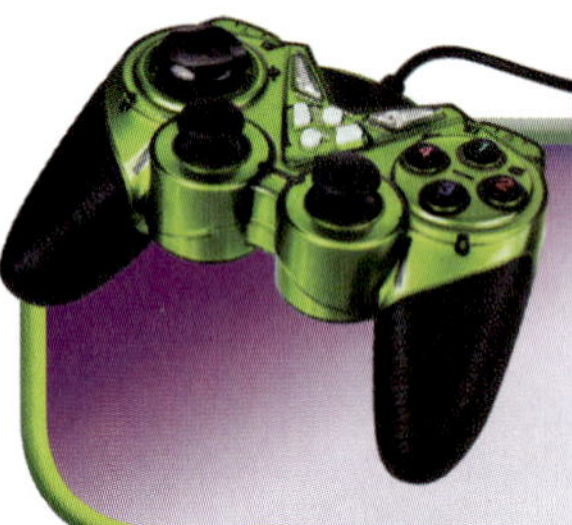

CHEAT CODE: PROTAGONIST

The protagonist is the main character of the story. The player sees the action in the game happening to the protagonist.

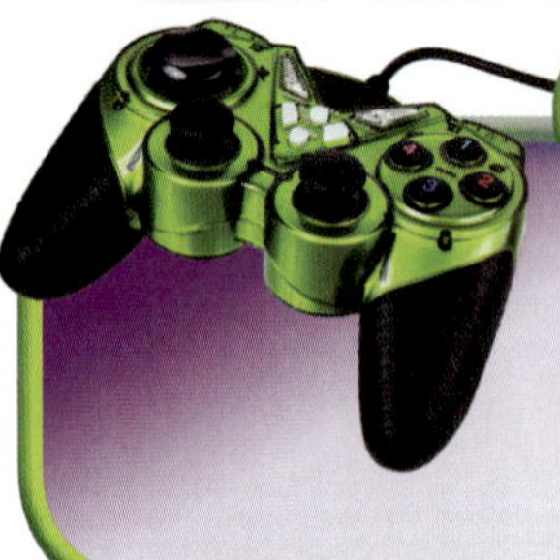

CHEAT CODE: ANTAGONIST

The antagonist is the main adversary or opponent to the protagonist. The antagonist tries to prevent the protagonist from reaching his or her goals.

The physical shape of a character need not look like a human. In the classic game *Frogger*, the **protagonist** character is a frog, as shown in **Figure 2-3.** The frog is motivated to cross a traffic-filled street and a snake-infested river to reach the safety of the lily pads before time runs out. This game has other characters. Depending on the version of *Frogger* being played, the snakes could be considered hazards or characters.

If the snakes are programmed to follow, chase, or interact with the frog, then they are motivated characters. In this case, the snake characters are **antagonists.** These characters are significantly different from the other game objects. Objects like the cars on the road have the ability to destroy the frog, just like the snakes, except they are not *motivated* to do so. They are only hazards. If the frog happens to get in the way of a hazard, the frog is destroyed. However, a motivated character will pursue the protagonist.

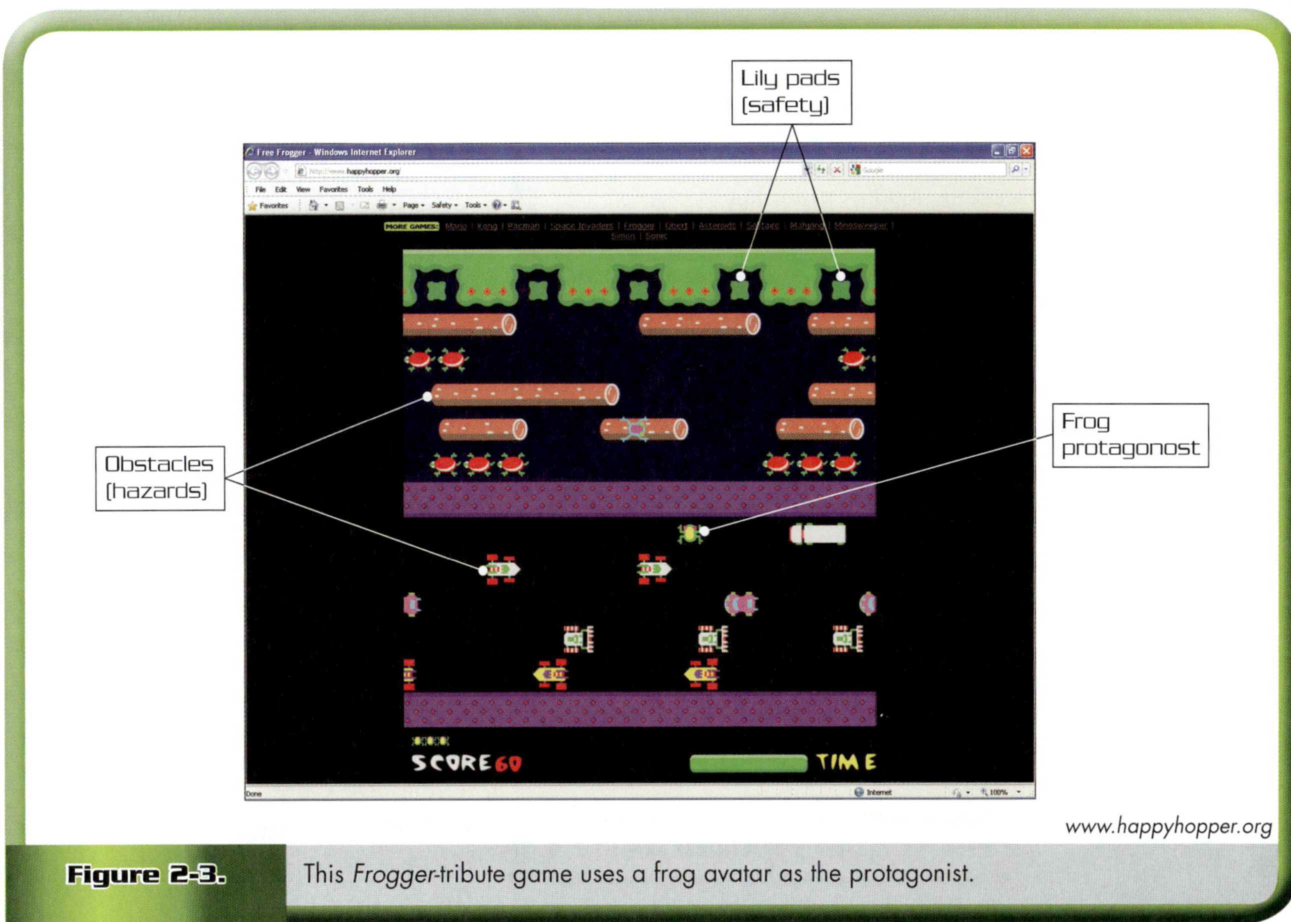

Figure 2-3. This *Frogger*-tribute game uses a frog avatar as the protagonist.

Player Character and Avatar

As seen in *Frogger,* a character can be controlled by the player (frog) or by the game (snakes). The character that is controlled by the player is called the ***player character (PC).*** In most single-player games, there is only one PC. However, in some games, one player may control more than one character. For example, in *Brothers in Arms,* the player must control a combat squad, moving the squad as a group or moving the individual characters in the squad to achieve the game objectives.

Many games allow the player character to be customized as a means of motivating the player. By winning levels or destroying enemies, players unlock perks or are rewarded points that can be used to purchase upgrades. ***Perks*** are attributes locked at the beginning of the game, but unlocked as the game progresses. For example, the player may need to collect certain items before a perk is unlocked. ***Upgrades*** are choices the player makes to obtain better equipment, weapons, magic, abilities, and so on. In *Star Wars Pod Racing,* the player must gain prize money from winning races to buy improvements to the racing pod. By allowing upgrades and providing unlockable perks, players are encouraged to practice and develop game skills to receive these rewards.

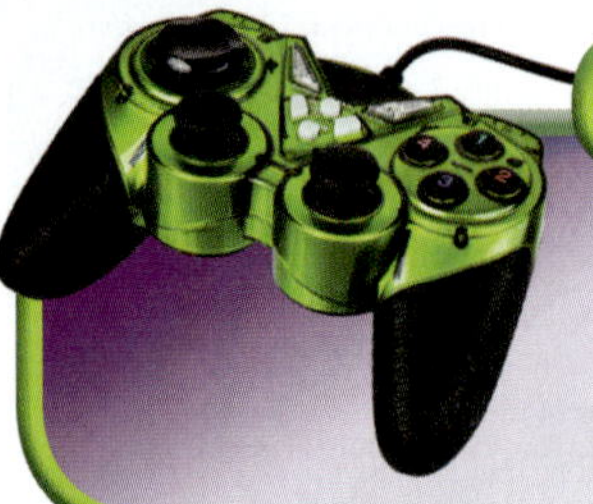

CHEAT CODE: SANSKRIT

Sanskrit is a classical language of India. It is of historical importance, especially to the religions of Hinduism and Buddhism.

In many games, the player can select an avatar for the player character. An ***avatar*** is an image used to represent the player in the game. In its original **Sanskrit** meaning, an avatar is the human form of a god. The use of this term in gaming likely originates from the abilities of all game characters to perform supernatural, godlike actions. These abilities range from laser vision and flight to basic game functions like regenerative health, multiple lives, and respawning. Customizing the avatar is a great way to increase player interest and immersion in the game. It is also an effective way to identify players in multiplayer games.

Player-Select Avatars

In a racing game, for example, a player may be able to choose between a dozen different images of the driver. Some of the avatars are males, while some are females. Some of the avatars are dressed in professional racing gear, while some are dressed in blue jeans and tee shirts. The avatar selected by the player has no impact on the gameplay, but reflects the player's mood or personality. These are called ***player-select avatars*** because the player can choose from a set of avatars. In the game *Arctic Thunder,* the player can also choose from several avatars. The player can choose to be a female rider, male rider, or even the yeti rider. This is also true of games like *Mario Kart* where players can choose their favorite character without having a **handicap** in the game.

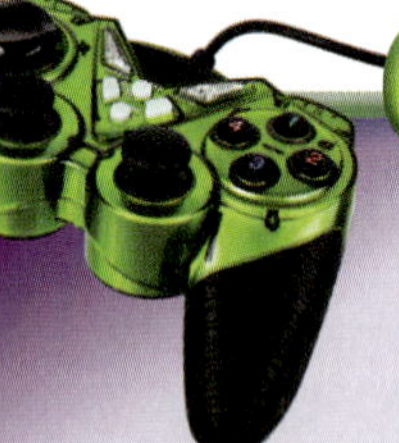

CHEAT CODE: HANDICAP

In terms of gaming, a handicap is an advantage provided to a low-level character or a disadvantage provided to a high-level character so all players are similarly matched. Often very good players take a handicap so they can play against lesser-skilled players. Without the handicap, the good player would quickly win and the game would not be much fun.

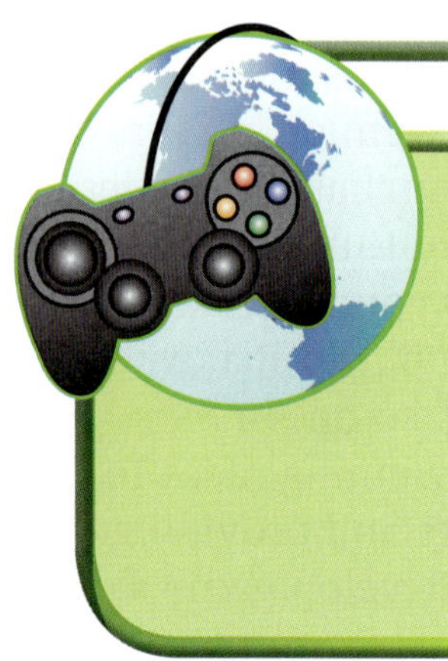

Green Gamer

Gamers usually have refreshments when playing games. Water is a healthy alternative to sodas and caffeinated drinks. Americans buy thousands of bottles of water each day. However, not only it is expensive to buy bottled water, disposing of the container contributes to landfill overuse. Try buying a reusable water bottle and filling it with purified tap water instead of buying a bottle of water at the store. You will save money and the environment.

Game-Select Avatars

Game-select avatars are provided by the game designers and cannot be changed. In many games, the player can choose between several different characters each with a unique avatar, but selecting the character alters the abilities available to the player. However, it is also common that the story in the game does not allow for the player to be any character other than one specific protagonist. In the game *Cruis'n the World,* the player selects a character, which is a car. Each character (car) has a unique avatar, but also has different abilities. For example, choosing a truck instead of a muscle car gives the player a different set of acceleration and handling features. The avatars in *Cruis'n the World* appear similar to real-world vehicles, but the characters have fictionalized names, as shown in **Figure 2-4.**

Cruis'n the World	
Character	**Real-World Vehicle**
ATV	AM General HMMWV (Humvee)
Banzai GTV	Mitsubishi 3000 GT
Bulldog	LTI Fairway (London taxi)
Conductor	AEC Routemaster (London bus)
El Niño	Chevrolet Bel Air
Enforcer	Chevrolet Caprice police interceptor
Exec	BMW 3
Grass Hopper	Toyota Dyna truck
Howler	Volkswagen Transporter Type II
Kamikaze AWD Mark IV	Toyota Supra
Monsta	Ford Adrenalin pickup truck
NY Taxi	Chevrolet Caprice taxi
Orca	Porsche 959
Rhino 4×4	Dodge Ram
Road King	Kenworth T-600 semitruck
Rocket	Willys Model 77
Sardine Extreme	Piaggio Ape three-wheeled truck
Scarab	Volkswagen Beetle Type I
Serpent	Dodge Viper RT/10
Skool Bus	GMC B Series school bus
Speed Demon	McLaren F1
Stallion P6	Ferrari 456 GT
The Surgeon	Mercedes-Benz T1
Tommy	Austin Mini
Zombie Mark IV	Ford Mustang

Figure 2-4. The avatars in *Cruis'n the World* look similar to real-world cars and trucks

Goodheart-Willcox Publisher

Player-Designed Avatar

A more advance type of avatar is the player-designed avatar. As the name implies, a ***player-designed avatar*** is created by the player. This is a common feature in **MMO** games in which thousands of players need to look unique. By allowing different choices of body type, skin color, gender, hair, clothing, weapons, and more, thousands of different avatars are possible within the same game. For example, a shirt may be available in six styles, 20 colors, and eight patterns. This provides 960 different combinations for just this shirt ($6 \times 20 \times 8 = 960$). If there are 50 different custom attributes for a character each with multiple options, the possible combinations number in the millions.

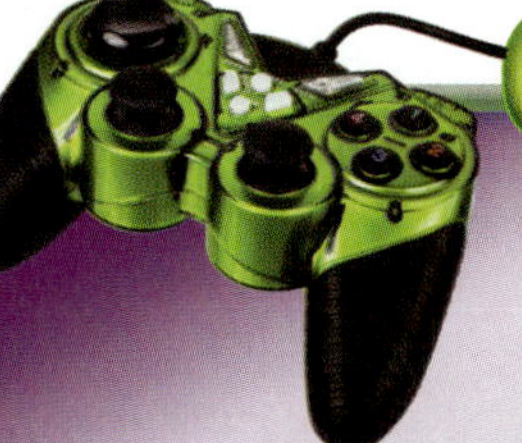

CHEAT CODE: MMO

An MMO is a massively multiplayer online game, like *World of Warcraft.* There are thousands of real people playing the game. *World of Warcraft* has around ten million registered users. Each person uses his or her own avatar and interacts with other players as the game is played online.

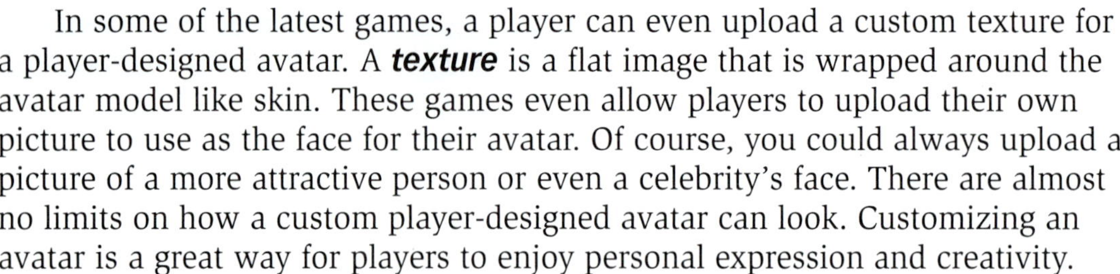

In some of the latest games, a player can even upload a custom texture for a player-designed avatar. A ***texture*** is a flat image that is wrapped around the avatar model like skin. These games even allow players to upload their own picture to use as the face for their avatar. Of course, you could always upload a picture of a more attractive person or even a celebrity's face. There are almost no limits on how a custom player-designed avatar can look. Customizing an avatar is a great way for players to enjoy personal expression and creativity.

In some games, changing the player-designed avatar is more than just for **aesthetic value.** In these games, skills or abilities are associated with specific attributes of the avatar. So, changing the avatar alters the gameplay. The player must alter the avatar, and the character, to meet the challenges of the game. In the racing game *RUSH 2049,* the player can modify the vehicle avatar with different tires, engine, and so on. These modifications not only alter the appearance of the avatar, they also change the ability of the character. The gameplay changes with changes to the avatar and character.

CHEAT CODE: AESTHETIC VALUE

Aesthetic value is the qualities of an object that provide decorative appeal. In other words, aesthetic value is the sense of beauty a person has for an object. The paint on a car has an aesthetic value, and that value is different from person to person.

Non-Player Characters

To create the story and challenges, a game needs many different characters with which the player can interact. Throughout any game, most of the characters are not controlled by the player. A ***non-player character (NPC)*** is any character controlled by the game instead of by the player. With the exception of MMOs, the majority of characters in a game are NPCs. A character controlled by another human player is an ***other player character (OPC).*** Depending on the game format, the NPCs and OPCs may be cooperative, competitive, or neutral.

Cooperative NPC

A ***cooperative NPC*** helps the player complete the game objectives. In many role-playing games (RPGs), the player is part of a team, also known as a *party* or *troop*. If the RPG is a single-player game, the other members of the player's party are all NPCs. When the team encounters an enemy, all characters in the party will battle the enemy. Together, they cooperate to achieve the victory.

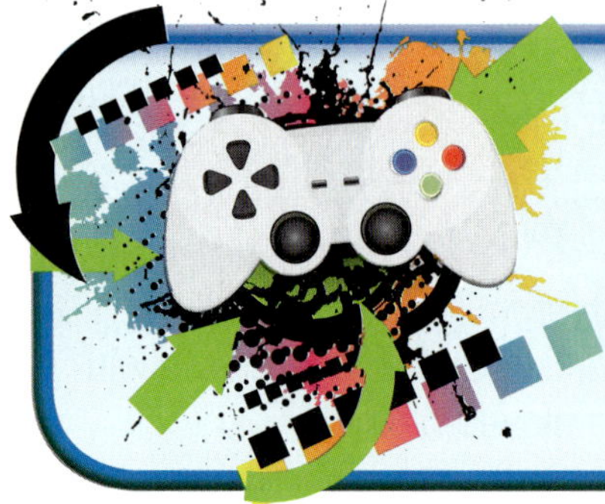

Ethical Gamer

It is unethical to misrepresent yourself on social media, which includes online gaming. Use good judgment and represent yourself in a respectable manner.

In a game like *Call of Duty* or *Star Wars Battlefront,* the player is part of a larger battle. One army seeks to defeat the other army. The player can recruit NPCs to aid in the battle. In addition to the NPCs that are working as part of the player's team, the rest of the player's army continues to battle the other enemy army. Each member of the same army as the player is a cooperative NPC.

A smaller version of the team or party is the sidekick. A ***sidekick*** is a companion who is **subordinate** to the player character. In a game with a sidekick, the player basically controls a two-character team. The sidekick always takes its instructions from the player and only advances with the player. In the comic book world, sidekicks are very common. One of the most popular of these is Robin, who is the sidekick of Batman, as shown in **Figure 2-5.** In the game world, one of the first games to incorporate an NPC sidekick was *Sonic the Hedgehog 2.* In that game, the sidekick character Tails could be operated either as a second player or as a sidekick NPC that followed Sonic.

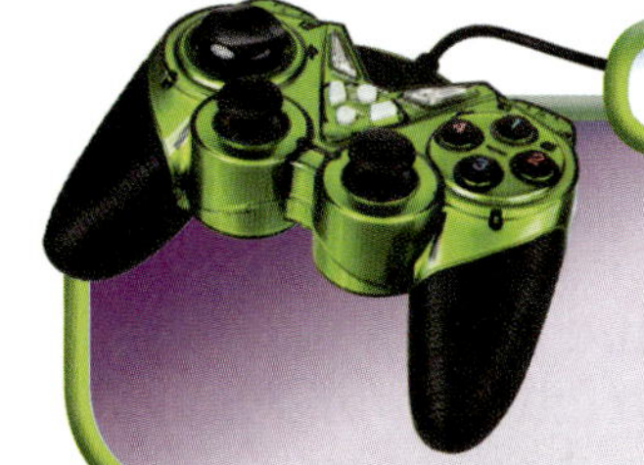

CHEAT CODE: SUBORDINATE

Subordinate means below, beneath, or lower. If value A is subordinate to value B, a character will follow value B before value A.

Competitive NPC

Of course, the player is also battling against an entire army that is trying to stop him or her from reaching the objective. Each of these enemies is a competitive NPC. A ***competitive NPC*** is any non-player character that is attempting to stop the player from completing an objective. Competitive NPCs operate independent of the player, but actively try to prevent the player from reaching the game goals.

The most significant role of a competitive NPC is that of antagonist. An antagonist is any character in conflict with the protagonist of the game. Since the player is the protagonist in the game world, all characters trying to beat the player are antagonists. Each competitive NPC is motivated to defeat the player.

In *Star Wars Battlefront,* the entire Republic army on the planet is a competitive NPC. Each army is trying to capture all of the command posts or destroy every member of the other army. In *Cruis'n the World* or *Need for Speed*, competitive NPCs are all of the other cars racing against you.

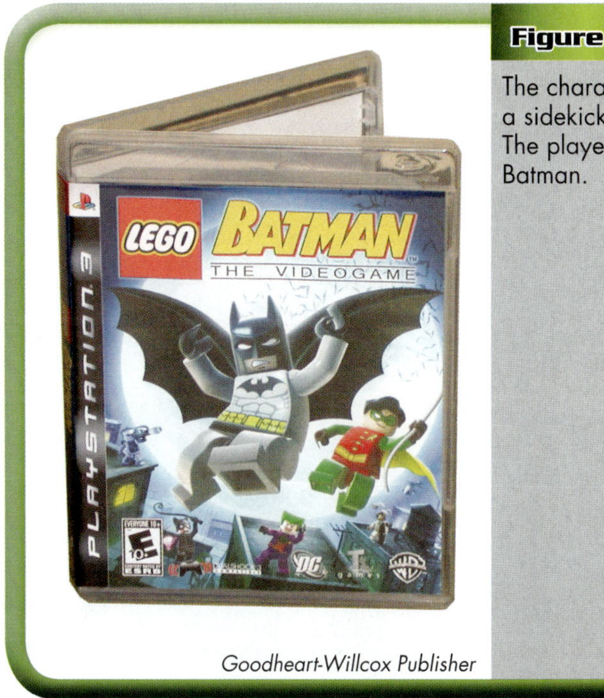

Goodheart-Willcox Publisher

Figure 2-5. The character Robin is a sidekick to Batman. The player controls Batman.

Competitive NPCs come in several standard classes. At the top of the competitive NPC hierarchy is the big boss. The ***big boss*** is the most powerful enemy in the game. Typically, this NPC is also the character that all other competitive NPCs work for. In the classic story of Star Wars, the big boss is Darth Sidious, the Sith master (Emperor Palpatine). All other competitive NPCs, like bosses and minions, work to protect the big boss and complete his or her objectives. These objectives are counter to the objectives of the protagonist (the player).

Bosses are the second-most powerful antagonists in the game. While defeating the big boss is the objective of the game, defeating a boss might be the major objective of a game level. In Star Wars, bosses include Darth Vader, Darth Maul, and General Grievous. Bosses are major characters within the game that are directly controlled by the big boss. Bosses usually control minions, as shown in **Figure 2-6.**

Minions are minor characters, like soldiers, and can come in several ranks, strengths, and abilities. Most competitive NPCs in a game will be minions. In Star Wars, minions include battle droids, storm troopers, droidekas, and super battle droids. Each character is motivated to battle with the protagonist and keeps him or her from reaching the objectives of the game.

Neutral NPC

Some NPCs may not be cooperative or competitive. ***Neutral NPCs*** are non-player characters that are not motivated by what the player is doing. Neutral NPCs are often used in simulations. They are often the objective or scoring feature of a simulation. Many other types of games have neutral NPCs. In any game that involves a large population, such as in a city, most of the NPCs in the game will be neutral NPCs. They have no motivation to help the player nor prevent him or her from achieving objectives. A game would be pretty easy if every character you saw was either helping you or an enemy.

In the game *School Tycoon,* all of the characters in the game are neutral NPCs. The player is not even a character in the game. The player can select different NPCs as teachers, custodians, and other staff, but they are not controlled by the

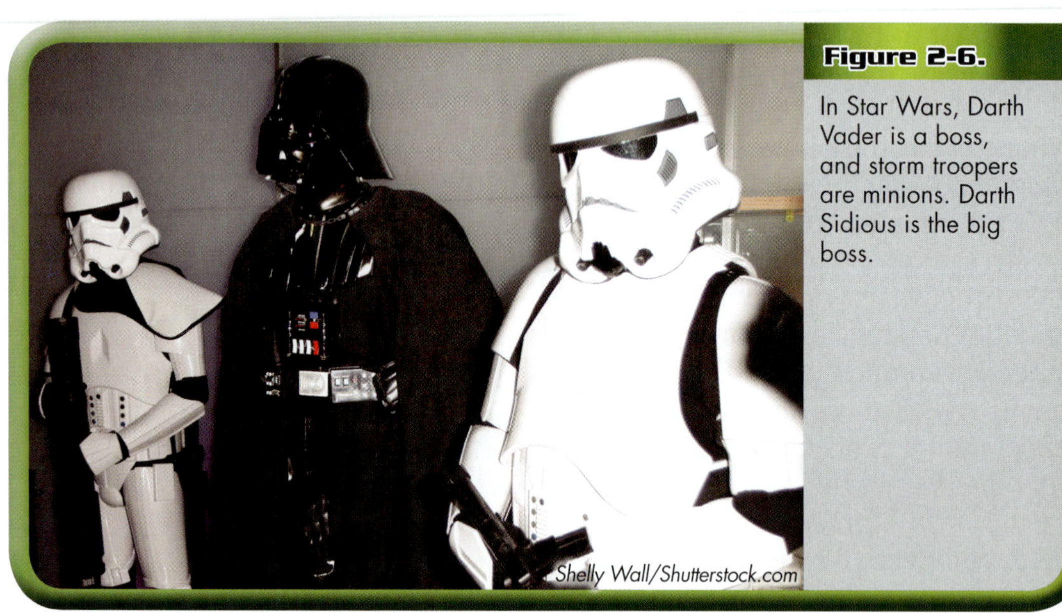

Shelly Wall/Shutterstock.com

Figure 2-6. In Star Wars, Darth Vader is a boss, and storm troopers are minions. Darth Sidious is the big boss.

player. The player merely gives them job assignments. The motivation for the NPCs is to do their job as well or as poorly as they have been programmed. The player can only hire or fire the employee to affect the outcome of the game. The students are also neutral to the objective of the player. They are programmed to react to the game environment and are motivated by their own needs and not by the player's objectives. The more satisfied the NPCs are, the more students attend classes and buy things. In *School Tycoon,* the player either meets or fails to meet the game objectives of satisfying the students.

Neutral NPCs also have individual will and personalities. Each NPC can be programmed with a unique set of needs and wants. These attributes drive their motivations. By varying the properties of NPC attributes, many NPCs can exist without creating a swarm. A ***swarm*** is a collection of characters that move, act, and behave as a single entity. A swarm is usually bad for gameplay, but in some cases it can be a desired action.

Think about a game like *Roller Coaster Tycoon.* If all of the NPCs were programmed the same, then they would all travel to the same ride at the same time. The group would be all thinking the same and would have the same movement within the game. Every time you opened a new ride attraction, the entire population at the theme park would immediately rush to fill the line of this new ride. This type of NPC would not be useful in the game. Instead, each NPC is free to choose to ride any attraction, use the bathroom, eat something, or otherwise fulfill a personal need or want.

Creating a swarm is not always a bad idea, as shown in **Figure 2-7.** In a war game, foot soldiers might be programmed to all act the same and pursue the same objective. Here, each soldier is just an advancing member of the army and need not have any other motivation than to follow the same order as all other soldiers. In addition to armies, other examples of swarms that may be good for gameplay include a flock of birds, school of fish, and bacteria or diseases. These NPCs will move toward a single objective with a single motivation.

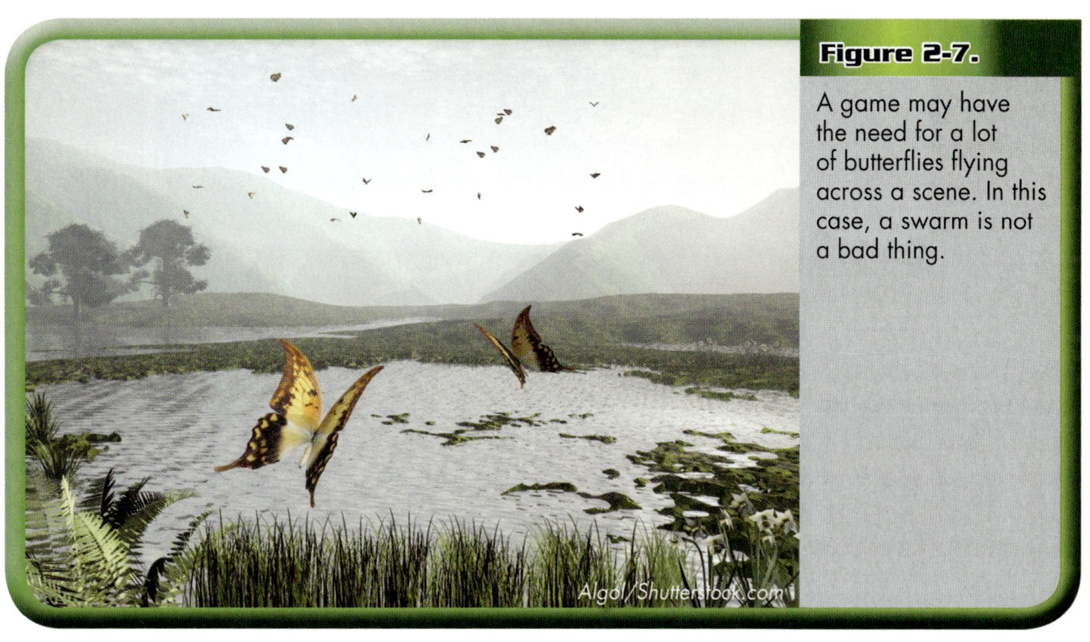

Figure 2-7. A game may have the need for a lot of butterflies flying across a scene. In this case, a swarm is not a bad thing.

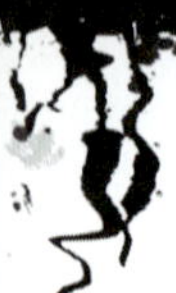

CASE STUDY

Neutral Non-player Characters in Simulation Games

Non-player characters are important to all video games, but they are a primary feature of simulation games. In tycoon-type simulation games, such as *Motorcycle Tycoon 2* shown below, the player controls resources and directions for non-player characters. In many of these types of games, the player never controls a character.

Motorcycle Tycoon 2 is a simulation game that has a construction and management component. The player must purchase parts for a motorcycle, hire and manage mechanics as they build motorcycles, and then race the motorcycles. The player can either race the motorcycle as a player character or hire a driver to race. The goal is to make a profit. The more races the player wins, the better the parts that can be purchased, and the better the motorcycle that can be built. As the player advances in the game and earns more money, additional technicians can be hired. These are all NPCs and must be kept supplied with parts and allowed to rest. The player must also manage the knowledge of the NPCs with repair manuals. If an NPC does not respond to rest and knowledge, then it may need to be sent home. The player must constantly interact with the NPCs in order to be successful at the game.

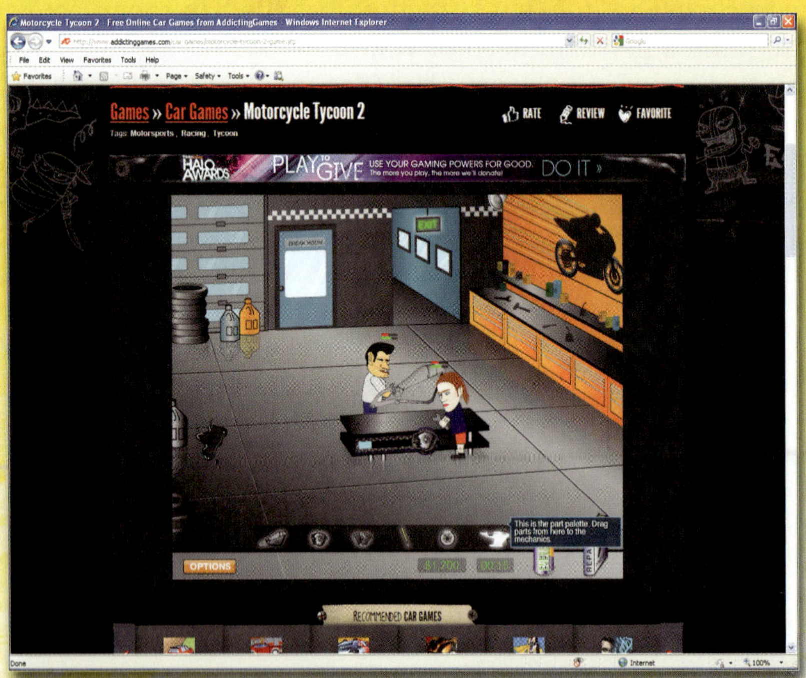

Disco Blimp/www.addictinggames.com

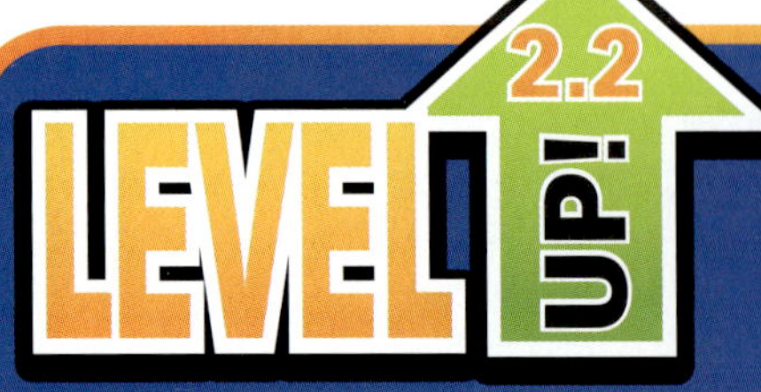

Consider the challenges and objectives of the simple game *Frogger.* Other than a frog, what animals would be believable characters for the game?

Driving Characters

Understanding the role and function of characters is very important when beginning to design character attributes. To understand the role and function, you must know the purpose of the character in the game. Characters will fall into one of two main purpose categories: gameplay-attributed characters and story-based characters.

Gameplay-Attributed Characters

A ***gameplay-attributed character*** is a game character that only needs the realistic physical features required to complete the game objectives. In other words, the attributes, or qualities, of the character are only what are required by the game objectives. These characters are the easiest to develop. They are motivated to complete a single, simple objective. Creating a gameplay-attributed character only requires balancing the character art with the abilities needed to accomplish the game objective.

Think about gameplay-attributed characters as empty vessels. They have **tangible features,** like strength, height, weight, and clothing, and the skill needed to perform in the game, but they have no emotion or associated story. These are characters just there to get the job done.

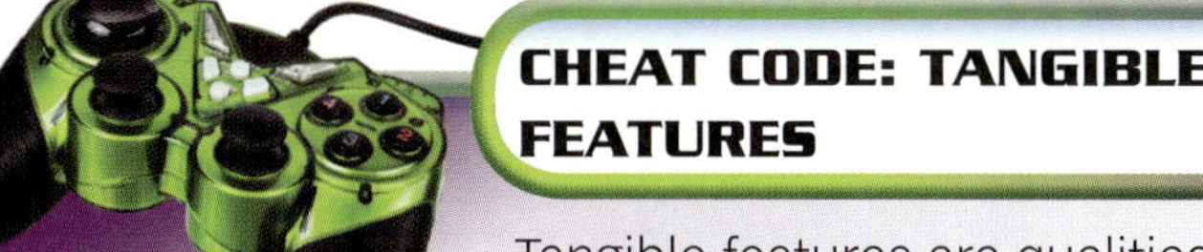

CHEAT CODE: TANGIBLE FEATURES

Tangible features are qualities of the character that can be seen or demonstrated. They are part of the functionality of a character. Tangible features include dimensions, like length, width, and height; speed; strength; agility; and pose.

Games that have gameplay-attributed characters focus on activity without a story. An example of this type of game is a car-racing game. The characters need to be cars, as shown in **Figure 2-8.** The characters should all look like cars and have tangible features that convey speed. These features may be big tires, flashy paint, a streamline body, a big motor, and flaming exhaust pipes. The motivation for the character is simple: to win the race. Little more needs to be known about each car.

Other gameplay-attributed characters may have human or animal form. The character in a golf game may be a featureless human in third-person perspective or even just a golf club in first-person perspective. Nondescript figures are acceptable for many sports-related games. These games focus on gameplay and increasing the skill of the player as the game progresses. Therefore, characters in these games only need to be built with tangible features that communicate the ability to complete the game objectives.

When creating gameplay-attributed characters, the designer is not required to build the character to fit a story. However, the designer must still create a congruous character to fit the game. *Congruous characters* look like they belong and fit the mood and theme of the game. *Incongruous characters* seem out of place or different than the rest of the game mood and theme, as shown in **Figure 2-9.** An incongruous character might not have the tangible features to overcome the game obstacles. For example, in a game where the protagonist character must run, jump, and smash the antagonist characters, a physically strong character is required. A character that is an elderly person who walks with a cane is incongruous and unbelievable to the player.

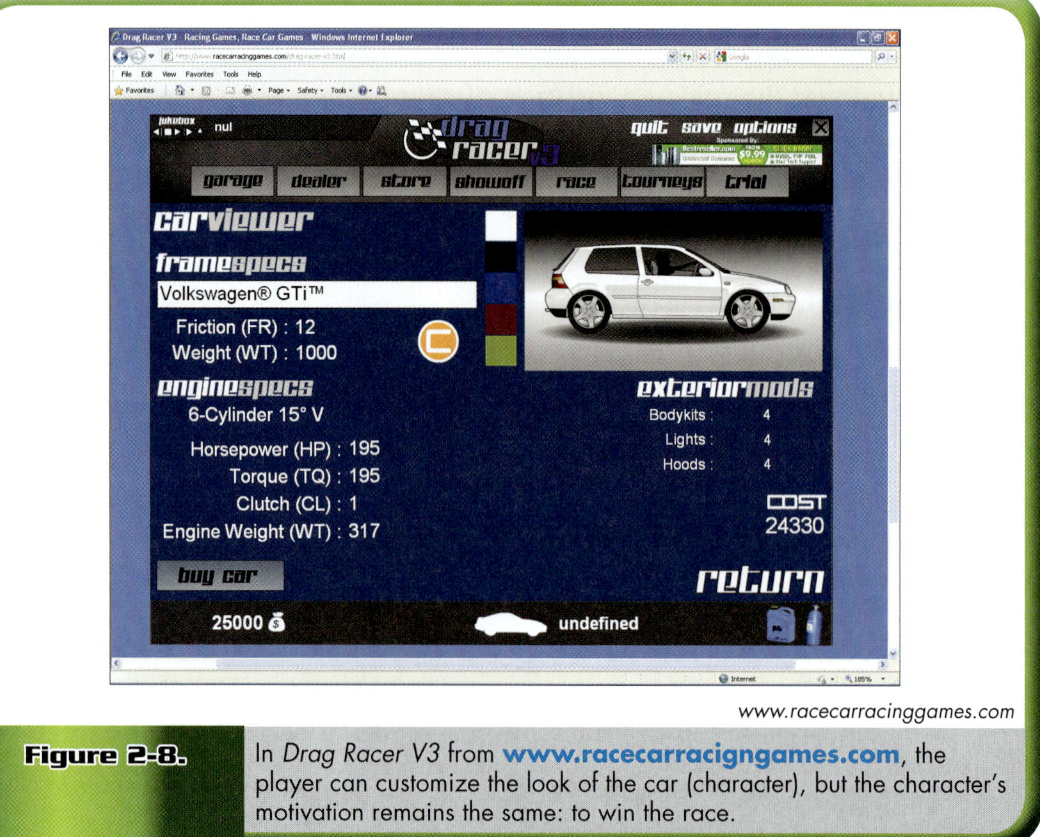

www.racecarracinggames.com

Figure 2-8. In *Drag Racer V3* from **www.racecarracigngames.com**, the player can customize the look of the car (character), but the character's motivation remains the same: to win the race.

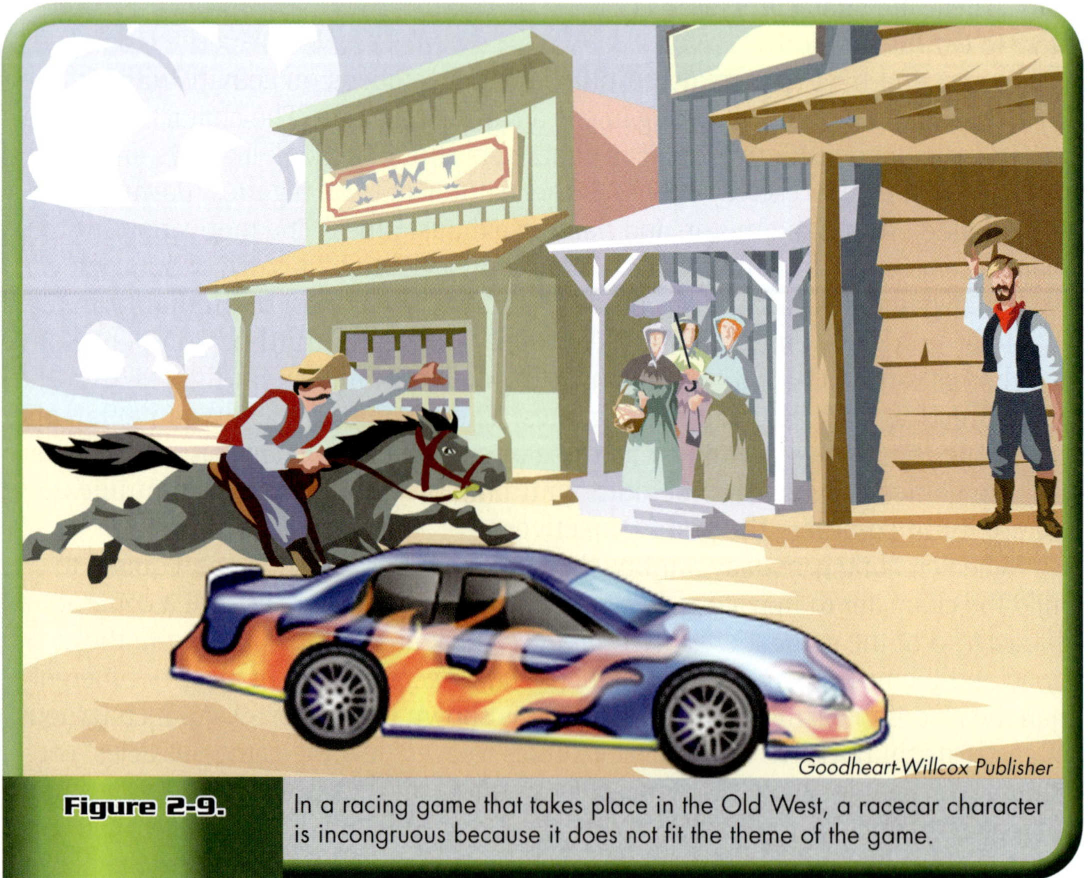

Goodheart-Willcox Publisher

Figure 2-9. In a racing game that takes place in the Old West, a racecar character is incongruous because it does not fit the theme of the game.

Story-Based Characters

A ***story-based character*** conveys some portion of the game story. The most important story-based character is the main character. The ***main character*** is the one around which the entire game revolves. The purpose of the story is to move the main character through the process of making decisions that will lead to completion of the game objectives. Unique to games is the idea that the player can make choices for the main character and live the adventure **vicariously**.

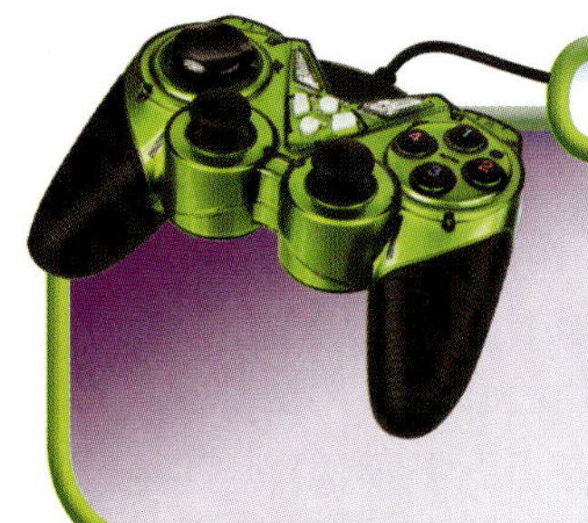

CHEAT CODE: VICARIOUSLY

When a player lives vicariously through the character, he or she imagines the experiences of the character as if they were happening directly to the player.

NPCs are also often story-based characters. While they are not main characters, they can be used to help tell the story. For example, NPCs may give the main character assignments, explaining what must be accomplished and why.

Throughout the game story, the main character faces choices. By the end of the story, the main character should have transformed, changed, or grown through situational enlightenment or self-enlightenment. ***Situational enlightenment*** is learning and understanding the cause of a problem that affects others. ***Self-enlightenment*** is learning and understanding problems and flaws within you.

Imagine a story about the owner of a paper manufacturer that is polluting the water supply. When the owner's son is born with cancer, the character experiences situational enlightenment that pollution from the paper mill is causing harm. Later, when the character feels personally responsible for trading profits for the health of the son and shuts down the paper mill, the character experiences self-enlightenment. Throughout the journey of the story, the main character makes choices so that by the end of a story, a character should change or grow somehow. This could be by learning something new or by growing in understanding of self.

The story only works if the player wants to see the character succeed in his or her quest for enlightenment. This means the designer needs to create a character that people will care about and want to solve the problems within the story. To create this experience, story-based characters need to have a richness and depth of character that is far beyond what is found in a gameplay-attributed character. The designer must incorporate intangible features.

Intangible features are those attributes that are part of the emotional or inner character, **Figure 2-10.** They are hard to measure and are only seen through the actions and choices of the character.

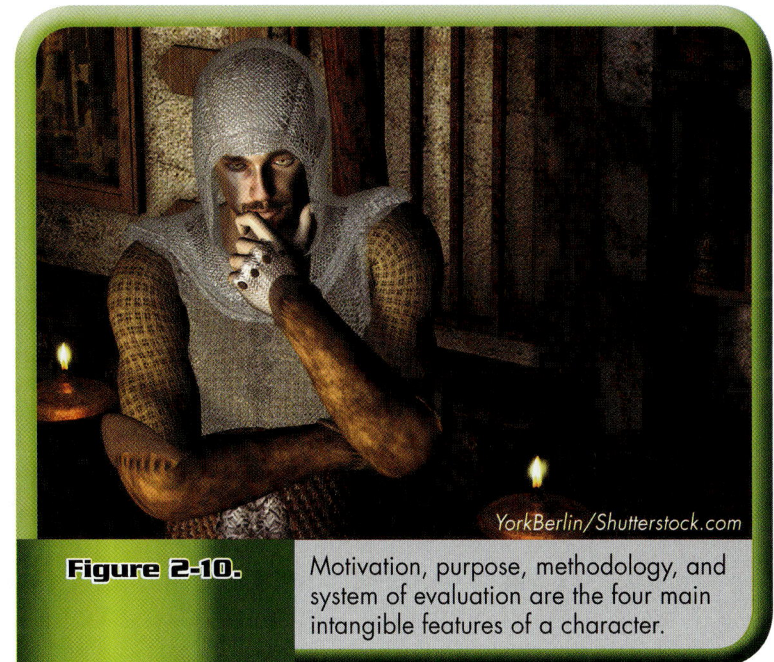

YorkBerlin/Shutterstock.com

Figure 2-10. Motivation, purpose, methodology, and system of evaluation are the four main intangible features of a character.

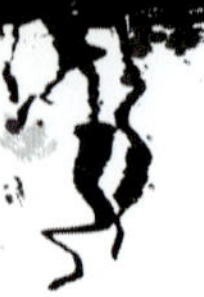

Intangible features include such concepts as mood, expression, emotion, motivation, and purpose. In video game design, intangible features are developed in the same way as a writer of a novel would develop the characters in the story. The four main intangible features of a character are motivation, purpose, methodology, and system of evaluation.

Motivation

Motivation is the cause for a character to begin an action. In the story Shrek, the motivation of trying to get the creatures to leave his swamp causes Shrek to move within the story. Initially, he travels outside of the swamp to find the cause of the problem. In Dulac, he is further motivated to rescue Princess Fiona in exchange for his swamp being cleared of trespassers. In the end, Shrek is motivated to again rescue Princess Fiona from marrying Lord Farquhar as his internal motivation changed from wanting to be alone in his swamp to finding the love of his life. At each critical moment in the story, the main character, Shrek, is motivated to action.

Purpose

Purpose is the character's reason for existing or primary duty. In a combat or RPG game, characters receive their purpose from their rank or class. This purpose defines their general authority to make decisions and the role they play in society. In a family simulation, a character purpose might be to serve as mom, dad, oldest child, or baby. Each of these titles is easily identifiable with the role and responsibility of a family member.

In cases where the character does not fall into a social category, one must be described to define the character's purpose. Returning to the story of Shrek, the purpose of an ogre is undefined. The designers needed to create a purpose of an ogre. They created the general purpose of an ogre as a strong, smelly outcast from society. As an ogre, Shrek's only purpose is to be feared and removed from civilized society.

Methodology

After the character's motivation and purpose are defined, its preferred methodology of resolving conflict and seeking resolution must be determined. ***Methodology*** is the general rules or principles on how a character does things. If the character is a fighter, then the character's methodology may be punching things that get in its way.

To apply the correct methodology, a character's actions must be believable and consistent with their purpose and motivation. Something unbelievable and inconsistent would be an error. Imagine a baby that is crying to get the attention of his mother who crawls out of the crib, smashes the refrigeration, and trashes the kitchen. This is an incorrect application of methodology.

Shrek's methodology is smashing through barriers, knocking out enemies, and generally using his size to achieve his objectives. This methodology is consistent with his motivation and purpose. If the same methodology was applied to his sidekick, Donkey, the actions would be unbelievable and incongruous. Donkey is too small to smash things. Instead, his methodology is using his skills at talking and annoyance to get his way. Therefore, Shrek's methodology is action based and Donkey's methodology is speech based.

System of Evaluation

In the end, the motivation, purpose, and methodology must be evaluated by the character and compared to a set of core values. The ***core values*** are the moral, ethical, and cultural rules that a person (or character) applies to his or her life. Designers need to understand how a character will view each situation and evaluate it against these core values. To begin understanding the evaluation process, the designer first needs to understand each core value. Additionally, a character in a game is often placed in situations where there is a conflict between core values.

Moral Values. The most basic value a character has is the knowledge of good and evil. ***Moral values*** are rules that a character uses to decide if something is good or evil. While this may sound easy, in practice it is much harder. Look at the graph in **Figure 2-11** that stretches from absolute good to absolute evil. All characters fall somewhere within that graph of morality. Notice that the graph is thickest at the neutral point and tapers to a point at both pure good and pure evil. This is because few characters approach pure good or evil. Even heroes and superheroes fail to approach pure good. Villains also are not pure evil. Rather, good characters have flaws that prevent them from being pure good. Villains also show some good, preventing them from being pure evil.

The character Mr. Burns from The Simpsons is on the evil side of the graph, but he is not pure evil character. Mr. Burns at times shows his good side. Marge Simpson, on the other hand, is basically good, but she still has flaws. She gets mad at Bart and Homer. If Mr. Burns were pure evil and Marge were pure good, they would not be as interesting. When designing your characters, picture where on the graph of morality between good and evil they will exist.

Ethical Values. Characters have to face ethical issues. ***Ethical values*** are rules that a character uses to decide if something is right or wrong. In most cases, ethical decisions are about how strictly the character will follow the law. For example, you see the person in front of you at the checkout counter drop some money on the floor without noticing. Do you let the person know he or she dropped some money? Or, do you wait for the person to leave and pick up the money for yourself? The answer depends on your ethical values, what you consider right (ethical) and wrong (unethical).

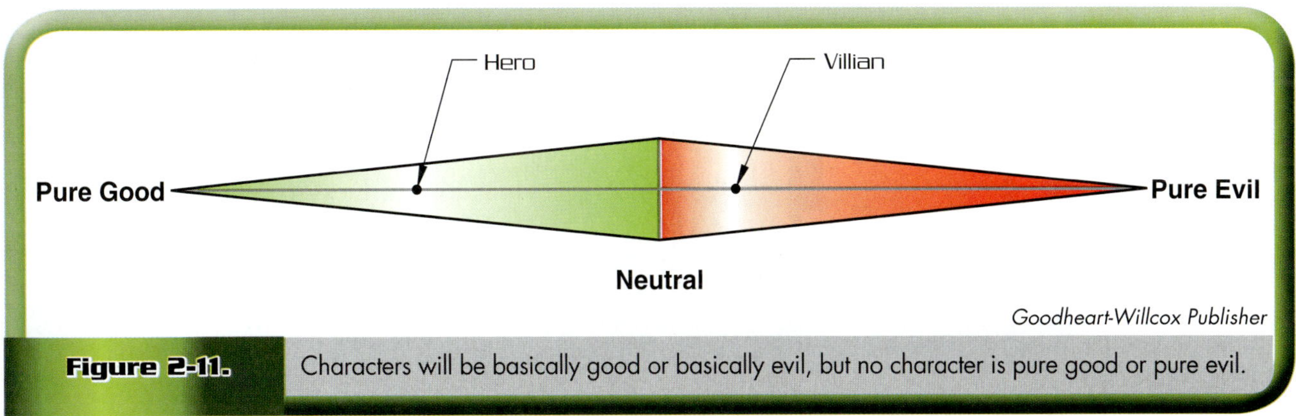

Goodheart-Willcox Publisher

Figure 2-11. Characters will be basically good or basically evil, but no character is pure good or pure evil.

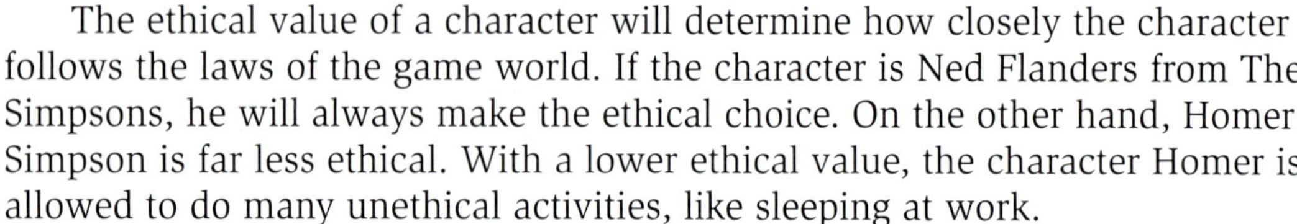

The ethical value of a character will determine how closely the character follows the laws of the game world. If the character is Ned Flanders from The Simpsons, he will always make the ethical choice. On the other hand, Homer Simpson is far less ethical. With a lower ethical value, the character Homer is allowed to do many unethical activities, like sleeping at work.

However, even though Homer does unethical things, he is still not an evil character like Mr. Burns. Homer has trouble determining what is right and wrong, but he is basically good. Mr. Burns is basically evil.

Cultural Values. Cultural values are the most detailed and varied. ***Cultural values*** are rules that a character applies as part of its ancestral heritage, religion, and family. Examples of cultural values are celebrating Thanksgiving, Christmas, Hanukah, or Kwanzaa. Celebrating Thanksgiving is a cultural value of a nation. Celebrating Christmas or Hanukah is a cultural value of religion. Celebrating Kwanzaa is a cultural value of heritage.

Cultural values can play a large role in the development of a character. Cultural values play a role in how characters dress and act according to customs and beliefs. It is important to fully research the historical period and cultural values of a character before you complete a character design.

Non-human characters also have cultural values. Dogs will travel in packs, fish swim in schools, and male lions hunt alone. Even the character Shrek has cultural values. One of the most obvious is the cultural value of marriage. Cultural values such as the duty of a prince and a father also play an important role in the story. Regardless of the physical shape of the character and whether or not it is based on real human form, the character must have a realistic cultural value system consistent with the purpose of the character.

Conflict of Values. Each time a character makes a decision, the choice must be consistent with the character's set of core values. However, many times the story writers place the character in a situation where a difficult choice must be made between conflicting core values. In this situation, the values will establish a hierarchy where the most important core value will win over a lesser core value. Consider an example where a character has a cultural value of attending temple every Sabbath. If the character's house is on fire, the cultural value of attending temple will fall subordinate to the ethical value of putting out the fire. A designer needs to understand how the character will evaluate each problem faced before deciding on the best action.

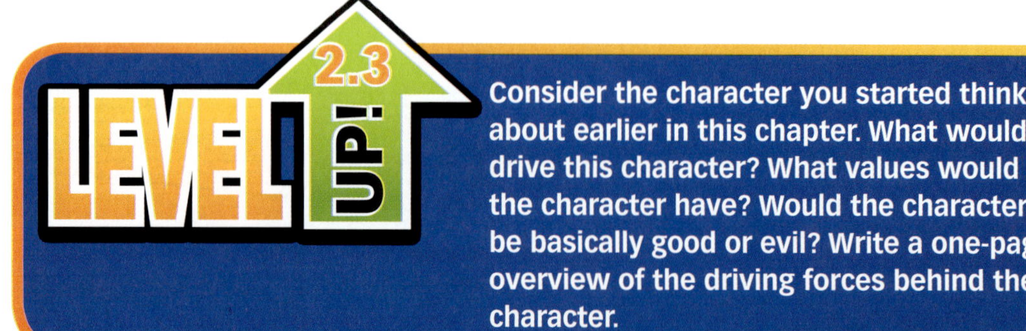

Consider the character you started thinking about earlier in this chapter. What would drive this character? What values would the character have? Would the character be basically good or evil? Write a one-page overview of the driving forces behind the character.

Designing Characters

Once a character has been given the basic motivation, purpose, methodology, and system of evaluation, depth and design can be added to the character. Adding depth is like putting the muscles on the metaphorical bones of the character. Adding design is like putting the skin over the muscles to create the artistic rendering of the character. When creating characters, designers pay attention to the background, conveying character, semiotics, and character archetypes.

Background

To build character depth, a character profile or background is created. A ***character profile*** is a question-and-answer document like an interview or matchmaking questionnaire. Answers to the questions provide the basic demographic information of the character, the likes and dislikes, and basic behavioral norms. This is where the character is described in specific details that will help lead to the eventual scale, shape, and texture of the character rendering.

Conveying Character

After the background of the character is created, it is time to start building a game character to match everything that has been defined for it. There are three ways in which game designers display character attributes. These are appearance and aesthetics, thoughts and conversations, and actions.

Appearance and Aesthetics

Appearance is how the character looks. Aesthetics is how pleasing to the eye the appearance is. The character appearance needs to fit the status and purpose of the character.

Status is the social standing of the character. Status might be the difference between a king and a peasant. The status will determine physical appearance such as clothing, cleanliness, mannerisms, facial expressions, and more. Purpose is, again, what the role of the player is in the game. Together, the game designer needs to create a character that looks right for the games. To accomplish the aesthetic role of character design, the artist will transform the idea of the character status and purpose into something that looks and dresses appropriately.

A character's appearance is the first visual clue to the player as to the role of the character. A large, muscular character is likely to be very strong. Suppose the character is dirty, wearing a leather apron, and carrying a large hammer. These visual elements serve as **context clues.** In this example, the context clues define the character as a blacksmith.

CHEAT CODE: CONTEXT CLUE

A clue is information that leads a person to a conclusion. Context is the surrounding environment or conditions. So, a context clue is a piece of information evaluated within the surrounding environment. In a game, if a player does not know the purpose of a character, certain elements of the character, such as the manner of dress or where the character lives, can be used to determine the character's purpose.

The quality of appearance can be applied to nonhuman characters as well. Look at the two cars shown in **Figure 2-12.** The car on the right is a high-end sports car. The car on the left is low-end basic transportation. Appearance defines the status and purpose of these nonhuman characters. In a game where the player must find a car to escape from enemies, the sports car would be the best choice. However, the game designers would likely make the low-end car easier to find. This makes the player choose between the easy-to-find, but slow car and the hard-to-find, but fast car.

Thoughts and Conversations

Thoughts are the character's internal dialog. These may be voiced to the player or appear on screen as printed text. Conversations are external dialog the character has with other characters in the game. What a character says, thinks, and feels helps convey character to the player. What a character says, how it is said, and to whom it is said are all very important.

The way the character delivers the spoken message can help the player determine the purpose of the character. A character that is a street thug will have a far different speech pattern than a good elf. In addition to the actual words used, the tone of the voice also has a lot to do with conveying character. Think about a big strong character who speaks with a high-pitched voice. A high-pitched voice or speaking slowly might show the player this character is a gentle giant that will help the player, not an enemy.

Syntax is how words are arranged into phrases and sentences. *Inflection* is the vocal tones of spoken words. A *dialect* is a variance in language found in a specific region or social group. The syntax, inflection, and dialect a character uses can provide context clues to the purpose of the character. A gangster will have a very different voice, manner of speaking, and pronunciation of words than a wise master. In video games, the wise master almost always has a very calm, slow, and thoughtful delivery of words. The gangster is loud, mispronounces words, and uses incorrect grammar.

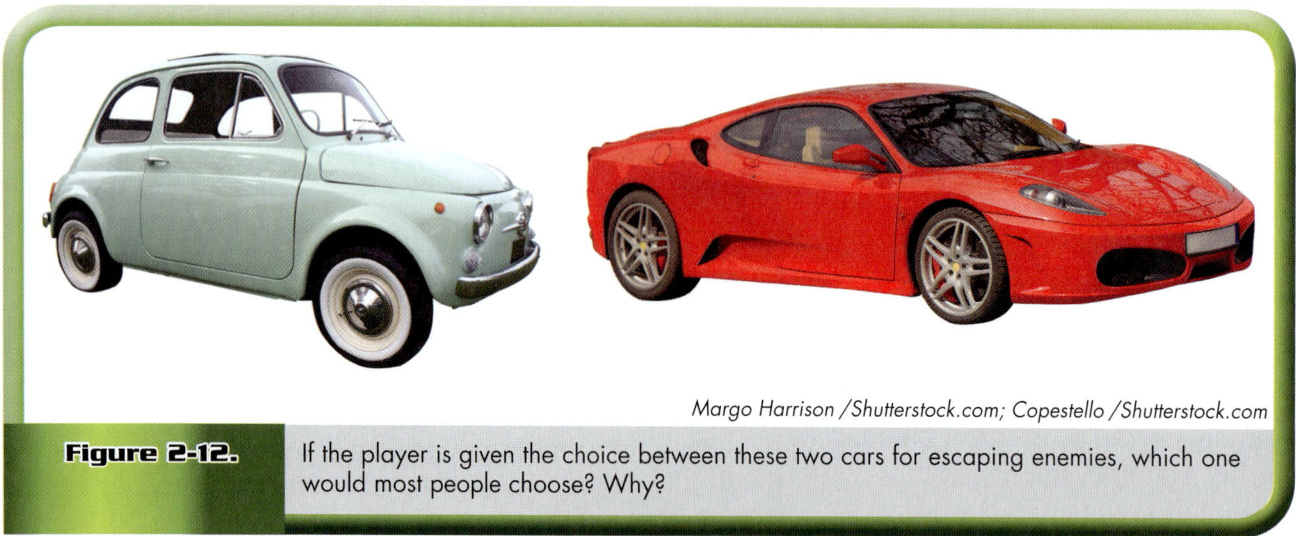

Margo Harrison /Shutterstock.com; Copestello /Shutterstock.com

Figure 2-12. If the player is given the choice between these two cars for escaping enemies, which one would most people choose? Why?

What other characters say or think about the character also provide context clues. When other characters speak in a **cut scene** or inside the game, they may be speaking about the PC or an NPC like the big boss. This dialog may provide clues to hidden strengths and weaknesses of the character. Additionally, the other characters to whom a character speaks provide context clues to the character's motivations, purpose, methodology, and system of evaluation. If a character associates with known enemy characters, then it is likely also an enemy. If a character associates with known cooperative NPCs, then it may be a cooperative NPC as well.

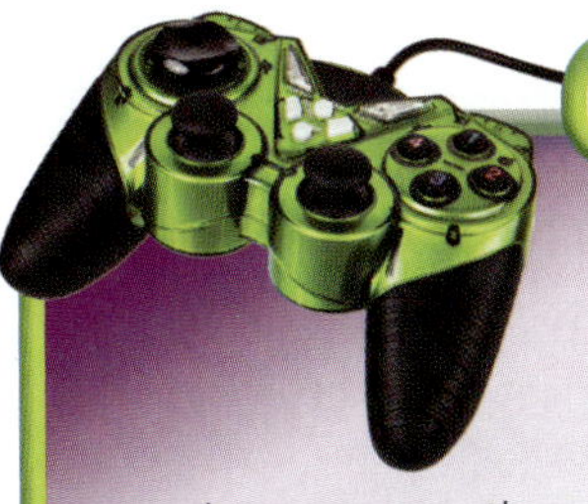

CHEAT CODE: CUT SCENE

A cut scene is a short video presentation. This is usually placed between levels or at checkpoints within a level. Often, a cut scene is used to occupy the player while the game loads a new portion of programming.

Actions

Actions are what the character does. Inactions are what the character does not do. Actions and inactions can be classified as action context clues or expressive context clues. Action context clues and expressive context clues help convey character to the player.

Action context clues are the moves and abilities a character has. As a designer, you have to imagine what moves a character will be able to do. Will it climb walls, drive a car, wield a sword, or conjure magic? Each move or ability provides context clues to the player as to the character's motivation, purpose, methodology, and system of evaluation.

In many games, the character's moves and abilities can increase as the game progresses. When this occurs, the character will level up. To ***level up*** means the character increases in game status by one level and acquires more abilities. When a change in game status takes place, the character appearance and speech does not change, but its allowable actions and abilities can change greatly. Having additional moves, powers, or weapons helps the player move the character farther through the game.

Expressive context clues appear in the body language of the character. This includes facial expressions. If the player sees a character with its arms crossed, an angry look on its face, and tapping its foot, the mood of the character can be inferred. The character is upset. In that same manner, an enemy pointing a weapon at the PC is conveying very different character than an enemy with its hands up.

One of the greatest expressive context clues is a facial expression. You have seen how teachers or parents can tell you how they feel just by the look on their faces. In older games, the technology to develop different facial expressions was limited. Designers of these games used different colored faces or symbols over the character's head to imply facial expressions. An angry character might have been shown with a red face or have an exclamation point (!) appear above its head. A character that loved the PC might have been shown with a pink face and have a heart above its head. In either case, the player had a clue to the motivation, purpose, methodology, and system of evaluation of the character. In today's games, true facial expressions can be

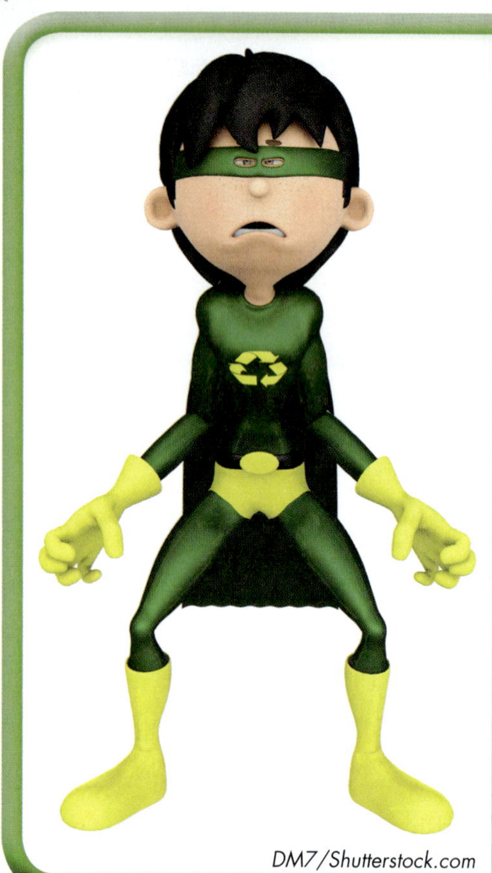

Figure 2-13. What expressive context clues can you use to determine this character's motivation? His mouth is curled down, his arms are open, and his fingers are curled in. This character may be angry about something happening in the game, or he may be surprised. Further context clues are needed to determine the exact motivation.

DM7/Shutterstock.com

used on characters to convey information, as shown in **Figure 2-13.** When designing characters, think about the moods and feelings they will have during gameplay. Then, design different facial animations to help convey this information.

Semiotics

In addition to developing a character through the use of a character background and attributes, game designers use semiotics. ***Semiotics*** is the science dealing with the meaning and relationship of symbols and features. Semiotics within the physiology of a character will provide the player with context clues to the purpose of the character within the game. ***Physiology*** is the physical shape, characteristics, and traits of a character.

A classic semiotic is the black hat. In the classic westerns movies of the 1950s, the good guys always wore white hats and the bad guys always wore black hats. In this way, the semiotic of hat color conveyed a meaning to the audience. Similarly, villains are often portrayed wearing black leather jackets or outfits, sometimes with chains and spikes. Some common semiotics of video game characters are shown in **Figure 2-14.** Remember, however, these are clues in video games. In real life, a person cannot be judged by his or her appearance.

There are many universal images and symbols that can be used to develop a character. Additionally, a game can employ its own semiotic images to add meaning. Something as simple as a uniform can symbolize allies and enemies. Other semiotics can also be applied. Regardless of the facial features or other physical characteristics, a character who carries a bow and arrows is always an archer.

Character Archetypes

In the early 20th century, the Swiss psychiatrist Carl Jung developed a set of psychic structures known as archetypes. An ***archetype*** is a universal character that is easily identifiable by any culture. Each culture describes these archetypes through the presentation of stories, myths, legends, literature, religion, and more. This makes examples of archetypes unique to each culture, but recognizable by every other culture and throughout every generation. In video games, the standard archetypes are hero, shadow, mentor, helper, guardian, trickster, and herald.

Trait	Meaning
Large muscles	Strong character; may be a PC or NPC
Long legs	Fast character; may be a PC or NPC
Pointy ears	Mythical or fantasy character; may be a PC or NPC
Old	Wise character; often a cooperative NPC
Young	Learner; often the PC
Tall	Leader; often a cooperative NPC
Short	Follower; often a sidekick NPC
Crown	Royalty or higher class; may be a PC or NPC
Dirty clothes	Common or lower class; may be a PC or NPC

Figure 2-14. In a video game, semiotics can give the player clues as to the motivation, purpose, methodology, and system of evaluation for a character. In the real world, a person cannot be judged by his or her appearance.

Goodheart-Willcox Publisher

Hero

The *hero* is the main character in the story and represents good. This character faces the challenges and drives the story. The hero typically begins the game as a regular citizen and develops skills and talents to become a hero as the game progresses. The hero may also exist in society using an alter ego to blend in with other citizens, such as Bruce Wayne and Batman. Context clues to identify the hero are usually young, healthy, and strong. Costumes to show a healthy physique are typical of the superhero games.

Shadow

The ***shadow*** is the villain or enemy of the hero and motivates the hero to do good. This character is often the equal of the hero in ability and strength. Context clues to identify the shadow often include wearing a hood, face is obscured, and skulls adorning clothing. The shadow may also be the mentor of evil characters. As such, it may also combine context clues associated with a mentor.

Mentor

The ***mentor*** teaches moral lessons and skills to the hero and directs the hero on the quest. This character is typically older and wiser than the hero. Context clues to identify the hero often include symbols of wisdom such as being elderly, wearing a long beard, and moving slowly. Due to superior skill, the mentor may often move very little in a battle.

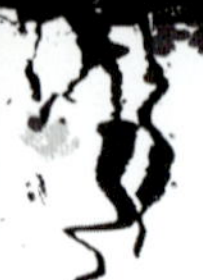

Helper

A *helper* is any character that gives vital information to the hero when the hero is trying to make moral and ethical decisions, is undergoing internal changes, or needs direction on the quest. In video games, the actions of the helpers move the story and direct the action of the hero. A helper may also be a sidekick, companion, or troop or party to help in battle. Context clues to identify a helper include being smaller, thinner, younger, and weaker than the hero.

Guardian

A ***guardian*** is a protector of an area, object, or objective. This character defends and blocks the path the hero must take to achieve victory. To defeat a guardian, the hero must usually outsmart it rather than overpower it. Context clues to identify a guardian include being a large, but unintelligent creature charged with a simple task.

Trickster

The *trickster* tries to distract the hero from the objective. This character likes to play pranks and cause mischief. The trickster also helps lighten a story and add elements of surprise. Context clues to identify a trickster include odd costumes, odd walking style or gait, highly expressive facial and body poses, and bright colors to draw attention and distract the hero.

Herald

The ***herald*** brings news to the hero or narrates the story. Using a herald is a good way to start the game story. The herald can report the situation to motivate the hero at the beginning of the story. Throughout the game, the herald can continue to provide updates of vital information to motivate the hero to complete each level. Context clues to identify the herald include: transportation items, such as wings and shoes; letters or books; writing supplies; trumpets or other devices for making announcements; and battle scars.

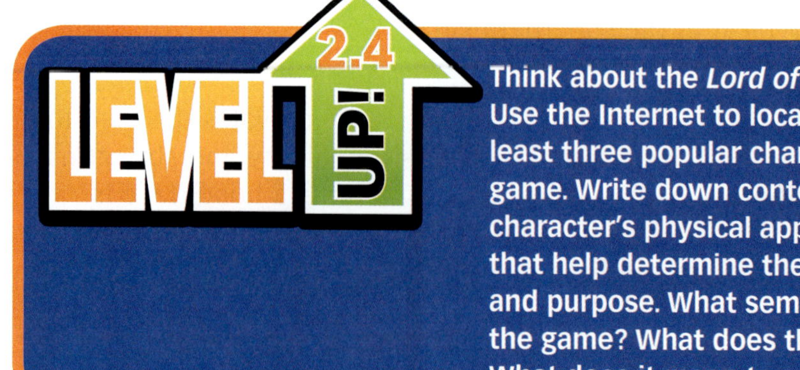

Think about the *Lord of the Rings* game. Use the Internet to locate images of at least three popular characters from that game. Write down context clues from the character's physical appearance and dress that help determine the characters' status and purpose. What semiotics are used in the game? What does the ring symbolize? What does it mean to carry the ring?

Character-Design Process

It is finally time to start making the character. In the formal design process used by most design studios, there is a series of steps to creating a final character. The specific steps and sequence will vary from one studio to another. The following are the steps a studio might use to create a final game character.

1. Create concept art.
2. Create model sheets.
3. Create movement sketches.
4. Create expression sketches.
5. Create sketches for weapons and accessories.
6. Create mockups.
7. Create renderings.

This chapter focuses on the creation of the physical form of the character. Later chapters will discuss fully developing the dialogue and story of the character.

Creating Concept Art

Concept art is the first iteration of the visual appearance of a character, background, or other element of the game. With concept art, the designer hopes to capture most of the physical attributes for the character in a basic sketch. When all of the main characters and backgrounds have been sketched as concept art, the designer will examine all of the sketches to make sure they fit the theme and mood of the game. After revising sketches as needed, the concept art moves to the next design phase, which is creating model sheets.

Creating Model Sheets

Model sheets show sketches of different poses and viewing angles for a single character. Typically, a character is posed on a single model sheet. The purpose of the model sheet is to give the rest of the design team an understanding of what the character looks like from many angles. This is important since many artists may be involved in creating different movements and renderings of the character. All of the members on the design team need to understand what the character looks like to properly place it in the scene.

Creating Movement Sketches

A ***movement sketch*** is a simple sketch of a few frames of animation to show what movement for the character looks like. It is important for each team member to know how each part of the character should move and how the character strength and ability is to be represented visually.

Movement sketches can contain both sketches and written notes. Notes are attached to let the artists identify the character move being shown and to list other possible movement sets that would use similar actions. For example, a movement sketch of a right leg kick might have notes to use similar movement for a left leg kick, roundhouse kick, or back flip. Since the animations are similar, there is no need to resketch each similar animation. This saves time and money.

Creating Expression Sketches

Expression sketches show a set of body positions and facial expressions for each emotion needed, as shown in **Figure 2-15.** Notes may also be attached to these sketches. Often, similar features are used to show similar expressions during the game. For example, an angry expression sketch may have notes detailing small changes in the body language and face to show frustration. By basing the frustration emotion on the angry emotion, time is saved. Other notes as to the amount of movement of the eyebrows or lips may also be included on expression sketches.

Creating Sketches for Weapons and Accessories

Just as important as the art for the character is the art for its weapons and accessories. This might include sketches of the character with, for example, his or her horse. The horse or whatever vehicle used needs to match the player's motivation and purpose. Additionally, weapons need to be appropriate to the character. Accessories the character will pick up as the game progresses, like different types of armor, also need to be sketched. All of the weapon and accessory sketches are used by the game artists to properly render the objects needed by the character.

Creating Mockups

Depending on the complexity of the character, a mockup may need to be created, as shown in **Figure 2-16.** A ***mockup*** is a physical representation of the character or game element. The mockup is used by the game artists along with the sketches to create the final renderings for the game. In many cases, the mockup may even include a full wardrobe and arsenal of weapons. In other cases, the designer might just go to the store and buy an action figure similar to the character, then change out costume parts and pieces.

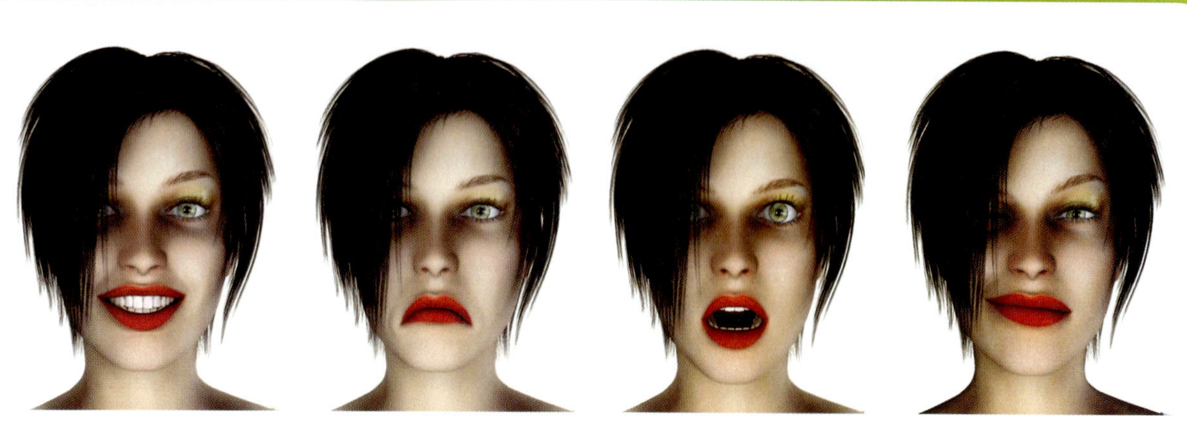

DM7/Shutterstock.com

Figure 2-15. Expression sketches show the facial features for the character's emotions. Artists use these sketches to create the final renderings, as shown here.

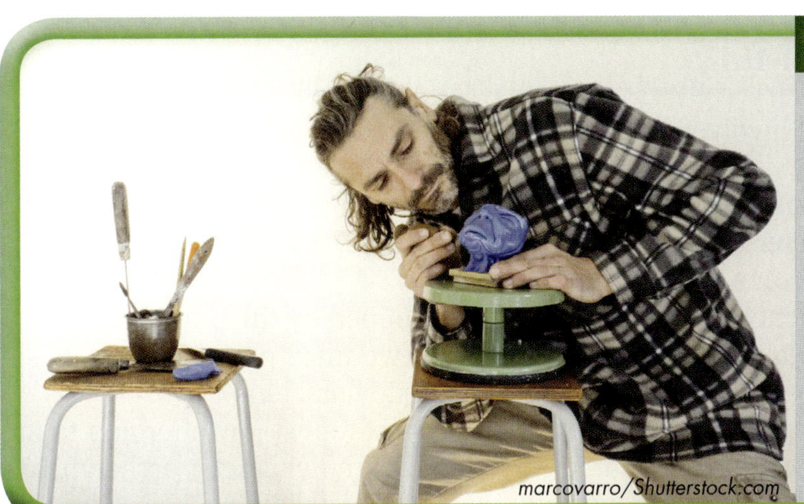

Figure 2-16.

Many times a detailed character mockup is created to help the artists visualize the character when creating the electronic artwork for the game.

Creating Renderings

When all sketches are approved, the art team begins to render the character images. All of the paper artwork and physical mockups are finally put into digital form and a computer-generated character is created. ***Rendering*** is applying colors and textures to create a final image as shown in **Figure 2-17**. In video game design, renderings are created using a computer and software such as 3ds Max, Maya, Photoshop, or Illustrator.

Since this step is the most detailed and time consuming, the design team needs to have the character fully detailed before beginning this step. If major changes are made to the character after it has been modeled and rendered, the entire model may have to be rebuilt and rerendered. This could waste a lot of time, effort, and money.

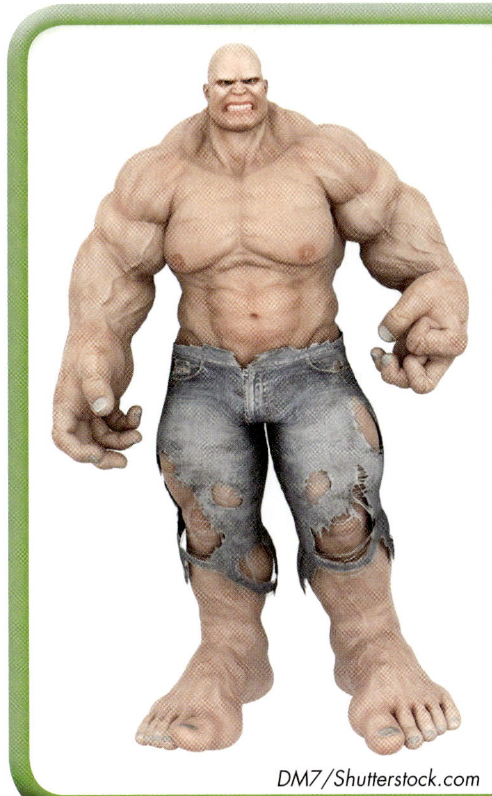

Figure 2-17.

This is a final rendering of a game character. It is the result of developing character, providing a driving force for the character, designing the character, and creating sketches of the character.

LEVEL UP! 2.5

Take the character you have been developing. Using software or by hand, sketch several designs for how the character may look. Include tools and other accessories the character may need.

Chapter Summary

- Character design involves artists, writers, programmers, and game designers.
- Dominant characters that stand apart from other characters in similar games are characters that embody emotions, flaws, and a human condition that make them come alive for the player.
- The role and function of a character are determined by the purpose of the character in the game which falls into one of two main purpose categories: gameplay-attributed characters and story-based characters.
- The important aspects of characters that designers must pay attention to are the background, conveying character, semiotics, and character archetypes.
- The character-design process typically includes the following steps: 1) create concept art, 2) create model sheets, 3) create movement sketches, 4) create expression sketches, 5) create sketches for weapons and accessories, 6) create mockups, and 7) create renderings.

Check Your Video Game IQ

Now that you have finished this chapter, see what you know about video game design by taking the chapter posttest.

www.m.g-wlearning.com

www.g-wlearning.com

Review Your Knowledge

On a separate sheet of paper or in a word processing document, match the following terms with the definition that fits best.

A. avatar
B. minions
C. central premise
D. sidekick
E. protagonist
F. texture
G. non-player character (NPC)
H. antagonist
I. semiotics
J. character

1. The science dealing with the meaning and relationship of symbols and features.
2. The main character of the story.
3. Any character controlled by the game instead of by the player.
4. The makeup of talents, skills, abilities, and physical attributes needed to achieve the victory condition.
5. A flat image that is wrapped around the model like skin.
6. The main adversary or opponent in the story.

7. The basic idea or situation of the story.
8. Minor characters, like soldiers, who can come in several ranks, strengths, and abilities.
9. An image used to represent the player in the game.
10. A companion who is subordinate to the player character.

On a separate sheet of paper or in a word processing document, answer each of the following questions.

11. What is the term for the main idea or situation the story is about?
12. Define protagonist.
13. Which type of characters are programmed by the game designers and not controlled by a player?
14. What is the difference between a game-select avatar and a player-designed avatar?
15. Define rendering.
16. Define sidekick.
17. What is the purpose of the story?
18. What is character purpose?
19. Define context clues.
20. Define archetype.

Apply Your STEM Knowledge

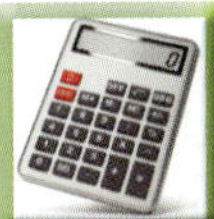

Mathematics

1. Custom avatars can be very unique. By multiplying the number of options for each attribute by the number of options for all other attributes, the total possible combinations for creating a custom avatar can be calculated. Use this mathematical concept to solve for the answers and fill in the table below.

Object	# of Styles	# of Colors	Total Combinations
Gender	2	4	8
Hair	12		192
Shirt	8	16	
Pants/Skirt		16	320
Shoes	9	16	
Total Unique Character Combinations			

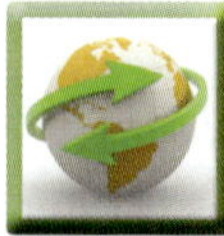

Social Studies

2. Research the total current population of humans living on planet Earth. List the total global population, your source, and date recorded. Is the total unique character combination for our custom avatar generator diverse enough for everyone to have a different avatar?

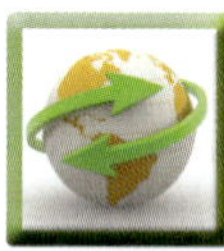

Social Studies

3. Research ten popular characters in recent game releases. Use a spreadsheet to create a table similar to the one below. List the characters and rate each on a scale from 1 to 10 where 1 is Good and 10 is Evil. Rate the character again on a scale from 1 to 10 where 1 is Ethical and 10 is Unethical.

Character	Evil Rank	Unethical Rank

Language Arts

4. Use the charting feature on the spreadsheet created in the Social Studies question above to create a stacked column chart to visually display the results of your rankings. Write a one-page paper to discuss your data.

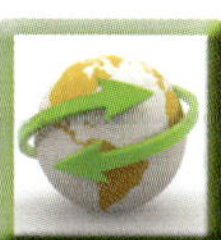

Social Studies

5. Play a recent game release. Observe the main character's movements, facial expressions, and other nonverbal communication. List each emotion displayed and describe the context clues that provided evidence to support your conclusion. With permission, photograph a person displaying the character's nonverbal communication and create a PowerPoint presentation to provide visual representation of each emotion described.

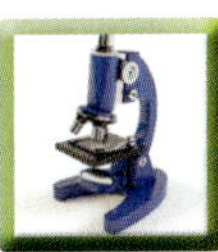

Science

6. Facial expressions provide context clues to the emotions of a character. These expressions are used in an expression sheet for character development. Research how the muscles of the face are used to create a smile. Note the total number of muscles involved. Explore how a complex system of muscles is used to make this simple expression. Create a PowerPoint presentation of at least ten slides to explain your research.

Working in Teams

In teams as assigned by your instructor, brainstorm ideas for a character. Prepare a PowerPoint presentation of up to ten slides (five to seven minutes) to present to the class explaining the character, describe its motivation, and show ideas for the appearance of the character. Include text, pictures, video, animations, slide transitions, and sound effects as appropriate to help explain your positions.

Gamer Portfolio

Your instructor may provide you with a checklist of components that should be included in your portfolio. If not, create a checklist that works best for you. Before you begin collecting information for your portfolio, write an objective related to creating the portfolio. An objective is a complete sentence or two that states what you want to accomplish. It should contain enough detail so that you can easily judge when it is accomplished, such as "I will complete one completed character sketch for each week of class." Creating a clear objective is a good starting point for beginning work on your portfolio.

1. Create a checklist to use as an ongoing reference as you create your portfolio throughout this class.
2. Decide on the purpose of the portfolio you are creating—temporary or short-term employment, career, or college application.
3. Do research on the Internet to find articles about writing objectives. Also, look for articles that contain sample objectives for creating a portfolio.
4. Write an objective for creating your portfolio that will be used in applying for a job or to a college. Include objectives for both a print portfolio and an e-portfolio.

G-W Learning Mobile Site

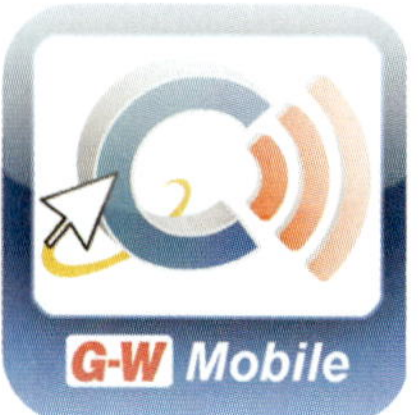

Visit the G-W Learning mobile site to complete the chapter pretest and posttest and to practice vocabulary using e-flash cards. If you do not have a smartphone, visit the G-W Learning companion website to access these features.

G-W Learning mobile site: www.m.g-wlearning.com

G-W Learning companion website: www.g-wlearning.com

Common Core

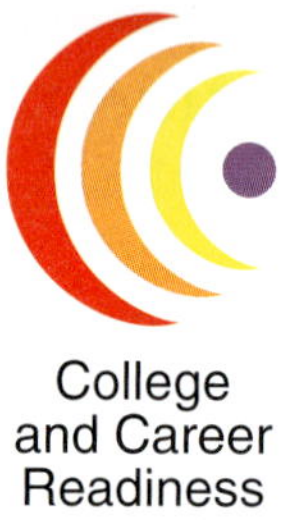

College and Career Readiness

CTE Career Ready Practices. Go online and search for desirable workplace skills. Then, conduct another search for top academic skills. Create a Venn diagram showing the overlap between the two lists.

Writing. Using the Internet, research the advice that experts have for people who want to become video game designers. Make sure to look at, among other sources, newspaper and magazine articles, scholarly reports, and public addresses from prominent video game designers. Write a final research report in which you cite the sources that you used and the strengths and weaknesses of each. Be sure to consider the background and point of view of the sources that you find.

Speaking and Listening. Research the features of some of the three-dimensional modeling software that is available. Compile information about the benefits and other aspects of each software, such as how easy it is to use, what image types your work can be saved in, and the cost. Use this information, along with what you already know about 3D modeling software, to analyze which software would be best suited to your needs. Using various elements (visual displays, written handouts, technological displays), present your choice to the class. Explain why you chose the software you did.

Event Prep: Prejudged Computer Game

Creating a computer game is a competitive event that may be offered by your Career and Technical Student Organization (CTSO). This may be an individual or team event. There may be two parts to this event: the prejudged program and the performance portion. The event calls for the development of a computer game as outlined by the organization. The topic will be detailed on the organization's website. Students are given an opportunity to create a game that shows creativity, programming skills, and meets the definition of a video game. To prepare for creating a game:

1. Read the guidelines provided by your organization. Visit the organization website early in the school year so you will have plenty of time to create your game. Make certain that you ask any questions about points that you do not understand immediately after you review the guidelines.

2. Create a checklist of the guidelines for the event.
3. There will be specific directions given as to the topic how the game should be created and presented to the judges. The prejudged portion of game creation will be submitted before the competition. Read the submission rules for the date, number of copies, and so on. These rules must be followed in order to qualify for the event.
4. The organization may specify a programming language or game engine to use or leave it to the participant's choice. Make certain you are clear on what can be used before beginning the process.
5. Creating a game can take a lot of time to properly prepare, therefore, it is important to start early. Set a deadline so that you can create the game at a comfortable pace.
6. After you create your first playable level, ask your teacher to review it and give you feedback.
7. Once you have the final iteration of your game, review the checklist. Make sure you have addressed all requirements. You will be penalized if a direction is not followed exactly.

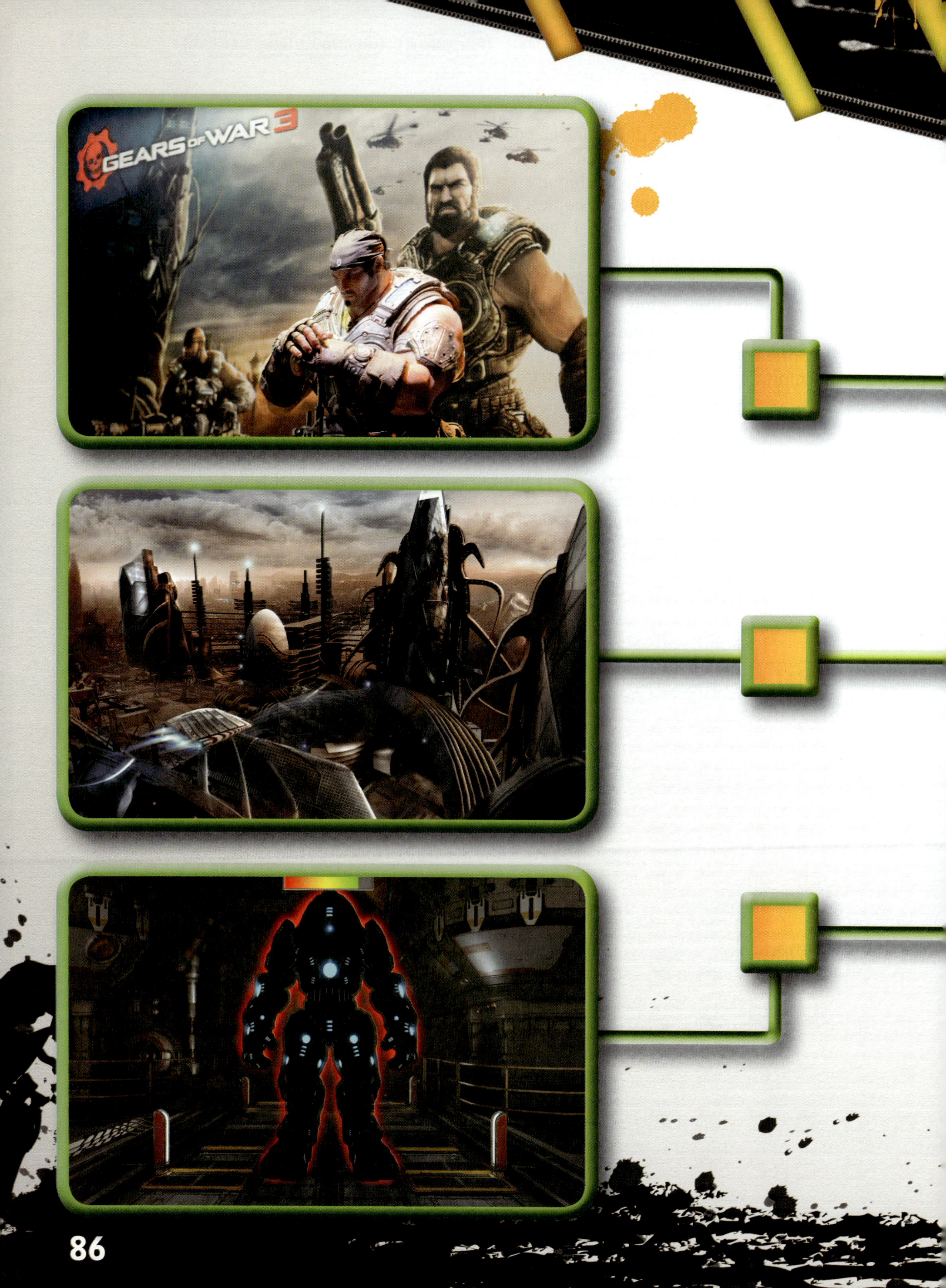
GEARS OF WAR 3

Chapter 3
Story Composition

Many video games are interactive stories. The player can become involved with the main storyline. There are several different ways a story can be added to the game, some of which allow the player to choose a path within the story. Add a story only if it will help make the game more meaningful to the player. This chapter explores how a story is assembled and how a game can be designed to tell a story.

Check Your Video Game IQ

Before you begin this chapter, see what you already know about video game design by taking the chapter pretest.

www.m.g-wlearning.com

www.g-wlearning.com

College and Career Readiness

Reading Prep. Before reading the chapter, skim the photos and their captions. As you are reading, determine how these concepts contribute to the ideas presented in the text.

Objectives

After completing this chapter, you will be able to:

- Determine when to add a story to a video game.
- Outline the basic creative writing procedures.
- Differentiate between a linear and a nonlinear structure for interactive story delivery.
- Explain how level design mimics the story design and differentiate between level designs for linear and nonlinear games.
- Define the essential elements of a level.

To Add or Not to Add a Story

A story illustrates a series of events that describe the process of a character resolving a problem or conflict. The *plot* is the plan or map for the story. It is total sequence of events needed to get to the final resolution.

Not every game tells a story. Think about early arcade games, like *Pong* and *Break Out*. These games were able to entertain without an underlying storyline. The gameplay alone was able to carry the game to success.

As games advanced, the need to differentiate between similar game actions led to the inclusion of a story. One of the first to add a simple story was the original *Donkey Kong*. Mario was motivated to rescue Princess Peach from Donkey Kong. It was a simple story, but allowed the player to connect to the gameplay and player motivation.

Today, some games still do not need a story for the player to connect to the game. Sports games usually do not have a story. However, most games must have a story for the player to connect to the game. A role-playing game (RPG), for example, depends on a story to motivate the player to undertake quests and seek higher player status.

In general, a story should be added to a game for one of five reasons:

- add entertainment to the game
- define the audience
- keep player attention
- differentiate the game
- integrate with marketing

Adding a story to the game should fit within the gameplay and add to the entertainment. Adding a thin and poorly developed story to a game will not make it a success. Game designers must properly apply a story to a game when appropriate. It is important to keep in mind that you should always be looking for things that will be fun for the player. If that thing is a story inside the game, then give the player a great story with interesting characters.

Add Entertainment to the Game

A story that allows the player to feel a sense of progression as problems are solved through gameplay adds to the entertainment value of the game. Without this progression, the gameplay may seem repetitive or meaningless without the need to make it to the end. Often, the story continues throughout a series of games. Think of the story of Altair in *Assassin's Creed* or Jack in *BioShock*, as shown in **Figure 3-1.** The stories in these games are an integral part of the gameplay.

Define the Audience

In some cases, the story is needed to make the gameplay appealing to a specific audience of players. Younger players may be attracted to the simple gameplay of a platform game. An older audience may need the game to have a strong story so they can connect with the player character. Also, the intensity and content of the story help determine the game rating. Games with mature stories will receive ratings like teen (T), mature (M), or adult only (AO). This helps define for whom the game is designed.

Keep Player Attention

For games that take tens of hours to complete, the player needs to feel motivated to continue to play. If the player is not motivated to play to the end, he or she will not like the game or feel it was worth the purchase price. Simple online games that seek only a high score as a reward do not need to keep the player's attention for very long. A strong story is not needed. However, a game like *Call of Duty* takes many days to complete. In *Call of Duty,* the gameplay at the beginning of the game is very similar to that in the middle and end of the game. The gameplay would get boring very quickly if not for the story. The game is broken down into missions to motivate the player to complete a segment of the story and eventually reach the end. Additionally, the player may encounter new players throughout the game. The story keeps the player's attention throughout the long gameplay.

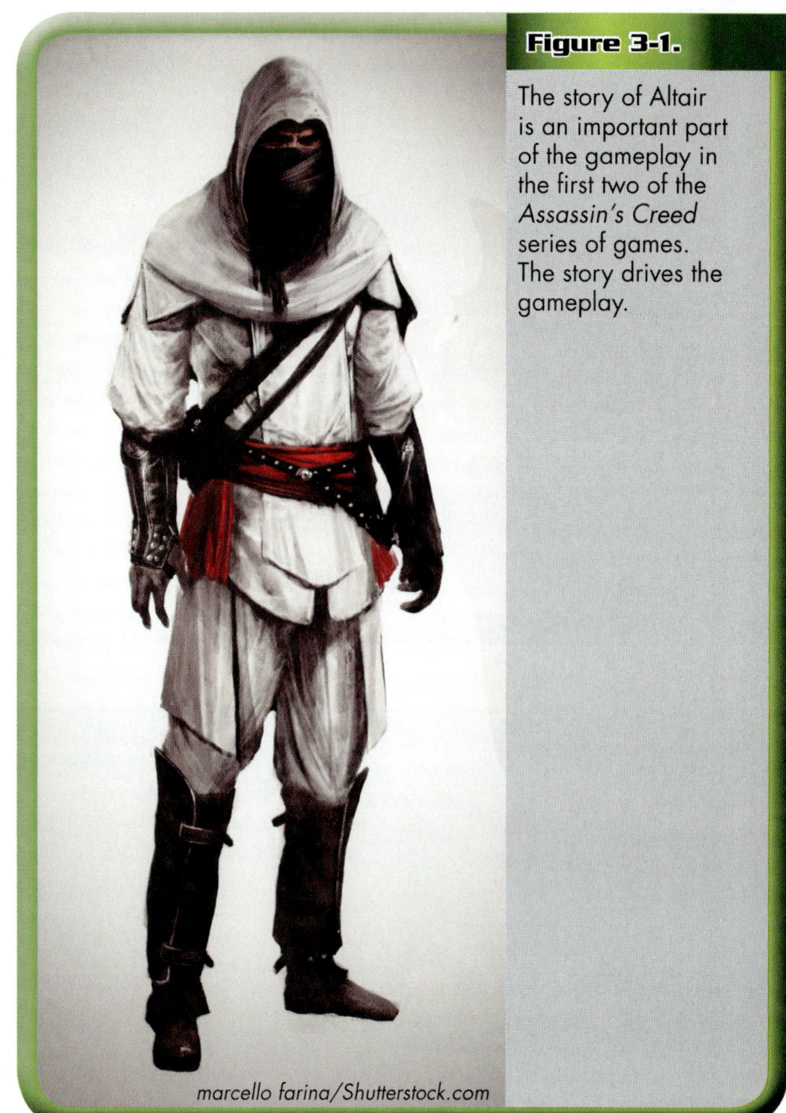

Figure 3-1. The story of Altair is an important part of the gameplay in the first two of the *Assassin's Creed* series of games. The story drives the gameplay.

marcello farina/Shutterstock.com

Differentiate the Game

With several games using the same or similar gameplay, a strong character and story will help buyers decide which game is best for them. There are several car-racing games that have almost the same gameplay. They all involve maneuvering the vehicle through a course, avoiding crashing, and getting to the finish line first. A story will help the player connect to one racing game over another.

It is also important for games in a series to have different stories, as shown in **Figure 3-2.** For example, the basic story in the *Halo* series of games is that of the alien alliance, Covenant, fighting a holy war against humans, whose primary defenders are super soldiers, known as Spartans. However, each game in the series tells a new part of the larger story. Each game in the series can be thought of as a chapter in a book that tells the story of the Covenant versus the Spartans. Without the story differentiating each game in the series, there would be little reason for a player to continue purchasing new *Halo* games.

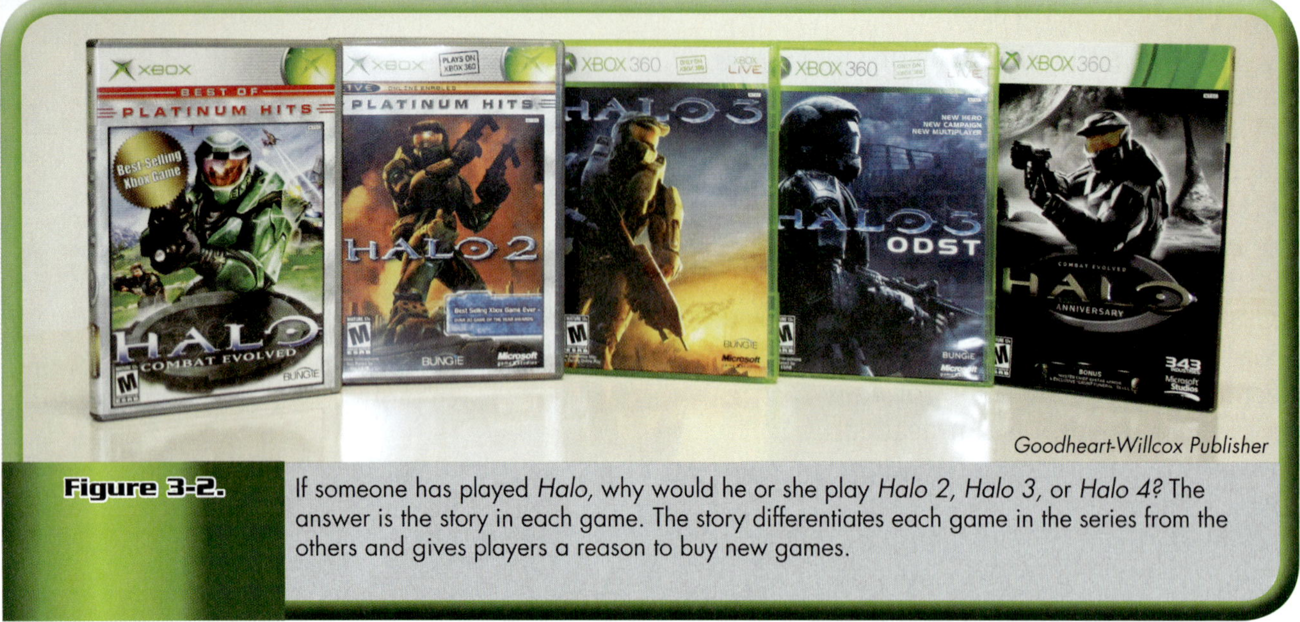

Goodheart-Willcox Publisher

Figure 3-2. If someone has played *Halo,* why would he or she play *Halo 2, Halo 3,* or *Halo 4*? The answer is the story in each game. The story differentiates each game in the series from the others and gives players a reason to buy new games.

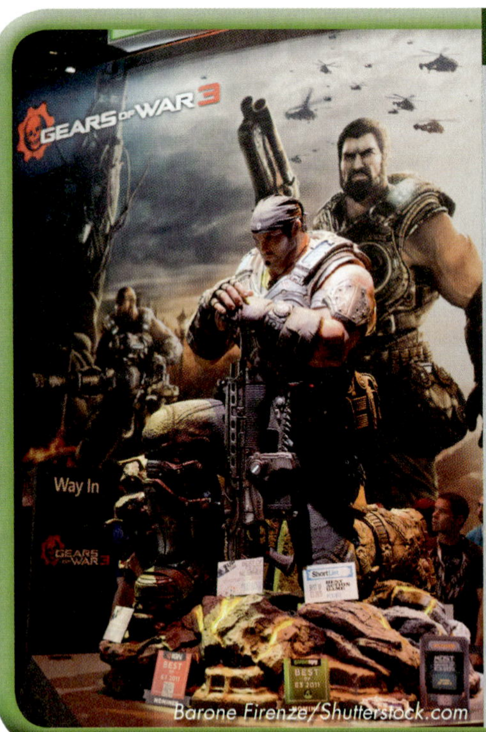

Barone Firenze/Shutterstock.com

Figure 3-3. The story of Marcus Fenix, the main character in *Gears of War 3,* becomes an integral part of the marketing effort for the game. Here, an oversize statue is displayed at a large video-game expo.

Integrate with Marketing

To effectively market a game and make it profitable, the producers may require the use of a story or character to help publicize the game. This might be true of a game like *Mario Kart.* A simple racing game is made far more marketable by the use of Mario and other familiar characters. Other games like *Gears of War* have very interesting characters and unusual storylines that can be used to help market the game, as shown in **Figure 3-3.** Attention-grabbing storylines and familiar characters help get the buyer's attention.

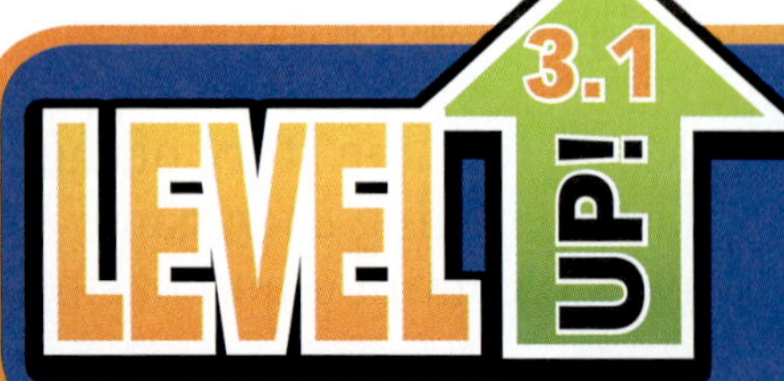

Play a favorite game that includes a story. Write a one-page paper describing the story in the game and which of the five reasons for adding a story were met.

Creative Writing

After the decision has been made that a story is needed for the game, you must come up with a good story. Creative writing is developing a work of fiction that tells a story with characters, places, and events. If you decide to become a game writer, you will have to develop skills to quickly expand stories and write dialogue to fit the story's central premise.

A good story has rising action, a climax, and falling action. These three things form the basic *dramatic arc* of the story, as shown in **Figure 3-4.** ***Rising action*** is the events that create the basic internal conflict of the story. The ***climax*** is the turning point of the story, which is the most dramatic part of the story. ***Falling action*** is the events that lead to the resolution of the basic conflict of the story.

While there are many different schools of thought on how to write a creative story, this textbook focuses on a simple outline to get the process started. The basics procedure for creative writing is:

- brainstorm ideas;
- determine the central premise;
- define the characters;
- create a primary conflict;
- structure the story; and
- develop an ending point.

The questions shown in **Figure 3-5** can be used to guide the writing process. In the end, you will need to develop a technique that works best for you. The final product is the important part, not the process used to achieve it.

Brainstorm Ideas

You will have to use your imagination to create new story ideas, characters, and plot points. ***Brainstorming*** is recording as many ideas as possible without sorting, editing, or eliminating any of the ideas. To begin brainstorming, write down things as you think of them. Do not try to sort the ideas as good, bad, or just plain silly. You can sort them out later. Write down the ideas on paper, key them into a word processing document, or even record them on your smartphone.

When brainstorming, think about game interactions or characters that are already defined. If the main character is a fish, start thinking about aquatic-themed ideas. Even if you come up with a silly idea about a fish living in the desert, write it down.

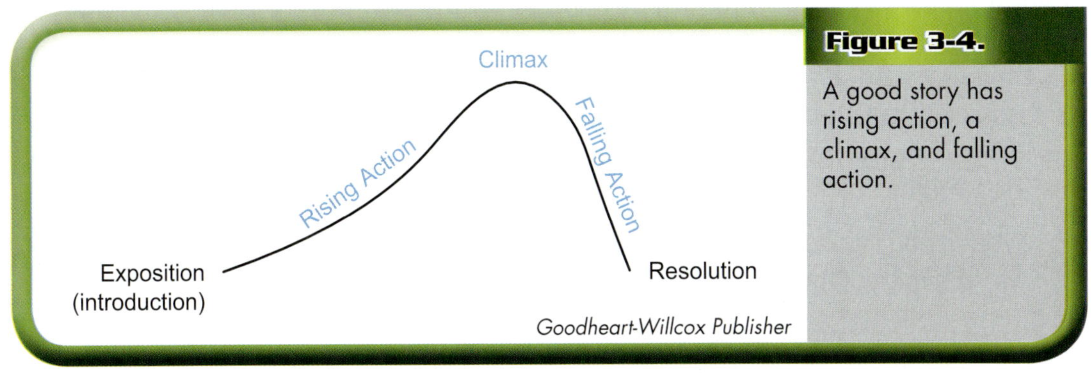

Figure 3-4. A good story has rising action, a climax, and falling action.

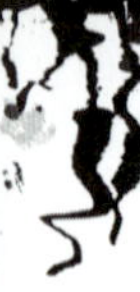

Requirements for a Good Story		
Topic	**Question**	**Yes/No**
Character resolution	Does the protagonist remain driven to seek the resolution?	
Character adaptation	Does the main character start doing something new and useful? Does the main character stop doing something old and useless?	
Player interaction	Is the story driven by the action and decisions of the main character?	
Story climax	Does the story build dramatic tension?	
Player success	Does the player have a reasonable chance of completing the story?	
Player emotion	Will the player end the game feeling good about the actions in the game or feel bad from disturbing images or events?	
Player immersion	Will the player become involved in the game world?	
Player support	Does the player have enough support from other characters to understand the story and how the resolution is to be achieved?	
Story credibility	Is the story believable? Is the player conflict important? Is the resolution adequate? Are rewards believable?	
Story cohesiveness	Do all elements of the story fit together? Are missions appropriate to the end result?	

Figure 3-5. These questions can be used to help make sure a story is well-developed.

Goodheart-Willcox Publisher

Crazier ideas have made people very wealthy. What about a sponge that lives in a pineapple under the sea and wants to cook hamburgers? That crazy idea turned into the SpongeBob SquarePants franchise. When brainstorming, there are no bad ideas. Record all your ideas and sort them later. You may come up with a real winner.

Determine the Central Premise

After brainstorming, sort through the list of possible ideas. Think about which ideas are the best. Discard the ideas that are not good. It is often helpful to start a new list and rewrite the ideas that you like best. When you have a list of good ideas, take the time to really think about each one. Which ideas have the best chances for success?

Develop a final list that includes the idea and a central premise for a story. As discussed in Chapter 2, the central premise is the basic idea or situation of the story. An idea might be travelling around the world. The central premise for this idea might be:

> What if you had to chase a criminal mastermind around the world and try to stop the theft of the cultural treasures of the world?

The central premise provides motivation for the characters and can be developed into a story. To make things easier to understand, try to follow these keys to a central premise.

- Be brief; about 30 words.
- Answers the question, "What if…?".
- Identify a character and a conflict.
- Reveal the setting for the conflict.
- Incorporate credible or believable events.
- Make sure it is easily understood by the target audience.
- Determine if it can be developed into a coherent or complete story.
- Be sure it contains elements that are different from other stories.

In many cases, a central premise can fit into a standard fill-in-the-blank model. **Figure 3-6** shows the fill-in-the-blank model.

Myths and legends can be used to generate ideas for the story's central premise. Myths and legends are important to society. Through myths and legends, a culture reveals the values of the society, including moral values, beliefs on the afterlife, patriotism, social bonds, the role of community, and the role of the individual. A society's myths and legends portray the example of what the ideal citizen would do when facing a value-based decision. These tales have a **moral**.

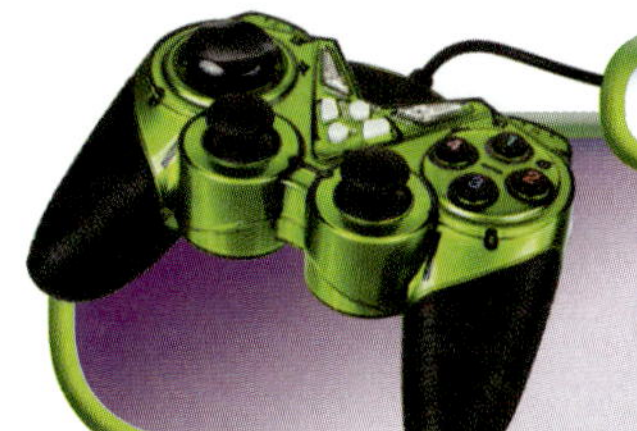

CHEAT CODE: MORAL

A moral is a lesson to be learned. Myths and legends communicate the right thing to do.

In many myths and legends, the sense of individual freedom is sacrificed for the betterment of the entire community. This might be demonstrated by a soldier heroically saving his unit by falling on a grenade or a mentor surrendering to the enemy to keep her apprentice safe. Each culture has developed a set of myths and legends that offer stories of the defenders of their way of life. However, throughout the world myths and legends have common themes and characters.

Model

What if TIME in PLACE, CHARACTER, had to CONFLICT or TASK to PURPOSE?

Examples

What if in the winter of 1925 in Nome, Alaska, the sled dog Balto had to cross the Arctic Sea to deliver the medicine needed to save the town?

What if once upon a time in a land far, far away, the knight Sir Joustsalot had to fight a fire-breathing dragon to rescue the princess?

Goodheart-Willcox Publisher

Figure 3-6. The fill-in-the-blank model can be used to construct the central premise of a story.

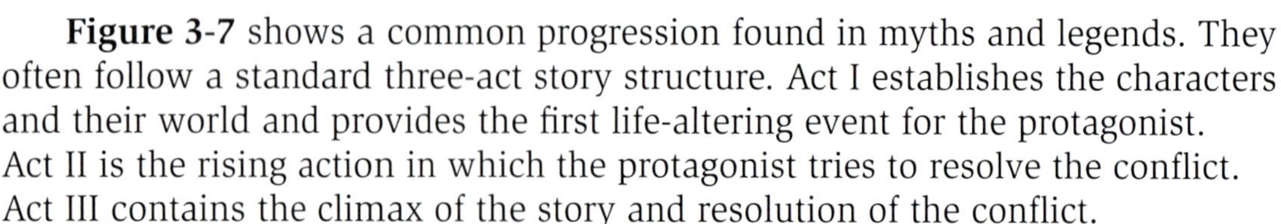

Figure 3-7 shows a common progression found in myths and legends. They often follow a standard three-act story structure. Act I establishes the characters and their world and provides the first life-altering event for the protagonist. Act II is the rising action in which the protagonist tries to resolve the conflict. Act III contains the climax of the story and resolution of the conflict.

Act	Stage	Stage Name	Description
	1	Ordinary World	Backstory; show the hero in his or her ordinary surroundings. The hero is often a misfit uncomfortable or unaware of his or her abilities or desires. The audience sympathizes with the hero's flaws.
	2	Call to Adventure	The first event that changes the life of the hero. This can be internal or external. The hero must notice the need for change, see the solution to the problem, leave the known ordinary world, and adventure to an unknown world to find the solution.
I	3	Refusal of the Call	An internal struggle begins where the hero experiences and displays his or her fears. This causes the hero to turn away or delay his quest. Another character may relate to the audience why no one else is willing or able to take the risks. A second event may be used to turn the hero back to the quest.
	4	Meeting the Mentor	The hero meets a specialist who offers training, weapons, equipment, and advice to help the hero on the journey. The mentor often requires a test of special knowledge or skill before the hero can continue on the quest.
	5	Crossing the Threshold	The hero commits to leaving the ordinary world and entering the special world where he or she is unfamiliar with the rules and customs.
	6	Allies, Enemies, and Heroic Tests or Deeds	The hero meets other characters that will prove to be either allies or enemies. The hero will also endure the tests of his skill and motivation. A battle with an enemy or partnering with an ally occurs here.
	7	Approach	The hero and allies prepare and plan for the major challenges of the special world. The unique skills of each ally will play a pivotal role in achieving the objective.
II	8	Ordeal	The hero assaults the inner sanctum of the special world and faces his or her greatest fear. This is a major turning point in the character development of the hero. The journey has changed from obtaining the physical treasure to the internal transformation or rebirth.
	9	Reward	The treasure is in hand, but there is a danger that it can be lost. This creates an urgency to return with the reward to the ordinary world.
	10	Road Back	The journey back to the ordinary world begins. The allies begin to leave the hero, either by returning home or a noble death in battle.
	11	Resurrection	The hero has traveled to the edge of the special world, but must face a major test. This is the climax. The hero seems resolved to accept his or her own death for the betterment of the ordinary world. This resolves the conflict from the inciting incident.
III	12	Return with the Treasure	The journey home with the treasure and victory continues. All remaining story elements are wrapped up as the hero crosses back into the ordinary world as a transformed and enlightened part of society.

Figure 3-7. Across all societies, myths and legends have similar heroes, heroines, and plots. Myths and legends can be a source of ideas for video game stories.

Goodheart-Willcox Publisher

CASE STUDY

The Hero's Journey

One of the most used story structures is the hero's journey. Twentieth century American mythologist Professor Joseph Campbell analyzed thousands of myths and found a group of common elements. He detailed a complete list of these elements in his books. The basic framework of just the most essential elements is discussed here to help you understand the role of the hero. This story framework applies well to video games and movies where a central hero is used.

The hero's journey describes the typical adventure for the hero archetype. The hero can be male or female as gender is not part of the hero's conflict. The hero must achieve an objective to save the tribe, city, civilization, or other group that makes up his world. When completed in order, the hero's journey is a cycle that returns the character home with both the world-saving elixir and a personal transformation or rebirth.

Similar to the hero's journey is the heroine's journey. In addition to all the same internal character development of the hero, the heroine must also battle and balance the elements of masculine and feminine traits or roles. Unique to the heroine is that she must remain a female throughout the story. To complete the quest, she must also master masculine skills as the hero. Use of *shape shifting* is a common element in the heroine's journey. Shape shifting is a change in the physical or outward appearance of a character. An example is a lycanthrope like a werewolf; the human form is shifted to the wolf form. Shape shifting allows the heroine to take on the persona of both the male hero and the female heroine.

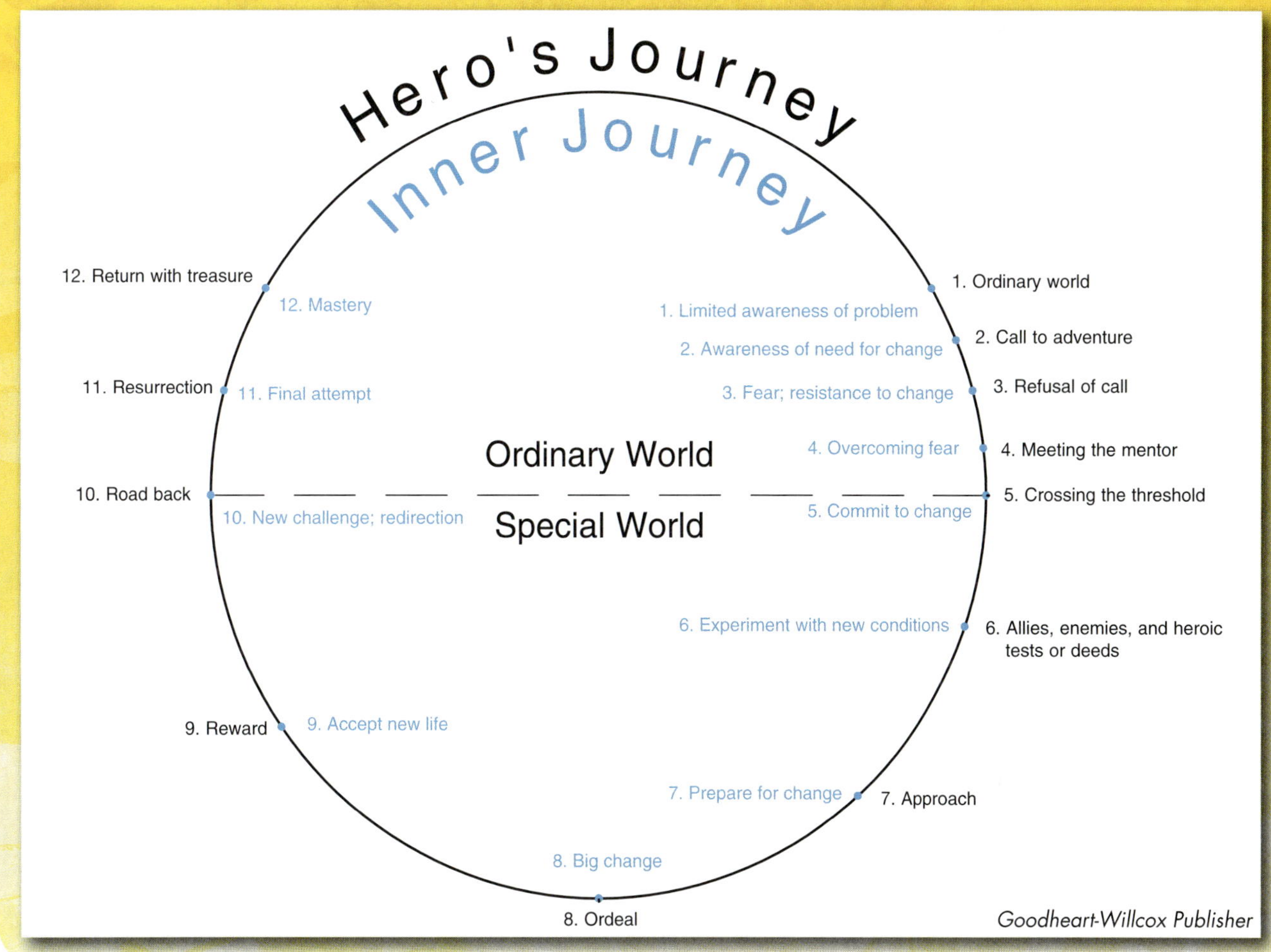

Goodheart-Willcox Publisher

Define the Characters

With a central premise established, the story needs to be filled with characters. Well-developed characters are very important to the story. Examine the central premise. Think about what type of characters might work best in that situation. You will have to decide if the characters will be round or flat characters.

Round characters develop and change throughout the story. These are the most interesting characters. The main characters of a story are almost always round characters. If the protagonist and antagonist are round characters, the player can have an emotional connection to them. The player wants good to happen to the protagonist and the antagonist to be defeated.

Flat characters do not develop or change throughout the story. These are typically stock or stereotyped characters. The player is not expected to make a connection with a flat character. The character is just in the game to fulfill a function.

Stock characters have standard traits and perform a standard role. This might be an infantry soldier, police officer, medic, or other character that performs a standard game role and looks like every other character of the same type in the game. Likewise, ***stereotyped characters*** perform a standard game role, but have very general characteristics that provide some variation among the same type of characters in the game. A stereotyped character might be, for example, a member of the pirate crew. Each crewmember looks different from the others, so they are not stock characters. But, each crewmember has general characteristics that immediately identify the character as a pirate. This may include a hook hand, wooden peg leg, black eye patch, or head bandana. Regardless of the physical differences, a pirate is just a pirate. Each pirate crew is expected to act in the same manner.

In addition to choosing between round and flat characters, a designer must also decide how to motivate the character. What rewards will the game present to increase the status of the character? What status attributes will be important to this type of character? The answers to these questions can help write good characters for the game story.

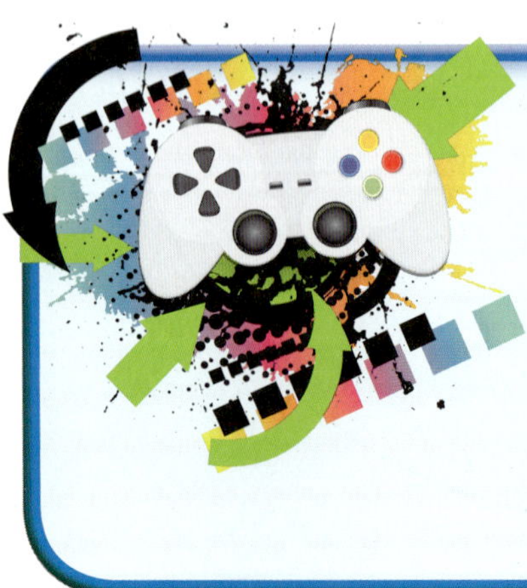

Ethical Gamer

Using age, gender, race, disability, or ethnicity as a way to describe others is unethical and sometimes illegal. Use bias-free language in all of your communication, whether verbal or printed, to show respect for those with whom you come in contact. For more information on unbiased communication, search the Internet to find out the latest information on the topic.

Create a Primary Conflict

To have a story, there needs to be a conflict. This conflict can be between the protagonist and antagonist, protagonist and the world, or even internally within the protagonist. The primary conflict is what makes a story a story. It makes the story interesting as the player wants to see how the conflict can be resolved. Other conflicts help move the story forward, but it is the primary conflict that connects players to the game and keeps them playing.

To create a primary conflict, put the character in a situation that has risk. Suppose the character must retrieve a golden crown from a cave. If the knight could just walk into the cave and get the crown, that would not be very interesting. There is no risk. But, what if there was a fire-breathing dragon in the cave curled up around the crown? Then there would be a risk for the knight in getting the crown. Now, what if the road to the cave is through a forest in which evil creatures live? There is greater risk to the knight. And, before traveling through the forest, the knight has to go to a seedy part of town to barter for tools and weapons. The greater the reward, the greater risk the character should experience.

The primary conflict must be great enough to propel the game story. It is the opposing objectives of the protagonist and antagonist. The protagonist wants to save the world, while the antagonist wants to destroy it.

Structure the Story

Once the story has a conflict, it needs to have dramatic tension, climax, and resolution built into it. ***Dramatic tension*** is a feeling of anxiety or anticipation related to the story being told, as shown in **Figure 3-4.** From the *exposition,* or introduction of the primary conflict, the dramatic tension builds to the climax. This is the *rising action* of the story. The highest point of dramatic interest occurs at the climax. At the *climax,* the action turns. After the climax, the level of dramatic tension begins to decrease as the conflicts are sorted out. This is the *falling action.* When the conflict is over, the story has reached a *resolution.*

A simple story will have a single conflict, climax, and resolution. More complex stories have many conflicts, many climaxes, and many resolutions. The story can be expanded with missions or episodes within the story. Each mission should have its own conflict, climax, and resolution. But, each mission should also move the main story forward to its climax and resolution, as shown in **Figure 3-8.** Mission-based episodes are a common way to build in more action within the game and allow for mini conclusion points throughout the game.

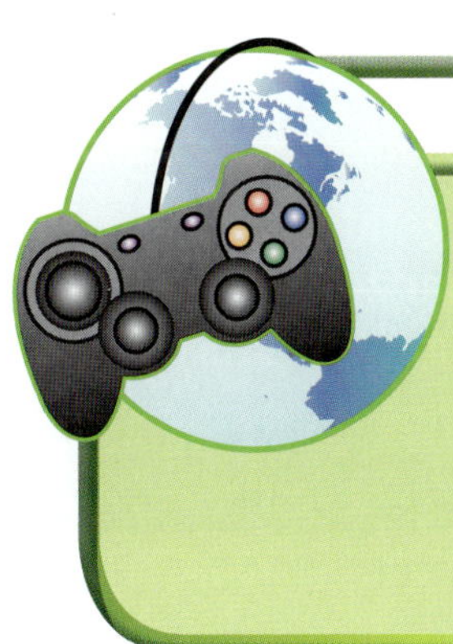

Green Gamer

As the need arises to purchase a new gaming computer, look for one made of environmentally-friendly materials. Manufacturers of technology equipment are doing their part to make better equipment with more ecofriendly materials. You can now find mercury-free computers and electronic devices built with components with reduced amounts of brominated fire retardants (BFR) and polyvinyl chloride (PVC).

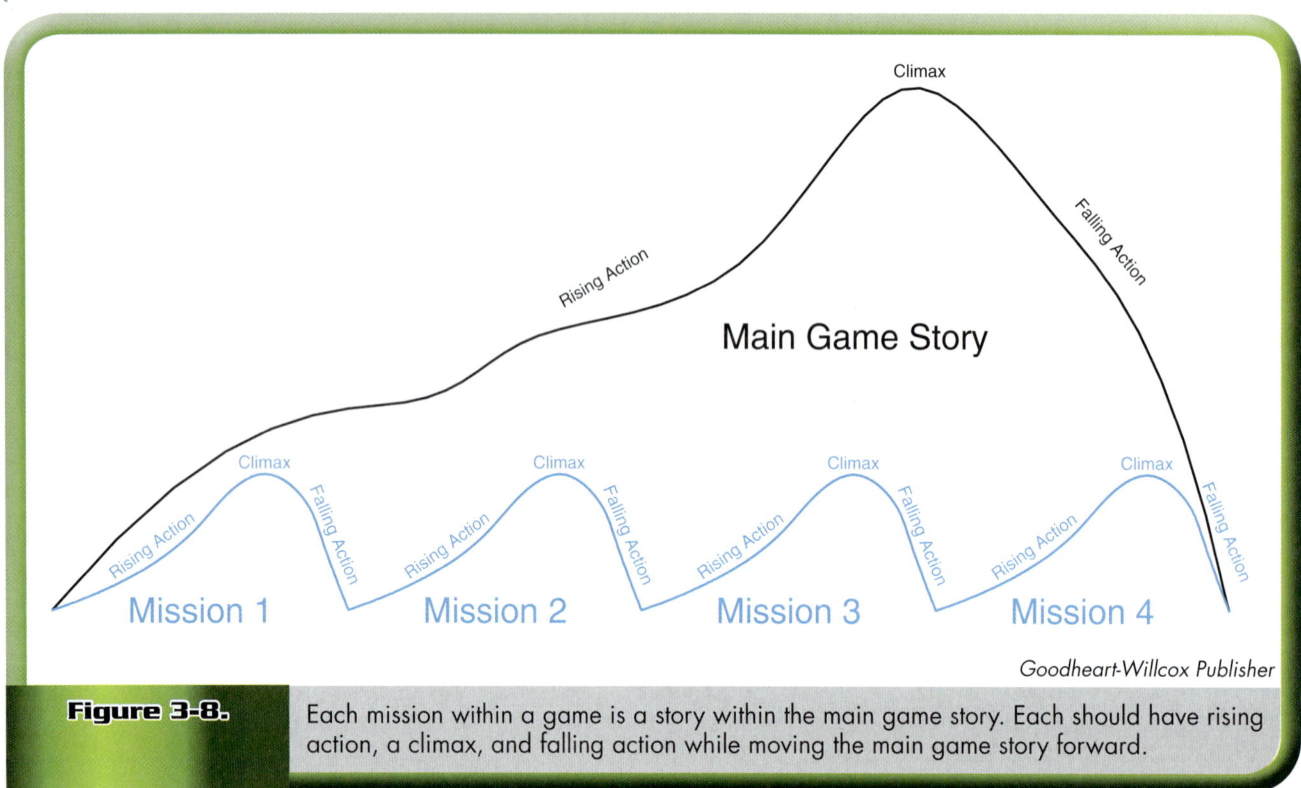

Figure 3-8. Each mission within a game is a story within the main game story. Each should have rising action, a climax, and falling action while moving the main game story forward.

Develop an Ending Point

After completing several missions, the player eventually can resolve the primary conflict and end the game. In many games, this involves defeating the big boss antagonist. All of the missions in the game lead the player to the battle with the big boss. When this conflict is finished, the game is over.

In the story of Shrek, the big boss is the tiny character Lord Farquhar. Shrek completes missions of rescuing Princess Fiona from the tower, battling the dragon, facing his fear of loneliness, and more. Each mission leads up to the final defeat of Lord Farquhar at the wedding. When the dragon eats Lord Farquhar, the primary conflict—trespassers in his swamp—can be resolved and the internal change where Shrek wants companionship has emerged. In the end, the trespassers became Shrek's guests at his wedding celebration. With all of the conflicts resolved, the story is over.

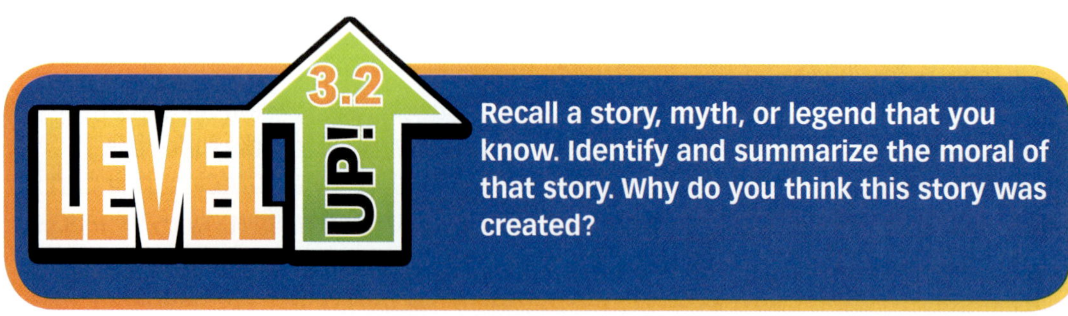

Recall a story, myth, or legend that you know. Identify and summarize the moral of that story. Why do you think this story was created?

Interactive Story Delivery

A game with a story is classified as an **interactive story**. The structure of the story will determine the path the player will follow and where each branch of the story will lead. Some games allow more freedom than others for the player to control the ending of the story. As a game designer, you have the power to create a game story with a single ending or multiple possible endings. The structure of the story within a game can be either linear or nonlinear.

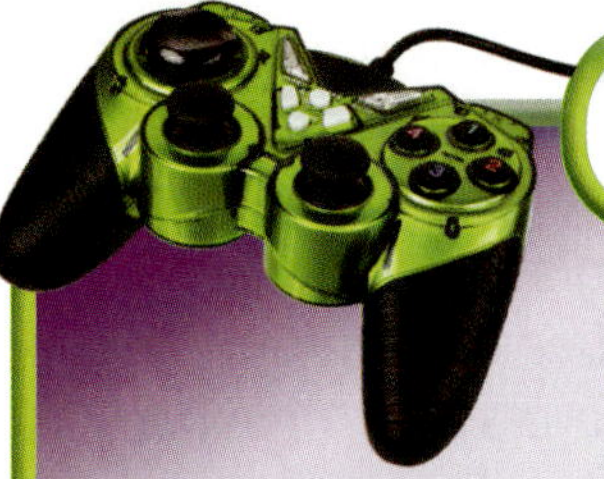

CHEAT CODE: INTERACTIVE STORY

An interactive story is a game in which the player performs the actions of the story. A player must complete actions and make in-game decisions as the story progresses. In many games, the player's decisions control the ending of the story.

Linear Structure

Stories with a ***linear structure*** follow a single path from beginning to end. The player must perform each task or mission in a specific order to win the game. Each completed task or mission makes another task or mission available. The player cannot go back to a previous task or jump ahead to any other task. Most novels are written as a linear story with a single path to the resolution.

Since the player only has a single way of completing the game, no programming is needed to allow for multiple story paths. With less programming come fewer chances for bugs and glitches. Beginning designers often start creating games with linear stories to build skill until they are able to implement the complex structure of a nonlinear story.

Nonlinear Structure

Stories with a ***nonlinear structure*** have more than one path from the beginning to the end, and there may be more than one possible ending. In a video game, the player can move between tasks or missions in any order. A key feature of a nonlinear story is that the game can be played several times completing it in a different way each time.

Nonlinear stories allow the player to make decisions that affect the way the game is played. Depending on the game, player decisions may lead to a single ending or to one of any number of possible endings. The two basic types of nonlinear stories are branching stories and foldback stories.

Branching Story

A ***branching story*** has several paths that branch from decision points. This is similar to a tree where the story starts at the base of the tree and the player can move along any branch of the tree to reach an ending. All nonlinear stories are categorized as branching stories. This is the most interactive of story models. It is similar to the "choose your own adventure" novels popular in the late 20th century.

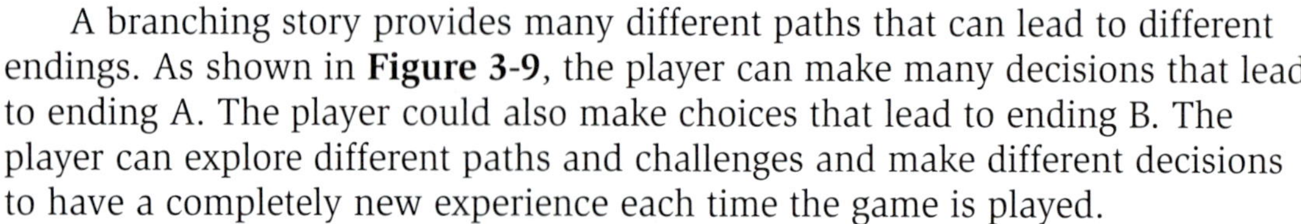

A branching story provides many different paths that can lead to different endings. As shown in **Figure 3-9**, the player can make many decisions that lead to ending A. The player could also make choices that lead to ending B. The player can explore different paths and challenges and make different decisions to have a completely new experience each time the game is played.

The benefit to a branching story is that the player is in control of the outcome. This leads to greater player immersion in the game. Drawbacks to branching stories include the complexities of programming, possibilities of more bugs, and writing more content than the player will experience in a single playing of the game.

Foldback Story

A hybrid of the linear and nonlinear structures is the foldback story. In a ***foldback story,*** the game branches and allows the player to make decisions, but all paths lead, or fold, back to the same end point. A foldback story may have several branching levels, but always has a single ending point, as shown in **Figure 3-10.**

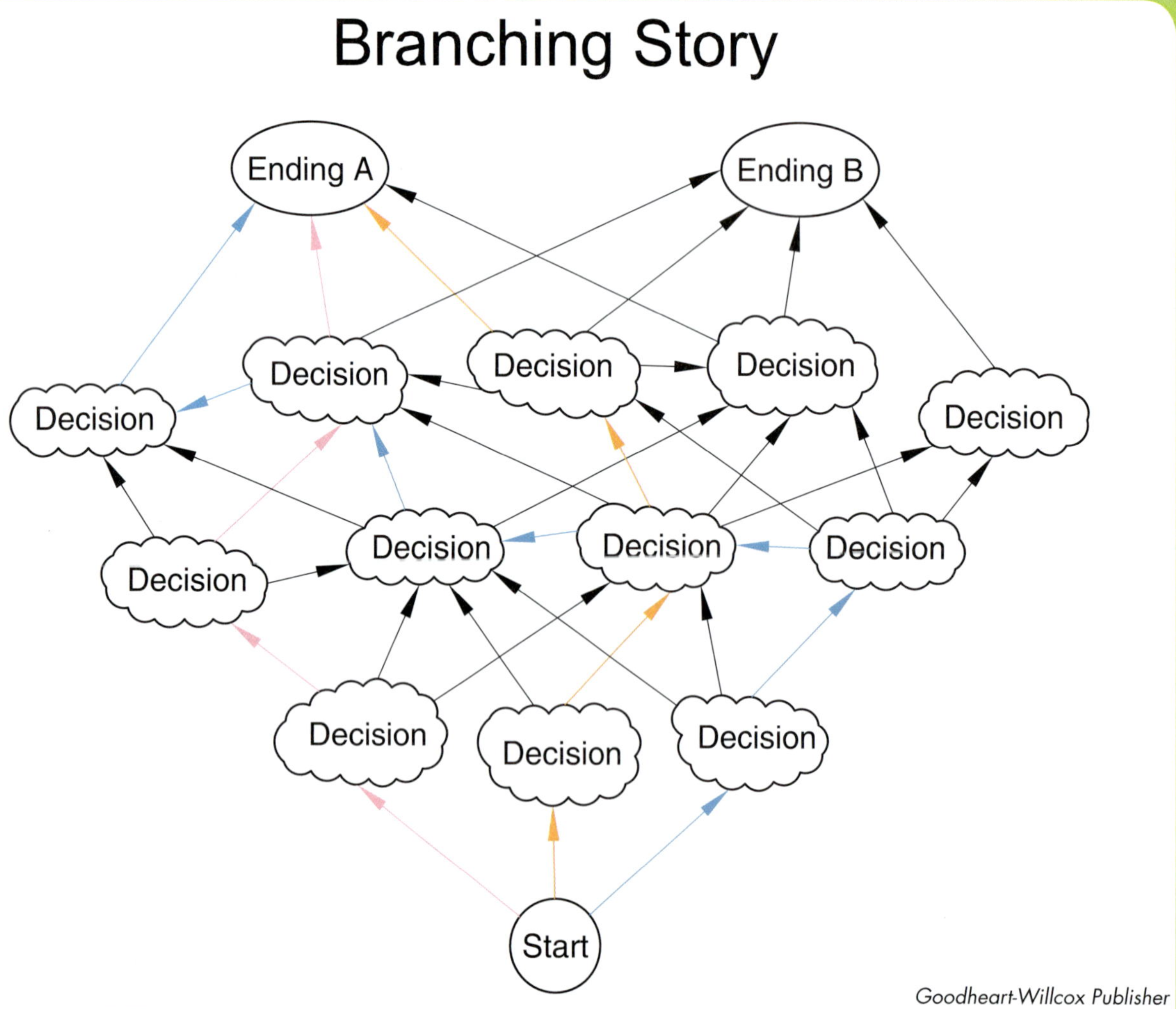

Branching Story

Ending A
Ending B
Decision
Start

Goodheart-Willcox Publisher

Figure 3-9. In a branching story, the player can take many different paths to reach the end of the game, and the ending may be different each time the game is played. Notice that three different paths are highlighted here, all leading to the same ending.

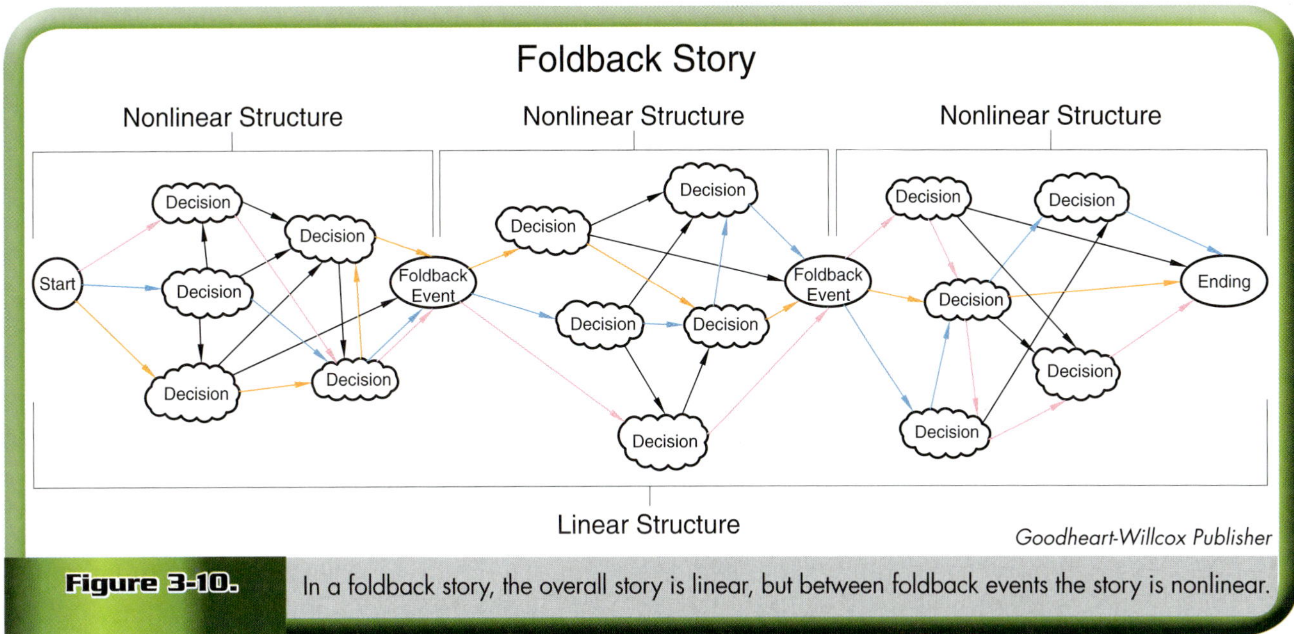

Figure 3-10. In a foldback story, the overall story is linear, but between foldback events the story is nonlinear.

A foldback story may also contain one or more foldback events. A ***foldback event*** is a resolution point within the game that the player must go through to move the story forward. A series of foldback events creates a linear structure, while the branching paths between foldback events create a nonlinear structure.

An example of a foldback event might be traveling to a riverside hut. The player has the choice to travel through the jungle by truck or boat. Traveling by truck will have certain obstacles and perils and require certain decisions. Traveling by boat will have different obstacles and perils and require different decisions. But, either choice for method of travel brings the player to the riverside hut destination.

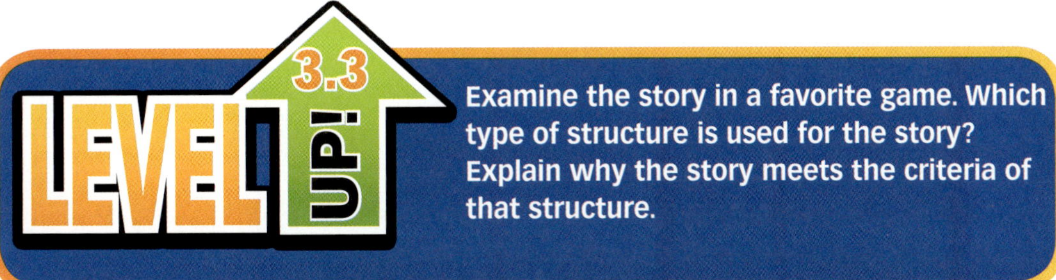

Examine the story in a favorite game. Which type of structure is used for the story? Explain why the story meets the criteria of that structure.

Design for the Story

When the story structure has been determined, you can design the layout of your game. The level design will mimic the story design and **rooms** will be organized in a similar layout to the story tree. There is one basic

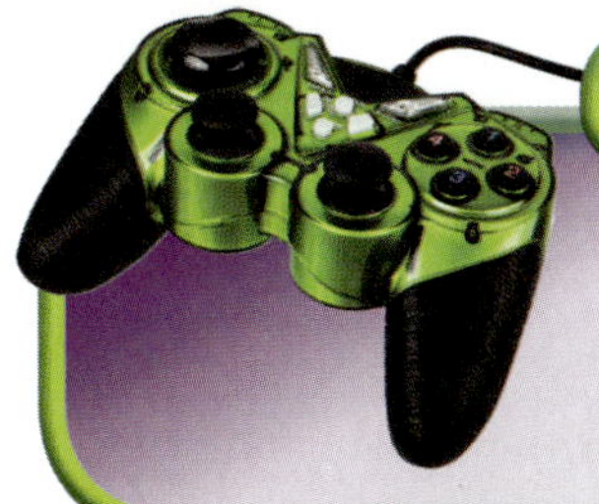

CHEAT CODE: ROOMS

In video game design, a room is a scene in a level. The player will travel from one scene, or room, to another in a pattern to match the story.

level design for a linear game and three basic level designs for nonlinear games, as shown in **Figure 3-11.**

- ***Linear level design*** has a single starting point and follows a single path to a single end point.
- ***Parallel-branching level design*** allows the player to start and make choices as to which room to enter to get to the end point.
- ***Hub-and-spoke level design*** allows the player to start in the center, complete a mission, and return to the center to choose another mission.
- ***Sandbox level design*** or network design allows the player to move freely without restriction from any room to any other room in the game.

Documentation of Story and Level Progression

The story must be properly documented to communicate the design to the team. There are several ways in which companies document story progression, but the most common is the use of a storyboard. A ***storyboard*** is a series of panels that contain sketches of the game action and a description of the actions in that room, as shown in **Figure 3-12.** It is similar to a comic book that shows a series of panels telling the story. However, a storyboard is not a complete detailing of the story. Rather, it is more like a visual outline of the story.

The idea behind a storyboard is to show the artists and designers a sample of what the complete game will look like. Each level should have a storyboard.

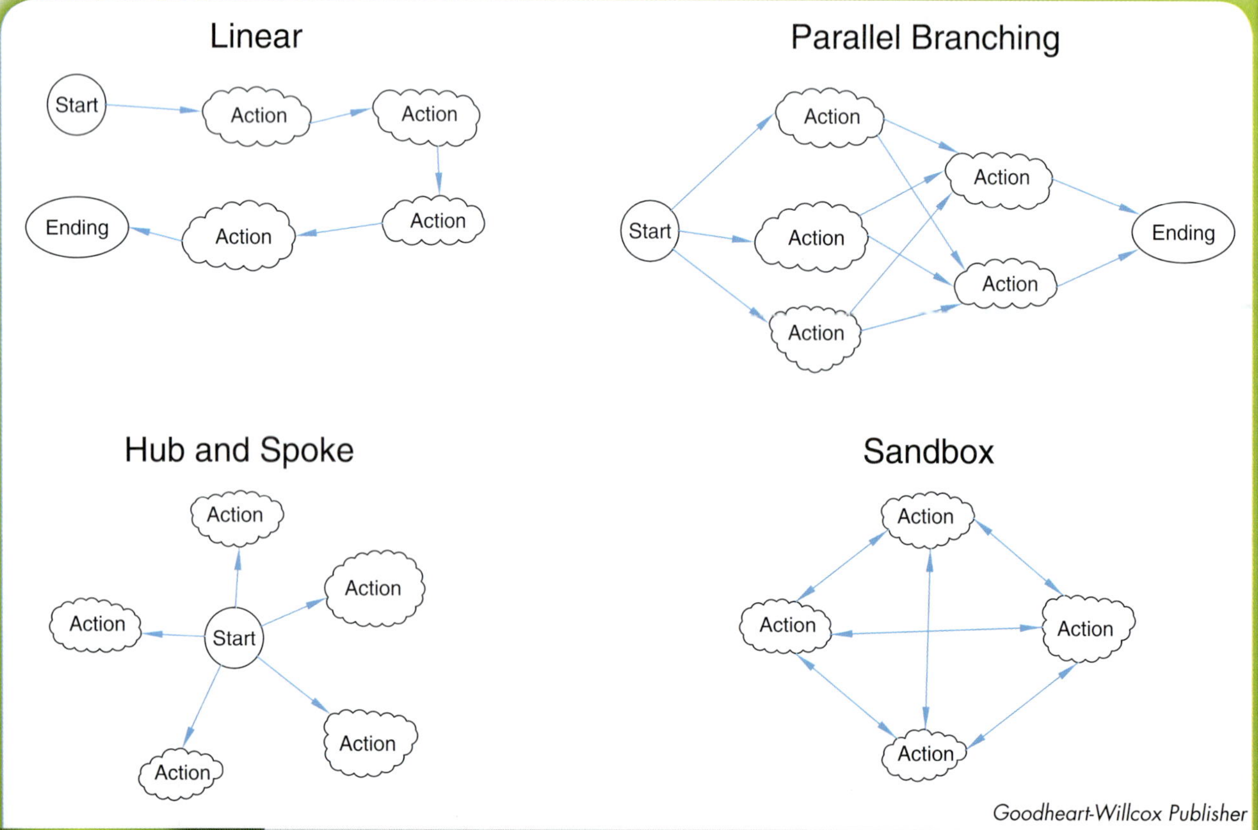

Goodheart-Willcox Publisher

Figure 3-11. There are four basic types of level design.

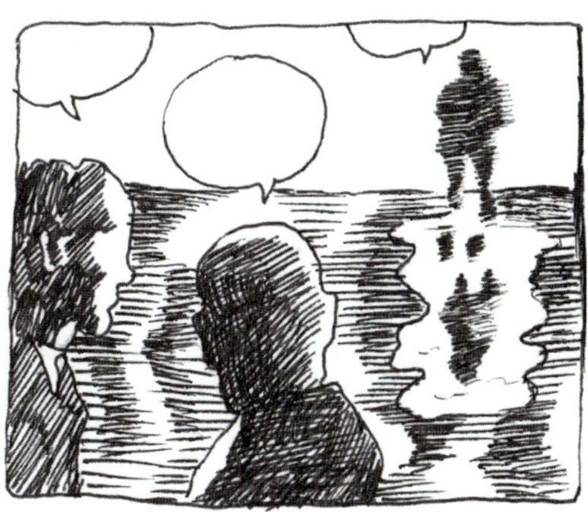

1. A mysterious stranger appears in town.

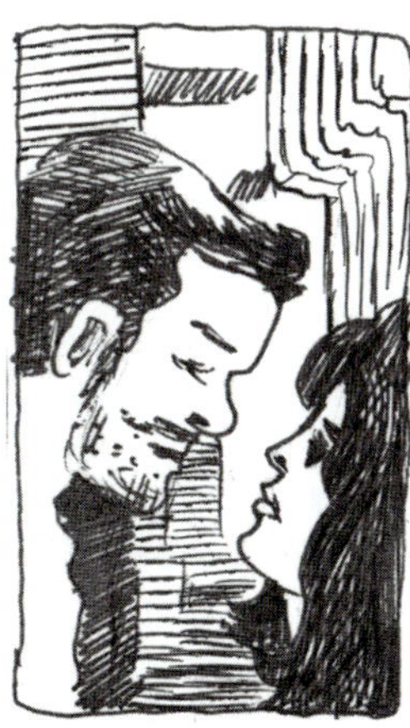

2. The hero meets a man with a secret past who needs help breaking a family curse.

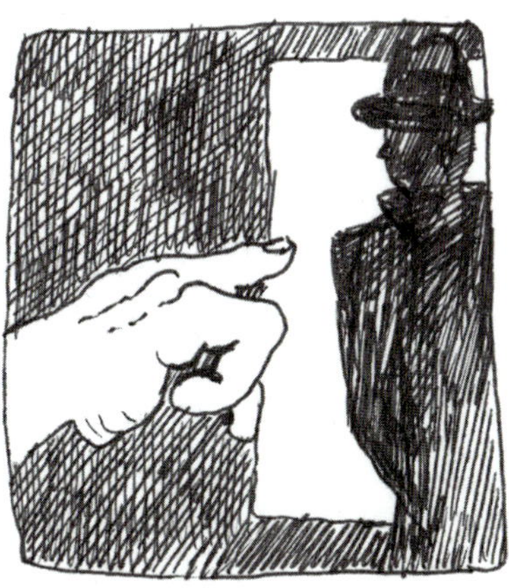

3. The mysterious stranger is revealed as the key to breaking the curse.

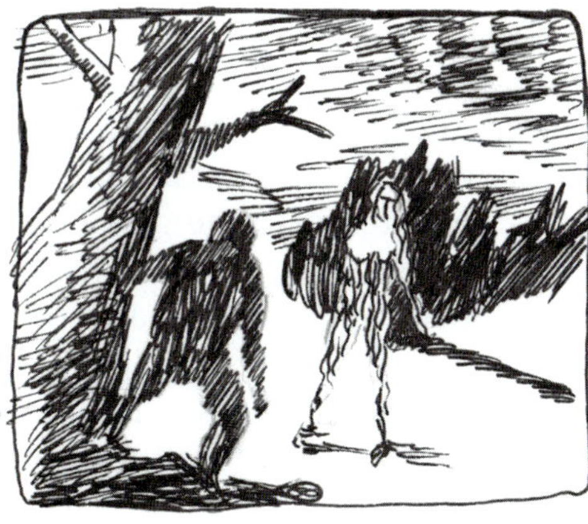

4. The final battle between the hero and the mysterious stranger.

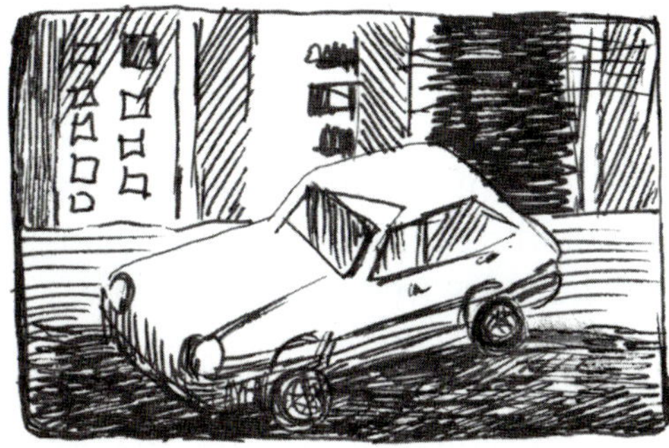

5. Escape from the henchmen of the mysterious stranger.

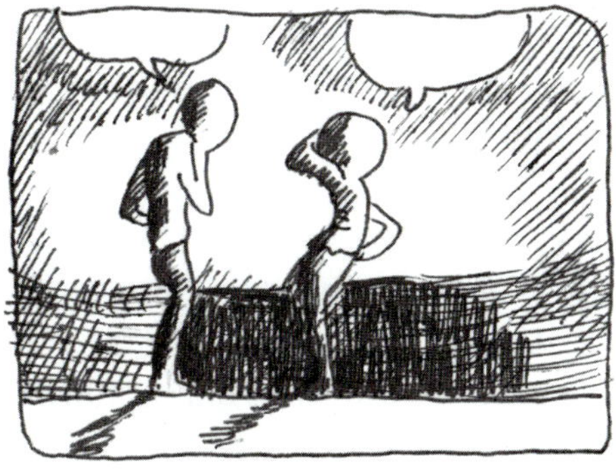

6. The hero tells the man his family's curse is broken.

Figure 3-12. A storyboard shows sketches of the action in a level or room.

Goodheart-Willcox Publisher; images: KUCO/Shutterstock.com

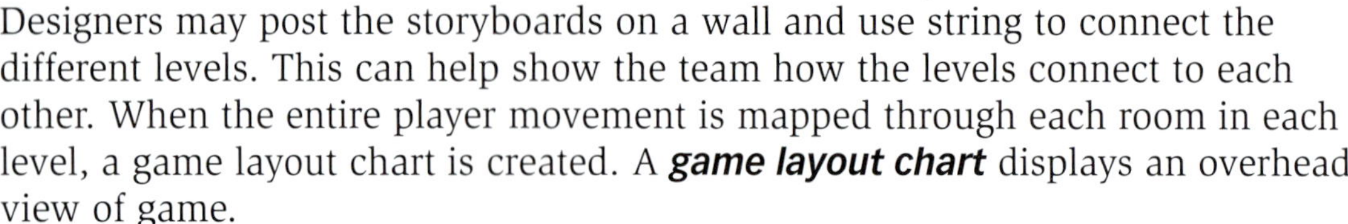

Designers may post the storyboards on a wall and use string to connect the different levels. This can help show the team how the levels connect to each other. When the entire player movement is mapped through each room in each level, a game layout chart is created. A ***game layout chart*** displays an overhead view of game.

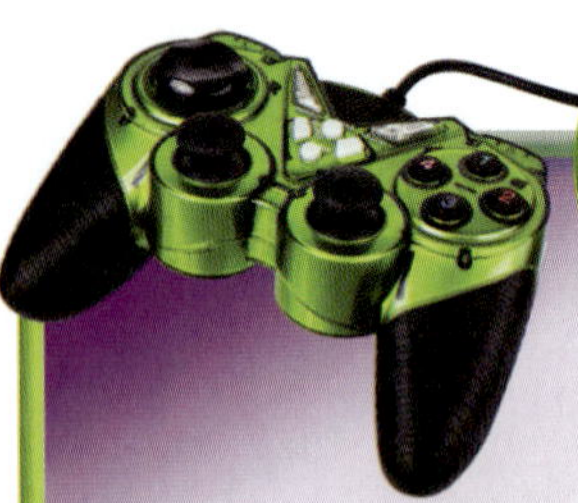

CHEAT CODE: PREDEVELOPMENT TOOL

Predevelopment tools are documents and other items used before the project is approved for design. In many cases, the predevelopment tools are used as pitch documents to sell the game to a publisher.

To show a video-game publisher the game concept, the storyboard panels can be artistically refined with color, clean lines, and typeset text. These display boards can be used as a **predevelopment tool** to help market the game and obtain financing. Showing the investors and clients the complete game story in graphical form helps them visualize how the final product will appear.

World-Design Document

In addition to the storyboards and game layout chart, the design team uses several other documents to convey the story. These documents together form the world-design document. The ***world-design document*** lists the items needed to create the game worlds. Each element of the game must match the theme and mood of the story. If a character or button looks out of place, it can ruin the conveyance of the story through the game. The design team uses the world-design document to ensure all elements of the game fit the story. Two documents commonly included in the world-design document are: 1) the environmental illustrations document and, 2) character design and model sheets.

Environmental-Illustrations Document

Creating the imaginary place that fits the mood, theme, and feel of the story can be a challenge. Each object must fit the original concept of the game when creating a scene. ***Environmental illustrations*** show the details of the virtual world in the game, as shown in **Figure 3-13.** Artist and game writers cooperate to create these illustrations, which are included in the environmental-illustrations document.

If the environment is not a real-world setting, the artists must imagine the environment from scratch. Creating drawings and features that have never existed before can be very exciting. The designers are free to create a new world. This world can have talking plants, a swirling sky, very hot or cold atmosphere, nonhuman characters, unusual dwellings, and more.

Concept sketches are created for original story ideas before the final artwork is created. The design team needs to sketch individual pieces of the game environment and sample scenes for approval. Each object and scene needs to be compared to the story to see how it will work in the story environment.

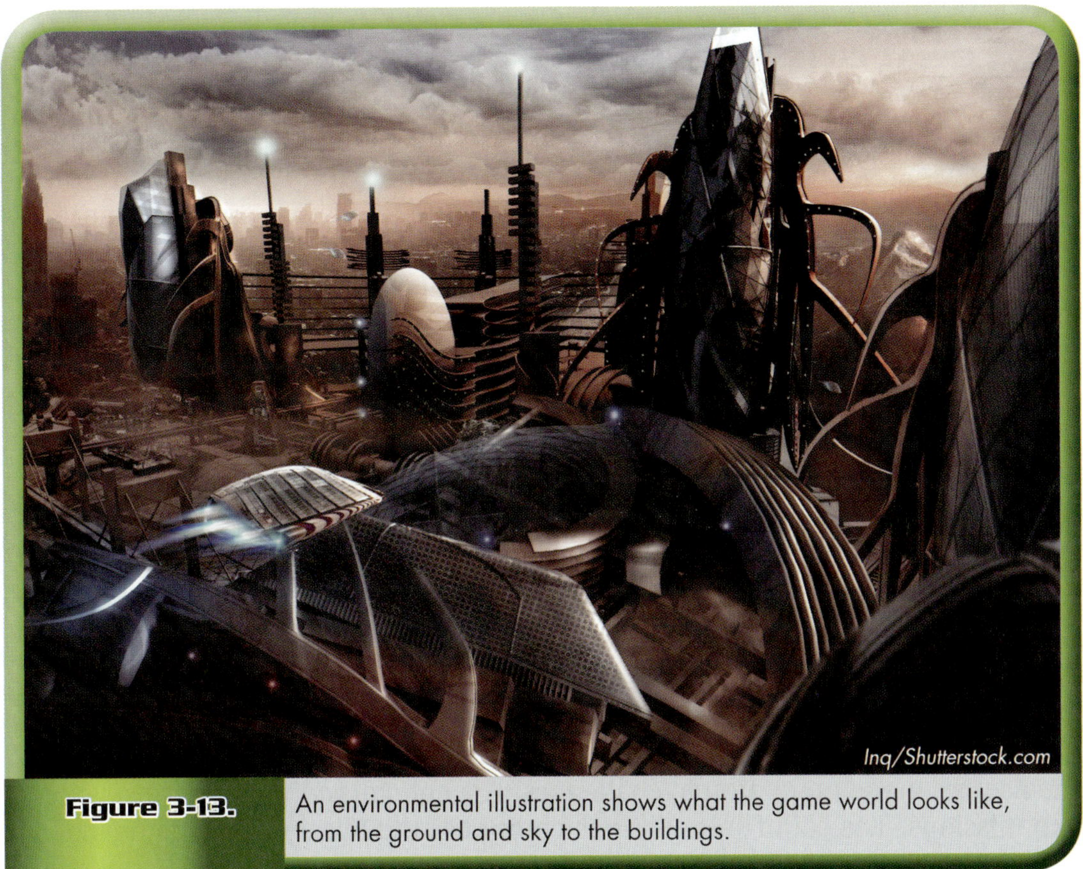

Inq/Shutterstock.com

Figure 3-13. An environmental illustration shows what the game world looks like, from the ground and sky to the buildings.

Character Design and Model Sheets

As discussed in the previous chapter, the characters must fit the story and also have the physical attributes needed to complete the game. The design team uses the detailed character descriptions and sketches to create final character artwork that matches the story setting. These are all included in the character-design document and reviewed as needed during construction. The ***character-design document*** contains all of the information needed to fully define the characters, from descriptions and attributes of each character to model sheets showing the character's appearance. The character-design document is included in the world-design document.

Level Design

Level design involves evaluating scenes, grouping the scenes together into levels, and setting the game objectives needed to convey the story. Each level must contain game action and the story elements that need to be completed before moving on to the next game level. This includes missions and sub missions.

Prototype scenes may be created as proof of concept and for functional testing. The idea is to design a part of the game to see how well the story concept translates into gameplay and how the player will attempt to achieve the story objectives. The tested scenes are reviewed by the design team and then compiled into levels.

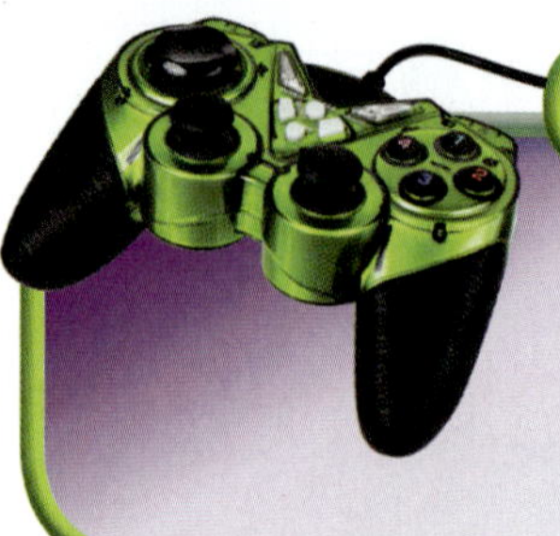

CHEAT CODE: MISSION

In a video game, a mission is a large assignment the protagonist must complete in order to reach the end of the game. A game typically has several missions.

Missions

Similar to the level design outlines, the design team puts the rooms together to create each level. Inside each room, the designers apply the story to create all the elements of the **mission.** By aligning the game actions with the story, the conflict from each mission will help bring the player to the final victory and ultimate goal of completing the game.

Within each mission, the designers break down each action needed to be performed by the player. An ***atomic challenge*** is the smallest component of the action. Just like the parts of an atom, these actions cannot be broken down any further. An atomic challenge might be as simple as having the player jump over a wall or open a chest. By combining atomic challenges, designers create sub missions and missions. Each level in a game is typically one mission.

Sub Missions

Sub missions are the series of activities that make up a mission and are themselves made up of atomic challenges. A single mission may have several sub missions. The set of sub missions completes the mission. In a game like *Star Wars Battlefront,* the mission might be to defeat the enemy on the planet Tatooine. A sub mission might be destroying the enemy tanks. Another sub mission might be capturing a command post.

GUI Design

A ***graphical user interface (GUI)*** is how the user will send and receive information with the computer. In a windows environment, the user has icons as graphics to activate programs. In the game, the GUI may use clickable buttons to interact in the game environment. In a dialogue, the GUI might display a YES or NO option. To activate it, the player will press the X button for YES or A button for NO. In other cases, the player will move the mouse to a clickable button.

HUD Design

The ***heads-up display (HUD)*** is a means of displaying information to the player during gameplay. In most games, the HUD displays more than just a score. It may also display a mini map, ammo count, lives, aiming crosshairs, or any other information that is overlaid on the game map. The HUD is always displayed during gameplay. This means the player does not need to stop the game action and check statistics.

A HUD must be designed to provide as much information as the player needs during gameplay, but it should take up as little space on screen as possible. If the HUD takes up too much space, then the area where the gameplay is displayed may be too small. The player may not be able to see enough of the room to detect approaching enemies or may need to excessively scroll around to move through the game.

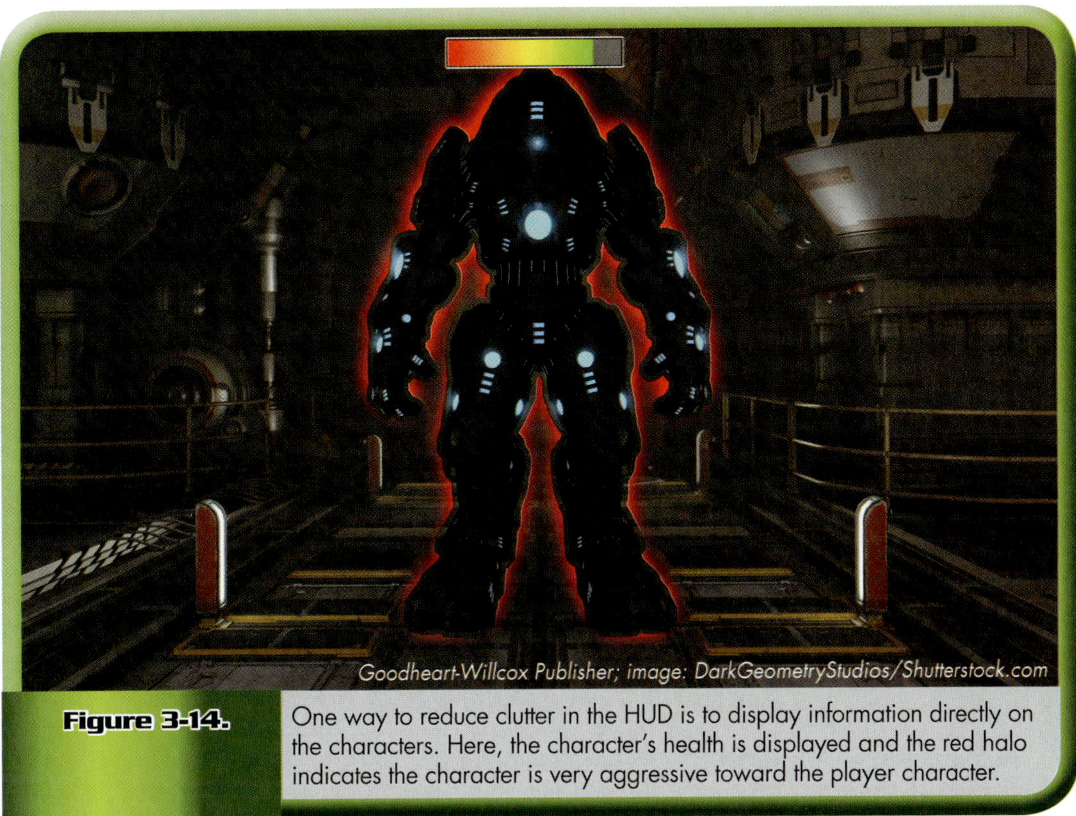

Goodheart-Willcox Publisher; image: DarkGeometryStudios/Shutterstock.com

Figure 3-14. One way to reduce clutter in the HUD is to display information directly on the characters. Here, the character's health is displayed and the red halo indicates the character is very aggressive toward the player character.

Placing some elements of the HUD directly on characters can help reduce clutter in the HUD. For example, if the health status of an enemy character is displayed on the character, then it does not need to be displayed on the edge of the screen. Other elements of the HUD can also be displayed directly on characters, such as the enemy's health bar shown in **Figure 3-14.** Part of the HUD in **Figure 3-14** is also the halo around the enemy character that indicates a level of aggression toward the player.

Also, the appearance of the HUD must match the game story. For example, if the game involves flying a spaceship, the HUD should look like the inside of a cockpit. If the game is an adventure game set in a fantasy world, the HUD should reflect the environment in the game.

The HUD takes up valuable gameplay area. A feature shown in the HUD should be more important than the amount of gameplay area it covers. By ranking game features by importance, a HUD can be designed that provides the player with needed information while allowing the focus to remain on the gameplay. Try to make the gameplay standout, not the HUD.

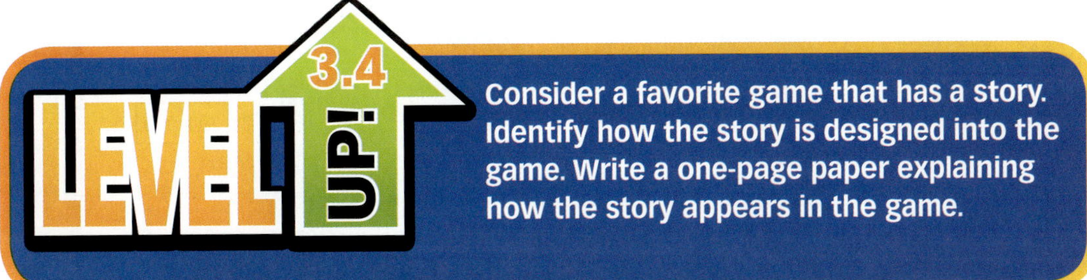

Consider a favorite game that has a story. Identify how the story is designed into the game. Write a one-page paper explaining how the story appears in the game.

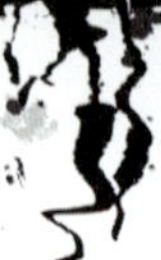

CASE STUDY

HUD Design

The game *Absolute Zero* by OceanBreezeGames is free to play online and can be found on many different gaming websites. Notice the HUD in the screen shot shown here.

The table below summarizes an evaluation of the HUD used with this game. The importance of each feature to gameplay is ranked on a scale from 1 to 10, with 10 being very important. The dominance of each feature is ranked to represent the size and space given to the feature, with 10 being a large space.

Notice that the navigation map is very small (dominance = 2), but is very important to playing the game and finding the objectives (importance = 9). The score takes up a lot of space, but is not very important to the gameplay.

Feature	Importance to Gameplay	Dominance on the Display
Navigation map	9	2
Health	5	8
Ammo	5	8
Score	1	8
New mission button	0	5
High scores button	2	5
Options button	0	5
Copyright info	0	8

Goodheart-Willcox Publisher

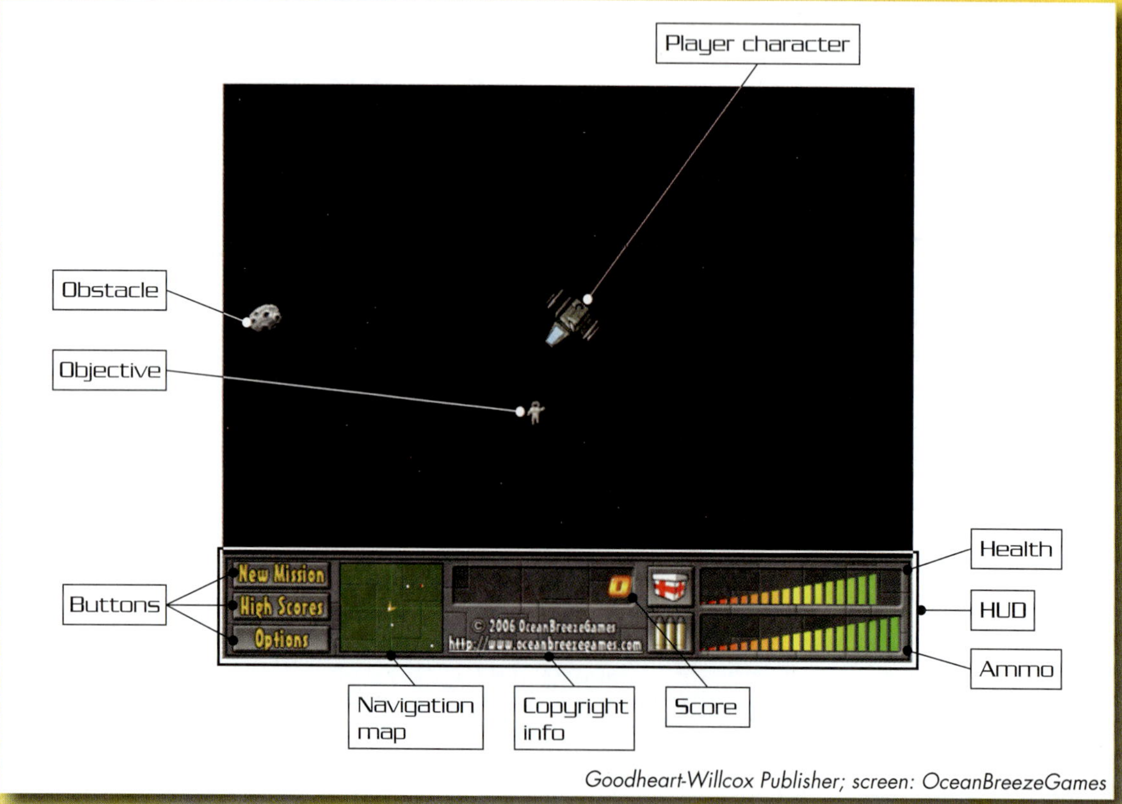

Goodheart-Willcox Publisher; screen: OceanBreezeGames

The score could be smaller to not take up so much gameplay area. Additionally, the HUD is cluttered with buttons and copyright information that are not important to the gameplay. These features could be placed on a title page that is shown before starting gameplay and a high-scores page that appears at the end of the game.

A great idea for features shown in the HUD is to make them semitransparent. This allows the player to see both the displayed data and anything underneath the HUD.

Below is one example of how the HUD for *Absolute Zero* may be improved. This redesigned HUD allows the player to see a larger gameplay area and minimizes the HUD elements as distractions. It allows attention to be focused on the gameplay and not design elements. Players will have an easier time identifying the most important gameplay data while staying immersed in the game action. Only the most important features relating to gameplay are displayed: ammo, health, navigation map, and score. The ammo status is displayed at the top-left corner. It is far less dominant, but still easy to read. Health status is displayed in the bottom-left corner. It remains similar to the first version, but is smaller and out of the way of the gameplay. The score is displayed in the bottom-right corner out of the way of gameplay. The navigation map is much larger and is semitransparent.

The size of each feature is determined by how important it is to see the data. Redesigning the HUD with a semitransparent navigation map allows the map to be larger while not hiding the obstacles and objectives underneath. The objects in the map itself are easier to see because they are larger.

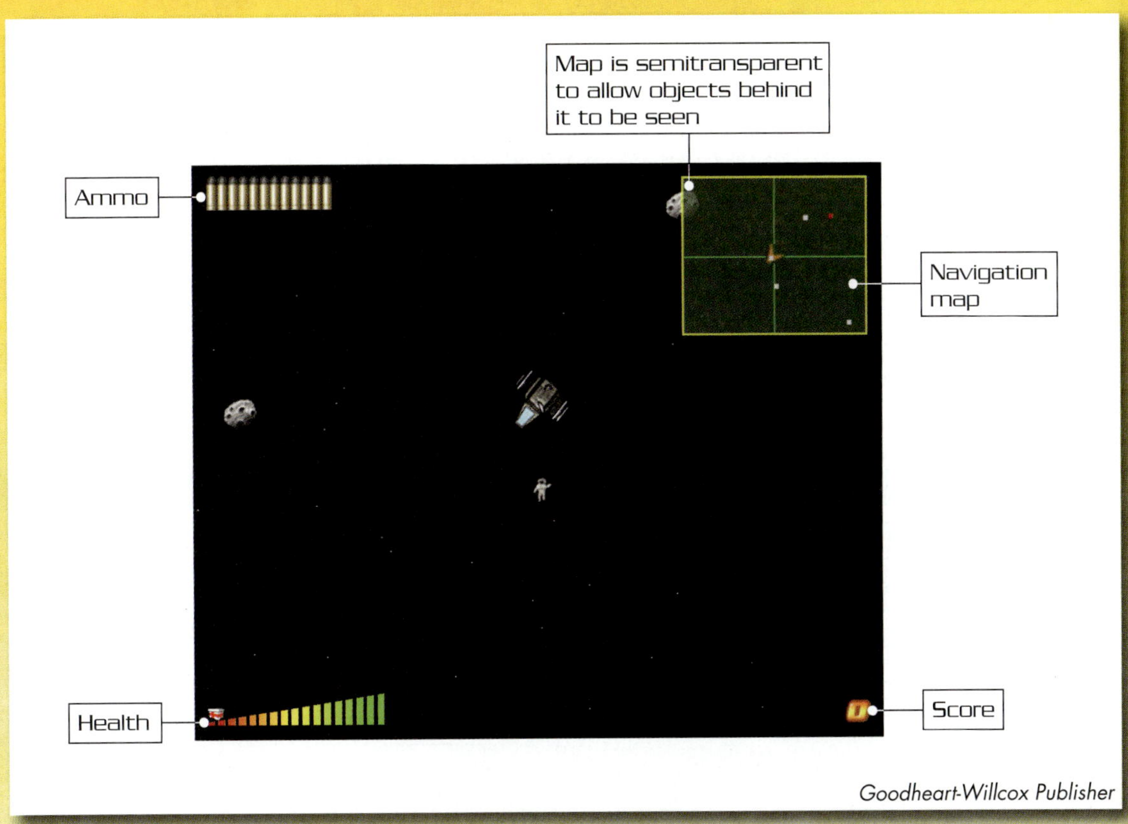

Goodheart-Willcox Publisher

Essential Elements of a Level

The characters are developed, the story is written, and the structure is set. Missions, sub missions, and atomic challenges have been identified. Character sheets, environmental illustrations, and other documents have been created and assembled into the world-design document. Now it is time to start building the levels for the game. There are five essential elements of a level:

- setting
- character motivation and emotional development
- purpose and goal
- dramatic action
- conflict and dramatic tension

Setting

Before levels are created, the setting needs to be established. The ***setting*** is the time and place of the action in the story. Often, the story determines the setting, but many times the story can be placed in any setting. In some games, the setting is the same for all levels. In other games, the setting changes from level to level. There are two components to the setting: time and place.

The time setting is when the action takes place. Will it take place in 10,000 BCE, modern times, or the future? The visual elements of the background and in-game objects will be very different depending on the time setting.

The place setting is the location where the action takes place. This also impacts the visual design of the scene. Will it take place in a historical village, modern city, or city on an alien planet? Each will have very different buildings, nature, people, and more.

Determining the setting for the level is important to developing its visual and audio elements. The grouping of related element of a scene is the theme. Each object that contributes to or conveys a theme is a ***thematic element.*** Objects such as buildings, roads, clothing, and technology all contribute to building a congruous theme. For example, if the game's setting is medieval times, the thematic elements listed in **Figure 3-15** may be included. Including objects such as a car or modern clothing would be incongruous with the theme and distract from the gameplay.

The emotional feeling of the setting is its ***mood.*** Mood is conveyed by use of color and shadow. A bright scene with pastel colors would convey a happy mood.

Buildings	Roads	Clothing	Technology
Huts	Forest path	Woolen and leather clothes	Horses and carriages
Castles	Wooden bridges	No zippers or buttons	Swords
Jousting stadium	Dirt carriage paths	Hats	Bows and arrow
Woodland camp	Stone roadways	Armor	No cannons
			Catapult

Figure 3-15. These examples of thematic elements would create a congruous theme for a medieval setting.

Goodheart-Willcox Publisher

A dark color palette with lots of black, gray, dark brown, or green would convey a mood of gloom or fright. Look at the examples shown in **Figure 3-16** to see how thematic elements can be changed to convey mood.

Character Motivation and Emotional Development

Each level needs to have elements to motivate the main character within the story and to emotionally develop the character. In many levels, the character needs to overcome a tragic flaw. In other levels, the character may simply be working on avenging a wrong from the enemy. An emotional change can be a very simple change from a stressful emotion in the heat of battle to a relaxed emotion in the safety of a checkpoint. A complex emotional change can be found in a story where the hero slays the dragon and rescues the princess. Here the high stress, angry emotional state is changed to living happily ever after.

Without character motivation and emotional development, a level in a first-person shooter is simply a shooting gallery with moving targets. Imagine your favorite first-person shooter (FPS) game. Does the character face decisions that cause an emotional change? The hero needs some motivation to achieve an objective. The hope is that by achieving the objective, the hero will experience an emotional status change.

Happy, Upbeat, or Cheerful		Gloomy, Foreboding, or Fearful	
Object	Mood Elements	Object	Mood Elements
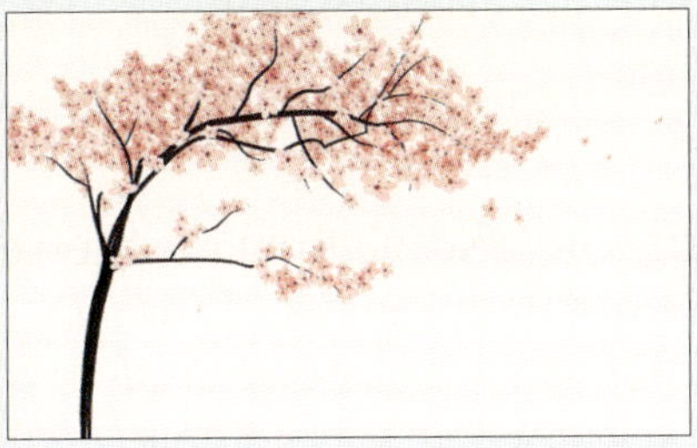	**Happy mood:** Pastel color palette; Natural lighting	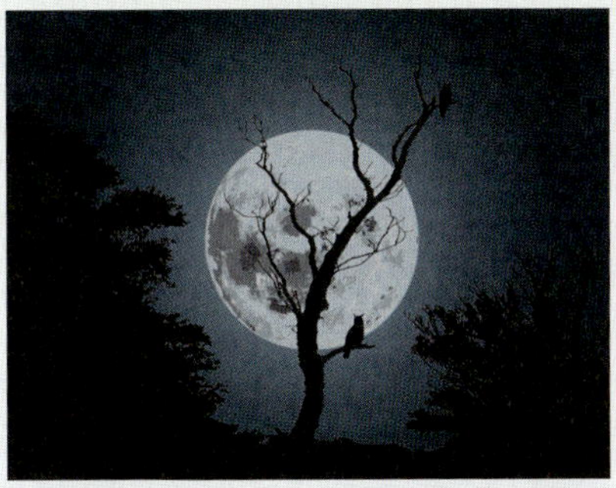	**Gloomy to fearful mood:** Dark color palette; Low light/ silhouettes
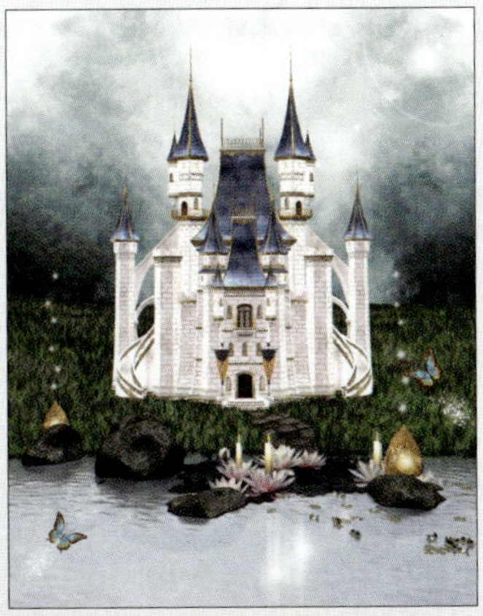	**Happy mood:** Bright color palette; Bright lighting	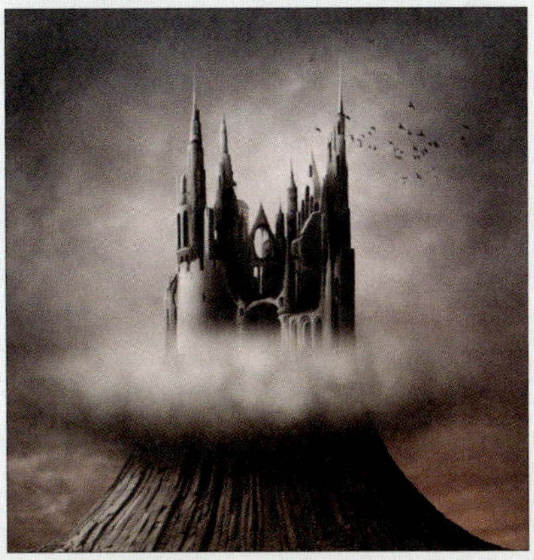	**Foreboding to gloomy mood:** Dark color palette; Subdued/muted lighting

Figure 3-16. Notice how visual elements can create a mood for the setting.

Goodheart-Willcox Publisher; images: rada80/Shutterstock.com, gasa/Shutterstock.com, Ellerslie/Shutterstock.com, Ann_Mei/Shutterstock.com

Purpose and Goal

For each level of the game, there should be a primary goal as well as smaller goals. The main character needs a purpose for being in that scene. It may be to find a mentor or acquire a new skill. The reason for playing the level is the purpose. What the player is to achieve in completing the level is the goal of the level.

The tasks to be completed on each level need to be nontrivial. ***Nontrivial tasks*** are those with purpose, like finding a potion to defeat an enemy. All tasks a player must complete should be nontrivial. ***Trivial tasks*** are those that have no point or purpose and do not move the game story forward. A player should never have to complete trivial tasks.

Dramatic Action

Recall that *dramatic tension* is a feeling of anxiety or anticipation related to the story being told. The ***dramatic action*** of the story is how the character reacts when faced with immediate conflicts or obstacles. Each level must have its own dramatic action. Along the journey needed to resolve the main conflict, the character encounters other minor conflicts and actions on each level to help move the story along.

Imagine an RPG where you go to rescue the princess, walk through a forest, knock on the castle door, the princess answers, and you ride away together. There is no dramatic action. There are no armies or dragons to defeat. There are no hidden traps or pitfalls. There are no keys, tokens, potions or amulets to acquire to open the door. There are no skills or experiences to build. Playing a level like this would be a trivial task.

On the other hand, imagine a racing game where the player must avoid crashes, restart the race after a crash, make pit stops, or even collect tokens. Each of these helps continue the action and give the player a reason to keep going. Completing a level like this is a nontrivial task.

Conflict and Dramatic Tension

Each level must have conflict and dramatic tension. In a scene from the movie Jaws, the dunt-*dunt*...dunt-*dunt* soundtrack provides dramatic tension. What is about to happen? The shark may be coming. The action is yet to be determined. There is dramatic tension because the viewer does not know what is going to happen. Will the shark surface? Will the person survive? Will they swim to the boat before the shark gets there? Move to the edge of your seat and wait for the action.

In the same way, each level in the game must have dramatic tension. A level that has something lurking in the shadows will help develop a sense of conflict and dramatic tension. A set of eyes that show through the trees in the forest or the noise of leaves rustling off-screen may suggest the presence of a beast. Is it going to see you? Is it a *big* beast? Is it a friendly beast like Shrek? All of these things run through the player's mind to build conflict and dramatic tension. Elements like dramatic action, conflict, and dramatic tension are what make a game exciting.

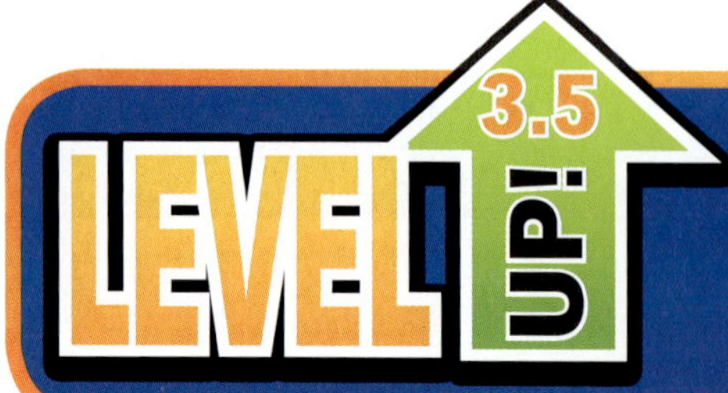

Consider a video game with a story. How are the five essential elements of a level applied to the game? Were the designers successful in applying the elements? Write a one-page paper describing your position.

Chapter Summary

- A story should be added to a game to add entertainment to the game, define the audience, keep player attention, differentiate the game, or to integrate with marketing.
- The basics procedure for creative writing is to brainstorm ideas, determine the central premise, define the characters, create a primary conflict, structure the story, and develop an ending point.
- The structure of an interactive story within a game, which determines the path the player will follow and where each branch of the story will lead, can be either linear or nonlinear.
- There is one basic level design for a linear game, which is linear level design, and the three basic level designs for nonlinear games are parallel-branching level design, hub-and-spoke level design, and sandbox level design.
- The five essential elements of a level are: setting; character motivation and emotional development; purpose and goal; dramatic action; and conflict and dramatic tension.

Check Your Video Game IQ

Now that you have finished this chapter, see what you know about video game design by taking the chapter posttest.

www.m.g-wlearning.com

www.g-wlearning.com

Review Your Knowledge

On a separate sheet of paper or in a word processing document, match the following terms with the definition that fits best.

A. stock characters
B. trivial task
C. climax
D. foldback story
E. flat characters
F. rising action
G. atomic challenge
H. stereotyped characters
I. falling action
J. dramatic tension

1. Action that has no point or purpose and does not move the game story forward.
2. Characters that have standard traits and perform a standard role.
3. The events that create the basic internal conflict of the story.
4. The smallest component of the action.
5. Characters that do not develop or change throughout the story.
6. The events that lead to the resolution of the basic conflict of the story.
7. A hybrid of the linear and nonlinear structures.
8. A feeling of anxiety or anticipation related to the story being told.

9. The turning point of the story.
10. Characters that perform a standard game role, but have very general characteristics that provide some variation among the same type of characters in the game.

On a separate sheet of paper or in a word processing document, answer each of the following questions.

11. List five reasons to add a story to a game.
12. How are characters and story used as part of the marketing effort of a game?
13. List the six procedures for creative writing.
14. How does determining the central premise differ from creating a primary conflict?
15. What does a female hero need to balance as she completes the heroine's journey?
16. How is a novel similar to a game with a linear story?
17. What story structure would be the best way to allow the player to choose a mission and start a different mission without having to finish the first?
18. What is the purpose of environmental illustrations in world design?
19. How do thematic elements create continuity of a scene?
20. What two items are most used to convey mood in a scene?

Apply Your STEM Knowledge

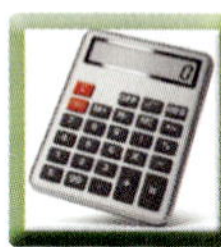

Mathematics

1. Solving for the number of probable outcomes requires the multiplication of the possible options for each draw. If you roll a single die three times and have the results of 6, 4, and 3, this creates a unique combination (6,4,3). The total number of possible outcomes for each throw is six. Each time the die is thrown, it can land on any of the six numbers. Possible outcomes could be (1,1,1), (1,1,2), (1,1,3), and so on. The total three-number combinations possible is found by multiplying the number of possible outcomes by the number of possible outcomes for every throw. In this case, it is: six (possible outcomes throw one) multiplied by six (possible outcomes throw two) multiplied by six (possible outcomes throw three).
   $6 \times 6 \times 6 = 6^3 = 216$
   This approach can be applied to find the total possible endings in a branching story. Assume the branches are "possible outcomes" and each level is a "throw." Use spreadsheet software to create the following table. Complete the table by determining how many possible endings this branching story can have.

Level 1	Level 2	Level 3	Total Endings
6	6	6	216
3	2	4	
2	4		40
5		5	75
	2	2	8

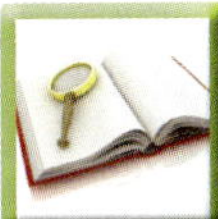

Language Arts

2. List all of the atomic challenges you perform for getting ready for school. Write a one-page paper describing each atomic challenge.

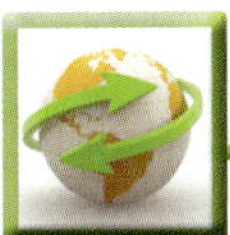

Social Studies

3. Research the historic "1925 Serum Run to Nome, Alaska". Identify a hero from the event. Write a one-page paper on how this event fits the hero's journey model.

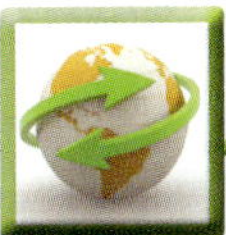

Social Studies

4. Research the Roman Empire. List the thematic elements needed for a video game scene set inside the Roman coliseum.

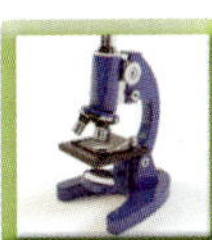

Science

5. Research the life cycle of a frog. Create a six-panel storyboard detailing a frog character that starts life as an egg and eventually becomes an adult frog.

Working in Teams

Working with the team assigned by your instructor, develop the story for a video game. The story should have three acts. Identify which part of each act will be covered on which levels. Create a PowerPoint presentation to illustrate the story to the class.

Gamer Portfolio

As you collect items for your portfolio, you will need a method to keep the items clean, safe, and organized for assembly at the appropriate time. A large manila envelope works well to keep hard copies of your documents, photos, game screen shots, awards, and other items. Three-ring binders with sleeves are another good way to store your information. Plan to keep like items together and label the categories. For example, store sample documents that illustrate your writing or artistic skills together. Use notes clipped to the documents to identify each item and state why it is included in the portfolio.

1. Select a method for storing hard copy items you will be collecting for your portfolio.
2. Write a paragraph that describes your plan for storing and labeling the items. Refer to this plan each time you add items to the portfolio.

G-W Learning Mobile Site

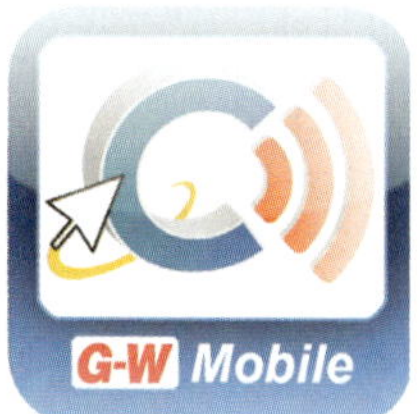

Visit the G-W Learning mobile site to complete the chapter pretest and posttest and to practice vocabulary using e-flash cards. If you do not have a smartphone, visit the G-W Learning companion website to access these features.

G-W Learning mobile site: www.m.g-wlearning.com

G-W Learning companion website: www.g-wlearning.com

Common Core

College and Career Readiness

CTE Career Ready Practices. Maintaining a healthy lifestyle has an impact on how you function physically and mentally. Choosing healthy foods in appropriate amounts is an important component of a healthy lifestyle. Use the US Department of Agriculture's MyPlate (www.choosemyplate.gov) to help you create a personal healthy eating plan. How do the MyPlate key behaviors align to the way you eat now?

Reading. Consider how the author uses the term *theme* throughout this chapter. How did your understanding of this term change as you were reading? Look up the word *theme* in the dictionary. How did the author shape this definition to fit the subject matter in this chapter? Write a few paragraphs about what the term *theme* means to you after reading this chapter.

Speaking and Listening. Research the use of dramatic tension in a variety of media (for example, plays, fictional stories, and movies). Compile information about the ways in which dramatic tension is used to move a story forward, how dramatic tension is created in these different media, and any other interesting information you find. Use this information, along with what you already know about dramatic tension, to storyboard a video game level. Using various elements (visual displays, written handouts, technological displays), present your storyboard to the class. Explain what would happen in the level and why players would be motivated to complete this level.

Event Prep: Computer Game Performance

Creating a computer game is a competitive event that may be offered by your Career and Technical Student Organization (CTSO). This may be an individual or team event. There may be two parts to this event: the prejudged program and the performance portion. To prepare for the performance portion of a presentation:

1. Read the guidelines provided by your organization. Make certain that you ask any questions about points you do not understand. It is important you follow each specific item that is outlined in the competition rules.
2. On your CTSO's website, locate a rubric or scoring sheet for the event.
3. Confirm the use of equipment or other visual aids that may be used in the presentation of the game and amount of setup time permitted.
4. Review the rules to confirm if questions will be asked or if the team will need to defend a case or business plan.
5. Make notes on index cards about important points to remember. Use these notes to study. You may also be able to use these notes during the event, depending on event rules.
6. Practice the presentation. Each team member should introduce himself or herself, review the game being presented, defend the game construction, and conclude with a summary.
7. After the presentation is complete, ask for feedback from your teacher. You may also consider having a student audience listen and give feedback.

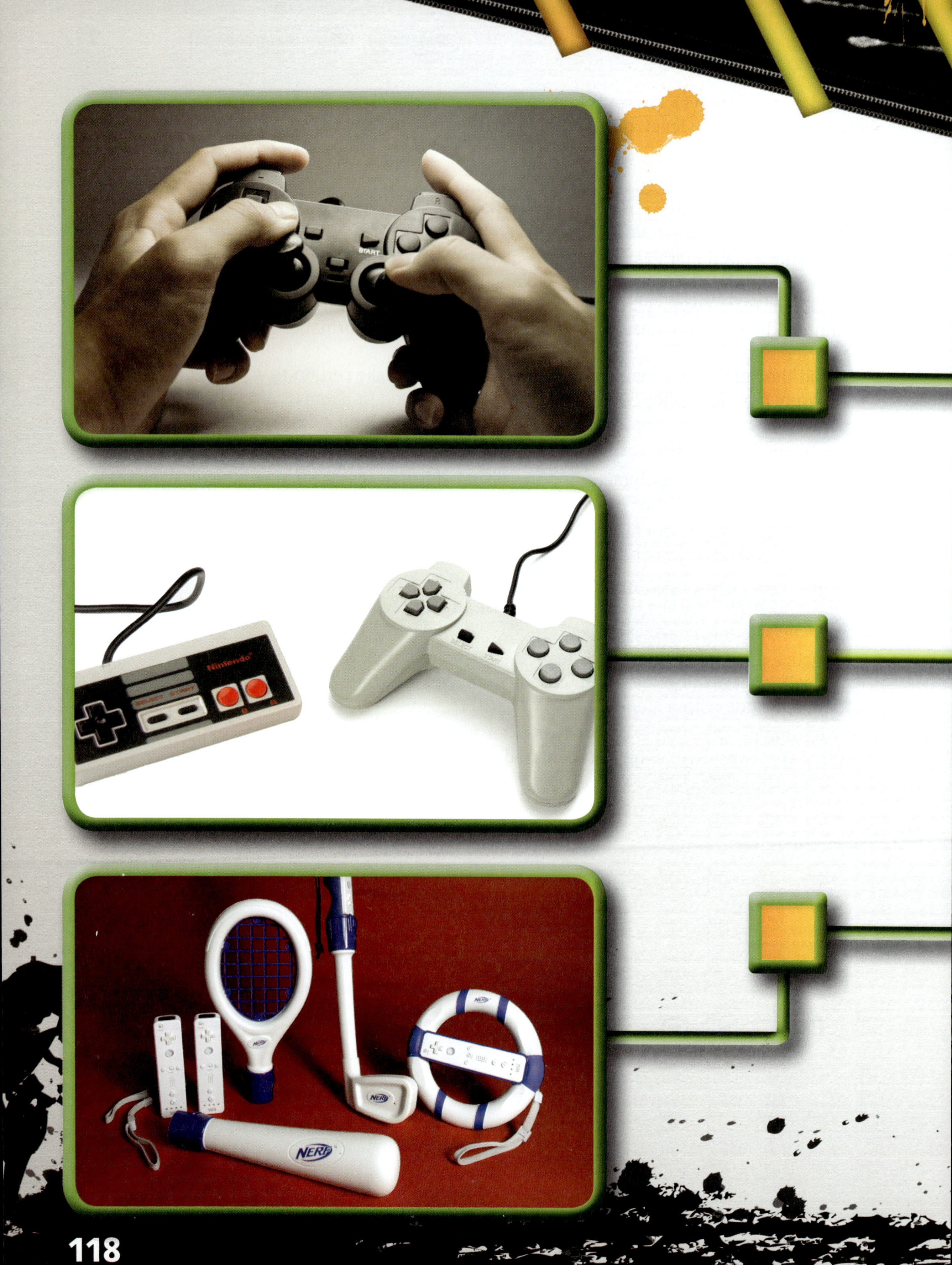
START
Nintendo
SELECT START
SELECT
NERF

Chapter 4

Interface Composition

One of the most important reasons for creating a video game is to entertain. A key to entertainment is interactivity and interaction with the game story. In a video game, the player becomes a character in the story. The player must have a way to control the character and drive the character through the story. In this chapter, the key components of interactivity and interaction with the interface are discussed.

Check Your Video Game IQ

Before you begin this chapter, see what you already know about video game design by taking the chapter pretest.

www.m.g-wlearning.com

www.g-wlearning.com

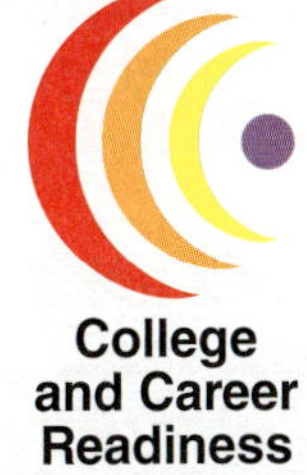

Reading Prep. In preparation for reading the chapter, think about what makes a video game successful? How is video game success measured? As you read, consider how the information in this chapter supports or contradicts your answers to these questions.

Objectives

After completing this chapter, you will be able to:

- Explain what is involved in player-centric video game design.
- Outline the four key topics related to player-centric immersion that have universal application, with a focus on the human-computer interface.
- Analyze and understand the ways to apply the human-computer interface to game design.

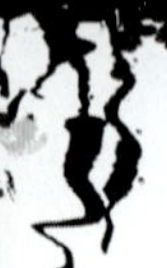

Player-Centric Design

The purpose of game design is to create an interactive environment that allows the player to become immersed in the gameplay. ***Immersion*** is the level to which the player feels he or she is actually experiencing the events of the game, or how well the player connects to the game world. ***Player-centric design*** involves understanding the player and centering the game design on what the player wants and needs. The elements of player-centric design listed below help designers focus their efforts on the player and to avoid common pitfalls of design.

- audience
- vicarious immersion
- typical player interest
- typical player dexterity
- typical player mental acuity
- audience sampling and surveys

The construction of the user interface is an important part of a player-centric game. This is discussed later in the chapter. However, before the user interface can be constructed, the designer must fully understand the process of player-centric design.

Audience

The first step in player-centric design is to define the audience. The ***audience*** is the group of typical players the game is targeted to attract. The audience is usually defined by demographics. ***Demographics*** are measurable characteristics of a person or group, as shown in **Figure 4-1.** Common demographics are age, income, language, country or geographic area, and gender. A designer will use demographics to create a typical player profile.

A ***typical player profile*** is a document that outlines the common characteristics of the group that is most likely to play the game. The characteristics are summarized in the typical player profile as if the group is a single player.

Player Profile

Age: 17
Gender: Female
Education level: 11th grade
Family Income: middle class
Language: English (American)
Country: USA
Likes: Puppies, cartoons, favorite color pink
Dislikes: Scary dogs, thunder, green peppers

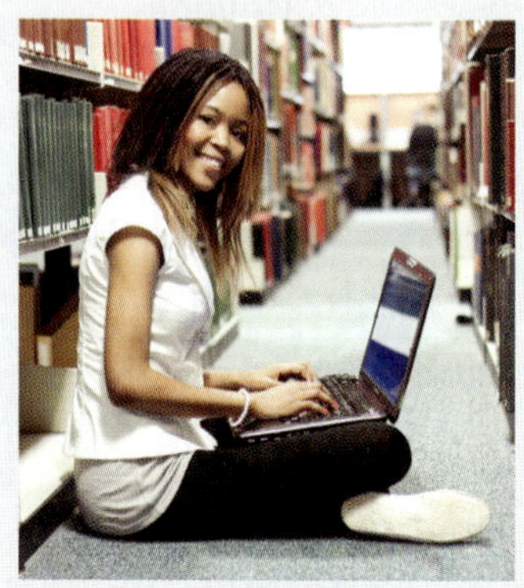

Figure 4-1. Demographics can be used to create a player profile.

Blazej Maksym/Shutterstock.com

This makes it easier for the design team to envision the typical player and how that player will behave. Designers focus on the player-centric needs of the typical player profile, even though the game may appeal to players who do not match the typical player profile.

When constucting the typical player profile, there are several demographics and other factors to consider. Keeping the following list of factors in mind when designing a video game helps lead to a good player-centric design.

- background: types and amount of life experiences the player has
- education: grade level of the player and his or her understanding of reading, math, science, and history
- motivation: why the player wants to play games
- training: experience the player has in a specific genre of gameplay or training in a simulated environment
- culture and language: ethnic-specific cultural influences and language differences of the player
- age: how old the player is
- gender: male or female
- physical abilities: coordination of the player and ability to input game information
- sophistication: socioeconomic status of the player may determine the level of refinement for the game

A game designed for 18-year old males would be very different from one designed for six-year old females. The audience consisting of 18-year old males may want a game with layers of story, lots of action, gore, and multiple button controls. The audience consisting of six-year old females may want games with a simple story, friendly cartoon or animal characters, simple controls, and a reward system that praises correct input.

The audience also has a big impact on the desired game rating. Imagine if a game designed for six-year old females gets an ESRB rating of T for Teen or M for Mature. This is a big problem and the game will probably be a commercial failure. Even a rating of E10 would miss the mark for the audience and cause problems in marketing and selling the game.

Another critical game component is the audience user interface, which must be appropriate for the audience. The original Xbox had a big problem in this area. The original controller was too big and bulky to be properly used by a large portion of the audience, as shown in **Figure 4-2.** After the Xbox was released, the controller was quickly redesigned to be smaller. This allowed a larger number of people to hold the controller comfortably.

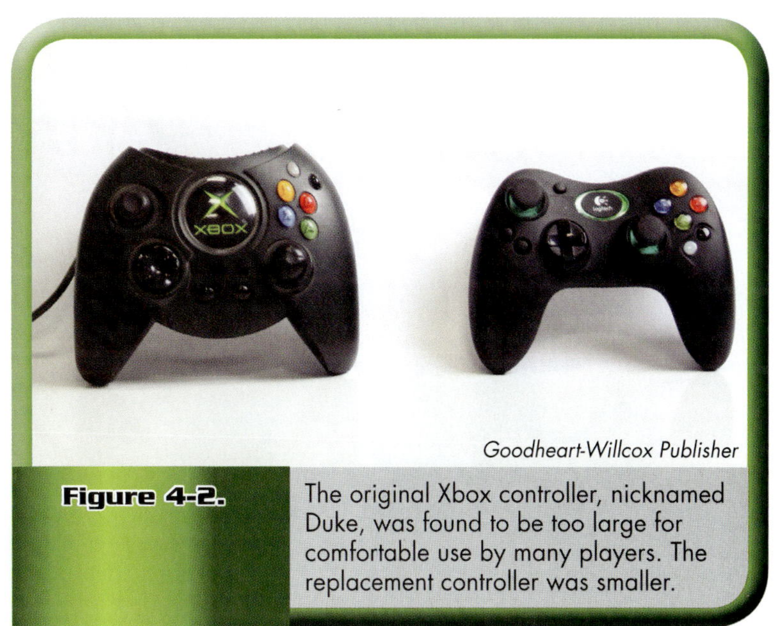

Goodheart-Willcox Publisher

Figure 4-2. The original Xbox controller, nicknamed Duke, was found to be too large for comfortable use by many players. The replacement controller was smaller.

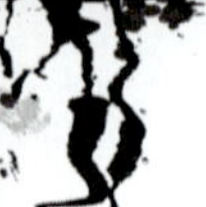

Vicarious Immersion

To adapt a game to the audience, a designer will need to imagine himself as the typical player. This technique is termed vicarious immersion. ***Vicarious immersion*** is the designer imagining himself or herself in place of the player to experience the gameplay. In order to engage in vicarious immersion, the designers need to get into the same mindset of the typical player.

To start getting into the same mindset as the typical player, designers need to research members of the audience. They interview the audience members to find out what they like and dislike. They also talk to the mothers and fathers of these audience members to find out what the parents see as appropriate for their kids. Remember, in many cases the actual game buyer is an adult.

Additionally, designers should study other successful products designed for the same audience. To really get into the mindset of the audience, a designer should play other games made for that audience. They should also watch audience members while they play other successful games and record anything that shows a positive or negative response by the audience.

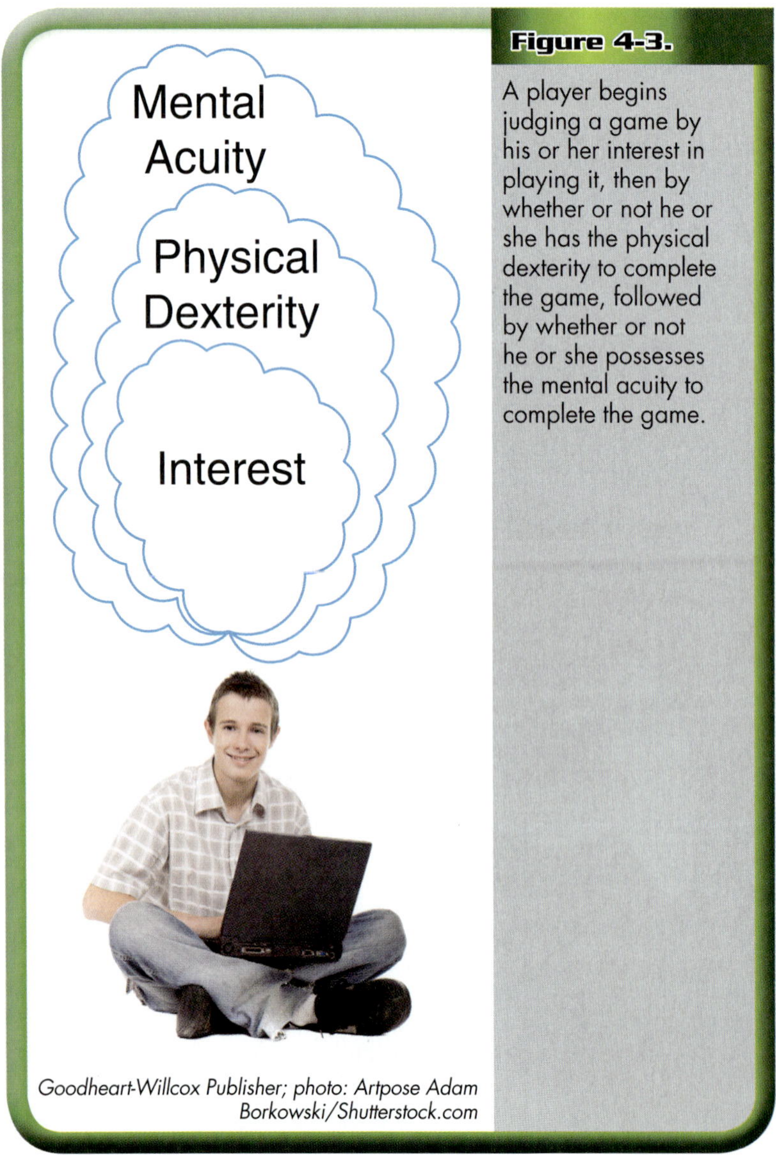

Figure 4-3. A player begins judging a game by his or her interest in playing it, then by whether or not he or she has the physical dexterity to complete the game, followed by whether or not he or she possesses the mental acuity to complete the game.

Goodheart-Willcox Publisher; photo: Artpose Adam Borkowski/Shutterstock.com

Since designers are not usually the typical players of the game they are building, it is important for them to have a deep understanding of the audience. By using vicarious immersion, a great game designer is able to take on the personality of the typical player and create a game for which the customer can experience immersion.

Typical Player Interest

With the audience defined and the designer in the mindset of the player, it is time to begin construction of the player-centric game. The next step in this process is to align to the typical player's interest. As shown in **Figure 4-3,** interest is the first step in a player's evaluation of a game.

An entertaining game will closely align the story, characters, and gameplay to the interests of the typical player. Remember, the story and characters have been defined. This is the time to revise the story and characters if needed based on the typical player profile.

Here is where the research pays off. Take the list of likes and dislikes from the audience and build in activities that the typical player will find entertaining. Have a list of items that the typical player expects to see in the game.

The gameplay also needs to be aligned with the interest expressed by the typical player profile. Both while designing and during the build process, designers should test play the game with players from the audience. Have the audience try a prototype of a game component. Make sure the audience finds that activity enjoyable and challenging, yet not too challenging that interest is lost. This testing is only for **audience appeal.** It is not the testing phase of game construction searching for bugs and errors. That occurs later.

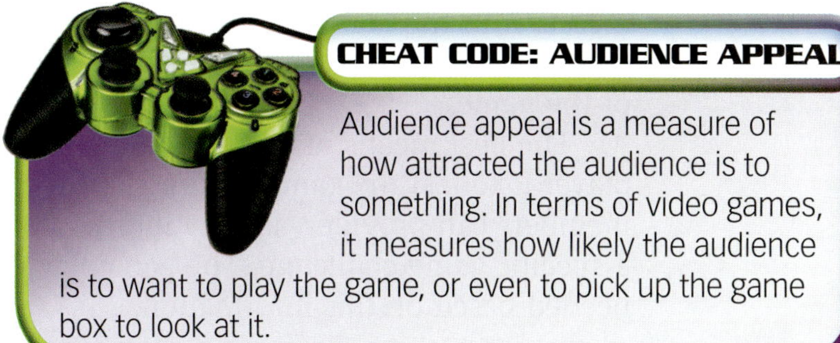

CHEAT CODE: AUDIENCE APPEAL

Audience appeal is a measure of how attracted the audience is to something. In terms of video games, it measures how likely the audience is to want to play the game, or even to pick up the game box to look at it.

Typical Player Dexterity

A player-centric design also must take into consideration the audience's **dexterity** to operate the user interface and game controls. Will the game use standard controllers for the game console or computer, or will game-specific controls be created? If the controller has tiny buttons placed close together, players with very small or very large fingers may have trouble using it. The input controls must meet not only the needs of the gameplay, but the dexterity of the typical player as well, as shown in **Figure 4-4.**

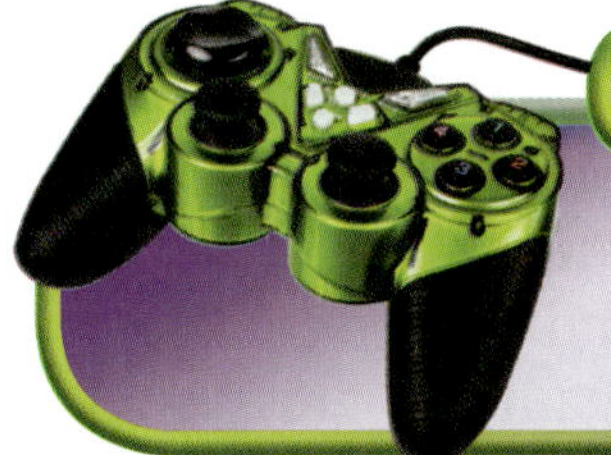

CHEAT CODE: DEXTERITY

Dexterity is readiness and skill in a physical activity, especially one involving use of the hands.

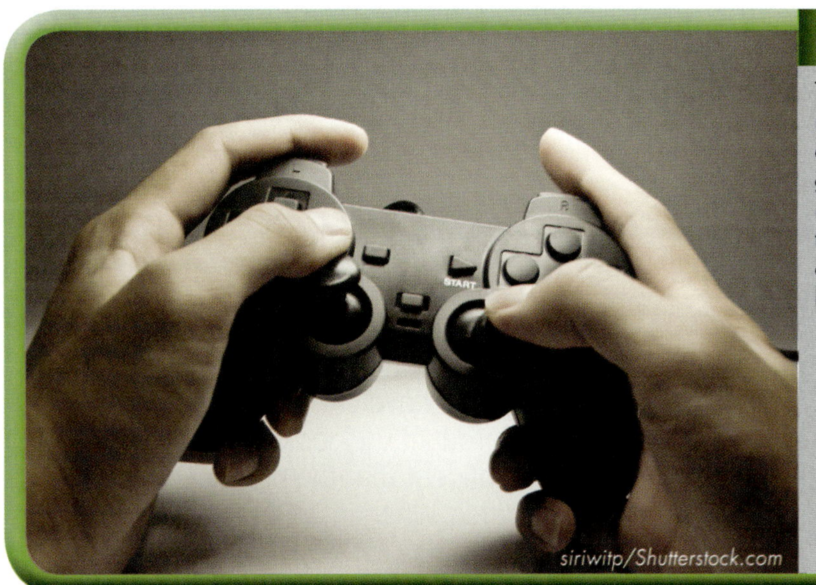

siriwitp/Shutterstock.com

Figure 4-4. The typical player must have the dexterity to use the game controllers and mental acuity to use the user interface in order for the game to be a success.

Another consideration related to dexterity is skill progression. If the skills needed to play the game do not increase throughout the game, the game will not allow for proper dexterity training. The first few levels need to have challenges that help the player build the muscle memory to perform a similar task again. ***Muscle memory*** is when a physical task has been repeated enough that the task can be completed without conscious effort. As the game levels progress, the physical skills needed to properly use the controls should increase. In the last levels of the game, the player should have use of the controls mastered to complete the very challenging tasks presented at the end of the game.

The best means of ensuring the game aligns with the dexterity of the typical player is to test the game on the audience. A *functionality test* using audience members can provide valuable information about the physical skills needed for a specific game challenge. The gameplay or the controllers can be revised as needed based on this information.

Typical Player Mental Acuity

The typical player must also have the mental acuity to complete game challenges. ***Mental acuity*** is a measure of focus, memory, and concentration. Mental acuity is *not* a measure of intelligence. The mental acuity needed to perform well at a photograph-matching challenge is different from that needed to follow a path on a map.

The challenges and tasks in the game need to be designed for the typical player. Often, as the game progresses the player must demonstrate higher levels of mental acuity. For example, as the player moves through a maze-style puzzle game, each new level of maze may require more focus and concentration to complete.

The need for mental acuity can be built into many components of the game. Examples include recalling facts from a mission briefing, recognizing the signal to a shortcut on a path, and seeing the slight differences between harmless and harmful game objects. The success of a game may depend on the audience being able to quickly solve these problems. What if the audience is unable to remember the difference between a neutral NPC and a competitive NPC, as shown in **Figure 4-5?** Then, the difference needs to be made more obvious.

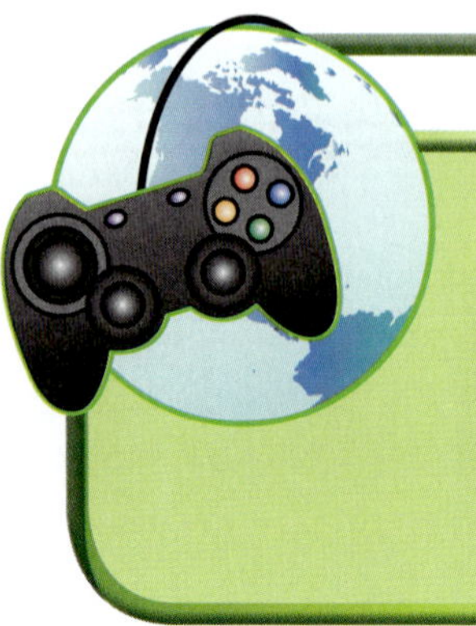

Green Gamer

Have you noticed the Energy Star label on products computers and other electronic devices? The EPA and the Department of Energy have created the Energy Star program to rate products. By looking for this label, consumers can be confident that the product meets environmental standards. When in doubt, check the website www.energystar.gov for information.

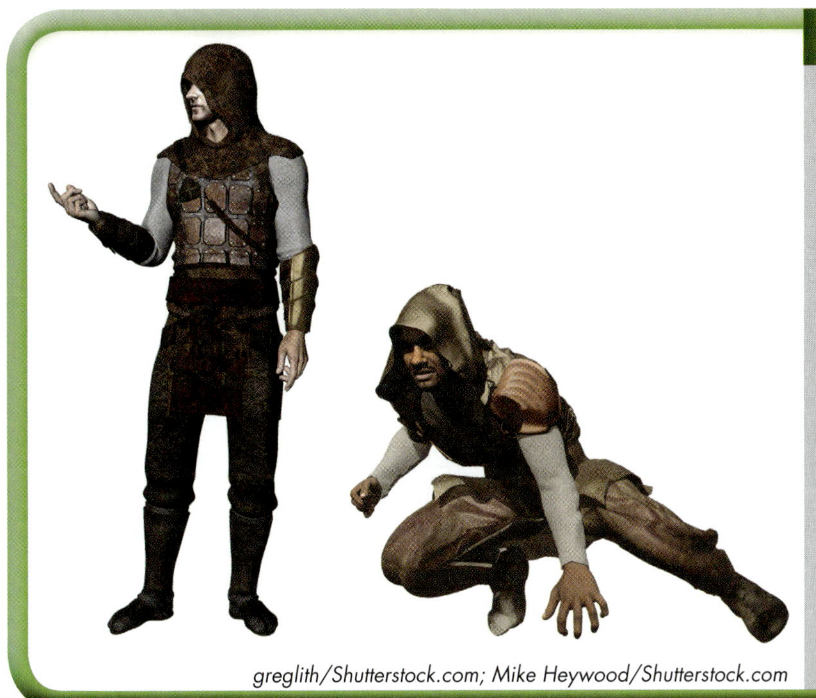

greglith/Shutterstock.com; Mike Heywood/Shutterstock.com

Figure 4-5. Is there enough difference between these NPCs for the player to use his or her mental acuity to determine which is friend and which is foe? Both are wearing similar clothes and both have hoods over their heads. Depending on functionality testing, this may be a case where the difference needs to be more obvious.

Audience Sampling and Surveys

As stated earlier, the ultimate measure of success for any player-centric game is to test it on the audience. During game construction and into a full prototype, the design team should be testing with the actual audience. If the game is going to fail with the audience, this should be known as soon as possible so changes can be made. Finding out at the end of the build that the audience cannot use the game's controllers or user interface would be time-consuming and expensive fix.

Sampling is taking a small group from the audience and asking them questions on their likes and dislikes. One way to do this is through the use of a survey. A *survey* is a questionnaire given to a group of people with the purpose of collecting data from that group. Another way to conduct sampling is to get a small group of the audience together in the same room and have them play the game. After they play, ask the group questions about the game and how to make it better. This type of a small group is called a *focus group*.

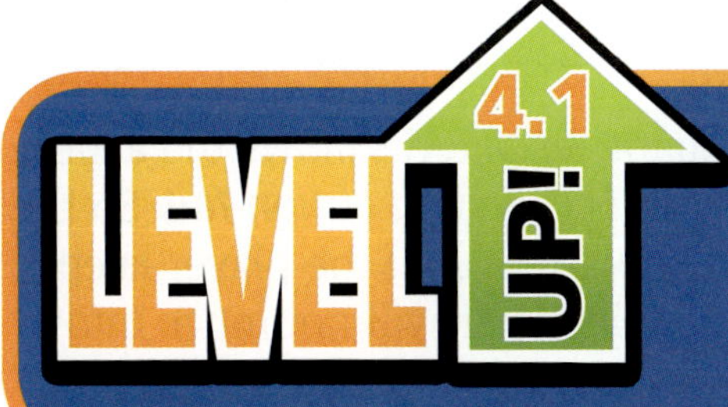

Consider your favorite game of all time. What is the audience for the game? Do you belong to that audience? Create a short PowerPoint presentation to describe the audience for the game.

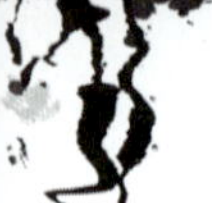

Player-Centric Immersion

Understanding the principles of player-centric design focuses the designer on the audience. Working with that focus, the designer needs to add elements to enhance player immersion and entertainment. Four key topics related to player immersion have universal application.

- human-computer interface
- elements of engagement
- elements of interest
- balance elements

The ***human-computer interface (HCI)*** is the connection and communication between the player and the game system. It is the focus of the rest of this chapter. Elements of engagement, elements of interest, and balance of elements are discussed in the following chapter.

At the core of a game is the ability for the player to input commands and receive feedback from the decisions made. This is done through a system of inputs and outputs. ***Inputs*** are instructions from the player sent to the computer. The method used for the player to input commands to the computer is termed the input-interaction model. ***Outputs*** are the information that the computer sends to the player. The method used for the computer to send information to the player is termed the output-interaction model.

Input-Interaction Model

An ***input-interaction model*** includes the player controls and the programming needed to interpret the button presses or other commands. An example of an interaction model is seen playing an online game using the computer keyboard as the controller. The [A] and [D] keys are used to move the character left and right respectively. In this case, the input-interaction model includes the [A] key on the controller (keyboard) and the programming used to move the character left. The model also includes the [D] key and the programming to move the character right.

The computer uses the core mechanics to interpret actions from the interaction model. Recall from Chapter 1, the core mechanics is the programming needed to enforce the rules of the game. In the earlier example, the player presses the [A] key to move the character left. The core mechanics checks this action against the game rules and then either allows or disallows moving the character left on the screen.

For example, say the character is standing to the right of a wall and the player tries to move the character left into the wall. The designers have written a game rule that states characters cannot pass through walls. The core mechanics state:

IF the character collides with a wall, **THEN** the character stops moving.

The core mechanics checks the position of the character and disallows the action of moving the character left. Disallowing the action is called an ***action-fail.*** So the character remains stopped, or standing next to the wall. Even if the player keeps pressing the [A] key to move the character left, the character will not move into the wall.

Another example is if the player presses the space bar to make the character jump. The core mechanics tests the game rule that the character must be touching the ground to jump and then allows or disallows the action.

When the character is touching the ground, the jump action is allowed. Allowing the action is called an ***action-fulfill.*** When the character is not touching the ground, an action-fail would end the action request.

Output-Interaction Model

The ***output-interaction model*** is the portion of the user interface that performs the action-fulfill commands and provides feedback to the player. As shown in **Figure 4-6,** the output-interaction model takes the results of game programming and converts them into information the player can see, hear, and touch. One of the requirements of a video game is a video display. This is an output device. However, the video display is not the only output device. Speakers may output sound. In some cases, the controller, which is primarily an input device, may shake or vibrate as a form of output. Each output device provides information to the user.

Computers process information at very high speeds. Commands can be quickly interpreted and the results are displayed in what the player sees as instantaneous. A computer processing information at 3.2 GHz cycles 3.2 billion times per second. Imagine breaking a single second into 3.2 billion parts. Since humans cannot perceive action that fast, it seems to happen instantly.

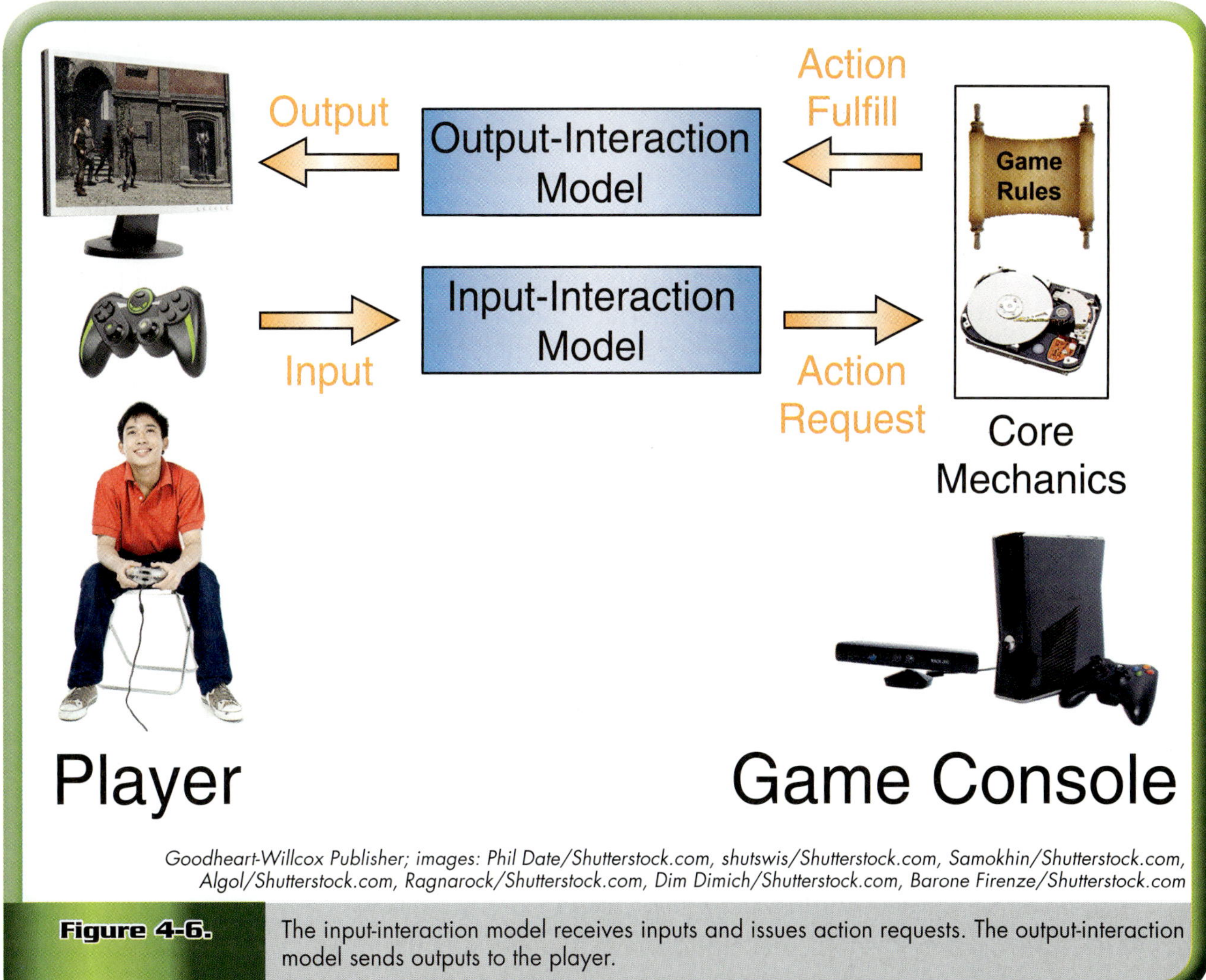

Goodheart-Willcox Publisher; images: Phil Date/Shutterstock.com, shutswis/Shutterstock.com, Samokhin/Shutterstock.com, Algol/Shutterstock.com, Ragnarock/Shutterstock.com, Dim Dimich/Shutterstock.com, Barone Firenze/Shutterstock.com

Figure 4-6. The input-interaction model receives inputs and issues action requests. The output-interaction model sends outputs to the player.

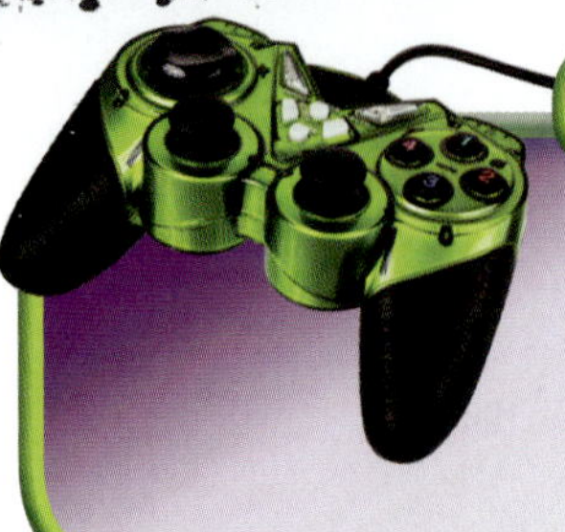

CHEAT CODE: CLOCK SPEED

The clock speed or clock rate is the speed at which the computer central processing unit (CPU) processes instructions. The higher the clock speed, the faster the computer.

The 3.2 GHz rating is a measure of the **clock speed** of the computer processor. With every tick of the clock, the computer can let in information and process a chunk. To put this into perspective, there are 31,536,000 seconds in one standard year. Round off this number to 32 million seconds. It would take the clock on the wall or your wristwatch 10 years to tick as many times as the computer processor ticks in only one second. That is why a computer can do so many functions that seem instantaneous. Game designers take advantage of the high speed of computers to create gameplay that includes animations, complex graphics, special effects, and other features.

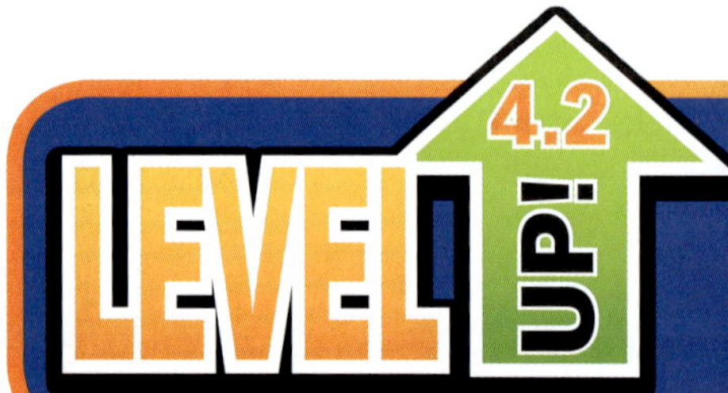

Consider games you have played. Select three games and make a list of the outputs associated with the game.

Applying the Human-Computer Interface to Game Design

The basis of the human-computer interface is the user interface of the game. It allows the player to input information and receive proper output from the computer. Understanding the needs of the typical player is critical to the proper design of the user interface. A real challenge occurs when dealing with players of different knowledge and proficiency levels. The user interface should be designed to allow for the frequent need of help that a new user will require, but also allow for the quick navigation required by an expert user.

While most games use the standard controller of the game console, designers are not limited to that input device. Many video games have modified controllers to make the gameplay more realistic and meaningful to the player. For example, games such as *Rock Band, Dance Dance Revolution,* and many of the Wii-based games have special controllers.

The eight golden rules of human-computer interface design are:

- strive for consistency;
- enable frequent users to use shortcuts;
- offer informative feedback;
- design dialogue to yield closure;
- offer simple error handling;
- permit easy reversal of actions;
- support internal locus of control; and
- reduce short-term memory load.

These rules have been applied to many computer systems. In this section, the focus is on how a game designer will apply these rules.

CASE STUDY

Eight Golden Rules of Human-Computer Interface Design

Ben Shneiderman's work on human-computer interaction at the University of Maryland led to the development of his eight golden rules of human-computer interface design. His work is detailed in the book *Designing the User Interface: Strategies for Effective Human-Computer Interaction.* The eight golden rules of computer interface design are summarized here as they apply to video game design.

Strive for consistency. Similar situations should have consistent sequences of actions. Identical terminology should be used in prompts, menus, and help screens. Consistent commands should be used throughout the game.

Enable frequent users to use shortcuts. As a user plays a game more frequently, the number of interactions should be reduced and the pace of interaction increased. This can be done through the use of abbreviations, function keys, hidden commands, and customization.

Offer informative feedback. For every action by the user, the game should provide feedback. For frequent and minor actions, the response can be minimal. For infrequent and major actions, the response should be more substantial.

Design dialogue to yield closure. Sequences of actions should be organized into groups with a beginning, middle, and end. Informative feedback at the completion of a group of actions should be provided to give the player the satisfaction of accomplishment, a sense of relief, the signal to drop contingency plans and options from their minds, and an indication that the way is clear to prepare for the next group of actions. This feedback can be in the form of character dialogue spoken to the player or on-screen messages displayed to the player.

Offer simple error handling. Try to design the game so the player cannot make a serious error. However, if the player does make an error, the game should detect the error and offer a simple and easy-to-understand way for the player to handle the error.

Permit easy reversal of actions. Provide a way for the player to undo actions. If the player knows that actions can be undone, exploration of the gameplay is encouraged. Depending on the game, the player may be permitted to undo a single action or a complete group of actions.

Support internal locus of control. Experienced players usually like to have the sense that they are in charge of the game and that the game responds to their actions. Design the game to make the player the initiator of actions rather than responding to game directions.

Reduce short-term memory load. There is a limit to what players can process and hold in short-term memory. The user interface should be simple. When possible, consolidate information on a single display. Reduce the amount of time a player must spend moving information elements, such as dialog boxes. Sufficient time should be provided through gameplay to allow the player to learn codes, mnemonic devices, and sequences of actions.

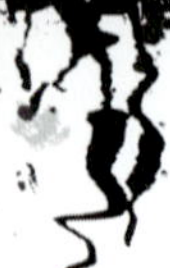

Consistency

Colors help maintain consistency throughout the display and between levels. Dramatic color changes should only occur when needed during gameplay. For example, changing color is an effective way to change the mood of the game. Otherwise, the basic color palette should be maintained throughout the game. A game should have readable text, overall consistency of layout, and functional consistency for both inputs and outputs.

Readable Text

Having text readable by the player is a critically important part of design. Stylized or decorative fonts are hard to read. A san serif font typically offers the best readability, as shown in **Figure 4-7.** In addition to the font, the size and color of the text need to be considered. The audience needs determine the correct size and color. Children and older adults require a larger text in a color that contrasts with the background. In early games, the text always appeared as black text on a white background or white text on a black background. Always test your text placement to see if it is readable during gameplay.

An important part of creating readable text is the contrast between the text and the background or game frame. Many games will display a text box with a high alpha channel value (transparency). Using transparency helps the player see through to the game frame, but hinders the readability of any text in the window. Using a transparent textbox may make it impossible for the user to read. Additionally, the text color should contrast with the background color.

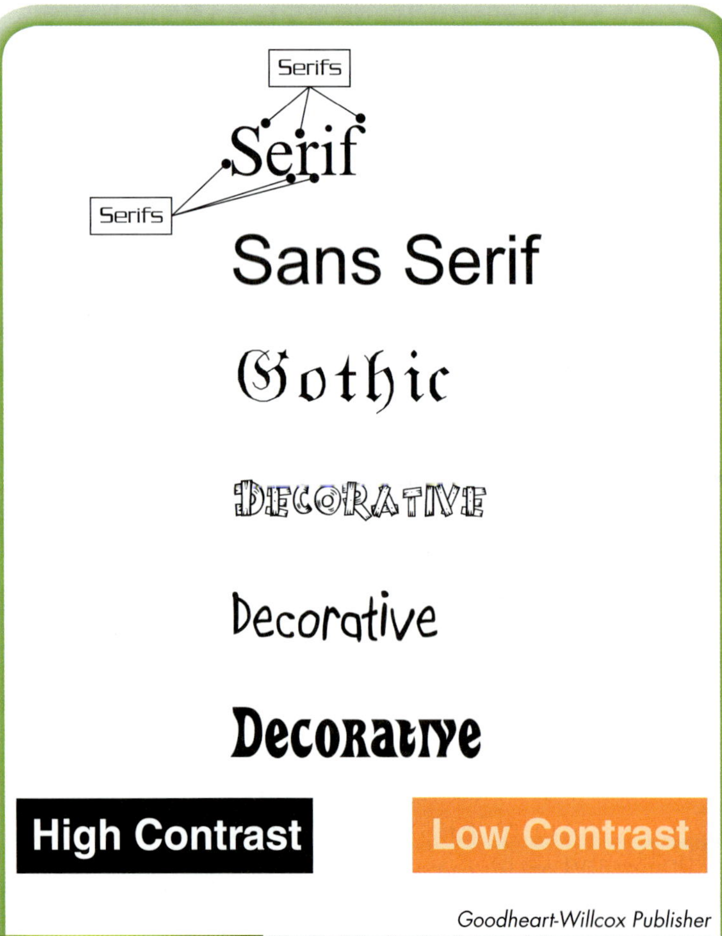

Figure 4-7. Text must be set in a font that is readable and must have enough contrast with the background.

Layout Consistency

The overall layout of the game should be both functional and navigable. The layout should remain as consistent as possible throughout the game so the player will not have to learn different locations for information. For example, if the minimap is in the top-left corner of the game for level 1, then the minimap should be in the top-left corner for all other levels. The minimaps are a critical feature in many games. A designer should always remember that a player looking at a minimap is not focusing on the game frame action.

This goes back to layout of the HUD. The HUD should be only as large as needed to properly display the needed information and should remain consistent throughout each level unless the game story dictates a change. When the story or gameplay changes, the HUD may change to give the best information required for that level. Even in this case, items that appear in the HUD on each level should be consistently located. If a new feature in the HUD is similar to one that is not needed on the new level, place the feature where the old feature was. This helps the player quickly learn the layout and use it efficiently.

Part of the layout should also help the player navigate the game. Using in-game signs, arrows, and other assets help the player know where to go. The minimap is also a common tool to help the player navigate levels. When navigation is wrong, there should be signals to indicate to the player that he or she is going the wrong way. Use of visual and sound clues will help the player properly navigate the game.

Functional Consistency for Inputs

For functional consistency of inputs, keep button-press actions the same as for similar actions in similar games. For example, most gamers have trouble converting from one game control system to another. When *Battlefield 3* was released in November of 2011, most *Call of Duty* players found the game hard to play. The frustration came from having to learn a new set of button-press action. *Call of Duty* players were familiar with using the [R2] button on the PlayStation 3 to activate a weapon. In *Battlefield 3,* the same [R2] button performs a crouch action. This lack of consistency across games caused expert users of one game to have difficulty in another. Whenever possible, controls should do the same game action as in similar games.

Functional Consistency for Outputs

For functional consistency of outputs, menus, colors, fonts, navigation, button locations, and overall game layout should be similar throughout the game. One of the most important areas of functional consistency is menu design. ***Shell menus*** are used for starting the game or for actions outside of gameplay, such as making screen and sound settings. In addition to shell menus, there are **shell screens,** as shown in **Figure 4-8.** These are called shell menus and screens because they exist as a shell surrounding the game world.

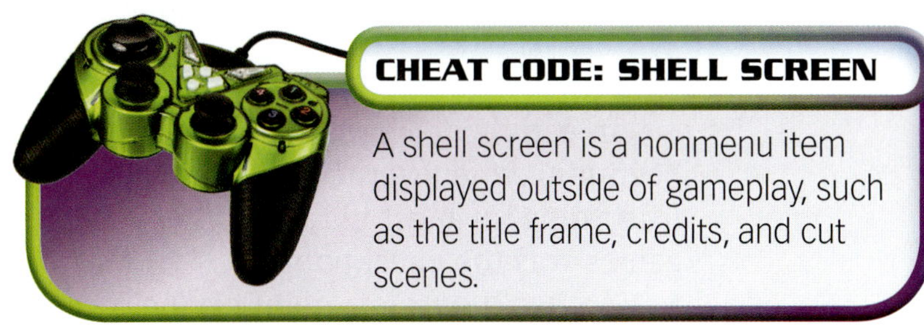

CHEAT CODE: SHELL SCREEN

A shell screen is a nonmenu item displayed outside of gameplay, such as the title frame, credits, and cut scenes.

Activities such as starting, loading, and saving are commonly done using a shell menu. Other activities that may be done using a shell menu include setting the volume for sounds, music, and dialogue; assigning custom controller buttons; specifying the HD-screen ratio; and selecting a display resolution. Game-specific shell menus include those to choose characters and customize game assets.

When constructing shell menus and screens, keep the style and layout consistent throughout the game. Choices that use the same menu should be visible every time the menu is selected. A choice can be grayed out to indicate it is not available at that point in the game, but the menu should look the same each time it is selected. Players get frustrated looking for menu commands and options. If a menu option is not shown because the player has not completed

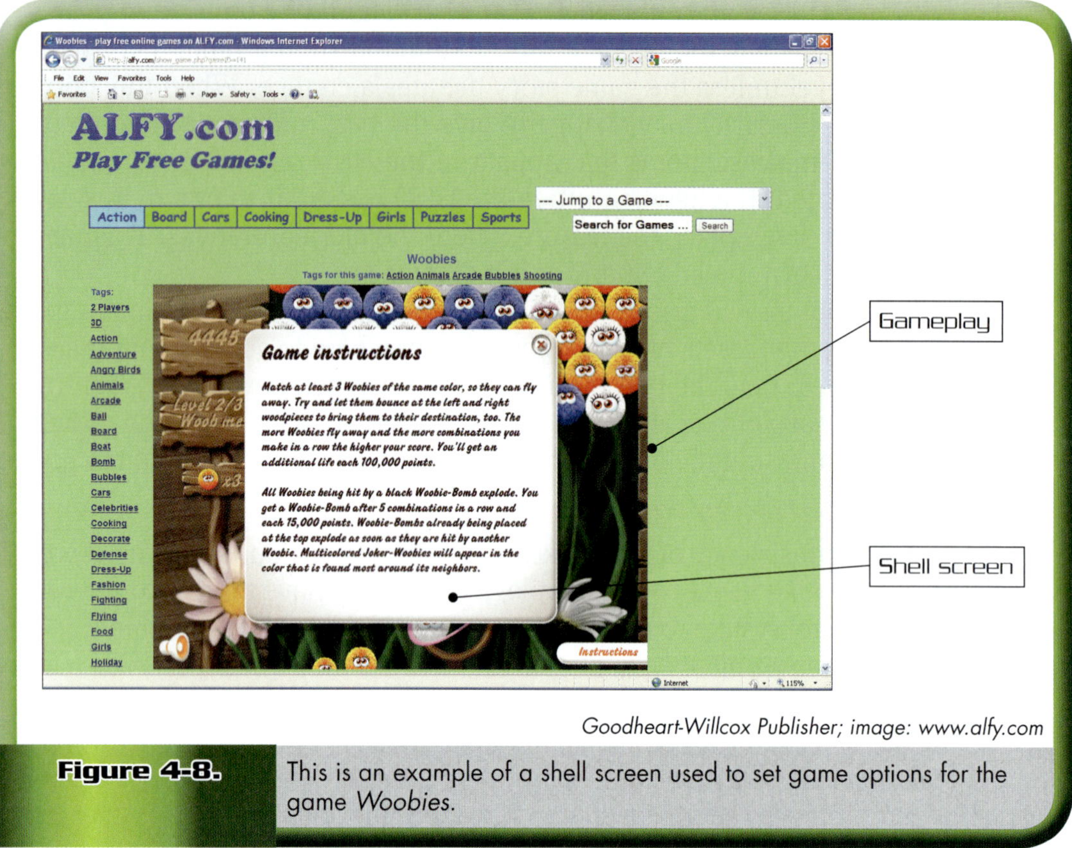

Goodheart-Willcox Publisher; image: www.alfy.com

Figure 4-8. This is an example of a shell screen used to set game options for the game *Woobies*.

a task to activate it, he or she will get frustrated looking for the option without knowing the error. It is better to gray out the menu option so the player knows something needs to be done to enable it. By keeping the menu consistent, the user is provided information to help better remember and navigate the menu.

Shortcuts

In early video games, players would have to restart the game from the beginning whenever they lost the game or a life within the game. This got very frustrating for most players. One of the first shortcuts to be added to video games was the checkpoint.

A ***checkpoint*** is a point on the gameplay timeline where the player will be returned if the player character runs out of health or life. A game typically has several checkpoints, usually after each difficult or time-consuming task has been completed. This keeps the player moving forward without having to start from the beginning if something goes wrong.

Many games have cheat codes and hidden commands. ***Cheat codes*** are commands used during game development so each part of the game can be properly tested without having to play the entire game. For example, a quality-assurance tester may need to test buying every item in the game. A cheat code to give unlimited gold makes that testing possible. Cheat codes are not typically intended for players to use, but they are usually leaked to the public or discovered by players. Some gamers use cheat codes and other hidden commands to gain an advantage over other players.

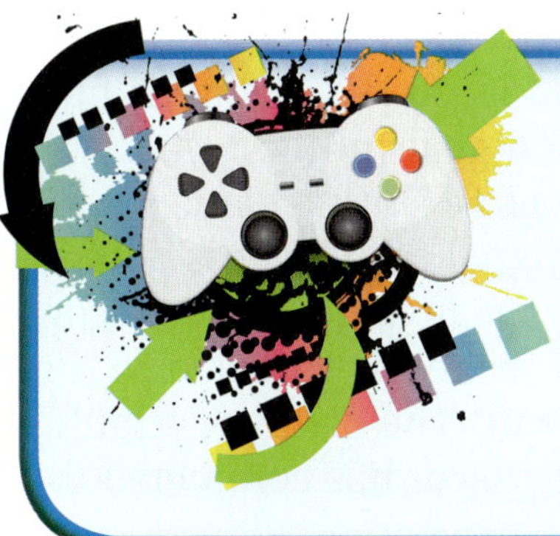

Ethical Gamer

Using cheat codes may be okay in a single-player game, but they should not be used in multiplayer games, especially online games. If used in a single-player game, the only person affected is the player using the cheat code. If used in a multiplayer game, cheat codes provide an unfair advantage over other players.

A new form of shortcut has appeared in some video games in recent years. It allows experienced players of a game franchise to jump past skill-building components of the game. For example, *Call of Duty Modern Warfare 3* awards tokens to players who had a specific prestige level in the previous game versions of *Modern Warfare 2* or *Black Ops*. This allows players to bypass the tutorial and early levels of the game designed primarily to build the player's skill level. It also allows for them to play online with other expert users without having to rebuild their skill level from scratch.

Designers should consider including shortcuts and other systems to allow expert players to get to challenging levels quickly. One way to provide the flexibility needed to allow both new players and experts to play the game is by having difficulty levels. Allowing users to select beginner, normal, difficult, and expert modes serve the same function as a shortcut.

Feedback

The player should receive some feedback, or output information, whenever an action is input. If the action is a jump, then a "boing" sound could be the feedback that the jump command was activated. Some games also provide feedback for the result of the PC's actions. A crowd cheering may indicate a good move. Booing may indicate a bad move. The more significant the outcome of the PC's action, the more substantial the feedback should be.

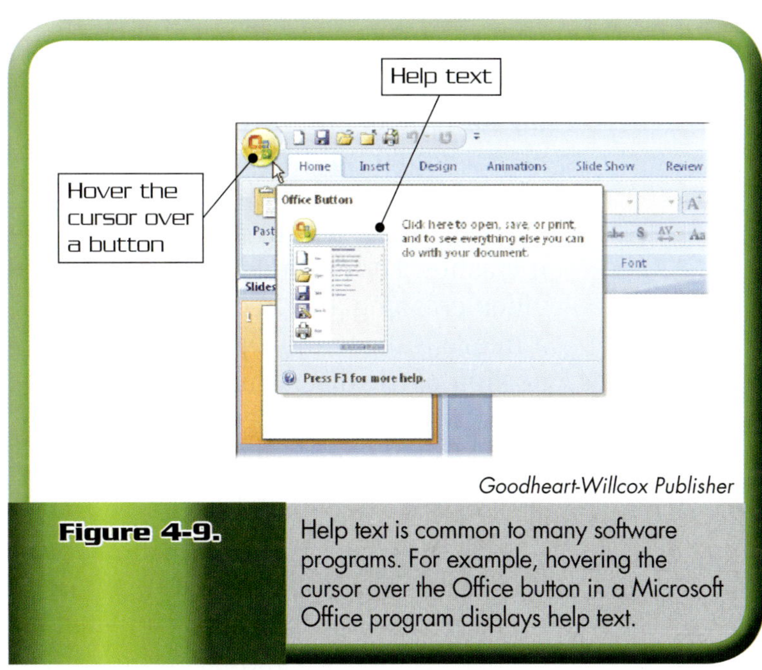

Goodheart-Willcox Publisher

Figure 4-9. Help text is common to many software programs. For example, hovering the cursor over the Office button in a Microsoft Office program displays help text.

Rollover help text is also a very common feedback feature. When the player moves the game pointer or cursor over a button or in-game icon, a text box appears to explain the function or purpose. This allows players to understand the interface and gameplay. As shown in **Figure 4-9,** rollover help text is common to many software programs. Game players will be very familiar with the feature before seeing it in a game.

Closure

Closure is a sense of conclusion to the game and its story. Closure is built into the game using the structure of the missions and goals of the game. The sequence of action should lead to a significant goal. During gameplay, dialogue between the game and the player should signal the player is going in the correct direction. In this sense, dialogue may mean actual speech from an NPC to the player or it may mean other types of feedback provided to the player. Eventually, each set of actions will need to end. The dialogue should bring closure to the game. In some games, after the player has completed the last objective and defeated the big boss, a cut scene plays to provide closure. It may sum up what has been accomplished in the game or provide an ending to the story.

Errors

It may be impossible to build a complex game system without any errors. As games advance, the processing power needed to run the graphics and input actions increases. This can lead to lag and crashes if not properly designed and tested. Games should be tested in an attempt to find all errors.

Output Error Prevention

During gameplay, the game should test for inactivity to make sure the player is not stuck. For example, in a car-racing game, if the player drives off road and hits a ditch, the car cannot move. The game should check to see if the car has not been moving for a period of time and, if so, reset the car to the nearest checkpoint without spending a life. A timeout feature would help eliminate player frustration with getting stuck in game obstacles.

A ***timeout*** is when the game resets after a period of player inactivity. When the player is inactive for a set period of time, the game resets the player to the nearest checkpoint. A word of caution: if a player who is not stuck gets a timeout, he or she will be upset. Find the amount of time where the typical player would not normally be inactive, or display a prompt for the player to press a button to continue or reset.

Additional output prevention should allow a system to automatically reset if it crashes. For example, DVD players have a system of multiscanning to prevent video crashing and freezing due to scratches and fingerprints on the discs. After a freeze is detected, a portion of the movie is skipped to avoid the damaged portion of the disc. This allowed the user to continue to watch the movie without having to take out the disc and restart the movie. The same function is found in video game consoles that use DVD drives.

Input Error Prevention

Error prevention must be designed into the game inputs. Simple error prevention may include marking forms fields as required and checking for number or text formats in completed form fields. Additionally, checking for proper user names and passwords is a component of error prevention. This makes sure the player is the correct player to access the game.

Additional input error prevention comes in the form of designing a controller with buttons spaced far enough apart to avoid pressing two buttons at the same time. Designs for input devices should follow

ergonomic design principles. Interface designers focus on six principles of interface ergonomics when creating input devices and displays.

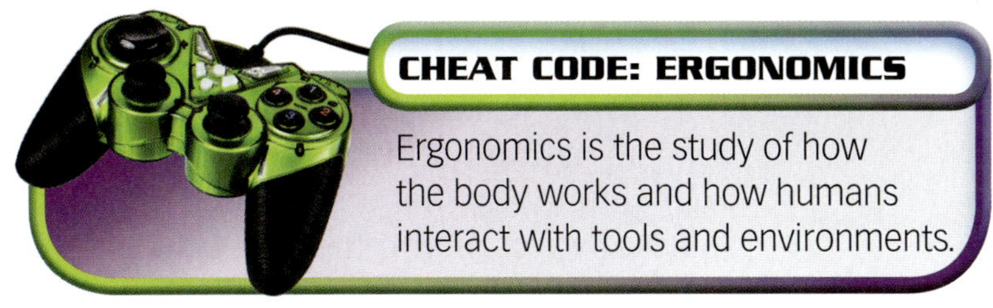

CHEAT CODE: ERGONOMICS

Ergonomics is the study of how the body works and how humans interact with tools and environments.

- design for comfort
- reduce force
- reduce reach
- limit excessive and repetitive motion
- reduce fatigue
- stretch the player

Figure 4-10 shows how a person should be positioned when using a computer workstation designed with ergonomic principles. The workstations in a game design studio and even at home should be designed to allow the user to sit in this position.

Design for Comfort. An input device should be designed so it can be easily held and moved. An important part of comfort is maintaining a neutral position. A neutral position is the shape of the body when it is relaxed and unstressed. Relax your hands and hold them in front of yourself with the palms facing each other. Notice that your wrists are straight, your fingers curl in without touching the palm, and the thumb rests on top of the index finger. This is the neutral position of the hands. Since most game controllers use the fingers, hand position is one of the most important design considerations for designers of input devices.

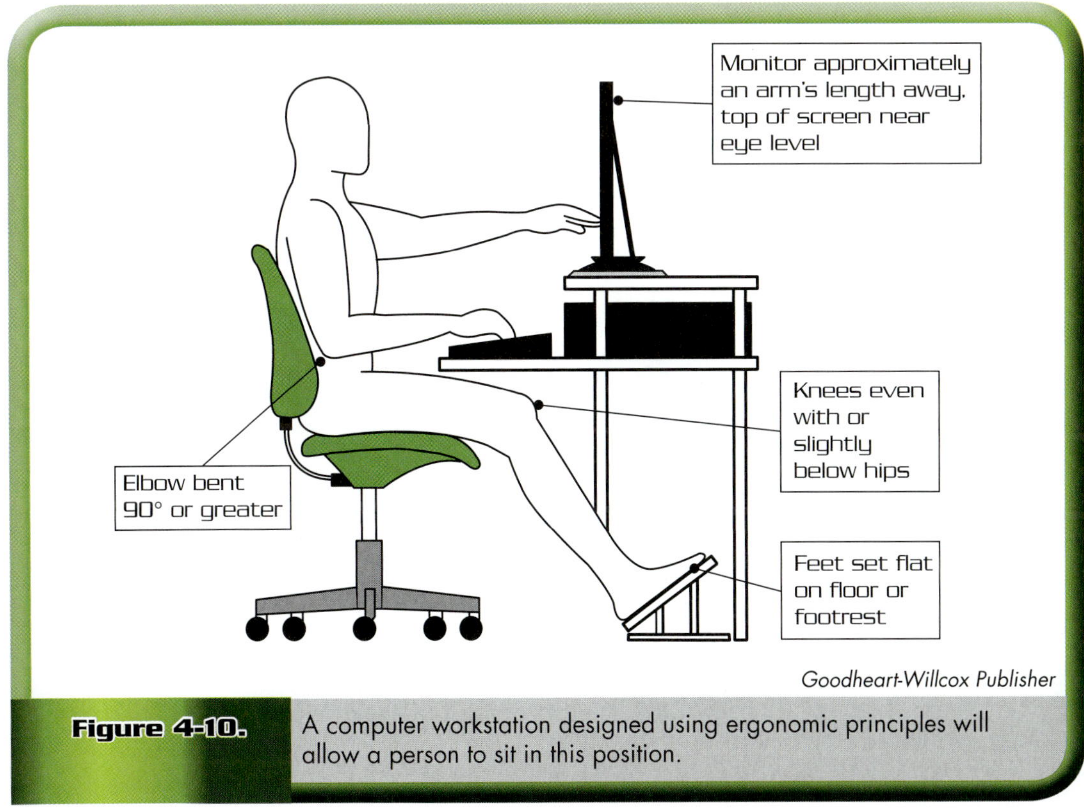

Figure 4-10. A computer workstation designed using ergonomic principles will allow a person to sit in this position.

The standard controller for many game consoles takes the neutral position into consideration with "wings" on the controller, as shown in **Figure 4-11.** The wings rest on the palm to support the weight of the controller. The fingers naturally curl around the wing to hold it firmly without any strain. The thumbs lay flat on the surface of the controller just as they would naturally rest flat on the index fingers. The controller keeps the hands about two inches apart. This is also a natural position. Because of the ergonomic design of the standard controller, the player can play for many hours without injury or fatigue.

One game console controller that is *not* ergonomically designed is the Wii remote. It has a rectangular shape that is difficult to hold and forces the fingers in unnatural position. This controller was designed to fit into many different accessories to create greater game immersion. When designing a custom controller, it must best fit a natural body position. The Wii accessories are ergonomically designed, but without them the controller is uncomfortable to use for long periods of time.

The Xbox Kinect and PlayStation Eye camera allow for no handheld controller. These controllers scan the player's body position and use actual body movement as input. When working with controllers like these, it is important to remember comfort during gameplay. An action requiring the player to lean left to turn left is good for a short period of time. However, if the player must hold a tilted position without anything to support his or her body, discomfort and even injury can result.

Reduce Force. A player pressing a button must exert force on the button to make it move. The button will have some resistance to the force and the ability to spring back into position when the pressing is complete. A button press is called ***trigger pull.*** The trigger pull on an input device must be sensitive enough to engage the control, but not so sensitive that the control

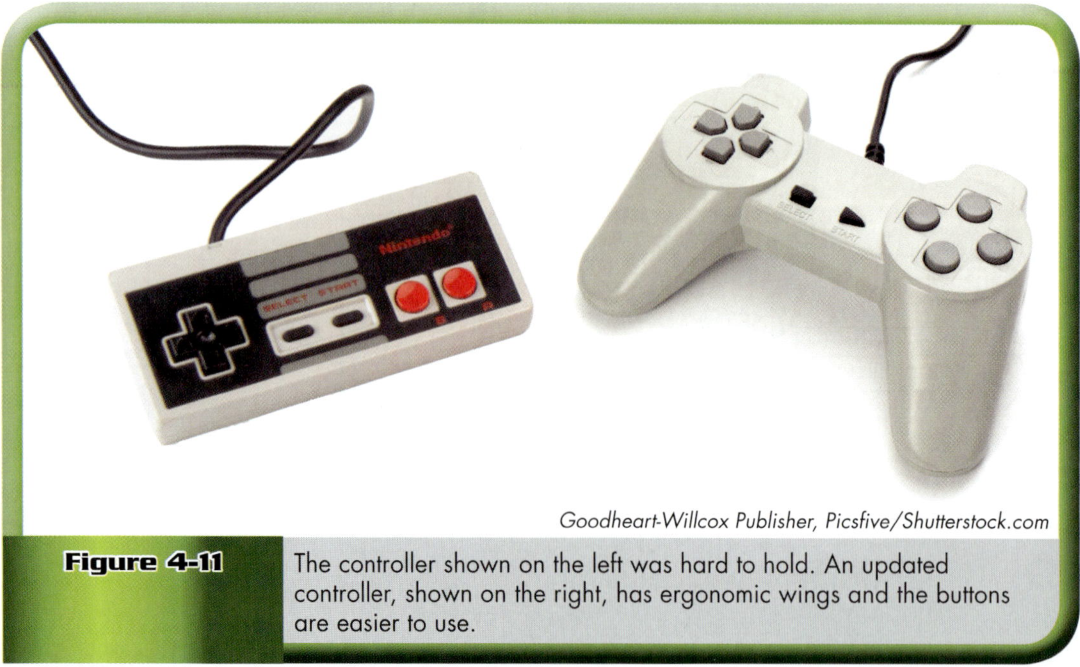

Goodheart-Willcox Publisher, Picsfive/Shutterstock.com

Figure 4-11 The controller shown on the left was hard to hold. An updated controller, shown on the right, has ergonomic wings and the buttons are easier to use.

engages when not desired. If designing a custom controller, buttons should support not only the weight of the button, but also the weight of the finger at rest on the button. A keyboard is a good example of this. Your fingers can rest comfortably on the keys without causing the keys to depress.

The principle of reduced force holds true for both button-press inputs and nonbutton inputs. A voice input should only require a force equal to a natural speaking volume. If the input requires yelling, the player may strain his or her vocal chords. A motion-based controller like the Kinect should not require excessive movement. Beyond the fact that a harsh force like a kick might throw off a shoe, the lack of contact with another object requires the body to apply opposing force to stop the movement. If you swing your arm quickly and try to stop it in front of you, you will feel the muscles in your shoulder tighten to stop the arm. This may lead to muscle strains.

Reduce Reach. All of the inputs on the controller should be within easy reach for the player. On the original Xbox controller, many players found it very hard to reach some buttons when needed. If designing a custom controller, locate buttons where the player can easily reach them.

Button combinations should be comfortable to use. A good button combination is to have the player press one button with the right hand and another button with the left hand. If the player has to press three buttons at the same time using just the left hand, he or she would probably drop the controller. By having each hand activate one button, the player can maintain a comfortable grip on the controller.

Buttons-press commands should also be programmed so the most frequent actions use the most natural positions. For this reason, most console controllers were designed with a thumb-controlled joystick or D-pad in the natural position of the thumb. As shown in **Figure 4-12,** the Nintendo 64–style controller has the joystick in an unnatural position. The player must hold the middle wing of the controller to use the joystick. This makes it impossible to press the [L] or [R] buttons while using the joystick.

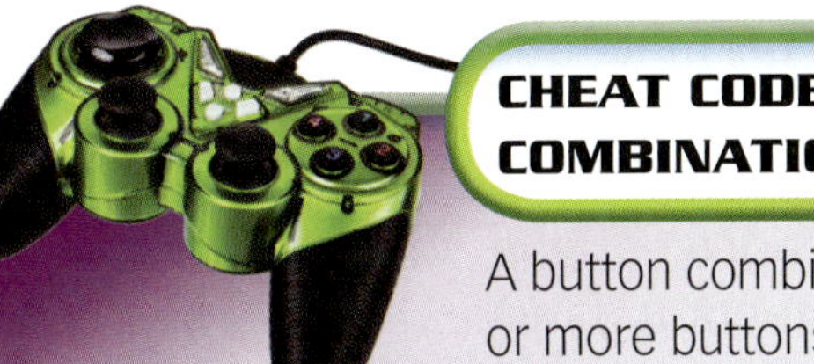

CHEAT CODE: BUTTON COMBINATION

A button combination is when two or more buttons must be pressed at the same time to activate a game command. By having both single-button commands and button-combination commands, the number of commands that can be executed with a single controller is increased.

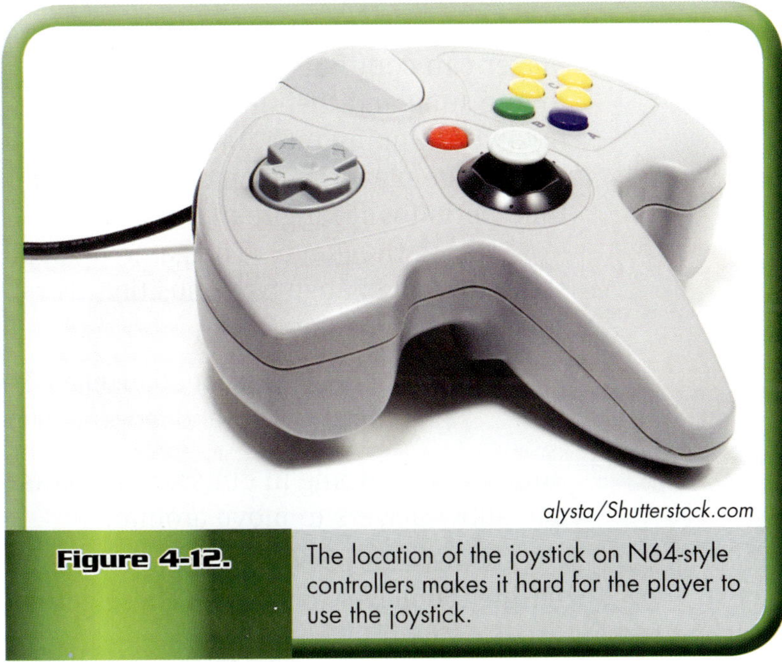

alysta/Shutterstock.com

Figure 4-12. The location of the joystick on N64-style controllers makes it hard for the player to use the joystick.

The purpose for design was to allow for both right- and left-handed players to use the single joystick, but this did not turn out to be the case. Revised designs of this controller include two joysticks, one for the right thumb and one for the left thumb. This improves the ergonomic design.

Limit Excessive and Repetitive Motion. Repetitive-motion injuries are common with players of video games. A ***repetitive-motion injury*** is an injury that occurs as a result of doing the same motion over and over. Imagine a game requires the player to press the [R] button to take a single step. The player's right index finger would become very tired after only a short amount of gameplay. This could lead to a strained finger muscle or damage to the finger joints. Instead, the game can be designed so that pressing up on the controller joystick moves the character forward. This eliminates the repetitive motion.

Many games require a button press to have the character throw or shoot. When designing the gameplay for these types of games, there should be breaks in the action to give the player time to rest. Instead of having the player use a thousand trigger pulls in a row, break up the action. Put the character in a situation that requires a few trigger pulls, and then have the character move to a new position before initiating more trigger pulls. This allows the player's hands and fingers an opportunity to rest in between trigger pulls.

Reduce Fatigue. Video game designers should consider ways to reduce the amount to fatigue the player will experience. The weight of the controller is a common factor of fatigue. Holding a heavy controller can get tiring. For the game *Guitar Hero,* a strap on the guitar controller makes it possible for the player to use a large, heavy controller for long periods of time without becoming fatigued from its weight.

Even using motion-capture controllers can lead to fatigue. For example, holding your arms above your head for only a few minutes is tiring even though there is no movement. Standing on one foot is another example of how fatigue can quickly occur without movement. Additionally, a game that requires full-body motion needs to have breaks in gameplay to make sure the player can continue the physical activity. A dance game may limit the dancing to one song and then have a break while the next song loads. A game that involves jumping may have a storyline with cut scenes the player must watch to give the player a chance to rest. Combining too many actions in a short time period will fatigue players.

Stretch the Player. The game must allow the player the opportunity to stand up and change body position. For example, the game may display a splash page that states:

> You have been playing for 30 minutes. The game will pause for two minutes. Take this time to stretch and move around.

Additionally, adding in cut scenes, status screens, and other pausing devices will allow players to move around.

Games that use motion-capture controllers can be more proactive in getting the player to stretch. These games run the risk of having players pull a muscle or incur another injury caused by not getting the muscles stretched and warmed up before use. When the game begins, the player can be required to complete a stretching or exercise sequence before gameplay begins.

Game designers should seek to add some component to gameplay that inspires players to take a break, move around, and change positions. This helps prevent conditions that occur from sitting too long, like the legs falling asleep.

Undo Actions

When players make an input error, they should be able to easily reverse, or undo, the error. During gameplay, the player may have selected the wrong weapon or armor for the quest. The player should be able to change the weapon or armor without having to restart the game. It may require going back to a merchant or using a selection menu, but the player should be able to realize the error and have the opportunity to correct it.

In many games, an automatic save is performed when the player reaches each checkpoint. This eliminates the chance that the player forgets to save the game. It also gives the player a point to return to if an error is made without having to replay the game from the beginning.

In cases where the game takes action to handle an output error, the player may be given the opportunity to reverse the action before the game resets. In *Mario Kart,* a race official using a siren and holding a sign that states wrong way is used to signal the player to turn around. If the player does not change direction, the game resets the player. Giving players clues to navigation errors will give them a chance to reverse course on their own.

Sense of Control

Players should feel like they are in control of the game and not just responding to game action. Much of this sense of control comes from the design of the obstacles and missions. The player should have the freedom to explore and make choices that effect gameplay. Additionally, the player should have an intuitive understanding of how to play the game. When the player needs to learn a new set of unfamiliar command and button presses, he or she can get frustrated. An ***intuitive controller*** needs little explanation on how to use it in the game. Intuitive controllers like the Wii accessories shown in **Figure 4-13** are similar to devices in real life and help add to the feeling of being in control.

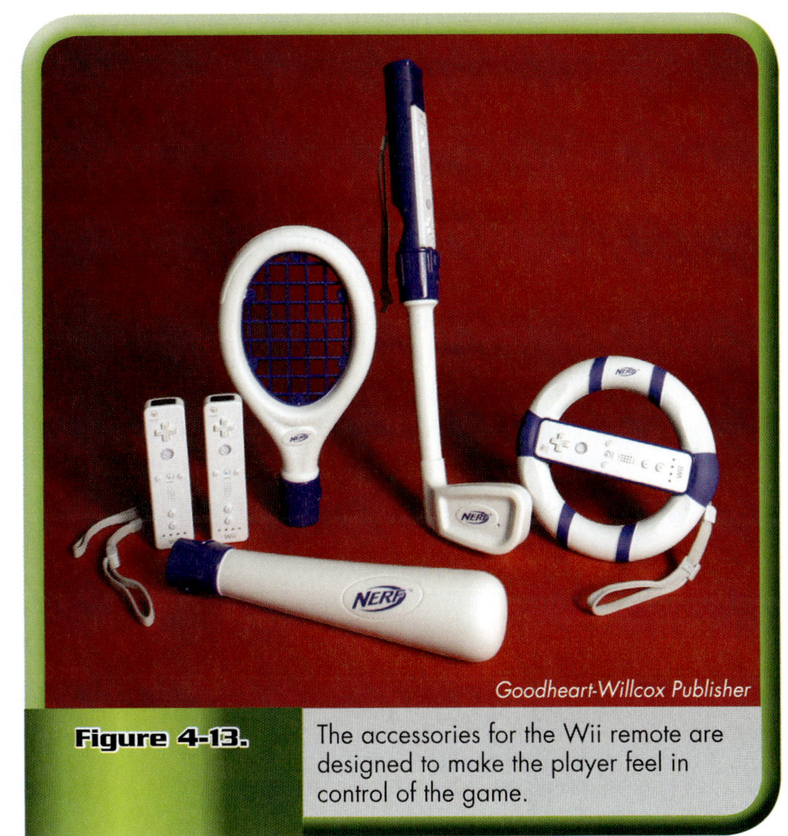

Goodheart-Willcox Publisher

Figure 4-13. The accessories for the Wii remote are designed to make the player feel in control of the game.

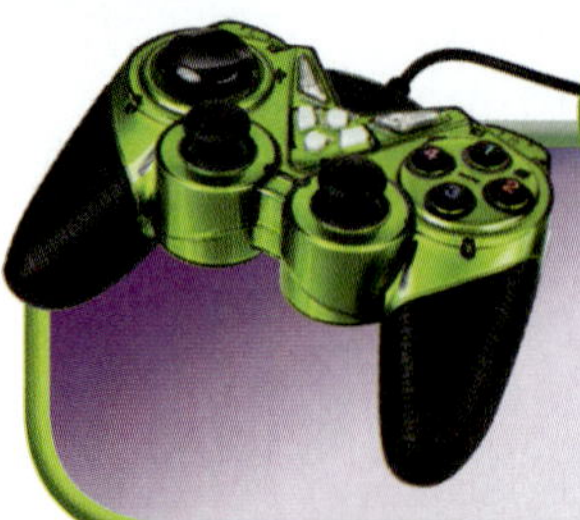

CHEAT CODE: NAVIGATION MAP

A navigation map is a small map in the corner of the game frame that displays relative locations of obstacles, enemies, and objectives.

Another common interface asset that allows the player to feel in control is a minimap or **navigation map**. This helps eliminate random wandering by the player looking for the objective. Other navigation tools, such as cooperative NPCs and directional clues, also aid in giving the player a sense of control.

Memory Overload

Video game designers must try to reduce the amount of information the player is required to remember. Tutorials will help the player get more familiar with the input and actions needed to be successful in the game. Additionally, by gradually increasing, or escalating, the tasks throughout the game the player is given the chance to learn the game in small pieces.

The game should also provide in-game information for the player to quickly recall objectives. In many games, a log book and an adventure map are used to reduce the amount of information the player must memorize. The player can review the log book to see clues already found. When the player gets to a new riddle or puzzle within the game, he or she can review the clues to solve the problem. The adventure map records which sections of the game the player has already completed. It may summarize actions the player took and the results of each section. The adventure map also generally provides clues to how much of the game is left to play.

To be able to navigate the game, a player typically must remember a lot of information. If the player takes focus off the gameplay to figure out where he or she is, the gameplay becomes secondary. Use of navigational aids, changes in game assets, and distinctive backgrounds will help the player recall where he or she is located within the game map. If the game has very similar buildings and backgrounds, the player may not be able to remember the path he or she is taking. Adding gameplay that allows the player to climb a building to get a view of the surroundings can take the place of a navigation map or be a way to supplement the navigation map.

In adventures that have puzzles integrated in the gameplay, use tokens, keys, amulets, or other game assets as rewards that unlock future gameplay elements. Do not force the player to remember a five-digit code that was deciphered in level one to unlock a door on level five. Instead, have the player find a key on level one that can be carried to level five to unlock the door. The door or gate obstacle that requires the key could also have a prompt, sign, or message telling the player what is required to open it.

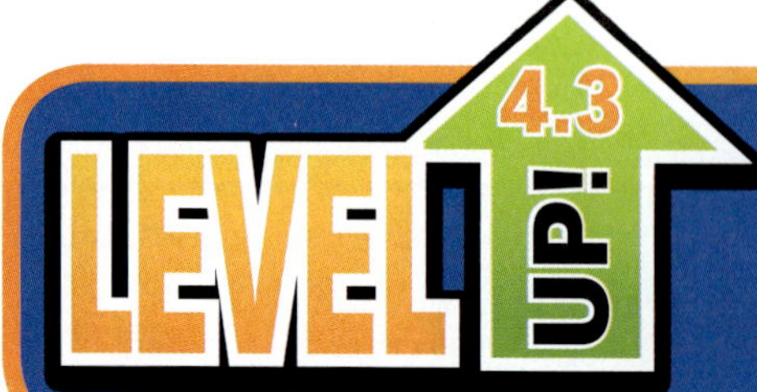

Select one of your favorite games. List the different ways in which the game provides feedback to the player.

Chapter Summary

- Player-centric design involves understanding the player and centering the game design on what the player wants and needs.
- Four key topics related to player immersion that have universal application are: the human-computer interface, elements of engagement, elements of interest, and balance elements.
- The human-computer interface allows the player to input information and receive proper output from the computer and should be designed to allow for the frequent need of help that a new user will require, but also allow for the quick navigation required by an expert user.

Check Your Video Game IQ

Now that you have finished this chapter, see what you know about video game design by taking the chapter posttest.

www.m.g-wlearning.com

www.g-wlearning.com

Review Your Knowledge

On a separate sheet of paper or in a word processing document, match the following terms with the definition that fits best.

A. demographics
B. output
C. immersion
D. dexterity
E. timeout
F. muscle memory
G. checkpoint
H. input
I. ergonomics
J. vicarious immersion

1. Readiness and skill in a physical activity, especially one involving use of the hands.
2. Instructions from the player sent to the computer.
3. The designer imagining himself or herself in place of the player to experience the gameplay.
4. When the game resets after a period of player inactivity.
5. The study of how the body works and how humans interact with tools and environments.
6. The level to which the player feels he or she is actually experiencing the events of the game.
7. The information that the computer sends to the player.
8. When a physical task has been repeated enough that the task can be completed without conscious effort.
9. Measurable characteristics of a person or group.
10. Point on the gameplay timeline where the player will be returned if the player character runs out of health or life.

On a separate sheet of paper or in a word processing document, answer each of the following questions.

11. In your own words, summarize the concept of player-centric design.
12. List the six elements of player-centric design.
13. How does muscle memory relate to player skill?
14. List the four key topics related to player immersion.
15. Explain the difference between an input and an output.
16. Explain how errors occur when similar games use common buttons for different actions.
17. List two ways feedback can be given in a game.
18. List the six principles of interface ergonomics.
19. List at least three possible solutions to prevent repetitive motion injury in a game requiring rapid fire.
20. How are navigation clues used for easy reversal of action?

Apply Your STEM Knowledge

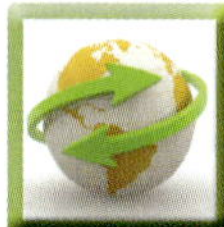

Social Studies

1. Use presentation software such as PowerPoint to create a typical player profile with yourself as the typical player. Include a picture and important demographics for yourself.

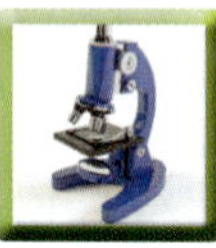

Science

2. In the Typical Player Mental Acuity section of this chapter, the text referred to an example of how a competitive NPC and a neutral NPC might look too similar. In nature, animals can mimic the colors and patterns or others such as the scarlet king snake and the coral snake. This makes them difficult to tell apart. Research these two snakes, along with other harmless animals that mimic a deadly lookalike. Find photo examples of each and create a PowerPoint presentation to explain the similarities and differences of each look alike pair.

Language Arts

3. Repetitive motion such as pressing the same controller button many times in a row can cause injury. Research the injury called gamer's thumb (also known as iPhone finger or Blackberry thumb). Write a one-page summary of the symptoms, causes, treatments, and prevention measures.

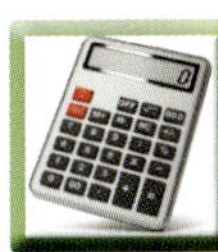

Mathematics

4. The user interface engineers need some specifications to construct the proper buttons for the player to push. Your team tested several of the typical players for the user interface devices listed in the table below. The engineers are waiting to get the data to set the spring tensions. While force is typically measured in Newtons (N), these small buttons need to be measured in dynes (dyn), which are 10^{-5} N (1 N = 100,000 dyn). Use spreadsheet software to create and complete the table below.

Button Type	Newton	Dyne
Pistol trigger	0.00006	
Pinky finger guitar fret		.8
Drum head	1.2	
Start button		4.5
D-pad up button	0.00013	

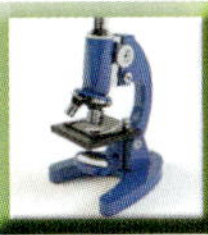

Science

5. The force needed to press a button on a controller can vary depending on which finger needs to press the button. Players can press with more force using their thumb than they can with their pinky finger. Each button has to allow for the correct finger to press while not accidentally depressing when the player gets tense or excited during gameplay. The research team has tested the strength of the typical player for the game you are building. Use spreadsheet software to create and complete the table below. Solve for the missing information using the formula:
   force = mass × acceleration
   For dyne calculations, the mass is in grams and the acceleration is in cm/seconds^2. Round all numbers to two decimal places.

Finger	Button Mass	Distance Moved	Time to Engage Button	Acceleration	Force
Thumb	2.00 g	1.00 cm	0.50 s	4.00 cm/s^2	8.00 dyn
Index	2.00 g	0.50 cm	0.50 s		
Middle	1.50 g	0.50 cm	0.70 s		
Ring	1.00 g	0.40 cm	0.80 s		
Pinky	0.80 g	0.03 cm	0.90 s		

Working in Teams

Working in with the team as assigned by your instructor, brainstorm ideas for the user interface of a video game that requires a special controller. Prepare a PowerPoint presentation of up to ten slides (five to seven minutes) to present to the class explaining the game and why a special controller is needed. Also describe the team's idea for a controller and how it would function. Include text, pictures, video, animations, slide transitions, and sound effects as appropriate to help explain your positions.

Gamer Portfolio

You will create both a print portfolio and an e-portfolio in this class. You have already decided how to store hard copy items for your print portfolio. Now you need to create a plan for storing and organizing materials for your e-portfolio. Ask your instructor where to save your documents. This could be on the school's network or a flash drive of your own. Think about how to organize related files into categories. For example, school transcripts and diplomas might be one category, awards and certificates might be another category, game builds in another, and so on. Next, consider how you will name the files. The names for folders and files should be descriptive, but not too long. This naming system will be for your use. You will decide in a later activity how to present your electronic files for viewers.

1. Create a folder on the network drive or flash drive in which you will save your files.
2. Write a few sentences to describe how you will name the subfolders and files for your portfolio.
3. Create the subfolders to organize the files using your naming system.

G-W Learning Mobile Site

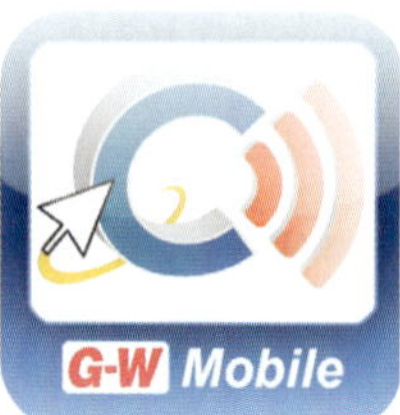

Visit the G-W Learning mobile site to complete the chapter pretest and posttest and to practice vocabulary using e-flash cards. If you do not have a smartphone, visit the G-W Learning companion website to access these features.

G-W Learning mobile site: www.m.g-wlearning.com

G-W Learning companion website: www.g-wlearning.com

Common Core

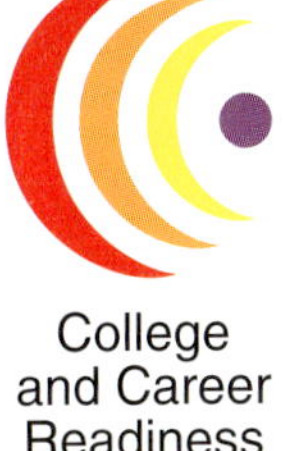
College and Career Readiness

CTE Career Ready Practices. Everyone has a stake in protecting the environment. Taking steps as an individual to be more environmentally conscious can help the environment and can also help a company be more profitable. Look at the Go Green feature in this chapter and those found throughout the book. What things do you think you can do to save energy or other resources?

Reading. Read a magazine, newspaper, or online article about the impact of technology on human-computer interfaces. Determine the central ideas of the article and review the conclusions made by the author. Provide an accurate summary of your reading, making sure to incorporate the *who, what, when,* and *how* of the article.

Writing. Research the history of the study of demographics. When did the concept of demographics originate? How is it used in the development and marketing of video games? Write an informative report consisting of several paragraphs to describe your findings.

Event Prep: Working in a Team

Some competitive events for Career and Technical Student Organizations (CTSOs) have a performance portion. If it is a team event, it is important that the team making the presentation prepare to operate as a cohesive unit. To prepare for team activities:

1. Read the guidelines provided by your organization. Make certain that you ask any questions about points you do not understand. It is important to follow each specific item that is outlined in the competition rules.
2. Complete the team activities at the end of each chapter in this text. This will help members learn how to interact with each other and participate effectively as a team.
3. Locate on your CTSO's website a rubric or scoring sheet for the event to see how the team will be judged.
4. Confirm the use of visual aids that may be used in the presentation and amount of set-up time permitted.
5. Review the rules to confirm if questions will be asked or if the team will need to defend a case.
6. Make notes on index cards about important points to remember. Team members should exchange note cards so that each evaluates the other person's notes. Use these notes to study. You may also be able to use these notes during the event.
7. Assign each team member a role for the presentation. Practice performing as a team. Each team member should introduce himself or herself, review the case, make suggestions for the case, and conclude with a summary.
8. Ask your teacher to play the role of competition judge as your team reviews the case. After the presentation is complete, ask for feedback from your teacher. You may also consider having a student audience to listen and give feedback.

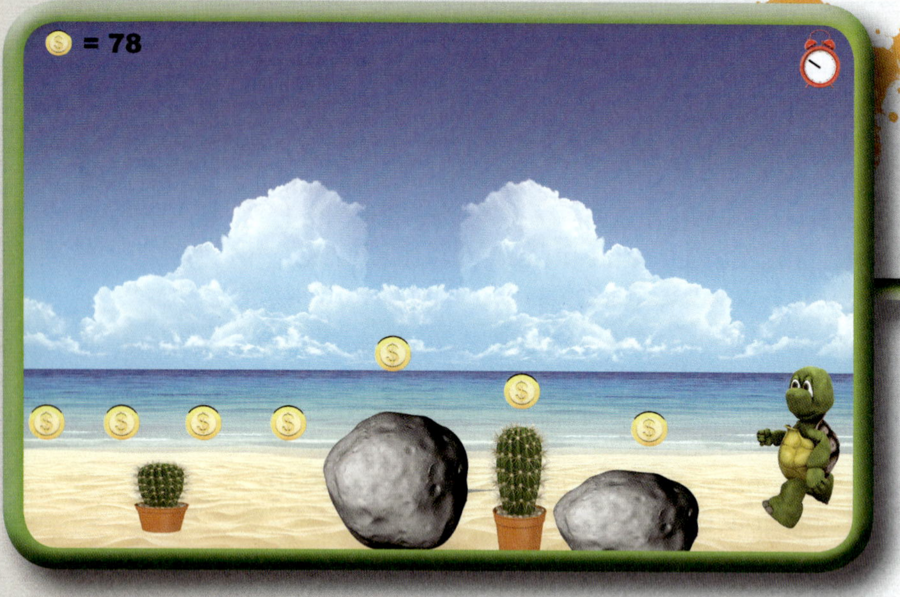

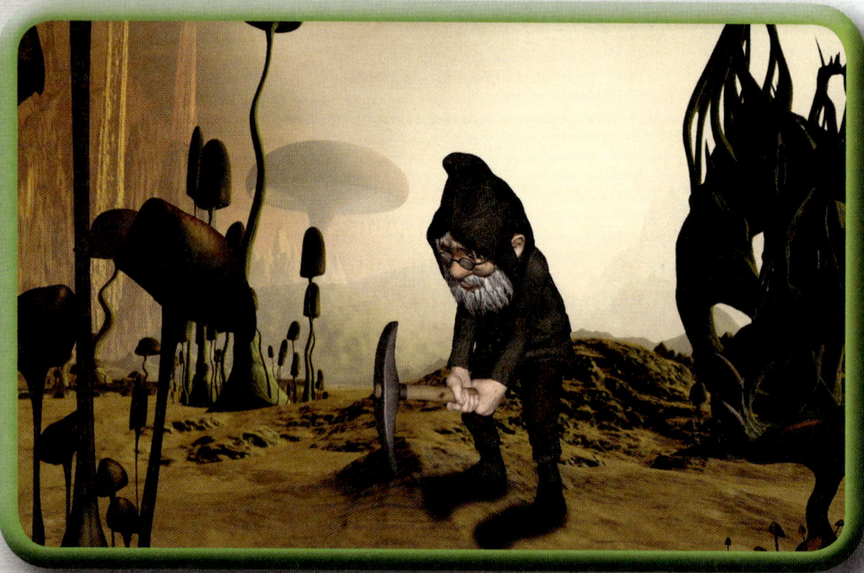

Beginner
Novice
Expert
Master

Chapter 5

Immersion Composition

The last chapter identified the four key topics related to player immersion. That chapter discussed in detail the element of the human-computer interface. An interface model alone will provide little enjoyment or immersion. The elements of engagement, elements of interest, and balance of elements must also be considered to create a player-centric game. These topics are discussed in this chapter. The techniques used to engage the player and keep the player immersed in the action are detailed.

Check Your Video Game IQ

Before you begin this chapter, see what you already know about video game design by taking the chapter pretest.

www.m.g-wlearning.com

www.g-wlearning.com

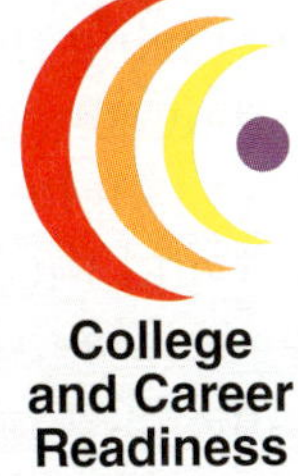

College and Career Readiness

Reading Prep. In preparation for the chapter, research Ray Kurzweil and his theory of technological singularity which is discussed in a case study in this chapter. Keep in mind what you learn about technological singularity as you read about the ways in which video games seek to create player immersion.

Objectives

After completing this chapter, you will be able to:

- Detail the elements needed to create audience-appropriate engagement.
- List the elements of interest that are aspects of a video game and draw the player to the game.
- Differentiate between balance and imbalance in a video game and identify the factors included in balancing elements.

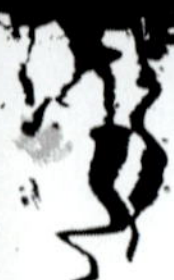

Elements of Engagement

Recall that *immersion* is the level to which the player feels he or she is actually experiencing the events of the game, or how well the player connects to the game world. Engagement and immersion are related. To experience immersion, a player must be engaged, or greatly interested, in the game.

To succeed in creating a player-centric design, the game must be designed for audience engagement. This means the typical player must be engaged in the game. Several elements need to be considered to create audience-appropriate engagement:

- genre
- story
- challenges
- success and escalation
- progress and feedback
- mental tasks
- sound effects
- narrations and voices
- competition model
- intuitive gameplay and physics

Genre

As discussed in Chapter 1, *genre* is a classification based on the type of gameplay. It is a major category of video game gameplay. A specific genre may have appeal to a specific audience. Part of the research into the typical player should ask about the games the player already enjoys. This is the genre likely to engage the typical player.

Imagine you are designing a game that you intend for an audience of ten-year-old males. The research you have done on this audience shows this group enjoys car-racing games. It would make sense to add actions to the game that are typical of other games in the sports genre that have a car-racing theme. This may help connect with the intended audience. Even if the game concept calls for the player to solve math problems, a car-racing component can be added. For example, a math problem can be displayed on a billboard and the answer choices are displayed as the street names at the next intersection, as shown in **Figure 5-1.** This allows the typical player to be engaged by the car-racing theme while solving the math problem.

Story

The first choice related to story is the choice of whether or not to have a story in the game at all. The factors related to this decision are discussed in detail in Chapter 3. If the game needs a story, then the typical player must be engaged by it.

To engage a player, the designer must create characters that the audience will connect to and understand. The characters need to be placed in situations similar to the background or life experiences of the typical player. The conflict must be one that the audience will understand. Finally, the designer needs to create resolutions and rewards that the audience will want to experience.

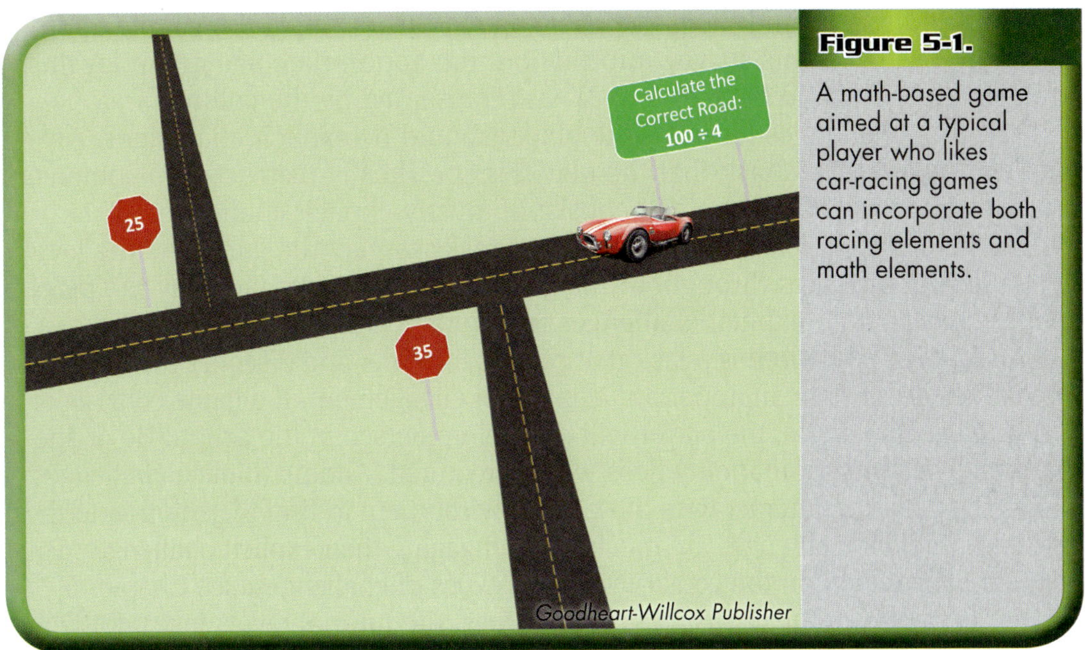

Figure 5-1. A math-based game aimed at a typical player who likes car-racing games can incorporate both racing elements and math elements.

Challenges

When constructing the challenges for the game, consider the physical and mental abilities of the audience. Determine if the challenges are obtainable and interesting to the audience. Challenges will always cause some stress for the player. The typical player must be able to deal with the stress and anxiety that the challenge creates. For an audience to be engaged in a game, designers must find the best balance between boredom and anxiety.

The graph in **Figure 5-2** measures the responses of players of different ages to a game challenge. At a very young age, simple challenges have low boredom and high anxiety. As the player's age increases, the same game challenge increases in boredom. The players are getting more mature. The life experiences and background information they gather with age create the desire and need for greater challenges. At the same time, anxiety and stress over facing this challenge decreases. A challenge must be both exciting and engaging. The ages to the right of the intersection of the anxiety and boredom lines

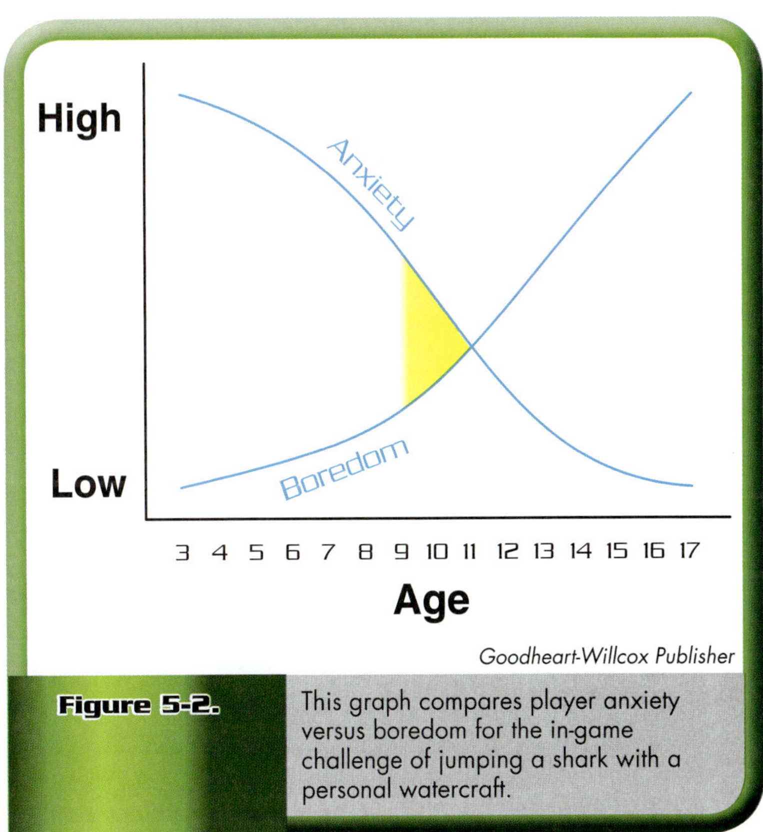

Figure 5-2. This graph compares player anxiety versus boredom for the in-game challenge of jumping a shark with a personal watercraft.

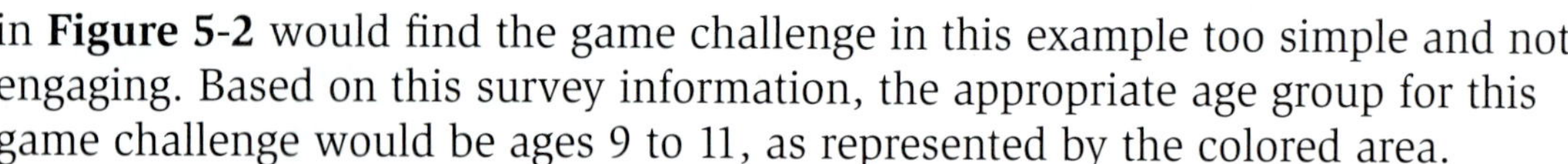

in **Figure 5-2** would find the game challenge in this example too simple and not engaging. Based on this survey information, the appropriate age group for this game challenge would be ages 9 to 11, as represented by the colored area.

The first challenges faced by the player should be explicit challenges. An ***explicit challenge*** is a task that the player is specifically instructed to complete. The tutorial levels of a game will consist of mostly explicit challenges. This allows the player to learn how to complete tasks to play the game. As the level of challenges escalates throughout the game, the challenges faced by the player should change from explicit challenges to implicit challenges.

An ***implicit challenge*** is a task that players interpret and discover on their own. Implicit challenges are an important element of engagement. If a game consists of only explicit challenges, the player will not feel immersed in the action. He or she may feel like a puppet that only does what is required. Adding implicit challenges allows the player to interact with the game environment to find the solution to the problem. Implicit challenges are much more engaging than explicit challenges. For detailed information on the construction and types of challenges, see Chapter 6.

For example, in the *Assassin's Creed* games, the tutorial levels instruct the player to use poison on a target character and to use a bomb on a different target. These explicit challenges teach the player the benefits of using specific techniques in different scenarios. As the game progresses, the challenges become implicit. An assassin may be asked to eliminate five guards without being detected, but not told *how* to accomplish the task. The player is left to apply the skills learned from explicit challenges in solving the implicit challenge.

Success and Escalation

Success is a critical part of any challenge presented in the game. If the player cannot successfully complete a challenge, he or she will not be engaged in the game and will stop playing. Success should be properly rewarded. The reward should balance the risk taken and the difficulty of the challenge. If the challenge is of moderate difficulty, such as defeating a small group of minions, the reward for that success should be moderate as well, perhaps a new weapon or skill. A challenge of great risk should be rewarded with something of higher value. Successfully completing a challenge should bring some reward, but the greatest reward should be reserved for victory over a big boss.

Success should also help **escalate** the challenges to a different stage of difficulty. At the beginning of the game, the player should see mostly explicit challenges. Successfully completing these challenges should reward the player with new skills, equipment, or knowledge to be used in later challenges. Additionally, the skill needed to complete each task should escalate in complexity, mental acuity, or physical dexterity. The challenges should escalate throughout the game so the final levels have mostly implicit challenges that require the player to use skills and knowledge gained from earlier challenges.

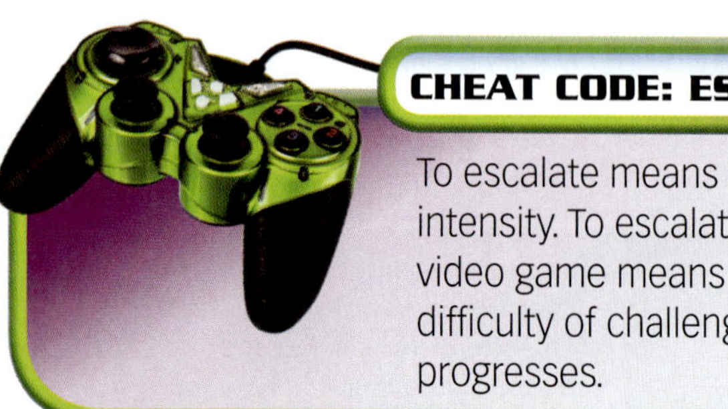

CHEAT CODE: ESCALATE

To escalate means to increase the intensity. To escalate challenges in a video game means to increase the difficulty of challenges as the game progresses.

However, continuously increasing the difficulty of challenges has some problems. The first problem is pushing the player from one intense activity to the next. Imagine an exhausting 20-minute battle to defeat a boss only to turn around and immediately face the big boss. This is probably too much for the typical player to comfortably withstand. Successful completion of every major challenge should be followed with a pause-and-relax activity. A ***pause-and-relax activity*** gives the player a chance to recover from the stress of a major challenge. This may come in the form of an exploration quest, cut scene, or other gameplay mode that is different from the challenge. Often changing from a skill challenge to a mental challenge can be a pause-and-relax activity that maintains immersion.

Another problem in increasing the difficulty of challenges is determining where in the game to have the increase. On the surface, it may make sense to increase difficulty after completion of a game level. However, this is often not the best place to increase difficulty. Many players find that the end of a level is a good stopping point for the day. When these players come back to the game, they may find the game too difficult. Because the player has not played the game for some time, he or she needs to get reacclimated to the gameplay before building on the skill and challenge from the previous level.

For these reasons, a sawtooth-challenge design is preferred for creating challenges in a video game. ***Sawtooth-challenge design*** allows for challenges to increase and then drop in difficulty, as shown in **Figure 5-3.** The skills are built back up and eventually become more difficult before dropping again. Using the sawtooth-challenge design also helps build in the pause and relax moments needed for sustainable gameplay.

A ***challenge retracement*** is when the player performs similar tasks from the previous challenge or challenges. Notice in **Figure 5-3** that each sawtooth has two parts. The first part of each challenge retraces much of the difficulty of the past set of challenges. This is the challenge retracement phase. After challenge retracement, is challenge escalation. A ***challenge escalation*** is when the player performs new tasks that are more difficult than in the previous challenge.

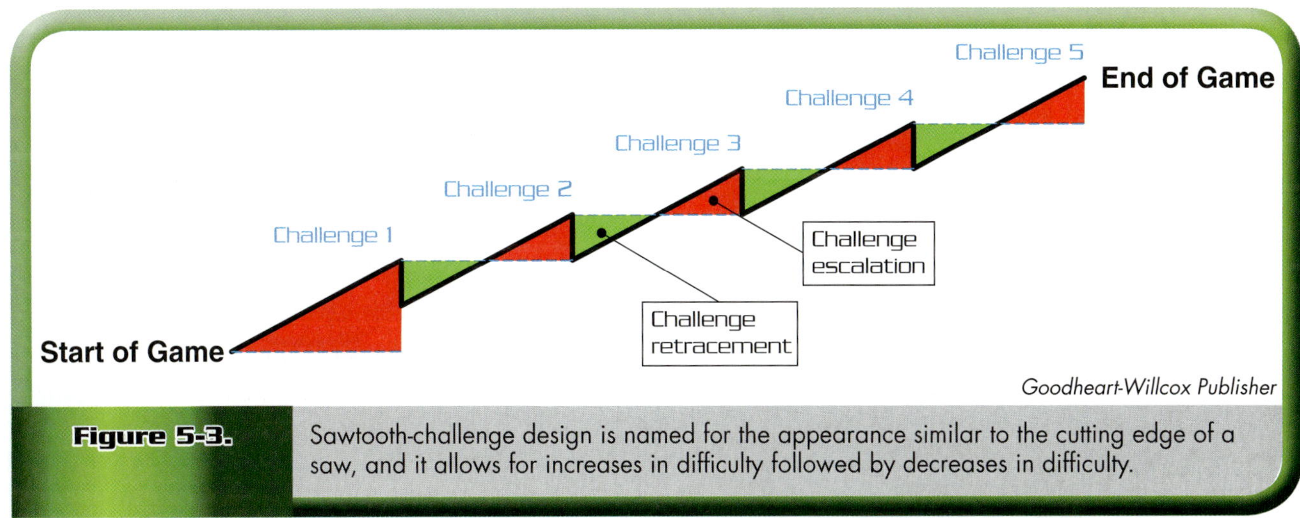

Figure 5-3. Sawtooth-challenge design is named for the appearance similar to the cutting edge of a saw, and it allows for increases in difficulty followed by decreases in difficulty.

Progress and Feedback

If the player cannot make sufficient progress or does not receive sufficient feedback, he or she will not be engaged in the game. Players must always know what they are supposed to do. If a player is not sure of what to do in the game, he or she will get frustrated and want to quit.

In many games, coins or other tokens are placed in the game world. The player's challenge is to collect as many coins as possible. However, the placement of the coins also leads the player in the correct direction, as shown in **Figure 5-4.** The number of coins collected might be displayed to give the player feedback on progress. If the player knows that 100 coins need to be collected within a time limit, for example, the display quickly indicates the player's progress. This feedback mechanism allows the player to explore and know how close he or she is to completing the objective.

The example of coins is only one way to provide the player with feedback and progress. The feedback mechanism can come in many forms. Many feedback mechanisms are part of the HUD, such as the minimap. This provides for easy access of the information by the player. A minimap, for example, often displays markers for game objectives. As the player achieves objectives, the markers are removed from the minimap. In this way, the player can see progression.

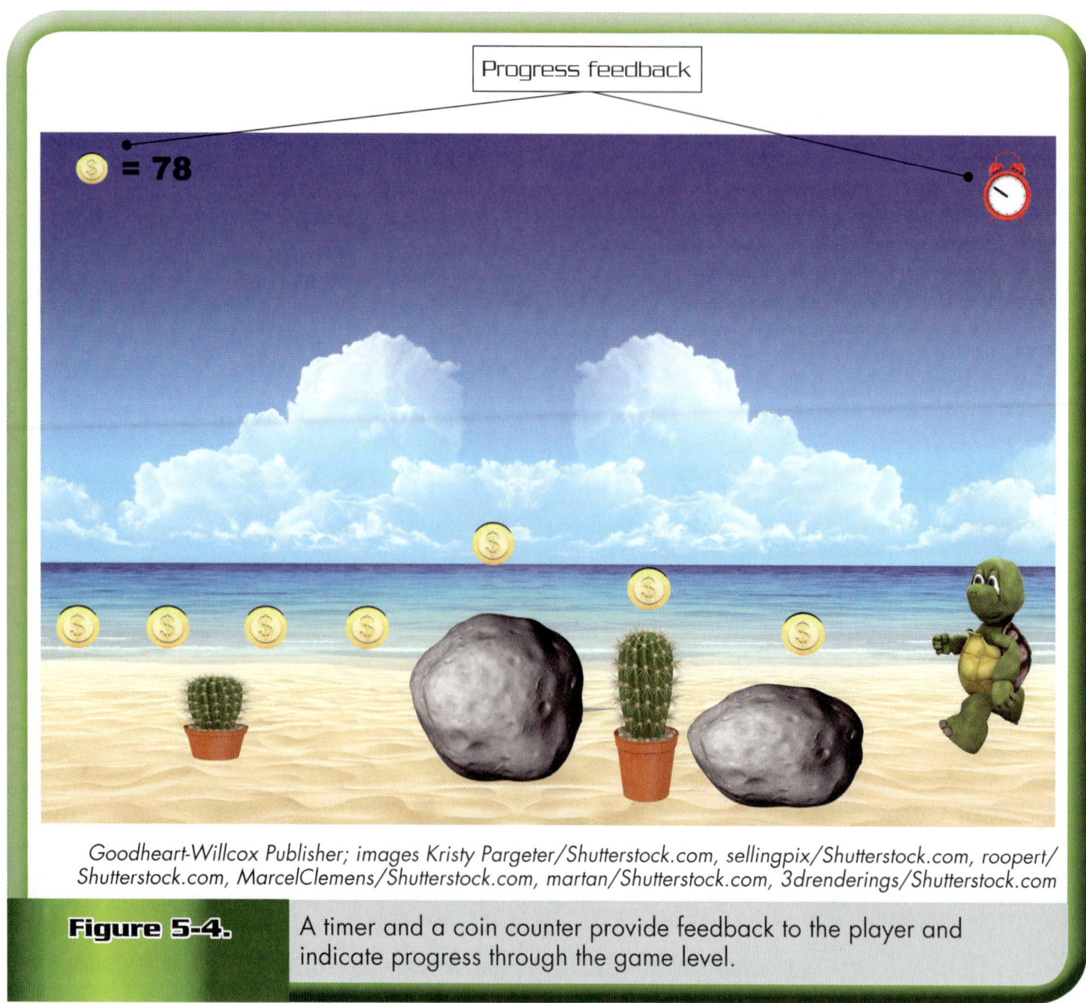

Goodheart-Willcox Publisher; images Kristy Pargeter/Shutterstock.com, sellingpix/Shutterstock.com, roopert/Shutterstock.com, MarcelClemens/Shutterstock.com, martan/Shutterstock.com, 3drenderings/Shutterstock.com

Figure 5-4. A timer and a coin counter provide feedback to the player and indicate progress through the game level.

Mental Tasks

Engagement is enhanced with mental tasks. Gameplay that requires physical skill and dexterity is interesting, but it may not be engaging. Physical gameplay without story and thought can get boring after a while. Imagine throwing a ball against the wall and catching it over and over. Before long, the physical activity gets boring without a challenge and mental stimulation. The use of puzzle elements and implicit challenges allow the player to achieve higher immersion. In a literal way, mental tasks get the player's mind in the game. For more on puzzle elements, see Chapter 7.

Sound Effects

Sound is an often overlooked element of engagement. Sound can help set the mood of the game. Sounds of birds chirping and waves splashing on the beach can set a calm mood. Sounds of gunfire, explosions, and characters screaming can set a tense or fearful mood. Use of these sounds help engage the player. It is difficult to create immersion and engage the player without paying attention to the sense of sound in the game. Chapter 9 has more detail about creating and editing sounds.

Ambient sounds are sounds in the background of a scene that seem to be coming from the scene. The ambient sound of a country scene may be birds chirping and leaves rustling as a breeze blows through the trees. The ambient sound of a city scene may be traffic noises, the murmur of people talking, and the sounds of commuter trains. Ambient sounds help set the scene and engage the sense of hearing for other in-game sounds.

Other in-game sounds may include sound effects and background music. ***Sound effects,*** or *sound FX*, are active sounds played in response to action in the game. They are small clips of sound that last just a few seconds. A water splash is an example of a sound effect in a game. Sound effects not only engage the player, they provide feedback to the player.

Background music is an artificial ambient sound. Ambient sounds are supposed be generated from the scene. Background music is provided to set the mood of the game when ambient sounds are not used. Fast-paced rock music will convey a much different mood than a slow-paced symphony.

Narrations and Voices

Included with the sounds of the game are **narrations** and all of the character voices. The use of the human voice is the most common communication method. This helps engage the player. Most games do not allow the player to communicate with the game using voice commands. However, it is very common for games to speak to the player. The player character also uses voice communication to interact with NPCs based on actions of the player. Whether presented in game action or through a cut scene, natural dialogue between players is a great way to maintain immersion while delivering information.

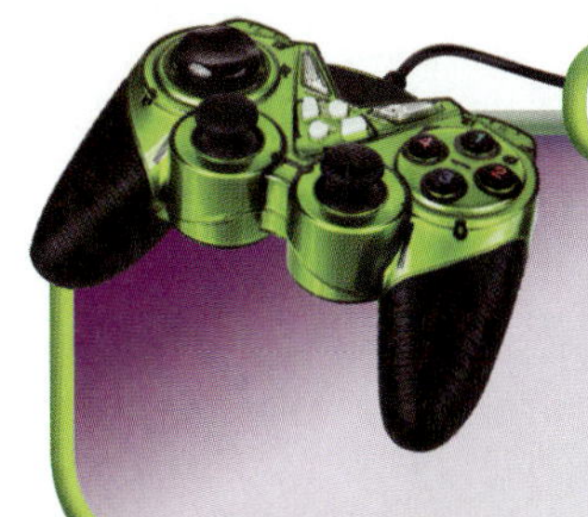

CHEAT CODE: NARRATION

Narration is any spoken details or commentary on the game. Typically, narration is not spoken to the player by a visible NPC. Rather, narration is only heard as a voice-over.

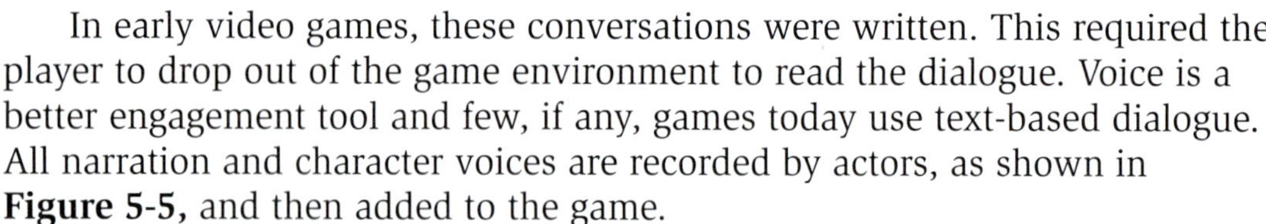

In early video games, these conversations were written. This required the player to drop out of the game environment to read the dialogue. Voice is a better engagement tool and few, if any, games today use text-based dialogue. All narration and character voices are recorded by actors, as shown in **Figure 5-5,** and then added to the game.

Dialogue between characters can be used both as a feedback mechanism and a mechanism for explicit challenges. For example, when the player is allowed to overhear the dialog of the NPCs, the player receives feedback. Clues provided to the player through character dialogue represent an important feedback mechanism. For example, a player can walk into a public area like a hotel lobby and overhear a conversation about a hidden treasure in the mountains. These types of interactions seem natural to the player.

NPC dialogue occurs when a non-player character speaks directly to the player. Clues, navigation, and rewards can all be conveyed with natural speech. For example, an action-genre game may have a wounded soldier say, "Give me a hand," as the player character walks past. The player will naturally turn toward that NPC to see what challenge, information, or reward is presented. The NPC may tell the player how to perform a task to resolve an issue. This would be a means of providing an explicit challenge. The voice interaction keeps the player engaged in the gameplay without having to read directions. This tactic leads to a high level of immersion.

Another voice communication in-game is multiplayer dialogue. ***Multiplayer dialogue*** is speech between human players. The use of microphones and the Internet allow players in different locations to form teams. Team members can talk to each other in the game and collaborate. They can plan their attacks and defenses as though they were in the same room. The use of voice also allows for communication without taking their hands off of the controls. In early video games, multiplayer dialogue was text based. The player would have to use the keyboard to enter text and then send the message. This not only required the player to take his or her hands off of the controls, it made a quick conversation impossible. Today, players can quickly communicate with each other in a voice format.

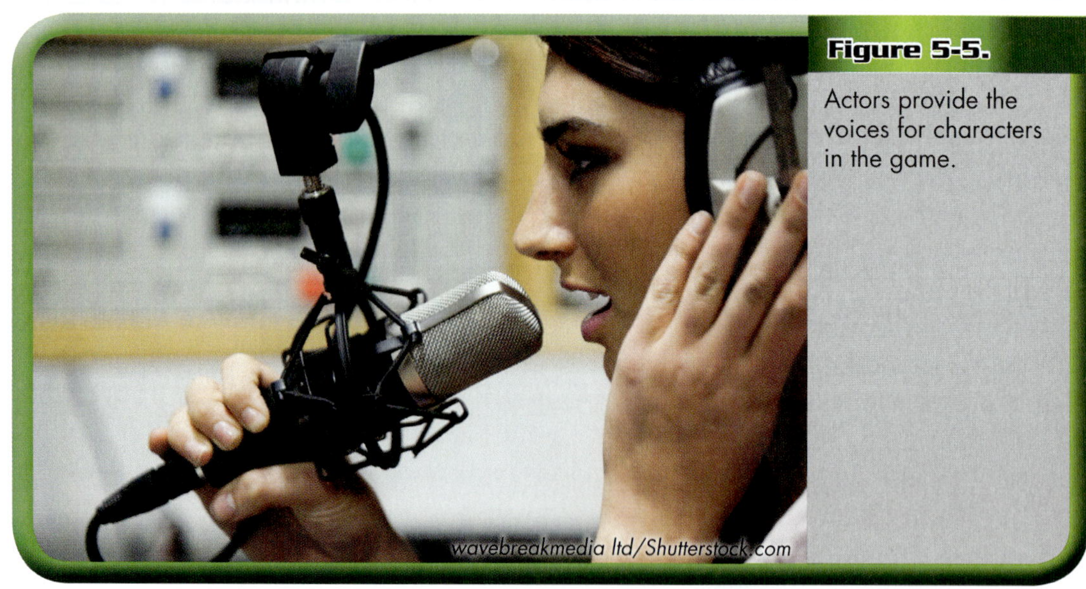

wavebreakmedia ltd/Shutterstock.com

Figure 5-5.

Actors provide the voices for characters in the game.

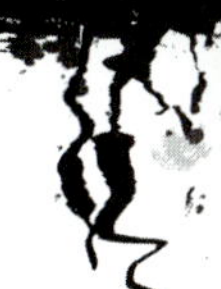

Competition Model

The ***competition model*** is how the player will interact with the game to complete it. There are seven standard competition models, as shown in **Figure 5-6** and listed here.

- player versus game
- multiplayer versus game
- cooperative play versus game
- player versus player
- unilateral competition
- multilateral competition
- team competition

In the player versus game model, the player attempts to defeat the game on his or her own. An example of this mode is *Solitaire.* There is only one player in the game. There are no NPCs.

In the multiplayer versus game model, many players attempt to defeat the game on their own. The players are competing against the game, not each other. Many car-racing games have this competition model.

In the cooperative play versus game model, a team of players works together to defeat the game. The players are competing against the game. However, unlike the multiplayer versus game model, the players must work together to defeat the game. Each player is not on his or her own.

In the player versus player model, there is direct competition between one player and another. However, the players are not competing against the game. The game becomes a vehicle for the competition between human players. A game like *Wii Tennis* is a good example of a player versus player game. This competition model is also known as head-to-head competition.

In the unilateral competition model, a single player tries to defeat other human players in the game. This is similar to the player versus player model, except one player is in competition with several other players that act as one. The game allows the competition to happen, but it is not a player in the competition. This is like the survival mode of many games. One against all.

In the multilateral competition model, three or more players try to defeat each other to win the game. This is similar to the player versus player model, except that more than two players are in competition. Examples of this model are the games *Monopoly, Sorry,* and other turn-based, themed board games.

In the team competition model, one group of players tries to defeat another group of players. Sports games like soccer or football use this model. This model is also very common in online combat games such as *Call of Duty* and *Halo.*

Intuitive Gameplay and Physics

For the player to be engaged in the game, the gameplay must be intuitive and the game physics realistic. Intuitive means it can be understood without explanation. This occurs because of prior knowledge the player has. Physics is the laws of physical properties of matter and energy.

Using a game interface that is similar to the real-world equivalent allows the player to have prior knowledge, and, therefore, the control would be intuitive. For example, having a guitar-shaped controller, racket-shaped controller, and motion-capture controller are all great ways to make an intuitive interface.

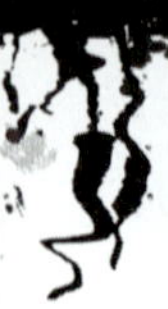

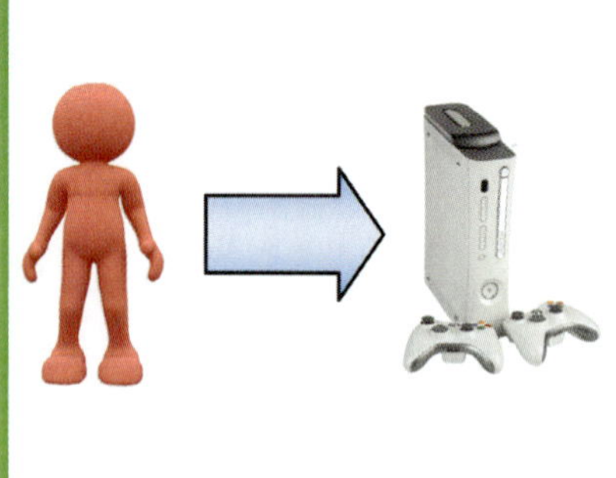

Player versus Game

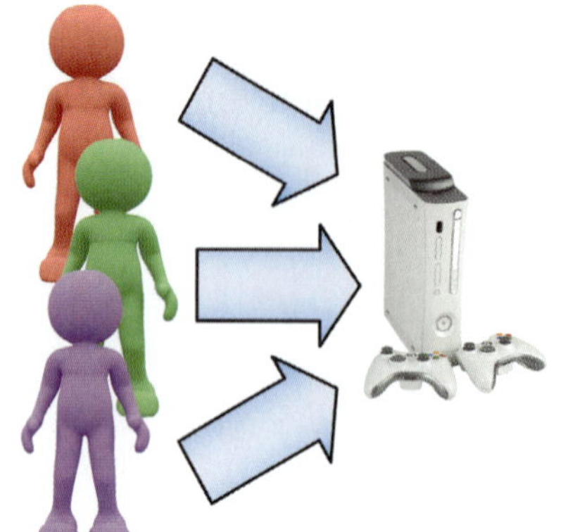

Multiplayer versus Game

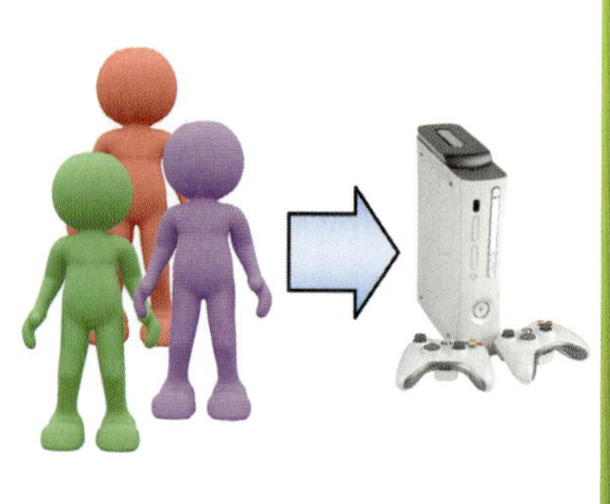

Cooperative Play versus Game

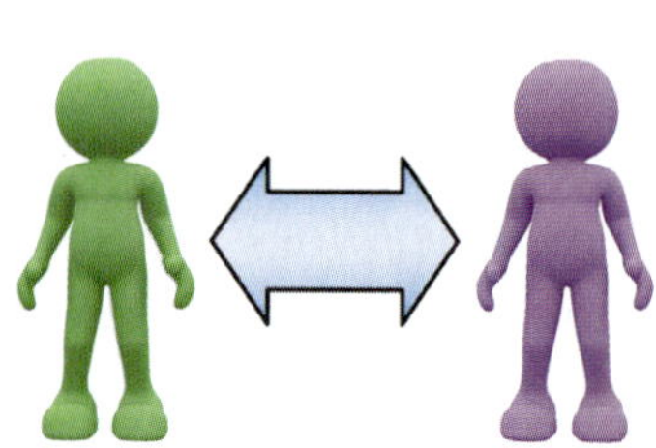

Player versus Player

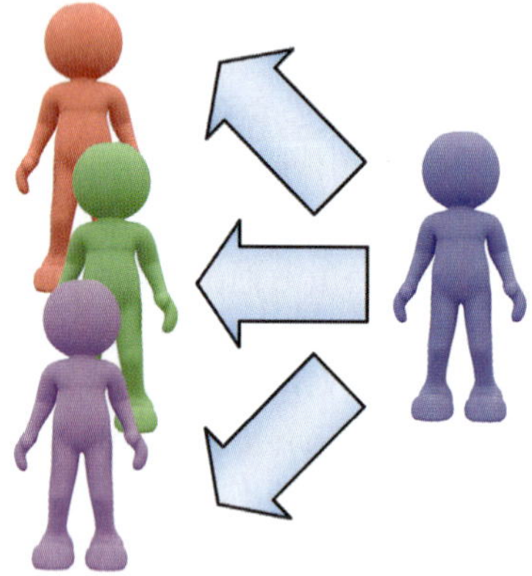

Unilateral Competition

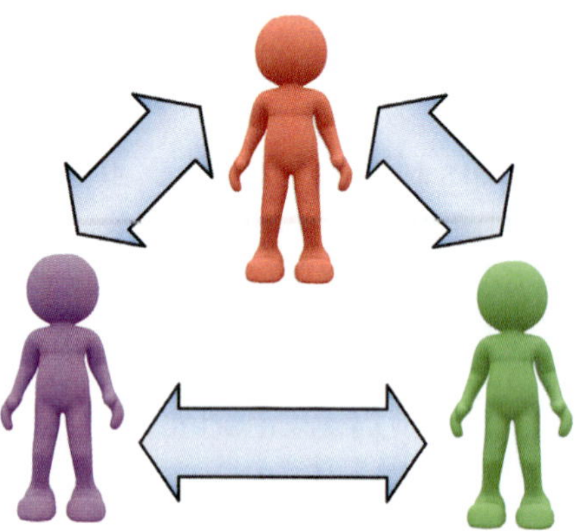

Multilateral Competition

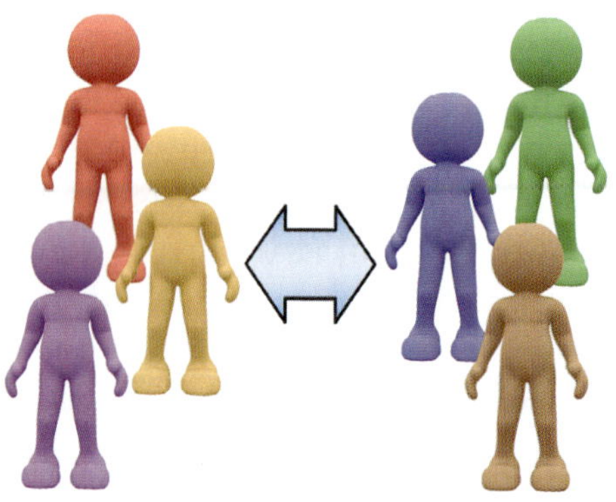

Team Competition

Goodheart-Willcox Publisher, CoraMax/Shutterstock.com

Figure 5-6. There are seven standard competition models for video games.

In addition to intuitive controls, the gameplay should be intuitive. Having aspects of the real world in the game world allows players to access prior knowledge and use it in the game world.

With the use of motion-capture controllers, gameplay has become very intuitive. Virtual reality allows players to experience the gameplay all around them in the real world. Systems like Xbox Kinect and PlayStation Move provide players with very intuitive controls where the player's body movement is translated into movement in the game. These systems border on virtual reality and have very immersive gameplay.

Having real-world physics in the game allows the player to understand how to properly jump, climb, and even in some cases fall. The upward force of the jump overcomes gravity for a period of time, and then gravity pulls the player character back down. Game physics do not need to be identical to real-world physics, but must be realistic within the game setting.

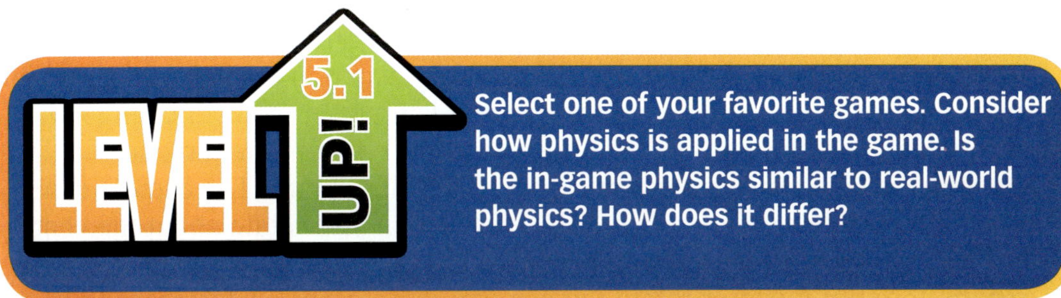

Elements of Interest

Elements of interest are aspects of the game that draw the player to the game. These elements include:

- camera view (perspective);
- scope;
- customization;
- NPC interaction;
- multiplayer environment;
- physical tasks;
- difficulty;
- visual elements; and
- background music.

Elements of interest are closely related to engagement. If the player finds an element of the game interesting, he or she is more likely to be engaged in the game.

Camera View

The choice of the camera view will provide interest to the gameplay. The ***camera*** provides the **perspective** of the game that is shown to the player on the screen. The two most common perspectives in video games are first person and third person. Both add an element of interest to the game.

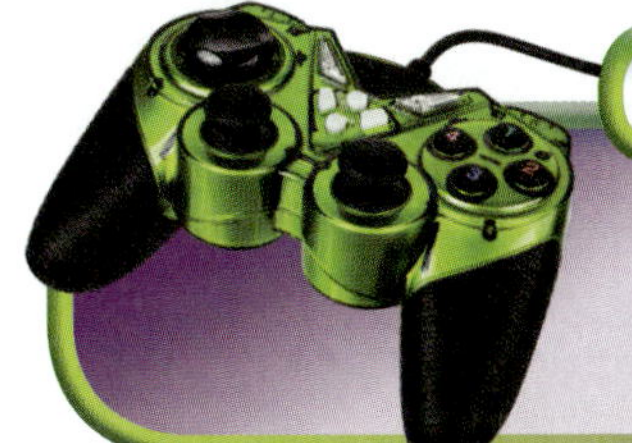

CHEAT CODE: PERSPECTIVE

The perspective is the point of view from which the game action is viewed.

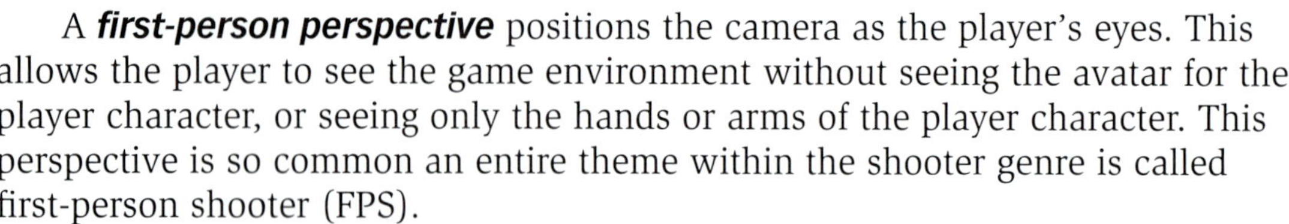

A ***first-person perspective*** positions the camera as the player's eyes. This allows the player to see the game environment without seeing the avatar for the player character, or seeing only the hands or arms of the player character. This perspective is so common an entire theme within the shooter genre is called first-person shooter (FPS).

A ***third-person perspective*** positions the camera as a spectator that is looking at the player character. The player can see the entire player character, often from behind or from the side.

A rarely used view is second-person perspective. A ***second-person perspective*** uses the eyes of the opponent as the camera position. If you have ever watched your player character on your opponent's screen, you have viewed a game in second-person perspective.

Allowing the player to change the camera to look around the game environment provides interest to the gameplay. A camera can move in seven directions. These are outlined in **Figure 5-7** along with gameplay examples of each.

Translation is when the camera moves on the game map. This occurs when the player walks in the game environment and is represented by a change in the X (left-right), Y (forward-back), or Z (up-down) coordinate direction.

Rotation is when the camera pivots about a central point. The camera can rotate left and right or up and down. The camera can also rotate about the center of the view. This is called a roll and is common in flight simulator games.

Zoom does not move or rotate the camera; it increases or decreases the magnification of the view. Since there is no translation or rotation, the camera position is said to be static.

Scope

The ***scope*** is the area of the game map displayed by the camera. If an object is visible by the camera, it is in scope. If the object is outside of the area displayed by the camera, it is out of scope. The way scope is used in the game can add an element of interest.

Movement Name	Description	Movement Type	Gameplay Example
Dolly	Forward and backward	Translation	Stepping forward
Crane	Up and down	Translation	Jumping or crouching
Truck	Left and right	Translation	Stepping to one side
Pan	Swivels left and right	Rotation	Shaking head "no"
Tilt	Swivels up and down	Rotation	Nodding head "yes"
Roll	Swivels about the screen center	Rotation	Barrel rolling a plane
Zoom	Enlarges or decreases view	Static	Using binoculars

Figure 5-7. There are seven basic ways to change the view in a video game by moving or zooming the camera.

Goodheart-Willcox Publisher

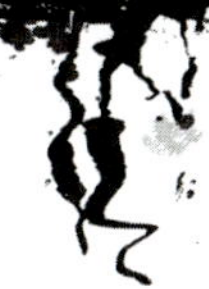

Game action can occur in scope and out of scope. In-scope action is the game action displayed on the video screen at any given time. Obstacles and threats can exist out of scope as well. Out-of-scope action is game action not currently displayed on the video screen. If the player character is being chased by an enemy, it may be damaged by out-of-scope action. The player sees the game map in front of the player character, but the attack is from behind. Out-of-scope action is important in many games to allow continuous action on a large game map. The NPCs that are not in view by the player still affect the outcome of the mission.

Minimaps can aid the player in understanding action that is out of scope. Use of HUD features and pop-up messages will help the player decide where on the map his attention should be placed. This will allow the player to maintain an interest in activity outside of the limited view of the game map displayed.

Important game actions should take place in scope. This makes the player feel as though he or she has contributed to the action. It also helps keep the player from being confused by the result of actions that were not seen. For example, if a major victory was achieved out of scope, the player may not understand the success. However, to keep the gameplay interesting and exciting may require many interactions outside of the scope. When actions must occur out of scope, they should be only minor actions that are needed to move the story forward.

Customization

Allowing the player to change controls and game features makes the game more personal. To many players, this is a very important element of interest. When a player is able to customize his or her avatar, difficulty level, background music, and other game features, he or she is able to obtain better immersion and higher interest. Imagine a player able to change the ethnicity of the characters or the urban setting.

Another powerful customization is a mod. A ***mod*** is an alteration of the gameplay of an existing game, typically done by players, not the game studio. *Modding* is the act of creating a mod. *Partial-conversion mods* only add content to the game. These mods can be as simple as providing a new weapon, character, enemy, or music to the existing gameplay. Advanced partial-conversion mods create a new game level or gameplay mode. Some mods result in an entirely new game. When a mod exists as a new game, it is referred to as a *total-conversion mod.*

Green Gamer

Presentations typically consist of slide shows, website demonstrations, and handouts of important points for the audience. However, not everybody in the audience will take handouts with them. The unused handouts represent a waste of paper, ink, and energy. Instead of handouts, post information on YouTube, Facebook, or other website.

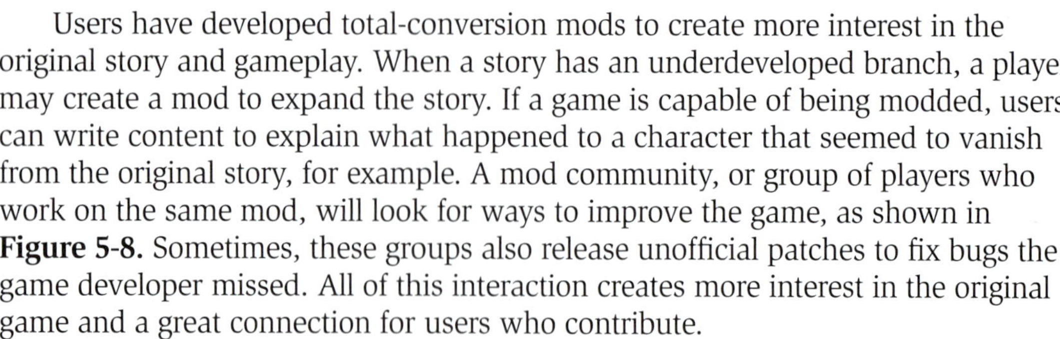

Users have developed total-conversion mods to create more interest in the original story and gameplay. When a story has an underdeveloped branch, a player may create a mod to expand the story. If a game is capable of being modded, users can write content to explain what happened to a character that seemed to vanish from the original story, for example. A mod community, or group of players who work on the same mod, will look for ways to improve the game, as shown in **Figure 5-8.** Sometimes, these groups also release unofficial patches to fix bugs the game developer missed. All of this interaction creates more interest in the original game and a great connection for users who contribute.

By supporting mods, some game-development companies improve sales and even release new spin-offs. A spin-off occurs when a character or story branch is disconnected from the original game and used to start a new game series. One such spin-off mod is *Counter-Strike.* This mod of the original game *Half Life* has expanded into a series of game releases that have collectively sold over 25 million copies. Mod customization of *Half Life* allowed the players to contribute content, which makes the game more interesting to them.

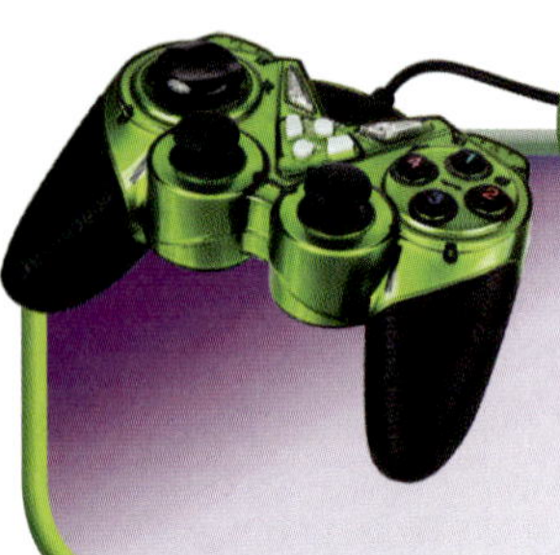

CHEAT CODE: HACKS

Hacks are the programming created to alter the original functions of the game. There are also hardware hacks that alter the hardware of the gaming system or smartphone.

A negative side of custom mods is hacking. ***Hacking*** is a means of cheating by creating **hacks** that change the gameplay

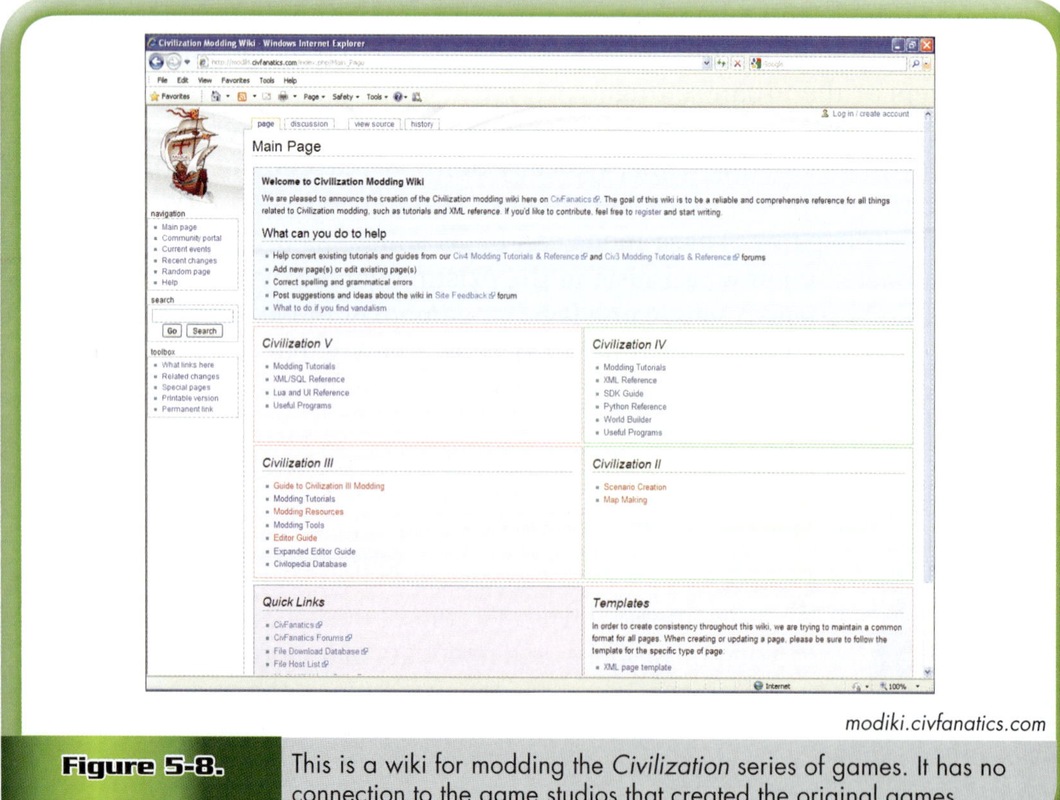

modiki.civfanatics.com

Figure 5-8. This is a wiki for modding the *Civilization* series of games. It has no connection to the game studios that created the original games.

to give a player an advantage. Some in-game hacks give a slight advantage. Examples of these may include a wall hack that allows the player to see through walls or a recoil hack that takes away a weapon's recoil. Other major in-game hacks can drastically alter gameplay or even make the game unplayable. A nuke hack that arms and drops a nuclear weapon or massive ordnance air blast (MOAB) bomb on the other team makes it impossible to continue playing. The game ends just as soon as the hacker uses the hack because the entire opposing team is instantly destroyed. This ruins the game and players no longer want to play.

Other forms of hacking are more destructive than in-game hacks. Some hacks steal player identities, money, or status. Joining a game where a hacker takes your identity and empties your wallet is frustrating to the player and a liability to the game developer. Stealing money and personal information is a crime. The game developer must stop these hacks to avoid having to repay the stolen funds and having players requesting refunds on defective games.

In the summer of 2011, the PlayStation Network (PSN) shut down as a major hack was deployed against the network. Players had online funds stolen through the hack and credit card information was compromised. To avoid further damage, PSN was shut down until the hack could be purged from the system and a firewall constructed to prevent a future hack of this kind. A ***firewall*** is a computer program or physical device that prevents users or information from entering a computer network.

NPC Interaction

The more realistic the gameplay, the more interesting the game will be to most players. One major component to this realism is the interaction of the player with NPCs, part of which is controlled by artificial intelligence. ***Artificial intelligence (AI)*** is computer science and engineering to make machines think and behave on their own. In the real world, AI appears in robots. In video games, AI appears in the mechanics of the game and the NPCs and is an important element of interest in the game.

AI is very complex. The programming to create real or even simulated thought is very extensive and prone to many errors. True artificial intelligence would allow a computer to write new programming for itself and modify existing computer code. While dramatic advances have been achieved in AI, a true AI has not yet been invented.

Many movies and books have been created to demonstrate the danger of computers taking over the world when given a true AI. Science fiction writer Isaac Asimov contemplated this conflict over creating a machine that could overpower the human race. He established the Three Laws of Robotics. The ***Three Laws of Robotics*** are:

- a robot may not injure a human being or, through inaction, allow a human being to come to harm;
- a robot must obey the orders given to it by human beings, except where such orders would conflict with the first law; and
- a robot must protect its own existence as long as such protection does not conflict with the first or second law.

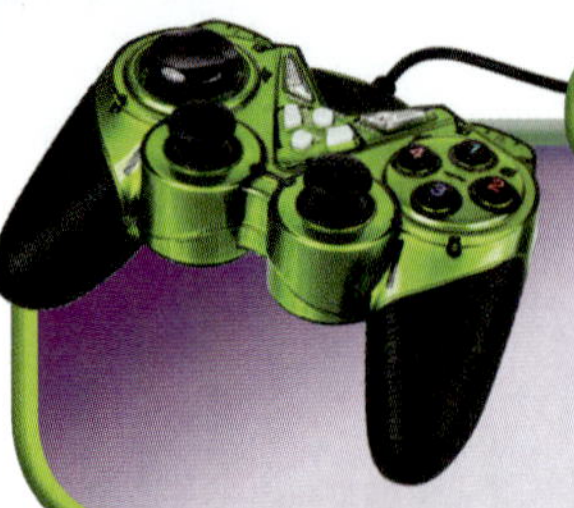

CHEAT CODE: BOT

Bot is short for *robot.* In video games, a bot is a program that controls the movement and actions of a game character.

Video games apply AI in the virtual world. To apply AI in a game, the designer seeks to have an NPC act as if it was a real person. Sometimes, characters are designed to act as if they were being controlled by a human player. This type of AI is used to create a **bot.** In some games, players can create bots to control the player character when the player is not controlling it on his or her own.

A ***multiuser domain (MUD) bot*** is often used to perform trivial tasks while the player is doing other things. A MUD bot might be set to cut wood or perform some other resource gathering while the player engages in combat with a foe. This is seen in the *Civilization* games where the player assigns tasks to worker units, such as building roads or clearing forests, as shown in **Figure 5-9.** While workers are performing these tasks, the player does other things in the game, such as allocating research, tax, and entertainment quotas.

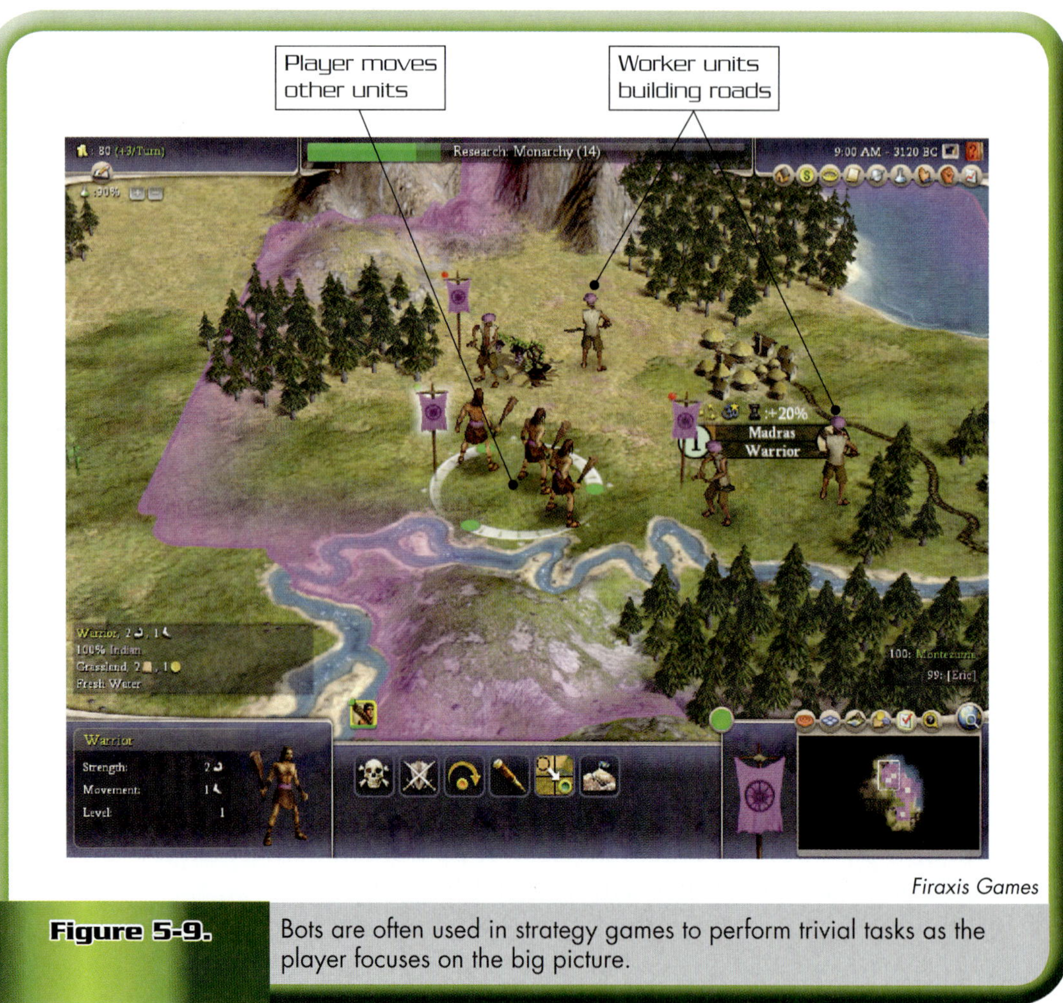

Firaxis Games

Figure 5-9. Bots are often used in strategy games to perform trivial tasks as the player focuses on the big picture.

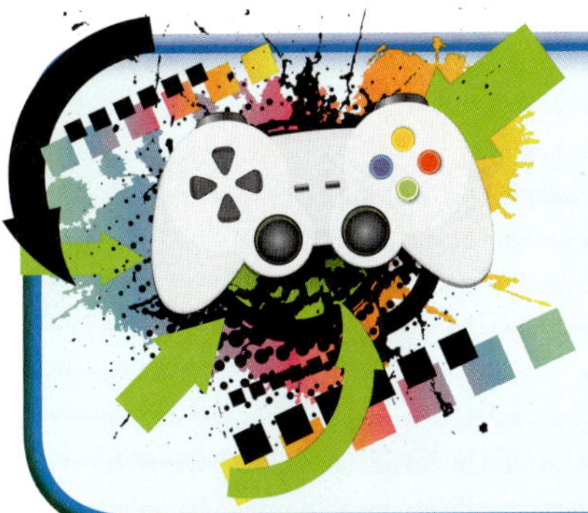

Ethical Gamer

In most massively multiplayer online (MMO) games, use of player-created bots is prohibited. Unethical gamers may use bots to keep playing even while they are at school or sleeping. This gives them an unfair advantage over other players who follow the rules of the game.

Designers create bots to control the interactions of NPCs. An AI program may call for a competitive NPC to attack the player character if the PC gets within 300 pixels of it. More advanced bot programming is used to control the attack style, movement, weapon use, and more. A cooperative NPC may follow the player throughout the game world to provide support and tactical advantage. Bots for cooperative NPCs are more difficult to program as they must interpret the moves the player makes and take actions to help.

Additional AI programming is used to control the emotional content of NPCs. Movements, facial expressions, and animations are all triggered by the bot programming. Having multiple facial animations and other movements requires programming to properly engage each action. Adding a sad expression to an NPC's face when it is failing or an angry expression during battle makes a game more interesting.

In addition to NPC interaction controlled by AI is the NPC's interaction with the physical game world through motion. The use of real-world physics to control character movement allows for more interesting gameplay. Realistic skin and costume textures create a visual connection to realism, but the movement of the character is what the player will notice most throughout gameplay. Having a character that looks realistic move with a jerky motion destroys the illusion of realism. This limits the element of interest in the game.

The football game *Backbreaker,* released in 2010, featured advanced physics and movement to control player movement. Using the Euphoria animation engine, the game allowed for dynamic animation instead of the same animation for each motion. This allowed the developer to advertise "no two tackles are the same." The game *Battlefield 3,* released in 2011, used new animation technology called ANT. This technology allows for more realistic movement, such as an NPC turning its head before its body turns and moves in that direction. Combined with AI, the natural physical movement of these advanced NPCs created a more realistic player interaction and a greater element of interest.

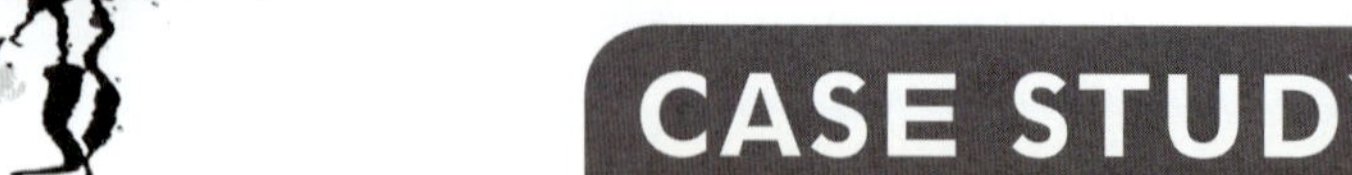

CASE STUDY

Moore's Law and the Technological Singularity

Moore's law states that the speed and performance of computers will double every 18 to 24 months. Moore's law is attributed to Gordon E. Moore, the cofounder of Intel Corporation. Moore noticed that the number of components in integrated circuits had doubled every year from the invention of the integrated circuit in 1958 until 1965 and predicted that the trend would continue.

It has been proposed that through the application of Moore's law a desktop computer with the same processing power of the human brain will be available by the year 2029. A leader of this idea is Ray Kurzweil. He proposes that humanity will eventually reach a point he calls the technological singularity where technology can augment human physical and mental abilities through a combination of genetics, nanotechnology, and robotics (including AI). This proposition is controversial. Some opponents assert that a machine will never be able to replicate the complex biomolecular existence of intelligence in the human brain.

Multiplayer Environment

Many players are interested in games that offer multiplayer environments. Multiplayer environments allow many players to play the game in cooperative and competitive modes. Online play increases the diversity of players able to join the game. Because the online players are always changing, the game itself is different each time it is played. This is more interesting because one player can play the same game map with different other player characters (OPCs). Even though the map is the same, the game is different each time it is played due to the multiplayer interactions that change with each new set of players. This also allows the game to continue to be fun and interesting after the campaign mode and other modes are completed.

Additionally, the multiplayer environment adds a social component to the game. Players can communicate with each other during gameplay through voice or text. Often, players gather at a single location to hold a LAN party. A ***local area network (LAN) party*** is where players connect to a single local computer network to play with or against each other. A simple LAN connection might be completed by plugging in several PlayStation 3 consoles to the network switch at your house. The connections can be made wirelessly if the switch has a wireless connection. This is a great way for friends to see each other and talk about the game and the gameplay action.

Online play also allows players from all over the world to connect and challenge each other using the server computers provided by the game developer. The *Madden Ultimate Team* server architecture is shown in **Figure 5-10.** Massive computer networks to support over 70,000 simultaneous players were constructed to send, receive, process, and store game data.

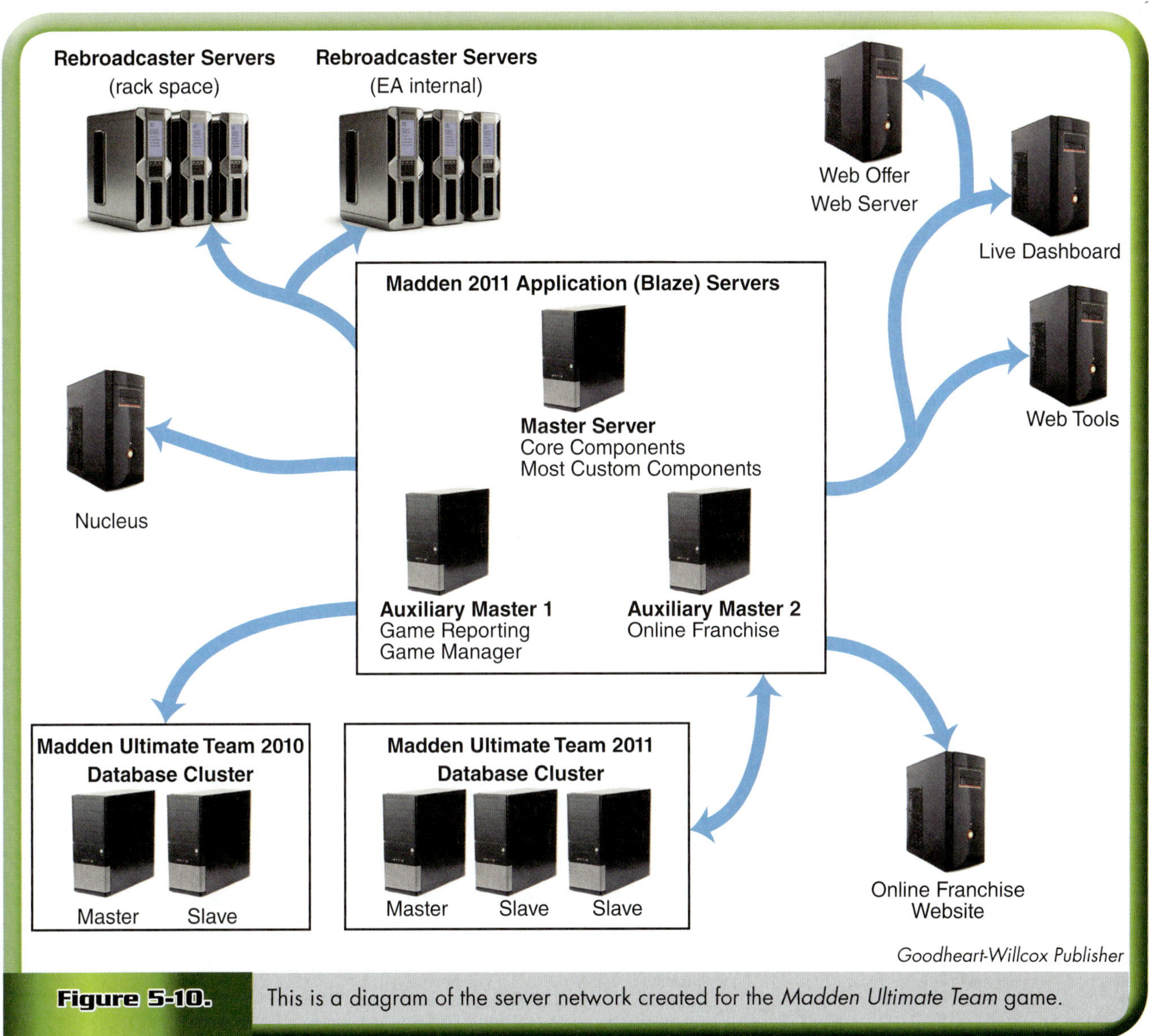

Figure 5-10. This is a diagram of the server network created for the *Madden Ultimate Team* game.

Physical Tasks

A variety of physical tasks adds a greater element of interest than a single task repeated over and over. Combining different movements and skills allows players to keep from overusing muscle groups as well as keep their minds alert. In a game that has a large game map and requires travel from one side to the other, a designer might change the mode of transportation. Instead of requiring the player to continuously hold down the left D-pad button to run from one side of the map to the other, integration of other actions will make the movement more interesting. Another option is to add some other physical tasks along the way. Simple actions like riding an elevator, swinging on vines, or even using a transporter will mix up the action enough to keep the player interested while on the quest. Hazards like a small river or stream to jump across are a start. Or, the player might slide down a zip line or jump from rooftop to rooftop to make the journey more interesting. Including a time constraint provides some dramatic action to the task.

Difficulty

The basic way to provide an element of interest with difficulty is to offer gameplay modes such as easy, basic, difficult, and expert. The difficulty increases with each level. Some players are expert gamers, while some are new to games. Expert players are probably not interested in a game that only has an easy level. On the other hand, new players may not have the skills needed to play a game that only has an expert level and their interest in the game will be very low. Unique in-game mental and physical tasks also provide difficulty.

To understand difficulty, it is important to first understand intrinsic skill. ***Intrinsic skills*** are those essential to complete a task. If you cannot perform the intrinsic skill properly, you will fail at the game. ***Extrinsic skills*** are not essential skills to complete a task. Intrinsic skills should be used to develop difficulty in games. Extrinsic skills should be minimized in importance to prevent trivial tasks from gaining importance. An example of increasing intrinsic skill might be changing the ability to throw five water balloons at once to only being able to throw one at a time. The intrinsic skills of aiming and accuracy are made more important.

Another technique for adding an element of interest with difficulty is to increase stress. The easiest way to increase stress is to add a time limit to the task. For example, being able to swim is an intrinsic skill, but being able to swim fast enough to escape a shark adds stress to the task. Time limits are handled in many different ways in video games. The time limit can be as simple as a countdown clock that runs as the player tries to get to a checkpoint before time runs out. Time limits can also be complex, like landing a plane before running out of fuel or outrunning a collapsing bridge. Time can also be character based such as defeating a swarm of replicating NPCs. The longer the player takes to eliminate them, the more new NPCs are spawned. As a game designer, you get to choose the cool ways to add time-based difficulty to your games.

Stress can also be increased without a time limit. For example, adding more risk of loss to the task increases the level of stress. The stress of the player having to crash-land a plane filled with rescued soldiers is greater than the stress of crashing an airplane filled with freight. Use engaging story elements to help create the immersion needed for the player to connect with the risk of loss. Interest is increased with difficulty by keeping the player challenged.

Visual Elements

Graphics or images usually provide a better element of interest than text or numbers. Using graphical displays, such as a red and green health bar, is more appealing than a counter that displays the number of health points remaining. Icons are also more interesting than text. An icon-based GUI or HUD is typically quicker and easier to read than a menu bar or pause menu. An added benefit of a well done graphic display is that it is language independent, which means a player can speak any language and understand the display. Using icons of ammunition and health on the HUD allows the player to see how much is remaining without having to read any words or numbers, as shown in **Figure 5-11.**

Use of high-quality images is not a requirement of success. Many games, such as *Angry Birds,* do not rely on high-quality images. Interest in *Angry Birds* would not be increased by using high-quality images. Keeping the visual elements in-line with the gameplay is more important than ultra-realistic images.

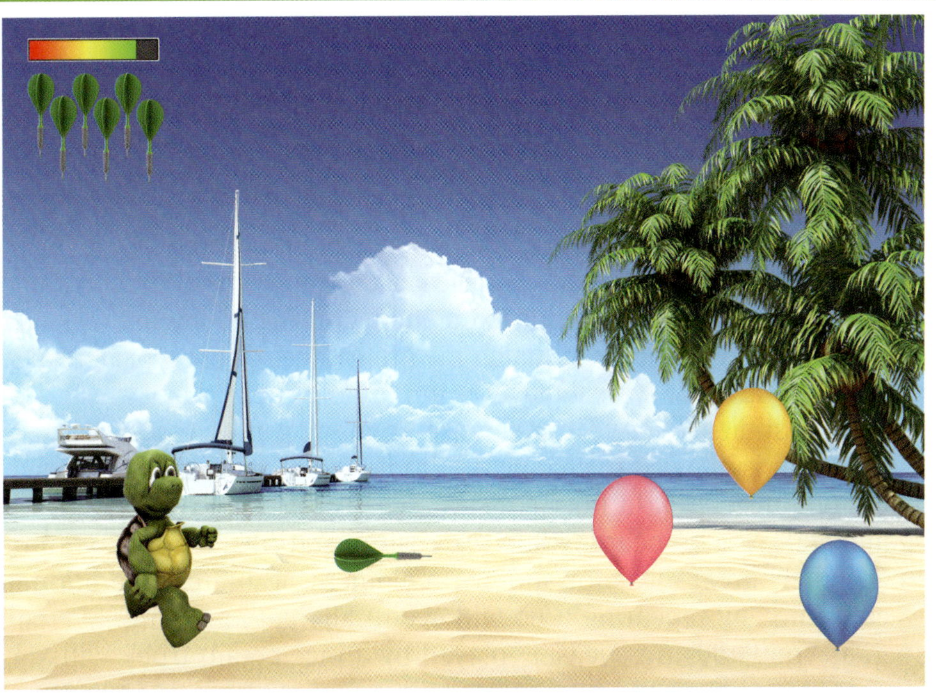

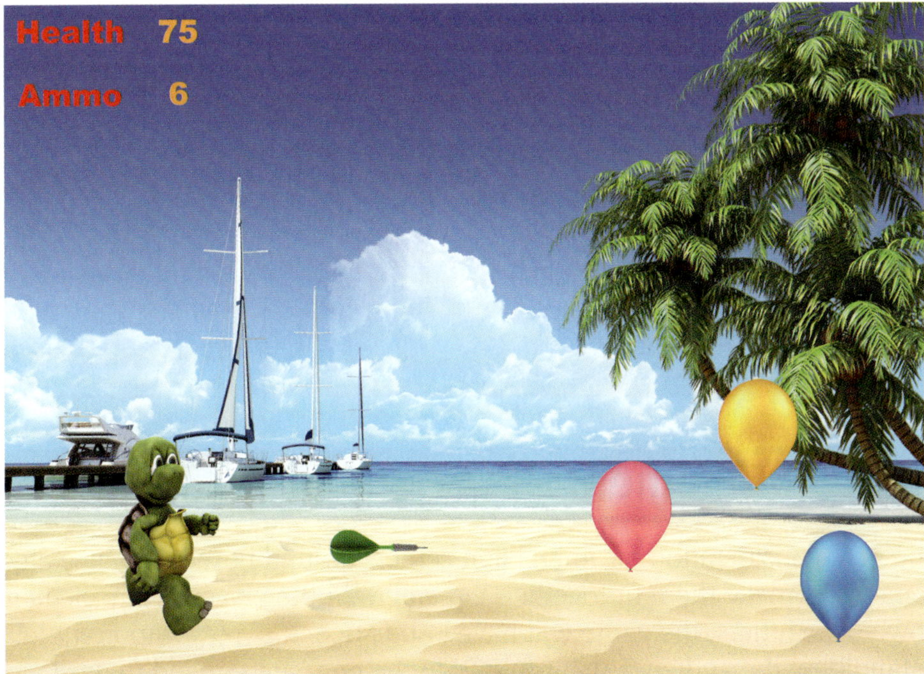

Goodheart-Willcox Publisher; images Kristy Pargeter/Shutterstock.com, sellingpix/Shutterstock.com, RN3dARTS/Shutterstock.com, More Trendy Design here/Shutterstock.com

Figure 5-11. The health and ammo display in the screen on the top can be recognized by any player. In the screen on the bottom, the display is a combination of text in English and numbers. Some players may not be able to recognize the meaning.

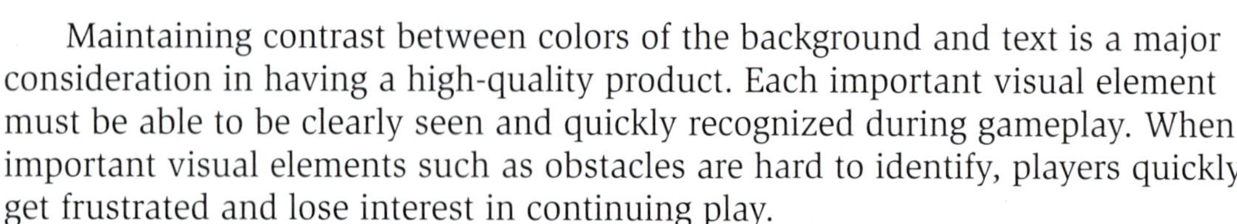

Maintaining contrast between colors of the background and text is a major consideration in having a high-quality product. Each important visual element must be able to be clearly seen and quickly recognized during gameplay. When important visual elements such as obstacles are hard to identify, players quickly get frustrated and lose interest in continuing play.

Background Music

Background music is a great way to add an element of interest, excite a player, and set the pace of the game. A slow musical score can be used to relax the player, while a fast upbeat tune may provide extra energy during an intense task. The choice of background music must match the preferences of the typical player. This is where research into the typical player is important. The types of music are nearly as varied as the audiences have a preference. In many games, especially car-racing games, the player is allowed to change the "radio" to music he or she likes.

Generally, music should not be distractive and kept low enough in volume for in-game action to be heard. Allowing custom settings to adjust volume and rhythm are likely great ideas for adding an element of interest. Additionally, using a continuously repeating tune will eventually get annoying. Even a happy tune such as "pop goes the weasel" played by an ice cream truck will annoy the player if played over and over. After only a few minutes, the player may be distracted from gameplay by attempting to find a way to rip the speaker from the truck.

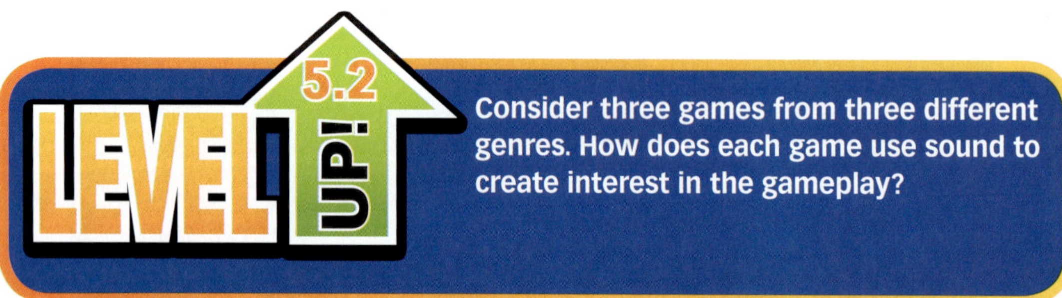

Consider three games from three different genres. How does each game use sound to create interest in the gameplay?

Balance of Elements

The final consideration for immersion centers around how to balance all of the elements to make them fit together and entertain the player. If any element overpowers the others, the game will have **imbalance**. It is very important to understand how the audience will respond to the engagement and interest elements of the game. What works for one audience may not work well for a different audience. Balancing elements includes these factors:

- maintaining interest
- automation of tasks
- vary the difficulty of challenge
- reward and praise
- frustration
- age to skill

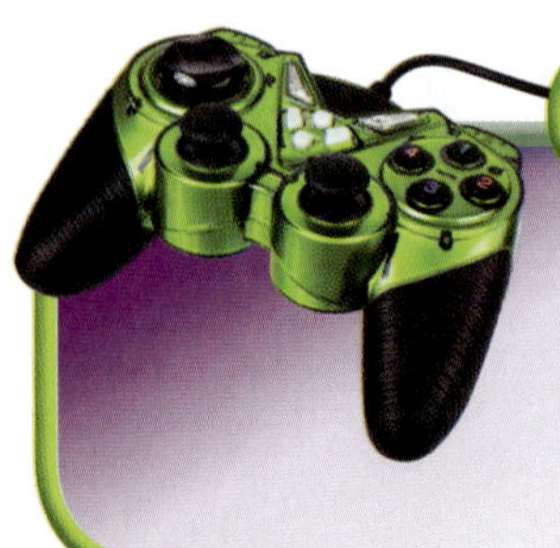

CHEAT CODE: IMBALANCE

Imbalance is a state of being out of proportion. If the background music is too loud, for example, that element is out of proportion to the sound effects and character dialogue.

In each area of balance, proper testing with the intended audience will help determine the best mix of options for a player-centric design. Taking time to test the likes and dislikes of the audience will save time and money in the long run. Success is not having a game that only you like to play and everyone else hates. Success is not making a game so hard that nobody can beat it. Success is having people enjoy your game and telling others to play it. Game on!

Maintaining Interest

An engaged, interested, and entertained player will have a good experience with the game. However, maintaining interest must be balanced with the technical aspects of the game. If the game fails to meet the quality and functionality expected by the player, the player will simply stop playing. Testing the game with members of the intended audience will help ensure that the game feels complete and unified to the audience. The previous section discussed many elements of interest. How the game designer applies each element will determine if the audience will maintain an interest in the gameplay and game story.

Automation of Tasks

Tasks must be balanced between those the game completes and those the player must complete. Whenever possible, automate trivial tasks in the game. Imagine a resource-gathering activity such as chopping wood or mining for minerals, as shown in **Figure 5-12.** The player needs to do this activity to

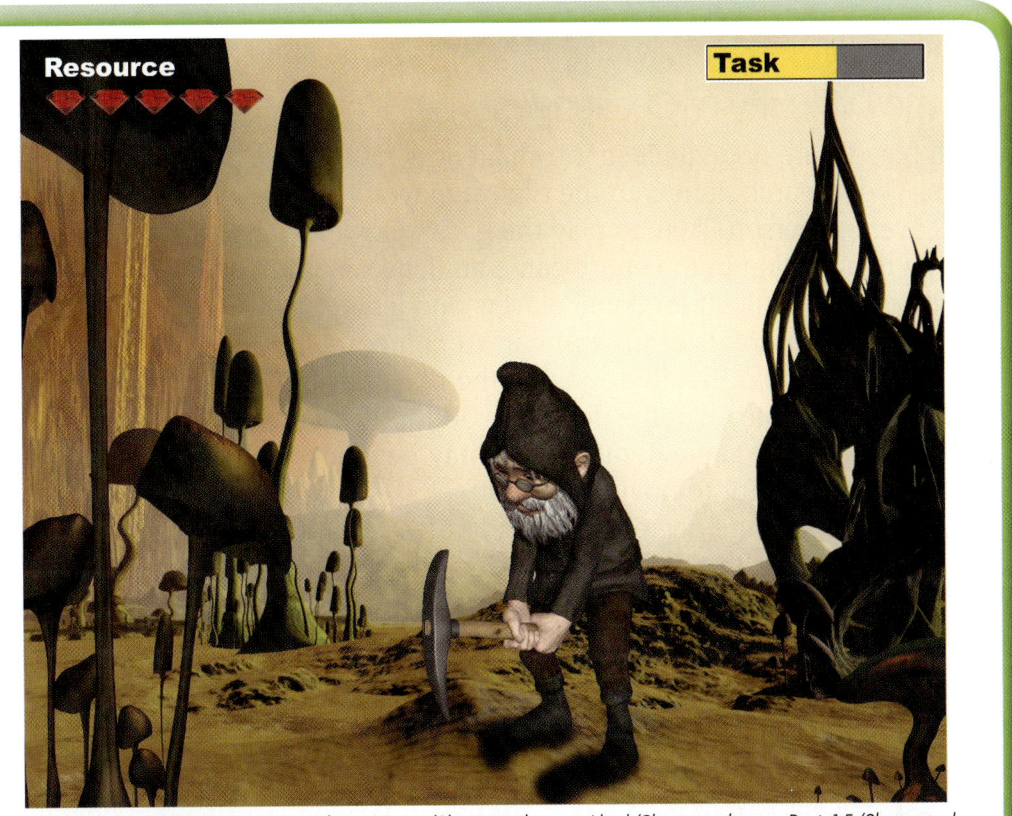

Goodheart-Willcox Publisher; images: Andreas Meyer/Shutterstock.com, Algol/Shutterstock.com, Boris15/Shutterstock.com

Figure 5-12. A trivial task such as mining for minerals or gems should be automated so the gameplay is balanced.

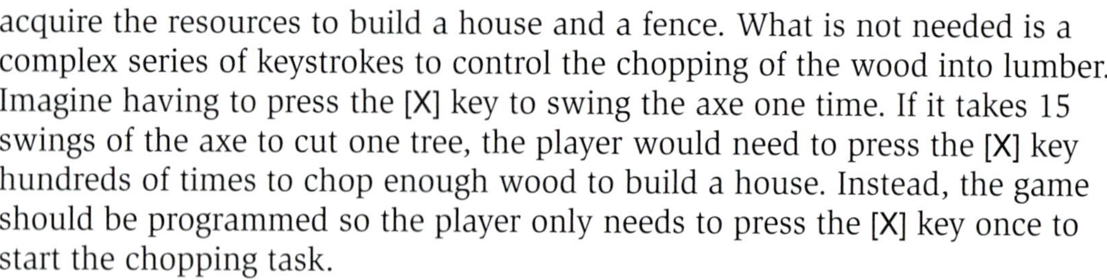

acquire the resources to build a house and a fence. What is not needed is a complex series of keystrokes to control the chopping of the wood into lumber. Imagine having to press the [X] key to swing the axe one time. If it takes 15 swings of the axe to cut one tree, the player would need to press the [X] key hundreds of times to chop enough wood to build a house. Instead, the game should be programmed so the player only needs to press the [X] key once to start the chopping task.

As motion-based controllers become more common, there is a greater need to automate trivial actions. One of the biggest advantages of these controllers is the ability for the player to be immersed in the game by physically moving in the game. However, in-game actions need not mirror real life to the point of frustration. Also, the player may become fatigued or develop soreness with a repetitive motion, so if the task is trivial it should be automated.

CHEAT CODE: BACK-OFFICE TASKS

In the business world, a back-office task is an activity needed to keep the business running, such as creating products and administrative activities. In a video game, back-office tasks are administrative activities and tasks such as keeping score and tracking the health level of the player character.

Additionally, tasks such as calculating status, keeping score, adding points, and even calculating remaining hit points during a battle should be automated. These **back-office tasks** take away from immersion. The game should do these tasks so the player can focus on the primary gameplay.

Vary the Difficulty of Challenges

All players are not equal, so the challenges must be balanced to appeal to all players. The research done into the typical player helps get the game in shape for the average person likely to play the game. However, the typical player profile will only fit a portion of the entire game audience. With this in mind, challenges need to be more difficult for some players and less difficult for others.

The ideal solution is to program an AI component to track the player's success and set the difficulty to match the player's ability. For most games, this is not practical. Instead, game designers add to the game hints, navigation aids, and other helpful in-game items. These may be ignored by advanced players, but can be very useful to novice players.

To determine if the degree of difficulty is accurate, test the game with several players from the target market. Include several players similar to the typical player, but slightly different. A great game will still need broad appeal. Test to make sure the game is challenging to most of the audience expected to purchase the game.

Reward and Praise

Reward and praise must be balanced with failure. A great game will praise often and criticize infrequently. However, the player should not be able to go through the game and complete each task on the first try. If the player cannot fail, the game is not fun to play.

There are polite ways of letting someone know they made an error. Nobody likes to be told that they are unskilled or a terrible player. In addition to being rude to the player, the fear of failure will eventually make the player stop trying to succeed. Let the players feel good about their progress without feeling bad about errors and failing to complete objectives. A message stating, "Nice try! You can make it next time," is much better than "You stink!" Remember, the player has paid for the opportunity to enjoy your game. Do not make him or her regret doing so.

Frustration

Stress and frustration are part of the learning and skill-building components of the game, but they must be balanced with success and satisfaction. Causing too much stress and overwhelming frustration will cause the player to quit. Frustration is a difficult element to balance. The obstacles should challenge the player to do his or her best. This is a great idea, but only if the player will continue to face the obstacles and not give up. There should be some way of tracking failures and build in rewards to keep the player trying.

Successful car-racing games like *Cruis'n the World* place NPC cars as the last few cars on the track to perform poorly. This allows the player to almost always finish in a place other than last, which helps the player feel less frustrated and less like a failure. The player still needs to finish in first or second place to pass the level, but finishing in third lets the player feel like he or she almost made it and can try again. This concept of ***just barely fail*** allows the player to believe that his or her next attempt may be the one that provides victory. Many gambling games use the just barely fail concept to keep players engaged and playing. The belief that if the last attempt had only slightly changed the player would have been the big winner is almost addictive. It provides hope that there will be a success in the near future.

Elements that increase frustration are red herrings, dead ends, and cookie-cutter designs. A ***red herring*** is a task that takes the player in the wrong direction. While red herrings can add interest to the game story, the player will get frustrated if he or she follows the misdirection for too long. There should be a way for the player to recognize the misdirection and then to quickly get back on track. Dead ends are similar to red herrings and are equally frustrating. A dead end occurs when the player completes a task without receiving a reward or moving the story forward. If the game has too many dead ends, the player will quickly lose interest and stop playing the game. Finally, **cookie-cutter designs** can be used to build a game quickly and economically, but will also make the player feel like the same level is being played over and over.

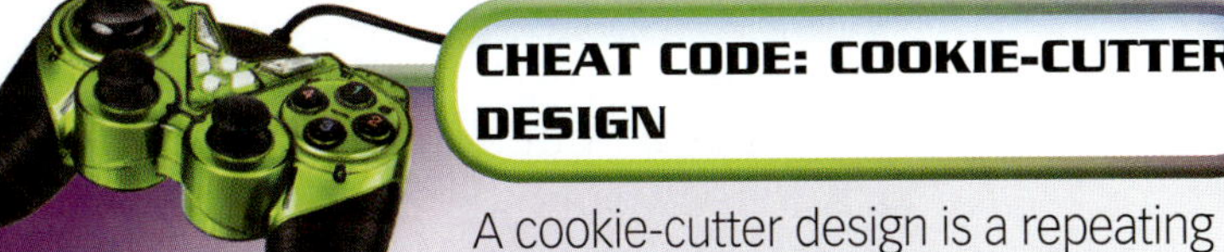

CHEAT CODE: COOKIE-CUTTER DESIGN

A cookie-cutter design is a repeating design. Early arcade games like *Pac-Man, Space Invaders, Asteroids,* and more used cookie-cutter designs. These games only modified the speed of the obstacles to create new levels. The same graphics and objectives were used on each level.

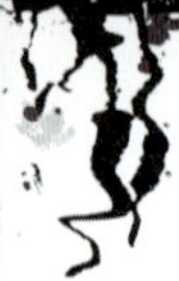

Age to Skill

There must be a balance between age and skill within the game. While it is possible for young children to be very skilled and older players to be poorly skilled, generally older players are more skilled than younger players. This is generally due to maturity and improved physical dexterity that comes with age. The game should provide the player with options for selecting a difficulty setting, as shown in **Figure 5-13.**

Regardless of their skill level, players may be reluctant to select the easy mode or the expert mode. For online games, the age of the player can be read from the log-in profile. Using this information, the game can prompt the player to select a difficulty typical for his or her age. For example, the default selection can be placed on the most appropriate difficulty setting. Another method of directing the player to an appropriate difficulty level is to name the options in a way that encourages selection of a proper difficulty setting. For example, if the player should not play on the hardest setting, perhaps name that setting "No Way to Win."

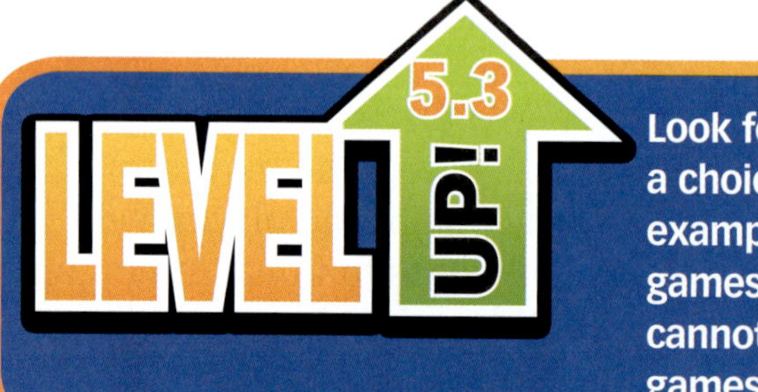

Look for games that do not offer the player a choice of difficulty settings. How many examples can you find compared to those games that offer a choice? If the player cannot choose a difficulty setting, how do the games balance the player age and skill level?

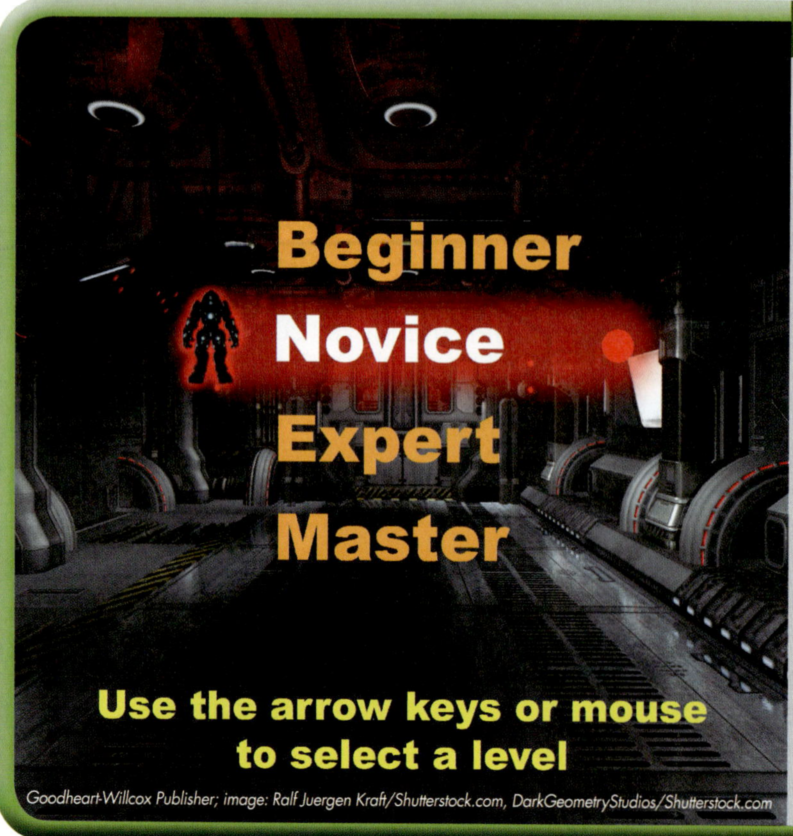

Goodheart-Willcox Publisher; image: Ralf Juergen Kraft/Shutterstock.com, DarkGeometryStudios/Shutterstock.com

Figure 5-13. An easy way to balance player age and skill is to provide an option for selecting a difficulty setting.

Chapter Summary

- The elements needed to create audience-appropriate engagement include: genre, story, challenges, success and escalation, progress and feedback, mental tasks, sound effects, narrations and voices, competition model, intuitive gameplay and physics.
- The elements of interest that are aspects of the game and which draw the player to the game include: camera view (perspective), scope, customization, NPC interaction, multiplayer environment, physical tasks, difficulty, visual elements, and background music.
- If any element overpowers the others, the game will have imbalance; balancing elements include: maintaining interest, automation of tasks, vary the difficulty of challenge, reward and praise, frustration, and age to skill.

Check Your Video Game IQ

Now that you have finished this chapter, see what you know about video game design by taking the chapter posttest.

www.m.g-wlearning.com

www.g-wlearning.com

Review Your Knowledge

On a separate sheet of paper or in a word processing document, match the following terms with the definition that fits best.

A. background music
B. intrinsic skill
C. explicit challenge
D. red herring
E. first-person perspective
F. implicit challenge
G. second-person perspective
H. extrinsic skill
I. ambient sound
J. third-person perspective

1. Sounds in the background of a scene that seem to be coming from the scene.
2. Uses the eyes of the opponent as the camera position.
3. A task that players interpret and discover on their own.
4. Positions the camera as a spectator that is looking at the player character.
5. Skill essential to complete a task.
6. Sounds provided to set the mood of the game.
7. A task that the player is specifically instructed to complete.
8. Positions the camera as the player's eyes.
9. A task that takes the player in the wrong direction.
10. A skill not essential to complete a task.

On a separate sheet of paper or in a word processing document, answer each of the following questions.

11. Why are implicit challenges used more at the end of a video game than the beginning?
12. How are ambient sounds used to create mood?
13. Why is verbal communication by an NPC to the player highly immersive?
14. List the seven common competition models for games.
15. How is first-person perspective different from third-person perspective?
16. Why is hacking a video game bad?
17. Why should game objectives focus on intrinsic skills?
18. How can stress be added to a situation without time pressure?
19. List six elements of balance to maintain immersion.
20. How does a just barely fail keep a player from quitting the game?

Apply Your STEM Knowledge

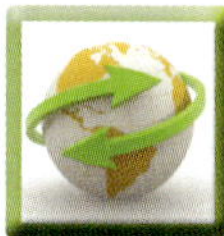

Social Studies

1. Refer to the graph in **Figure 5-2.** Describe how a four-year old player would experience the task. Describe how a 14-year old player would experience the task. Speculate why there is a change in how the different-aged audience would experience the same task.

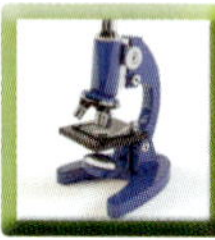

Science

2. Game design should include pause-and-relax activities to allow a player to recover from stress. Research psychological stress, its effects on the human body, and mechanisms for coping with stress. Write a one-page summary of your research.

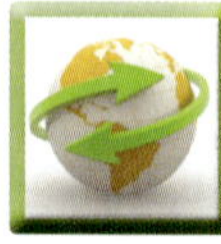

Social Studies

3. In human society, laws and consequences for breaking laws maintain civilization. If robots were part of human society, how could these same laws be enforced? For example, if a robot was speeding while driving a car, how could a penalty be enforced? Write a paper explaining your position. Consider the Three Laws of Robotics in your answer.

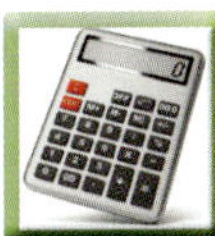

Mathematics

4. Apply Moore's law to find the solution to the following scenarios. Assume a doubling every 24 months and in 1965 a chip contained 60 components and cost $400 to produce.
   A. How much would it cost to make a chip with the same function in 1985?
   B. How much would it cost to make a chip with the same function in 2005?
   C. How many components would a chip costing $400 in 1967 have?
   D. How many components would a chip costing $400 in 2015 have?
   E. How much would a chip costing $400 in the year 2001 have cost to make in 1965?

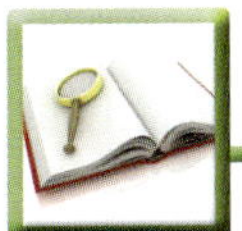

Language Arts

5. Research the debate concerning the singularity. Create a PowerPoint presentation that explains all sides of the debate. Form an opinion based on your research and include it as the conclusion to the presentation.

Working in Teams

Form into seven teams as directed by your teacher. One competition model from this chapter will be assigned to each team. As a team, research the competition model. Prepare and present a PowerPoint presentation that includes the competition model and description, examples of physical games using that model, examples of video games using that model, a list of specific reasons why this model is beneficial in creating player engagement, and an explanation of how this model could be used in an RPG.

Gamer Portfolio

Your e-portfolio may contain documents you have created. Scanned images of items, such as awards and certificates, may also be included. You need to decide which file formats you will use for electronic documents. You could use the default format to save the documents. For example, you could use Microsoft Word format for letters and essays. You could use Microsoft Excel format for worksheets. Someone reviewing your e-portfolio would need programs that open these formats to view your files. Another option would be to save or scan documents as PDF (portable document format) files. These files can be viewed with Adobe Reader software and some other programs.

Having all of the files in the same format can make viewing them easier for others who need to review your portfolio. Also have a plan for providing your game builds to others. In most cases, you will provide game builds as executable files.

1. Search the Internet and read articles to learn more about PDF documents. Download a free program that opens these files, such as Adobe Reader.
2. Practice saving a Microsoft Word document as a PDF file. Note: Use the Save As command. Refer to the Help link, if needed.
3. Create a list of the formats you will use to store your electronic files.

G-W Learning Mobile Site

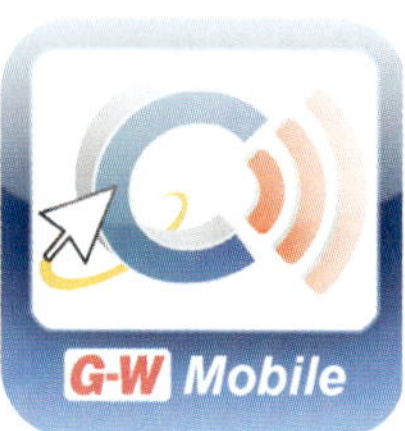

Visit the G-W Learning mobile site to complete the chapter pretest and posttest and to practice vocabulary using e-flash cards. If you do not have a smartphone, visit the G-W Learning companion website to access these features.

G-W Learning mobile site: www.m.g-wlearning.com

G-W Learning companion website: www.g-wlearning.com

Common Core

College and Career Readiness

CTE Career Ready Practices. Whether you see problems as challenges or opportunities, they often require creative thinking to solve them. Many new inventions come about from trying to solve a problem. Describe a situation in your life or in history where a problem led to the creation of a new way of doing things or a new invention.

Writing. Conduct a short research project to answer the question, "Who was Isaac Asimov and how did he influence the views and expectations of artificial intelligence?" Using information from multiple sources, write a report on your response to this question.

Speaking and Listening. Perform an Internet search on the use of music to set the mood or tone of a movie. Look for various views on what works and what does not work. After reading a few expert opinions, use this information to form your own opinion. Discuss your findings and reasoning with the class. As you listen to your classmates' opinions, evaluate your own position. How does their reasoning contribute to your view of the use of music? Does your opinion change or is it strengthened?

Event Prep: Objective Test

Some competitive events for Career and Technical Student Organizations (CTSOs) require that entrants complete an objective part of the event. This event will typically be an objective test that includes terminology and concepts related to being a video game designer. Participants are usually allowed one hour to complete the objective part of the event. To prepare for the concepts portion of the objective test:

1. Read the guidelines provided by your organization. Make certain that you ask any questions about points you do not understand. It is important you follow each specific item that is outlined in the competition rules.
2. Visit the organization's website and look for video game concepts tests that were used in previous years. Many organizations post these tests for students to use as practice for future competitions.
3. Look for the evaluation criteria or rubric for the event. This will help you determine what the judge will be looking for in your presentation.
4. Review the checkpoint questions at the end of each section of this text.
5. For additional practice, review the end-of-chapter activities.
6. Create flash cards for each vocabulary term with its definition on the other side. Ask a friend to use these cards to review with you.
7. Ask your instructor to give you practice tests for each chapter of this text. It is important that you are familiar with answering multiple choice and true-false questions. Have someone time you as you take a practice test.

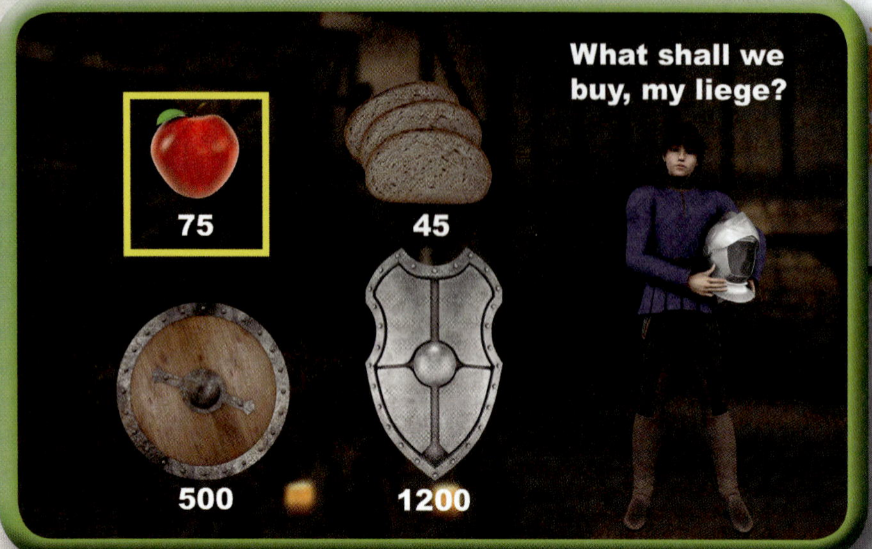
What shall we buy, my liege?
75
45
500
1200

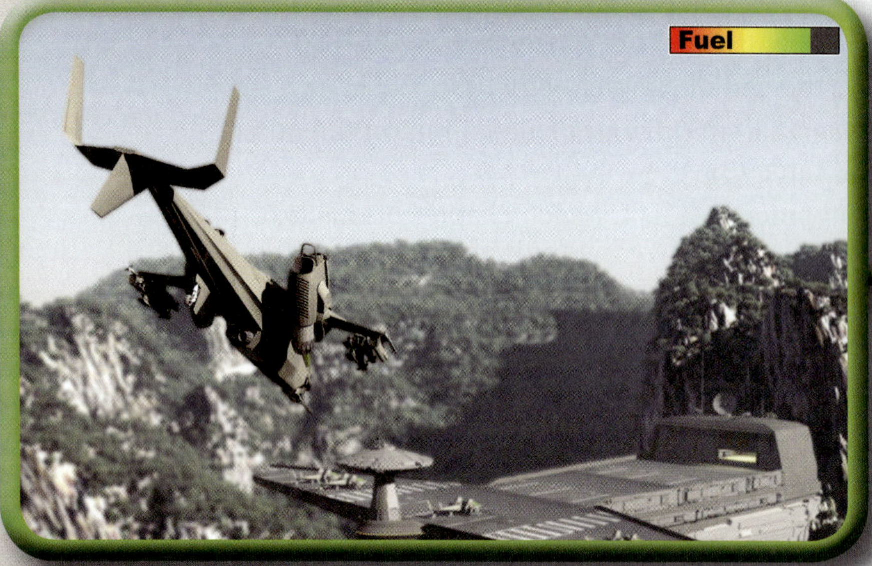
Fuel

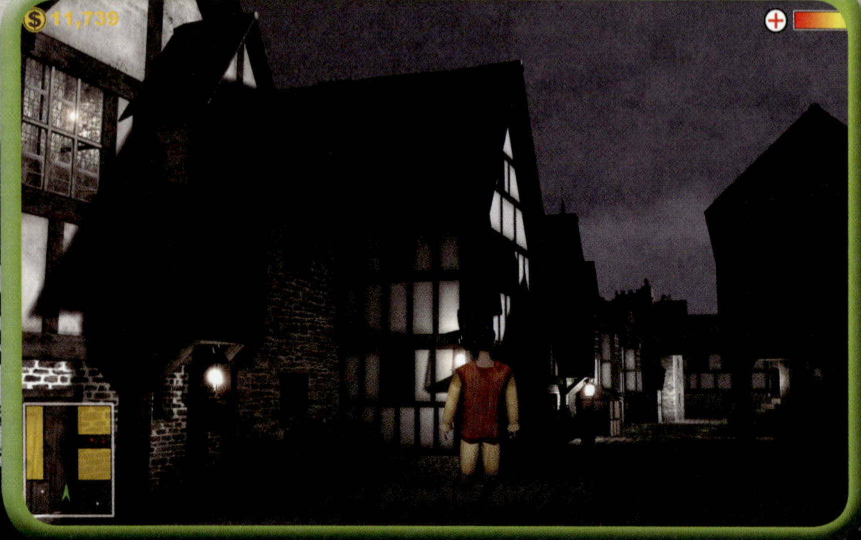

Chapter 6
Strategy Composition

As competition advanced in games, the idea began to emerge that *planning* an attack would give an advantage to the player. These plans developed into strategies and tactics. From the beginnings of strategy games based on battlefield maneuvers to the advanced components of a game-based virtual economy, play has evolved to closely mirror reality. In this chapter, you will explore the origins and key mechanics of strategy and tactics used in video games.

Check Your Video Game IQ

Before you begin this chapter, see what you already know about video game design by taking the chapter pretest.

www.m.g-wlearning.com

www.g-wlearning.com

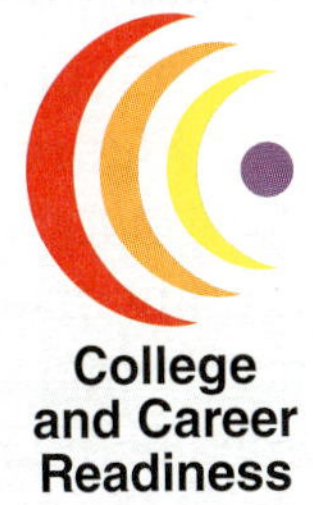

College and Career Readiness

Reading Prep. As you read the chapter, determine the purpose of the author. What aspects of the text help to establish the purpose?

Objectives

After completing this chapter, you will be able to:

- Differentiate between strategy and tactics.
- Outline the five key mechanics of strategy games.
- Summarize the factors that must be considered for game flow in a strategic game.
- Identify the importance of proper feedback in a strategic game to let the player understand his or her progress, success, and failure.

Strategy and Tactics

When the game world consists of planning and attacking an enemy force, strategy and tactics become an important component of the game. *Strategy* is the plan for defense and offense. *Tactics* are the methods of achieving a strategy. For example, a strategy might be to defend the castle. The tactic might be to hire more archers and build a moat.

Strategy is used in almost every competitive game. Even a game like billiards uses strategy. A player facing a very difficult shot may decide to miss the shot to place the opponent in a very difficult or impossible position. Likewise, a player will use spin and speed to make sure the cue ball moves to a good shooting position for the next shot. Other players choose to leave a ball near a pocket as a defense move. This both blocks the opponent from using the pocket and sets up an easy shot for later.

Strategy games have been a hit with audiences from the beginning. Players could control the game instead of simply overcoming obstacles. To make this happen, the game designers had to build a system that required a balance between risk, reward, and chance. Take the simple strategy board game of chess. The player needs to balance the risk and reward by moving parts so he or she can both attack and defend. Commit too many pieces to the attack strategy and the king may be left undefended, allowing the opponent to win. Commit too many pieces to the defense strategy and the player may never win because he or she never attacked. The final element to this balance is chance. In chess, the chance is if the opponent sees your imbalance and takes advantage. You may have implemented an attack and left a weakness in your defense. If the opponent sees that opening, it could be the end of the game if he or she chooses to attack the weakness. If the opponent attempts to fortify defenses when you attacked, you get away with the risk and take an advantage.

Game designers advanced from early board and skill games to create games with advanced-strategy game mechanics. A great advancement in design of games was dice. The dice are used to manage the chance component of a strategy game, as shown in **Figure 6-1**. In a board game like *Monopoly,* the dice help to randomly distribute the game assets since the players will land on and purchase the properties randomly. This random distribution means that player strategy to spend limited cash must become part of the decision process for each turn. The other mechanics of the game allow for more strategy elements. These mechanics established by earlier games evolved over time to become the key mechanics of strategy games and, hence, of strategy-based video games.

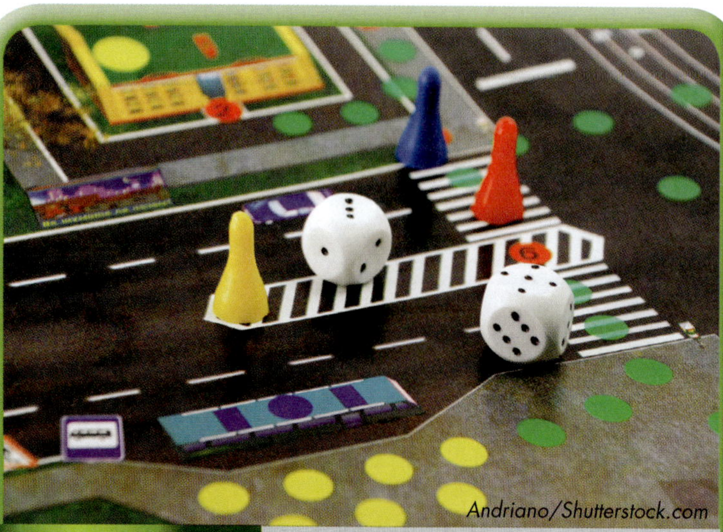

Andriano/Shutterstock.com

Figure 6-1. Dice add the element of chance to board games. The more dice rolled, the greater the randomness of the results.

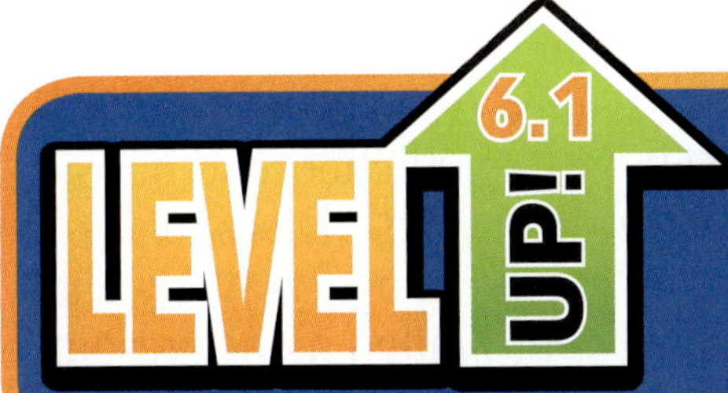

Select one of your favorite games. Describe how strategy and tactics are used in the game.

Five Key Mechanics of Strategy Games

Up to this point in developing your game, the storyline has been created, the plot has been cast, and rich character personalities have been worked out. Now, the task is to develop game mechanics that will allow the player to participate and compete in the story. Player strategy and choices will determine winning and losing. Here, the player is finally in control of the game. The options you build for the player to choose will allow him or her to plan a strategy to defeat the in-game enemies, challenges, and other players.

In creating a strategy component to a game, in-game choices must have purpose. Consider the game rock-paper-scissors and the choices the players make. Each choice is a guess. No information from each previous battle yields any information or advantage for the next round. Each player cannot build up defenses or manage resources to gain an advantage. This makes rock-paper-scissors a game of chance, not a strategy game. To create a strategy game, consider each of the five ***key mechanics of strategy***:

- resource management (strategic management)
- dissimilar assets (arms race)
- maneuvers (risk/reward)
- pacing (speed and recovery)
- economy (gains and drains)

Resource Management

At the core of tactical gameplay is **resource management.** The fact that the player has limited resources, such as money, means he or she must make choices to effectively manage those resources. Resource management becomes a game challenge. If the player has unlimited ammo, he or she can simply keep the trigger button depressed and spin in a tight circle to create a 360 degree spray. Nothing can get close enough to damage the player character and the game quickly gets boring. By limiting the ammo resource, the player must make tactical choices, which helps create immersion in the game.

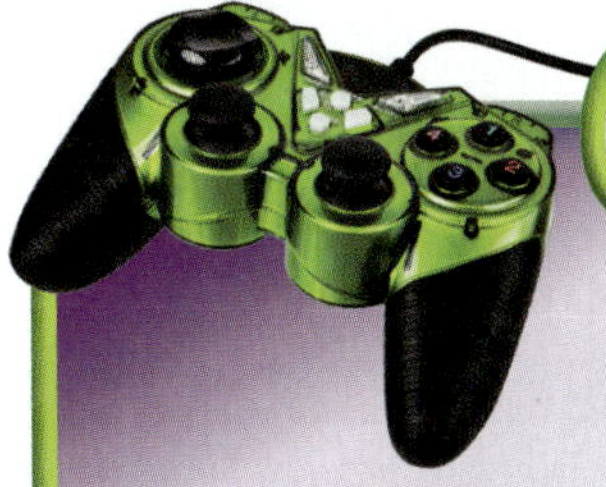

CHEAT CODE: RESOURCE MANAGEMENT

Resource management is using limited resources effectively to achieve a goal. The ability to do the most with limited resources is a key to winning many strategy-based video games.

Resource management in a video game is a simulation of the real world. In the real world, you have limited resources. For example, you have to make choices on how to spend your money, which is a limited resource. Imagine that you received $60 for your birthday. With that $60, you could choose to buy a video game, a bicycle, or new shoes. You have to evaluate the choices to see what you need or want most. Since there is a hole in your shoes, that is what you need most. The decision you make is to spend your limited money resource on shoes instead of the bike or video game. Life involves making decisions on how to allocate limited resources. Resource management in a video game allows the player to make the same economic choices.

The ***game economy*** determines which resources are available, in what amount, and at what cost. The more resource options available, the more variations there are to the gameplay. With each choice, the game is customized and different from previous attempts. Each player can enter the same game, make different choices, and have a completely different game experience. Common game resources are time, money, energy, land, team members, weapons, health, and lives.

Resources are specific to the game being played. As shown in **Figure 6-2,** a role-playing game (RPG) may have resources of gold, weapons, potions, spells, hit points, and health. Each resource must be maintained to reach

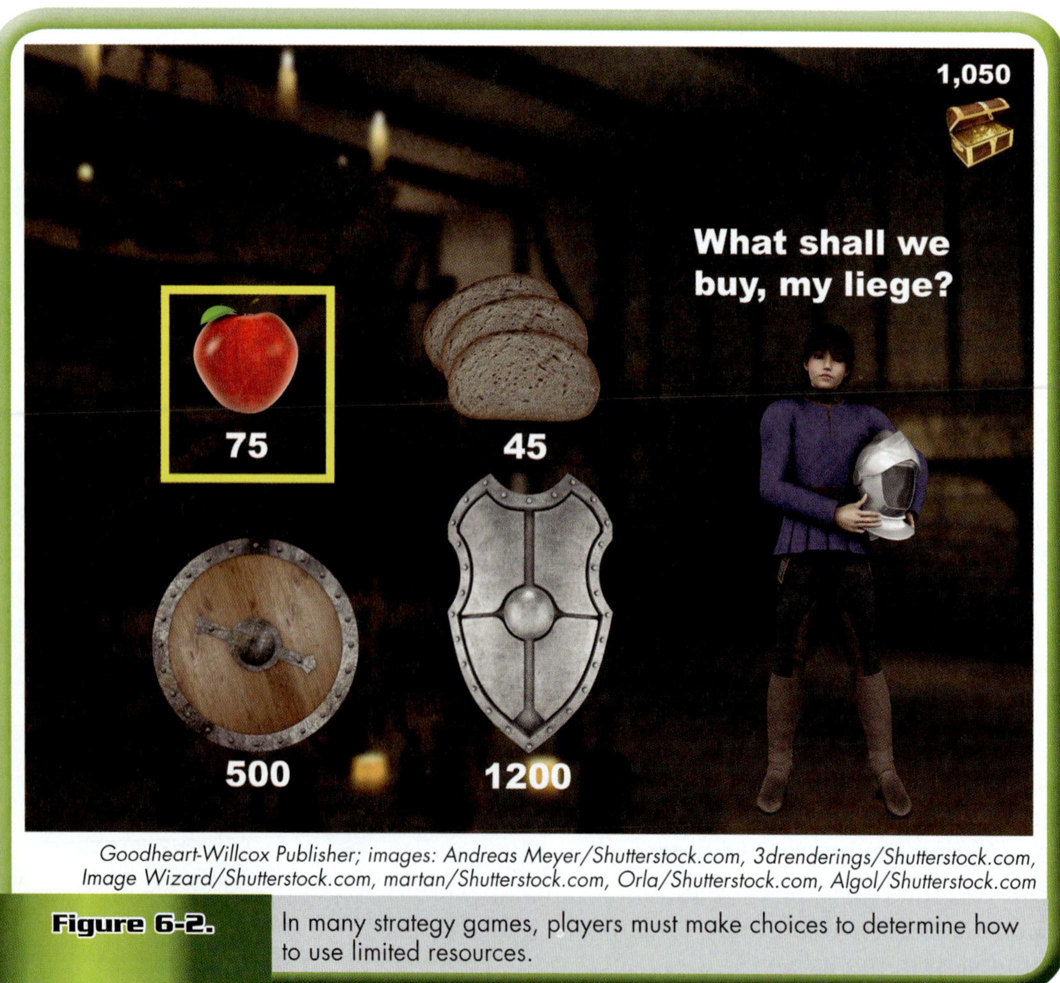

Goodheart-Willcox Publisher; images: Andreas Meyer/Shutterstock.com, 3drenderings/Shutterstock.com, Image Wizard/Shutterstock.com, martan/Shutterstock.com, Orla/Shutterstock.com, Algol/Shutterstock.com

Figure 6-2. In many strategy games, players must make choices to determine how to use limited resources.

the objective of the quest. The player can decide to spend gold on defensive armor or an offensive weapon. The player may be limited to a certain number of spells cast per day or per quest. The player can decide if the health status is great enough to enter a battle or if food or a regeneration potion needs to be purchased.

CASE STUDY

Resource Management in *Civilization*

There are many games in which management of resources is a primary gameplay element. One of the most popular of these types of games is the *Civilization* series, shown below. In the **Civilization** games, the player must seek and manage certain resources in order to build units and buildings, discover technologies, and win the game.

In the recent releases of the series, resources have taken on extra importance because certain technologies reveal certain resources on the game map, and certain resources are required to build certain units and buildings. For example, in *Civilization V,* when the player discovers the ironworking technology, the iron resource is revealed on the map. The player must then build a road through that resource and into a city in order to build certain units in the city, swordsman units for example.

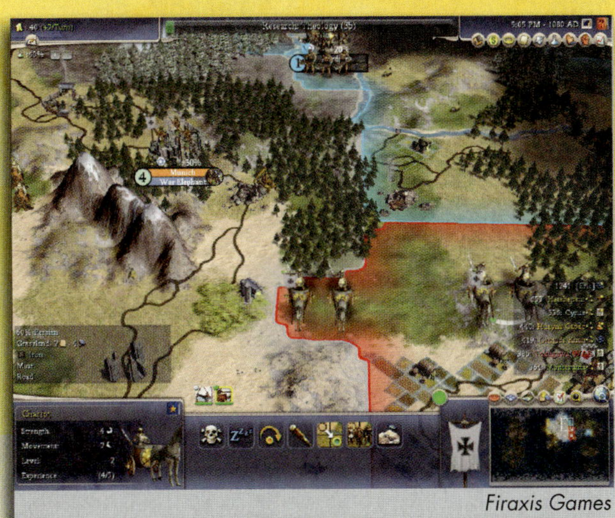

Firaxis Games

If the player does not have an iron resource in his or her territory or does not connect the resource to a city, then all units and buildings requiring iron cannot be built. The player must either trade for iron with other players or conquer territory that contains the resource. Toward the beginning of the game, this may not seem like a great undertaking. However, as the game progresses, other players will need the same resources and will be seeking to acquire them through diplomacy or conquest. Without access to and control over resources, the player will not be able to win.

In addition to resources such as iron, the player must manage taxes, science research, and happiness (luxuries). These are also game resources. All three resources are set as a percentage, and the total percentage cannot exceed 100. Buildings and units cost money to maintain, so taxes may need to be raised to keep from running out of money. This means that either science research, luxuries, or both need to be lowered to balance the increase in taxes. However, with a lower rate of science research, the player will not discover new technologies as quickly and may fall behind opponents. The entire game of *Civilization* is about managing resources to be in a position to win the game.

Dissimilar Assets

Dissimilar assets are in-game objects that have unique characteristics. An all-terrain vehicle has different characteristics than an aircraft. One is driven on land and the other is flown through the air. Because each asset has differences, the strategy options change based on which vehicle the player is using. Each asset has a unique set of strengths and weaknesses that make the choice of asset important. A winning strategy should require a combination of dissimilar assets to defeat an opponent. Each side has to use its resources to acquire the best assets for achieving victory. The use of different assets and the combination of different assets makes a game very interesting.

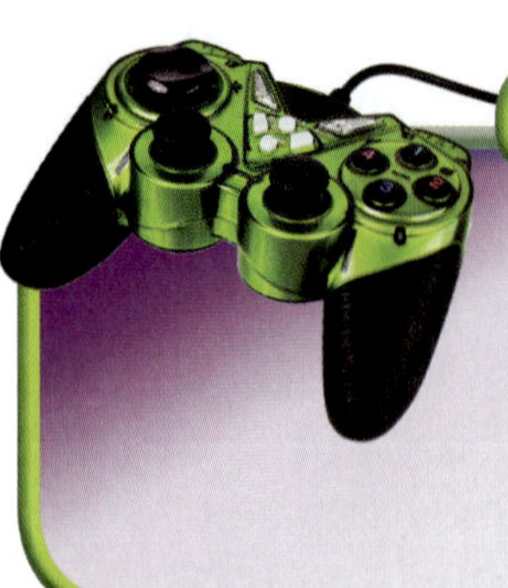

CHEAT CODE: COMBINED ARMS

Combined arms is a combat strategy that uses dissimilar assets to complement each other in specialized units. These combined-arms units are then deployed as part of a battle plan.

In a real-life war game simulation, the study of **combined arms** is applied using dissimilar assets. The combined arms of infantry, artillery, aircraft, missile units, reconnaissance units, naval patrols, and more are deployed to overpower enemy forces. As part of the overall strategy, tactical divisions are deployed to meet specific objectives. These objectives support the overall goal, not the goal of an individual or unit.

Look at the dissimilar assets of the game rock-paper-scissors, as shown in **Figure 6-3.** It is easy to identify the strength and weakness of each asset. In video games, character classes and weapon choices can similarly provide a tactical advantage. Designing a wizard class that can defeat an orc class is a simple rock-paper-scissors design—build a set of parameters that determine the outcome of a battle.

Item	Strength	Weakness
Rock	Crushes scissors	Covered by paper
Paper	Covers rock	Cut by scissors
Scissors	Cuts paper	Crushed by rock

Game Rules

1. Two players each take five note cards.
2. Players choose five assets by writing down Rock, Paper, or Scissors on each note card.
3. Players select one card and place it on the table face up.
4. The losing card is discarded and the winning card is returned to the player. In the case of a tie, players pick up the cards and throw again.
5. Repeat steps 3 and 4 until one player is out of cards. The winner is the player who has cards remaining.

Goodheart-Willcox Publisher

Figure 6-3. Rock-paper-scissors is a simple game that uses dissimilar assets.

For example, consider a wizard character that has 50 battle points and carries a spell with a multiplier of five against muggles, ten against orcs, and three against clerics. If the enemy is a muggle with 300 health points, the wizard could not defeat the muggle with the current spell.

50 battle points × 5 multiplier = 250 damage
250 damage < 300 health points

A different spell would have to be obtained to defeat this muggle. On the other hand, the wizard could defeat an orc that has 300 health points with the current spell.

50 battle points × 10 multiplier = 500 damage
500 damage > 300 health points

Avoid creating a single great weapon or great character class. If a class or weapon does not have any weakness, it cannot be defeated. The first player to achieve the class or find the weapon will always win. An undefeatable weapon or class negates dissimilar assets in a strategy. For example, add a firecracker to the game of rock-paper-scissors. If firecracker explodes rock, paper, *and* scissors, then all players would always choose firecracker because nothing beats it. Within the system for dissimilar assets that you create, balance strengths and weaknesses to ensure fair play.

Maneuvers

With all of the choices for assets, the player may quickly lose interest in the game without a gameplay component. Maneuvering is the heart and soul of tactics. ***Maneuvering*** is positioning resources at their most needed or beneficial location. This starts with making the best choice for resources, as discussed earlier. If the player has the best resource, then the resource needs to be in the best position at the best time to be fully maximized.

In the game of chess, the players begin with the same game resources. Only through maneuvering of these resources does one player get into a position to win the game. Each move adjusts the position of the pieces to be at the right position at the right time. Of course, this is an ever-changing game world in which forces can be changed and moved. When the opponent makes moves, the other player's tactics must be adjusted to defend or attack.

When designing a video game, include mechanics for players to maneuver. The more attack and defend maneuvers you design, the richer the strategic gameplay will feel. For example, if an attack is on a castle, then allow for multiple points of attack. Simply limiting the attack to the front gate may make the game easier to program, but allowing for a sneak attack from the rear will add strategy such as creating **diversions.** Diversions are a fun element of a strategy game that can give a much weaker force an advantage over a larger force.

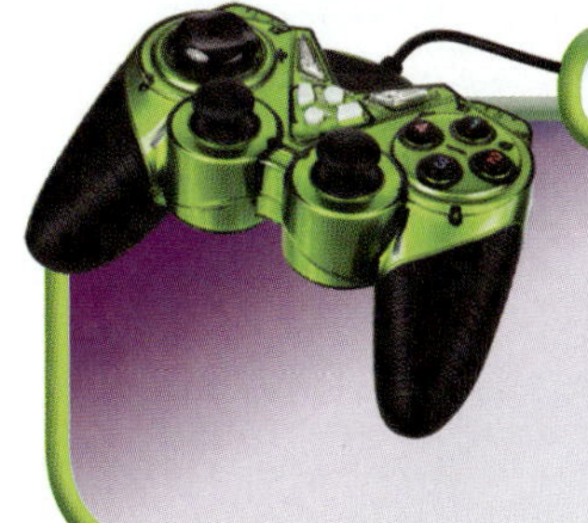

CHEAT CODE: DIVERSION

A diversion is a strategy that involves drawing the attention of the opponent to one location so an attack can be made in a different location.

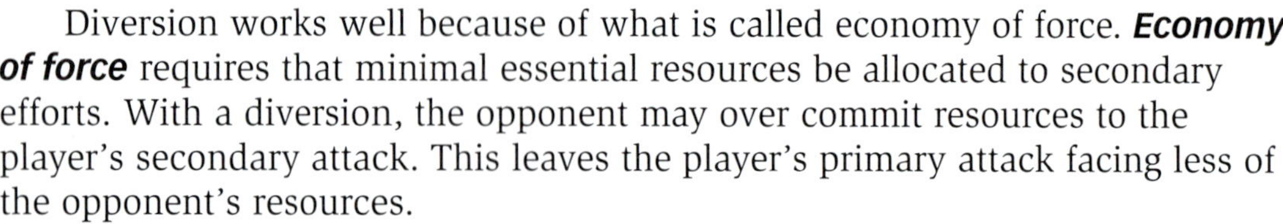

Diversion works well because of what is called economy of force. ***Economy of force*** requires that minimal essential resources be allocated to secondary efforts. With a diversion, the opponent may over commit resources to the player's secondary attack. This leaves the player's primary attack facing less of the opponent's resources.

The main idea of economy of force is for the player to discover primary tasks and assign the bulk of his or her attention to these tasks. But the player must not ignore the secondary tasks. Failing to address an attack from the side would lead to defeat. The player must address all secondary tasks with enough attention to deal with them, but not so much attention as that the primary task fails.

The game environment can be designed to help the player make maneuvering part of the strategy. A game environment that includes rivers, mountains, forests, buildings, and more can allow players different modes of transportation to maneuver within the terrain, as shown in **Figure 6-4.** If the player has to cross a river obstacle to complete an objective, then he or she must think of a strategy for crossing the river. If the PC jumps in the water to walk across, it may lose health, be slowed down, or become an easy target for opponents.

Additionally, design terrain to be obstacles and cover. Cover is an area to hide from attack. Areas of cover can also play into the design of the pause-and-relax time needed to keep the player from being overwhelmed. Obstacles are areas of openness or difficult crossings where risks must be taken to proceed. Allow character movement such as crawling or a stealth mode to provide the player with a way to maneuver the risky terrain.

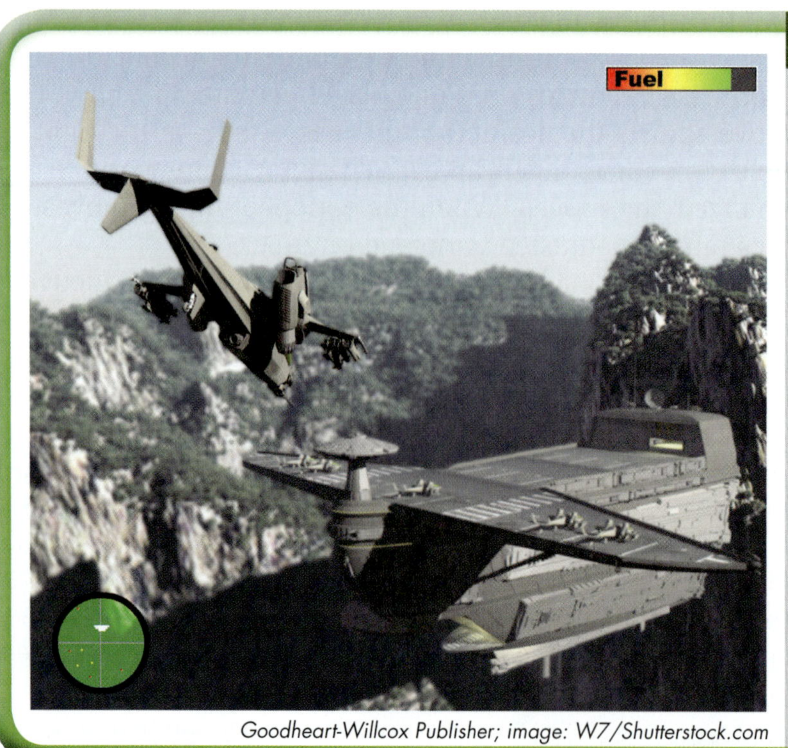

Goodheart-Willcox Publisher; image: W7/Shutterstock.com

Figure 6-4.

This game provides the player with aircraft to maneuver through mountainous terrain.

The tactics of maneuvering cause the player to make many risk-reward decisions. These decisions have the player weigh how much loss the move will create verses how much gain will be made. In many cases, retreat is the best option. The player can avoid the current risk and plan a new set of strategies and tactics. To move the game forward, the game designer must provide a reward large enough to keep the player wanting to take the risks.

Pacing

Pacing adds another level to decision making and creates advanced tactical gameplay. ***Pacing*** is the rate at which a player must make decisions. A game like checkers allows a player as much time as needed to make moves. This can be very frustrating to the opponent who is waiting to take a turn. Everyone wants to have enough time to make a good decision, but not too long to hold up the game. The balance between thinking time and game delay is often very difficult to achieve. Sports games like football and basketball have a play or shot clock to control pacing. This is a way to make the game exciting and fun while allowing time for strategy.

When designing a video game, pacing must be configured to keep the game moving. Pacing can be controlled by something as simple as a timer in the game. However, this may not be a good choice. Timers are not typically something seen in the real world and can work against immersion in the game. Instead, use meaningful elements of the game story to control pacing. For example, the rate at which flood waters are rising could set the pacing for a player task of building a dam. The sun rises in the morning and the characters must move under the cover of darkness to avoid detection. These examples show how pacing can be set without using an artificial element like a timer.

However, using timers to control pacing is not always a bad idea. There are many aspects of strategy gameplay in which timers are very useful. Health regeneration is one of the most common examples in which a timer is used. After a set period of time without damage, the PC's health increases. In another timer example, after being bitten by a snake, the PC has limited movement until the venom timer expires. It is perfectly fine to use timers when they are integrated into gameplay and do not break the player's immersion in the game.

Pacing can be integrated into the tactical system as well. The speed of building resources, such as stone cutting or foraging for food, should be consistent with the need to plan and acquire assets. If you could quickly mine iron ore and forge it into weapons and armor, then the need to save gold to purchase these items would be decreased. Additionally, there should be a pacing mechanism to keep the player from always mining. The gameplay needs to force use of the asset or at least the need to travel out of a safe zone to continue acquiring the limited resource.

Early video games used the difficulty setting to control pacing. In these skill games, obstacles would move faster and faster as the levels increased, so the pace increased on each level. Similarly, in strategy games, allowing the player shorter and shorter time between decisions makes the game more difficult. However, instead of decreasing the amount of time a player has to make decisions, increase the complexity of the implicit challenges. More resources, more choices, and more maneuvering will lead to more difficulty. This allows for a steady pace of action and decision making, while increasing the difficulty of the game levels.

Economy

The previous four mechanics are combined to create the structure for gameplay. These work behind the scenes to manage the virtual world. The economic system of the game regulates and manages the other four mechanics in a system of gains and drains.

Gains occur when the player receives something like a resource, skill, or knowledge. ***Drains*** occur when the player has something taken away. A simple example of this is fuel in a car. The player starts the game with a full tank of fuel. As the player drives around in the game, the fuel is burned, which is a *drain* on the fuel resource. Eventually, the player must refuel, which is a *gain* on the fuel resource, to avoid running out.

Using the mechanic of limited resources might be as simple as allowing a player character to carry only enough water to fill a canteen. As shown in **Figure 6-5,** this may be indicated by thirst. As the temperature in the game world rises, the player needs to stop and drink water more frequently. The player must manage how far and when to travel in order to manage the water resource. Traveling at night will create less thirst because the temperature is lower, but there are more dangers because thieves and villains are out at night. This allows gains and drains to become part of the strategy model for the player.

The more complex the economic system, the more complex the system of gains and drains needs to be. Imagine a massively multiplayer online (MMO) game that launched a year ago. Players who started playing when the game was launched have already found gold, but new players need to find gold to keep playing and competing.

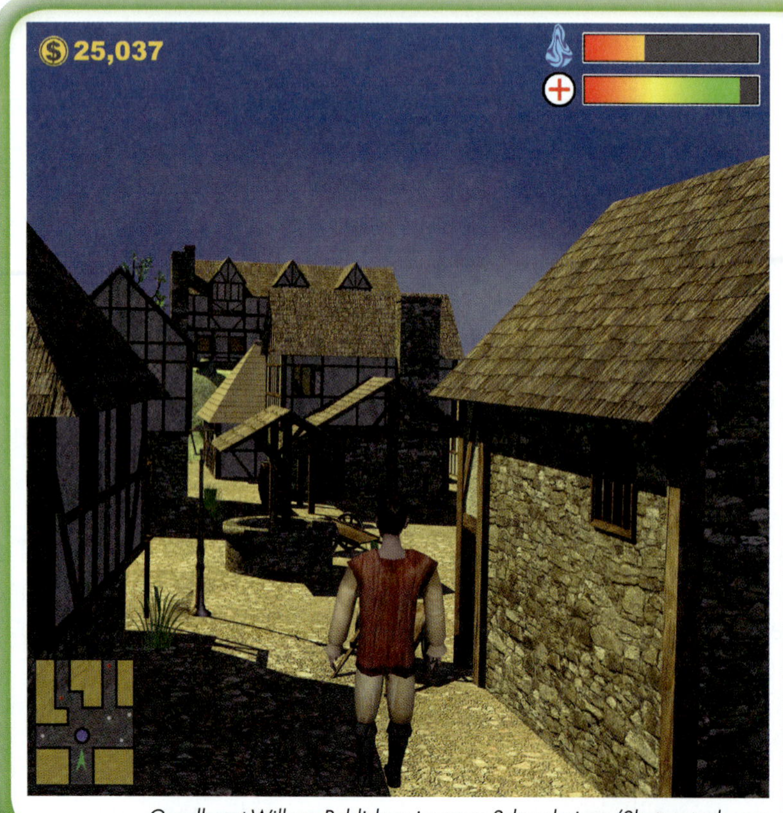

Goodheart-Willcox Publisher; images: 3drenderings/Shutterstock.com

Figure 6-5.

In this game, the player must monitor the thirst level while traveling through the game. Many games use thirst or hunger as a way to force players to use limited resources of water or food. As an added element, the rate of thirst or hunger may be altered based on environmental conditions. As shown here, the PC has a dangerous thirst level, so the player may need to see if the well contains water.

The economic system in the game needs to have ways for new players to acquire, or *gain*, gold and cause advanced players to spend, or *drain*, gold. This becomes even more important in games where players can exchange assets without using the game-world store. A player and his or her friends could give all the gold to one player if there is nothing built into the economic system to prevent that unfair advantage.

Each asset created for the game must have a gain and drain component built in along with the strength and weakness of dissimilar assets. If food spoils, the player will need to find other food in another part of the game. When the player spends gold at the game-world store, gold is removed from that player's assets and returned to the unused gold resource in the game.

In the end, the gains and drains of the economic system must comply with the five contributing factors to establishing a **sustainable community**. The five factors are:

- regulating factors;
- provisioning factors;
- cultural factors;
- health factors; and
- supporting factors.

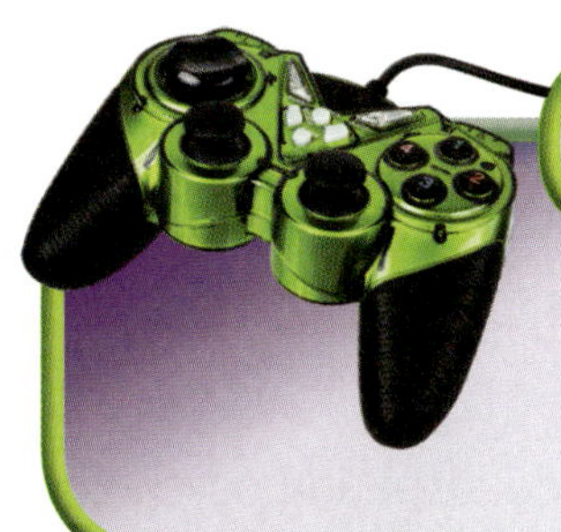

CHEAT CODE: SUSTAINABLE COMMUNITY

A sustainable community is one that has or can obtain the resources needed to keep meeting the needs and wants of its citizens.

Regulating factors of the community are those components that control the environment and interactions. These can include the climate, terrain, resource distribution, carrying capacity, and more. In real-world nature, these factors include climate, nutrient balance, and water filtration, among others.

Provisioning factors of the community are those components that are consumable by the player. These factors can include food, medicine, potions, minerals, money, and more. In the real-world, these factors include food, medicine, clothing, and minerals. Generally, anything that is part of the resource management is a provisioning factor.

Cultural factors of the community are those components that contribute to setting, tradition, player classification, character types, and more. In the real-world, these include science, spiritual, ceremonial, recreation, and aesthetic factors. Additional cultural factors come from the players. The player skill, the ability to level up, and knowledge from previous versions can contribute to the application of cultural factors. Recent games such as *Call of Duty: Modern Warfare 3,* shown in **Figure 6-6,** allow players to skip levels based on their skill from previous versions.

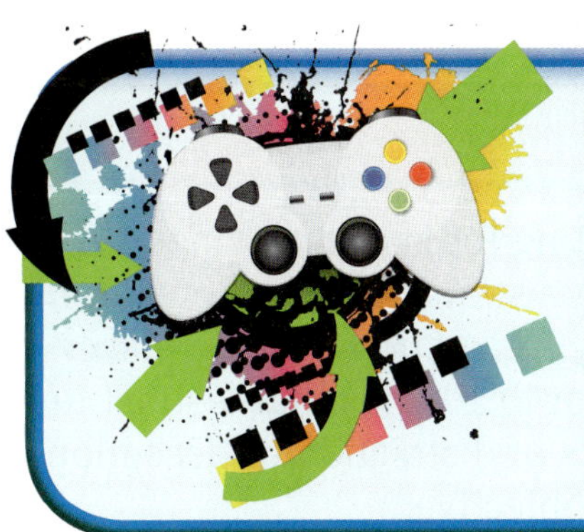

Ethical Gamer

When playing MMOs or any multiplayer game that allows transfer of assets between players, consider the impact on other players of transferring assets. This can be considered a form of cheating that hurts the gaming community and causes problems for new players when they join.

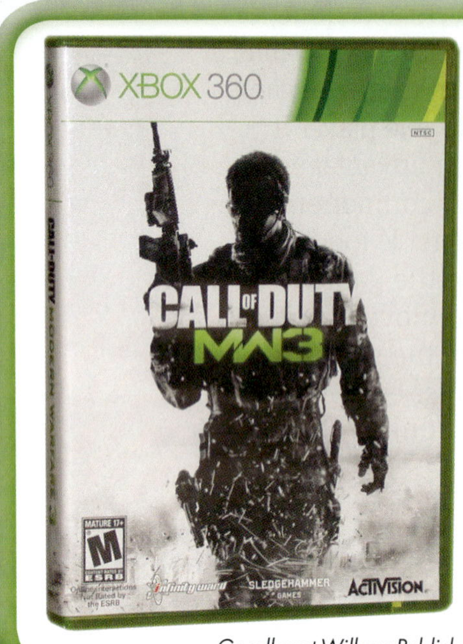

Goodheart-Willcox Publisher

Figure 6-6. *Call of Duty: Modern Warfare 3* allowed a player to skip early game levels based on his or her skill. In this way, experienced players did not have to play levels designed to build skill.

Health factors of the community are those components that determine strength, damage, and recovery. Health can be measured in many ways, such as physical health, emotional health, and psychological health. The most obvious use of health is physical health. A game character can gain and drain health in many ways. Artificial health indicators such as health points or bars give a value to the total health of the character. More realistic health meters show the character missing parts, wounded, sick, or otherwise physically hindered. In this way, health is not displayed as a number, but rather physical attributes display injuries to indicate health. More difficult to display in a game are levels of emotional and psychological health. In the *Civilization* series of games, the player must keep the citizens happy. If the emotional and psychological health of the citizens in a city drops low enough, the city will revolt. If the player does not address the situation quickly enough, the government may collapse and the player will need to play through several turns of anarchy.

Supporting factors of the community are those components that allow resources to be exchanged and recycled to maintain balance. In nature, this is best demonstrated by leaves falling from trees that eventually decompose and turn into nutrients in the soil for the tree. In video games, the game rules and game systems created by the designers are the support for the community.

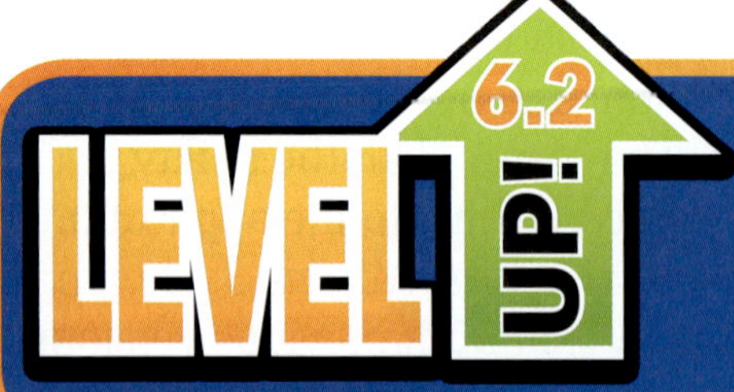

List three strategy games. Consider how each game implements the five mechanics of strategy games. Do any of the games use all five mechanics?

Strategic Game Flow

In the previous section, the focus was on creating the mechanics needed for a strategy game. This section focuses on designing a strategic game flow. ***Game flow*** is a design of levels, processes, and gameplay integration that the player should follow. Game flow is also the red herrings or dead ends that distract the player. If the game does not include some elements of distraction or deception, the player will be able to easily find a path to the objective.

Strategy games require the player to explore and make choices. This means that part of the design of levels needs to foster exploration and include challenges in areas that are not part of the victory condition. In strategy games, trivial tasks help add to the overall challenge of discovery. In other types of games, inclusion of trivial tasks is discouraged. Factors that must be considered for game flow in a strategic game include:

- goals;
- application of rules;
- prediction;
- deception;
- causal chain; and
- computerized benefits.

Goals

The first element of strategic game flow is setting goals. As you have learned, setting goals is a critical element in every type of game. Strategy games are no different. Goals and objectives need to guide the player throughout the storyline. As such, the player will act as the agent of change in the game world. As an ***agent of change,*** the player is the main game element that changes the outcome of the game. In a strategy game, the decisions and choices of the player determine how victory is achieved.

In strategy games, nested victories are very important. ***Nested victories*** are the smaller victories that lead to the ultimate victory condition. When designing the game plan, create an outline that shows what objectives the player should achieve to demonstrate enough skill to level up. In multiplayer games, the goals need to be skills the player demonstrates through battle with other players.

Application of Rules

The design of the strategic game flow needs to incorporate how the rules are applied. Strategy games typically have complex rules. This is true of video games as well as board games. The design of levels and obstacles should give an advantage or disadvantage to special weapons, vehicles, skills, and characters. This can create many special circumstances that make the rules complex or difficult to understand. The application of rules can be broken down into three areas of **complexity:** concept, mechanics, and mass.

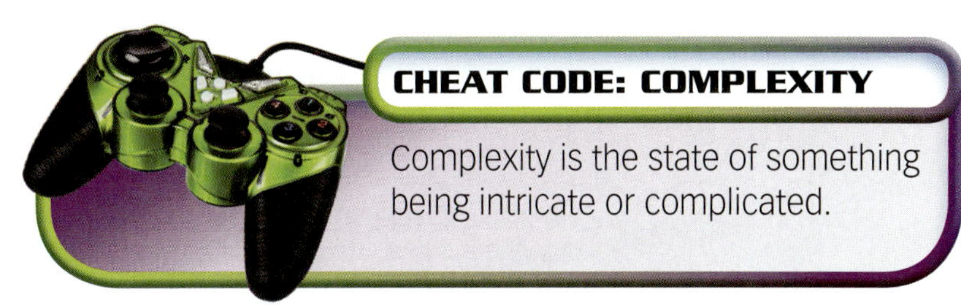

Complexity of Concept

Complexity of concept takes into account all possible outcomes or maneuvers. A simple board game like chess has a high complexity of concept. In the game concept, the moves are simple, but the millions upon millions of possible combinations of moves make the game very complex. The open-ended design of chess highlights player choice because the player has many pieces and the freedom to move any piece. This also makes discovering the opponent's strategy very hard. Each player must track multiple game pieces with different attack properties.

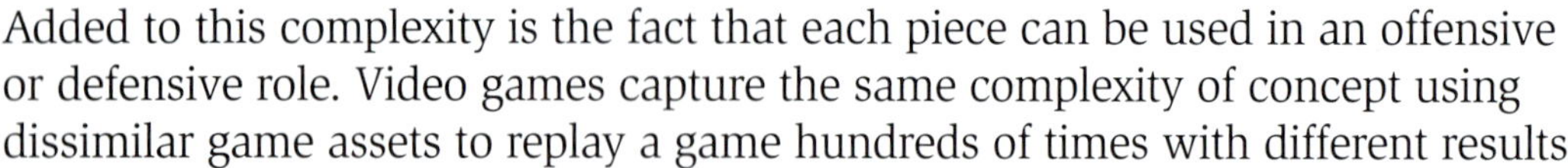

Added to this complexity is the fact that each piece can be used in an offensive or defensive role. Video games capture the same complexity of concept using dissimilar game assets to replay a game hundreds of times with different results.

Complexity of Mechanics

Complexity is additionally found in the mechanics of the game. The example of chess shows how the simple mechanic of movement can result in complexity. In a role-playing game, the mechanics of a move may be far more complex than in the game of chess. It may take many mathematical calculations to determine the strength of a sword strike. Imagine the variables for a simple sword strike to determine how much damage was done to a player, such as location of the strike, attack weapon, force of strike, and defense of strike. Refer to the sample calculation shown in **Figure 6-7.** The rule mechanics in that example are simple, yet a sword strike can have a very complex result. Notice the two very different results obtained by a sword strike. Rules can be much more complex than this example.

Complexity of Mass

Complexity can be found in the large number of special situations and the application of rules in each special situation. This is referred to as complexity of mass because the rule book for the game can be very large. Consider the tabletop role-playing game *Dungeons and Dragons.* The person who is the dungeon master deals with a high complexity of mass because he or she must design the quest, manage all of the NPCs, assign rewards and penalties, and many other tasks all while following the extensive rules of the game. Complexity of mass is simplified in video games because the computer can perform the calculations for each special scenario. However, understanding the benefit the player will receive from each possible scenario is still very complex.

Players enjoy games that have complexity of mass because the games allow for many choices and the prestige of mastering the game. This "knowledge is power" dynamic plays out in games that have complexity of mass where the most skilled are those who know more game secrets. In video games, knowledge of cheat codes, shortcuts, or **Easter egg** locations is often a closely guarded secret. Players who have that knowledge feel they have an advantage over other players who do not. Understanding complex rules can give a master player the same advantage over the average player.

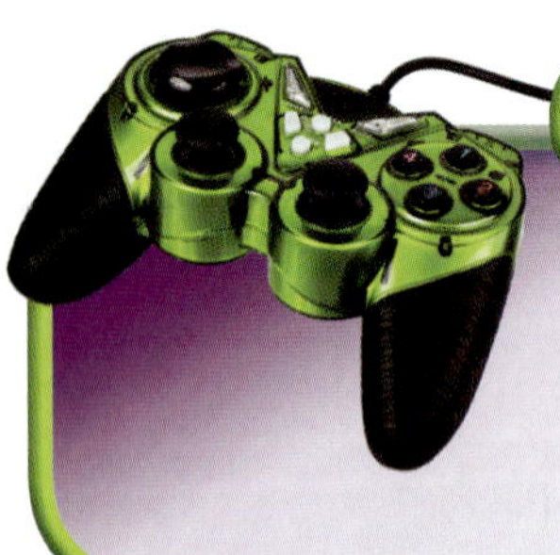

CHEAT CODE: EASTER EGG

An Easter egg is a hidden message or special feature. In a video game, an Easter egg may unlock a special ability or display concept art used in developing the game, for example.

Prediction

An important part of the game flow in a strategy game is the ability for the player to predict the moves of opponents. ***Pattern recognition*** occurs when a player can observe repeating actions or conditions and use that to predict future game movements and events. Having patterns that the player can recognize is an easy way to help with prediction. Randomness eliminates any patter recognition that may occur, so be sure to avoid randomness when programming patterns for the player to recognize.

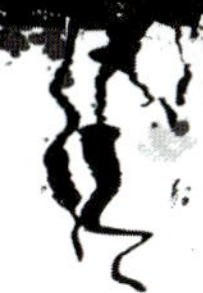

Location Damage

IF the strike is to the head, **THEN** subtract 10 hit points.
IF the strike is to the body, **THEN** subtract 8 hit points.
IF the strike is to the leg, **THEN** subtract 4 hit points.
IF the strike is to the arm, **THEN** subtract 2 hit points.

Weapon Damage

IF the strike is by a crystal sword, **THEN** subtract 25 hit points.
IF the strike is by a steel sword, **THEN** subtract 15 hit points.
IF the strike is by an iron sword, **THEN** subtract 10 hit points.
IF the strike is by a copper sword, **THEN** subtract 6 hit points.
IF the strike is by a wooden sword, **THEN** subtract 2 hit points.

Force of Strike Damage

IF the strike speed is 1, **THEN** use a multiplier of 1.
IF the strike speed is 2, **THEN** use a multiplier of 2.
IF the strike speed is 3, **THEN** use a multiplier of 3.
IF the strike speed is 4, **THEN** use a multiplier of 4.
IF the strike speed is 5, **THEN** use a multiplier of 5.
IF the strike speed is 6, **THEN** use a multiplier of 6.

Armor Damage Reduction

IF the strike is on golden armor, **THEN** divide the damage hits points by 3.
IF the strike is on steel armor, **THEN** divide the damage hits points by 2.
IF the strike is on leather armor, **THEN** divide the damage hits points by 1.5.
IF the strike is on cloth armor, **THEN** divide the damage hits points by 1.1.
IF the strike is on no armor, **THEN** divide the damage hits points by 1.

Location	Weapon	Strike Speed	Armor
head	crystal sword	5	leather

$((-10 - 25) \times 5) \div 1.5 = -117$ hit points removed from character

Location	Weapon	Strike Speed	Armor
body	copper sword	3	golden

$((-8 - 6) \times 3) \div 3 = -14$ hit points removed from character

Goodheart-Willcox Publisher

Figure 6-7. Look at the conditions of an attack, then examine how the hit points are calculated.

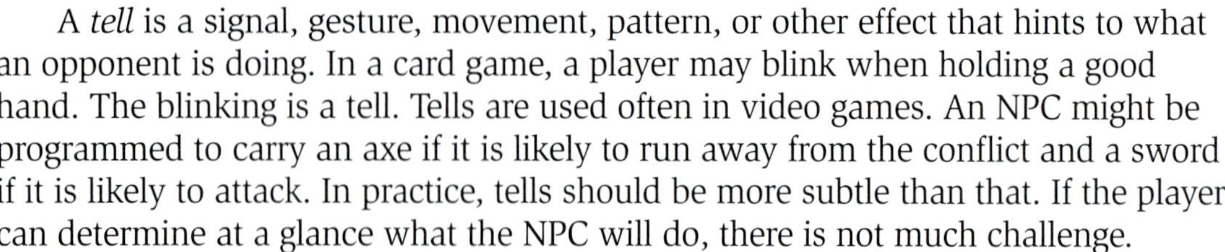

A *tell* is a signal, gesture, movement, pattern, or other effect that hints to what an opponent is doing. In a card game, a player may blink when holding a good hand. The blinking is a tell. Tells are used often in video games. An NPC might be programmed to carry an axe if it is likely to run away from the conflict and a sword if it is likely to attack. In practice, tells should be more subtle than that. If the player can determine at a glance what the NPC will do, there is not much challenge.

Reconnaissance is a form of prediction in a video game. Reconnaissance, or *recon,* is the ability to spy on the opponent. Specialized characters, such as scouts or drones, can be created for the game to allow the player to perform recon activities. Minimaps also play a part in reconnaissance. Showing the relative location of the objectives and enemies on the minimap helps the player predict enemy movements, attacks, and defenses. The player can predict the best path to take to avoid or engage enemy combatants.

Deception

The counterpart to prediction is deception. Deception tactics are used to spoil the opponent's predictions. Critical to a strategy game is the ability of the player to deceive opponents as to attacks and defenses. A strategy game needs to provide for hidden movements and hidden decisions. Hidden movements might include use of cover from a forest, buildings, tunnels, smoke, or invisibility spells. As shown in **Figure 6-8,** darkness can also be used to allow for hidden movements. Hidden decisions are more complex as they are meant to deceive. Effort taken in game design to limit lines of sight with fog, artificial horizons, terrain, or other conventions will allow for hidden decisions and deception. If the game does not support these types of tactics, it limits the player's ability to think and plan strategic maneuvers.

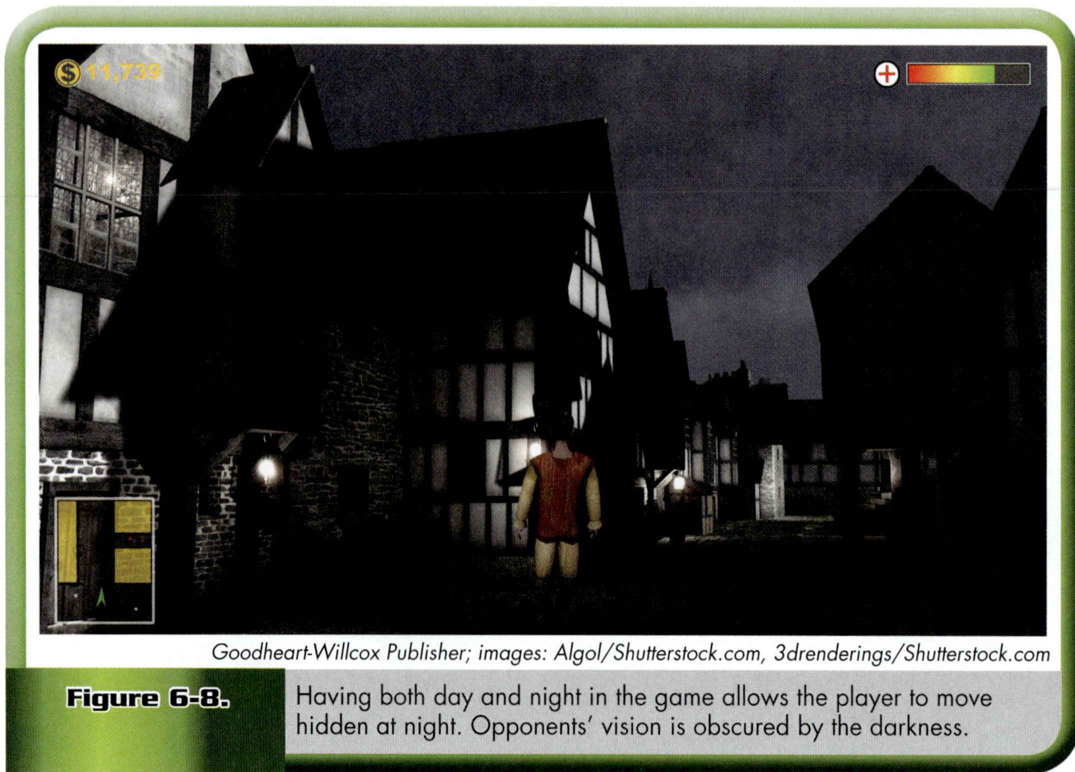

Goodheart-Willcox Publisher; images: Algol/Shutterstock.com, 3drenderings/Shutterstock.com

Figure 6-8. Having both day and night in the game allows the player to move hidden at night. Opponents' vision is obscured by the darkness.

Additionally, sound can play an important role in deception. Allowing a player to make a sound in one direction, such as throwing a rock or setting of an explosion, can draw the opponent there. This can allow the player to sneak past or attack another location. Programming sound for footsteps or the movement of metal armor, for example, is also a great way to add immersion to the game.

Causal Chain

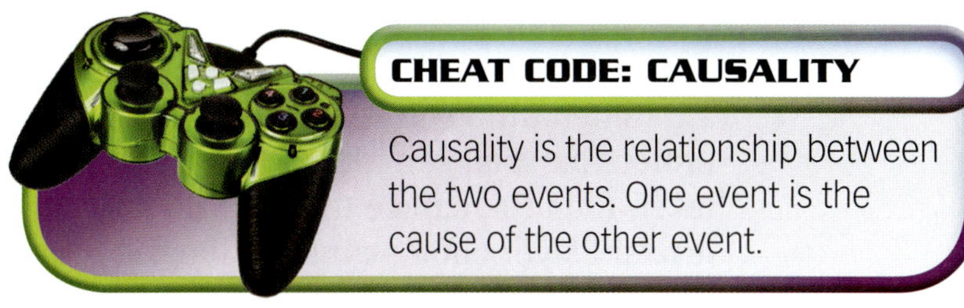

CHEAT CODE: CAUSALITY

Causality is the relationship between the two events. One event is the cause of the other event.

Causal chain relates to a series of cause-and-effect events that form an ordered sequence. The second and subsequent events have **causality.** Many people tend to think of the causal chain as the casualties or losses during a battle. While managing these losses is an important element of any strategic decision, this is not the definition of a causal chain. Do not confuse the words *causality* and *casualty.*

In a strategy game, the tactics a player takes to achieve the strategic plan make up the causal chain. These tactics may create a short chain of events or a very long chain of events. There must be enough interactions designed into the game to allow the causal chain to be formed and implemented. An example of a causal chain may be:

1. Create deception in the east.
2. Draw the opponent to the eastern attack.
3. Retreat from the eastern attack.
4. Allow the opponent to pursue eastern forces.
5. Use reconnaissance to verify opponent has committed a majority of forces to the eastern attack.
6. Attack from the west with a large force.
7. Capture the castle.

Computerized Benefits

One part of the definition of a video game is that the game be computerized. Computers allow games with complex rules and scenarios. This offers players more opportunity to experience high quality strategy gameplay. Constructing computerized gameplay is a complex design process. The causal chain needed to win should be dynamic and not a single linear path. The computer can do the math quickly and easily, so the complexity of mass and concept place little burden on the player. This frees the player to make many complex decisions in the causal chain to lead to a successful outcome. When constructing the game, the designer must provide meaningful player choices, prevent errors, expand the decision model, and maintain player immersion.

Provide Meaningful Player Choices

Depending on the design of the game, the player may face thousands of choices during gameplay. With so many variables, multipliers, and combinations, the total possible solutions could number in the millions. Allowing player choice and the freedom to experience gameplay that is not

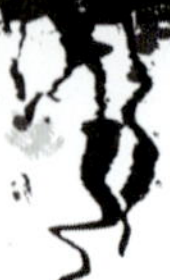

typical are great ways to entertain the player. However, the choices presented to the player must be meaningful to the game story. Even though the computer can handle the calculations needed for thousands or millions of player choices, the player should only be offered choices that help move the game forward or provide red herrings.

Many designers do not like to talk about limiting player choices, but it is a common practice. Player choice can be limited if the player action is not matched to the purpose of the game. For example, suppose a game has a haunted dungeon level. If it is discovered that the player choice of using a protection spell can allow the PC to move unharmed throughout the entire level, then the choice to select the protection spell must be limited to other levels. Player choice must be limited to options that do not interfere with the proper functioning of the game.

Prevent Errors

Computers and network gameplay allow for an amazing amount of data to be collected. This includes bug detection, error locating, and much more. During the time period after releasing the game, the support team has to monitor gameplay for any errors, hacks, or unsuitable options. The most effective means of monitoring for these errors is by evaluating metrics.

Metrics are measurable parameters that can be analyzed for performance and behavior. With game metrics, statistical data are captured as the game is played, as shown in **Figure 6-9.** The computer can collect and store a huge amount of data on everything that occurs in the game. The entire volume of

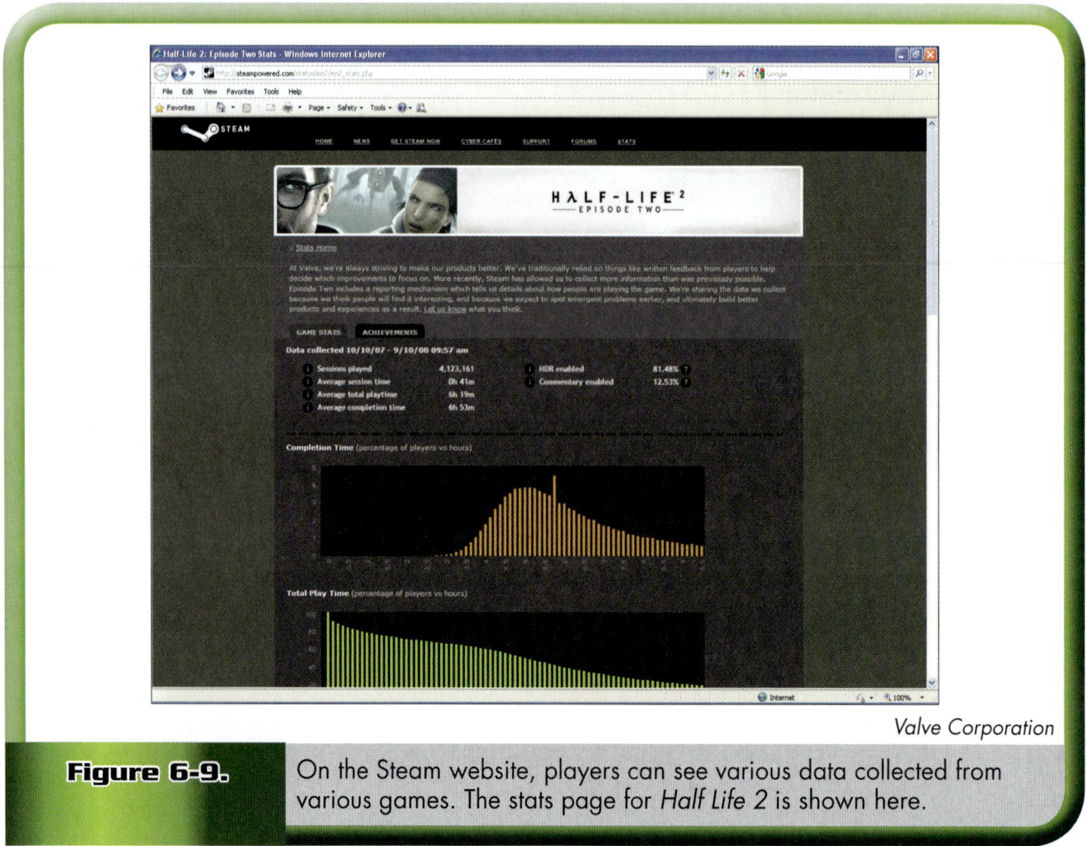

Valve Corporation

Figure 6-9. On the Steam website, players can see various data collected from various games. The stats page for *Half Life 2* is shown here.

data is analyzed to see what the players are doing in the game. ***Data mining*** is the process of discovering patterns from a set of raw statistical information. When patterns are discovered, metrics are assigned for the interaction and the data are tracked for specific results. Metrics for games are typically separated into game-focused or player-focused data.

Game-focused statistical data are the easiest to capture and understand. Recording how much time it takes for players to complete a level or a specific task is easy to collect. With a large sample of players, the support team can determine how long the average player would take to complete the task. If these time data seem to suddenly shift lower, then the metrics have discovered unexpected results. The player movements and inputs can be observed and recorded to see what condition is making what should be a two-hour task take only five minutes. A patch can be constructed to fix this error if needed. Many of the hacks and cheats are discovered using game-metric analysis such as this.

Player-focused statistical data are used in an attempt to understand the typical player and identify preferences, experiences, and ways in which players can get around the rules. Some data for this analysis are captured while the player is engaged in the game. Measuring how many players use a specific item, such as a vehicle, can identify common behaviors. These are important to understand as a given solution may be too common. Additionally, player choices such as character types and movement paths can also be captured. Some of these data can help designers balance game components. A metric for player choice might identify that 70 percent of players choose the knight character and only 2 percent choose the wizard. With information like this, the design team can limit the number of knight characters to avoid having an MMO filled with knights. Another path designers might take is to give the wizard character better assets to influence player choice. Maybe just allowing the wizard's staff to slash and bash like the knight's sword will cause players to think the wizard is cool and select it more often.

The in-game environment can be modified based on game-focused and player-focused data. Weather effects, terrain, and other environmental components can be modified to balance gameplay and player movement based on the metrics data. Placing a mountain or wall in the game to force players in another direction may help eliminate errors in navigation and avoid player frustration. Another approach to correcting similar issues is to change the point system for taking risks. Allowing bonus points for longer interactions, harder moves, or more skillful use of a certain item can influence players to engage with less used items or areas of the game map. Additionally, changing the NPC count and distribution can help correct unintended shortcuts, unbalanced weaponry, or other game items that may be too hard or too easy.

Visualizing metrics makes the data easier to understand. A simple **histogram** or chart can make data trend far more recognizable than a page full of numbers. Even better visuals like color-coded maps make player-focused and in-game data easier to understand.

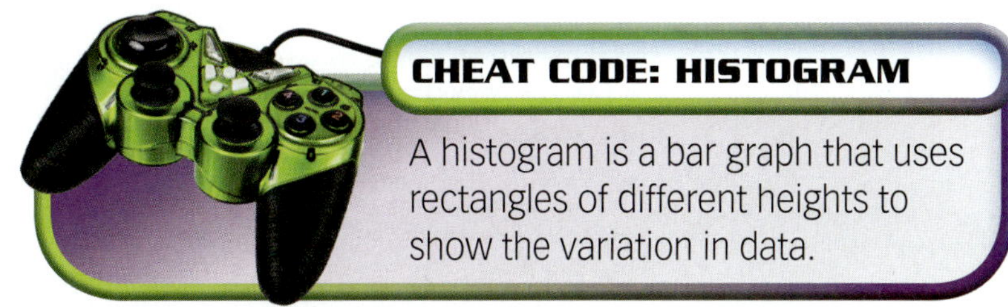

CHEAT CODE: HISTOGRAM

A histogram is a bar graph that uses rectangles of different heights to show the variation in data.

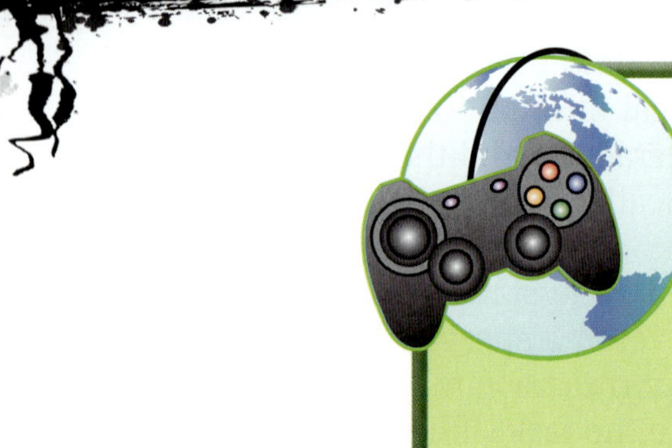

Green Gamer

What kind of lightbulbs are in the lamps in your gaming room at home? Compact fluorescent lamps (CFL) use 80 percent less energy than regular incandescent lightbulbs and last up to 10 times longer. This not only saves money, but reduces the carbon footprint of creating and powering lightbulbs. However, CFLs contain mercury, so they must be disposed of properly to protect the environment.

Expand the Decision Model

A strategy game should capitalize on all of the capabilities of a computer and network to expand the decision model. The computer will allow for a long causal chain and application of complex rules. Combining these elements will allow the player more options and decisions. In a strategy game, this combination is most likely found in a conflict strategy model. The ***conflict strategy model*** requires players to engage each other in conflict or battle. The basic components of the conflict strategy model include the distribution of assets known as units or factories.

Units are any maneuverable game asset. A unit can be a single character, aircraft, car, ship, or any other movable game asset. Units can also be assembled into larger units of dissimilar assets, such as a battalion consisting of infantry, cavalry, archers, artillery, and tanks.

Factories are any nonmaneuverable game asset with some strategic value. A factory can be a building, such as headquarters, munitions dump, gold mine, or any other nonmovable asset. The strategic value each factory has will determine if the enemy wants to destroy it or capture it. A strategic decision might include capturing a gold mine. The player or an opponent might not want to destroy the gold mine so it can be overrun and the gold taken. Having several types of factories will increase the strategic decisions by all players.

Another decision model used in strategy games is the resolution strategy model. A ***resolution strategy model*** requires players to negotiate a diplomatic solution. Players use spies and other information-gathering tactics to convince the opponents to yield to their demands. In general, diplomacy through emissaries and alliances is used to gain **boon.** Strategy games with gameplay that focuses on trading use the resolution strategy model. Players with an excess of one type of asset exchange the excess for more powerful or valuable items. The *Civilization* series of games makes use of the resolution strategy model in its trade function. The dissimilar assets are used to make negotiation and trading important to achieving the goals of the game.

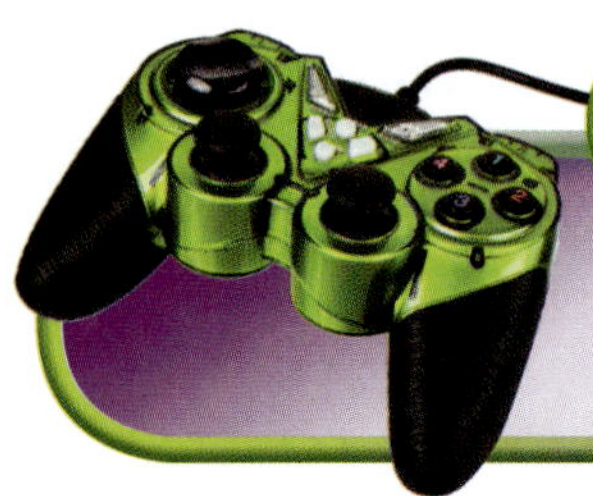

CHEAT CODE: BOON

A boon is a benefit or favor granted in response to a request.

A favored component of the resolution strategy model is the use of allies. ***Allies*** are other players, either NPCs or human players, who agree to join forces to achieve victory over a common enemy or gain a common goal. Allies can be a very interesting part of the gameplay because they may not stay allies for the entire game. In order to win the game, allies may need to eventually combat each other in a final episode. Also, a player may act as an ally, but really be a double agent and try to get other opponents to fight each other.

The resolution strategy model is much more difficult to program and implement than the conflict strategy model. However, it can provide a much richer game with intellectually stimulating content. Combining both the conflict strategy model and resolution strategy model into a single game gives players significantly more decision options. The *Civilization* series of games is an example of combining the two models in one game.

Maintain Player Immersion

Player immersion can be achieved at a much higher level using computers. Immersion is the level to which a player is connected to the imaginary game environment. Computer graphics, motion controls, 3D realistic environments, and speaking characters all help create this connection to the game environment. New computer capabilities bridge the gap between real and virtual environment through highly realistic simulations, as shown in **Figure 6-10.**

A highly realistic simulation may include a 360 degree video screen, 3D graphics, realistic handheld controller, multidirectional treadmill, motion-sensing camera, multiple speakers, and projectile cannons. Everything in the game environment is included in the virtual environment. One such undertaking was performed using *Battlefield 3.* A domed screen projected the game environment all around the player. The player carried a realistic gun controller that accurately targeted in the game. Every movement of the player was captured using multiple Xbox Kinect cameras. This allowed the player to move freely in the real world under the domed screen and have the movements appear in the game environment. Finally, there were multiple paintball guns that fired to deliver the same blow as the virtual bullets in the game.

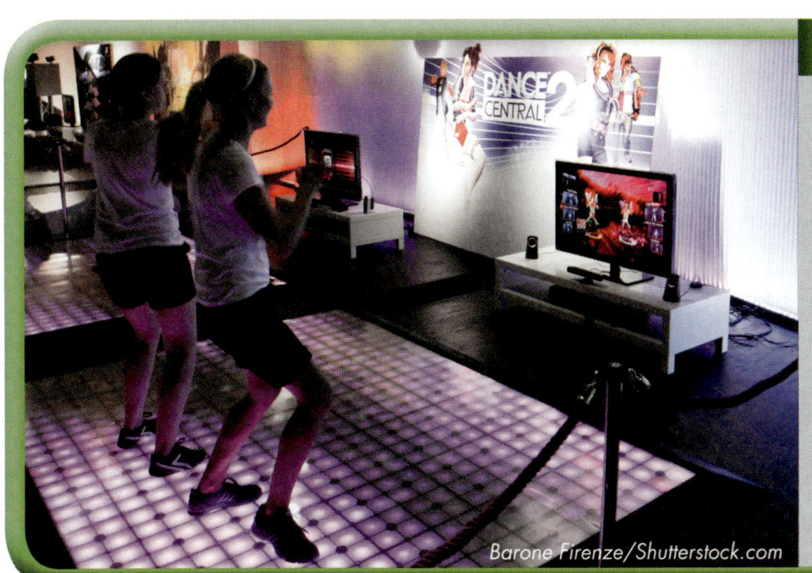

Barone Firenze/Shutterstock.com

Figure 6-10.

Motion controls such as those used on the Xbox Kinect allow the player to be more fully immersed in the game, making the gap between the virtual world and the real world smaller.

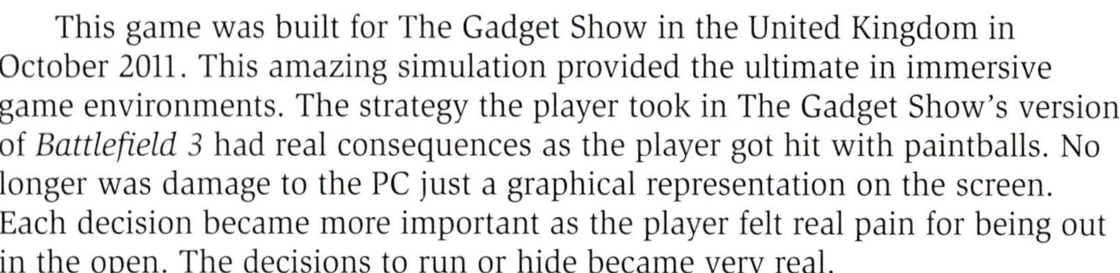

This game was built for The Gadget Show in the United Kingdom in October 2011. This amazing simulation provided the ultimate in immersive game environments. The strategy the player took in The Gadget Show's version of *Battlefield 3* had real consequences as the player got hit with paintballs. No longer was damage to the PC just a graphical representation on the screen. Each decision became more important as the player felt real pain for being out in the open. The decisions to run or hide became very real.

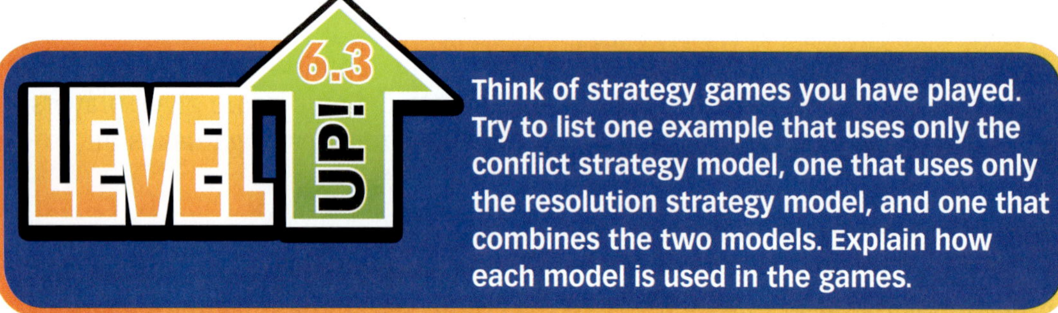

Think of strategy games you have played. Try to list one example that uses only the conflict strategy model, one that uses only the resolution strategy model, and one that combines the two models. Explain how each model is used in the games.

Strategic Feedback

With all of the complexities of strategy games, it is very important that the game have proper feedback to let the player understand his or her progress, success, and failure. In a game with a conflict strategy model, the total number of enemy remaining may be an appropriate measure of success. The player may be able to see the units remaining and determine if he or she has more units or fewer units than the competition. This feedback will lead to better decisions by all players.

As a designer, it is important to provide resources that will give the player clues. Clue finding can occur in overt or covert ways. ***Overt clues*** are those such as purchasing the satellite image or viewing a navigation map. Overt clues are easy to find and understand. More interesting clues are covert. ***Covert clues*** are hidden or hard to read. A riddle is a covert clue. The player must decipher the riddle to understand the information. Covert clues are puzzle elements that add mystery and intrigue to the game. More detailed information on puzzle composition is covered in the next chapter.

Other in-game statistics will help players make better decisions. These statistics need not be free. The player may have to pay for espionage to get the information. Paying for a satellite image of the battlefield will display unit deployment of opponents. Information needs to be very expensive in terms of the game economy to force the player to make a thoughtful decision to spend money on a satellite image or a weapon upgrade.

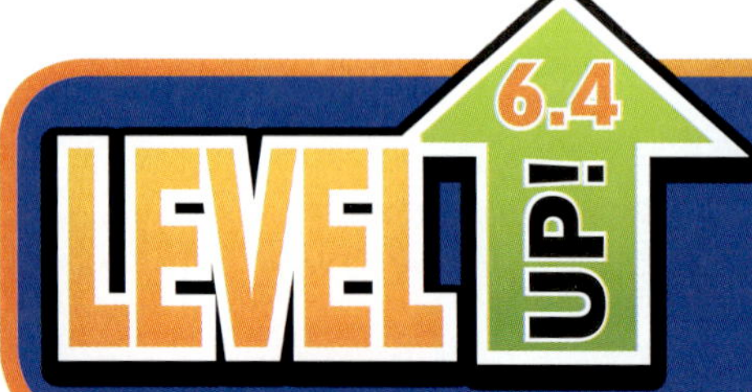

Play three of your favorite video games. For each game, make a list of at least five overt clues and five covert clues.

Chapter Summary

- Strategy is the plans of defense and offense, while tactics are the methods of achieving a strategy.
- The five key mechanics of strategy games are: resource management (strategic management), dissimilar assets (arms race), maneuvers (risk/reward), pacing (speed and recovery), and economy (gains and drains).
- Factors that must be considered for game flow in a strategic game include: goals, application of rules, prediction, deception, causal chain, and computerized benefits.
- Proper feedback in a strategic game, through overt and covert clues, is very important to let the player understand his or her progress, success, and failure.

Check Your Video Game IQ

Now that you have finished this chapter, see what you know about video game design by taking the chapter posttest.

www.m.g-wlearning.com

www.g-wlearning.com

Review Your Knowledge

On a separate sheet of paper or in a word processing document, match the following terms with the definition that fits best.

A. factories	F. maneuvering
B. resolution strategy model	G. conflict strategy model
C. overt	H. covert
D. metrics	I. pacing
E. units	J. data mining

1. Decision model that requires players to engage each other in conflict or battle.
2. Any maneuverable game asset.
3. Process of discovering patterns from a set of raw statistical information.
4. Positioning resources at their most needed or beneficial location.
5. Clues that are easy to find and understand.
6. Measurable parameters that can be analyzed for performance and behavior.
7. Any nonmaneuverable game asset with some strategic value.
8. Decision model that requires players to negotiate a diplomatic solution.
9. The rate at which a player must make decisions.
10. Clues that are hidden or hard to read.

On a separate sheet of paper or in a word processing document, answer each of the following questions.

11. What is the difference between a strategy and a tactic?
12. List the five key mechanics of strategy.
13. Describe two ways to set pacing without using a timer.
14. Allowing food to spoil is an example of which part of the game economy?
15. Which part of the game economy includes components that control the environment and interactions?
16. What is the purpose of red herring and wild goose chase elements of the game?
17. List the three areas of rule complexity.
18. How does pattern recognition aid in prediction?
19. Which strategy best describes an army that constructs many empty tents and builds large fires to make the opponent think the fighting force is larger than it really is?
20. Describe the difference between overt clues and covert clues.

Apply Your STEM Knowledge

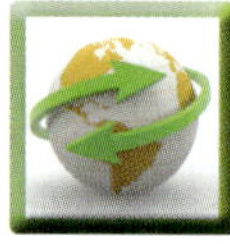

Social Studies

1. Research the Cold War between the United States and the Soviet Union. Explain how dissimilar assets moved military technology forward in an arms race. Create a PowerPoint presentation to show images and descriptions of the dissimilar assets and improvements made to better the other country's technology.

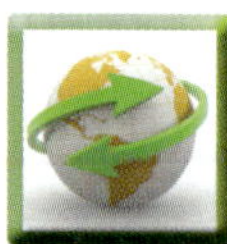

Social Studies

2. Research the diversion tactics of the Allies in World War II from the D-Day invasion of Normandy. Evaluate which diversions were successful and how each helped enable victory at Normandy. Write a one page paper to explain your conclusions.

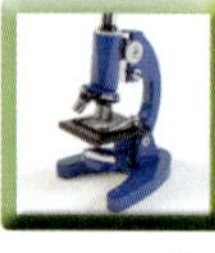

Science

3. A linear causal chain of events can be like a row of dominoes where one falls and causes another domino to fall. This rippling effect from one action causes many other actions to occur. This leads many to refer to a linear causal chain as a domino effect. To stop the last domino from falling, any one domino can be stopped before the reaction reaches it. Research the topic of potential energy and write a brief summary of how potential energy allows the domino effect to occur.

Language Arts

4. Examine the strategy causal chain given in the Causal Chain section in this chapter. Identify which event is the easiest to stop. Write a one-page summary of how you would break the causal chain and prevent overtaking of the castle.

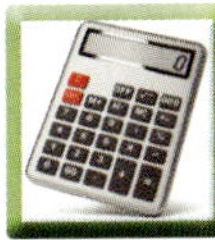

Mathematics

5. The table below is used by the programmers to calculate damage for each attack. Using the information provided, solve for the attack total. Use the following formula. Round to the nearest whole number.
[(location + weapon) × strike] ÷ armor = total damage

Location	Damage Value
Head	–10
Body	–8
Leg	–4
Arm	–2

Weapon	Damage Value
Sword	–20
Spear	–15
Arrow	–10
Knife	–5

Armor	Damage Factor
Steel	5
Chain Mail	4
Bronze	3
Padded Leather	2
None	1

Location	Weapon	Strike Speed	Armor	Total Damage
Head	Sword	4	Steel	
Body	Knife	8	Padded Leather	
Arm	Spear	5	Bronze	
Leg	Arrow	3	Chain Mail	
Head	Knife	6	None	

Working in Teams

Working with the team as assigned by your instructor, create a causal chain that starts with a flat tire on your school bus in the morning and ends with your school's football team losing a first-round playoff game. The causal chain should have at least five, but no more than ten, events. Create a PowerPoint presentation with one slide for each event and a slide that presents the team's conclusion.

Gamer Portfolio

You have identified the types of items you might place in your portfolio. You will begin adding items in this activity and add other items as you continue this class. Locate certificates you have received. For example, a certificate might show that you have completed a video game design workshop. Another certificate might show that you have passed an exam on a certain programming language. You might have a certificate that you received for taking part in a community project. Include any certificates that show tasks completed or your skills or talents. Also create a document that lists each certificate along with when you received it. Briefly describe your activities, skills, or talents related to each certificate.

1. Scan these documents to include in your e-portfolio. Use the file format you selected earlier.
2. Using the naming convention you created earlier, give each document an appropriate name. Place each certificate and the list in an appropriate subfolder for your e-portfolio.
3. Place the hard-copy certificates and list in the container for your print portfolio.

G-W Learning Mobile Site

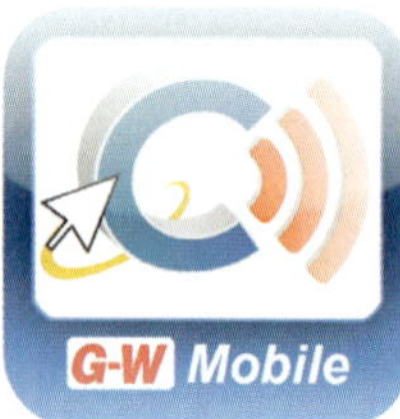

Visit the G-W Learning mobile site to complete the chapter pretest and posttest and to practice vocabulary using e-flash cards. If you do not have a smartphone, visit the G-W Learning companion website to access these features.

G-W Learning mobile site: www.m.g-wlearning.com

G-W Learning companion website: www.g-wlearning.com

Common Core

College and Career Readiness

CTE Career Ready Practices. What do you think the old adage, "necessity is the mother of invention" means? Find examples of how the need for something has sparked something new.

Reading. Using independent research and the information contained in the text, write a report in which you analyze how the strategic flow of a game is established by the game designers. What decisions do they make that impact game flow? How do these decisions allow for greater player immersion? Cite specific evidence from the text and your research to support your understanding of this topic.

Speaking and Listening. Perform an Internet search on the use of player deception in strategic video games. Look for opinions for and against its use. After reading a few expert opinions on this topic, use this information to form your own opinion. Discuss your findings and reasoning with the class.

As you listen to your classmates' stances on this topic, evaluate your own position. How does their reasoning contribute to your understanding of the use of deception in strategic video game composition? Does your opinion on the degree to which it should be used change or is it strengthened?

Event Prep: Communication Skills

Competitive events may judge participants' communications skills. Presenters must be able to exchange information with the judges in a clear, concise manner. This requirement is in keeping with the mission of Career and Technical Student Organizations (CTSOs): to prepare students for professional careers. Communication skills will be judged for both the written and oral presentation. The evaluation will include all aspects of effective writing, speaking, and listening skills as applied to the gaming environment. To prepare for the communications portion of the event:

1. Visit the organization's website and determine specific communication skills that will be evaluated.
2. Spend time reviewing the essential principles of communication, such as grammar, spelling, proofreading, capitalization, and punctuation.
3. If you are making a written presentation, ask a teacher to evaluate your writing. Review and apply the feedback so that your writing sample appears professional and correct.
4. If you are making an oral presentation, ask a teacher to review your presentation and listen for errors in grammar or sentence structure. After you have received comments, adjust and make the presentation several times until you are comfortable.
5. Review the reading, writing, speaking, and listening activities that appear at the end of each chapter of this text as a way to practice your skills.

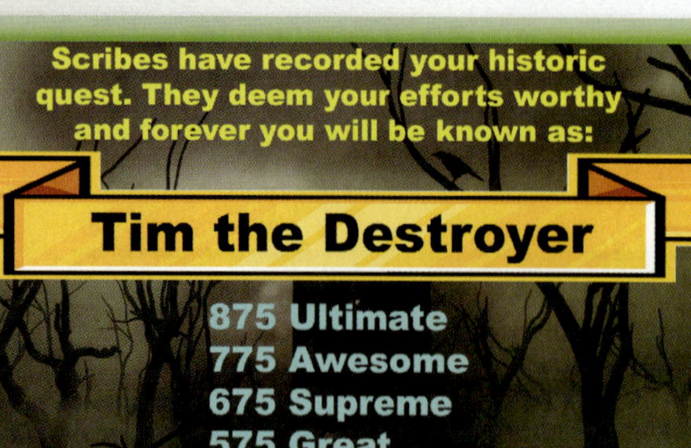
Scribes have recorded your historic quest. They deem your efforts worthy and forever you will be known as:
Tim the Destroyer
875 Ultimate
775 Awesome
675 Supreme
575 Great
475 Conqueror
375 Destroyer
275 Able
175 Imposter
75 Forgotten

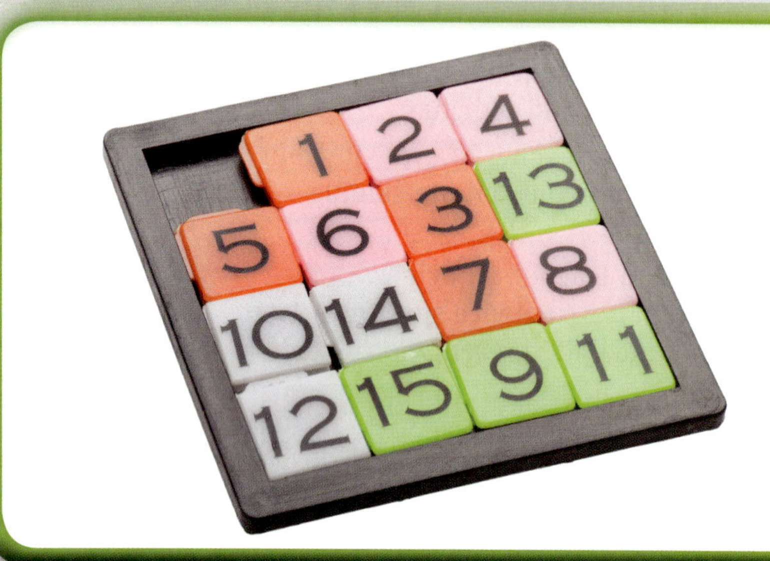
1 2 4
5 6 3 13
10 14 7 8
12 15 9 11

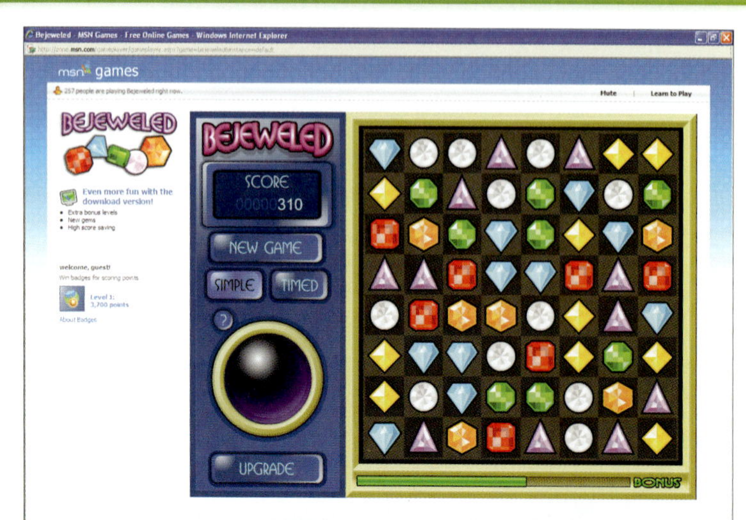
msn games
BEJEWELED
SCORE
310
NEW GAME
SIMPLE
TIMED
UPGRADE
BONUS

Chapter 7
Puzzle Composition

Whether overt or covert, puzzle elements are integrated into most computer games, regardless of the genre. From simple game unlocks to complex puzzle plots, game designers integrate classic puzzle elements that have entertained for centuries. Understanding the human need to solve problems and how puzzles are constructed will help a game designer create great video games that entertain players.

Check Your Video Game IQ

Before you begin this chapter, see what you already know about video game design by taking the chapter pretest.

www.m.g-wlearning.com

www.g-wlearning.com

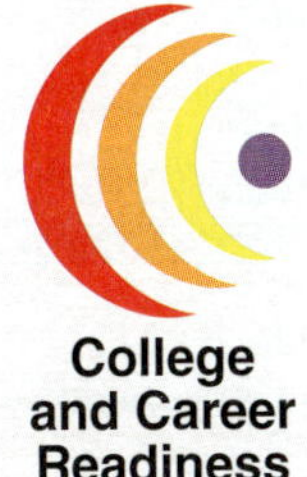

College and Career Readiness

Reading Prep. In preparation for reading the chapter, read a newspaper or magazine article on the use of puzzles in video games. As you read, keep in mind the author's main points and conclusions.

Objectives

After completing this chapter, you will be able to:

- Explain why adding puzzles as objectives in a story can enhance a video game.
- Outline the key steps to puzzle design.
- List the main themes within the puzzle genre.
- Compare and contrast traditional puzzles and computerized versions of puzzles.

Puzzle Design

At the core of creating adventure games is including puzzles. ***Puzzles*** are mental challenges whereby the player must find a solution to a problem. While puzzle games without any story, like a Sudoku puzzle, are fun to play, adding puzzles as objectives in a story can create greater purpose of play. This also helps the player engage in thinking while applying the navigational and action-based skill of gameplay.

Imagine a quest in which the hero must protect citizens and vanquish the enemy. After a few hours the physical gameplay of swordplay may become boring to the player. However, if the game contains puzzle elements, the player can experience other action and may have a reason to keep playing. For example, the hero may need to gather information from the enemy by capturing mechanical parts, diagrams, or maps. Each new objective adds to the solution of the puzzle. In this case, it may be the location of the secret base where the enemy is building a new weapon. The player must collect and interpret the clues beyond the routine action of combat to be successful in the game.

Elements of puzzle design are found in almost every genre of game. Discovering the weakness of a big boss, navigating a maze to find an amulet, stacking furniture to escape a room, or listening to a sound pattern to press the correct buttons to disarm the missile are all ways designers have added puzzle elements to games. To properly add puzzle elements, a designer must first know the key steps to puzzle design. With understanding of the key steps, the designer can structure the elements into adventure and a meaningful story.

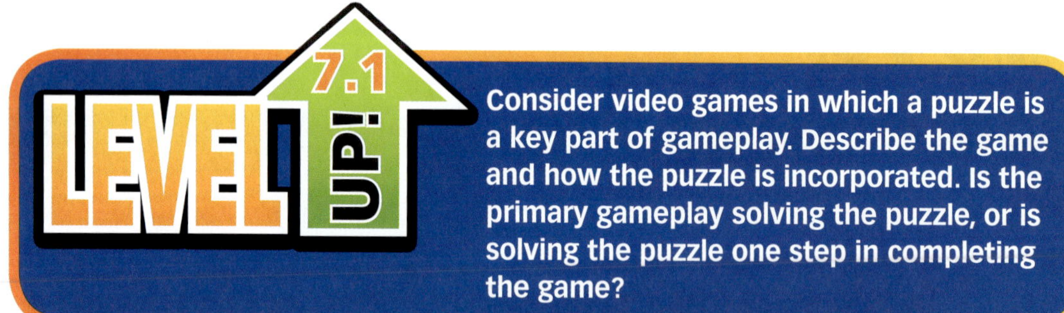

Key Steps to Puzzle Design

The expert in modern puzzle creation is Scott Kim. Mr. Kim has refined the process of puzzle creation. He is well known for his eight steps to puzzle creation and the thousands of puzzles he has created. Mr. Kim is a frequent presenter at conferences such the Game Developers Conference (GDC). There he shares the secrets he uses to create new puzzle games.

An examination of Mr. Kim's first puzzle shows how a simple puzzle is both a challenge and a solution to a problem. Look at the puzzle shown in **Figure 7-1.** This is a folded-paper puzzle that forms a letter when unfolded. The problem is determining what the letter is. The challenge is to unfold the paper just once to reveal the letter. The solution, since the rules disallow the letter L, is the letter F.

Mr. Kim's eight steps to puzzle creation represent a comprehensive approach to building a puzzle from concept to market. Below is an adaptation of Mr. Kim's eight steps as applied to traditional puzzles, computer puzzles, and games.

1. Be inspired.
2. Simplify.
3. Build with a construction set or an editor.
4. Plan and document.
5. Complete the level design.
6. Integrate player aid and hinting.
7. Test.
8. Refine the presentation.

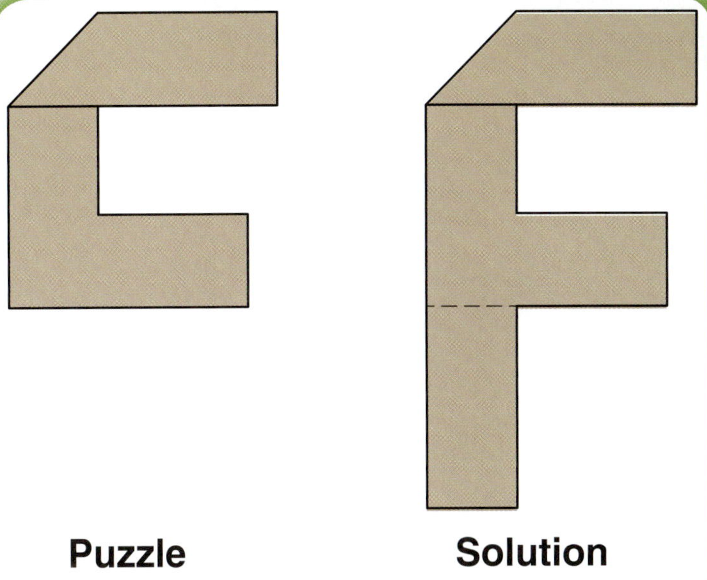

Figure 7-1. This piece of paper has been folded just once. When unfolded, it is a letter of the alphabet. Which letter is it? It is not the letter L.

Be Inspired

Before applying any design elements, the idea for the puzzle must be developed. ***Inspiration*** suggests or influences an idea or motivates a particular thought. Inspiration is a practice in observation. Seeing things move and react and putting things in different configurations are great ways to find inspiration for puzzles. Think of a magician. Each magic trick is a puzzle. An illusion, or trick, will appear magical to the audience who does not know the solution to the puzzle. The magician uses skill to conceal movements and props that help achieve each trick. By observing the way things normally move and react, the magician can assemble an illusion of the unexpected or impossible.

In this same way, you can observe interactions from the real world, stories, or art and begin to imagine your own version of a puzzle. Inspiration is everywhere. Play other games, observe complex machines, watch a crowd of people, and so on. Watch how all parts and pieces move in and around each other. Brainstorm ideas and see what amazing creations you have yet to build.

Simplify

The next step is to take the inspiration and make it workable. Just like the magician, you need to keep the puzzle as simple as possible. Taking a long time to make the person disappear from the box would give away the secret of the illusion. The magician needs to find a simple way of quickly getting the person out of the box unseen by the audience. You need to make similar refinements in your puzzle concept to make it playable. Follow these four steps to help simplify the puzzle design.

1. Identify the essential tricky skill.
2. Eliminate irrelevant details.
3. Use uniform objects of similar sizes.
4. Simplify the controls.

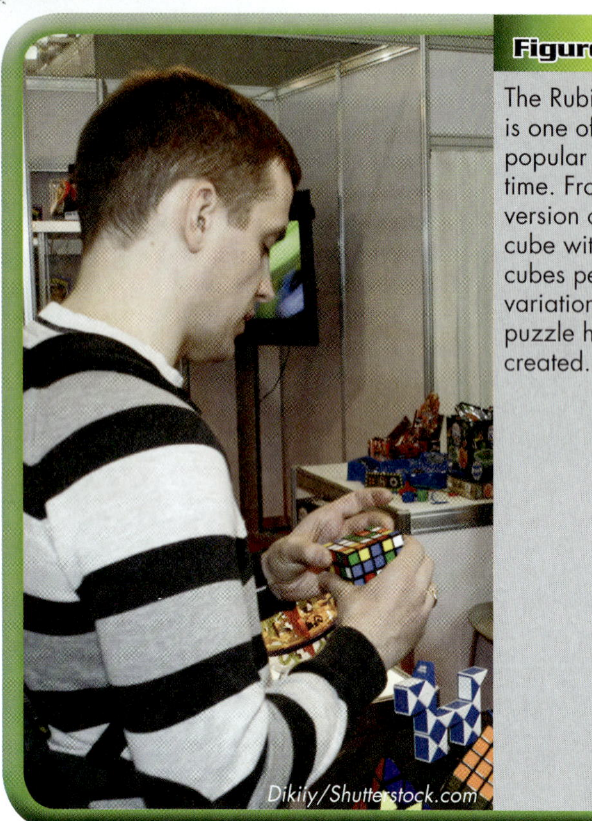

Figure 7-2.

The Rubik's Cube is one of the most popular puzzles of all time. From the original version of a large cube with nine smaller cubes per face, many variations of the puzzle have been created.

The Rubik's Cube is a very successful puzzle. To solve the Rubik's Cube puzzle, the player must twist the cube segments until all the faces are a single color, as shown in **Figure 7-2.** Examine how the steps of simplification could have been applied when developing Rubik's Cube the puzzle.

1. The essential tricky skill is aligning the smaller cubes so all faces of the large cube are a single color.
2. Do not number the smaller cubes so the player must get the colors correct *and* the numbers in sequence.
3. The smaller cubes are all the same size.
4. The player can rotate a single plane to move nine smaller cubes at a time. Each smaller cube is not moved independently.

Build with a Construction Set or an Editor

Build a construction set prototype as a proof of concept to make sure the puzzle will work. Before making a virtual puzzle, try it out with a paper mock-up. Using simple physical items such as note cards, paper, scissors, and a pen can save hours of computer time. A mock-up construction set will also help you define the rules and see possible areas where a player could cheat. On the other hand, there are many times when a physical mock-up may not be appropriate due to the complexity of the puzzle. There are also elements of some puzzles that cannot exist in the physical world.

An ***editor*** is a computer program that allows the designer to prototype the gameplay. In many cases, the same editor is also used to create finalized game levels. Just like the physical construction set, the editor will allow the designer to test rules and techniques that work best and limit cheating. The idea here is to quickly test the rules. No art or details are included. Basic components and wireframe work great for this stage of development. If the same editor is used for the proof of concept and creating the game, the gameplay programming can be saved as the core mechanics for the finished game.

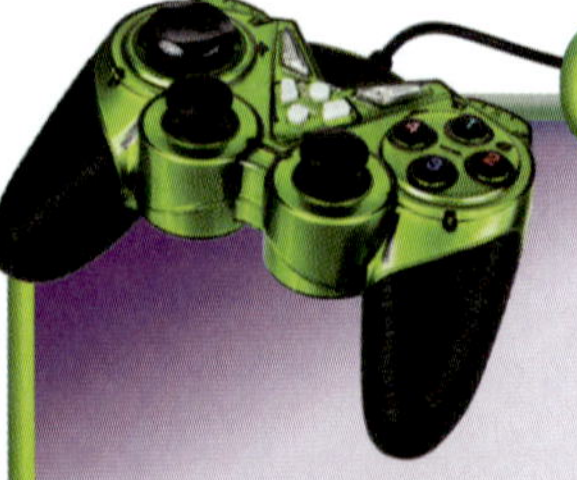

CHEAT CODE: RUBE GOLDBERG

Rube Goldberg was an American cartoonist who became famous for his drawings of machines that were overly complex or over engineered to perform very basic tasks. His name has become a synonym for overly complicated.

Image a game where the player must create a **Rube Goldberg** contraption similar to the board game *Mousetrap* or the video game *The Incredible Machine,* shown in **Figure 7-3.** Suppose the player must make a ball drop, trigger dominoes falling, which in turn trigger a mouse trap, which then flips a cookie into the target of a giant's mouth. It may be fun to set that up in physical form, but it may not be as practical as building it in a virtual environment. The virtual environment in the computer allows all of the interactions to be tested and retested.

With either a physical construction set or computer editor, the end result of this stage is to have the rules set for the puzzle. Defining the rules is the most critical part of puzzle design, as it is with most games. The rules will eventually become the logic statements that allow or disallow moves. When testing with the construction set or editor, make a list of the rules and add new rules as needed to get the correct solution. When creating rules, define rules for each of the four major components of the puzzle:

- map
- parts
- moves
- victory condition

Combining the four major components of a puzzle with good rules helps create player immersion.

Map

The map for a puzzle is the play environment. It can be either physical or virtual space. Look at the game *Tetris.* The map is a 2D wall along which the player stacks pieces, as shown in **Figure 7-4.** In chess, the map is a checkerboard grid.

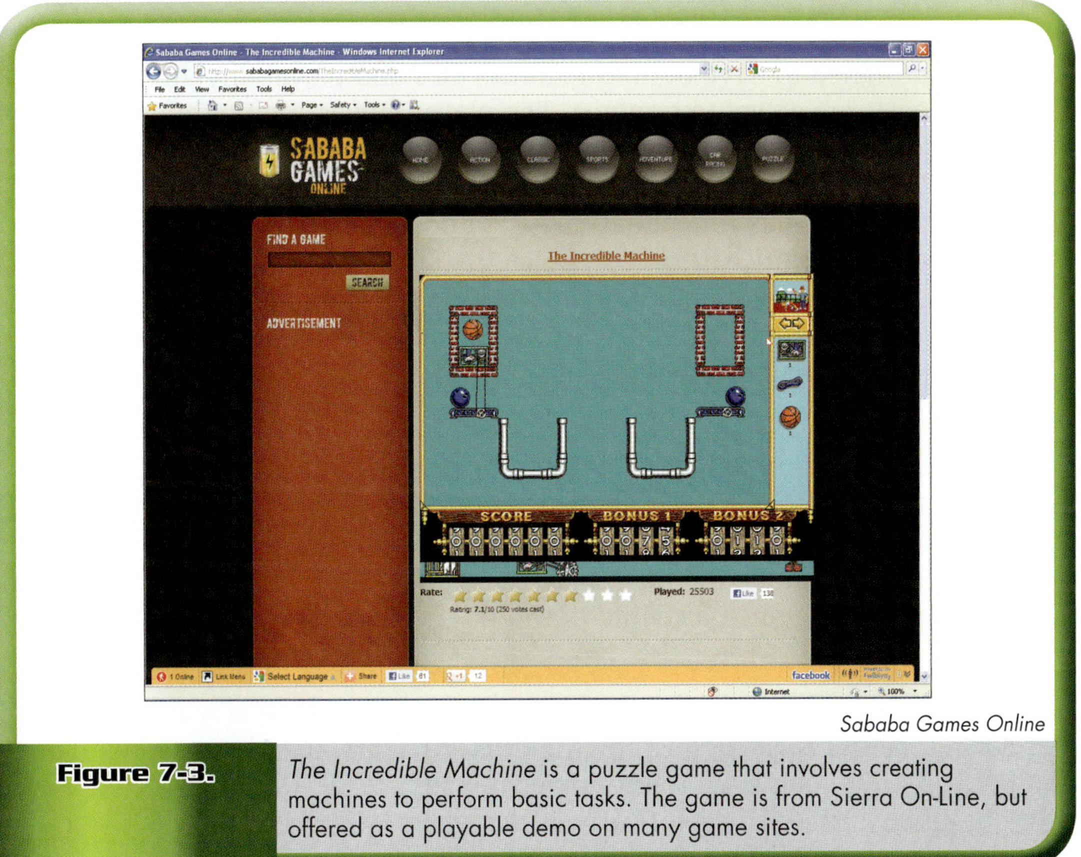

Sababa Games Online

Figure 7-3. *The Incredible Machine* is a puzzle game that involves creating machines to perform basic tasks. The game is from Sierra On-Line, but offered as a playable demo on many game sites.

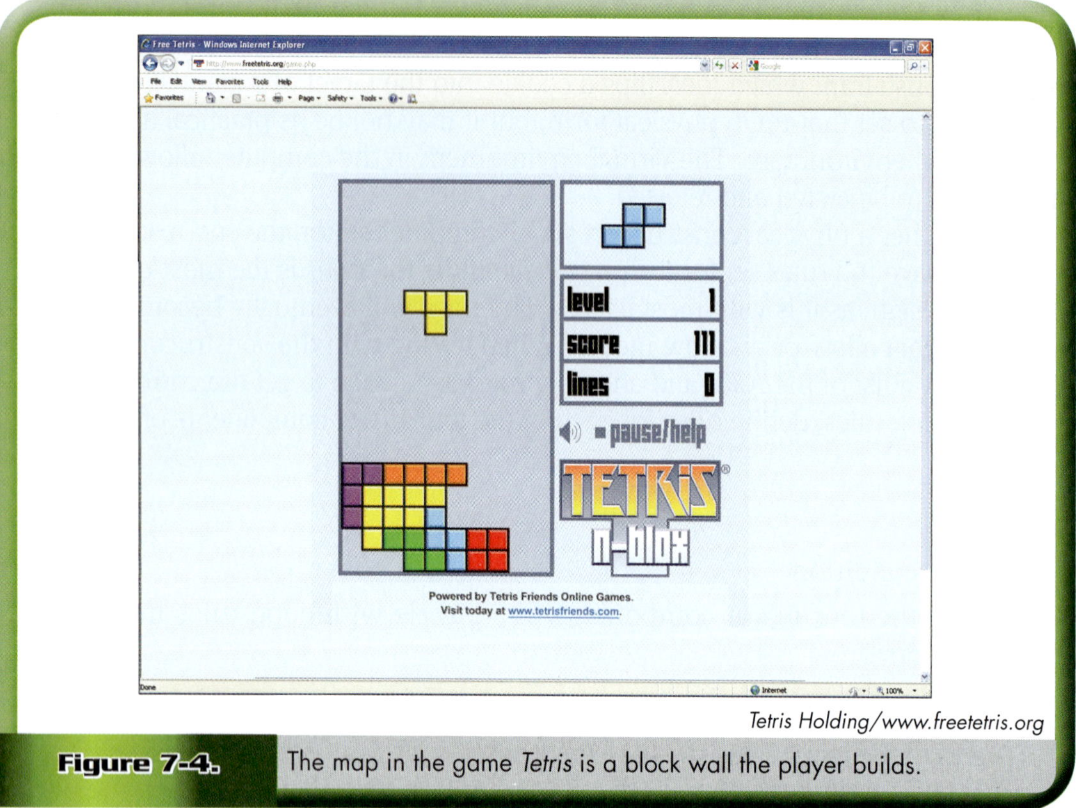

Tetris Holding/www.freetetris.org

Figure 7-4. The map in the game *Tetris* is a block wall the player builds.

Parts

In a puzzle, the ***parts*** are the pieces manipulated in the game. The parts should be designed to have both functional rules and playability attributes. In *Tetris,* the parts are called tetrominos. The player moves each tetromino into position as it moves down the map. ***Functional rules*** control how each part works. In *Tetris,* each part has a unique shape that fits into the stacking puzzle. In chess, each piece has functional rules that define special movements. Each part also has ***playability attributes,*** which help the player to recognize each piece and maneuver it into place. In *Tetris,* each tetromino has a color to help quickly identify it and to better see how it fits in the stack. In chess, each piece has the team color and character design.

Moves

The moves determine how the gameplay proceeds. In *Tetris,* the parts can be rotated and moved left and right as they drop from above. As soon as one part has dropped to the bottom, another part drops from the top so the moves are continuous. In chess, the moves are sequential and turn based. Each player takes a turn to move one piece into position.

Victory Condition

Finally, the puzzle must have a victory condition, which is when the player has solved the puzzle as defined by the rules. In *Tetris,* the player manipulates the parts to form completed rows. The goal is to have all rows be formed without empty spaces so each row will be removed. In chess, the rules state that the game is over when checkmate occurs.

Plan and Document

The initial testing with the construction set or editor fleshes out most of the rules and components needed to assemble and play the puzzle. The next step is to record all of these decisions in the puzzle design specifications document. Just like all other aspects of game design, decisions need to be recorded in design documents so all members of the team can understand how to properly contribute to the project. The ***puzzle design specifications document*** is like a smaller version of the governing game design document (GGDD) discussed in Chapter 1. The puzzle design specifications document for a computerized puzzle consists of seven sections:

- concept: a description of the four major components of the puzzle (map, parts, moves and goal)
- overview: a description of the build constraints, such as audience, platform, interface, competing or similar puzzles, and sophistication of typical player
- art assets: a list of art assets, asset names, quantities, sizes, sketches, and samples or mock-ups
- sound assets: a list of sound assets, asset names, sound functions, and file size limits or other specifications
- story: guidelines story elements, thematic elements, character development, and so on.
- script: details the story and game action
- backstage: porting issues, compatible software versions, deadlines, and workflow requirements

Complete the Level Design

After completing the planning and documentation, it is time to construct an individual puzzle to the first playable milestone. Unless the game is strictly a puzzle unto itself, the larger context of the story must be built into the problem and path to the solution. This is the time to make the puzzle fit the theme of the story. However, this is not the time to begin assembling the larger game. Here, the focus is on a single puzzle component of the game and building it. This is like assembling a sub mission for a game level to later integrate into the complete mission.

The puzzle may be a simple three-digit combination to open a door. If the game is set in ancient Egypt, the art assets must match that theme. This might include stone blocks with geometric shapes or symbols instead of numbers. Similarly, an educational game might require the assembly of an electrical circuit to power a lightbulb. The player might need to gather wire, a battery, and a lightbulb during gameplay, but the puzzle component is a separate gameplay mode. The puzzle component requires the assembly of gathered parts into the working wiring diagram and is not the quest to find the parts.

Variables to the puzzle control the difficulty and skill needed for each level. Changing the speed variable for all obstacles and changing the probability variable for each chance selection are common means of altering difficulty. Each puzzle component and interaction needs to be tuned and tested to fit properly in the correct position in the overall game.

It is important to remember the concept of flow when creating and placing puzzles in a video game. As defined by psychology professor Mihaly Czikszenmihaly, ***flow*** is a state of immersion in the task or activity being undertaken. Flow is

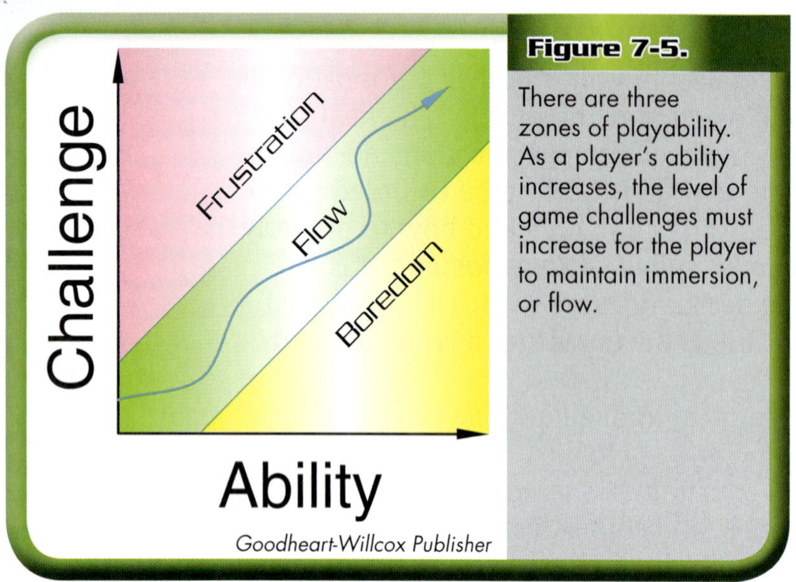

Figure 7-5. There are three zones of playability. As a player's ability increases, the level of game challenges must increase for the player to maintain immersion, or flow.

Goodheart-Willcox Publisher

commonly known as being "in the zone." **Figure 7-5** shows a diagram of flow based on a diagram presented in Czikszenmihaly's book *Flow: The Psychology of Optimal Experience.* The diagram shows three zones of playability: frustration, boredom, and flow. If the player's ability is too low for the challenge, the player is in the frustration zone. If the player's ability is too high for challenge, the player is in the boredom zone. For the player to maintain flow, game challenges must escalate as the player's ability increases.

Integrate Player Aid and Hinting

Even when designing for the typical player, steps need to be taken so those more or less experienced than the typical player can enjoy the game. The designer needs to develop a system to keep the game moving forward. A puzzle may not have a means of gradually increasing player skill. A single-use puzzle may not have variables that can be lessened for different player sophistication. The typical player sophistication may be the only available means of adjusting the puzzle element. The techniques used to adjust elements for varying player sophistication are similar to those used in action games. This involves use of sequencing, hinting, and **self-leveling.** **Figure 7-6** shows a chart of how these three elements can be used in a game.

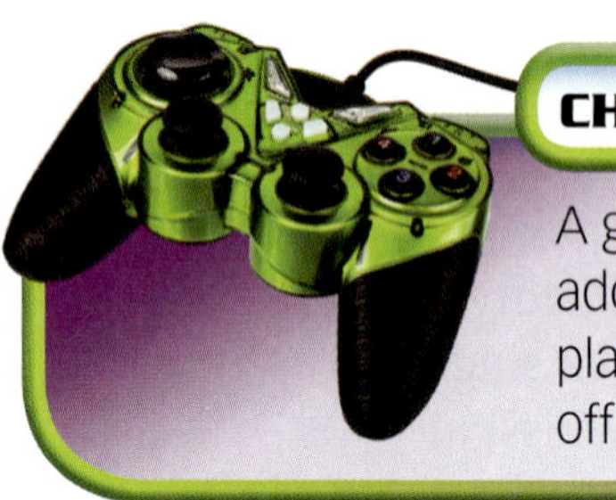

CHEAT CODE: SELF-LEVELING

A game that is self-leveling provides additional help for less-skilled players that can be ignored or turned off by more-skilled players.

Player Aid Techniques

	Before Gameplay	During Gameplay	After Gameplay
Sequencing	Linear structure guides the player through the game from easiest puzzle to most difficult	Branching structure allows player to choose from multiple paths and difficulty	Sandbox structure allows player to complete puzzle in any order of difficulty
Hints	Tutorial, game manual, demo	Navigation aids, camera views, dialogue, inventory	Undo and checkpoints
Self-leveling	Player selects difficulty level for gameplay	Alternate paths, shortcuts, cheat codes	Positioning player score in a ranking

Figure 7-6. Sequencing, hinting, and self-leveling can be applied in different ways in a video game.

Goodheart-Willcox Publisher

Sequencing

Figure 7-7 outlines different ways the puzzles can be sequenced in a video game. Using a linear sequence keeps the player always aligned to the game and moving properly through the designed plan for the game. Using this design is a way to control the sequencing before the game begins. Branching and foldback events allow the player to reverse decisions and choose a harder or easier path. These designs allow the player to control sequencing during gameplay. If the level is a sandbox style, the player can solve individual puzzles in any order. This design allows the player to not only control sequencing, but also go back to uncompleted puzzles after the main gameplay victory condition has been achieved.

The storytelling in the game impacts sequencing of the puzzles. In a linear story, the player must discover the purpose for the puzzle through previous gameplay. Throughout the gameplay, the pieces to the puzzle are gathered or assembled. The solution to the puzzle may be the victory condition of the mission or something that unlocks more gameplay.

An interesting application of a linear or escalating progression is the metapuzzle. A ***metapuzzle*** is a single, large puzzle made up of smaller puzzles. Typically, the player must complete puzzle missions and challenges that form the larger puzzle solution to achieve the victory condition. For example, in a mission the player may need to solve the combination of a door. The reward behind the door is a piece to a larger puzzle, which is the victory condition of the game. In this way, each puzzle mission or sub mission is part of the larger game objective. Sometimes video games that feature minigames require puzzle solutions that provide partial solutions to the larger puzzle. Other metapuzzle games are like a crime scene investigation (CSI) or detective story. The solutions to the smaller puzzles provide the player with clues to the large whodunit puzzle.

	Escalating	Difficulties continuously increase.
	Linear	Puzzle elements are used as the solution to each level in a linear story; each puzzle solution is the conclusion to a level.
	Sawtooth	Pause and relax integration of puzzle elements; puzzle elements may be repeated on each level of the game to move story forward.
	Foldback	Foldback points serve as the linear backbone of the story, while paths between foldback points can be used to provide skill differentiation by offering easy and difficult paths.
	Sandbox	The player can jump between puzzles without any sequential order; players choose the difficulty of their liking.
	Metapuzzle	An ordered collection of puzzles that contribute to a larger puzzle; the larger puzzle is the victory condition of the game.

Figure 7-7. Puzzles can be sequenced in different ways in a video game.

Goodheart-Willcox Publisher

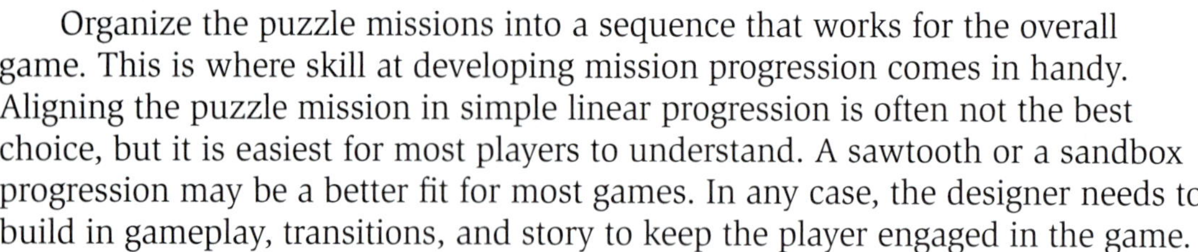

Organize the puzzle missions into a sequence that works for the overall game. This is where skill at developing mission progression comes in handy. Aligning the puzzle mission in simple linear progression is often not the best choice, but it is easiest for most players to understand. A sawtooth or a sandbox progression may be a better fit for most games. In any case, the designer needs to build in gameplay, transitions, and story to keep the player engaged in the game.

Hinting

Instructions, demos, tutorials, or walkthroughs can give the player hints to the gameplay and logic needed to complete the puzzles before he or she begins playing the game. During the game, hints can be provided through overt and covert means. Overt hints include navigation aids, highlighted items, cooperative NPCs, or other interactions that directly communicate the hint. The key is the hint is directly communicated to the player. Covert hints include information overheard in NPC dialogue, camera angle or view, suggestions for tools, or other interactions that help lead the player to the answer without providing the answer.

Most players find covert hints to be more fun. Imagine an adventure game where the player must solve an ancient code to open a pyramid. The player must search the area around the pyramid for artifacts that have ancient symbols. Along the way, the player might talk to a vendor at the local marketplace who knows a riverbank where eerie and mysterious items seem to wash ashore. Or, a letter from a previous explorer might direct the player to a shopkeeper who sells maps to the location of ancient ruins. These are covert hints because they direct the player to the eventual discovery or purchase of the artifacts needed to solve the puzzle. With the quest items in hand, the player can return to the pyramid and press the correct carved images to open the pyramid. The original puzzle idea may have been a simple three-digit-combination puzzle or other means of opening the door. By adding covert clues discovered throughout gameplay, the designer creates a story and motivation for the character.

It is not easy to design covert hints. The player should be mentally engaged to find the solution, but flow also needs to be maintained. If the player does not find the answer within the first few attempts or within a reasonable amount of time, he or she will quickly lose flow and end up in the frustration zone. For example, the game may be programmed to track the number of times a puzzle has been attempted. On the first attempt, the player may not be offered any hints. On each later attempt, increasing hints may be provided. On the second attempt, the area where the solution is located may be the focus of the camera. On the third attempt, not only is the camera focused on that area, the solution is highlighted.

The undo and checkpoint functions in a video game can be thought of as a means of providing hinting after gameplay. Both allow the player to attempt the puzzle, or complete the gameplay, and then try it again if unsuccessful. By learning from previous mistakes, the player can eventually solve the puzzle. Undo is reversing the last action. A checkpoint is a saved point, either automatic or manual, that can be loaded to return the player to a previous point in the game. Both may be needed depending on gameplay. These are also very important human-computer interface (HCI) attributes.

Self-Leveling

A game can be self-leveling before gameplay starts by allowing the player to select a difficulty setting. In most games, players can select easy, medium, or hard levels. Selecting a difficulty setting determines the skill attributes of the game. Puzzles are inserted in the game to best match the selected difficulty.

During gameplay, difficulty can be adjusted using programming that compares the player's actions against a standardized set of action metrics. The programming can adjust the puzzles and obstacles to better match the player's changing abilities. Diverting the player to a different story branch or automatically leveling up or down are covert methods of dealing with player skill that does not match the metrics needed for the level. Overtly, the game could display a message telling the player the puzzle was solved quickly or slowly and suggesting a more appropriate skill level. Overt self-leveling tends to break immersion, but may be needed in some cases.

The multiple pathways in a foldback story allow the player to select a more difficult mission. The path may be shorter, but the puzzles may be more difficult. A longer pathway may have many easier puzzles. In this way, the player can reverse the decision and backtrack to the easier pathways if stuck. The problem with this type of design is many items must be created, and most of them will not be used. That is both time-consuming and expensive.

After completion of a puzzle or level, scoring can identify accuracy. Instead of a simple win-loss resolution, the score could measure the time or number of clicks needed to solve the puzzle. Or, the player's progress or score can be placed in a status list ranked with other possible status results, as shown in **Figure 7-8.** The player can be a winner without a perfect solution. This will challenge the player to do better and master the puzzle.

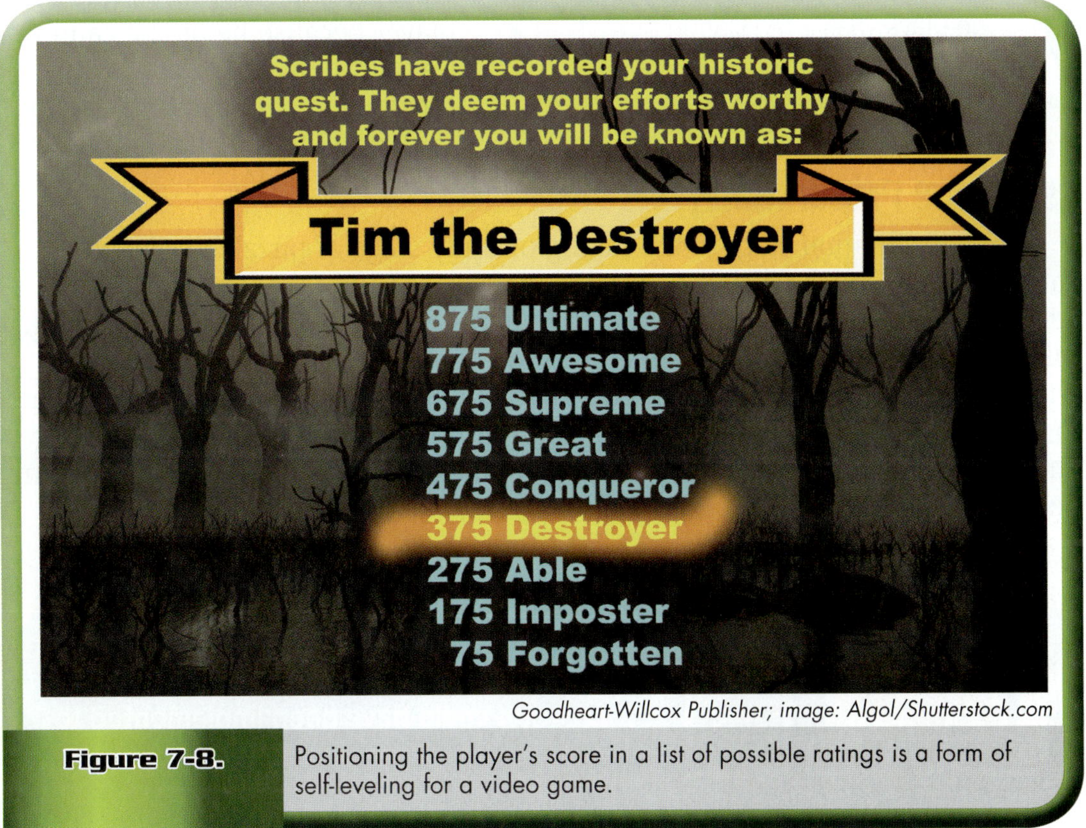

Goodheart-Willcox Publisher; image: Algol/Shutterstock.com

Figure 7-8. Positioning the player's score in a list of possible ratings is a form of self-leveling for a video game.

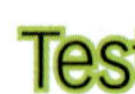

Test

With the individual puzzle element built, it must be tested to make sure it fits the needs of the game and audience. Just as the overall game is beta tested, the puzzles within the game need to be beta tested. It is a good idea to do this testing before the puzzle mission is inserted into the larger game. Test the concept of the puzzle to see if it fits the main idea and if the audience understands what they must do to solve the puzzle. Test the aesthetics of the puzzle to see if the graphics are acceptable and that the pieces can be identified.

Test the functionality of the game to make sure the target audience can find the solution. Be sure all of the rules are enforced. Also, determine if there are solutions to the puzzle other than the intended solution. Test for the actual victory condition and not your expected path to the solution. Players are ingenious at finding solutions the designer never anticipated. For example, if the victory condition is escaping a cage, then test the position of the player character in relation to the cage, not if the cage door is open. Maybe the player found a way of squeezing through the bars or dug a tunnel under the doorway. Fix any bugs, but it may be okay to allow for solutions other than what the designer originally intended.

Finally, test for replay value. The puzzle should have enough replay value to keep the typical player interested in as many attempts as it takes to find the solution to the puzzle. At some point during the thought process of solving the puzzle, the player should experience an **aha moment**. Randomizing the solution is often a poor means of adding replay value. Doing so can frustrate the player because he or she cannot learn from mistakes made in previous attempts and, therefore, cannot get to the aha moment.

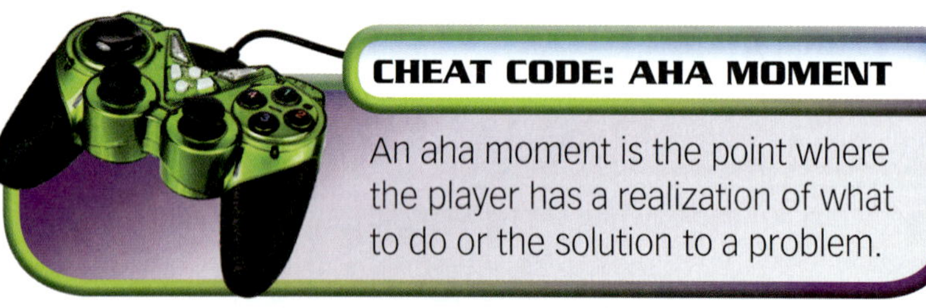

Refine the Presentation

The presentation stage is the tuning or unity stage of puzzle design. All game elements, such as sound, animation, scoring, and user interface, are added to the puzzle. For example, if the puzzle is to create an electrical circuit, this is the stage where the designer will add an electrical zapping sound for when the switch is turned on and animate the lightbulb to glow. Take your time to expertly integrate all game elements and make a complete game. All timing and gameplay of the puzzle needs to be complete before taking care of the extra details for a great game presentation.

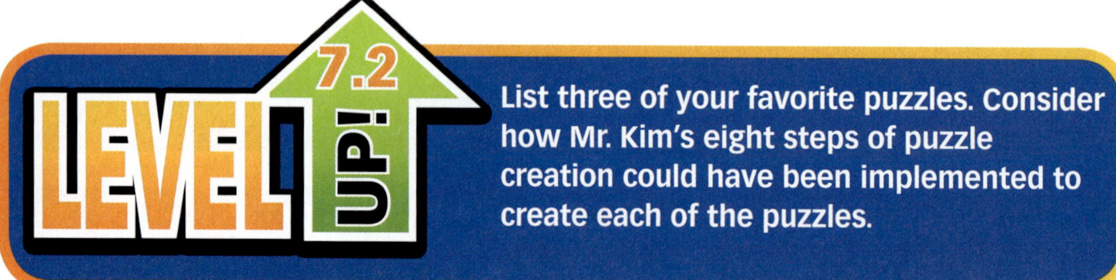

Types of Puzzles

The puzzle genre of video games can be separated into five main themes:

- guessing game
- logic puzzle
- mechanical puzzle
- transport puzzle
- word puzzle

Each theme may have multiple variations. While this is not a universal segmentation of the puzzle genre, it covers the majority of applications within the genre.

Guessing Game

Guessing games are high risk as the player takes a blind guess as the first step in the solution. Look at the classic word game *Snowman*. The player starts the game knowing only the number of letters composing each word in the puzzle. The player must take a guess as to a letter that may be in one of the words. If the player guesses wrong, a large snowball is added as the bottom of the snowman. The player then takes another guess. If correct, the letter is placed in the puzzle, but if wrong another snowball is added to the snowman. Based on letter positioning and the length of the word, the player builds confidence as the parts to the puzzle are filled in with guesses.

Another guessing game is *Battleship*. The player takes a guess at where a hidden ship is located on a grid, as shown in **Figure 7-9.** If the player guesses

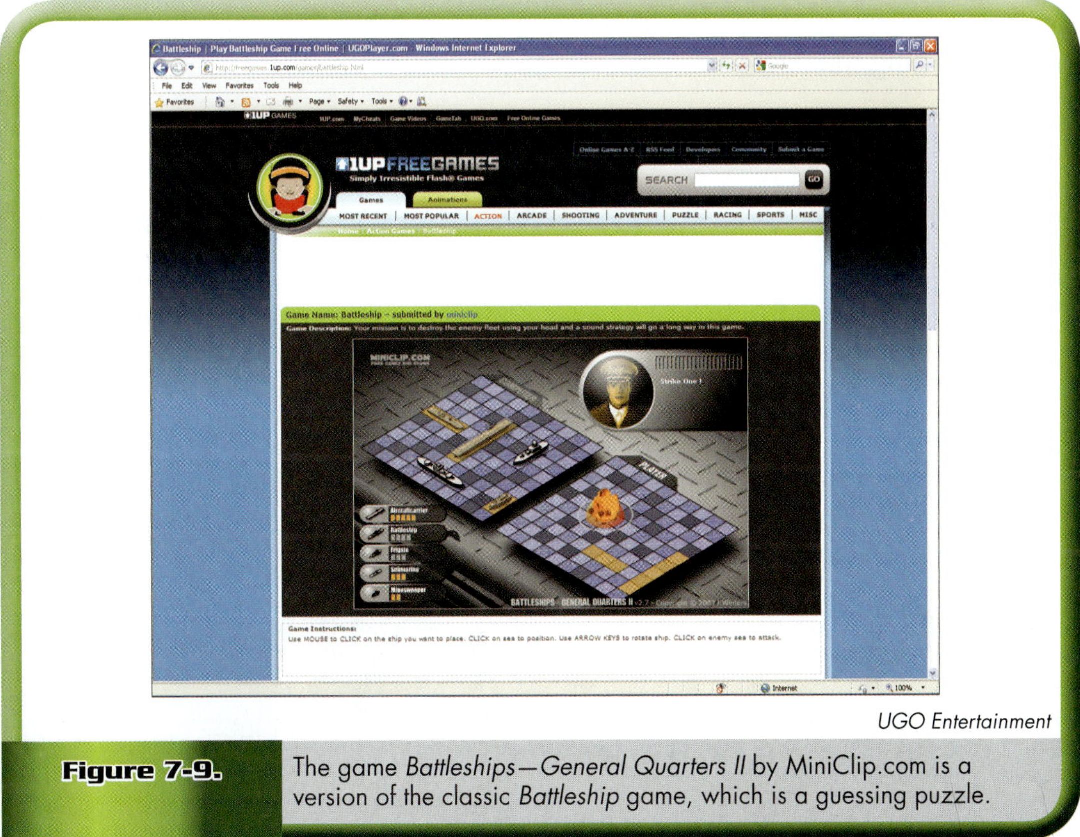

UGO Entertainment

Figure 7-9. The game *Battleships—General Quarters II* by MiniClip.com is a version of the classic *Battleship* game, which is a guessing puzzle.

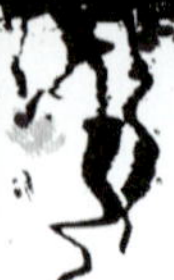

correctly, a part of the ship is revealed as a hit. Since the ship is positioned in a straight line, the player can then make a better guess as to the next hit location. When a ship is hit a certain number of times, it sinks. The first player to sink all of the opponent's ships wins the game.

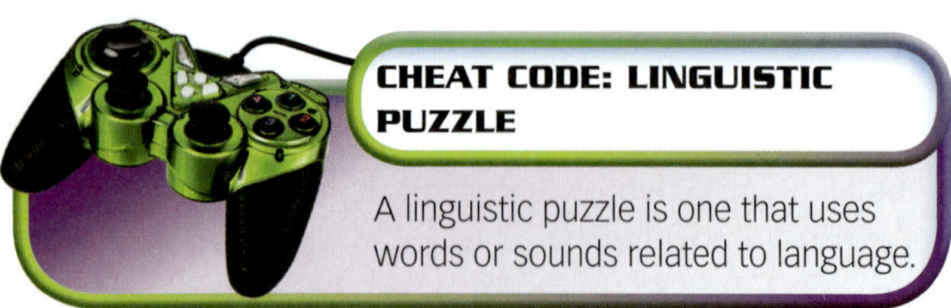

CHEAT CODE: LINGUISTIC PUZZLE

A linguistic puzzle is one that uses words or sounds related to language.

There are two major variations on the guessing game theme: riddles and situation puzzles. ***Riddles*** are **linguistic puzzles** solved with wit and skill. These puzzles often use tricks like double entendres and homophones to mislead the player and hide the solution. A double entendre is a phrase or word that can have more than one meaning. A homophone is a word that sounds like another word. An example of this would be the character names Miss Turkey (mis-tur-key) or Mister Key (mis-tur-key). Both are spoken the same, but have clearly different references. The same effect is created with a rebus puzzle. A ***rebus puzzle*** is a picture puzzle that contains pictures that when combined sound like a word. **Figure 7-10** shows two rebus puzzles.

In a ***situational puzzle,*** or lateral-thinking puzzle, the player must find the solution to a riddle by looking at the puzzle from a different and often obscure angle. *Lateral thinking* describes the process of thinking along a different line to find the solution. This type of puzzle begins by describing to the player a specific situation or set of events. Next, the player can ask a limited number of questions that can only be answered yes or no. Based on the initial information and the answers to the questions, the player must use lateral thinking to solve the puzzle. The popular games of *Mind Trap* and *Brain Camp* use situational, or lateral-thinking, puzzles.

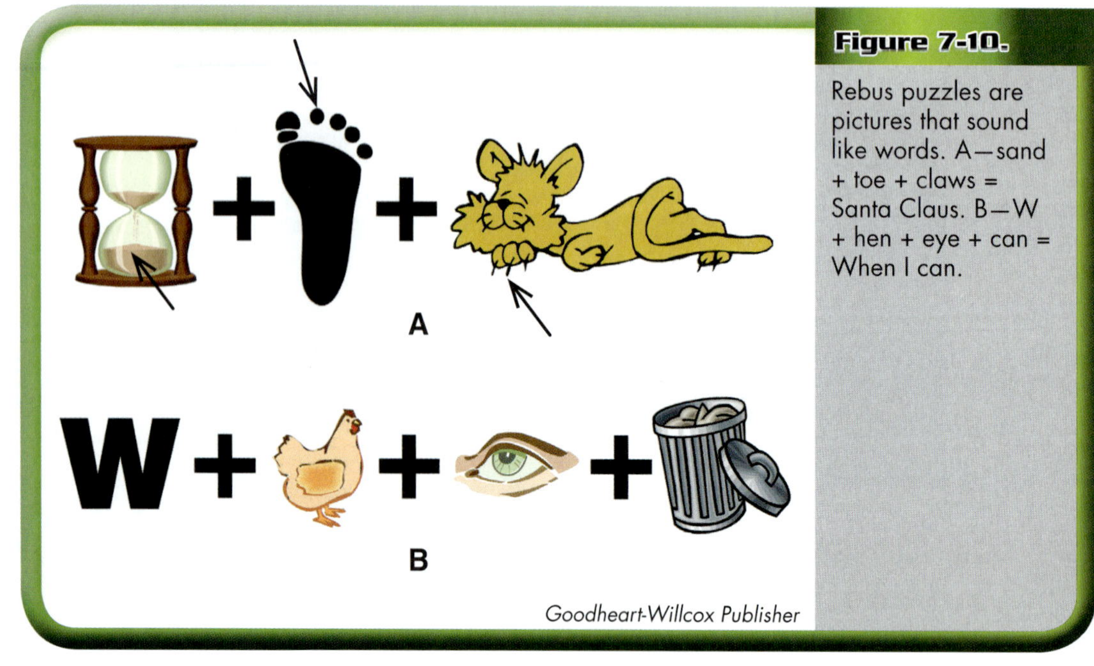

Figure 7-10. Rebus puzzles are pictures that sound like words. A—sand + toe + claws = Santa Claus. B—W + hen + eye + can = When I can.

CASE STUDY

Situational Puzzles

Situation: A man fell from the roof of a tall building. He fell 70 floors and is alive and unharmed.

Puzzle: How is he still alive after falling that far?

Questions:
Did he have a parachute? No.
Did he hit anything while going down? No.
Is he freefalling? Yes.
Does he require medical attention? No.
Is he still falling? Yes.

Answer: The building is taller than 70 stories.

Situation: A girl fell out of a window of a 20-story building and hit the ground. She is alive and unharmed.

Puzzle: How is this possible?

Questions:
Is she still falling? No.
Did she have a parachute? No.
Did she hit anything while going down? No.
Was the window on the top floor? No.

Answer: She fell out of a first-story window.

Logic Puzzle

Closely related to a situational or lateral-thinking puzzle is a logic puzzle. In a ***logic puzzle,*** the player applies reasoning to determine the correct answer. These puzzles are commonly used as tests, such as the law school admissions test (LSAT) and other similar admissions tests. There are many types of logic puzzles, but most fit into a four main categories: dissection, induction, logic grid, and recursive or self-reference.

Dissection Puzzle

The object of a ***dissection puzzle*** is to take a geometric shape that has been cut into a certain number of pieces and reassemble the shape. This type of puzzle may be used in math classes to teach geometry and logical thinking. These puzzles come in both 2D and 3D varieties. A twist to this type of puzzle is to also fit the pieces together to build a specific shape. The tangram shown in **Figure 7-11** is an example of this. Dissection puzzles may also be known as transformation or Richter puzzles.

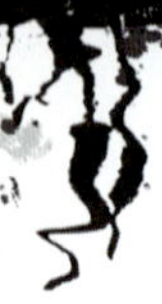

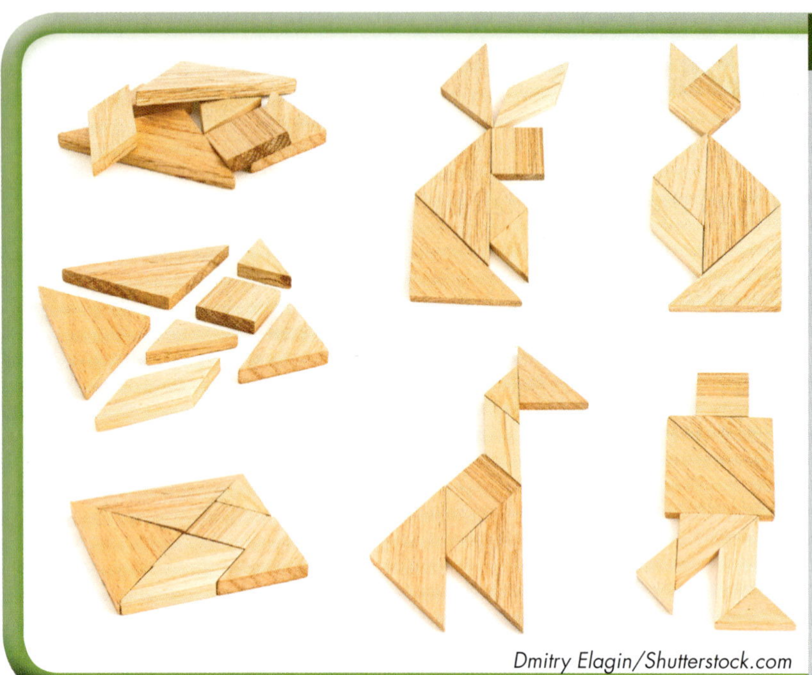

Figure 7-11. A tangram is a type of dissection puzzle. The pieces of the puzzle form a square, but can be used to create different shapes as well.

Dmitry Elagin/Shutterstock.com

Induction Puzzle

An ***induction puzzle*** requires deductive reasoning from a limited amount of information about the opponents with no information about the player. The solutions to most induction puzzles involve reading and interpreting the actions of others. The puzzle may have a few solutions based on the action or inaction of the other players. The **Nash equilibrium** is applied to game theory to determine how much benefit members of a group would receive from cooperation or competition. Since the choices of all participants help determine the outcome, sometimes it is better to cooperate than compete. The Nash equilibrium can be clearly seen in the possible actions of the Organization of Petroleum Exporting Countries (OPEC). Suppose OPEC group has set the price of oil at $100 a barrel. If one county defects from OPEC and charges $10 less per barrel, more people will buy oil from that country. This seems like a good move to sell more and make more money. But, the other countries in OPEC do not want to lose customers, so they immediately match the price drop. Now all countries are getting less money for their oil. Since they all lose when one country defects and acts separately, they all make more money through cooperation and maintaining the same price.

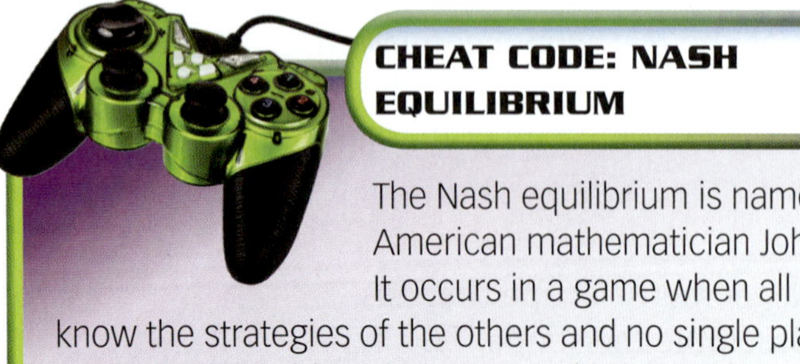

CHEAT CODE: NASH EQUILIBRIUM

The Nash equilibrium is named after American mathematician John Nash. It occurs in a game when all players know the strategies of the others and no single player can gain when only his or her strategy is changed.

Logic-Grid Puzzle

In a ***logic-grid puzzle,*** the player is given certain clues to the solution, which the player then organizes into a grid to determine the solution. Many detective scenarios use logic puzzles to determine who committed the crime. The grid helps organize the different pieces of information. The basis of this puzzle is the process of elimination. If all other parts are accounted for, then the item unaccounted for must be the answer. In many cases, the initial question contains very important information about the solution. Without the question, the player would not be able to figure out the solution to the puzzle.

Readers of the novel *Harry Potter and the Sorcerer's Stone* saw a logic-grid puzzle when Harry and Hermione must find the bottles that contain magic potions. The most famous logic-grid puzzle is the *Zebra Puzzle*, or *Einstein's Puzzle*. A very simplified version of that puzzle type is shown in **Figure 7-12.** Notice how the process of elimination is applied and mapped out in the logic grid. Additionally, note that without the information from the question, the options for milk and German would not have been available. The answer is derived from the given information and the question.

Situation

1. There are three houses next to each other and only one of the houses is yellow.
2. The third house is red.
3. The Italian lives directly to the right of the water drinking person.
4. The Italian drinks juice.
5. There is one house between the brown house and the house the Spaniard lives in.

Puzzle

What color is the German's house?
Who drinks milk?

Solution

A grid is used to organize the information and find the solution.

		House 1	House 2	House 3
Colors	red			X
	brown	X		
	yellow		X	
Drink	water	X		
	juice		X	
	milk			X
Nationality	Italian		X	
	Spaniard			X
	German	X		

Goodheart-Willcox Publisher

Figure 7-12. Using the grid, the solution to the puzzle is that the German lives in the first house, which is brown, and the Spaniard drinks milk.

Recursive Puzzle or Self-Reference Puzzle

A ***recursive puzzle*** or ***self-reference puzzle*** is one that contains the solution as part of the puzzle. These are mostly used as numerical solutions, but may also be created using words. Recursive puzzles are a little tricky and best shown through an example:

There are _____ Es in this sentence.

The solution is recursive since it is part of the solution set. Recursion is used in computer programming to create smaller equations or methods. ***Recursion*** is when a method calls itself as part of the solution.

The above example is complicated even more since the answer could be written as a number or expressed longhand. If the number 7 is written in the blank, it is the correct answer. However, if the word seven is written in the blank, that would actually make the answer nine Es, so seven is incorrect. If nine is written in the blank, the answer becomes eight. If eight is written in the blank, the answer is eight. However, if the number 8 is written in the blank, it is incorrect.

In a recursive solution, the answer can vary based on any changes to the original statement. Sometimes this results in *circular logic* where the solution keeps changing the statement, which, in turn, changes the solution. Circular logic in a computer program causes the computer to freeze. The computer will continue to work the problem forever.

CASE STUDY

Prisoner's Dilemma

The *Prisoner's Dilemma* is a classic logic puzzle. Logic puzzles have practical applications outside of games. Look at the following scenario.

Situation: The police have arrested two suspects and taken them to separate rooms. The police do not have enough evidence to convict anyone for the murder and need information from the suspects to build the case. If one suspect testifies against the other, the police will have enough information to convict the other suspect and close the case. Currently, the police only have enough evidence to put each suspect in jail for one year on a lesser charge.

Puzzle: The police offer each suspect a deal, that testifying against the other suspect will result in a one-year sentence instead of spending 15 years in prison. The choice will remain hidden from the other suspect until the investigation is completed.

Solution 1: One suspect takes the deal and receives a one-year prison sentence. The other receives a 15-year prison sentence.

Solution 2: Both suspects refuse the deal and each receives a one-year prison sentence.

Solution 3: Both suspects take the deal and each receives a 15-year prison sentence.

You are one of the suspects and do not know if your partner will cooperate. What would you do?

Mechanical Puzzle

A ***mechanical puzzle*** is solved by physically linking, unlinking, or maneuvering pieces. Many puzzles of this type are used in illusions where something like a set of metal rings can be joined or separated by the magician. Once these puzzles are solved, the player has little desire to replay the puzzle or even reassemble it for others to disassemble. A mechanical puzzle can be simulated in a video game, but the simulation is not technically a mechanical puzzle.

Common types of mechanical puzzles are disentanglement, assembly, disassembly, folding, locking, and sequential movement. A locking puzzle is shown in **Figure 7-13.** The Rubik's Cube is a sequential-movement puzzle. It requires a sequential set of steps called an algorithm to solve the puzzle. Regardless of how the cube is scrambled, the algorithm will solve the cube.

Mechanical puzzles can involve many feats of physical dexterity, trial and error, and visualization in three dimensions. In video game design, simulations of mechanical puzzles are not bound by the laws of nature. Since the virtual world can allow unrealistic moves, mechanical puzzles are a hard sell to game players. The puzzles should make use of the alternate reality provided by the gaming environment. For example, to solve a mechanical puzzle, maybe the player must take a simple wooden torch underwater to burn through a rope. That task obviously cannot be completed in the real world. But, if the rules of the game environment allow that action, the player may expect to be able to complete the task.

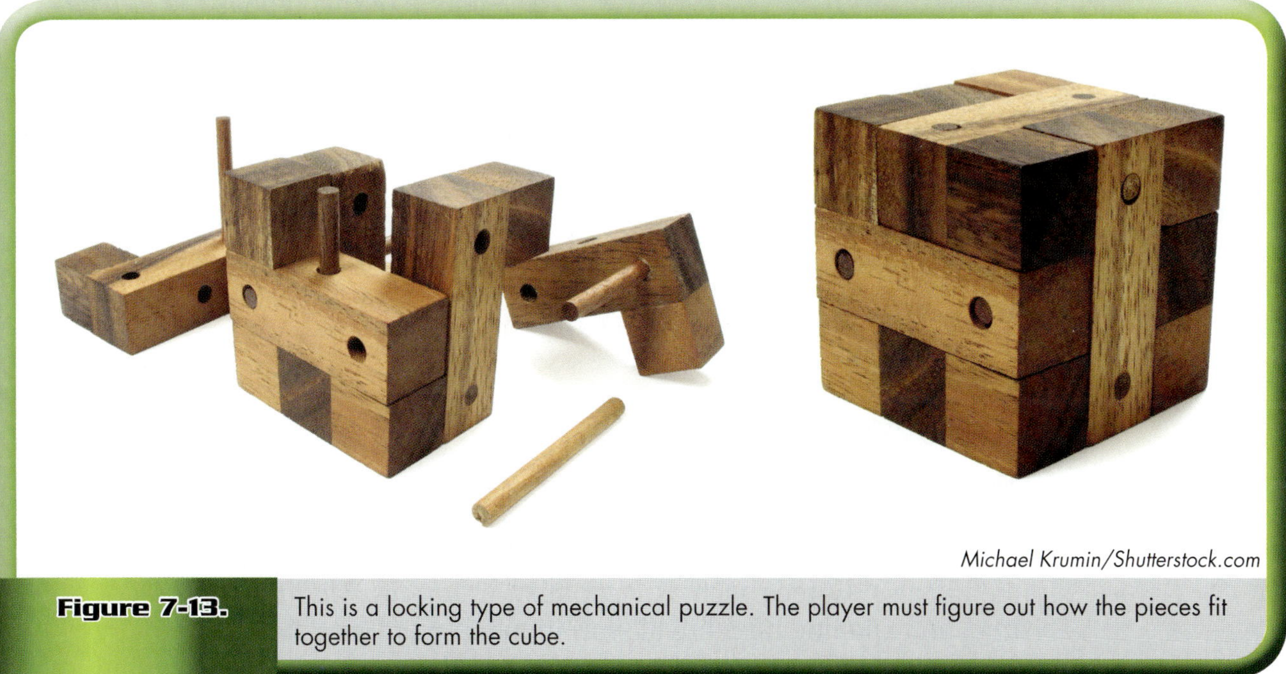

Michael Krumin/Shutterstock.com

Figure 7-13. This is a locking type of mechanical puzzle. The player must figure out how the pieces fit together to form the cube.

Transport Puzzle

A type of puzzle that is popular in video games is the transport puzzle. ***Transport puzzles*** require the player to move pieces within the confined space of the game board. No pieces are removed, but they can be rearranged to create a clear path or sequential arrangement. The most common form of a transport puzzle is a simple maze. By drawing the correct path from start to finish, the puzzle is solved.

A variation of the simple maze puzzle requires the player to move, spin, or otherwise position objects such as walls, tunnels, or bridges to reorganize the maze environment. This was very popular in the video games *Pipe Dreams* (or *Pipe Mania*) and *Lemmings.* A variant of *Pipe Dreams* was used in *BioShock.*

A logic maze is another variation of the simple maze. A ***logic maze*** is a simple maze with some additional rule to increase the difficulty. A marble maze that requires the player to tilt the iPad to move the marble through the maze is an example. Other logic mazes might contain numbered tiles. The player must solve the math problem or other problem that shows the solution to the correct path. Microsoft Windows contains the game *Minesweeper,* which is this type of maze. The player uses probability to solve a path through a minefield.

Sliding puzzles that require the player to move and arrange the puzzle into the correct pattern are popular adaptations from physical to video games. The most popular game of this type is the *Fifteen* puzzle, as shown in **Figure 7-14.** The player must unscramble the numbered tiles and put them in order. The pieces can slide within the game board, but not be removed. A common variation of this puzzle is created by placing a picture on the tiles instead of numbers. The player must arrange the tiles to assemble the picture.

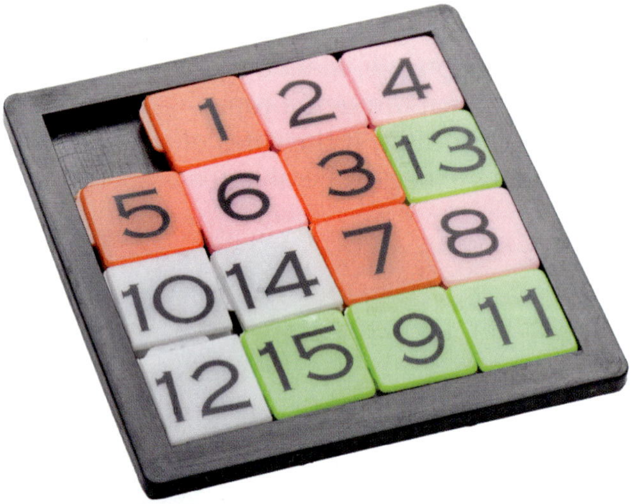

Ugorenkov Aleksandr/Shutterstock.com

Figure 7-14. The *Fifteen* game is a transport puzzle in which the player must slide the numbered pieces to arrange them in sequence from 1 through 15.

Word Puzzle

Word puzzles are constructed of written or spoken words. Crossword puzzles, word searches, and word jumbles are common applications of creating or finding word patterns. However, word puzzles are far broader than these simple puzzles. Games such as *Pictionary, Charades, Mad Libs, Wheel of Fortune,* and spelling bees are all variations of word puzzles.

Word puzzles can be found in video games that have code words within gameplay. Other games in the educational/edutainment genre are specifically designed to train the player on spelling, synonyms, nouns, and other uses for words.

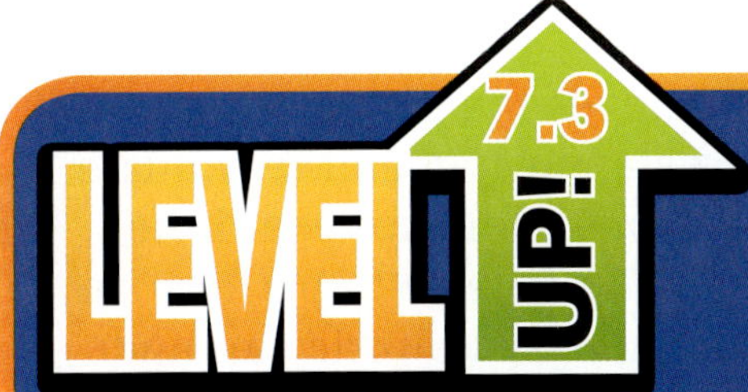

Identify your two favorite types of puzzle. Think of a new puzzle that you could create for each of the two types.

Computerized Puzzles

Creating a computer-based puzzle game allows many improvements over traditional puzzle games. Even if the computer puzzle is a simple electronic version of a traditional puzzle, the computerized version may have many benefits. Benefits include:

- application of rules;
- reversal of actions;
- randomizing and leveling;
- instant feedback and rewards;
- multimedia;
- dangerous and impossible moves; and
- competition and collaboration.

Many of these benefits align with the eight golden rules of human-computer interface design discussed in Chapter 4. They are each described in greater detail in the next sections.

Application of Rules

The computer enforces the rules to keep the player from cheating. A computer will always enforce the rules, while a traditional puzzle requires the player to self-enforce the rules. Some players become frustrated trying to solve a Rubik's Cube puzzle. It would be easy to simply take off the stickers and rearrange them on the correct face of the cube. The cube is in the victory condition, but the player has cheated by not following the rules. A similar computerized puzzle would not allow the player to cheat in this manner.

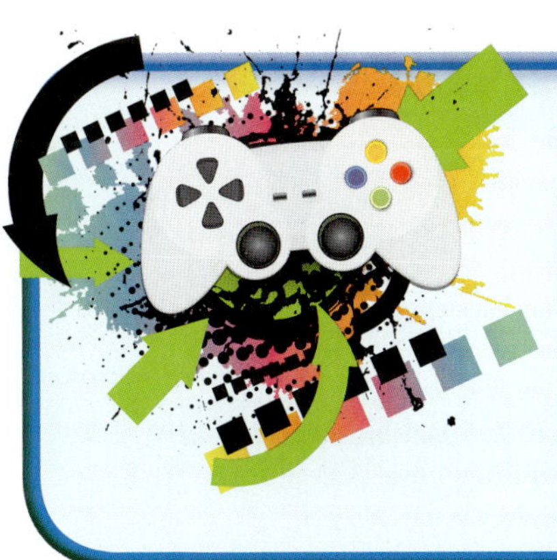

Ethical Gamer

Cheating is unethical. It places other players at an unfair disadvantage. Cheat codes can be found for most video games, but using them to defeat the game is unethical when playing with others. Even when playing a game as a single player, using a cheat code to defeat the game is not *really* defeating the game.

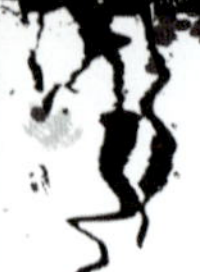

Reversal of Actions

Computerized puzzles can store all of the moves the player makes. This allows the player the opportunity to go back a step or two and reevaluate choices. In many physical puzzles, the player would need to record the moves on a sheet of paper and then do the steps in reverse to perform an undo. With a simple click, the player of a computerized puzzle can undo and redo moves. This allows the player less risk when solving through trial and error. For example, when solving the Rubik's Cube, it would be a great benefit to have the ability to undo a few moves when the player realizes an error was made.

Randomizing and Leveling

A computerized puzzle can be refreshed as a completely different puzzle or even set as easy, intermediate, or difficult. This would be like resetting the gems in a game of *Bejeweled,* which is shown in **Figure 7-15.** Randomizing allows for a game that is easy to learn and involves simple mechanics. A physical puzzle often has a solution set of only one solution.

Instant Feedback and Rewards

A computerized puzzle can display hints and tutorials when the player moves in the wrong direction. A physical puzzle cannot do this. Additionally, the game software can lock parts of the puzzle when correct or

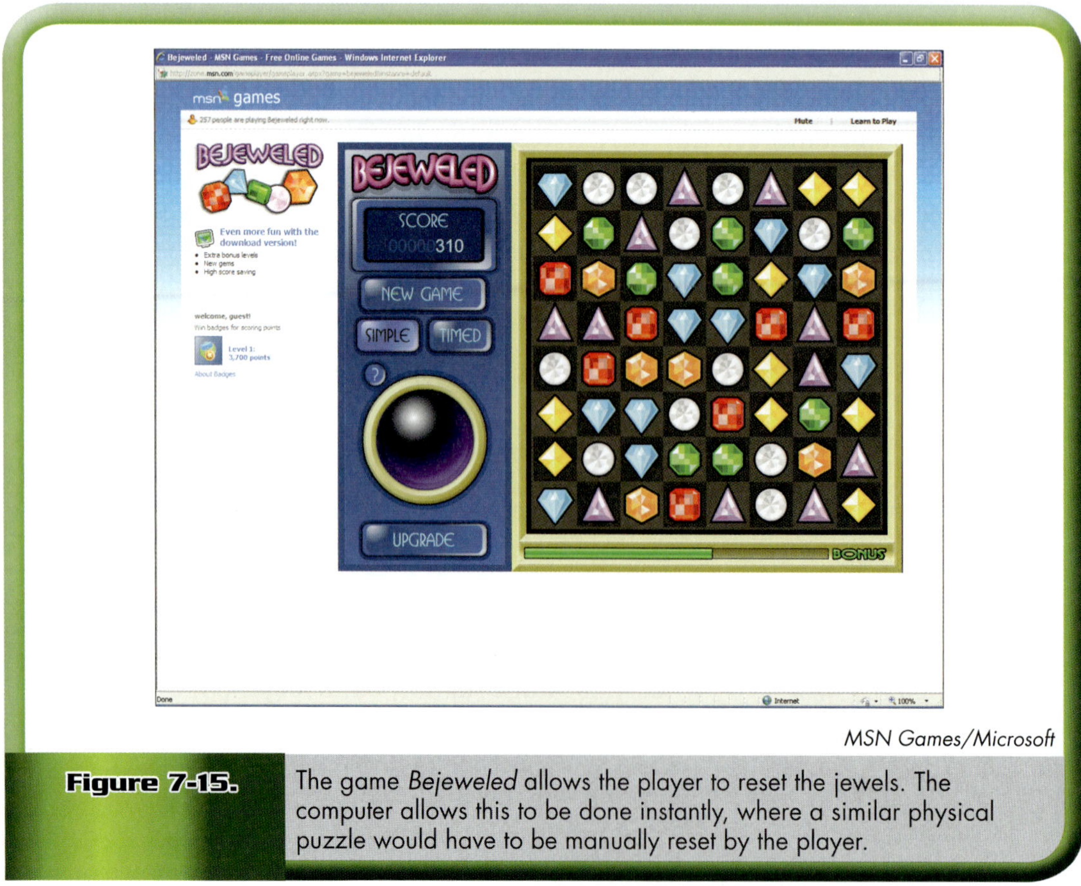

MSN Games/Microsoft

Figure 7-15. The game *Bejeweled* allows the player to reset the jewels. The computer allows this to be done instantly, where a similar physical puzzle would have to be manually reset by the player.

use animation, color, or sound to show a correct move. In the video game *Tetris,* the filled row blinks and a sound is played to show that a bonus has been applied.

Complex metapuzzles can be structured with a reward component to build a story and larger puzzle elements. In the video game *I Spy Spooky Mansion,* hidden images in the puzzle glow and are animated when properly selected. Also, the riddle changes color to indicate that portion has been solved. Furthermore, the player solves hidden-image puzzles to earn a puzzle piece that will solve the metapuzzle needed to exit the spooky mansion. The reward from each puzzle within the game would not be available in the I Spy book on which the game is based.

Multimedia

A computerized puzzle can use sound, animation, color change, and more to make the game experience better for the player. The video game *I Spy Spooky Mansion* has multimedia effects that are not present in the printed book. A voice-over narration gives directions and reads the riddles. In the game *Dr. Seuss' The Lorax Marshmallow Munch,* shown in **Figure 7-16,** the puzzle includes animations and sounds when the player breaks a piece of wood or glass to make the marshmallow fall. These elements add to the fun and immersion in the game and would not be available in a physical puzzle.

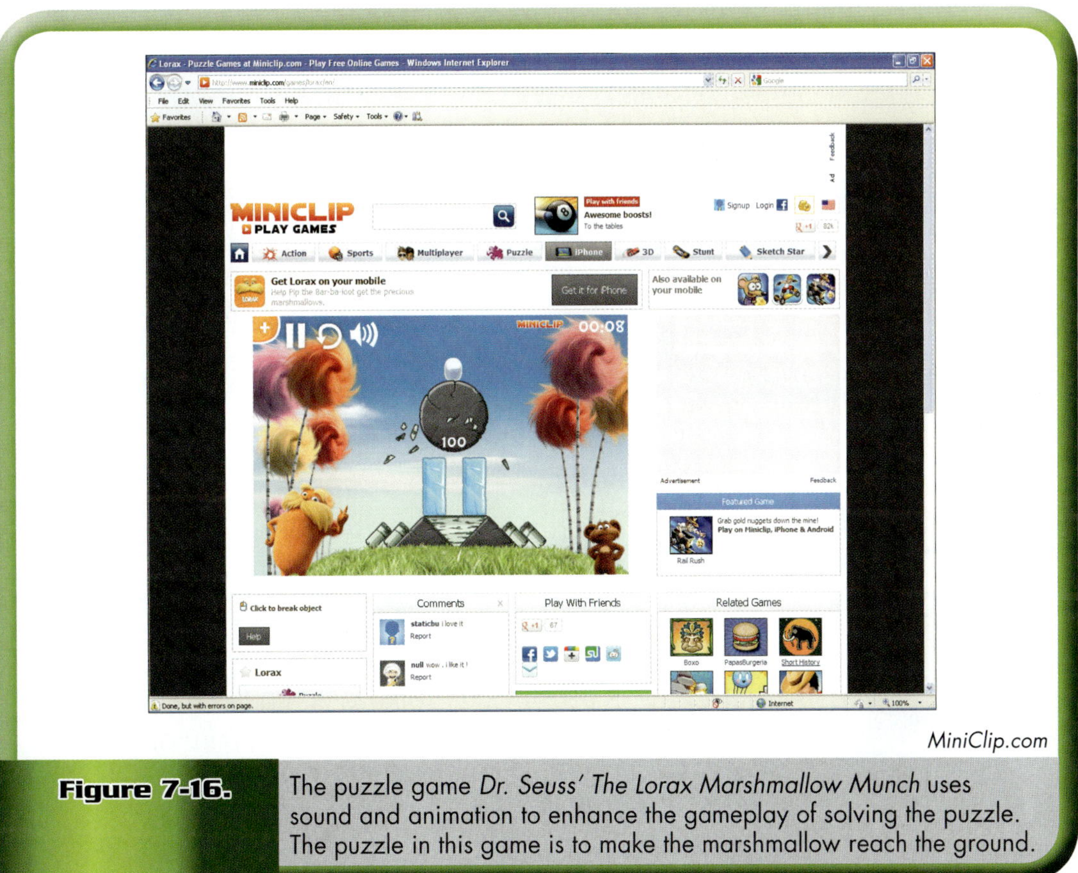

MiniClip.com

Figure 7-16. The puzzle game *Dr. Seuss' The Lorax Marshmallow Munch* uses sound and animation to enhance the gameplay of solving the puzzle. The puzzle in this game is to make the marshmallow reach the ground.

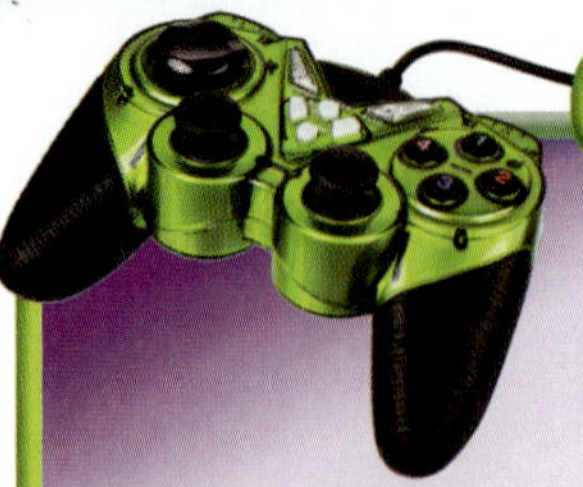

CHEAT CODE: SHOCK WAVE

A shock wave is the pulse of energy moving through a medium as the result of a shock, explosion, earthquake, and so on. For example, the shockwave of an explosion can shatter windows outside of the blast zone.

Dangerous and Impossible Moves

A computerized puzzle can allow moves that cannot exist in a physical puzzle. Moves that require dangerous actions, like riding the **shock wave** of an explosion, are safely done in a video game. Additionally, changes to the puzzle such as loss of gravity, rotating the entire world, lighting the path, color changes, or even removal of a layer such as occurs in *Tetris* are easy to do in computerized puzzles, but hard or impossible to do in the physical world. Imagine a video game containing a puzzle that the player must solve to defuse a bomb. If the player gets it wrong, a checkpoint can be reloaded. In the real world, one mistake means the bomb explodes—without a chance to do over.

Competition and Collaboration

A computerized puzzle can provide competition by posting a leader board with the fastest times or even a real-time online event. Players can compare results or compete as a team in an online competition. Using on online connection, players can work together to build the solution. In the social media video game *Farmtown,* players can even send their friends a tree, plant, or other game asset they might need. Players can also exchange game assets, as in the game *Pokémon.* Many online scavenger hunt–style riddles and puzzles use a team to find the missing items. These teams are also competing against other online teams.

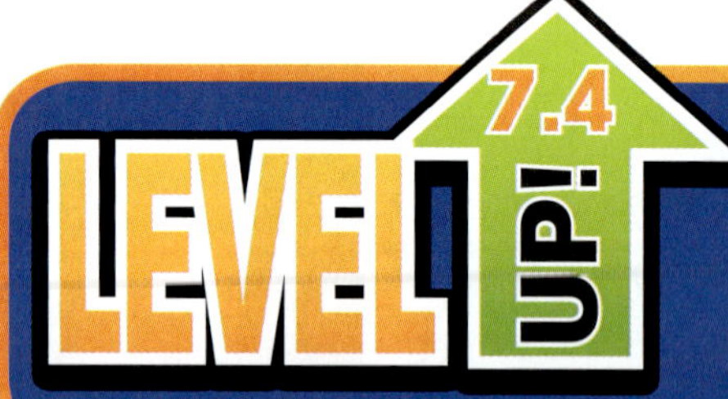

List five video games that have puzzles within the gameplay. For each game, identify the type of puzzle and explain how the puzzle is part of the gameplay.

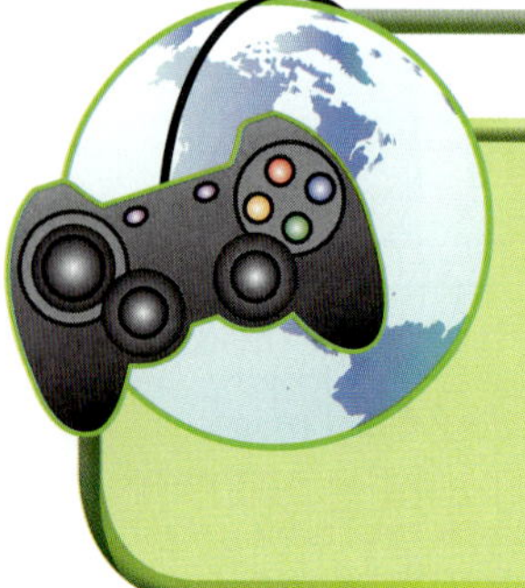

Green Gamer

It is a common practice in Europe to unplug equipment that is not in use, including lights, computers, and gaming devices. Up to 25 percent can be saved on energy costs by just turning off and unplugging equipment at the end of the day. Less energy usage also reduces negative effects on the environment.

Chapter Summary

- Adding puzzles as objectives in a story can enhance a video game by adding greater purpose of play and help the player engage in thinking while applying the navigational and action-based skill of gameplay.
- The eight key steps to puzzle design are: be inspired, simplify, build with a construction set or an editor, plan and document, complete the level design, integrate player aid and hinting, test, and refine presentation.
- The five main themes within the puzzle genre are guessing games, logic puzzles, mechanical puzzles, transport puzzles, and word puzzles.
- Computer puzzles have many benefits over traditional puzzles, including: application of rules, reversal of actions, randomizing and leveling, instant feedback and rewards, and competition and collaboration.

Check Your Video Game IQ

Now that you have finished this chapter, see what you know about video game design by taking the chapter posttest.

www.m.g-wlearning.com

www.g-wlearning.com

Review Your Knowledge

On a separate sheet of paper or in a word processing document, match the following terms with the definition that fits best.

A. induction puzzle
B. logic maze
C. rebus puzzle
D. recursion
E. situational puzzle
F. Rube Goldberg
G. transport puzzle
H. Nash equilibrium
I. dissection puzzle
J. flow

1. A state of immersion in the task or activity being undertaken.
2. A puzzle that requires deductive reasoning from a limited amount of information about the opponents with no information about the player.
3. The object of this puzzle is to take a geometric shape that has been cut into a certain number of pieces and reassemble the shape.
4. A simple maze with some additional rule to increase the difficulty.
5. Occurs in a game when all players know the strategies of the others and no single player can gain when only his or her strategy is changed.
6. A picture puzzle that contains pictures that sound like a word.
7. A puzzle that requires the player to move pieces within the confined space of the game board.
8. When a method calls itself as part of the solution.
9. A synonym for overly complicated.
10. A lateral-thinking puzzle in which the player must find the solution to a riddle by looking at the puzzle from a different and often obscure angle.

On a separate sheet of paper or in a word processing document, answer each of the following questions.

11. List the eight steps to computer puzzle creation.
12. Which stage of puzzle design involves building a prototype?
13. List two common ways to increase puzzle difficulty.
14. List the five major puzzle themes.
15. Which puzzle type involves reasoning and deduction to solve?
16. Describe the puzzle of the Prisoner's Dilemma.
17. Which benefit of computerized puzzles protects the player from actual explosions?
18. Which benefit of computerized puzzles allows players to work together from remote areas to find solutions?
19. Which benefit of computerized puzzles limits the player's ability to cheat?
20. Which benefit of computerized puzzles allows replay of the same puzzle without getting bored?

Apply Your STEM Knowledge

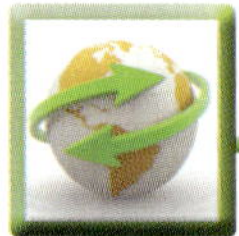

Social Studies

1. Research OPEC and the 1979 energy crisis. Describe how game theory can explain how cooperation by member nations helped raise the world oil prices to $39.50 per barrel from $15 per barrel. Hypothesize what would have happened if a large OPEC member, such as Saudi Arabia, would have defected and sold at a reduced price. Write a one-page paper to explain how your findings and hypothesis relate to game theory.

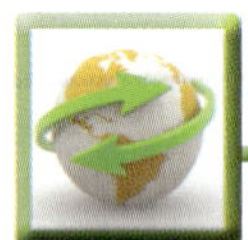

Social Studies

2. Research the inflation-adjusted historical price of oil. What was the inflation-adjusted price of oil in 1978, 1980, and the current year? In what year was the lowest inflation-adjusted price? Hypothesize what happened between 1980 and the year of the lowest price to cause the drop. Write a one-page paper to explain how your findings and hypothesis relate to game theory.

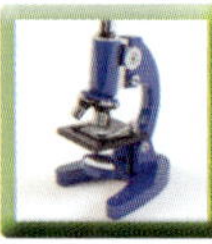

Science

3. Scientific experimentation is much like the solution to a puzzle. By observing the clues and formulating a hypothesis on why things happen, a scientist solves the puzzle of different systems. In astronomy, scientists

observe the characteristics of planets and other celestial objects looking for patterns. These patterns are clues to the puzzle of the universe. When something does not match an expected pattern, the astronomer must create a hypothesis of how the interactions function. Research the topic of black holes. Explore how these hypothetical objects are the solution to a puzzle. Create a PowerPoint presentation of five to ten slides to describe the clues, puzzle, and solution that may lead to the discovery of a black hole.

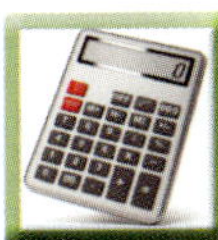

Mathematics

4. Create the logic grid shown below on paper or in spreadsheet software. Use it to solve the following puzzle.
   Situation: Shizuko had friends Alvaro, Betty, and DaSean over for a video game party. When the friends went home, Shizuko found three games that were not hers. Which game belongs to which friend?
   Known information:
   Alvaro owns only rated M games.
   Puzzle Land is a rated E game.
   DaSean loves his PS3.
   Puzzle Land will not play on the Xbox 360.
   Sports World is only available on the PS3.
   RPG City is a rated M game.
   There is one game that is rated T.
   A. Which game is rated T?
   B. Who owns an Xbox 360?
   C. Which game belongs to Betty?
   D. Who owns a Wii?

	Games			System			Rating		
	Puzzle Land	Sports World	RPG City	Xbox 360	PS3	Wii	E	T	M
Alvaro									
Betty									
DaSean									

Language Arts

5. Using the vocabulary words in this chapter, create a crossword puzzle. Write proper definition for each term to use as clues. Create the puzzle on a sheet of graph paper or use a puzzle-maker website. Exchange your crossword puzzle with a classmate and complete.

Working in Teams

Working with the team assigned by your instructor, brainstorm ideas for a game that incorporates a puzzle as a main part of the gameplay. Solving the puzzle may be the main objective of the game or it can be an obstacle to the main objective. Create a PowerPoint presentation explaining the team's idea, how the puzzle is incorporated into the gameplay, and what type of puzzle is used.

Gamer Portfolio

Community service is an important quality that interviewers expect in a candidate. Serving the community shows that the candidate is well rounded and socially aware. In this activity, you will create a list of your contributions to nonprofit organizations. Many opportunities are available for young people to serve the community. You might volunteer for a community clean-up project. Perhaps you enjoy reading to residents in a senior-living facility. Maybe raising money for a homeless-animal shelter appeals to you. Whatever your interests, there is sure to be a related service project. Plan to update this list when you have new activities to add.

1. List the service projects or volunteer activities in which you have taken part. Give the organization or person's name, the dates, and the activities that you performed. If you received a certificate or award related to this service, mention it here.
2. Give the document an appropriate name, using the naming system you created earlier. Place the file in your e-portfolio.
3. Place a copy of the list in the container for your print portfolio.

G-W Learning Mobile Site

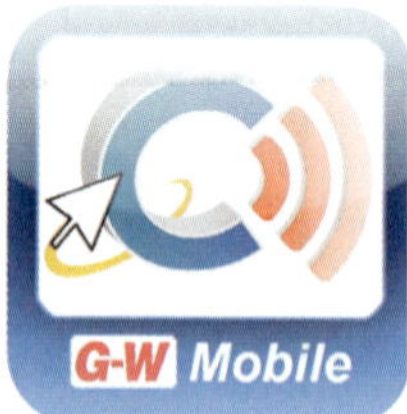

Visit the G-W Learning mobile site to complete the chapter pretest and posttest and to practice vocabulary using e-flash cards. If you do not have a smartphone, visit the G-W Learning companion website to access these features.

G-W Learning mobile site: www.m.g-wlearning.com

G-W Learning companion website: www.g-wlearning.com

Common Core

CTE Career Ready Practices. You will have a number of options to consider when thinking about your future plans. Approaching the different options available to you in a logical way, helps in the decision-making process. One simple way is create a pros and cons chart. Create such a chart showing the pros and cons of pursuing a career that requires additional schooling after high school. Place all of the good or positive things about it on the left under on the "pro" side and all the negative things on the right, or "con" side. Circle the items on your list that you consider the most important when considered rationally. Put a star or asterisk by all those you consider important emotionally. Reflect on what the items on the list mean to you. Has the list helped you come to a decision? Why or why not?

Reading. Research information on the Nash equilibrium. Who was John Nash and how did this come to be named after him. Does the Nash equilibrium apply to modern games and, if so, in what way? Write a report in which you analyze the ways in which the Nash equilibrium applies to games (past and present), using information from your research and this text. Present your opinions to the class.

Writing. Using the Internet, research the advice that experts have for incorporating puzzles into video games. Make sure to look at, among other sources, newspaper and magazine articles, scholarly reports, and public addresses from prominent video game designers. Write a final research report in which you cite the sources that you used and the strengths and weaknesses of each. Be sure to consider the background and point of view of the sources that you find, as well as any bias that the author may bring to the issue.

Event Prep: Essays

Writing an essay may be a competitive entrepreneurship event offered by your Career and Technical Student Organization (CTSO). This may be an individual or team event with two parts: the written essay and the oral presentation of the essay. The essay may be focused on careers or selected topics. Good writing and communication skills are very important to present the research completed on the assigned topic. Completion of the essay may be required prior to the event or at the event. Written events can be lengthy and take a lot of time to prepare. Therefore, it is important to start early. To prepare for writing an essay:

1. Read the guidelines provided by your organization. There will be specific directions on how the essay should be presented. In addition, all final formatting guidelines will be given, including how to organize and submit the final paper. Make certain that you ask any questions about points that you do not understand.
2. The CTSO may give a topic for you to research. If a topic is not given, select a topic related to video game design that is of interest to you.
3. Do your research early. Research may take days or weeks, and you do not want to rush the process.
4. Visit your CTSO's website and create a checklist of the guidelines for the event.
5. Set a deadline for yourself so that you write at a comfortable pace.
6. After you write your first draft, ask a teacher to review it and give you feedback.
7. Once you have the final version of your essay, review your checklist. Make sure you have addressed all requirements. You will be penalized on your score if a direction is not followed exactly.

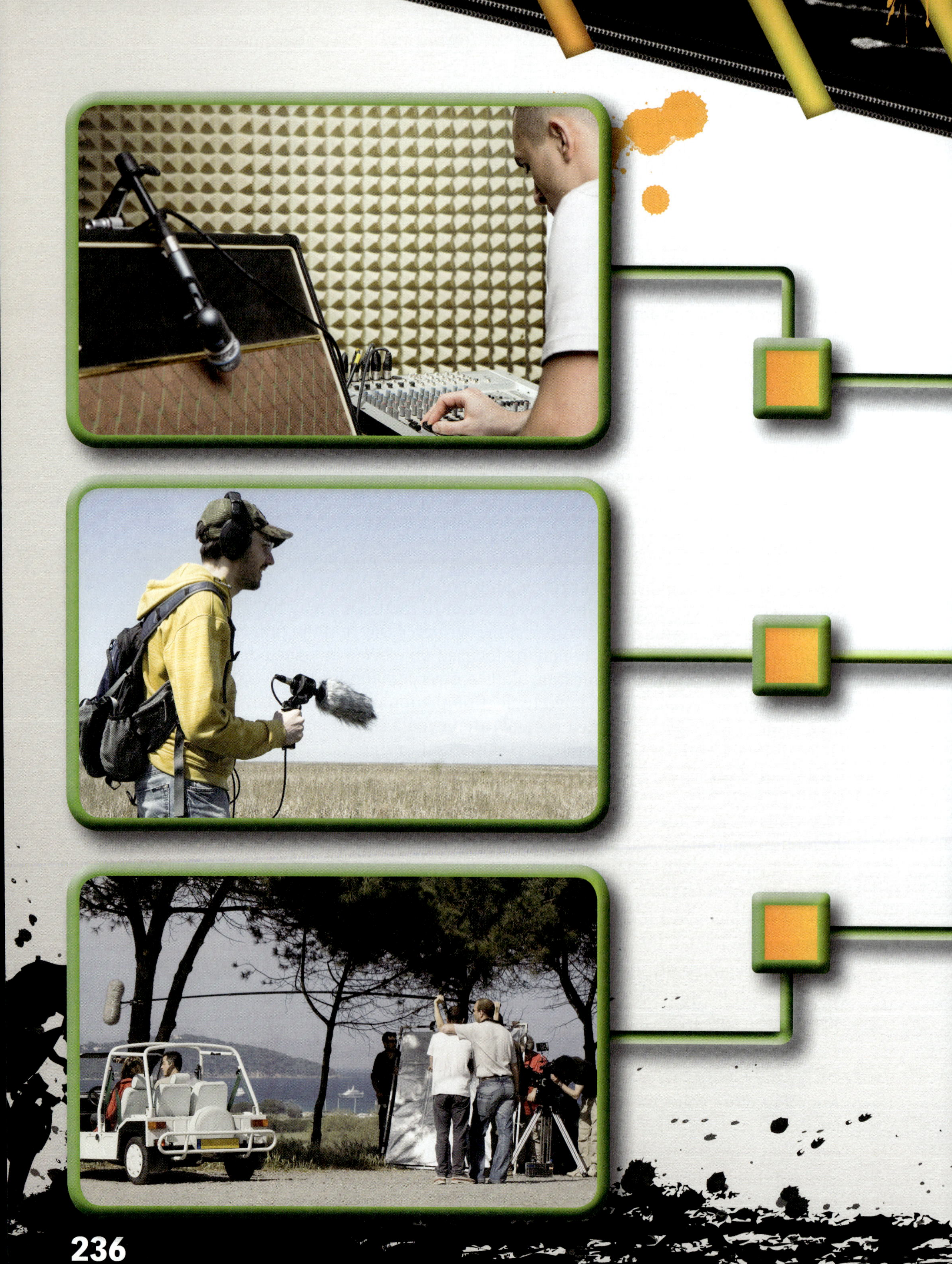

Chapter 8
Sound FX Composition

This chapter explores the basic components of sound engineering needed to create, mix, and edit natural or synthetic sounds. Additionally, you will learn how to create the art animations and other special effects to match these sounds. Get ready to sync up your brain to the active learning in this chapter. Crank up the knowledge and "mix" it up!

Check Your Video Game IQ

Before you begin this chapter, see what you already know about video game design by taking the chapter pretest.

www.m.g-wlearning.com

www.g-wlearning.com

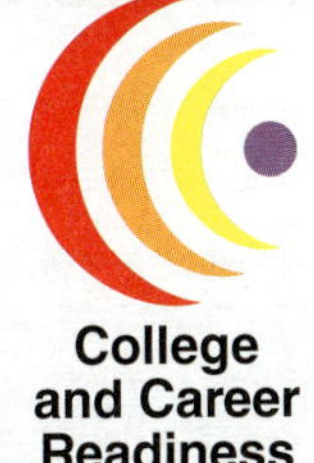

Reading Prep. Think about what you already know about sound technology. What do you think the future holds for digital sound? As you read, evaluate how the ideas presented in the text compare to your own.

Objectives

After completing this chapter, you will be able to:

- Describe the work and responsibilities of a sound engineer.
- Identify a sound asset and define the elements of a sound asset entry.
- Explain what a sound library is and how it can be used.
- List common recording equipment used to create sounds for video games.
- Summarize the process of sound rendering.
- Outline the use of sound effects in video games.

Sound Engineer

Sound is an important part of most games. In a simple game, it helps set the mood for the game. However, in many games, sound is a critical part of gameplay. For example, in a point-of-view (POV) game, sound can be used to indicate an approaching unseen enemy, tell the player when the situation is safe or dangerous, or provide feedback as to the condition of a vehicle. All of these sounds are called sound effects. Sound effects, or ***sound FX,*** are audio game assets used as content or artistic enhancements within gameplay.

Sound production is a key aspect of video game design. This part of the design process involves creating and managing sound assets, the sound library, recording equipment, and rendering of sound.

The ***sound engineer*** is the team member responsible for sound production. A sound engineer is shown in **Figure 8-1.** Sound production encompasses creating and managing everything related to the sound in a video game. A sound engineer has five major responsibilities:

- Identify sound context.
- Generate sounds to specification of the asset.
- Record and edit voice (dialogue).
- Optimize sounds for the game platform.
- Mix sounds.

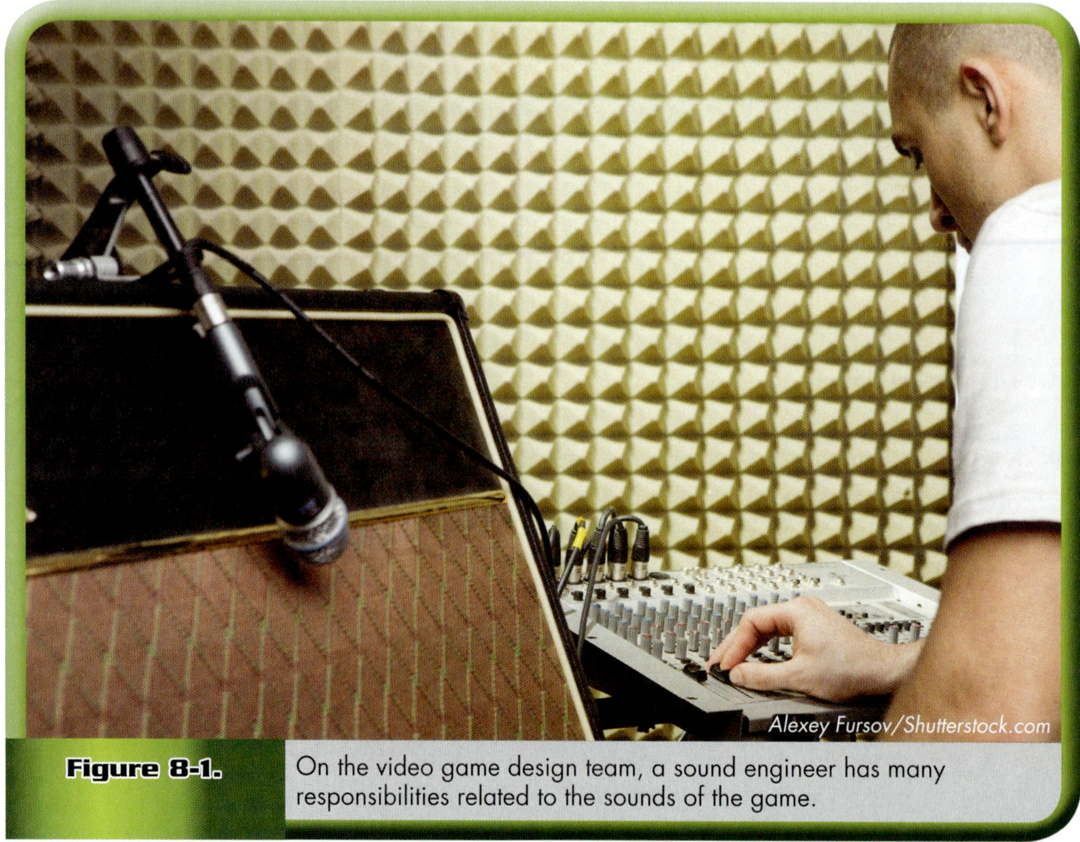

Alexey Fursov/Shutterstock.com

Figure 8-1. On the video game design team, a sound engineer has many responsibilities related to the sounds of the game.

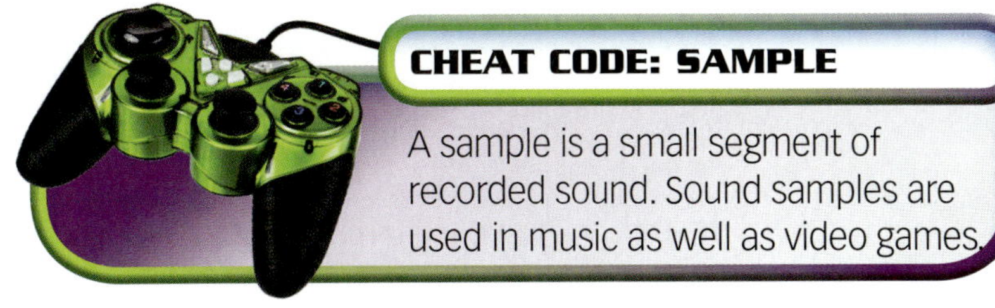

CHEAT CODE: SAMPLE

A sample is a small segment of recorded sound. Sound samples are used in music as well as video games.

The two main branches of sound production are sound engineering and composing.

Sound engineering is the art and science of creating, editing, mixing, and synchronizing sounds. A sound engineer will typically work with **samples.** Samples are used for many items in a video game, from the sound of a laser blaster to the roar of a lion or the click of a button. The sample of dialogue from a voice actor is larger than the sample for a button click. In video game design, the sample size is typically kept very small so the sample will load quickly and not cause the game to lag. For example, a two-minute long sample of dialogue, which may not seem very long, would be cut into smaller samples. This allows the sound to begin playing in the game before the entire two minutes is loaded.

In terms of sound production, ***composing*** is creating music. Music is a collection of sounds or tones arranged in a rhythmic pattern. These sounds can be assembled from instruments, voice, or digital sources. The music a composer creates is used for background sound to add mood and feeling to the game.

Identify Sound Context

The first job of the sound engineer is to research the sound context. ***Sound context*** is a description of what and where an action is occurring. The sound engineer will read the design documents to find out the sound context for each sample needed.

The sound asset list may state, "hero's sword clashes with boss' sword". The sound engineer will need to research the type of weapons used, identify an appropriate sound, and determine how that sound will fit with the scene. This means reviewing the design documents to see the concept art for the swords. A different clanging sound may need to be created for each type of material the hero's sword can contact. If the sword hits another sword, a sample of a high pitched clang may be appropriate. If the sword hits a wooden table, a sample of a dull thud may be appropriate. If the sword hits armor, a sample of a hollow clunk may be best. The sound context of each collision must be researched before the sample can be created.

Generate Sounds to Specifications

The sound engineer has quite a bit of freedom in creating sound samples that he or she thinks are appropriate for the game interaction. The sounds must make sense, match the action occurring, and fulfill the specifications of the sound context. However, the sound does not need to be the actual sound made in the real world for the same interaction. In fact, in many cases, sounds must be created for interactions that do not exist in the real world, such as a phaser blast. The sound of a broken tree branch may be simulated with a sample of a pencil breaking. The sample for the whirr of a projectile flying through the air might be created by using a rubber band to launch a washer past a microphone. Creativity is the key.

Samples can be saved in many different file formats, as shown in **Figure 8-2.** The sound engineer must make certain that the sample is saved in the correct sound format. The correct format may be specific to the device and platform on which the game will play.

Format	Name	Compression	Benefit
WAV	Pulse Code Modulation Wave	None	Standard PCM format for Windows
AIFF	Apple Interchange File Format	None	Standard PCM format for Apple.
MP3	Motion Picture Experts Group Layer 3	Lossy	Very compressed format; popular format due to the typically small file size
AAC	Advanced Audio Coding	Lossy	iTunes format similar to MP3
MPEG4	Motion Picture Experts Group Layer 4	Lossless	Compression eliminates silence data without loss of sound data

Figure 8-2. These are some common sound file formats.

Goodheart-Willcox Publisher

The sample must meet the specification for file size and upload speed. If the sample is for game on a handheld device, the requirement may be a very small file size. Also, on most game platforms, samples must be preloaded to play smoothly. *Preloading* is when the sound sample is loaded into the computer memory before it plays. If the sample is not preloaded, the game may lag as the computer loads the sound into memory. For this reason, many sound files are compressed just as images are. Online games and handheld games are most sensitive to file size and upload speed. In some cases, game consoles may be powerful enough to allow sound samples to be played without preloading.

Record and Edit Voice

For many games, much of a sound engineer's time is spent working with voice actors. A ***voice actor*** is a person hired to be the voice of a game character. The voice actor reads the lines of **dialogue** adding inflection and tone to create meaning beyond just the words. The sound engineer can suggest how a line should be read by the voice actor. A line that states, "Halt! Who goes there?" should be spoken loud and with force to get attention. Other lines might need to be whispered. The voice actor must match the vocal tones to the action in the game. This can be a challenge because the dialogue is recorded before the animations are created. The voice actor must imagine the scene since there is nothing to look at except perhaps some character sketches.

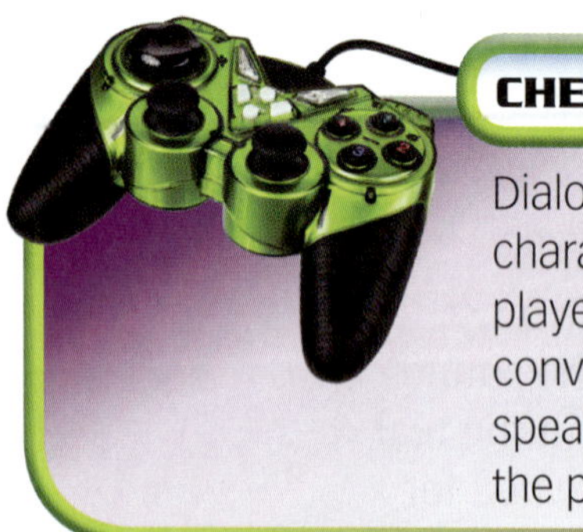

CHEAT CODE: DIALOGUE

Dialogue is a conversation between characters. In video games, the player may be an implied part of the conversation, such as when an NPC speaks a warning about an action the player is taking.

Typically, the sound engineer records many samples of the same dialogue from the voice actor. Then the best version is selected for editing. The first edit is to cut the needed sound from all other parts of the recording. This takes the large sound file with many lines and cuts it into samples. The samples are then mixed and edited to get the best sound for that point in the game. For example, the volume of the voice actor's dialog may need to be increased to be heard over other sounds in the scene. In other cases, the voice actor's dialogue will be adjusted using sound FX, which are detailed later in this chapter.

Optimize Sounds

The platform on which the sound sample will be played determines how a sound is optimized. ***Optimizing*** involves formatting the audio so it sounds best from the playback device. Sound for a theater that is enabled for Dolby Surround sound will be processed using the Dolby technology. The engineer will edit the sound and adjust speaker output so the audio sounds best in a theater. The sound engineer may have to split the sound between ten different speakers so the sound will not echo and can be heard properly.

This will not be the case if the sound playback is through a set of headphones. The sound will be split between two speakers and will be optimized for the range of sound a typical headphone speaker can reproduce. The range of a speaker is the spectrum of sound waves that device can produce. A small headphone speaker is good at replaying high-pitched sounds. However, headphone speakers generally cannot reproduce low-toned bass sounds. Reproducing bass requires a larger speaker to move a large volume of air. When optimizing sound for headphone speakers, the lowest tones can be removed since these speakers cannot reproduce bass. Removing the range that cannot be reproduced also allows the file size to be smaller.

Mix Sounds

Sound engineers often must mix sounds to create new and unique sounds. ***Mixing*** is the process of combining two or more recorded sounds into a single sound. Most mixing can be done "in-the-box," which means on a personal computer. Software and a personal computer have replaced many of the large mixing boards and audio workstations of the past. This combination is a very convenient and inexpensive way for sound engineers to mix sounds for video games. **Figure 8-3** shows a comparison of some available mixing software.

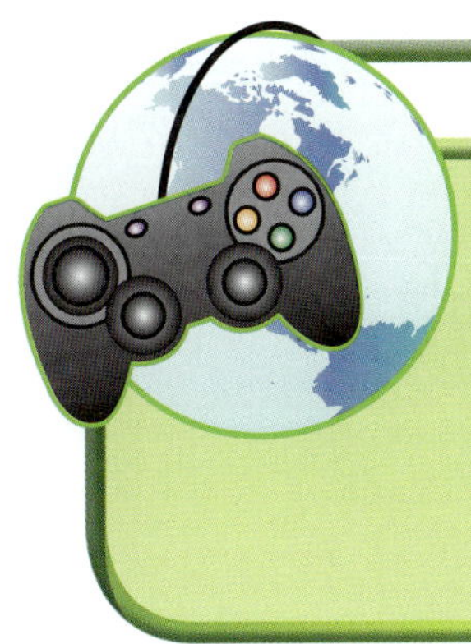

Green Gamer

When you go to the store to buy a video game or other items, consider bringing along a reusable bag. Reusable bags save thousands of pounds of landfill waste every year. While there are different schools of thought on this topic, it is generally accepted that plastic bags take nearly 1,000 years to degrade. Additionally, discarded plastic bags can pose threats to wildlife and contaminate the soil.

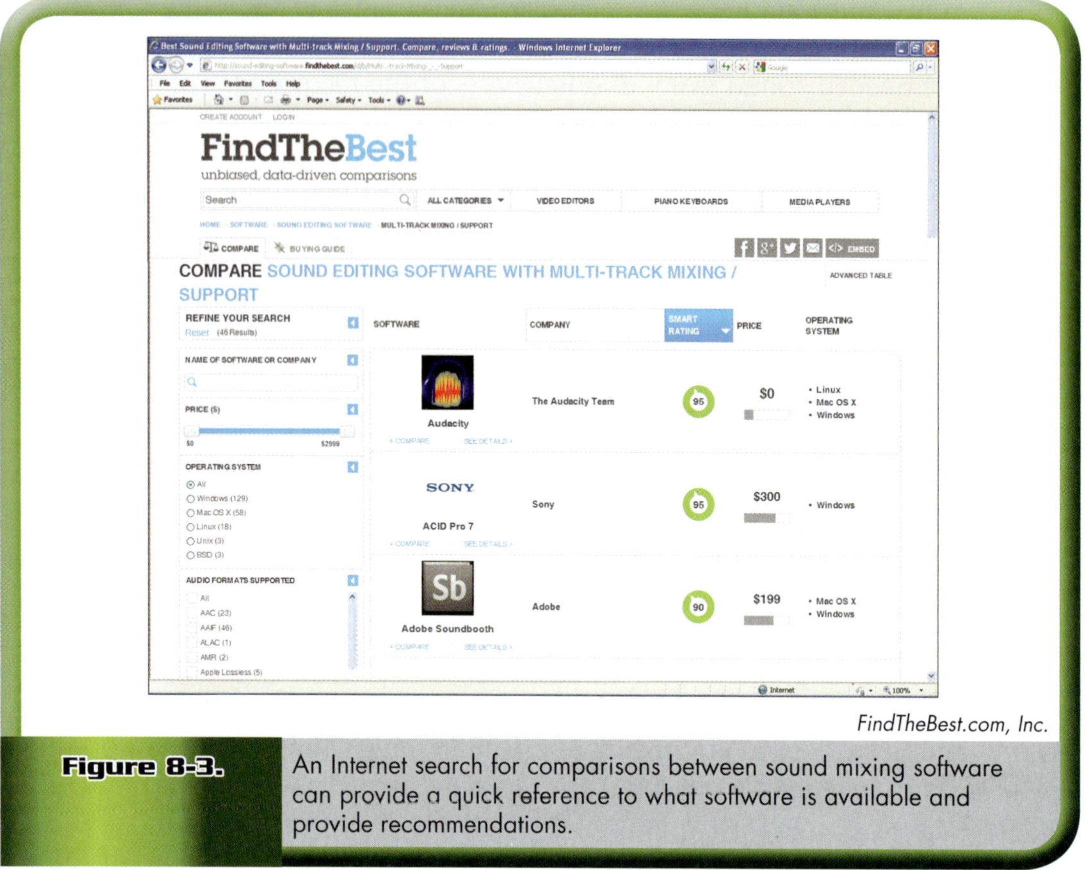

FindTheBest.com, Inc.

Figure 8-3. An Internet search for comparisons between sound mixing software can provide a quick reference to what software is available and provide recommendations.

When mixing sounds, adjustments are made to each sound so it matches the other sounds in the mix. Volume and signal levels of the source can be corrected during mixing. Additionally, special effects can be added to the mix to create cool sounds. Multitrack or multiple recorded sound tracks can be condensed into one or two channels. A sample with a single audio channel is called a mono sound. The more typical sample has two channels and is called a stereo sound. The number of tracks that can be mixed depends on the software or mixing board being used. Eight- and sixteen-track mixers are common, but some mixers may have 50 or more tracks.

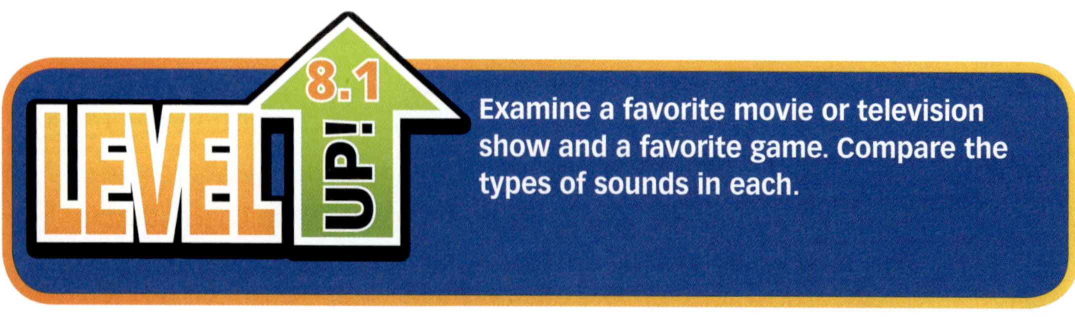

Examine a favorite movie or television show and a favorite game. Compare the types of sounds in each.

CASE STUDY

Getting Started as a Sound Engineer

The first thing to remember about being a sound engineer is that you may not always work in video games. Many sound engineers work on projects from movies to live stage performances. Each project carries a unique set of challenges and rewards. The skills and experience gained in each project will make you a better sound engineer. To get started in sound engineering, focus on education, experience, contacts, gear, and software.

Education is one of the best ways to get ahead in this business. You can begin with classroom instruction by taking music, principles of computer music, sound recording, orchestration, harmony, and other related courses found in a high school, tech school, or college. The knowledge gained in these classes form the foundation for all skills you will develop through experience. Do not just focus on sound engineering courses. Many successful sound engineers also get a degree in electrical engineering or electronics technology. You will be running many wires and making many connections. It is not absolutely necessary to be an electrical engineer, but it may help.

Experience is the best teacher. Without experience, finding paying jobs may be difficult. Look around school, church, athletic stadium, concerts, or other places where sound equipment is being used. Find someone who is hooking things up and offer to help. Make friends with the sound crew at a local concert venue. Look for places to volunteer or apprentice.

Not only do these opportunities give you experience, they also allow you to start making contacts in the business. A network of contacts often can provide leads and recommendations for jobs.

To learn more about equipment, use the Internet to research sound gear. Look at the websites of the companies that make the gear. Study these tools of the trade so you will have an idea of what they do when you see them.

Editing software comes in many different varieties. Fortunately, many software companies have free trials or demo versions. Start using the software at home for your own projects. Get comfortable with the features and tools as they are very similar between programs. Some software to look for include Digital Performer, ProTools, Live, and Cubase.

As a final note, protect your ears! Use earplugs with adjustable attenuation when working with loud sounds and music. You only have one set of ears in your lifetime, so start protecting your hearing now.

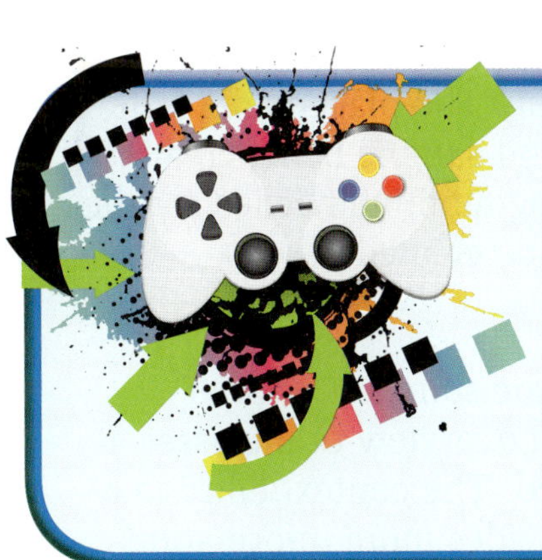

Ethical Gamer

It is unethical to use a school or work computer, without permission, for personal means such as playing games, shopping, or other activities that are outside of your assignments. It is also unethical and may be illegal to access confidential information, download copyrighted material, or harass others.

Sound Assets

A sound asset must be created for each interaction in the game that requires an associated sound. The design documents list the sounds needed and give the specifications for the sounds. The sound engineer will create the sounds and add them to the sound **database**. The database is used to manage the sound library, which is discussed in the next section.

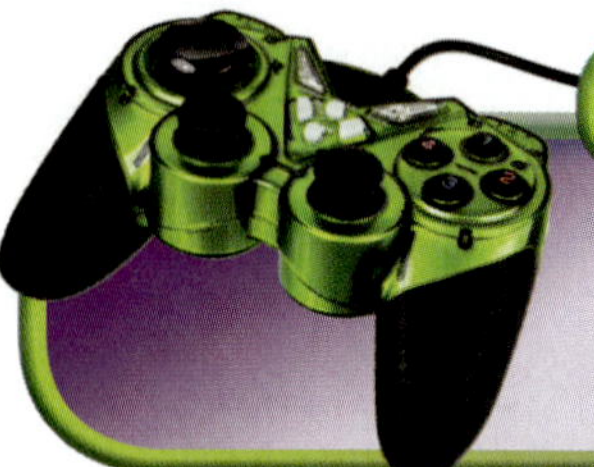

CHEAT CODE: DATABASE

A database is an organized system of storing information that allows for searching and retrieval of the data.

A database makes it easy for a designer to find the correct sound and contains information on how to properly format it. There are many different sound database programs used by game design studios. Microsoft Excel and Microsoft Access are examples of database software. A given studio may have the sound entered into the database in a slightly different manner than what is shown in **Figure 8-4.** The entries in the database list the information needed to design and store the sound. The information the sound engineer needs to research and complete the asset is contained in the context, category, and cue columns. By putting together all the information from the database details and the design documents, the sound engineer can create the best sound for the interaction.

Name and Asset Number

Most entries in a sound asset database start with a name and asset number. The name of the asset is the name of the file and is created using a file-naming convention. A ***file-naming convention*** is a standardized way of naming an asset. The file name can be quite long to make sure the asset is easily identifiable. An asset name usually follows a format such as *class_object_effect*. Since spaces can cause serious problems in some programs, it is important to use the underscore (_) or hyphen (-) character to separate the words. If the sound is for the hero's sword hitting armor, the name might be HERO_Sword_Armor-Hit. This naming convention is also used for art and animations.

The asset number is used for keeping track of the sound in the project. A programmer will start building the game using a placeholder for the sound. A ***placeholder*** is a substitute for the asset that is being created. The placeholder is simply replaced with the actual sound sample once the asset is finished.

For example, a programmer may insert a generic sound like a beep as a placeholder for the sound sample of a door opening. The placeholder will have the same name and asset number as the sound sample being created. This allows the programmer to finish all of the programming needed for the interaction without waiting for the actual asset to be created.

Context

The context entry gives a brief description of the sound. The brief information in the context column simply gives an overview of the asset. It is not a full description of what needs to be created. The context entry may reference a page in the design documents that provides more information.

Name	Asset#	Context	Category	Cue	Specs	Loop	Link	Due	Status
HERO_run.wav	4352	Level 3 running footsteps for hero	Character	Run animation	44.1 kHz, 16 bit, stereo	Yes	//level3/characters/ animations	5/23	In progress
HERO_Sword_Hit_ Boss_Sword.wav	4353	Sword hit on boss sword	Weapon	Collision with boss sword	44.1 kHz, 16 bit, mono	No	//level_1/hero/ weapon	5/18	Redo
HERO_Voice_ Intro_Scene2.mp3	4354	Intro cut scene	Voice	Hero Running away, panting and scared	96 kHz, 24 bit, stereo	No	//Intro/Cut-scene2/ hero	5/10	Delivered
HUD_Menu_ Pause_Click.wav	4355	Pause menu open in level 4	Menu	Click Options tab	44.1 kHz, 16 bit, mono	No	//HUD/Menu/ Pause	4/28	Accepted
	4356	Start button click	Button	Click Start button	44.1 kHz, 16 bit, mono	No		5/23	Not Begun
	4821	Level 2, scene 4 background for enter forest	Music	Enters forest	96 kHz, 24 bit, stereo	Yes		4/28	Deferred
AMBIENT_Forest_ Level2_Scene4.wav	4826	Level 2, scene 4 in forest	Ambient	Enters forest	32 kHz, 16 bit, stereo	Yes	//level_2/ Scene_4/ Forest/ Ambients	4/28	Ready

Figure 8-4. This is a partial example of a sound assets database.

Goodheart-Willcox Publisher

Category

The category entry provides the major classification for the asset. In a large game, several assets may have similar uses, names, and characteristics. Use of a category may help the sound engineer look up the art for that asset and get a better idea of what sound it might make.

Cue

The cue entry indicates when in the game the sound will occur. A ***cue*** is a trigger for an action, such as playing a sound sample. The cue is usually a collision. For example, a cue might be when the player's sword hits the armor of an enemy. One of the actions triggered is playing the sound sample, which may be named something similar to HERO_Sword_Hit_Armor.wav.

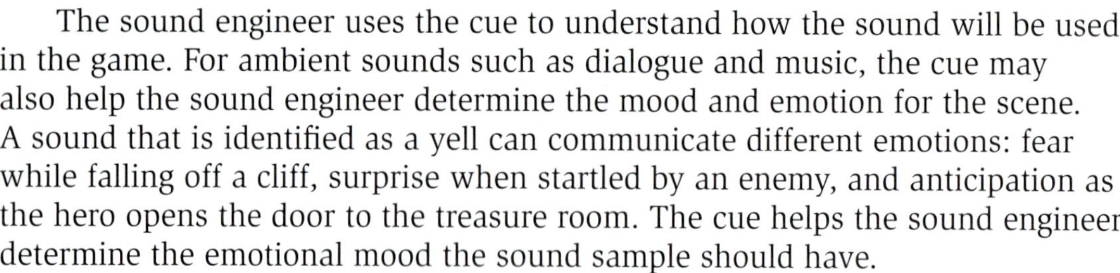

The sound engineer uses the cue to understand how the sound will be used in the game. For ambient sounds such as dialogue and music, the cue may also help the sound engineer determine the mood and emotion for the scene. A sound that is identified as a yell can communicate different emotions: fear while falling off a cliff, surprise when startled by an enemy, and anticipation as the hero opens the door to the treasure room. The cue helps the sound engineer determine the emotional mood the sound sample should have.

Specs

While all of the information in the database is important, the specifications, or specs, entry is critical. The specs entry details the file size, file type, sound quality, and playback media. The sound engineer must know this information to properly construct a sound to fit.

The file size is very important information for a sound sample. Many devices do not have enough processing power or memory to handle large sound files. Early video games did not include recorded sounds because the game consoles could not store and process even simple sounds. The sounds were beeps and clicks generated by the game console itself. Later, when these early game consoles became more powerful, games could include recorded sounds, but the file size of the sound was still a concern. One early example of the sound issue is the game *Quadrun* for the Atari 2600 game console. This was one of the first games to have voice. The sound file to say only "quadrun" maxed out the memory of the system. Because the system could not play the sound and create screen images at the same time, the screen had to blink on and off. Today, similar problems can be seen as **lagging** gameplay in online and handheld games containing large sound files.

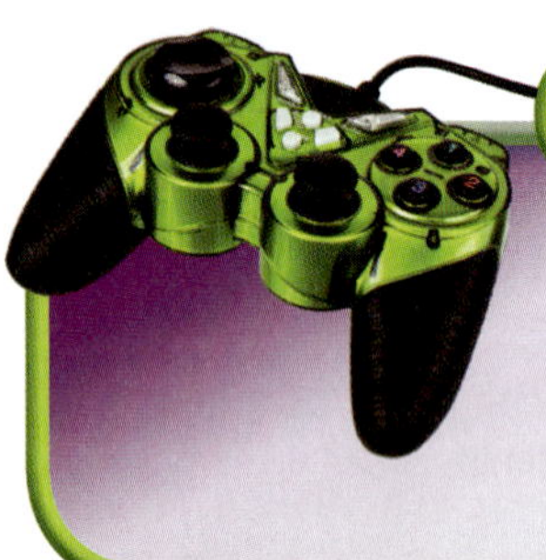

CHEAT CODE: LAGGING

Lagging means falling behind or happening later than intended. When gameplay is lagging, the sound playback or rendering of graphics causes the gameplay to slow down.

Sound samples are recorded and stored based on frequency and bit rate. ***Sampling frequency*** is how many times per second the sound data are recorded. Frequency is measured in Hertz. As shown in **Figure 8-5,** one Hertz is one cycle per second. Hertz is the unit of measure for many different things, including:

- sound waves;
- computer processor speeds;
- electrical power line frequency; and
- recording rates (sampling frequency).

The common recording rate for compact disc (CD) audio is 44.1 kHz. This means that the sound-recording device makes 44,100 samples each second. The time between each sample is 1/44,100th of a second. Higher-quality sound is recorded at a much higher rate, usually 96 kHz or greater. The more samples per second, the smoother and cleaner the reproduction of the sound will be.

Another quality setting for recording audio is bit rate. The ***bit rate*** is the number of bits of data transferred per second. A bit is a single memory storage unit for a computer. If your cell phone can download ten bits per second,

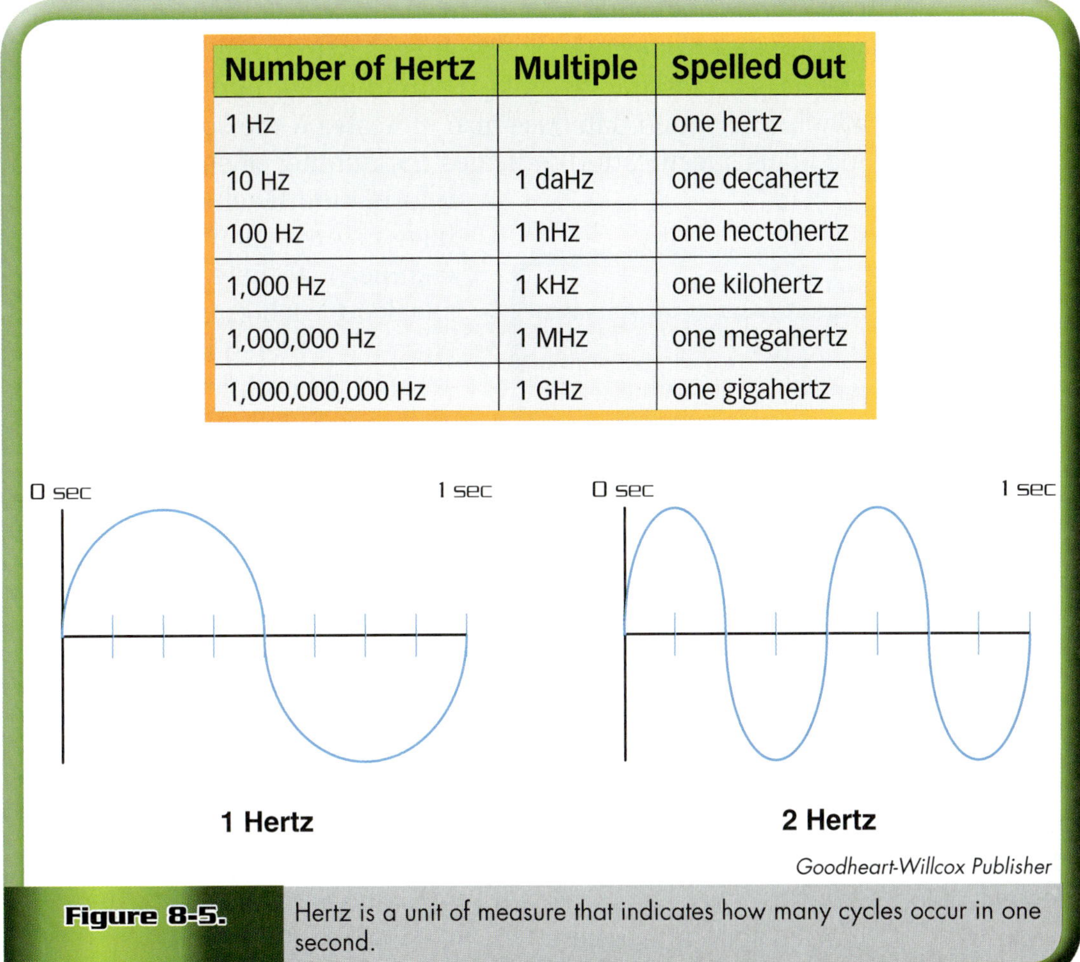

Number of Hertz	Multiple	Spelled Out
1 Hz		one hertz
10 Hz	1 daHz	one decahertz
100 Hz	1 hHz	one hectohertz
1,000 Hz	1 kHz	one kilohertz
1,000,000 Hz	1 MHz	one megahertz
1,000,000,000 Hz	1 GHz	one gigahertz

Figure 8-5. Hertz is a unit of measure that indicates how many cycles occur in one second.

or a bit rate of ten, then it would take one minute to download 600 bits of information. In terms of a sound recording, *bit rate* refers to the number of bits of information recorded for every unit of time, such as bits per second (bit/s).

For example, suppose a sound is recorded at 44.1 kHz. The unit of time for the bit rate is 1/44,100th of a second. If the bit rate is 16, then 16 bits of data are recorded every 1/44,100th of a second. That means a sound sample one second in length recorded with these specifications contains 705,600 bits of information.

16 bits per second × 44,100 samples per second = 705,600 bits
705,600 bits ÷ 8 bits per byte = 88,200 bytes = 88.2 kilobytes

Most game consoles, like the PS3 and Xbox 360, use the Red Book standard. ***Red Book standard*** refers to specifications for the physical properties of compact discs and for the digital audio on the discs. The audio must be two channels recorded at 44.1 kHz with a bit rate of 16. In video games, the file format is generally WAV or AIFF. Red Book audio is not typically used on handheld devices and cell phones because the file sizes are too large and playback quality of the sound exceeds what can be reproduced by small speakers.

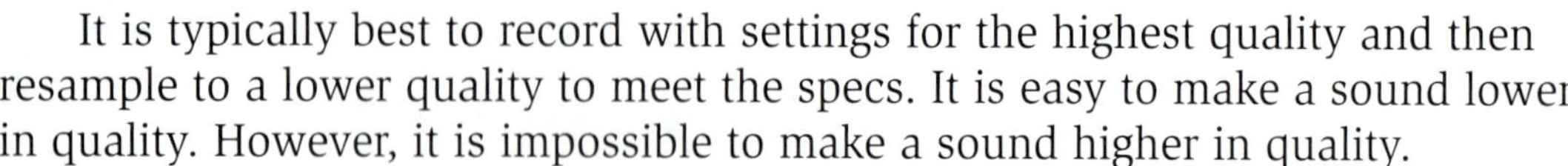

It is typically best to record with settings for the highest quality and then resample to a lower quality to meet the specs. It is easy to make a sound lower in quality. However, it is impossible to make a sound higher in quality.

The specs entry in the sound database also indicates if the sound is **mono,** stereo, or surround. This specification indicates the number of speakers to send information. Each speaker will have its own channel. Mono is channel 1. If there are multiple speakers, each one receives channel 1. Stereo is channel 1 and 2 for both left and right speakers. Surround sound can support several speakers. Most home surround sound units have eight channels.

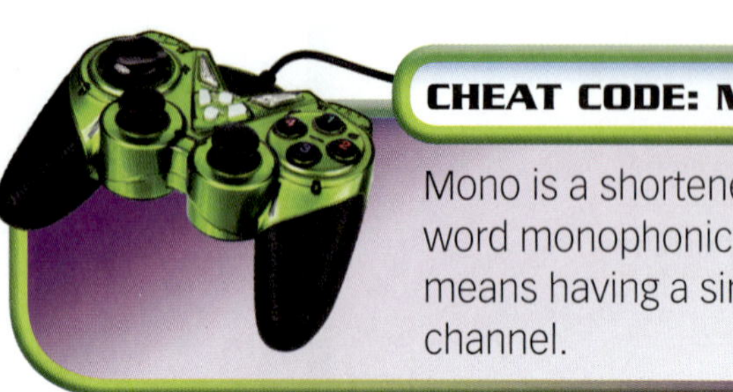

CHEAT CODE: MONO

Mono is a shortened version of the word monophonic. Monophonic means having a single audio channel.

Stereo or surround sound can be a really cool feature for a game. If the sound engineer knows that an enemy will be entering from the left, the sound engineer can mix the sound so the footsteps sound plays only in the left-hand speaker. This adds to the gameplay as the player receives a sound clue to the direction of an approaching enemy.

Loop

The sound engineer can limit the file size of a sound by looping the sound. ***Looping*** is when the sound or animation restarts at the end of playing. For this reason, a loop must be a complete cycle with the same ending and starting points. The waveforms shown in **Figure 8-5** are complete cycles because the ending and starting points are on the same horizontal line. Police sirens and car alarms are common sound loops of a single cycle.

In a video game, the sound for footsteps can be a single cycle of a foot hitting the ground. Then, this cycle can be looped to create the sound for a character walking. This allows for a very small file size. As shown in **Figure 8-6,** the sound file for a single footstep looped ten times is ten times smaller than the sound file for ten footsteps.

Link, Due, and Status

The link, due, and status entries in the sound database are workflow identifiers. ***Workflow identifiers*** are items and information that help keep the work moving forward.

The link entry states where the sound asset is stored. This is the location on the server. An asset may have more than one name entered in the Name column. This can be done to identify a sound that is used on multiple levels or for multiple effects. To best identify the sound, each name follows the naming convention to match each condition. This might seem to be clumsy, and you might think it requires the sound to be saved multiple times. However, this is not the case. There is only one link entry for all of the names. The programmers use the link entry to program the game to retrieve the sound from one file.

The due date is a very important part of the sound database. The design documents lay out all of the milestones or stages of completion. The due date for each asset is assigned to meet the deadline for each milestone. The lead

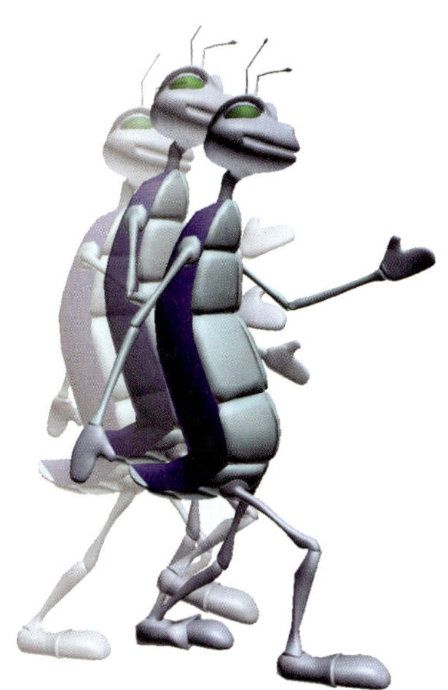

One Footstep

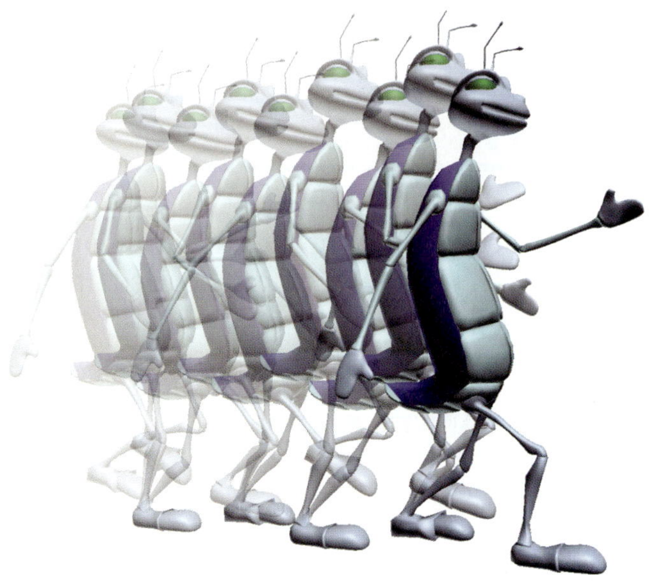

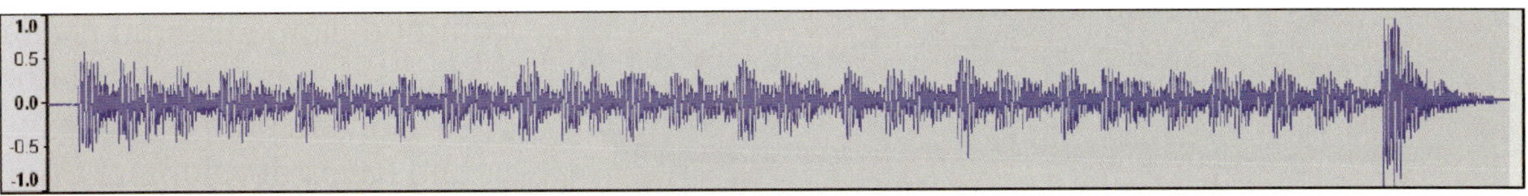

Multiple Footsteps

Goodheart-Willcox Publisher; model Autodesk

Figure 8-6. The sound file for one footstep is much smaller than the file for multiple footsteps.

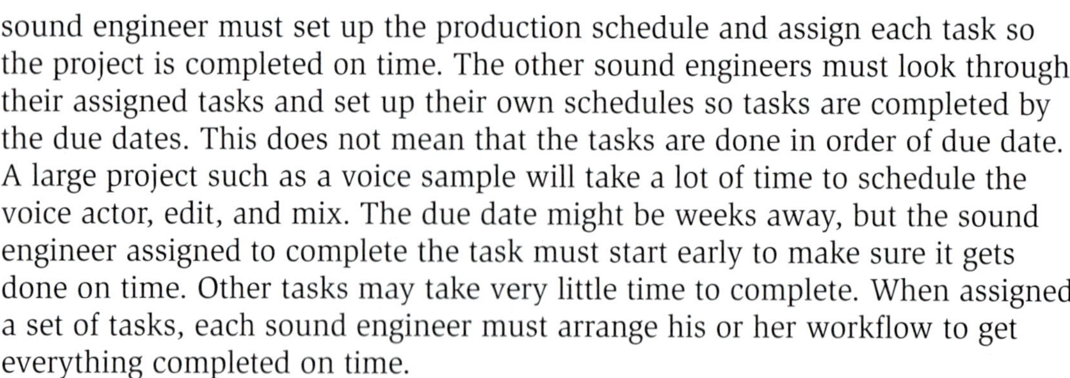

sound engineer must set up the production schedule and assign each task so the project is completed on time. The other sound engineers must look through their assigned tasks and set up their own schedules so tasks are completed by the due dates. This does not mean that the tasks are done in order of due date. A large project such as a voice sample will take a lot of time to schedule the voice actor, edit, and mix. The due date might be weeks away, but the sound engineer assigned to complete the task must start early to make sure it gets done on time. Other tasks may take very little time to complete. When assigned a set of tasks, each sound engineer must arrange his or her workflow to get everything completed on time.

When a sound is finished, the sound engineer changes the status entry for the sound asset from "in progress" to "delivered." The asset is then inspected by the lead sound engineer for approval. Then, the status entry is changed to either "accepted" or "redo." Accepted assets will be inserted where the placeholder was. Assets that must be redone did not meet the needs for the scene and will have to be corrected and delivered again.

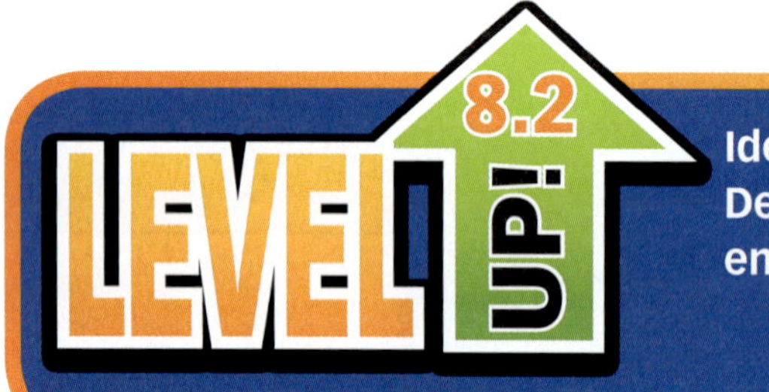

Identify a sound from a favorite game. Describe how that sound asset may be entered into a sound database.

Sound Library

As more and more sounds are created, a sound library is developed. A ***sound library*** is a collection of completed sound samples that are available for use. The sound assets in one game can be used in another game. Reusing sound assets is an inexpensive and time-saving way to add sounds to a game.

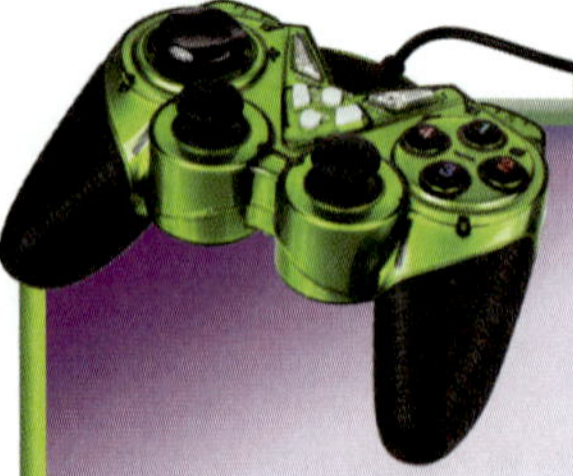

CHEAT CODE: CANNED SOUND

The term *canned sound* comes from the physical metal containers that were used to store tape recordings. When a soundtrack or film was completed, it was said to be "in the can," and the terminology continues to this day.

Some games are designed using canned sound. **Canned sound** or a canned track is a previously recorded generic sound. Canned sound may be purchased or taken from the company's own library. A common canned sound is a laugh track, which is often used on television sitcoms. Using canned sound saves development time. A canned sound library can be purchased or licensed so an entire game can be built without the need to record any new sounds. If canned sound is purchased or licensed for redistribution, the original creator of the sound holds the copyright on the sound. Without permission, the sound cannot be used or redistributed.

Many sound engineers build and maintain their own sound libraries of raw and edited sounds. Raw sounds are the original field recordings without any editing, balancing, or mixing. A ***field recording*** is made by a sound engineer using a microphone and recording device outside of the studio, as shown in **Figure 8-7.** Many sound engineers carry a set of quality microphones and a recorder at all times. There are interesting sounds everywhere in nature, cityscapes, homes, and more. The ability of a sound engineer to hear something and imagine how that sound can be used to simulate something in a game comes from an understanding of sound art and experience.

A famous field recording was made for the original Star Wars movie. A sound engineer noticed the twangy "pee-ooo" sound made when a guy wire was struck with a metal hammer. Guy wires are the cables that brace towers and telephone poles. The sound was recorded and used in the movie for the sound of all laser blasters. When the movie came out, kids everywhere were tapping guy wires with sticks to recreate that cool laser sound right outside their homes.

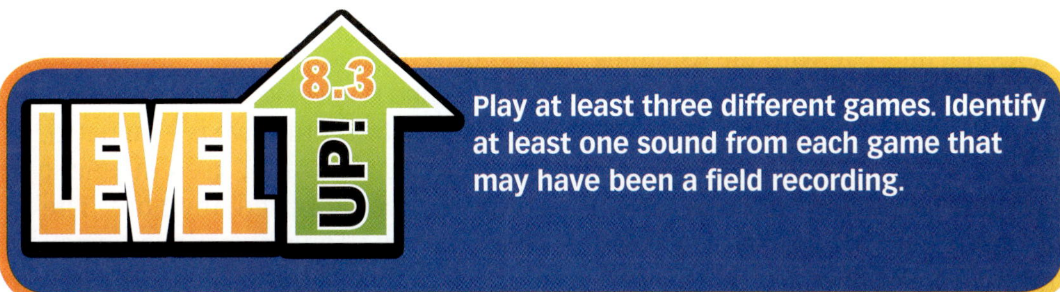

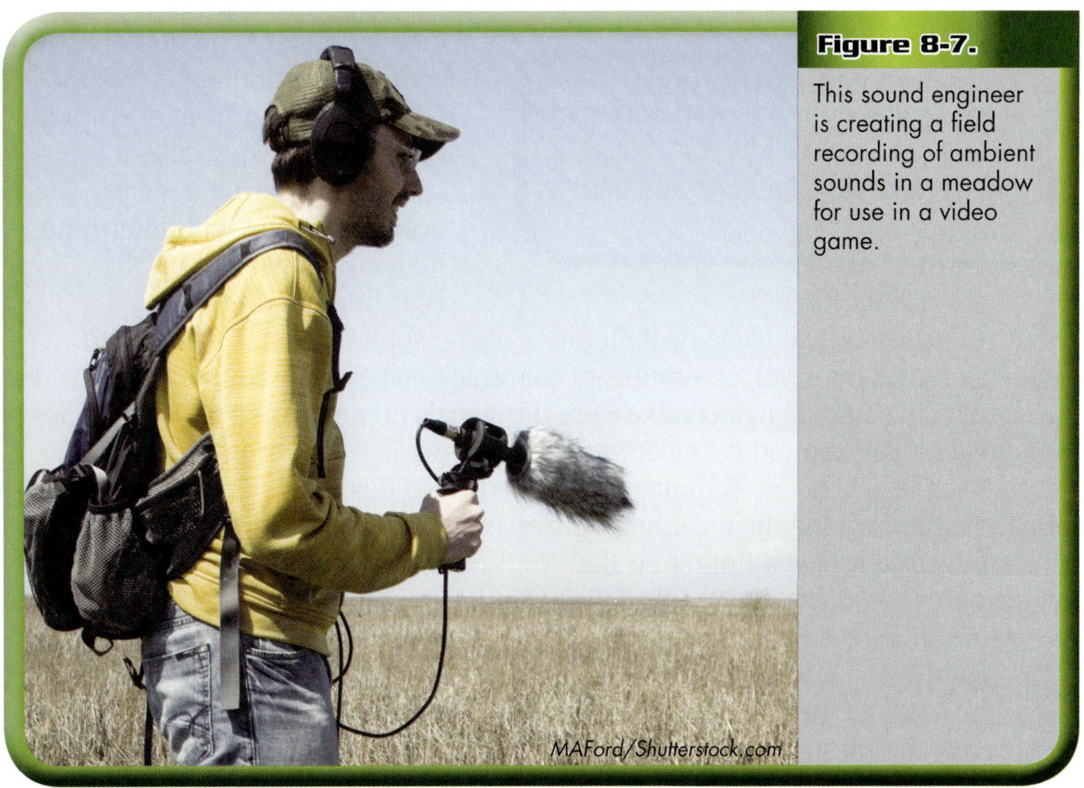

Figure 8-7.

This sound engineer is creating a field recording of ambient sounds in a meadow for use in a video game.

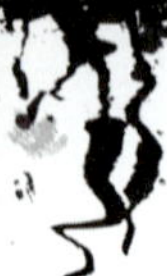

Recording Equipment

Some standard equipment is needed to capture and record sounds. Typical equipment includes:

- recording device;
- microphone;
- windscreen (when required); and
- mount (when required).

At a minimum, a microphone and recording device are needed. A windscreen is often used in field work, but may not be used in studio work. A mount is used in studio work and sometimes in field work.

Recording Device

The ***recording device*** is the piece of equipment that takes the electronic signals from the microphone and stores them on a media. Most sound engineers work with recording devices that store sound data digitally on a hard drive or in flash memory. Flash memory is quickly replacing the hard drive in many recording devices because it does not interfere with the recording. A hard drive makes noise as it stores and accesses data. Flash memory has no moving parts and makes no noise when storing the data. With flash memory, the whirr and ticking of the hard drive is eliminated.

In the past, field recordings were done with recorders that used magnetic tape to store analog sound data. Few of these devices are used anymore. The process of writing and reading data on magnetic tape could introduce noise into the recording. Digital recording devices allow for nearly flawless recording. Additionally, the digital recording can be instantly transferred to a computer for editing and mixing. An analog recording on magnetic tape must be first **digitized** before it can be edited on a computer. The digital field recording technology available today can range from a simple iPhone app to specialized sound engineering devices. The recording needs will determine the features needed on the recording devices.

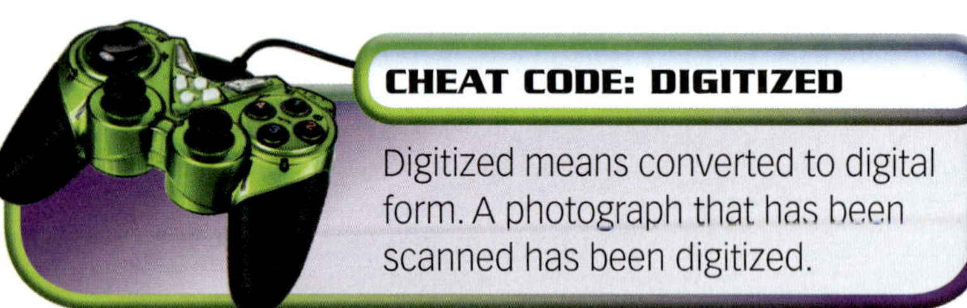

CHEAT CODE: DIGITIZED

Digitized means converted to digital form. A photograph that has been scanned has been digitized.

A sound meter will likely be built into a digital sound recorder. The ***sound meter*** measures the level, or volume, of sound in decibels. The sound level must be adjusted by the sound engineer to assure the signals do not exceed the capabilities of the recorder. If a sound is louder than the recorder is set to record, a buzzing or clipping sound will occur. You may have experienced this if you have ever yelled into a microphone and the recording buzzes and hums at the point where you yell.

The recorder uses a limiter so that loud noises are eliminated from the recording to avoid errors. Additionally, a limiter might be set to record only a certain range of sound frequencies. For example, an explosion produces sounds with very low frequency. These may be beyond the capability of the microphone to capture. Instead, a distorted sound will be recorded. The limiter either clips data outside the set range or alters the data to be within the range.

Microphone

Microphones detect sound, convert it to an electrical signal, and transmit the signal to an output. The output is connected to a recording or amplifying device. Microphones are one of the most important and expensive components for a sound engineer. Several microphones are shown in **Figure 8-8** along with a chart listing types of microphones.

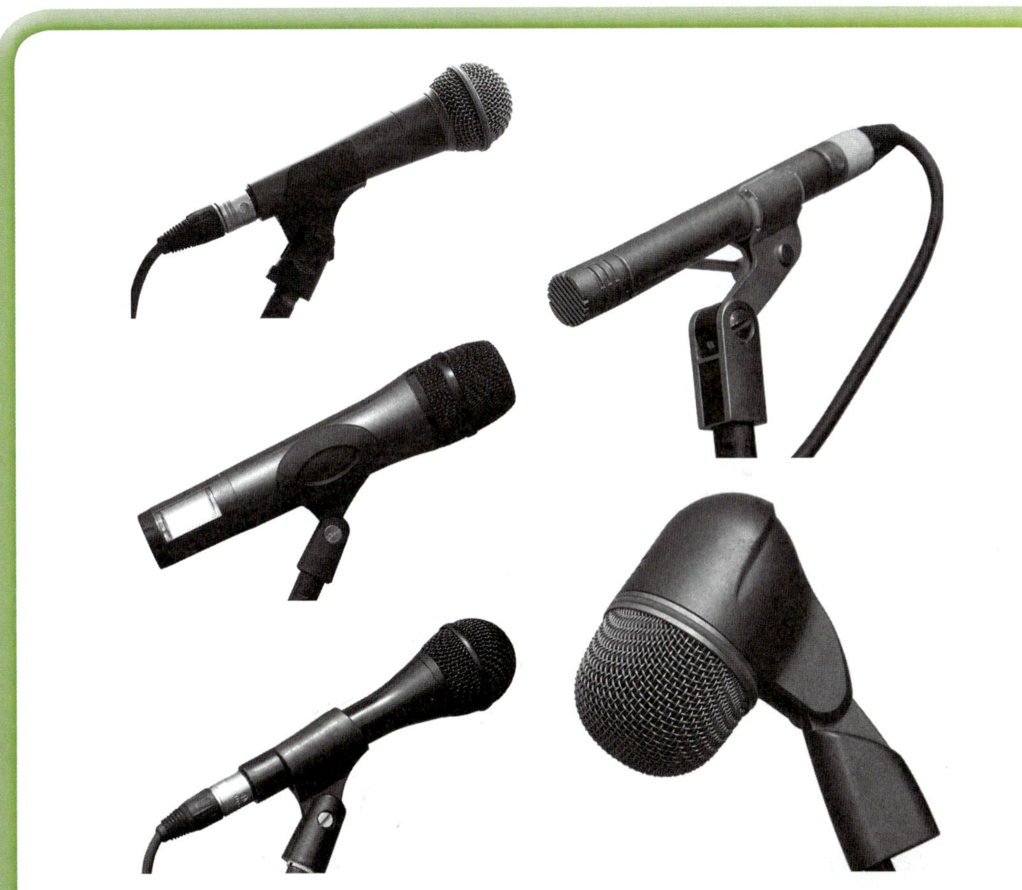

Type	Directivity	Application
Condenser	Omnidirectional	Lavalier (small, neck microphone)
Dynamic	Unidirectional	Wireless
Ribbon	Cardiod	Contact
Carbon	Bi-Directional	Parabolic
Fiber optic	Shotgun	Noise canceling
MEMS	PZM	Stereo

versh/Shutterstock.com

Figure 8-8. There are several types of microphones each with different properties. Select the type that best suits the needs of the recording.

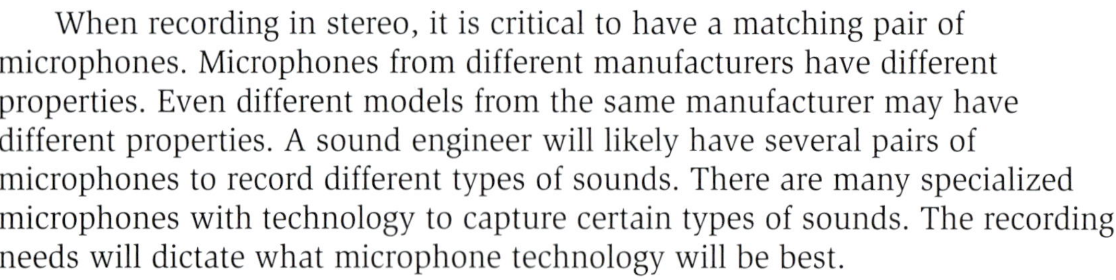

When recording in stereo, it is critical to have a matching pair of microphones. Microphones from different manufacturers have different properties. Even different models from the same manufacturer may have different properties. A sound engineer will likely have several pairs of microphones to record different types of sounds. There are many specialized microphones with technology to capture certain types of sounds. The recording needs will dictate what microphone technology will be best.

Windscreen

Microphones usually need some attachments to work best. A common attachment is a windscreen, or windsock. A ***windscreen*** is a foam or furry cover over the microphone that reduces wind noise detected by the microphone. A windscreen is shown in **Figure 8-7.** Windscreens are made for different conditions and recordings. Outdoor recordings typically need some type of windscreen to keep away the whoosh sound created by the wind blowing over the microphone. Even on a calm day, the movement of the microphone itself can produce wind noise.

Voice recordings may use a different type of windscreen to reduce the interference caused by a voice actor's breath. The human body uses strong air pressure to create voice and other sounds. Some sounds, like the popping P sound when speaking the word *puppy,* create a sharp air pressure on the microphone. To combat these issues, a small ***pop screen*** is placed in front of the microphone to diffuse the air pressure created by the voice, as shown in **Figure 8-9.** Another reason to use a pop screen for voice recordings is to limit mouth spray. More than just being gross, droplets of mouth spray can thump against the microphone and be detected as sound.

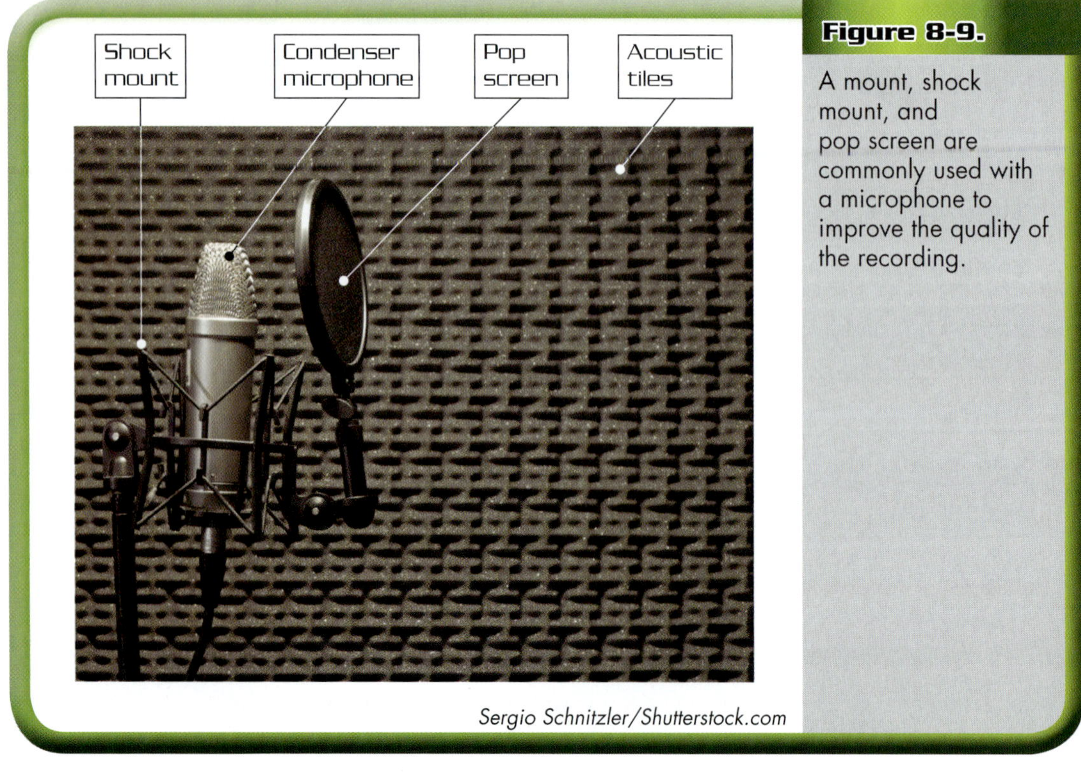

Sergio Schnitzler/Shutterstock.com

Figure 8-9. A mount, shock mount, and pop screen are commonly used with a microphone to improve the quality of the recording.

Mount

Another microphone attachment is the mount. A ***mount*** is a device used to hold and place a microphone. Having the microphone on some type of mount or stand will help keep vibration interference from the recording.

A ***shock mount*** suspends the microphone on rubber or springs so any vibration from the main mount will not interfere with the recording. A shock mount is shown in **Figure 8-9.** When practical, use a shock mount. Holding a microphone in your hand will pick up the vibration of your movements and even the pulse in your hand, depending on the sensitivity of the microphone.

For extra reach and portability, a boom mount is necessary. A ***boom mount*** places the microphone at the end of a long overhead pole so the microphone can be placed above the source being recorded. Boom mounts are commonly used in television and movie productions to capture the voices of the actors, as shown in **Figure 8-10.**

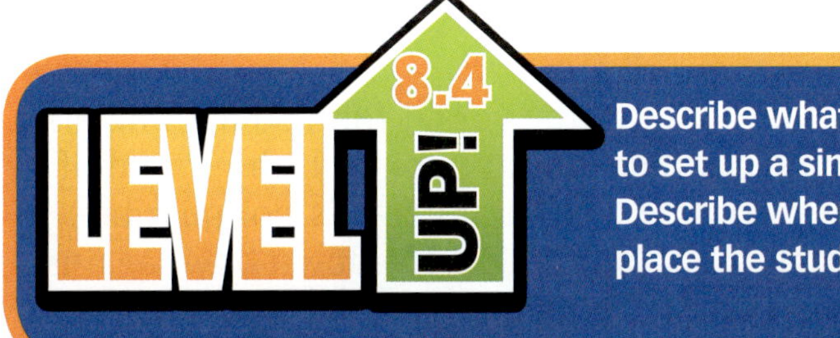

Describe what equipment could be used to set up a simple home recording studio. Describe where in your home you would place the studio and how you would set it up.

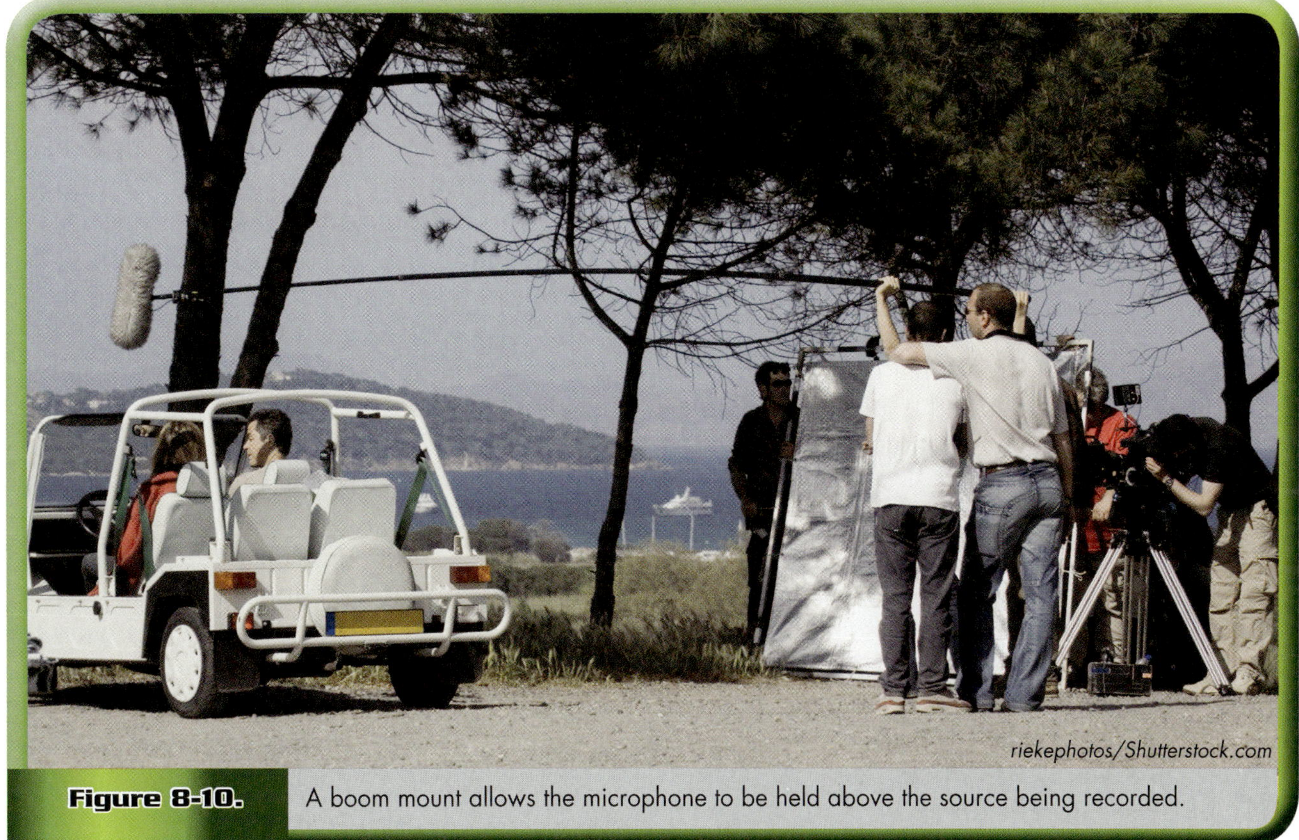

riekephotos/Shutterstock.com

Figure 8-10. A boom mount allows the microphone to be held above the source being recorded.

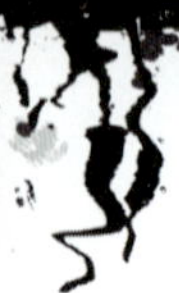

Rendering

Sound rendering is the process of using sound to communicate feelings, effects, and acoustic reality in a virtual world. For example, seeing an NPC character that is twice as tall as the player's avatar tells the player the NPC is powerful. But, adding thunderous sounds for footsteps, perhaps even including crackles of splintering wood, helps tell the player just *how* powerful the character is. Sound engineers record actual sounds, similar sounds, and composite sounds and then render them to create the final result.

Actual Sound

An ***actual sound*** is the sound made by a real object, animal, or person. If the game has an electric can opener in a scene, then record an actual can opener. If the character rides a horse in the game, record the sounds of a horse's hooves on various surfaces, such as dirt, stone, and leaves.

Similar Sound

A ***similar sound*** is a sound that imitates the sound from something else. Old radio shows used many similar sounds in storytelling. If the sound of a horse's hooves is needed, but recording an actual horse is not possible, record a similar sound. The sound of tapping an upside-down bowl against a table makes a similar sound to a horse's hooves on a road. By matching the rhythm of a walking horse, the bowl sound can simulate the footsteps of the horse.

Composite Sound

When actual and similar sounds do not meet the needs, composite sounds must be created. A ***composite sound*** is several sound assets mixed to render a single sound. For example, when a horse walks across a cobblestone road, there is the sound of the hooves on the road surface, creaking of the leather saddle, snorting breath of the horse, and chomping of the horse's teeth on the bit. These sounds do not occur sequentially. Rather, they all occur at the same time. The rendered sound must be a composite sound in order to present the player with the full impact of the action in the game.

Creating a composite sound is what most people think of as a typical job for a sound engineer. It requires an understanding of equipment and software and their features. Sound-editing software can have very specific features to attract buyers. These features might make it easier for the sound engineer to create new and original composite sounds. While features **differentiate** software for specific use, most sound-editing software includes the standard features shown in **Figure 8-11.**

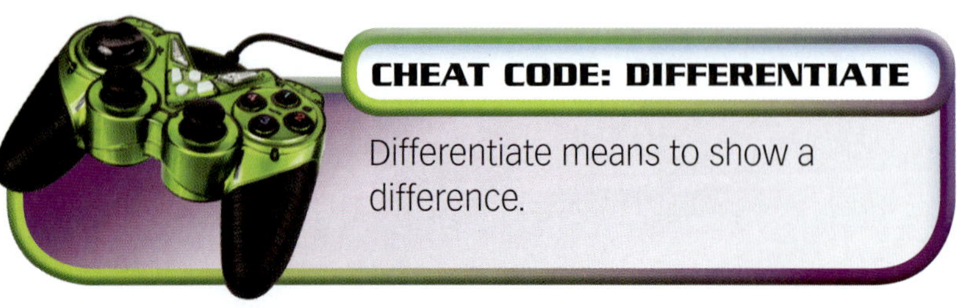

CHEAT CODE: DIFFERENTIATE

Differentiate means to show a difference.

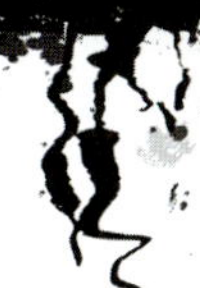

Feature Name	Function	Use
Cut	Edit by trimming the head (beginning) and tail (end) from a sample	Cuts off unneeded parts of the recording
Fade In Fade Out	Edit the head and tail of a sample by gradually increasing the volume from zero to full volume or vice versa	Allows sound to gently enter and leave; disguises a harsh cut
Time Stretch Time Compression	Modify a sound so it plays slower or faster without changing pitch	A faster sound creates a sense of urgency; a slower sound creates a sense of tension, like a door hinge creaking open; also fits a sound to the animation length
Pitch Shift	Change pitch of a sample without changing time	Higher-pitch sounds for smaller characters, like a talking chipmunk; lower-pitch sounds for larger characters, like an evil boss
Gain	Adjust volume	Set the sample volume to match the volume of the scene
Reverse	Play sound backward	Create echoes and odd sounds
Merge	Combine two or more samples	Blend actual and similar sounds to create a composite sound
Crossfade	Fade out one sample as another sample fades in	Create a smooth transition between two sounds
Conversion	Change file type or specification settings	Change from a WAV to MP3 format; downgrade the quality settings to match the game system performance
Effects and plug-ins	Change original sound into a different sound	Makes samples for similar sounds; add richness to original sound

Figure 8-11. Sound-editing software generally has these common features.

Goodheart-Willcox Publisher

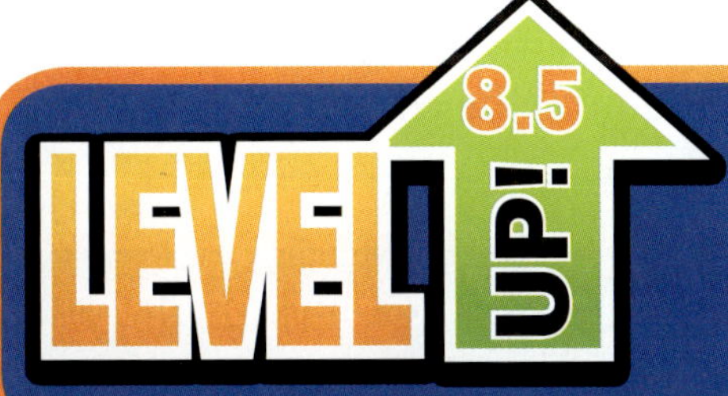

Play a game with a fantasy or science fiction theme. Identify at least three sounds in the game for interactions that do not exist in the real world. Describe how you would create the sounds.

Sound Effects

One of the most exciting parts of sound editing may be using sound effects. Sound FX in a game are sounds used to enhance the artistic presentation of the game. Sound FX in relation to sound recording and rendering are enhancements to sound samples. Two interesting sound effects are reverb and chorus. While most sound-editing software ships with a standard collection of effects, other effects may be available as plug-ins.

Reverb

Reverb is an echo effect that makes the sound full by simulating the reflecting of sound waves off of walls and objects. Reverb levels can be adjusted to create echo effects to simulate closed environments. If the game interaction is in a large cave, the reverb should have a lot of echo to simulate the sound bouncing off of the rock walls. An empty warehouse is another location where reverb can help simulate the environment. In a space scene, there sound should have little or no reverb to simulate the quiet vacuum of space.

Chorus

Chorus is similar to reverb except it adds a delay to the sound to simulate more than one sound source. Just like the name suggests, chorus changes the sample much like the difference between a solo singer and a chorus of singers. For example, if the character must use a keyboard, chorus may be added to the sound sample of key clicks to simulate very fast finger movement. In other cases, the chorus effect may be used to help blur a sharp sound.

Plug-Ins

A ***plug-in*** is software that enhances another program by extending its capabilities. Three major plug-ins are DirectX, Audio Units (AU), and Real-Time AudioSuite (RTAS).

Some plug-ins include interface equipment like a synthesizer or sampler. A *synthesizer* creates artificial sounds from pure tones. Some electronic keyboards work well as a synthesizer. Synthesizers can create interesting sounds like beeps and notes. These same keyboards can work as samplers as well. A *sampler* can record a sound and then play it back at different pitches. With a sampler, you could record your dog barking and play it back in pitches from low to high. This can create some really fun songs, like playing Jingle Bells using dog bark notes.

A *musical instrument digital interface (MIDI)* is used to connect musical instruments to a computer using a cable connection. The instrument must be MIDI enabled. Instruments like drums, guitars, pianos, and more can be plugged into the computer to record digital music. A talented musician could record MIDI-enabled instruments on different channels. When all the tracks are combined, a one man orchestra would be playing the entire musical score from the computer.

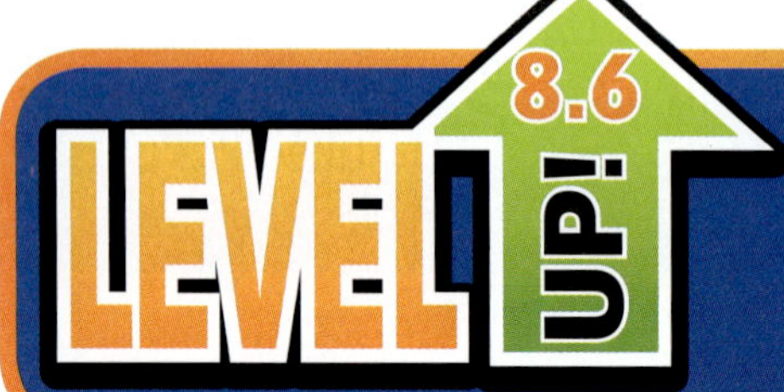

Think about sound effects that you have heard in video games. Describe how the effects enhanced the emotion or sensation of the sounds.

Chapter Summary

- The sound engineer is the team member responsible for sound production, the part of the design process that involves creating and managing sound assets, the sound library, recording equipment, and the rendering of sound.
- A sound asset must be created for each interaction in the game that requires an associated sound and then be added to the sound database; the entries in the database list the information needed to design and store the sound.
- A sound library is a collection of completed sound samples which can be used in multiple games; reusing sound assets is an inexpensive and time-saving way to add sounds to a game.
- Standard equipment needed to capture and record sounds includes: a recording device, a microphone, a windscreen (when required), and a mount (when required).
- Sound rendering is the process of using sound to communicate feelings, effects, and acoustic reality in a virtual world through the use of actual sounds, similar sounds, and composite sounds that are rendered to create the final result.
- Sound effects in a game are sounds used to enhance the artistic presentation of the game; they are enhancements to sound samples.

Check Your Video Game IQ

Now that you have finished this chapter, see what you know about video game design by taking the chapter posttest.

www.m.g-wlearning.com

www.g-wlearning.com

Review Your Knowledge

On a separate sheet of paper or in a word processing document, match the following terms with the definition that fits best.

A. actual sound	F. canned sound
B. windscreen	G. shock mount
C. composite sound	H. similar sound
D. pop screen	I. bit rate
E. sampling frequency	J. boom mount

1. A microphone mount that places the microphone at the end of a long overhead pole so the microphone can be placed above the source being recorded.
2. The sound made by a real object, animal, or person.
3. The number of bits of data transferred per second.

4. A foam or furry cover over the microphone that reduces wind noise detected by the microphone.
5. A sound that imitates the sound from something else.
6. Several sound assets mixed to render a single sound.
7. A microphone mount that suspends the microphone on rubber or springs so any vibration from the main mount will not interfere with the recording.
8. An object placed in front of the microphone to diffuse the air pressure created by the voice.
9. A previously recorded generic sound.
10. How many times per second the sound data are recorded.

On a separate sheet of paper or in a word processing document, answer each of the following questions.

11. List five major responsibilities of a sound engineer.
12. Describe the process for recording dialogue.
13. What is the difference between mono and stereo sound?
14. How did early video games overcome the need for large sound files?
15. How frequently is sound sampled for CD quality?
16. How does creating a sound library help save time and money?
17. List four common pieces of sound recording equipment.
18. Which feature of sound editing software allows the engineer to eliminate unwanted parts at the beginning or end of the recording?
19. What type of device would allow you to record your cat's meow and play the sound back as notes in a song?
20. What is the interface that allows a musical instrument to connect to a computer or other digital recording device?

Apply Your STEM Knowledge

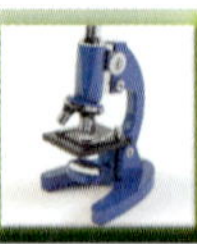

Science

1. Research the Doppler effect. Write a one-page paper to include a description of the Doppler effect and how it can be applied in video game design sound context and as a clue to off-screen action.

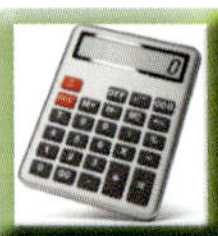

Mathematics

2. Use a word processor or spreadsheet program to recreate the following table. Solve for the missing data.

Sample	Recorded Frequency (kHz)	Recorded Bit Rate (bits)	Spec Length (seconds)	Mono File Size (bits)	Mono File Size (kilobytes)	Stereo File Size (kilobytes)	Spec File Size (kilobytes)
Cat meowing	44.1	16	1.2	846720	105.840	211.68	250
Man screaming	96	16		4300800			1000
Door creaking		8	3.0			716.8	720
Bomb exploding	8		0.9	57600			250
Laser firing	44.1	16	0.3				30

Language Arts

3. Review the sound sample table in question 2. Notice that there are some samples that exceed the specifications for file size and others that are far below the requirements. Write a one-page paper to list each sample and state if it meets specifications, is above specifications, or is below specification. For each that does not meet specification, explain how to modify the sample to meet file size specifications.

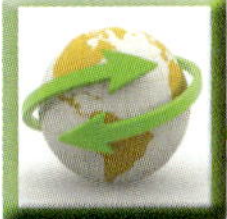

Social Studies

4. Recreate the table below using a word processor or spreadsheet program. Using a website such as the one for the Bureau of Labor Statistics, research salary data for the popular video game sound design careers listed in the table. Complete the table.

Job Title	Annual Salary	Years of Experience Required	Location of job
Senior Sound Designer			
Sound Engineer			
Assistant Sound Engineer			
Sound Editor			
Sound Tech			

Language Arts

5. Using the Cheat Codes and bold italic key terms from this chapter, create a crossword puzzle. Write proper definition for each term to use as clues. Create the puzzle on a sheet of graph paper or use a puzzle-maker website. Exchange your crossword puzzle with a classmate and complete.

Working in Teams

Working with the team assigned by your instructor, select one video game and make a list of sounds contained in the game. Identify ways in which each sound can be created and recorded. Prepare a class presentation to describe your findings.

Gamer Portfolio

Your portfolio should contain items related to your schoolwork. These items might include report cards, transcripts, or honor roll reports. Diplomas or certificates that show courses or programs you completed should also be included. At some point, you will likely apply for a particular job or volunteer position. At that time, you should list the classes you took that helped prepare you for the job or volunteer position. Describe the activities you completed or topics you studied in these classes that relate to the job or volunteer duties. This information will be helpful when you apply for the position by letter or talk with an interviewer.

1. Identify a job or volunteer position for which you could apply. Write a paragraph that lists the classes you took and activities completed that relate to the position. You can use this document as a model when you are actually ready to apply for a position.
2. Scan other documents related to your schoolwork, such as grade reports, transcripts, and diplomas. Place the model paragraph and other documents in your e-portfolio.
3. Place hard copies in the container for your print portfolio.

G-W Learning Mobile Site

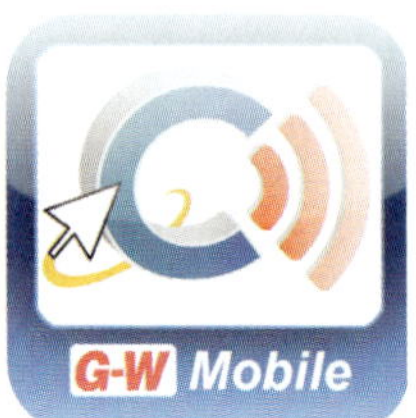

Visit the G-W Learning mobile site to complete the chapter pretest and posttest and to practice vocabulary using e-flash cards. If you do not have a smartphone, visit the G-W Learning companion website to access these features.

G-W Learning mobile site: www.m.g-wlearning.com

G-W Learning companion website: www.g-wlearning.com

Common Core

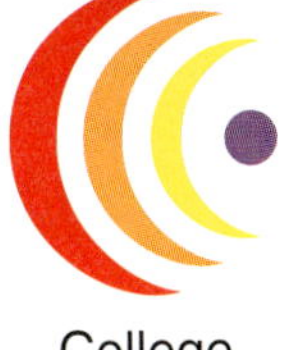
College and Career Readiness

CTE Career Ready Practices. Read the Ethical Gamer features presented throughout this text. What role do you think ethics and integrity have in decision making? Think of a time when you used your ideals and principles to make a decision. What process did you use to make the decision? In retrospect, do you think you made the correct decision? Did your decision have any consequences?

Writing. Perform an Internet search for the sound design of Star Wars to find out how these classic movie sounds were created. Write an informative report, consisting of several paragraphs, to describe your findings.

Speaking and Listening. Research the features of some of the sound editing software used in video game design and movie production. Compile information about the aspects and features of each that help sound engineers perform their jobs more effectively. Include any other interesting information you find. Use this information, along with what you already know and what you learned in this chapter, to choose the software that you would like to have. Using various elements (visual displays, written handouts, technological displays), present your choice to the class. Explain why you chose the software you did.

Event Prep: Extemporaneous Speaking

Extemporaneous speaking is a competitive event you might enter with your Career and Technical Student Organization (CTSO). This event allows you to display your communication skills of speaking, organizing, and making an oral presentation. At the competition, you will be given several topics from which to choose. You will also be given a time limit to create and deliver the speech. You will be evaluated on your verbal and nonverbal skills as well as the tone and projection of your voice. To prepare for the extemporaneous speaking event:

1. Read the guidelines provided by your organization. Make certain that you ask any questions about points you do not understand. It is important you follow each specific item that is outlined in the competition rules.
2. Ask your instructor for several topics on video game design so you can practice making impromptu speeches.
3. Once you have an assigned practice topic from your instructor, jot down your ideas and points you want to cover. An important part about making this type of presentation is that you will have only a few minutes to prepare. Being able to write down your main ideas quickly will enable you to focus on what you will actually say in the presentation.
4. Practice the presentation. You should introduce yourself, review the topic that is being presented, defend the topic being presented, and conclude with a summary.
5. Ask your teacher to play the role of Competition Judge as your team reviews the case. After the presentation is complete, ask for feedback from your teacher. You may also consider having a student audience to listen and give feedback.
6. For the event, bring paper and pencils to record notes. Supplies may or may not be provided.

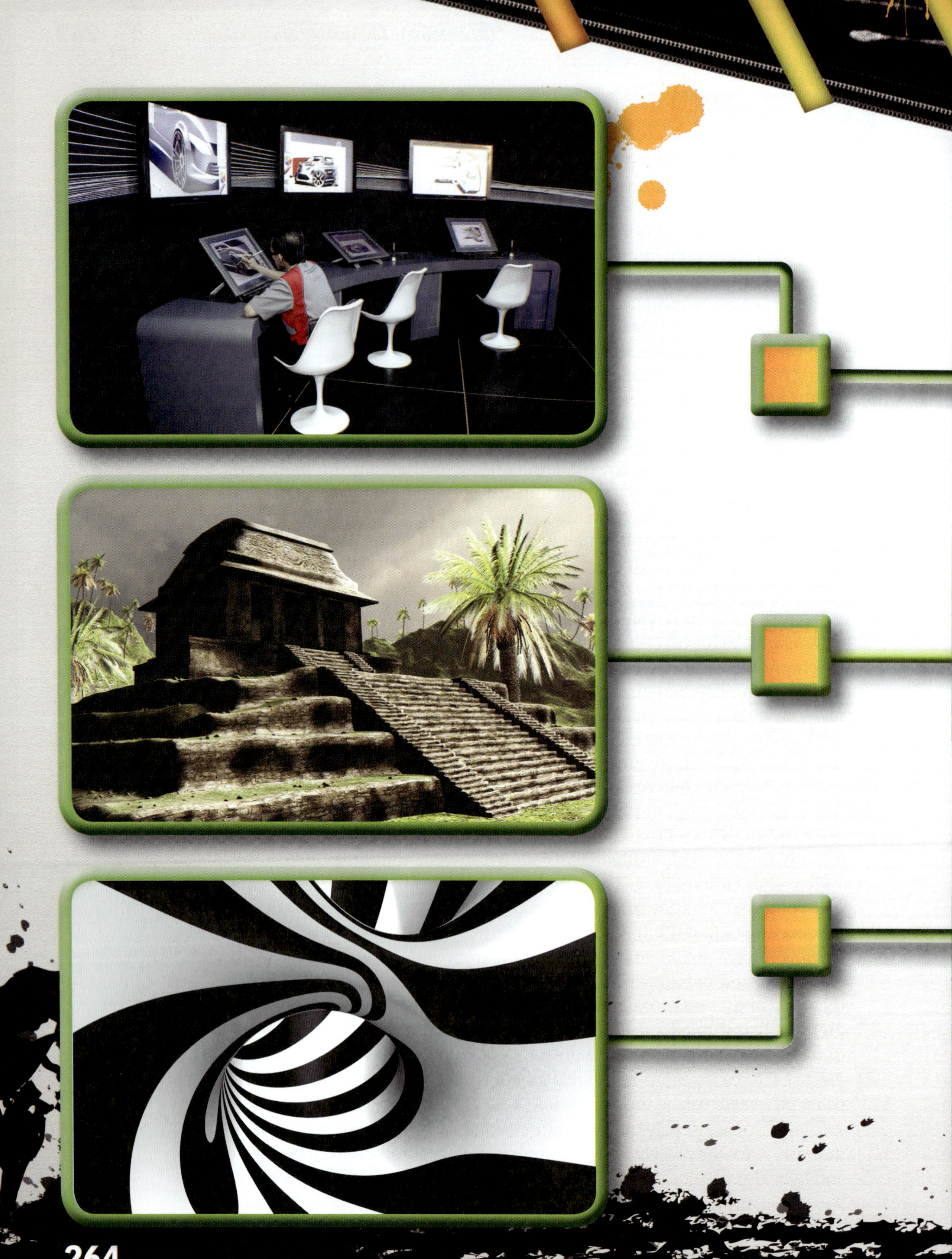

Chapter 9
Art Composition

This chapter discusses the basics needed to create great art, animations, and special effects. In addition to a story, the art, animation, and special effects are what make the game come alive. Without these assets, the game would be just text and code. The artistry of the game creates the immersive multimedia game environment that connects the player to the gameplay.

Check Your Video Game IQ

Before you begin this chapter, see what you already know about video game design by taking the chapter pretest.

www.m.g-wlearning.com

www.g-wlearning.com

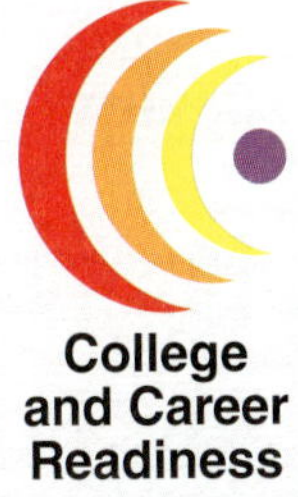

College and Career Readiness

Reading Prep. In preparation for this chapter, use the Internet and printed materials to locate advertisements for video games. What catches your attention in the advertisements? Is there one element that stands out from the rest? What colors are used? Think about these advertisements as you read the chapter and consider how art composition applies to each.

Objectives

After completing this chapter, you will be able to:

- Consider the impact that art has on video game design.
- Assess how the art in a video game will be viewed or experienced.
- Outline the elements of art and the principles of design that apply in imagery for video games as well as other art forms.

Art Influences

Image design is usually more art than science. A person skilled in traditional art, such as painting or sculpture, may have a better chance at developing great skill in game art and animation than a computer programmer. It can take an artistic eye to see how all parts of an object will be formed and combined to give the correct surface needed for an object, as shown in **Figure 9-1.**

This does not mean that only an artist can create valuable game art and animations. Since computers are used extensively to create game art, most technology-savvy students can acquire skills to design quality game art. Many of the skills you have already mastered will be used in making game art.

On a design team, a game artist is the specialist who creates the visual elements of the game. A specialist is an expert with strong skills in a certain area. Specialists in art have strong skills in drawing, coloring/rendering, and sculpting/modeling. They should also have a strong background in art history and the cultural influences in art. With these specialist skills, a game artist is prepared to create game assets that fit the historical and cultural theme of the game.

Art history and culture should be considered when creating game art. Art history is the major trends and innovations in art. Historical periods of art include medieval, renaissance, mannerism, baroque, neoclassicism, romanticism, realism, modern art, and contemporary art. In each historical period there are subcategories called art movements to help sort the art of the period. An ***art movement*** is a particular dominant style or technique. For example, the period of modern art includes the art movements of cubism (art with hard lines and primitive shapes), expressionism (distorting images to exaggerate emotion), surrealism (use of unusual, shocking, and surprising content), and pop art (use of common items as art).

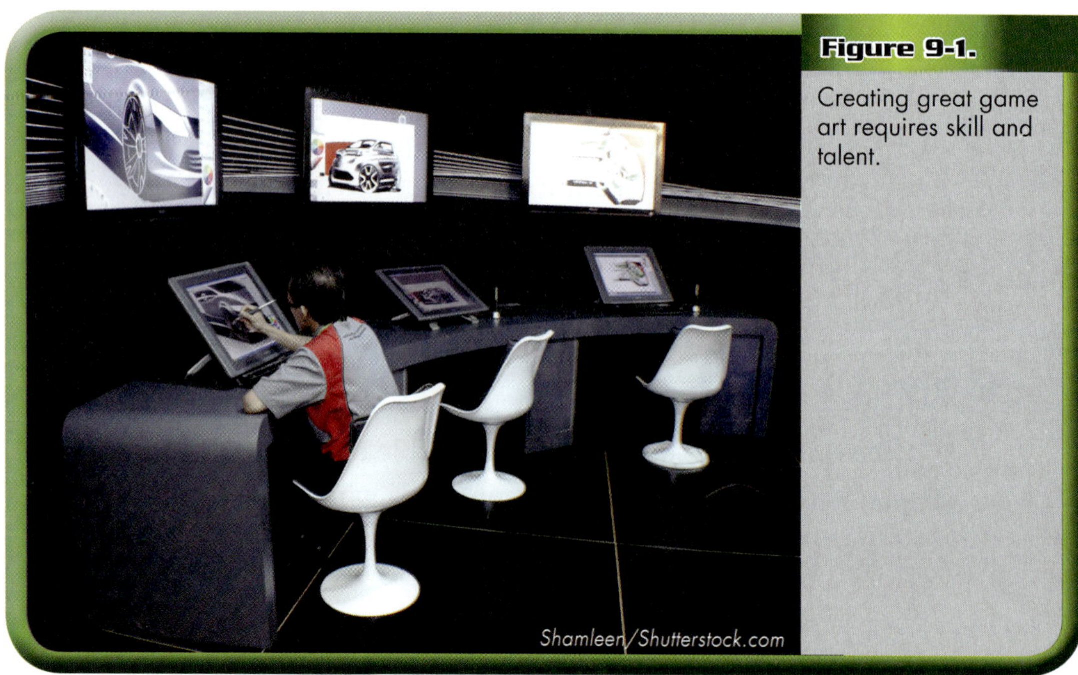

Shamleen/Shutterstock.com

Figure 9-1. Creating great game art requires skill and talent.

Often, within the study of art is the reason for making the artwork. In many cases, art was the only way to record history. A piece of medieval art might be a sculpture or pottery design that showed how invaders were defeated. In these cases, the reason for the art is to record the history of the battle. The **Bayeux tapestry** is a good example of this. In other cases, art is used to display the feeling or emotion of the society. The famous piece of pop art Campbell's Soup Cans by Andy Warhol is 32 separate silkscreened paintings of soup cans. This artwork may be trying to convey that visual art and design are part of everyday life and everyday objects. Throughout time, artists have been capturing the beliefs, values, emotions, and events from their community in their artwork.

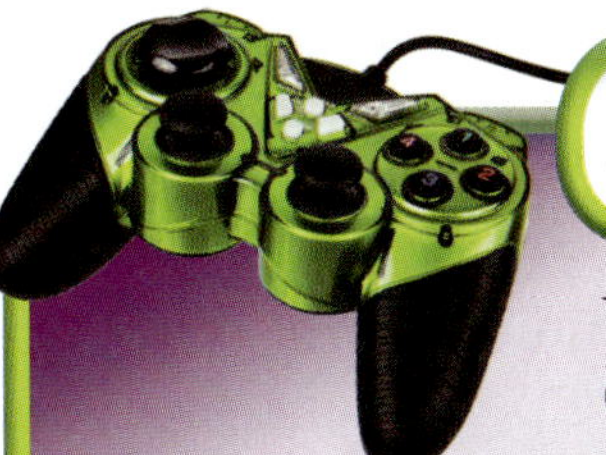

CHEAT CODE: BAYEUX TAPESTRY

The Bayeux tapestry is a famous embroidered cloth nearly 230 feet long that records the battle of Hastings in which the Normans successfully invaded England in 1066.

Much of what an archeologist will find and use to learn about an ancient society is its artwork. This is not only because the art captures the historical and emotional content of the society, but also captures the cultural influences. ***Cultural influences*** are those characteristics unique to a geographic region or the people of that region. Common cultural influences in art are religion, family, government, natural resources, environment, and activities.

Look at the historical artwork from two different cultures shown in **Figure 9-2.** Look at the details and how the art can be used to compare and contrast the two different cultures. The Egyptian artwork shows a horse-drawn chariot, while in the Indian artwork an elephant is the mode of transportation. Additionally, the manner of dress is significantly different between the two cultures. The cultural influences displayed in each of these works of art show how much an artist must know to match the details of a game with reality.

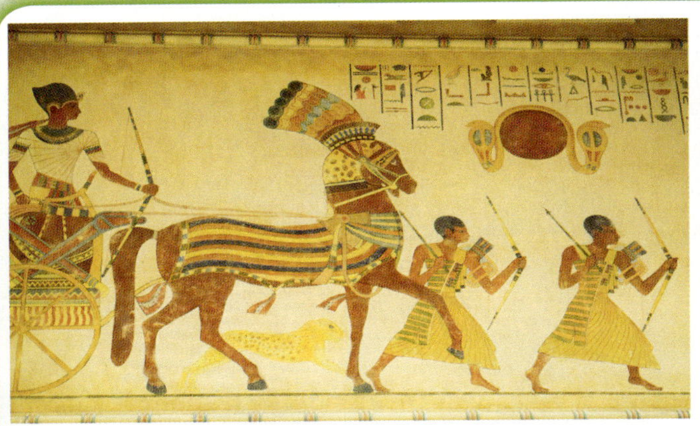

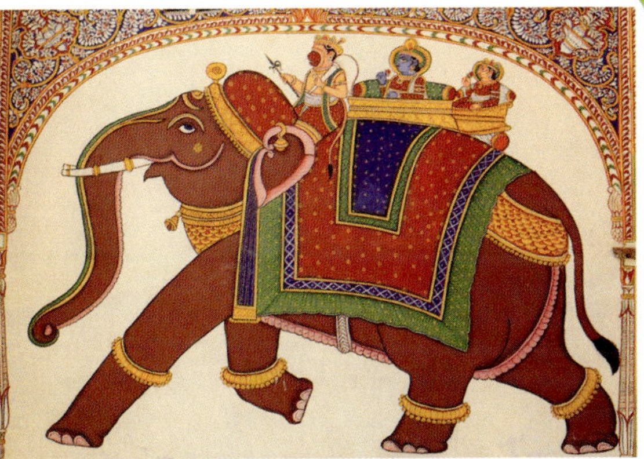

Elnur/Shutterstock.com; Rafal Cichawa/Shutterstock.com

Figure 9-2. In the historical artwork on the left from Ancient Egypt, the mode of transportation is a horse-drawn chariot. In the historical artwork on the right from Ancient India, the mode of transportation is an elephant.

If you were in charge of creating a game in which the victory condition is conquering the world, you would need to create game art to match each culture. This is true whether the world is historically accurate or a fantasy world. Each culture will likely have different clothing, weapons, environments, and much more. When creating game art, the game assets must match the time period and location being used in the game world. The story of the game, whether real or fantasy, determines what is accurate. Understanding traditional artwork such as paintings, sculptures, architecture, and drawings from real historical periods and locations will prove important when creating digital game art.

Since a video game world is an imaginary world, some of these historical elements can be combined to make a new and interesting world unlike anything on Earth. This makes a game artist the creator of worlds. Adapting history and culture to new worlds is a great way to connect the reality of the human past with the bold new world in the game. Look at **Figure 9-3.** What historical and cultural influences are used in this game world?

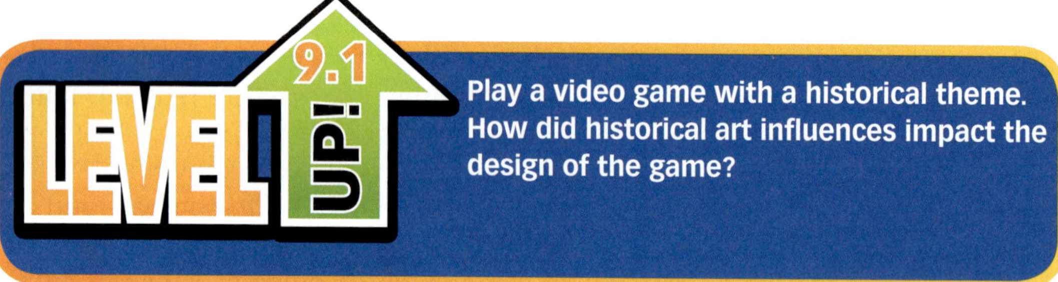

Play a video game with a historical theme. How did historical art influences impact the design of the game?

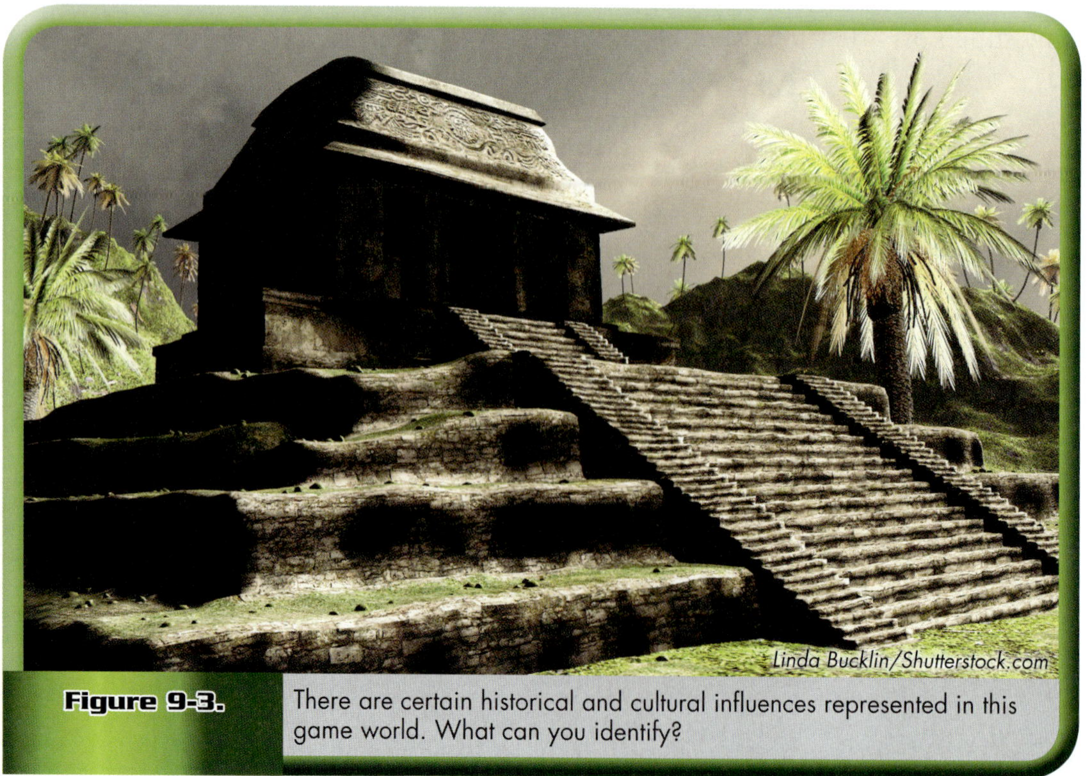

Figure 9-3. There are certain historical and cultural influences represented in this game world. What can you identify?

Art Presentation

The first step in creating artwork is to understand the presentation. ***Presentation*** is how the art will be viewed or experienced. The purpose of the artwork will help guide the presentation. If you are creating something that people will see from high above, then you will need to have a large presentation area on the surface of the Earth. The Nazca lines, some of which are shown in **Figure 9-4,** are ancient drawings that cover almost 200 square miles. The presentation of the Nazca lines was from high above the drawings, perhaps from the surrounding mountains. The presentation of artwork in a video game is a considerably smaller format. Once the presentation is determined, the designer must reverse engineer the artwork to fit the format. The old adage, *form follows function,* applies here.

To match the artwork to the presentation, two additional decisions are required: the choice of medium and tools. The medium is the material used to create the artwork. Tools are the devices used to create the artwork. **Figure 9-5** shows various artwork or items and how the presentation determines the media and tools needed.

A game artist may typically work with digital media and tools. However, concept art, sketches, textures, and mockups may be completed using the media and tools of traditional art. The background of a virtual world may be a scene photographed from the real world. Motion-capture devices and 3D scanners are also commonly used to record the real movements of a person or to convert a real object to a digital model. These may be some of the tactics the designers use to help the player be immersed in the game world.

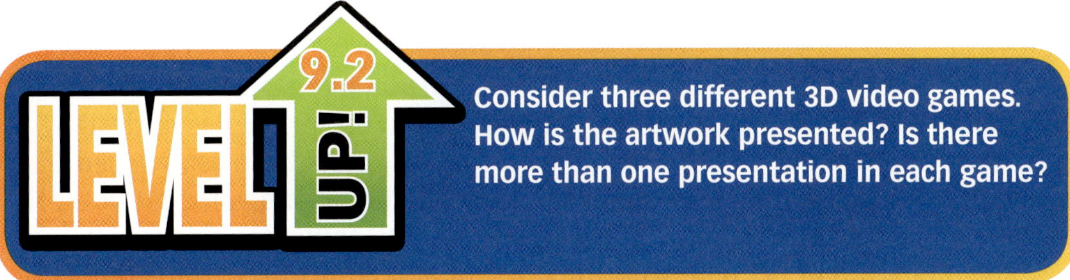

Consider three different 3D video games. How is the artwork presented? Is there more than one presentation in each game?

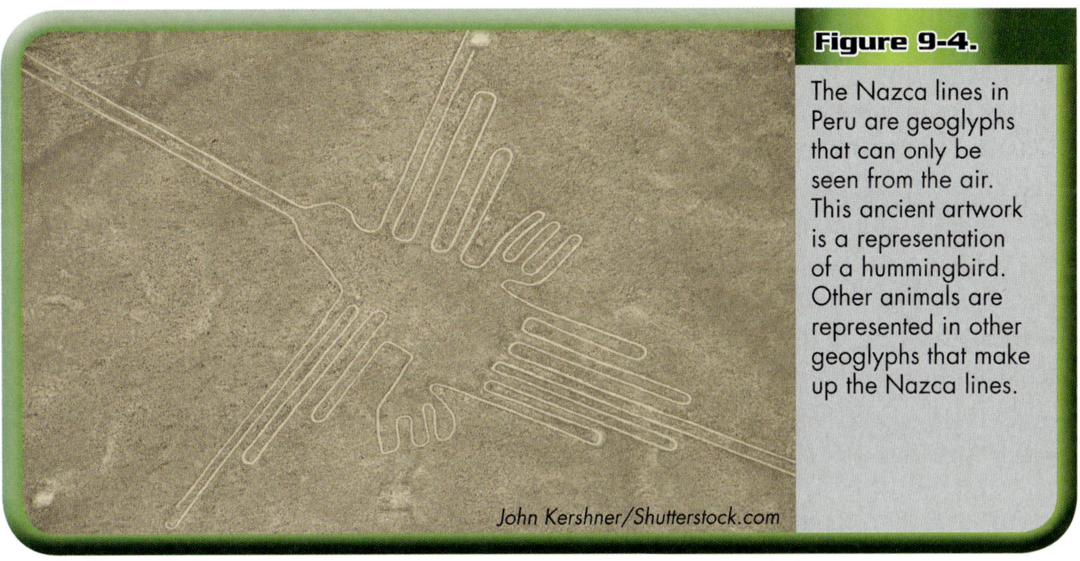

Figure 9-4. The Nazca lines in Peru are geoglyphs that can only be seen from the air. This ancient artwork is a representation of a hummingbird. Other animals are represented in other geoglyphs that make up the Nazca lines.

Item	Presentation	Medium	Tools
Nazca lines	View from above	Desert floor and stones	Shovel or rake
Painting	Framed and hanging on wall	Canvas and paint	Paint brushes
Photograph	In a photo album or collage	Paper and ink	Camera, computer, and printer
Sculpture	In a courtyard, garden, or room	Marble	Hammer and chisel
Dance	In a theater	Visual or performance	Costumes and dancers
Song	In concert, on the radio, or from an MP3 player	Recording media or sound system	Microphone, sound booth, stage, and a recording device
Website	On a computer monitor, smartphone, or tablet	Web browser	Web developer software and imaging software
Video game	On a TV, computer monitor, smartphone, or tablet	Game console or computer	Game engine and imaging software

Figure 9-5. This table shows some types of artwork, the presentation, and possible media and tools needed to create the artwork.

Goodheart-Willcox Publisher

Elements and Principles of Art

Whether the artist is working with virtual media like a video game or physical media like a sculpture, the elements of art and principles of design hold true. Thousands of years of trial and error by artists have established these universal truths. To develop the skills needed to create game artwork, the elements of art and the principles of design must be applied.

The ***elements of art*** deal with the individual features needed to compose artwork. Each individual feature or element is constructed and arranged to create artwork. Artwork is an artistic work developed using a combination of art elements to create a visual scene, character, volume, or image. Artwork should also be developed following the principles of design. The ***principles of design*** govern how to effectively combine the elements of art to compose a pleasing work of art. Together, the elements of art and principles of design are used to create game art and artistic scenes.

Traditional artwork is created without the use of computer technology. Examples of traditional artwork include paintings, drawings, sculptures, pottery, and so on. ***Digital artwork*** is created using a computer. The artist inputs information into a computer program that helps create the artwork. The final artwork can be displayed in physical form or in virtual form. Digital artwork can be output in physical form such as a printed page or an object produced by molding, rapid prototyping machine, computer-guided lathe, or other computer-controlled output. Digital artwork in virtual form may be digital pictures or animations displayed on a computer screen.

Elements of Art

There are seven elements of art: shape, form, line, color, value, space, and texture. Each of these elements details an aspect of a single attribute of an object. These elements are universal and apply to both traditional and digital art. Below are brief descriptions of each element of art.

Shape

The black circle shown in **Figure 9-6A** is a shape defined by the edges of the black ink on the paper. Shape is a defined area in two-dimensional space. Shapes come in two different varieties: geometric and organic.

Geometric shapes are regular figures, like a square, circle, triangle, octagon, or trapezoid. Geometric shapes are also known as 2D primitives. ***Primitives*** are regular shapes and objects that are used to assemble more complex shapes or objects. For example, the robotic character shown in **Figure 9-6B** is constructed from 2D primitives: three circles, five rectangles, and one trapezoid.

Irregular shapes are known as ***organic shapes.*** Organic shapes describe things like a cloud, tree, blowing steam, or even an ergonomic computer mouse. Mostly, organic shapes are used to describe things in nature. In practice, organic shapes describe natural and unnatural shapes that have curved or irregular edges.

Form

The assembly of 2D shapes to represent a third dimension is ***form.*** Form shows measurable dimensions of length, width, and depth for an object. A traditional sculpture has form, but a computer-modeled character also has form.

Line

If you look at the basic robot in **Figure 9-6B,** each shape is defined by the boundary created by a solid black line. A line is the path between two points and most often used as a boundary to create a shape. Lines can be straight, curved, looping, or organic and can be solid or composed of dashes or other marks.

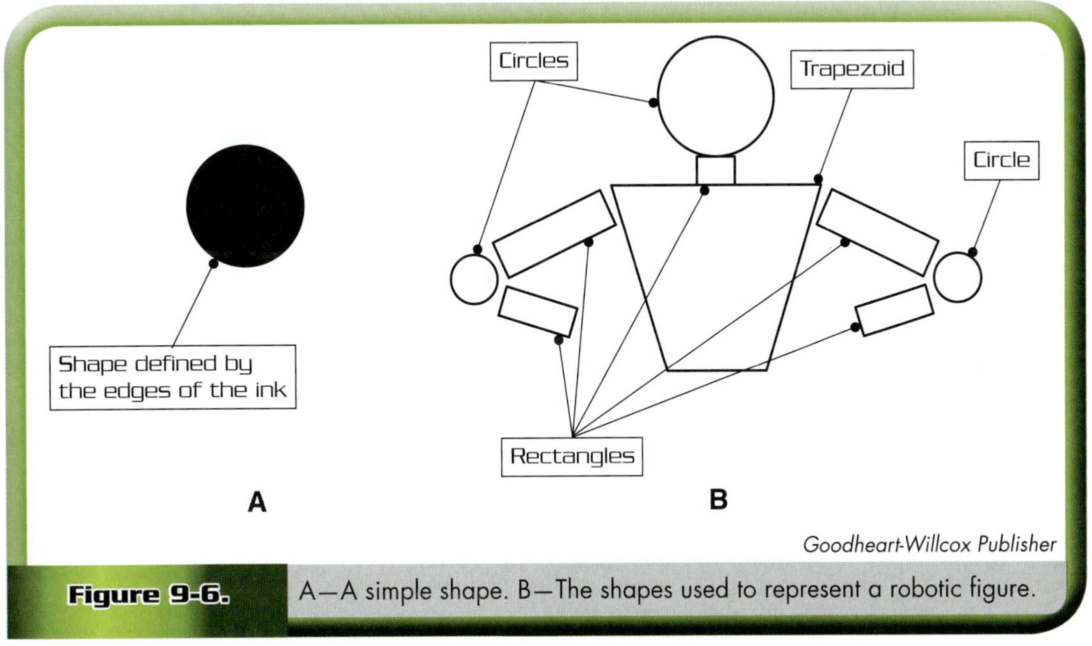

Figure 9-6. A—A simple shape. B—The shapes used to represent a robotic figure.

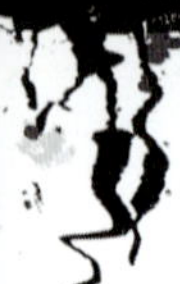

When a line is composed of dashes or other marks, it is an implied line, as shown in **Figure 9-7.** An ***implied line*** is the path the viewer's eye takes to connect the two endpoints of the line when it is not continuous. Basically, the viewer's eye connects the dots with an invisible (implied) line to complete the line path.

Color

The combination of hues applied to a line or shape is its color. In imaging software, the *line color* or *outline color* is applied to the border line only. The *shape color* or *shape fill* is color applied to the shape defined by the line. In most imaging software, the shape color can be applied only if the shape is completely enclosed by lines or the edges of other shapes. If there is a break in the line or the shape is not completely enclosed, the color will "leak out," as shown in **Figure 9-8.**

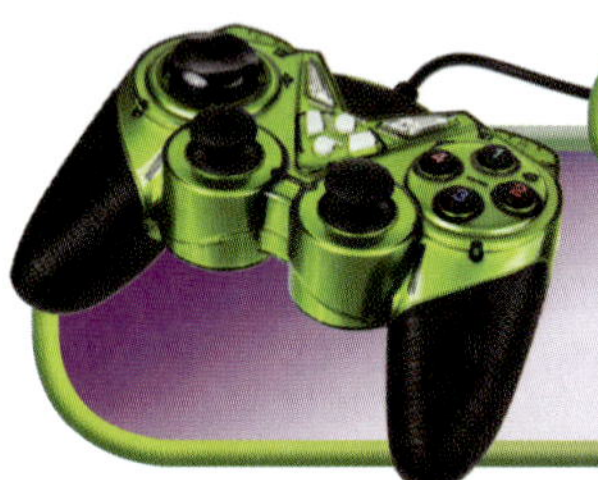

CHEAT CODE: COLOR MODEL

A color model is a way of mixing base colors to create a spectrum of colors.

Colors are defined using a **color model**. The RGB color model is the most common color model used in game design. The name comes from the three base colors used in the color model: red, green, and blue. All of the colors you see on a computer screen are made by mixing these three base colors. Other color models include hue, saturation, luminescence (HSL) and cyan, magenta, yellow, and key (CMYK). Hue is the pigment color, saturation is how dark or rich the color is, and luminescence is how much light is shining on the color. Cyan, magenta, and yellow are process colors. The most detail in a printed image appears in the key color, which is almost always black.

The total spectrum of colors a given model can create is called the ***gamut.*** Colors are assembled or blended using an additive or subtractive method. The *additive method* starts with no color, or black, and colors are added to create

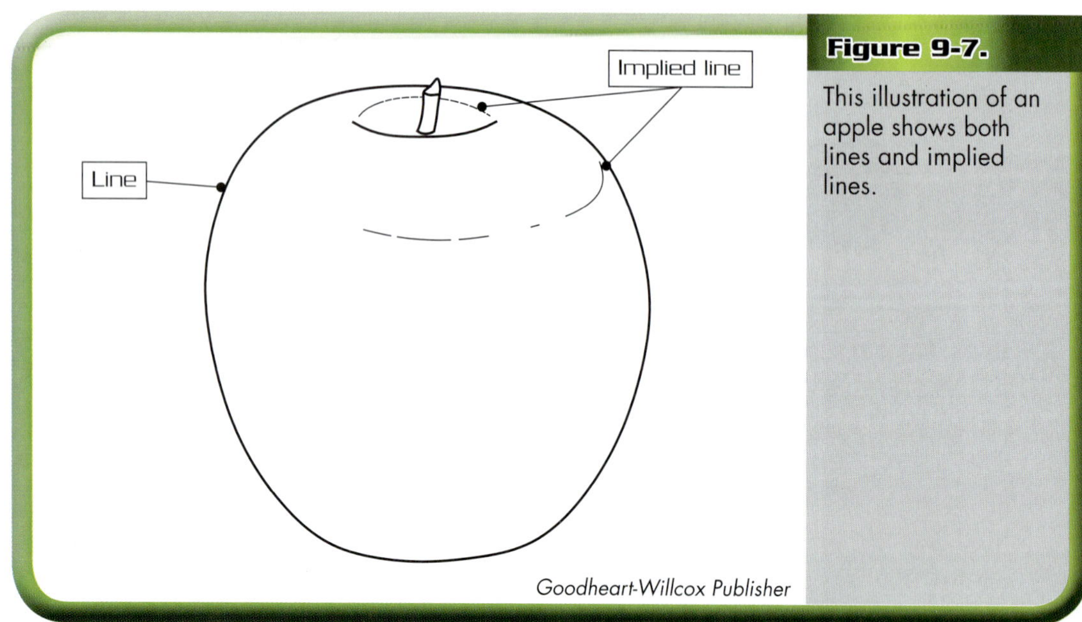

Figure 9-7. This illustration of an apple shows both lines and implied lines.

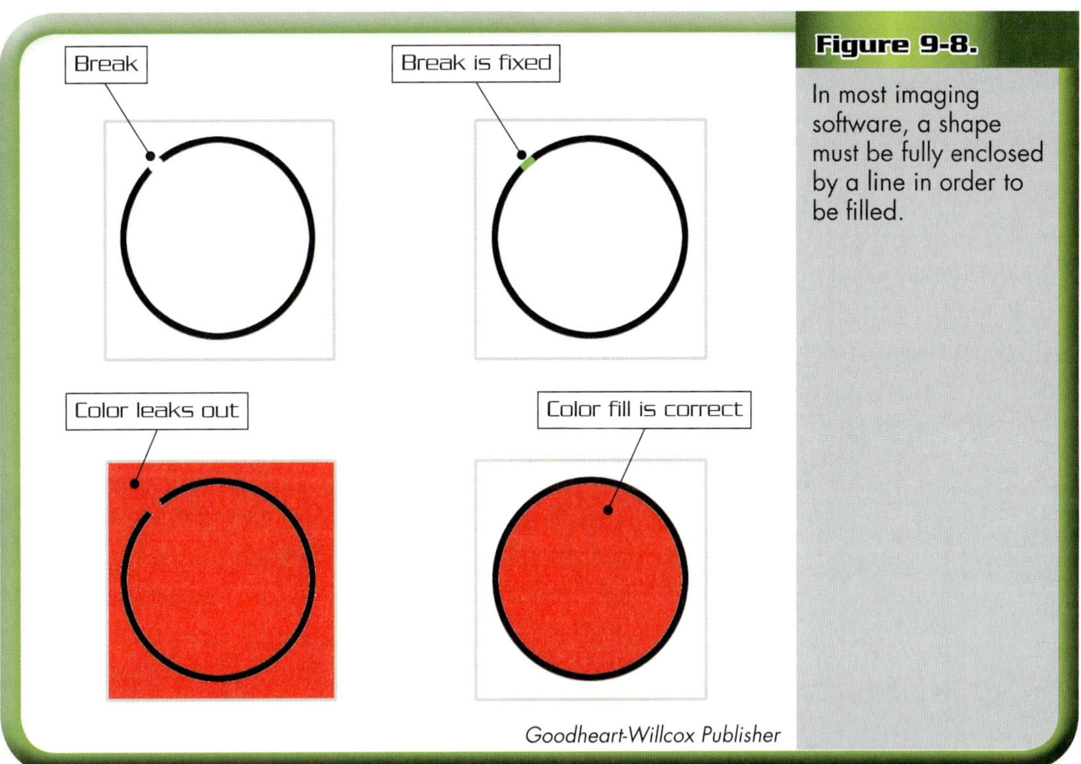

Figure 9-8. In most imaging software, a shape must be fully enclosed by a line in order to be filled.

the final color, as shown in **Figure 9-9.** White in an additive color model is the combination of all color wavelengths in light. In the RGB color model, black is red 0, green 0, and blue 0. This means no color is added to the black screen. White is red 255, green 255, and blue 255. This means the maximum amount of all three colors is added to the black screen.

The *subtractive method* starts with all color, or white, and colors are removed to create the final color. For example, when you look at a red object, all color wavelengths in the light are absorbed by the paint (subtracted) except for red. What you see is the red wavelength. White is the reflection of all color wavelengths, so no color is subtracted. Black occurs when no color wavelengths are reflected, so all color is subtracted. CMYK is a subtractive color model. **Figure 9-10** summarizes some common color models and whether they are additive or subtractive.

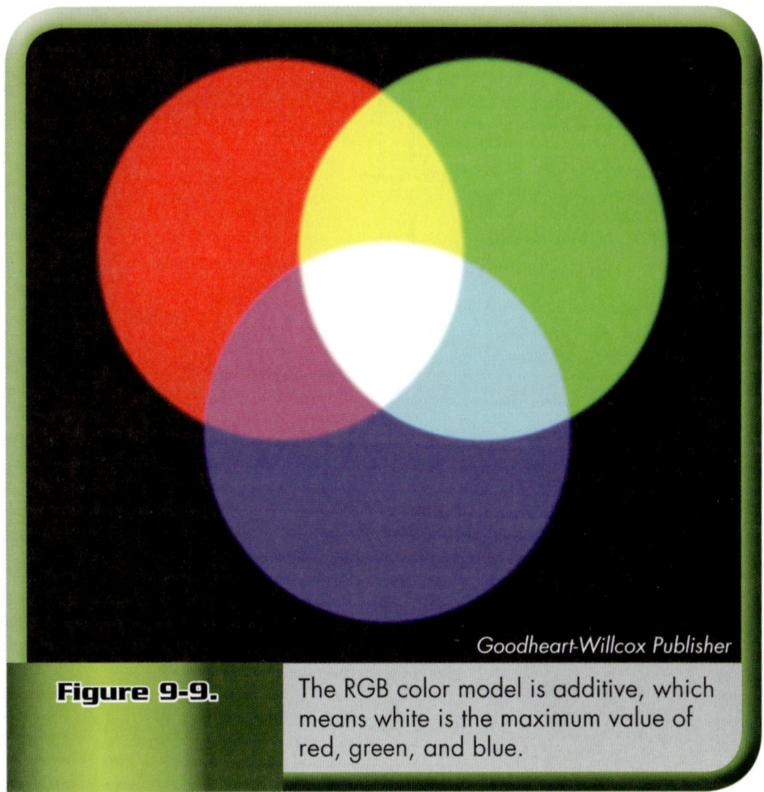

Figure 9-9. The RGB color model is additive, which means white is the maximum value of red, green, and blue.

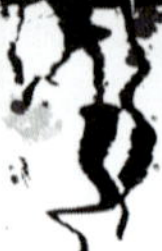

CASE STUDY

Color Wavelengths

Visible light is the portion of light that humans can see. This spectrum, or gamut, of light is displayed by the colors of the rainbow. The major colors are red, orange, yellow, green, blue, indigo, and violet. Colors are actually different wavelengths of light energy, as shown in the figure.

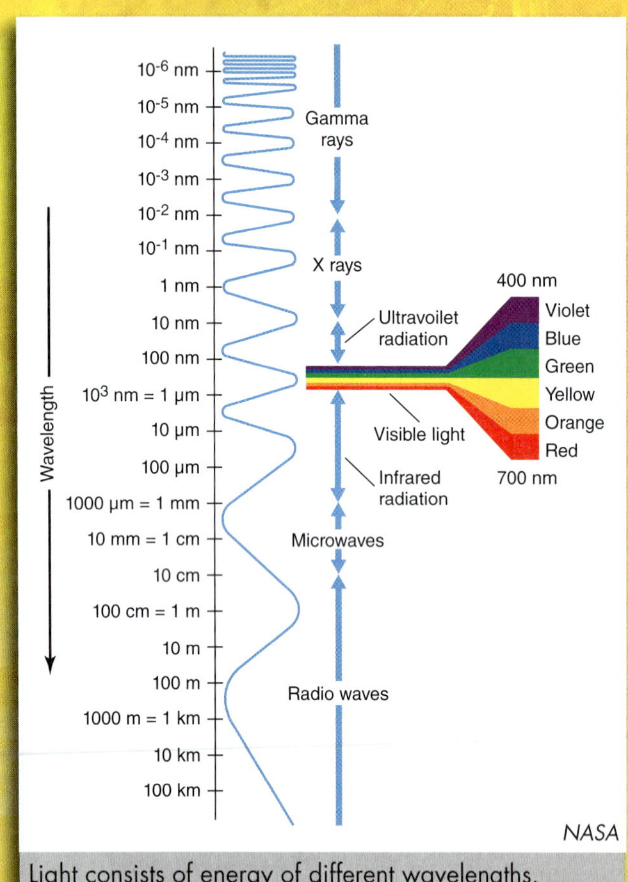

Light consists of energy of different wavelengths.

Red is the longest wavelength of light humans can see. Energy wavelengths longer than red are called infrared. Heat energy emits wavelengths in the infrared spectrum. The shortest wavelengths of light humans can see is violet. Energy wavelengths shorter than violet are called ultraviolet.

A wave of energy is measured by length, amplitude, and frequency, as shown in the figure. Length is the distance from one wave top to the next wave top. Amplitude is the height of the wave. Frequency is the number of complete waves per a time period, often one second. The wavelength determines the color of light. The amplitude determines the brightness of the light.

Since sounds are also waves of energy, the same terminology can be applied to sound. If the wavelength of sound is changed, the sound changes in pitch. If the amplitude is changed, the volume of the sound changes.

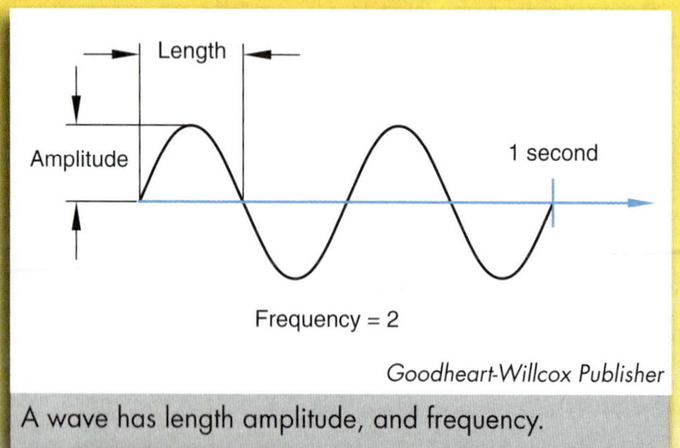

A wave has length amplitude, and frequency.

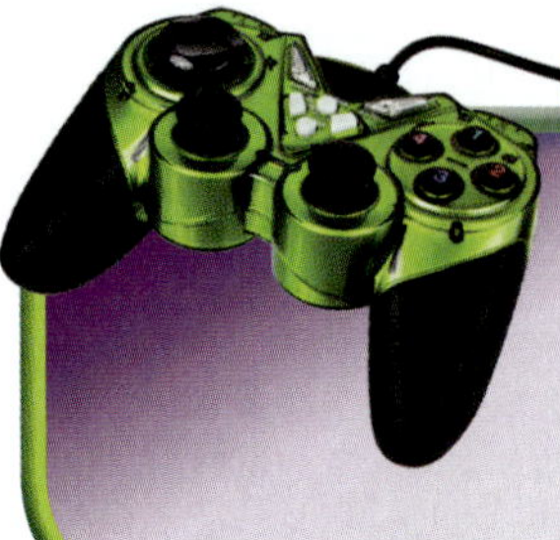

CHEAT CODE: MONOCHROMATIC

Monochromatic means only one hue is used on the image. The most common monochromatic image is a black-and-white image.

Value

Value is the use of light and dark to add highlight, shading, or shadows. If you look at a **monochromatic** image, the entire image is created based on the principle of value. Look at the image of the apple shown in **Figure 9-11.**

Color Model	Features	Method
HSL (also known as HSB or HSV)	Creates color by a combination of hue, saturation, and luminescence (or brightness or value). This model is popular in creating textures and surfaces for 3D models. Since 3D models require the use of light and shadow to define position relative to the light source in the game, using this color model allows the computer to leave the hue and saturation of the texture unchanged while adjusting the luminescence setting to be brighter on the surface facing the light source and darker on the surface facing away from the light source.	Additive
RGB	Creates color by a combination of red, green, and blue. Blending these three colors allows for over 16 million colors at 8-bit depth.	Additive
RGBA	The RGB color model with support for alpha channels. Alpha channels are transparency channels. The alpha channel sets the saturation of an RGB color from full opacity (not see through) to full transparency (completely see through).	Additive
Hexadecimal	An RGB color model in which the color is represented as a series of six letters and number. This color model is used in web page design. Many imaging software programs allow the user to limit colors to "web only," which are 216 colors universally compatible with web browsers.	Additive
CMYK	Creates color by a combination of cyan, magenta, yellow, and a key color that is almost always black. This model is used for printed materials. Each of the colors corresponds to one of the four printing plates on a printing press.	Subtractive
L*A*B*	The description of the L*A*B* color model is a bit complicated as the L is for lightness and the A and B components are derived from a nonlinear color matrix, similar to an X,Y coordinate graph. This model seeks to create natural looking colors. Additionally, L*A*B color model is used to convert RGB color models to CMYK color models or vice versa. L*A*B* color works for both video displays (RGB) and printed materials (CMYK) and is considered device independent.	Matrix of both additive and subtractive combinations

Figure 9-10. A comparison of common color models.

Goodheart-Willcox Publisher

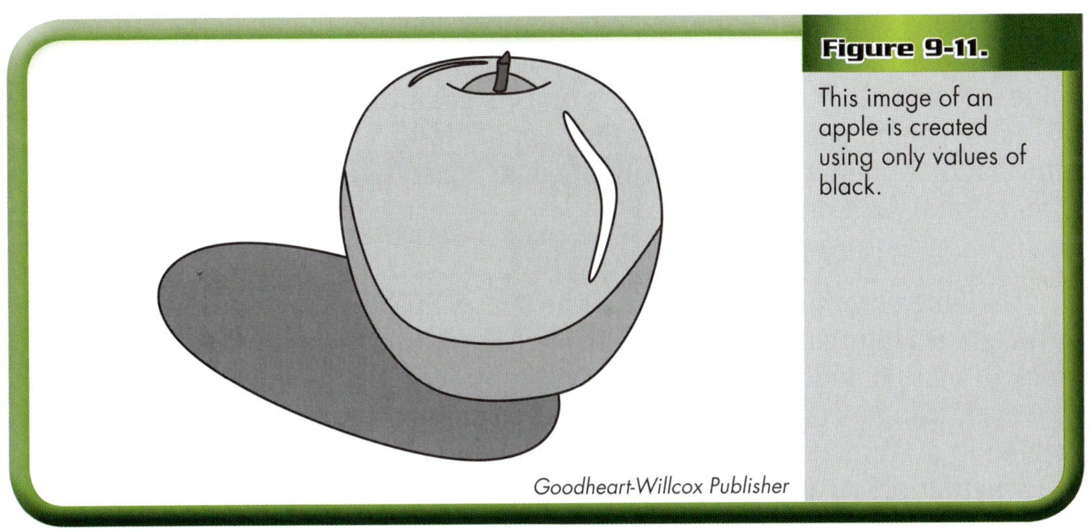

Goodheart-Willcox Publisher

Figure 9-11. This image of an apple is created using only values of black.

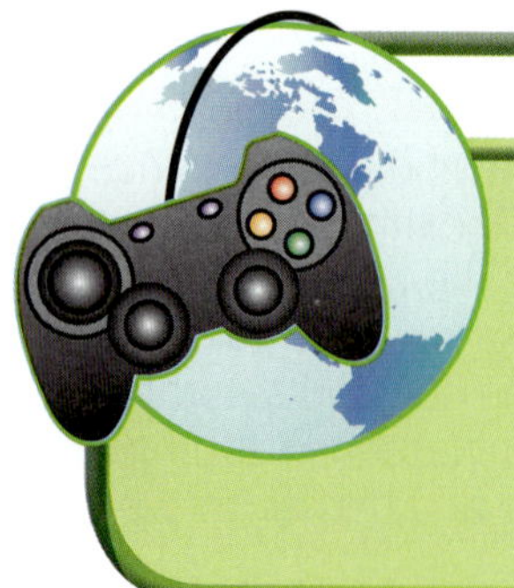

Green Gamer

Computers that are always on consume a lot of energy. Software is available to monitor how much energy and money can be saved by using a sleep and shutdown schedule for the computer. Taking advantage of these applications can save energy and extend the life of the equipment.

By using just the black hue, the image can have shape, line, and value. Value of the black hue is shades of gray. Depth is created around the stem of the apple by darkening that area. Near the top of the apple, depth is created by lightening the part of the apple that is closest to the light.

Artists use the term ***chiaroscuro*** to describe how value is used to create the illusion of depth, shape, and shadow. Form is defined in a chiaroscuro through the use of a range of value from highlights to shadows. A sphere rendered without value appears as a flat circle. As differing values are added to the sphere, it begins to take on the appearance of volume. A chiaroscuro gives the illusion of depth and volume to a shape.

A chiaroscuro is created by replicating the values seen on real objects. This includes the specular, diffuse, and ambient values, as shown in **Figure 9-12.** A ***specular color*** or value is the highlights, or shiny spots, on the object. The ***diffuse color*** is the main color or value of the object. The ***ambient color*** is the dark areas where the light source cannot provide direct illumination.

Value is also used to create contrast. ***Contrast*** is a comparison between the light and dark areas of an image. High-contrast images have great variations in value with bright areas and dark areas. Low-contrast images have little variation in value and details may be very difficult to see. Value can be used in a scene to create depth by adding shadow and light to create contrast between objects. Contrast coloring is discussed in more detail later in this chapter.

In video games, the game engine use pixel shading to create the illusion of depth. ***Pixel shading*** is the use of lighter and darker colors, or changes in value, to create light and shadow. As objects get farther from the light source, the game engine darkens them so they appear farther from the source. For information on applying value with 3D imaging software, see Chapter 10 Three-Dimensional Art Composition.

Space

The area or volume in a scene is the space. Space may be physical or virtual. A sculpture occupies physical space. An artist actually cuts into the block of marble and creates a statue with physical length, width, and depth. However, using a computer, an artist can create in virtual space. The object created in a 3D modeling program has virtual length, width, and depth. In 2D art, whether physical or virtual, space must be represented with illusion.

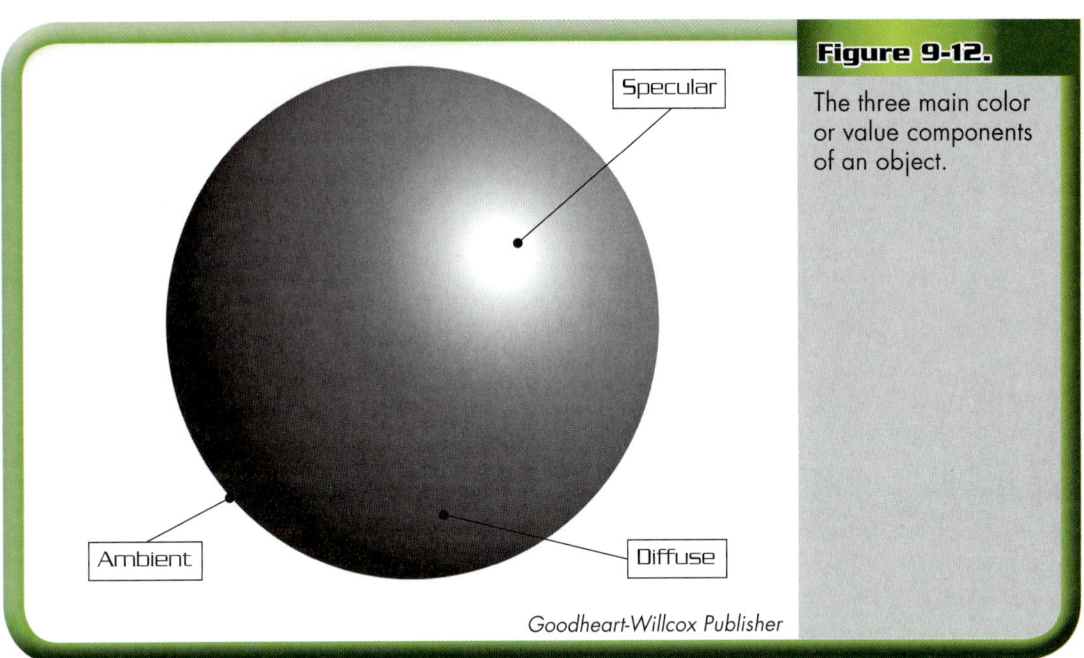

Figure 9-12.
The three main color or value components of an object.

Positive and negative space apply emphasis to the design. ***Positive space*** is the area or volume occupied by the primary objects. ***Negative space*** is the area or volume around or between the primary objects. An example of these can be found in a yearbook photo. You are the positive space in the portrait. The volume between you and the background is the negative space. The amount of negative space in a design can help provide contrast and emphasis to the primary objects. Imagine the yearbook photo is taken as a panoramic view in a stadium. While you are still a primary object, you are surrounded by hundreds of other objects. You are hard to identify as the primary object in the photo. This is because there is little negative space to separate you from everything else in the photo. Without any negative space, your image has less emphasis than it did in the portrait of just you in front of a background. Likewise, in game design, a scene can become cluttered if there is not enough negative space.

In three-dimensional space, length, width, and depth dimensions are used to create an object. When working with a 2D surface like a sheet of paper or a computer screen, the artist must trick the eye to create the illusion of 3D space. In computer rendering, artists apply both pixel shading and vertex shading to help create the illusion of 3D. ***Vertex shading*** is moving the points on an object to resize it such that the object appears smaller in the distance. The principle of visual perspective is applied during vertex shading.

Visual perspective is the proportional scaling of objects as they move toward a vanishing point. In **Figure 9-13,** notice how the parallel lines of the path angle inward until the lines meet in the distance. Of course, the sides of the path remain parallel. It is just the principle of visual perspective that makes the sides of the path appear to converge. Also, notice how the tree trunks appear to get thinner in the distance. Each object is scaled down as it moves toward the vanishing point. The point where parallel lines meet is the ***vanishing point,*** as shown in **Figure 9-13.** There may be one, two, or three vanishing points, but one- and two-point perspectives are the most common.

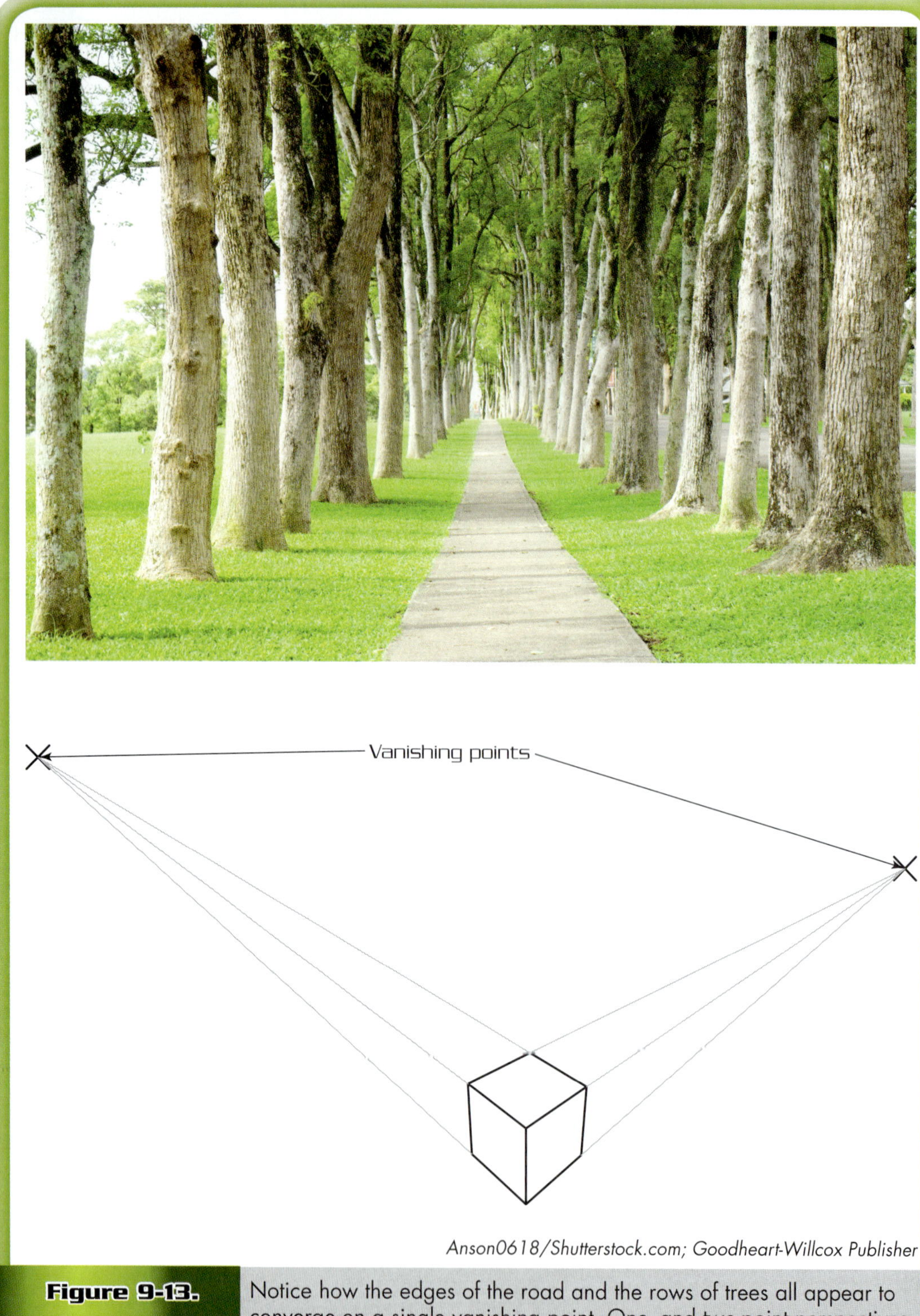

Anson0618/Shutterstock.com; Goodheart-Willcox Publisher

Figure 9-13. Notice how the edges of the road and the rows of trees all appear to converge on a single vanishing point. One- and two-point perspectives are the most common.

Also notice in **Figure 9-13** that the trees closest to the viewer appear to be in focus, while the trees in the distance appear out of focus. This effect can be applied in video game art to help enhance the illusion of depth. By adding a blur effect to an object in the distance, the **spatial** relationship of near or distant objects is enhanced.

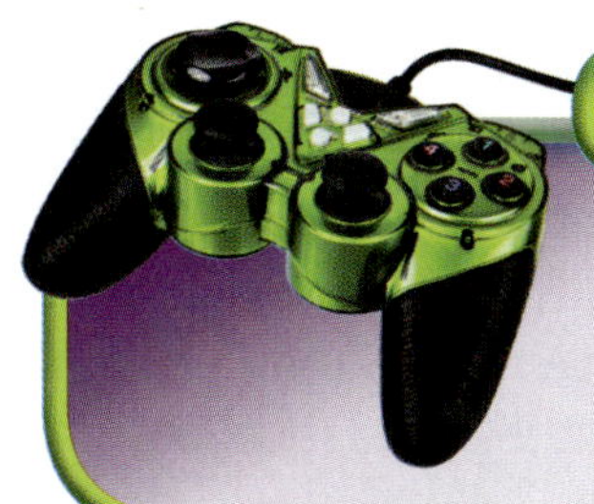

CHEAT CODE: SPATIAL

Spatial means having or occupying space. A spatial relationship describes how an object appears in space in relation to the viewer.

Texture

Variations in form and color create texture, which is an uneven surface. ***Tactile texture*** is an irregular surface that can be physically felt, like sandpaper. When you touch it, you feel the surface is bumpy or rough. This texture is a variation in surface depth to create a coarse physical sensation. ***Optical texture*** is creating variation in what you see. The skin of an orange has an optical texture because the color changes around the orange. The surface of the orange is not a single solid color. Additionally, the orange has tactile texture because the surface has physical bumps that can be felt.

Imaging software makes applying textures easy. Many programs allow for texture fills and filter effects. *Texture fills* are images that are wrapped around an object. The image of the texture creates the illusion that the shape is a real object. A texture such as a cloth texture can be applied to a shirt shape or an oak texture for a wooden boat. Other programs have filter effects to apply texture. *Filter effects* use the base image and alter it based on the definitions in the filter. As shown in **Figure 9-14,** these filters can simulate effects such as grain, mosaic tile, stained glass, plaster, canvas, brick, burlap, and much more.

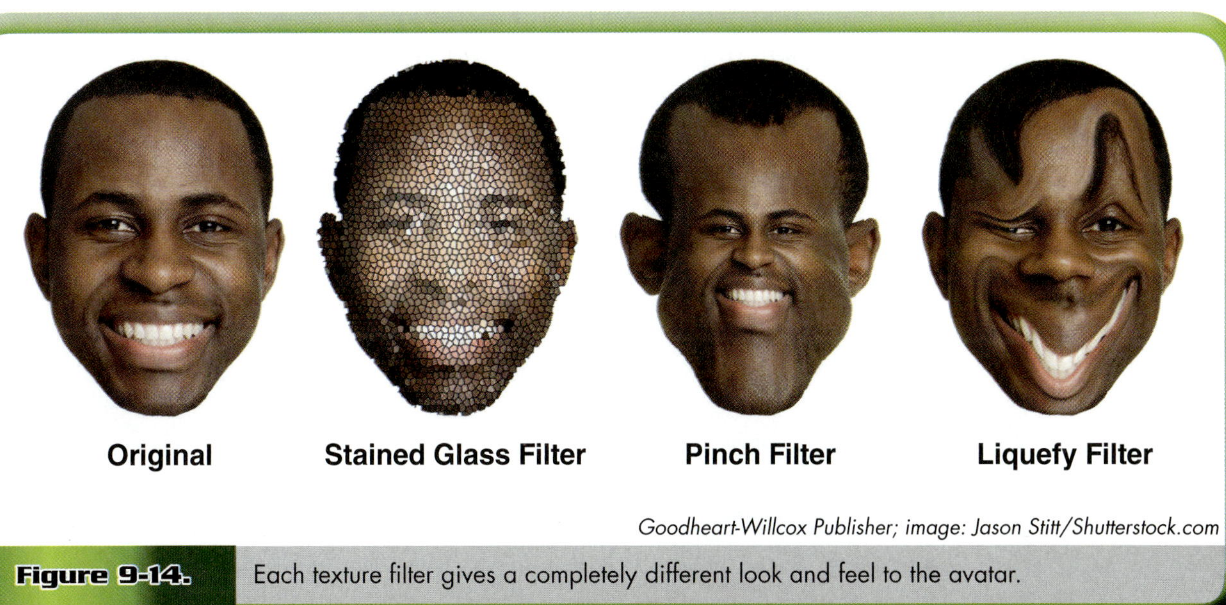

Goodheart-Willcox Publisher; image: Jason Stitt/Shutterstock.com

Figure 9-14. Each texture filter gives a completely different look and feel to the avatar.

Principles of Design

The principles of design are the set of rules or guidelines used to create artwork. The principles of design are specific to make sure you are creating effective layouts or art. Depending on the type of design (web, game, fine art, or other) the number of principles will change. For game design, the principles of design are movement, emphasis, harmony, variety, balance, contrast, proportion, pattern, and unity.

Movement

Applied action is movement. In traditional art forms, a static picture must convey movement. In game art, movement is typically done through animation. A game artist must understand and apply the movement principle, even if the object is going to be animated.

Look at **Figure 9-15** and see how movement is represented in the illustration. The tassels on the jacket are drawn to the right instead of straight down. This implies the snowboarder is moving to the left. Additionally, bits of snow are drawn to the right of the snowboarder, which also imply movement to the left. Lines are added to imply movement. Straight lines imply the leftward movement, while curved lines imply the legs and outstretched arm are moving. Finally, the position of the snowboarder implies movement. For the snowboarder to be in that pose, it is logical to interpret movement, and the fact that the character is looking to the left implies leftward movement. A game artist can use some of these same visual cues to help improve the movement of a character as it runs, jumps, draws a sword, or performs some other action.

Emphasis

When a designer draws attention to an object, the object is given ***emphasis.*** In game design, emphasis is typically accomplished by making an object larger, brighter, repeated, or moving. Having the object make noise is another way to add emphasis. The idea behind adding emphasis is that the player will understand the object is special in some way. The object may be a reward or it could be an obstacle that needs to be avoided. For example, if tokens are gold coins almost as large as the player character, the tokens are being emphasized. In this way, emphasis is giving a clue to the player.

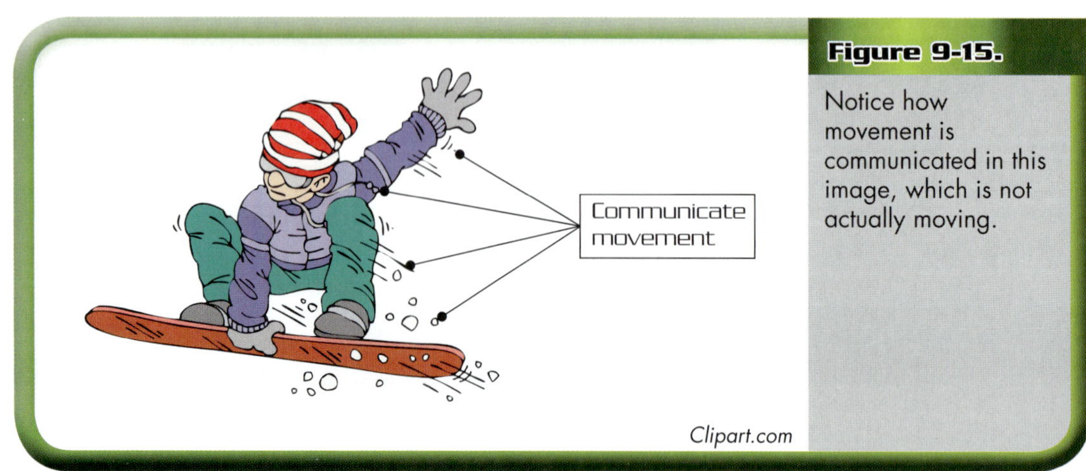

Figure 9-15. Notice how movement is communicated in this image, which is not actually moving.

Harmony

Using similar elements is the principle of ***harmony.*** Harmony helps hold the image or scene together. Imagine a dirty character dressed in old raggedy clothes, but wearing a gold crown. The gold crown just does not fit with the way the character is dressed. The design of this character is not demonstrating harmony.

Likewise, the elements of a scene need to have harmony. Objects that are out of place detract from the gaming experience. If the game has a **medieval** theme, all characters, buildings, vehicles, language, and so on, need to match the medieval setting. A scene in which knights are sitting around a table with a computer on it lacks harmony.

Harmony also needs to be maintained between levels in a game. Some characters, tools, and other game elements should move with the player to the next level to give the game a sense of harmony.

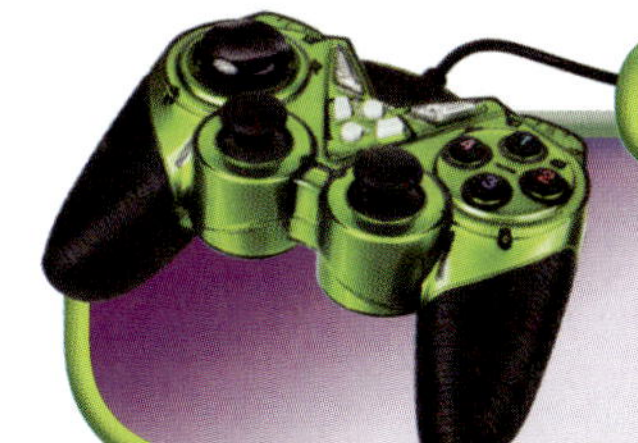

CHEAT CODE: MEDIEVAL

Medieval refers to the Middle Ages, the historical time period from about 400 AD to about 1400 AD.

Variety

The purposeful absence of harmony to create visual or contextual interest is the principle of ***variety*** (also known as alternation). This differs from emphasis in that the design is less obvious. Here the designer might want a clue that makes the player think or explore options. Imagine the classic dilemma of the two doors. Behind one door is a princess and behind the other is a tiger. To keep the player from making a guess, the designer may apply the principle of variety to the doors. Maybe the correct door has a few specs of glitter on the handle or the incorrect door handle has teeth marks. Possibly, one door is metal and the other is wood. Unlike applying emphasis, the clue is not obvious. It takes keen observations or thinking by the player to discover the clue.

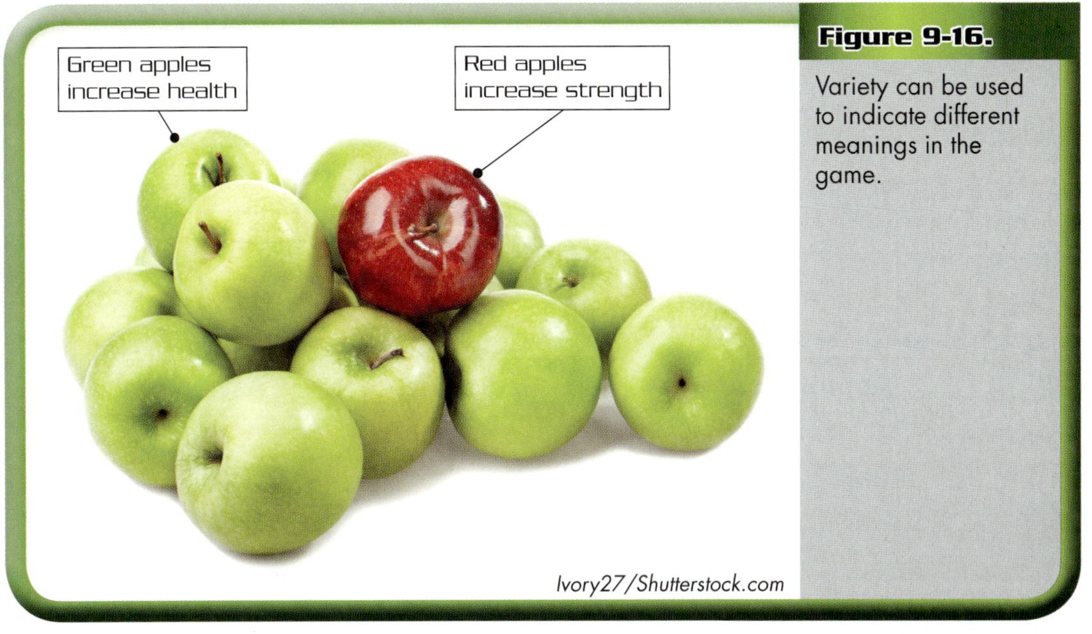

Ivory27/Shutterstock.com

Figure 9-16. Variety can be used to indicate different meanings in the game.

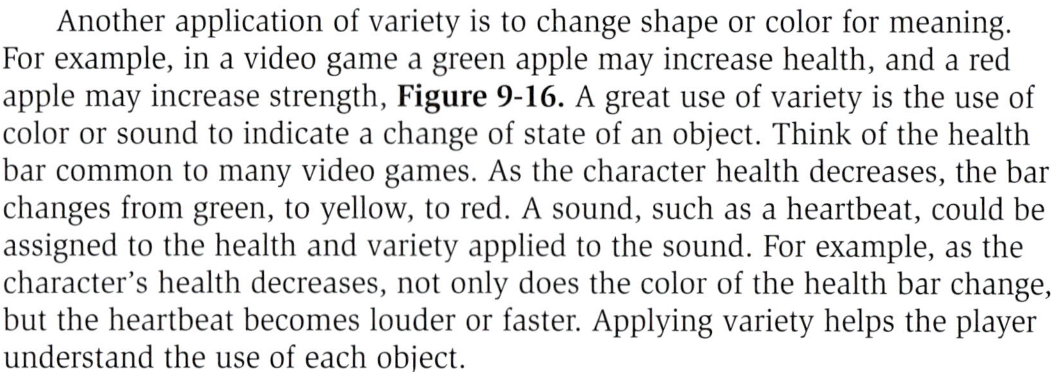

Another application of variety is to change shape or color for meaning. For example, in a video game a green apple may increase health, and a red apple may increase strength, **Figure 9-16.** A great use of variety is the use of color or sound to indicate a change of state of an object. Think of the health bar common to many video games. As the character health decreases, the bar changes from green, to yellow, to red. A sound, such as a heartbeat, could be assigned to the health and variety applied to the sound. For example, as the character's health decreases, not only does the color of the health bar change, but the heartbeat becomes louder or faster. Applying variety helps the player understand the use of each object.

In video game design, variety is not limited to just visual or audio elements. Variety may be changing the movement pattern of an NPC or using random elements. Random movement or obstacle generation also adds variety to the game. Randomness or chance adds unpredictability to the game. This might be something as simple as shuffling the cards in a game of *Solitaire* to make each game different.

Balance

Objects arranged such that no one section overpowers any other part is called balance. When constructing a work of art, the artist needs to divide the canvas into equal parts to measure balance. Balance can be established as either symmetrical or asymmetrical, as shown in **Figure 9-17.**

Symmetrical Balance. When the right and left sides, top and bottom, or all sides are equal, ***symmetrical balance,*** or formal balance, is created. If the image is split down the middle, both halves contain the same number and size of objects. An example of symmetrical balance is your eyes on your face. Your nose is in the center, and one eye on each side of your nose provides symmetrical balance. Since the right side of your face is a mirror image of the left side, this is called ***horizontal symmetry.*** Symmetry can also be established from a center point and radiate equally from that center. ***Radial symmetry*** is equal in length from a center point. An example of radial symmetry is the rings created by dropping a pebble into a puddle.

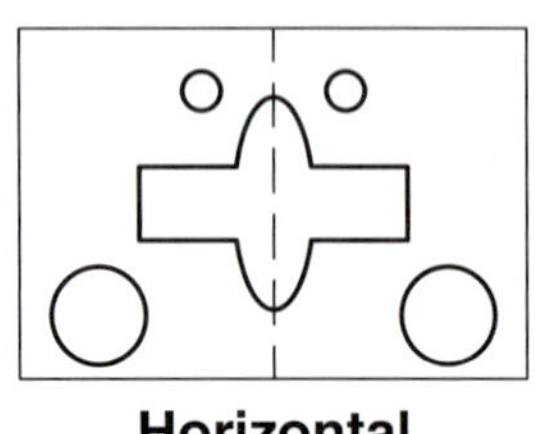

Horizontal Symmetry

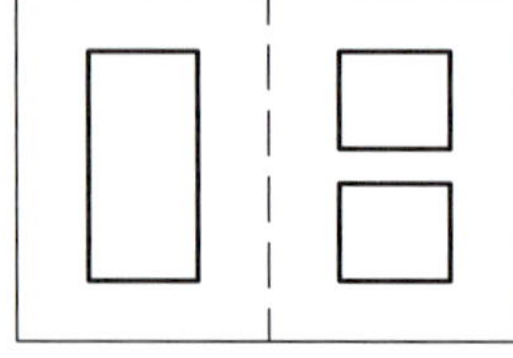

Approximate Horizontal Symmetry

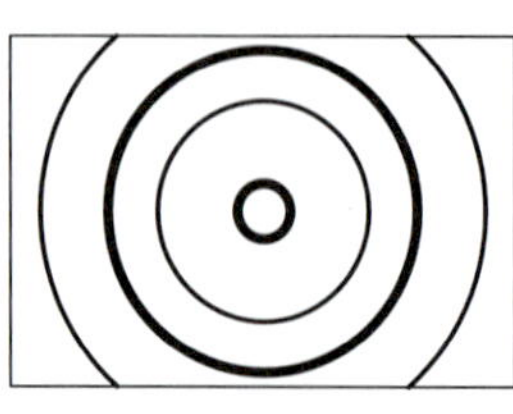

Radial Symmetry

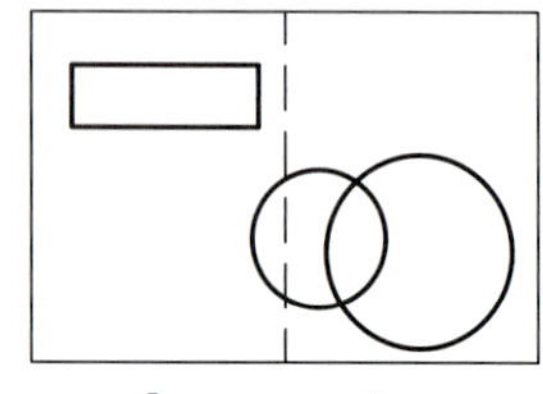

Asymmetry

Goodheart-Willcox Publisher

Figure 9-17. Symmetry and asymmetry can be used in the design of a scene.

Asymmetrical Balance. ***Asymmetrical balance,*** or informal balance, is the use of similar objects to create balance, or the use of color and light balance instead of object balance. Unlike symmetrical balance in which the right and left sides may be mirror images, asymmetrical balance can be seen in something like a book shelf. The shelves balance the amount of space taken up by the books, but the size, shape, color, and arrangement of the books differs on each shelf. The concept is that a lot of something small can balance a little of something big. A swarm of small bees provides asymmetrical balance to a single large beehive. This can work with color as well, where a small area of a vibrant color provides asymmetrical balance to a large area of a neutral color.

Asymmetrical balance is often confused with asymmetry. ***Asymmetry*** means that the work is not at all balanced. Placing objects off center or heavy to one side of a work can draw the viewer to an area of attention, as shown in **Figure 9-17.**

Proximity. The final element of balance is proximity. ***Proximity*** is how closely objects are arranged. In a social setting, placing characters close to each other conveys a meaning such as friendship, family, or **camaraderie.** Conversely, placing characters far apart conveys a meaning such as enemy, stranger, or rival. Proximity can help create tension. Placing an object such as a stick of dynamite near an open fire creates tension as these two elements will cause an explosion if combined. Proximity can also help show scale or relative size. Placing a character next to a building provides scale to the height of the character. If the character is taller than a tree, for example, the player understands the character is a giant.

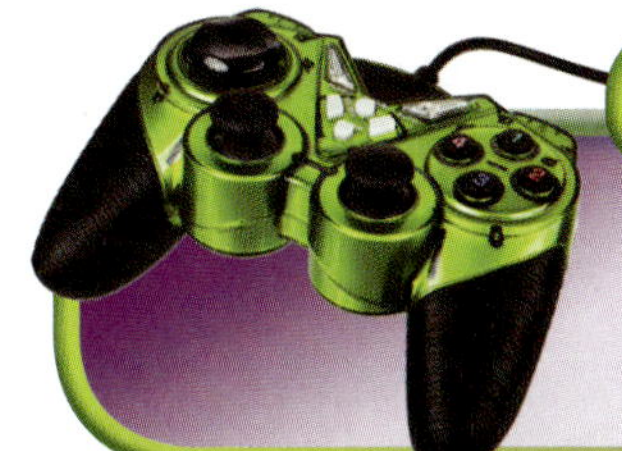

CHEAT CODE: CAMARADERIE

Camaraderie is a spirit of friendship between two or more people, who may or may not be friends.

Rule of Thirds. The rule of thirds can be used to help achieve balance. The ***rule of thirds*** is a guideline that states an image should be divided into three sections horizontally and three sections vertically to create nine areas. This is like putting a tic-tac-toe board on top of the image. Where the lines cross are the focal points for a scene. Placing the objects you want the viewer to focus on at these points will draw the observer's eye to those objects.

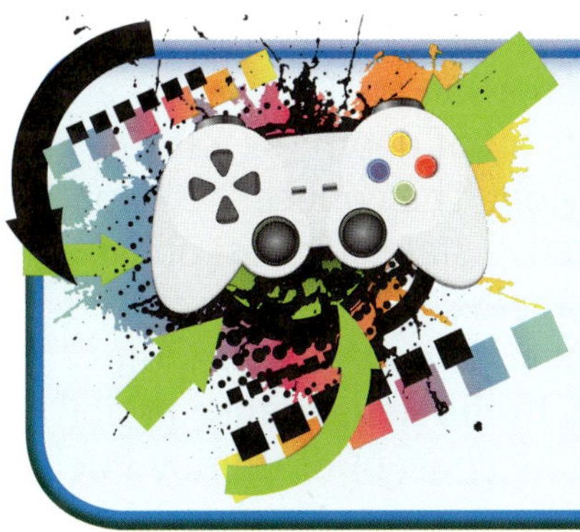

Ethical Gamer

A code of ethics outlines acceptable behavior when interacting with others, whether students, school personnel, coworkers, or customers. It is important to know the code of ethics for your school or workplace so you can behave in a correct manner.

Contrast

The variation of color and brightness to make objects stand out from each other is ***contrast.*** Contrast is very important in video game design. Imagine using blue text on a blue background. Players could not read the letters. The designer needs to select a color, such as yellow or orange, that contrasts with the blue background. Alternately, the brightness of the blue used for either the text or background can be varied to provide contrast. A light blue text on a dark blue background may provide enough contrast for the player to read the words. This same principle applies to game objects. Imagine using a red ball on a red background. The ball needs to contrast with the background to be seen easily.

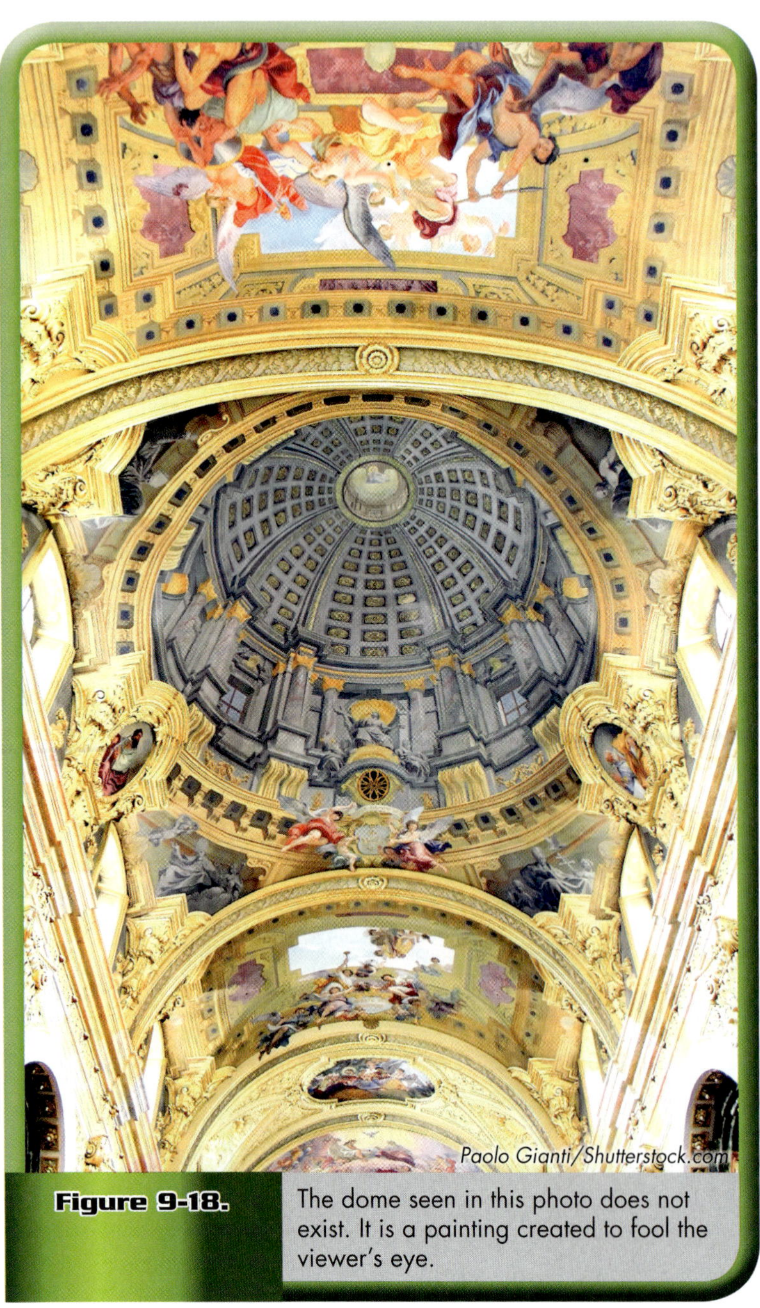

Paolo Gianti/Shutterstock.com

Figure 9-18. The dome seen in this photo does not exist. It is a painting created to fool the viewer's eye.

Proportion

Proportion is the size of an object in relation to the other objects around it. In game design, proportion may be exaggerated to make something more noticeable or prominent. A boss character may be much larger than the player character to communicate that the character is more prominent or more powerful. In other cases, the size of the game objects in relation to the player character may be reduced. In some games, the player character may be almost as large as the buildings. This exaggerated proportion is used to make the game easy to navigate and to show the character detail. If the player character is shown in proper proportion to the buildings, the character would be a small dot on the game map. When possible, a designer tries to show objects in proper proportion to the other objects in the scene. This gives the game a realistic look.

Proportion is also used to give the illusion of depth, or a third dimension. The concept of visual perspective states that an object looks smaller in the distance and gets larger as it approaches the viewer. In the Renaissance period of art, the concept of trompe l'oeil was applied to art. ***Trompe l'oeil*** translates to "fool the eye." Art of this type uses perspective, depth, and shadow to create ultra-realistic scenes. **Figure 9-18** shows the ceiling of the Jesuitenkirche (Jesuit church) in Vienna, Austria. The artist has made it appear as if there is a dome, but the dome does not exist. A painting of the trompe l'oeil type appears to the viewer as if looking out of a window at a real landscape or object. In a similar manner, game designers attempt to create realistic game art.

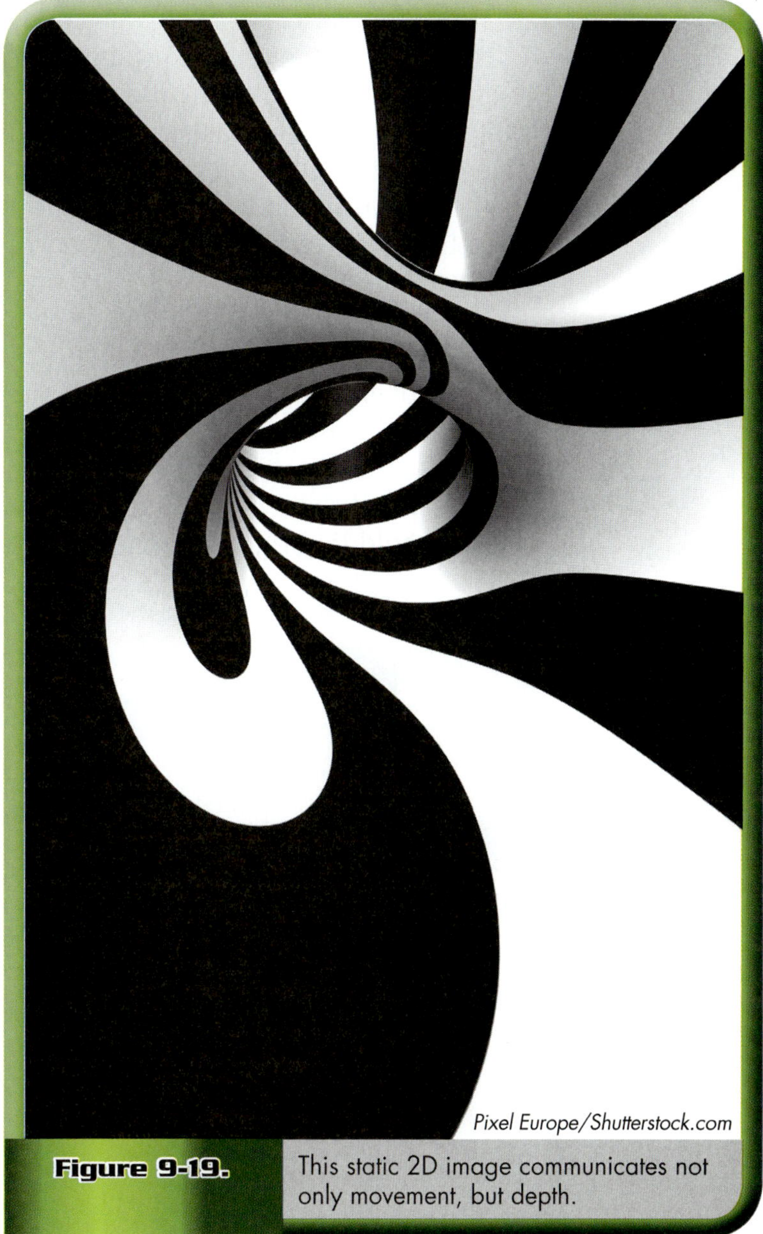

Pixel Europe/Shutterstock.com

Figure 9-19. This static 2D image communicates not only movement, but depth.

Pattern

When an element is repeated, a pattern is created. In video game design, patterns occur in both visual layout and in gameplay. Visually, pattern is applied in one of three ways: regular, flowing, and progressive.

A regular pattern has repeating objects of similar size and spacing, such as seen on a checkerboard. Flowing patterns have more organic shapes than regular patterns and mimic movement, as shown in **Figure 9-19.** A simple example of flowing pattern is an arrow or curve that leads to a point. The eye follows the curve from the thickest end to the point, which provides a feeling of movement or motion. Progressive patterns display a sequence or series of steps. This is a dominant visual pattern used in video game design, since it is used in animations. In static (not animated) art, a progressive pattern can simulate continuing motion or progression within a single frame, such as the image shown in **Figure 9-19.**

In gameplay, objects move in patterns. This patterned movement allows the player to navigate hazards that require timing. For example, a player may need to recognize the pattern of a swinging vine and jump at the right time to catch the vine and swing to the next platform. Pattern can also help set the pace of a game. For an animation of a running character, the artist must balance the pace of the animation with the movement of the background. If these are not synchronized, the animation will appear odd to the player.

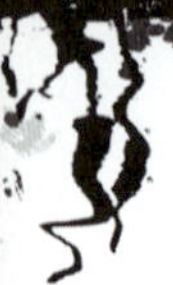

Unity

All of the elements and principles of art work together to create unity. When something has ***unity,*** it appears as a single piece and not an assembly of different parts. The easiest way to explain this is to look at a character. A game character might have a hat, whip, leather jacket, dark hair, large muscles, mustache, jeans, and boots. Each of these pieces is one part of the whole. When these pieces come together, a single character is created that has a sense of unity.

Unity also applies to the layout of a scene. Each component of the scene should look like it fits with the others. Many times, the unity of the entire project is overlooked. The artists get involved in creating each asset of the scene and forget to design simple things like start buttons and menus that properly match the scene. These elements should match the theme for the rest of the scene. If the overall theme is bright and cheery, then the buttons and menus should be bright and cheery.

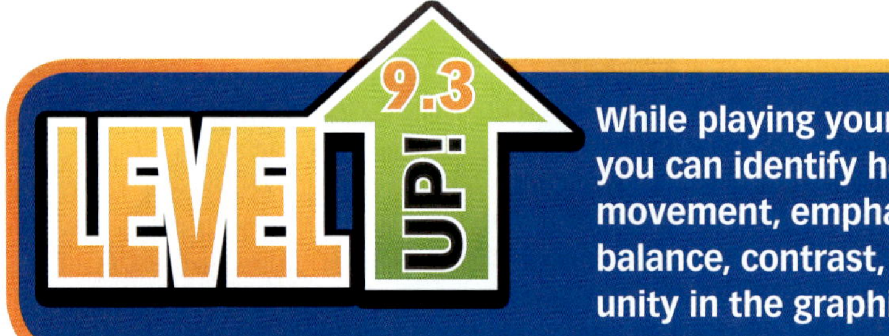

While playing your favorite game, see if you can identify how the designers used movement, emphasis, harmony, variety, balance, contrast, proportion, pattern, and unity in the graphics of the game.

Chapter Summary

- Since a video game world is an imaginary world, historical elements can be combined to make a new and interesting world using a variety of art techniques and forms.
- Presentation is how the art will be viewed or experienced; the artwork is guided by the purpose of the presentation.
- Whether an artist is working with virtual media or physical media, the elements of art (which deal with the individual features needed to compose artwork) and principles of design (which govern how to effectively combine the elements of art to compose a pleasing work of art) hold true.

Check Your Video Game IQ

Now that you have finished this chapter, see what you know about video game design by taking the chapter posttest.

www.m.g-wlearning.com

www.g-wlearning.com

Review Your Knowledge

On a separate sheet of paper or in a word processing document, match the following terms with the definition that fits best.

A. negative space	F. positive space
B. tactile texture	G. optical texture
C. horizontal symmetry	H. radial symmetry
D. symmetrical balance	I. asymmetrical balance
E. unity	J. proximity

1. When something appears as a single piece and not an assembly of different parts.
2. How closely objects are arranged.
3. The area or volume around or between the primary objects.
4. The use of similar objects to create balance, or the use of color and light balance instead of object balance.
5. An irregular surface that can be physically felt, like sandpaper.
6. Equal in length from a center point, such as is seen when a pebble is dropped in water.
7. The left side of something being a mirror image of the right side.
8. Creating variation in what is seen, such as the skin of an orange.
9. When the right and left sides, top and bottom, or all sides are equal.
10. The area or volume occupied by the primary objects.

On a separate sheet of paper or in a word processing document, answer each of the following questions.

11. Which design-team specialist creates the visual elements of the game?
12. List four art movements during the modern art period.
13. Why would a game artist create an imaginary world with elements from human history?
14. What are two devices commonly used to record real movements and convert them to a digital model?
15. List the seven elements of art.
16. List three common color models.
17. How does an artist add the illusion of form to a 2D drawing?
18. Explain how visual perspective is created.
19. In video game design, how can variety be used as a clue for the player?
20. Which principle of design mandates that the theme of the buttons match the theme of the gameplay?

Apply Your STEM Knowledge

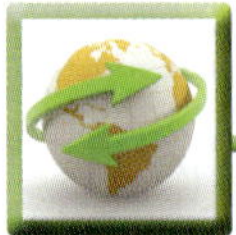

Social Studies

1. Research the cultural influences needed for a historically accurate game with ninja characters. Create a PowerPoint presentation to summarize your findings on art, religion, family, transportation, architecture, government, clothing, weapons, and geography.

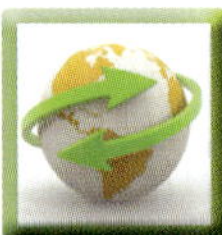

Social Studies

2. Research salary data for game artists. Create a table like the one shown below using a word processor or spreadsheet program. Complete the table.

Job Title	Annual Salary	Years of Experience Required	Location of job
Game art director			
Lead artist			
Concept artist			
Texture artist			
Animator			

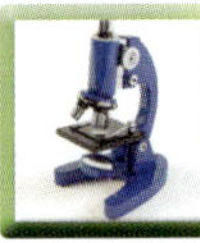

Science

3. The color you see is determined by the structure of your eyes. Research the human eye and its structure. Create a PowerPoint presentation of seven to ten slides to show the structure of the eye and how light is interpreted.

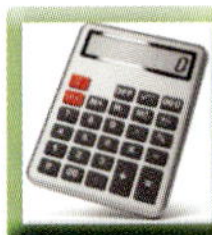

Mathematics

4. When creating a scene that uses visual perspective, the objects need to be scaled smaller as they approach the vanishing point. The level designers need art created for the scene below. Calculate the size needed for each of the trees. Using spreadsheet or word processing software, create a table similar to the one shown below and record the settings. The display screen will use 72 pixels per inch. Round to three decimal places.

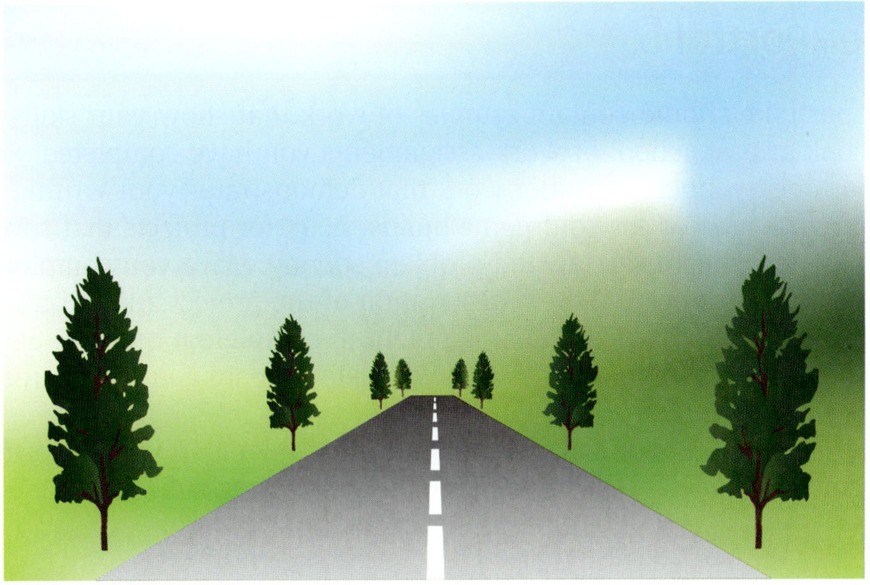

Mire/Shutterstock.com

Asset	Scale %	Height (pixels)	Width (pixels)	Height (inches)	Width (inches)
Tree_Left_Large	100	180	144	2.5	2
Tree_Left_Medium	75				
Tree_Left_Small		90			
Tree_Left_Tiny					0.5
Tree_Right_Large	100	250	200	3.472	2.778
Tree_Right_Medium	80				
Tree_Right_Small		125			
Tree_Right_Tiny			60		

Language Arts

5. Using the bold italic key terms and Cheat Codes in this chapter, create a crossword puzzle. Write proper definition for each term to use as clues. Create the puzzle on a sheet of graph paper or use a puzzle-maker website. Exchange your crossword puzzle with a classmate and complete.

Working in Teams

Working with the team as assigned by your instructor, brainstorm the basic concept for a video game that incorporates historical art and cultural influences. Base the game in a specific historical time and place. Present to the class the team's concept and explain which art and cultural influences are covered in the game. Explain how these influences are incorporated into the game.

Gamer Portfolio

Your portfolio should contain samples of work that show your skills or talents. Look at past school or work assignments you have completed. Select a book report, essay, poem, or other work that demonstrates your writing talents. Include artwork created for your game builds. Look for projects that show your skills related to critical thinking and problem solving. Have you completed a long or complex project? Write a description of the project and tell how you managed various parts of the assignment to complete it on time. Select completed work from other classes that will help prepare you for a career in the video game design industry.

1. Save the documents that show your skills and talents in your e-portfolio. Remember to place the documents in an appropriate subfolder.
2. Place hard copies in the container for your print portfolio.

G-W Learning Mobile Site

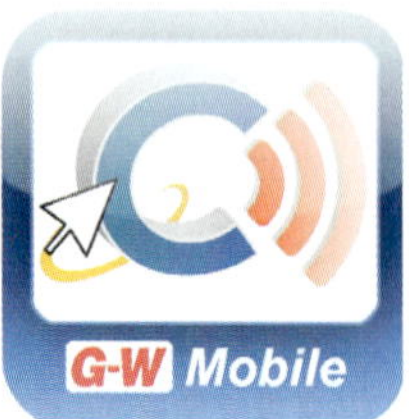

Visit the G-W Learning mobile site to complete the chapter pretest and posttest and to practice vocabulary using e-flash cards. If you do not have a smartphone, visit the G-W Learning companion website to access these features.

G-W Learning mobile site: www.m.g-wlearning.com

G-W Learning companion website: www.g-wlearning.com

Common Core

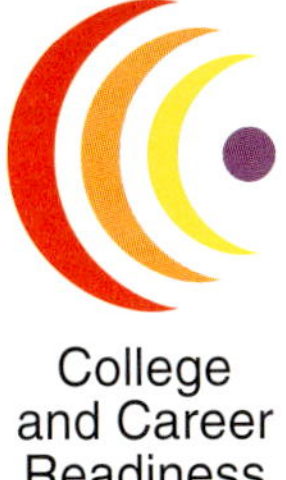
College and Career Readiness

CTE Career Ready Practices. Create a Euler diagram (a type of multicircle Venn diagram) to show the relationship between your career interests, your preferences, your goals, and requirements of your career choice. Where do the circles overlap? What do you think overlap signifies? What would a diagram with a lot of overlap tell you? What about one with little or no overlap?

Reading. Consider how the author uses the term *art* throughout this chapter. How did your understanding of this term change as you were reading? Look up the word *art* in the dictionary. How did the author shape this definition to fit the subject matter in this chapter? Write a few paragraphs about what the term *art* means to you after reading this chapter.

Speaking and Listening. Perform an Internet search on virtual (digital) art versus traditional art forms. Look for opinions for and against the use of digital tools in areas other than video games. After reading a few expert opinions, use this information to form your own opinion. Discuss your findings and reasoning with the class. As you listen to your classmates' opinions on the use of digital tools, evaluate your own position. How does their reasoning contribute to your understanding of the purpose and place for digital tools? Does your opinion change or is it strengthened?

Event Prep: Ethics

Ethics may be a competitive event you might enter with your Career and Technical Student Organization (CTSO). The competitive event may include an objective test that covers multiple topics. However, ethics may be one part of another event that may include objective questions or a presentation. Ethics may also be required as part of your game build presentation. To prepare for an ethics event:

1. Read the guidelines provided by your organization. Make certain that you ask any questions about points you do not understand. It is important you follow each specific item that is outlined in the competition rules.
2. Review the Gamer Ethics features throughout this text. Make notes on index cards about important points to remember. Use these notes to study.
3. Ask someone to practice role playing with you by asking questions or taking the other side of an argument.
4. Use the Internet to find more information about ethics and social responsibility. Find and review ethics cases that involve gamers, video games, or the video game industry.

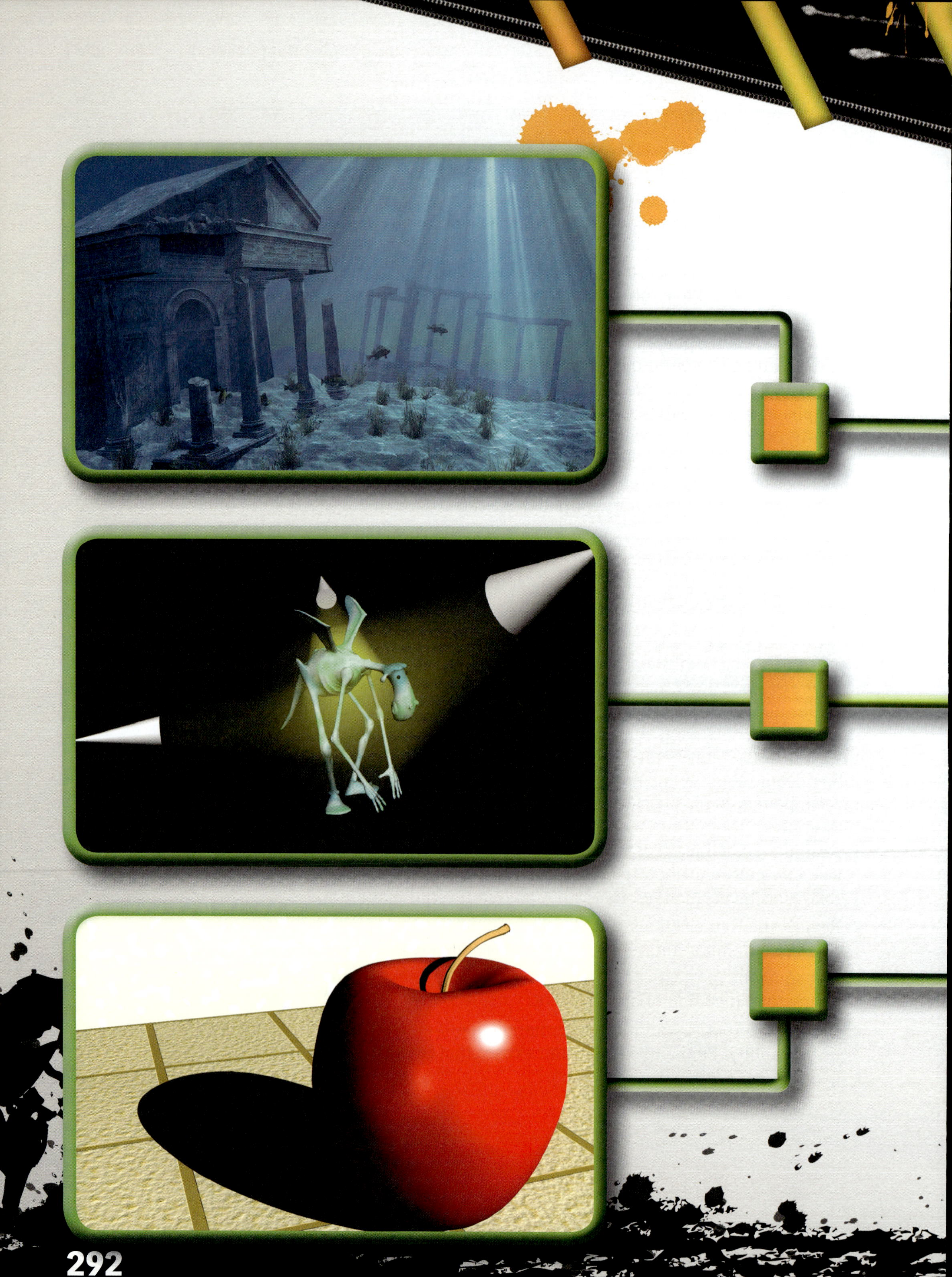

Chapter 10

Three-Dimensional Art Composition

There are two basic types of art for gaming, two dimensional (2D) and three dimensional (3D). Two-dimensional art is flat with length and width dimensions, like a photograph. Three-dimensional art has volume with length, width, and height dimensions. Of course, during gameplay, 3D art is projected onto a 2D screen. However, some games make use of technology that allows the user to see the art in three dimensions, such as wearing polarized or anaglyphic (red-blue) glasses. Three-dimensional art is created from 3D models.

Check Your Video Game IQ

Before you begin this chapter, see what you already know about video game design by taking the chapter pretest.

www.m.g-wlearning.com

www.g-wlearning.com

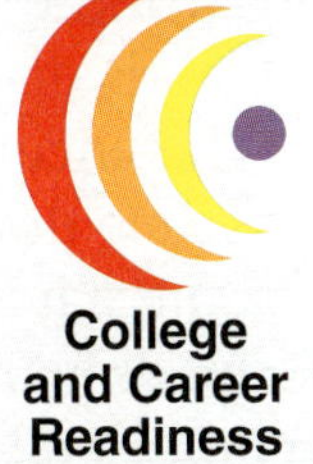

Reading Prep. As you read the chapter, think about the safeguards that both artists and video game designers use to protect their businesses from financial loss. Use what you learn to evaluate the protections most video game design companies use today.

Objectives

After completing this chapter, you will be able to:

- Describe the different video game design team roles available for people with art and animation skills.
- Outline the key elements of three-dimensional modeling.
- Compare and contrast raster images and vector images.
- Explain the legal rights an artist has in protecting artwork as well as steps taken by game designers and artists to physically protect content from being copied.

Game Art Team

There are many different team roles available for people with art and animation skills. In the game industry, there are many specialist careers in 2D and 3D art. These same skills are used in other industries, like motion pictures, advertising, web design, corporate marketing and branding, and countless others.

In most industries, there is a hierarchy of authority, and the game industry is no exception. A ***hierarchy*** is a structure where one person has authority and decision-making power over others. In other words, each person has a boss. In the military, the hierarchy might start with the privates and go up to a general. The general has authority over all others below. Ultimately, this hierarchy ends with the commander-in-chief at the top.

In the game industry, the highest-ranking artist is usually called the art director. An ***art director*** sets the vision for the game art and makes sure it is what is needed for the theme and story. An art director typically oversees several games under development at the same time. To keep all projects flowing well and to remember all decision on a game project, the major decisions are recorded in design documents. For the art department, the design documents include concept art, model sheets, world-design document, and animation sets.

To start an art project, concept art needs to be produced. ***Concept art*** is a series of simple sketches that show what a character or other major game asset might look like. These sketches are shown to the art director and other decision makers for suggestions and improvements. When the concepts are approved, the concept art is converted into model sheets. A model sheet is a detailed drawing of the final character and typically includes several poses and expressions. These poses and expressions help the digital artists create the correct animations for the character. Model sheets may also include items like the weapons and other accessories for the character.

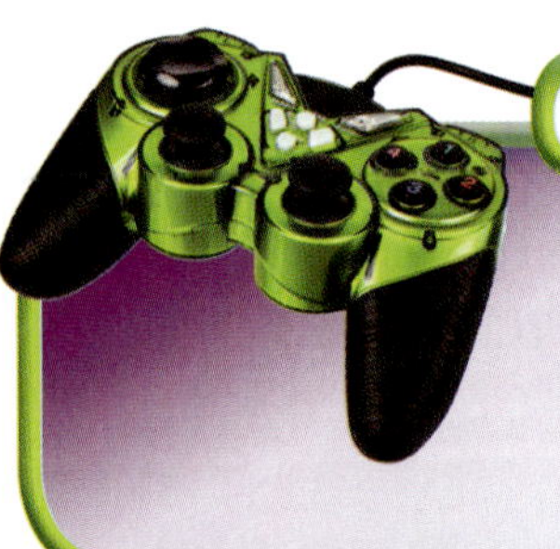

CHEAT CODE: COLOR PALETTE

The color palette is a standard set of colors used throughout the game. This may be a set of dark colors for a game with a gloomy mood or a set of pastel colors for a child's game.

The model sheets are used to compile the world-design document, which is discussed in Chapter 3. This includes the **color palette,** scene drawings, storyboards, game navigation, and more. Scene drawings show what the level or scene should look like in the game. Game navigation includes objects like signs, roads, flags or other parts added to a scene to help the player understand where to go in the game world.

There are many artists who work on a design team. The art director communicates the requirements for the game art to the lead artist. The ***lead artist*** manages the details of a single project and makes sure all art is designed correctly. This person is the one to assign tasks to individual specialists or groups. Some specialist jobs include concept artist, texture artist, environment artist, 3D modeling artist, video director, asset manager, and animator.

Each person on the team serves an important role in making the entire project look great. ***Concept artists*** are strong in creating new characters and objects that have never existed before. These artists have strength in imagination and drawing. ***Texture artists*** create 2D art using digital or traditional art media. These artists are strong in creating artwork that embodies all of the basic elements of art. ***Environment artists*** create scenes for the game world, such as the one shown in **Figure 10-1.** These artists are strong in use of color and landscape drawing. ***Three-dimensional modeling artists*** create game objects in 3D. These artists are strong in the use of 3D modeling software such as 3ds Max, Maya, Blender, or Rhinoceros. The ***video director*** creates the cinematic cut scenes between levels or records video for use in promotional materials. This role requires strengths in camera setup, lighting, and directing. ***Asset managers*** keep track of all art assets being produced and make sure each asset is designed to specifications, catalogued, and properly stored. They have strength in evaluating art and organizational skills. An ***animator*** is strong in rendering objects in motion. This role requires great technology skills to use animation software for 2D or 3D animation rendering.

Three-Dimensional Modeling

The first concept to master in 3D modeling is the idea that you are creating the outside of an object, not a flat surface. Almost like working in clay, you have to add or subtract pieces to make the basic shape of an object. The most basic of these shapes are called primitives. ***Primitives*** are standard building blocks used to create other objects. In 3D modeling, primitives include cubes, cylinders, planes, spheres, and other geometric forms. Each primitive can be made up of several polygons to form the sides and faces of the 3D shape, as shown in **Figure 10-2.**

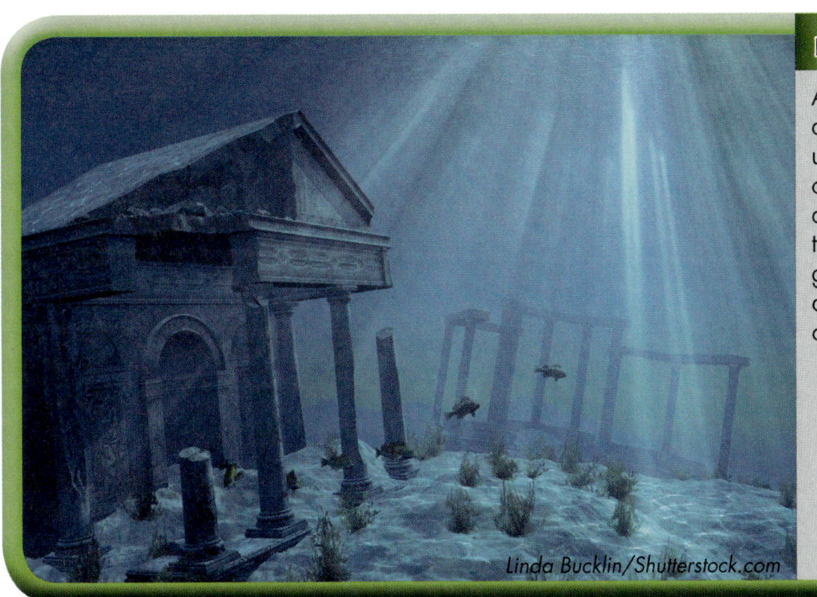
Linda Bucklin/Shutterstock.com

Figure 10-1.

An environmental artist created this underwater scene of a lost city. Other artists will create the remaining games assets, such as characters and objects.

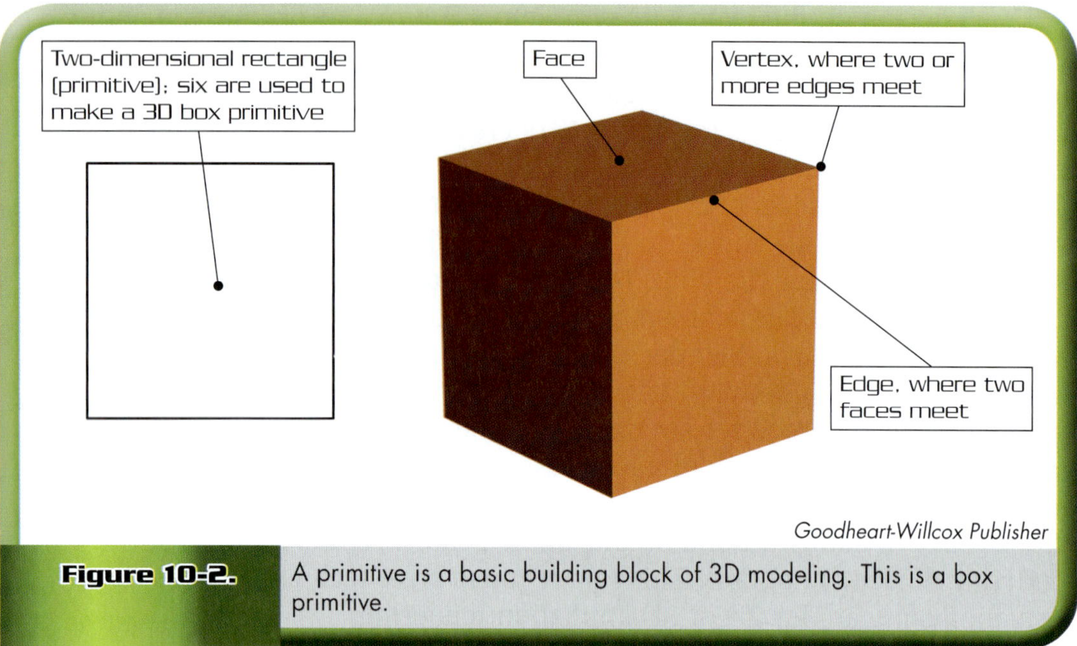

Figure 10-2. A primitive is a basic building block of 3D modeling. This is a box primitive.

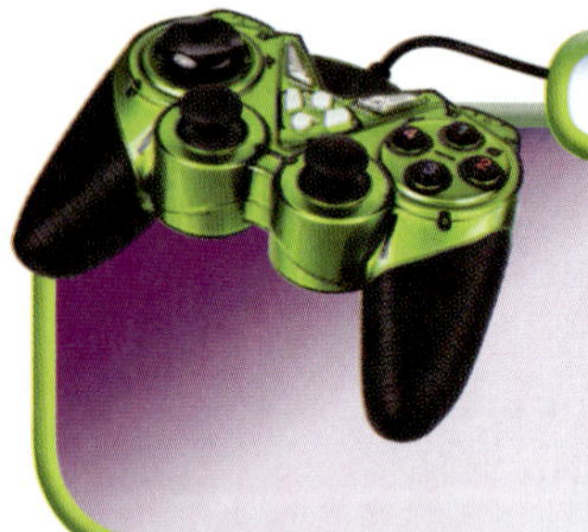

CHEAT CODE: DICE

Dice are cubes with numbered sides commonly used to randomize gameplay. Dice is the plural of die (one cube is a die). Some dice are not cubes and may have greater or less than six sides.

Meshes

A regular cube, like used for **dice,** has six faces that are all square polygons (or 2D primitives). These polygons are on different planes (left, right, front, back, top, and bottom). When all of these polygonal squares are touching edge-to-edge, a cube mesh is formed. A ***mesh*** is a combination of four or more polygons connected to make one piece. A designer can edit a mesh to change the size and shape of the mesh. For example, moving a vertex changes the size of the connected edges and the shape of the connected faces.

If you think back to your days as a child playing with Lego blocks, you can see the concept of building a 3D model with mesh primitives. Each Lego block is a standard primitive. You assemble the blocks to create a form that looks like an object. The end result of your efforts is similar to a 3D mesh. This same idea applies to 3D modeling. You add primitives and connect them to form a mesh that has the form of what you are trying to create.

Even a sphere is a mesh of polygons. Think about creating a ball out of rectangular Lego blocks. The ball is not perfectly smooth because flat rectangular faces represent the curved shape form. The same is true of 3D meshes. However, once a mesh is created, tools can be used to smooth the form.

A ***UV sphere*** is constructed of rectangular and triangular polygons. The mesh lines (edges of polygons) run in regular intervals from top to bottom and side to side, like the lines of latitude and longitude on a globe. A ***geodesic sphere*** is constructed of regular polygons such as triangles, pentagons, and octagons. This is similar to a soccer ball. Octahedrons, dodecahedrons, and icosahedrons are specific types of geodesic spheres.

Mesh Smoothing

By using primitives, a designer can quickly create the basic shape of a game object. After the primitives are assembled, the object may look jagged due to the flat faces. However, smoothing can be added. ***Smoothing*** takes a sharp edge between faces and applies a radius. This is not to be confused with increasing the polycount.

The smoother a mesh object, the more polygons (or polys) are used to create the form. ***Polycount*** is the number of 2D faces (polys) used to create the 3D mesh model. The form of all 3D mesh models is the result of how the polygons are arranged.

Think about drawing a curve with a series of straight-line segments, as shown in **Figure 10-3.** The curve can be made smoother by increasing the number of segments used to define the curve. However, this increases the polycount. On the other hand, applying smoothing allows a lower number of straight-line segments to be used while still achieving an end result that looks like a curve. This same concept is applied to the edges between faces. Smoothing is a mathematical calculation, so it helps increase the speed at which the computer can work with the model. This can lead to smoother gameplay. When smoothing and refining an object from a primitive mesh to a finished product, the designer needs to keep polycount and file size in mind.

The information or data needed to define the 3D model is stored in a computer file. The ***file size*** is the amount of storage space required for the file and it is measured in bytes, megabytes, or gigabytes. The computer must calculate all of the angles and lines needed to build the polygons in a mesh. The more polygons, the larger the file size and the longer it takes for the computer to process the information. If that time causes the game to lag, then the model and the game are both failures. As a designer, you must balance the desire to have a smooth model with the amount of data the computer must process during gameplay. This is where smoothing can help. Considerations for file types are discussed later in this chapter.

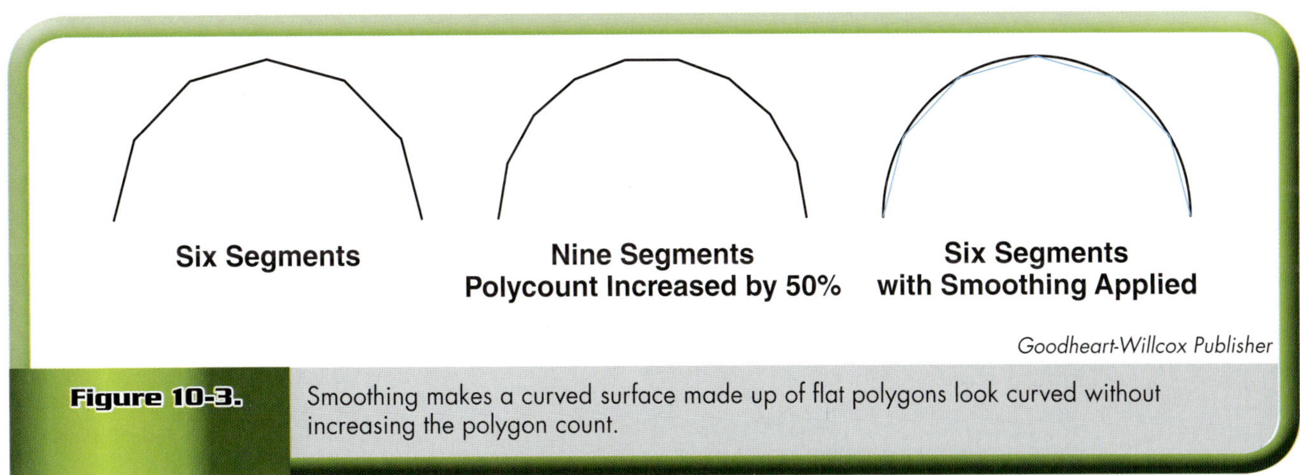

Figure 10-3. Smoothing makes a curved surface made up of flat polygons look curved without increasing the polygon count.

NURBS

Meshes are not the only way to create 3D models. A ***NURBS*** model is based on a mathematical calculation that creates a curve or surface from specified control points. NURBS stands for non-uniform rational basis spline. Because a NURBS model is based on a mathematical formula instead of polygons, it can be infinitely resized without becoming jagged. NURBS models are formed around a series of control points and a knot vector, not meshes. NURBS modeling is an important tool to understand when working with advanced modeling software, such as Maya or Rhinoceros 3D. NURBS models are often used to create organic, freeflowing objects such as characters.

The number and location of control points define the shape of the curve or surface, as shown in **Figure 10-4.** The more control points, the more detail can be added to the NURBS model. Each control point has a weight value that determines how much impact that control point has on the overall NURBS model.

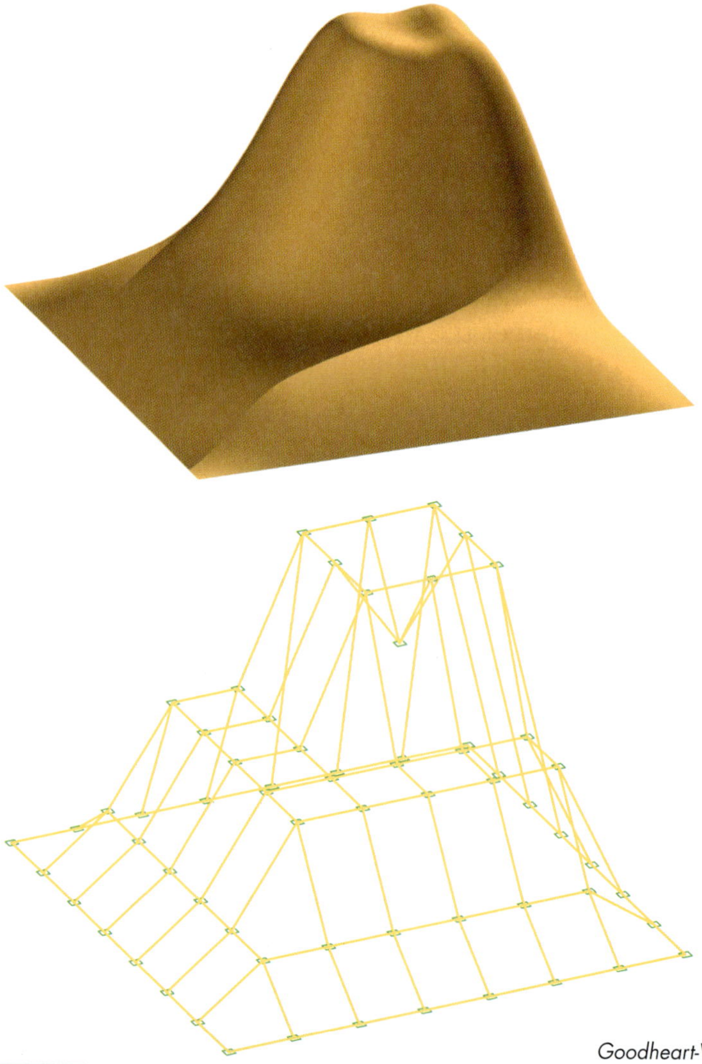

Goodheart-Willcox Publisher

Figure 10-4. The lattice of control points shown on the bottom is what defines the NURBS model shown on the top.

The knot vector determines where and how the control points define the shape of the NURBS model by dividing the model into intervals called knot spans. Each control point has at least one knot associated with it.

Lighting Composition

Whether taking a photograph or rendering a 3D scene, proper lighting is very important. A photographer will use several types of lighting from different angles. The photographer is trying to eliminate shadows in some areas, while adding shadows in other areas to show depth. Using the right lighting, the photographer can properly capture the subject.

When rendering 3D scenes, lighting is just as important. Shadows and shading are needed to show depth and edges. To accomplish the task of lighting, the 3D artist uses virtual light sources, called lights or lamps, to shine light in the correct direction and with the correct intensity and color. The types and names of lights vary depending on the 3D modeling program being used. Most programs have at least point, spot, and sun lights, although the names may be different.

Light Types

A ***point light*** is a light source that illuminates in all directions, like a common household lightbulb, as shown in **Figure 10-5.** It is mainly used to illuminate a small area to eliminate a shadow. Maybe the shadow of a character's nose covers the right eye. A point light could be placed on the right side of the character's face to lighten just that area and remove the shadow.

A ***spotlight*** projects light rays in a cone shape. It is used to shine a beam in a specific direction like the spotlights used in theatrical lighting or to search for airplanes. Applications for a spotlight include directional lighting, like simulating a sunbeam shining through a window or a streetlight at night. Spotlights are perhaps the most commonly used type of lighting. They form the basis of triangle lighting, which is discussed in the next section.

A ***sun light,*** or sunlight, is a light source that provides constant illumination in one direction. In other words, the light rays are parallel. A sun light acts like the real Sun. By the time rays of sunlight reach Earth, the rays are effectively parallel. The use of a sun light is primarily limited to providing the main illumination for a scene. A sun light is not used to eliminate shadows.

Lighting Theory

Triangle lighting is the traditional way to illuminate a scene. Triangle lighting consists of three lights, as shown in **Figure 10-6.** The ***key light*** provides the primary illumination. The ***fill light*** or *floodlight* is used to eliminate unwanted shadows or dark areas in the scene. The ***backlight*** is used to add a sense of depth to the scene by illuminating the back of the primary object. Depending on how these three lights are placed, the mood of the scene can be dramatically affected.

Placing lights may take some trial and error to get the correct illumination for the scene. In many cases, more time is spent lighting a scene and creating materials for it than modeling it. Lights can be moved, rotated, and animated just as any other object. That way the light can move to make a scene change from day to night or to follow a light source like a moving flashlight.

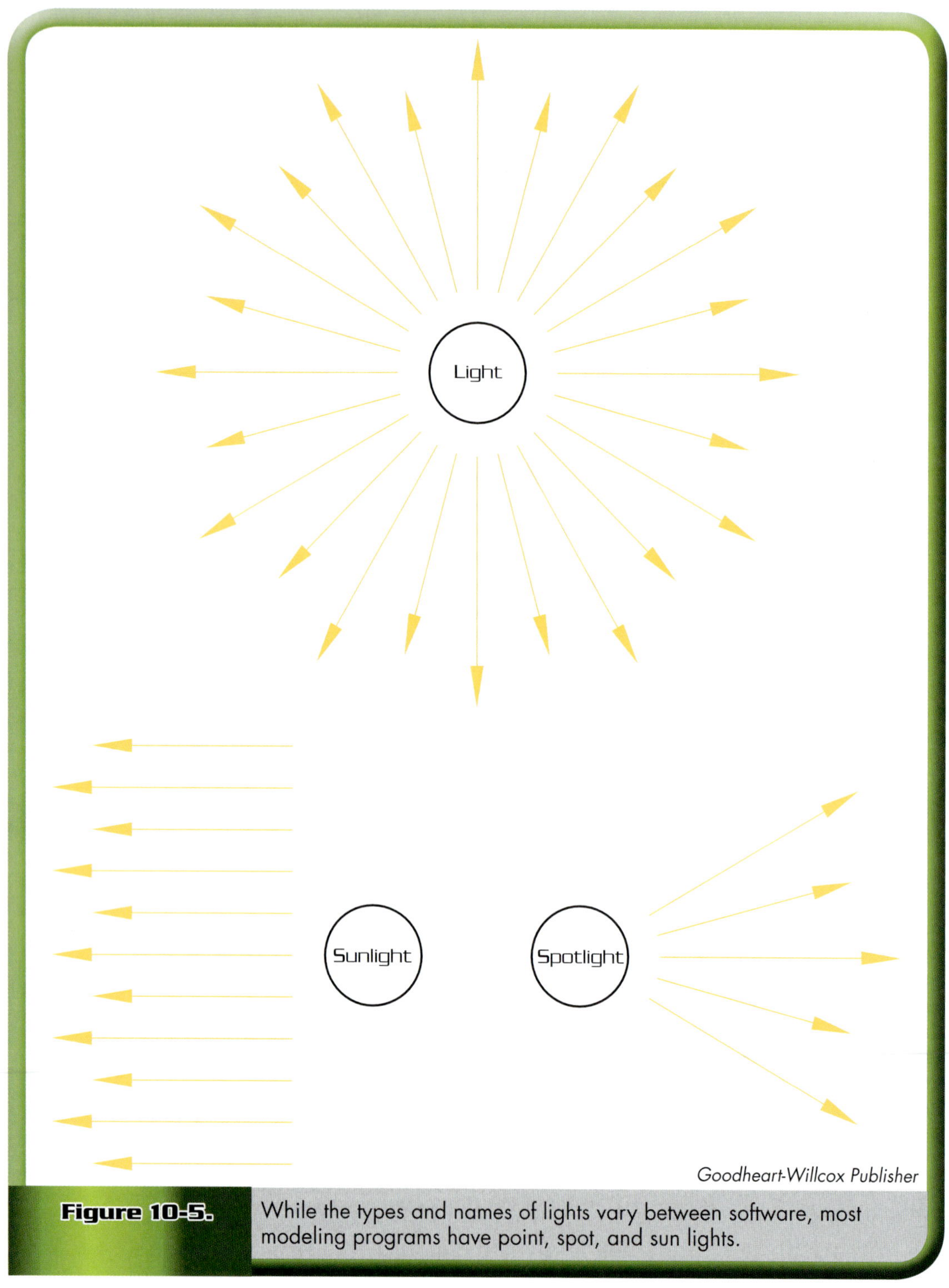

Figure 10-5. While the types and names of lights vary between software, most modeling programs have point, spot, and sun lights.

To get a brighter or more intense light, the energy or value setting of the light is increased. This setting is like the watt ratings of a lightbulb. In your home, there are probably lightbulbs rated at 60 watts to 100 watts. Watt is a unit of energy measurement. It tells how much energy the bulb is consuming. If there is a 60 watt bulb in your room and more light is needed, the bulb could be replaced with one that is more intense, or has a higher wattage rating. By putting in a 100 watt bulb, more light will be emitted.

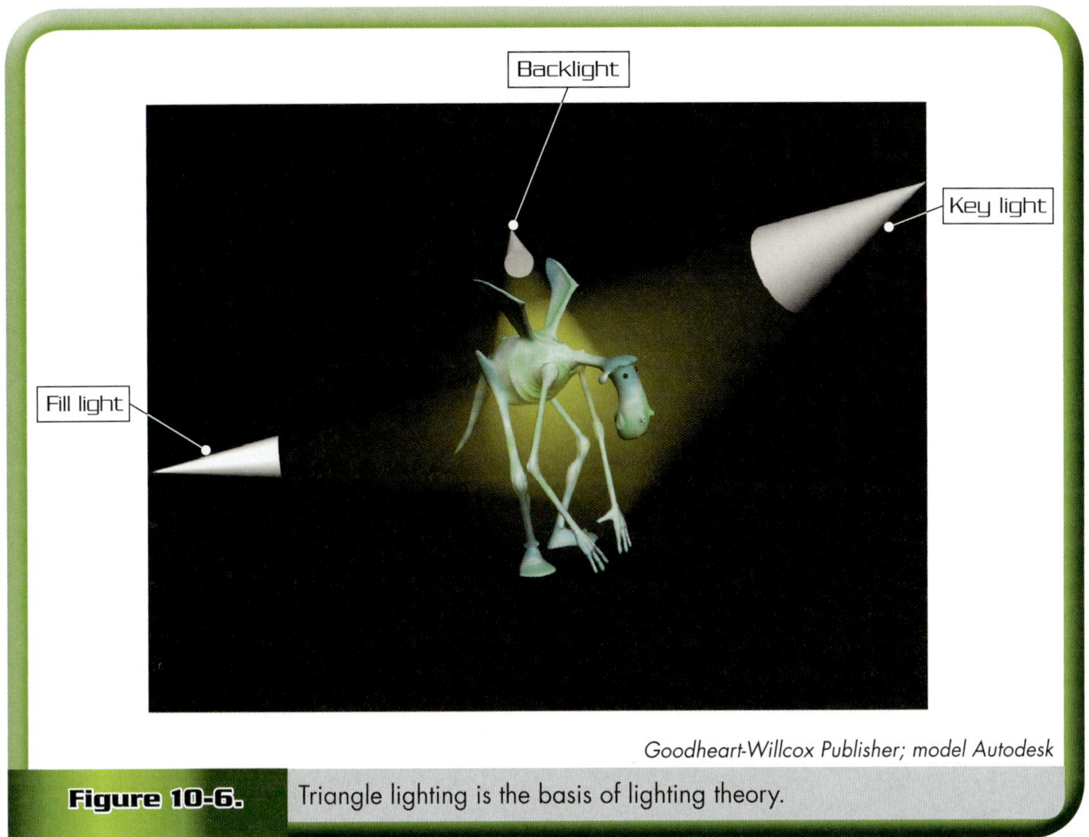

Goodheart-Willcox Publisher; model Autodesk

Figure 10-6. Triangle lighting is the basis of lighting theory.

Material Composition

Once a 3D model is created, materials must be added to the model. Sometimes the scene is lighted before materials are applied, and sometimes materials are applied before the scene is lighted. This usually depends on not only the preference of the designer, but also on the complexity of the material and model.

Materials

A ***material*** is simply an image stretched over the model to make it look as if it is made of wood, plastic, skin, or any other material. The "image" does not have to be a photograph, but a photograph can be used. The ability to create, edit, apply, and adjust materials varies by software. Some modeling programs are very good when it comes to creating and modifying materials. Other modeling programs may be best suited only for modeling. These programs are usually used with other software that is specifically designed for creating and modifying materials.

The three basic color components that define the overall color of an object are specular, diffuse, and ambient, as shown in **Figure 10-7.** The material editor in most modeling software includes these three color definitions for a material. Additionally, most material editors allow for different base material types, or templates, on which to build a material. For example, the software may allow a designer to start with basic settings for a metal material, standard material, raytrace material, composite material, or other type. From the basic settings,

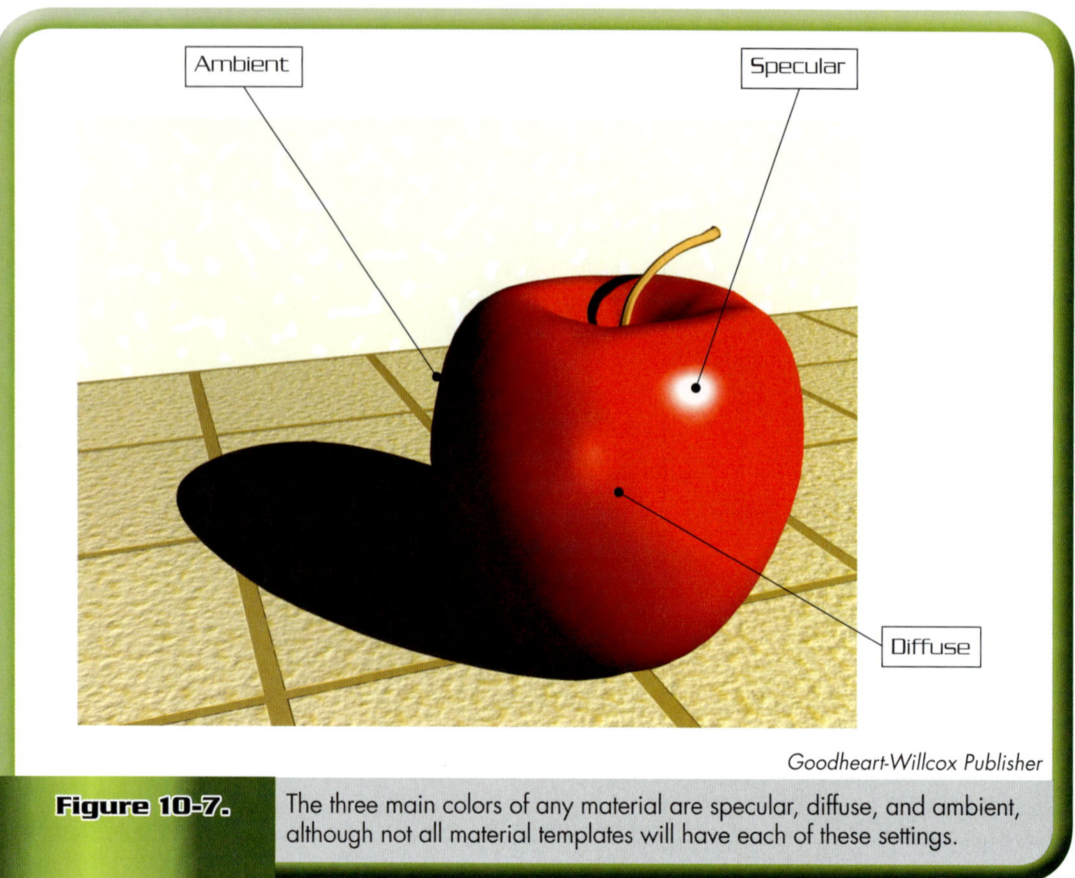

Goodheart-Willcox Publisher

Figure 10-7. The three main colors of any material are specular, diffuse, and ambient, although not all material templates will have each of these settings.

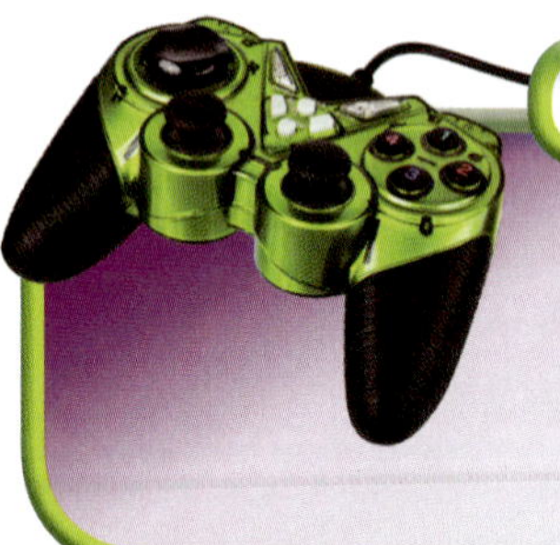

CHEAT CODE: OPACITY

Opacity is the quality of being see-through. A material that is opaque, or has maximum opacity, appears solid. A material with low opacity is semitransparent.

the designer alters color, shininess, **opacity,** texture mapping, and various other settings to achieve the final material. The specific color definitions available for a material depend on the material type. For example, a metal material type may have only definitions for specular and diffuse colors. The software uses these color definitions along with other specifications in the material definition to render the final material.

Once a material is defined, it is applied to objects in the scene. Usually, several adjustments need to be made to each material after a rendering is created. It is important to think of creating a material as an ongoing process. A first version of the material is created and applied to objects. Then, the scene is rendered to see how the material appears on the objects with illumination and shadows. The designer must evaluate this rendering to see what adjustments need to be made to the material definition and then make those changes. It is not uncommon for this revision process to be repeated dozens of times until the material appears correct in the rendering.

CASE STUDY

The Additive Color Wheel

The three primary colors are red, blue, and yellow. These three colors are mixed to create all other colors. A device called a color wheel is used to select colors that work well together. The three secondary colors are green, orange, and purple. These colors are made by mixing the two adjoining primary colors, such as yellow and red to make orange. The tertiary color wheel shown here contains the three primary colors, three secondary colors, and six tertiary colors. An infinite number of mixes means millions of different color combinations can be created.

Printers use a slight variation of the three primary colors. They use cyan, magenta, and yellow, along with a key color (CMYK), to blend all colors. Video equipment, such as computer displays and televisions, uses another variation of the three primary colors. This equipment uses red, green, and blue (RGB) color values to make all colors. RGB mixing can produce 16,581,375 color combinations at 24-bit color depth. Notice the color wheel from the software 3ds Max shown here.

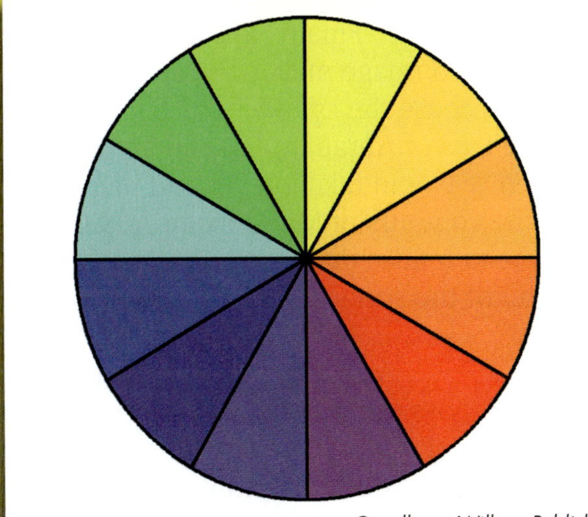

Goodheart-Willcox Publisher

A tertiary color wheel shows the primary, secondary, and tertiary colors.

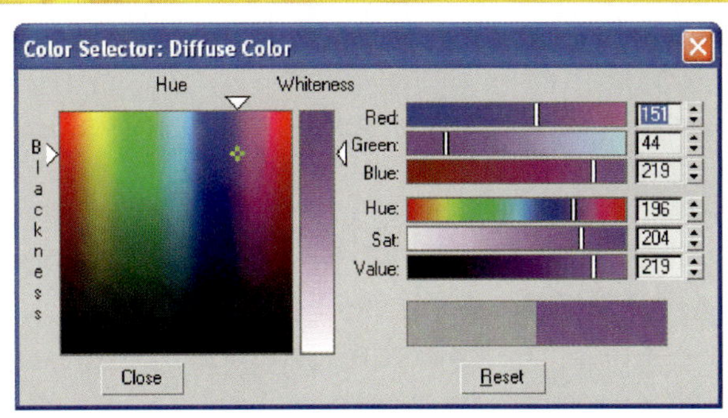

Goodheart-Willcox Publisher

Computer display uses a variation of the three primary colors, known as RGB.

Two basic principles of color are used to create a pleasing image. These principles involve the position of colors on the color wheel. Matching, or analogous, colors are next to each other. Opposing, or complementary, colors are across from each other.

A character or object should be created with matching colors to create maximum harmony for that design. Use of matching colors helps the entire object appear unified and not a mixture of many pieces. Contrast indicates how well one color looks against another. To create maximum contrast, use complementary colors directly opposite of each other on a color wheel. Contrasting colors need not be exactly opposite. But, the closer they are to opposite, the higher the contrast.

Look at the blue and purple boxes shown here. The color in the small boxes is the same.

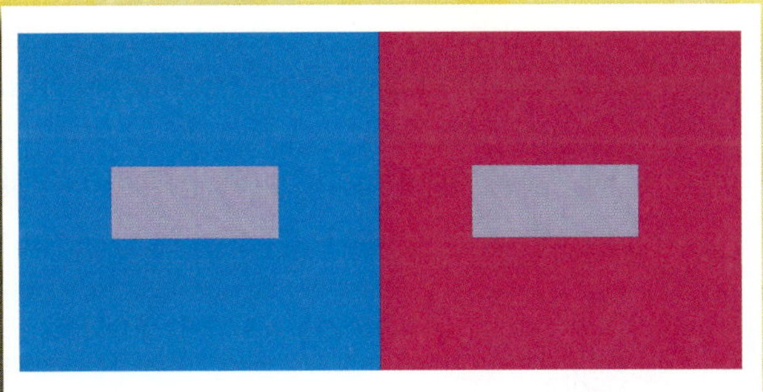

Goodheart-Willcox Publisher

Notice how color choice has a dramatic impact on how you see the small rectangle.

(Continued)

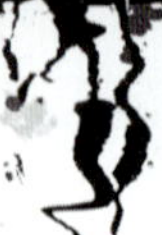

CASE STUDY (Continued)

Notice how the small box is easier to see in the large purple box. In this example, the blue box is a dominant color due to the large size when compared to the small box. Your eyes tend to focus on the contrasting color elements of the subordinate color in the small box.

Now, look at the blue and purple boxes with light-colored circles. All balls are the same size and color. The ball to the far left is the most obvious and easiest to see. The ball to the far right is the least obvious and hardest to see. Notice how the ball on the far right almost disappears as it gets farther away from the darker blue background.

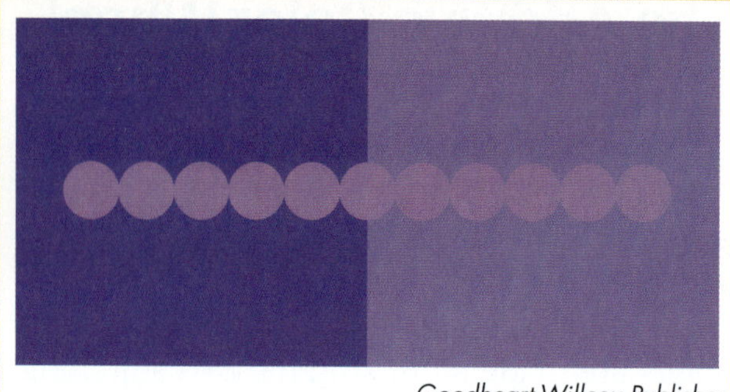

Goodheart-Willcox Publisher

The ball on the far left is easiest to see, while the ball on the far right is hardest to see.

Texture Mapping

A powerful tool of 3D modeling software is the ability to apply a texture map. A ***texture map*** is a picture or pattern assigned to an element of the material definition, as shown in **Figure 10-8.** A map may be assigned to the diffuse color, bump setting, opacity or transparency element, or any other part of the material definition as allowed by the software.

For example, to make a model of a penny, first create a short cylinder. Then, create a material with a picture of the front of the penny assigned to the diffuse color. This map would be called a *diffuse color map.* Finally, apply the material to the cylinder and render the scene. The rendered image may look good, but it will not have the same texture as a real penny because the cylinder has flat ends. A real penny has an uneven surface with the face of Abraham Lincoln **embossed.** To model the embossed features of the penny would take forever and involve thousands of polygons to exactly match the contours of Mr. Lincoln. Additionally, it would take an enormous amount of time to render the penny. Fortunately, there is an easier way to create the illusion of the surface of the penny using bump mapping and isosurfacing.

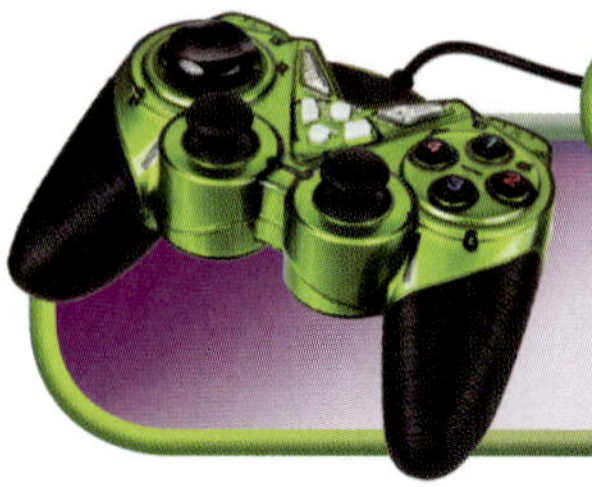

CHEAT CODE: EMBOSSED

Embossed means the image is raised above the background.

A ***bump map*** is a texture assigned to the bump property of a material. The light and dark areas of the texture create the illusion of raised and lowered areas on the model without actually physically adding features. The software adjusts the lighting and shadows to achieve the illusion. In the penny example, Mr. Lincoln and all other raised areas would be lighter colors in the bump map file, and flat or recessed areas would be darker colors. When the material is applied to the cylinder and the scene rendered, the bump map makes Mr. Lincoln appear to come out of the surface of the cylinder. However, the polycount of the cylinder remains unchanged.

The advantage of bump maps is that the geometry is not altered, but this is also a limitation. Since there is only the illusion of a raised surface, the shadow cast by the object is based on the mesh, not the areas that *appear* to be raised. This is not a problem with a penny, but what if the object has a wrinkled or hairy surface? A bump map could be used to create the wrinkles or hair, but the shadow cast by the object would show a smooth surface. When this is a problem, the model must have the actual polygonal shapes molded to the texture. This can be done through a process called isosurfacing.

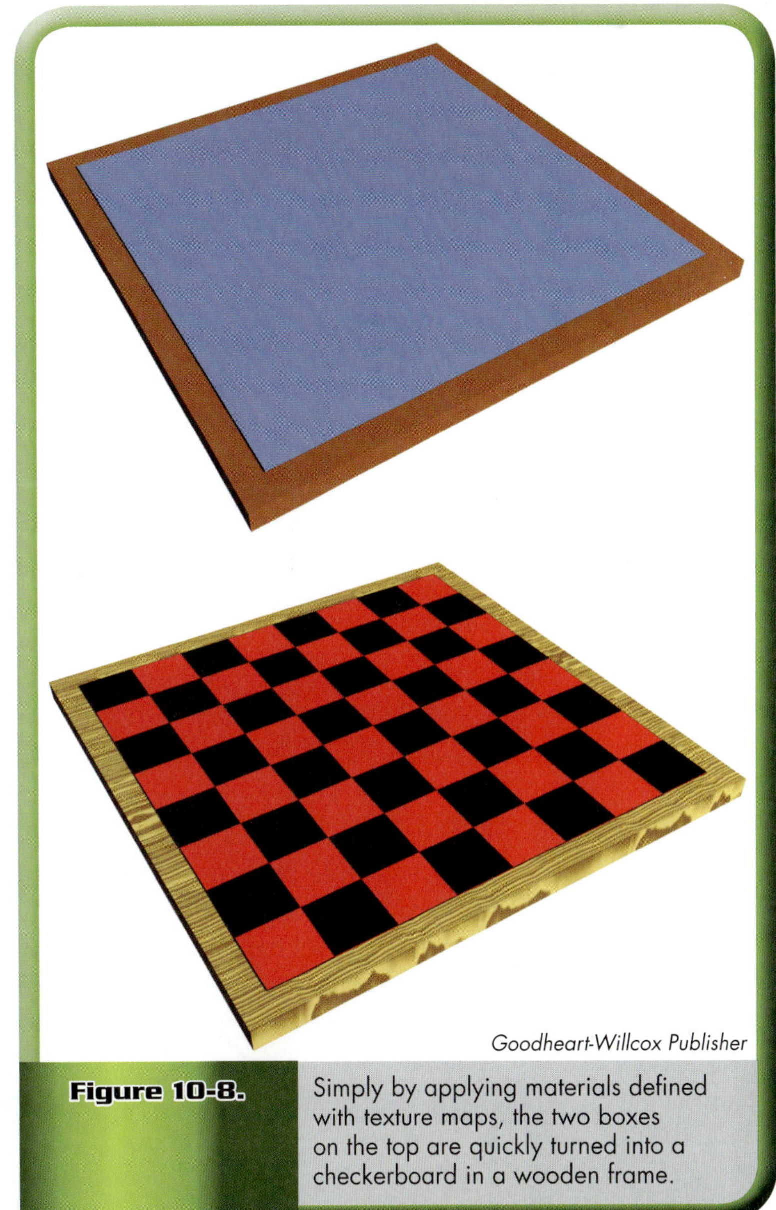

Goodheart-Willcox Publisher

Figure 10-8. Simply by applying materials defined with texture maps, the two boxes on the top are quickly turned into a checkerboard in a wooden frame.

Isosurfacing uses the light and dark regions of the texture map to create raised and lowered areas on the model, like a bump map. However, unlike a bump map, isosurfacing actually alters the mesh, generating triangular polygons to fill the spaces. Isosurfacing substantially increases the polycount and file size. The advantage of an isosurfaced object is that the shadow cast by the object will show the raised and lowered areas of the mesh.

Mapping is the process of determining how a material is positioned on an object. So, mapping controls how the texture map appears on an object, as shown in **Figure 10-9.** When applying a map to the model, the software tessellates the texture. ***Tessellation*** is the breaking up of the overall texture image so a part of the image can be applied to each individual polygon in the model. Much like a tile floor, the colors and textures applied to each polygon help to bring out the desired image. With a texture map in place, the rendered model will display the image flat on its surface. In **Figure 10-9,** tessellation is what allows the decal to be mapped onto the curved surface.

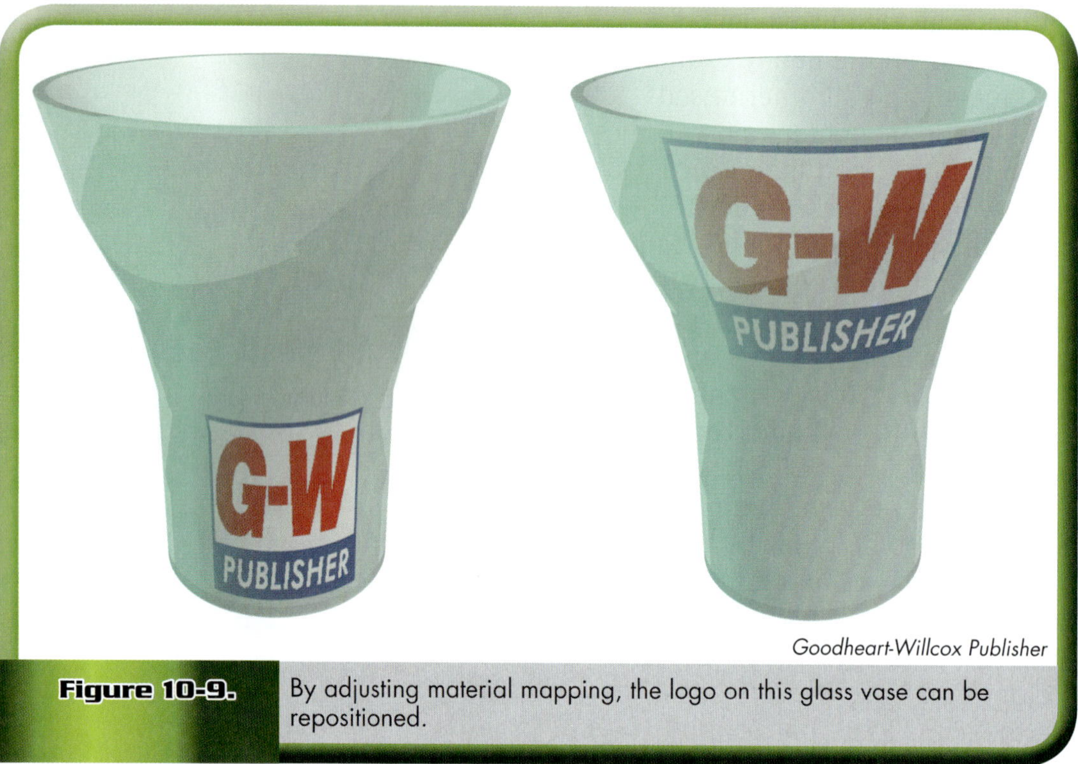

Goodheart-Willcox Publisher

Figure 10-9. By adjusting material mapping, the logo on this glass vase can be repositioned.

In the example shown in **Figure 10-8,** the checker texture map is a diffuse color map because it is applied to the diffuse color property. Mapping then specifies that the texture map, which is made up of two black squares and two red squares, repeats four times in each direction so the board is eight by eight.

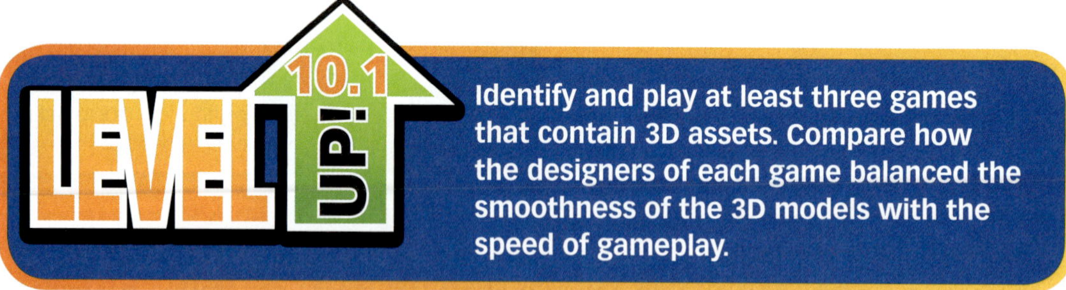

Identify and play at least three games that contain 3D assets. Compare how the designers of each game balanced the smoothness of the 3D models with the speed of gameplay.

File Formats

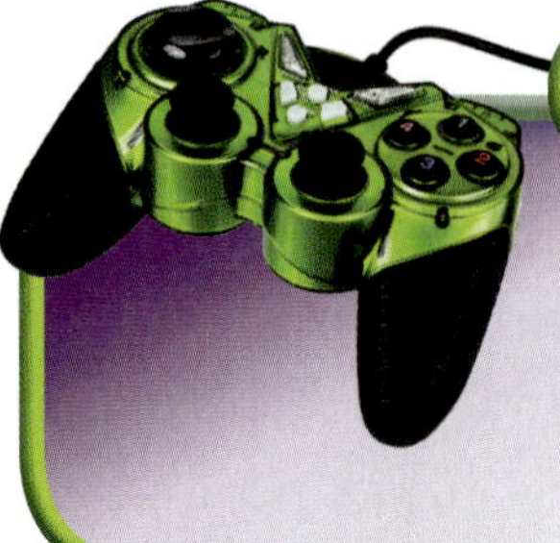

CHEAT CODE: BYTE

A byte is a unit of measure of storage capacity of computer data or information. One byte equals eight bits of information. One bit can be thought of as storing either a 1 or a 0.

File size is a major limiting factor in 3D modeling. The file size is the total of all computer data needed to store the image or model and is measured in **bytes.** A kilobyte (KB) is one thousand bytes, a megabyte (MB) is one million bytes, and a gigabyte (GB) is one billion bytes. The larger the file size, the longer it takes for the computer to process the information.

This can be a major concern in games, especially those games that render on the fly as the gameplay progresses. If the gameplay lags because the models are too large, then the models and game are both failures. Sometimes a model must be created that is not as smooth as the designer may want in order to reduce the number of polygons and the amount of data in the file. NURBS models may also be used since they are often smaller than similar mesh models.

Digital images, whether 2D photographs, 2D illustrations, or 3D renderings, can be stored in various file formats, as shown in **Figure 10-10.** File formats are a standardized way to organize the information of a digital image. The two basic image formats are raster and vector.

Raster Images

Raster images record the location and color of each picture element (pixel) of the image. If the image is enlarged or reduced, the number of pixels changes. As a result, raster images lose clarity when enlarged and reduced. When the image is enlarged, for example, new pixels need to be created in the space between the original pixels. The process of creating a new pixel is called *interpolation*.

Image Format	Name	Compression	Benefit
GIF	Graphic Interface Format	Lossless	Popular for use on websites; 256 colors and can be animated
PNG-8	Portable Network Graphic, 8-bit depth	Lossless	Same as GIF, but cannot be animated
PNG-24	Portable Network Graphic, 24-bit depth	Lossless	Same as PNG-8, but more colors and transparency options
JPEG	Joint Photographic Expert Group	Lossy	Generally offers the smallest file size
BMP	Bitmap	Run length encoded (RLE)	Device independent
RAW or CIFF	Camera Image File Format	None	Raw data at full uncompressed value
CGM	Computer Graphics Metafile	Vector	Can be used with many vector-imaging programs
AI	Adobe Illustrator	Vector	For use with Adobe Illustrator
EPS	Encapsulated PostScript	Vector	Generic vector format that can be used in any PostScript-enabled software

Figure 10-10. While there are over 100 different file formats for graphics, this table details some of the most popular.

Goodheart-Willcox Publisher

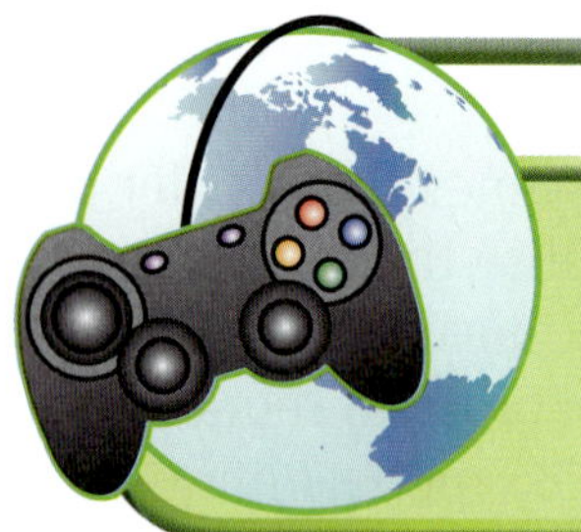

Green Gamer

Avoid chemical cleaners when removing the smudge marks from an LCD TV screen or computer monitor. Look for environmentally friendly cleaners that will not harm either the equipment or the environment.

The color of the new pixel is an approximation of combining the colors of the original pixels surrounding it. When an image is reduced, pixels need to be removed.

The file size of a raster image can be very large since each pixel must be recorded as data. To make the file size smaller, a compressed image format was developed. A computer algorithm is used to record the pixel data in a smaller file size and then uncompress the image when it is opened in image-editing software. The two most popular image-compression algorithms are lossy and lossless. The ***lossy compression algorithm*** compresses the image, but does not keep perfect image clarity. The image generally will have an acceptable appearance, but it will not be as clear when uncompressed as the original image. The ***lossless compression algorithm,*** or losslessly compression algorithm, compresses the image and keeps perfect clarity when uncompressed. However, the file size may be larger than the same image compressed with the lossy compression algorithm.

Photographs are raster images, as are renderings of 3D scenes. Animations are a type of raster image. In an animation, a series of raster images are displayed in sequence. There is a small difference between each raster image, which the brain interprets as motion. Think of the simple animations you may have created on the page edges of a notebook. When you flip the pages, the drawing appears to move.

Vector Images

Vector images store image data as a mathematical definition, not pixel-by-pixel data. A line in a vector image is stored as its mathematical definition, not as the data needed to display a series of pixels to create the line. As a result, vector images do not have the problem with loss of clarity when enlarged or reduced, as shown in **Figure 10-11.** If a vector image is enlarged, the software calculates the result based on the mathematical definition. This means that the image can be expanded infinitely without loss of clarity.

A standard computer monitor or television cannot display vector images. These devices can only display pixels or dots. For a vector image to be displayed, the software must **rasterize** the image before it is sent to the display device.

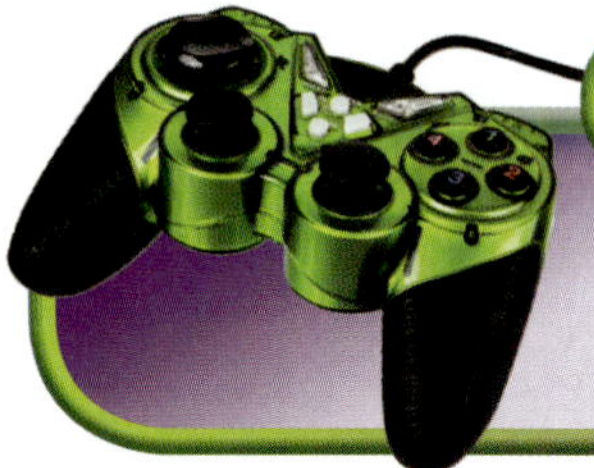

CHEAT CODE: RASTERIZE

To rasterize an image is to convert the existing image into a raster image.

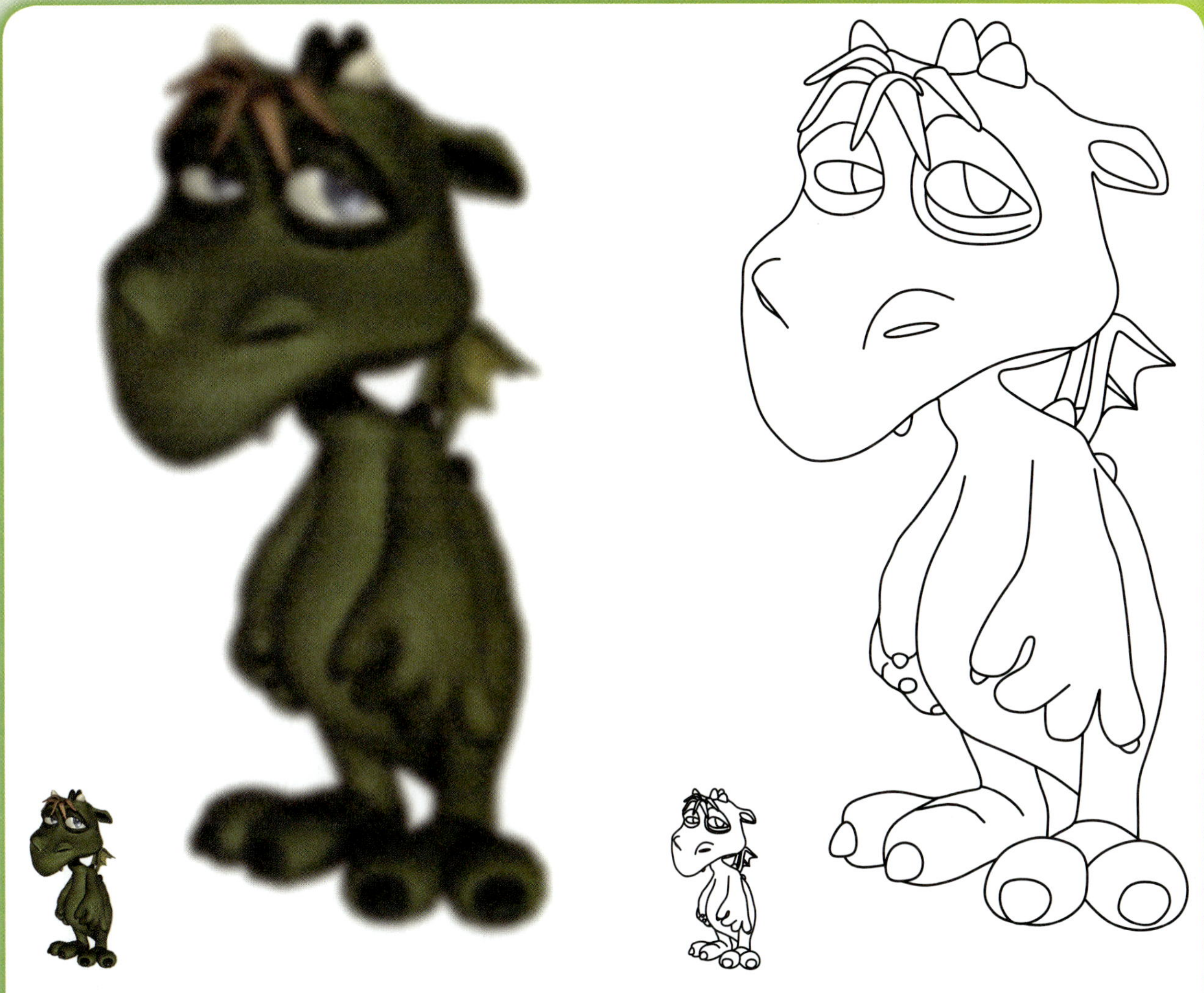

Goodheart-Willcox Publisher; image: Andreas Meyer/Shutterstock.com

Figure 10-11. Raster images become pixelated when enlarged, but vector images can be infinitely scaled without loss of clarity.

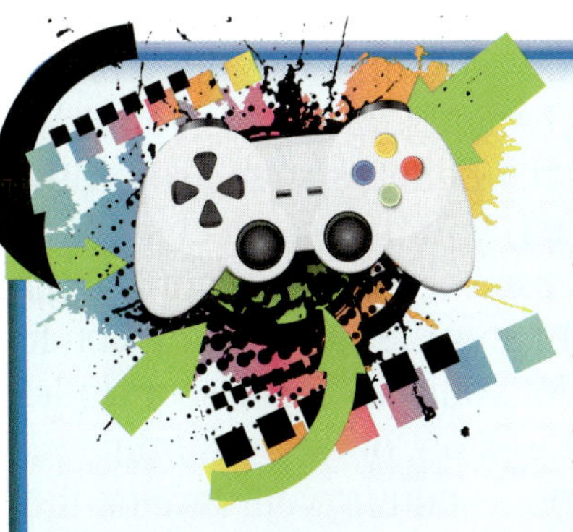

Ethical Gamer

Plagiarism is a form of theft where you copy somebody else's material without permission. Under copyright law, as soon as something is in tangible form, it is automatically copyrighted. Just about everything you see in print, all music you listen to, any images you see on television or movie screens, and almost all information on the Internet is copyrighted. If you copy any of this material without the permission of the copyright holder, you have committed theft.

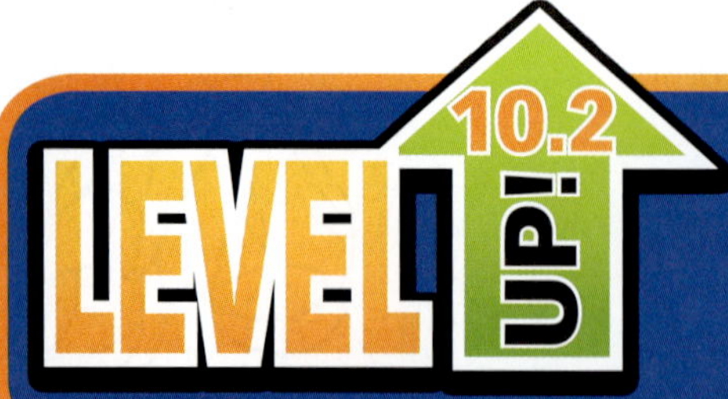

There have been games that displayed vector graphics. Conduct research to find at least one game with vector graphics and describe the game.

Legal Issues

Some of the most important information an artist or game designer should understand is related to copyright and ownership. There are several legal rights an artist has in protecting artwork. Equally important are those steps taken by game designers and artists to physically protect the content from being copied.

The most critical legal standing is ownership. When you make a new and original game or piece of artwork, you are the owner…sometimes. If you paint a picture and no one has asked you or paid you to do this, you are the owner. However, if someone has paid you to paint the picture, then that person is often the owner, depending on the contract between you and the other person. The difference is the contract.

When you are hired at a game design studio, you will likely be required to sign a contract. That contract will lay out the rules for what the company owns and what you own. The wording of the contract may even give ownership to the company of something you create at home on your own time. This may sound harsh, but think of it like homework. When you do homework, the intent is that the work will be turned over to your teacher. That holds true for most work you do from home for a company that hires you. Your contract will likely state that the company has exclusive rights of ownership of any works you produce on behalf of the company or of a derivative work.

In some cases, you may not be hired as an employee of the company. Instead, you may be a freelancer engaged in a work-for-hire contract. A ***work-for-hire contract*** states what you are expected to produce, the starting and ending dates of the work, and what you will be paid. The contract should also state the company owns the work you produce and if you may use the work in any way. The work-for-hire contract will state any benefits to be received. In most cases, a freelancer will not receive any company benefits such as vacation or health insurance. If it is not stated on the contract, you do not receive it.

An ***exclusive right*** allows the creative work to be used or reproduced only by the person or company who owns the contract, or to whomever they give permission to do so. That means you are not even allowed to use it for yourself. This also includes any derivative works. A ***derivative work*** is anything based on, or derived, from any part of the original. An example of a derivative work is putting your face on the game character Master Chief. The original character is the original work. You used part of the original work to make a new character. That makes the new character a derivative of the original. So, if you work for a game design company and build a really cool game, you cannot just change the name and sell it on your own.

A good working knowledge of copyrights and other means of protecting your work is important to ensure you keep possession of your creative works or are paid for your work. Make sure you read and understand all parts of a contract before you sign it. If you do not understand something, ask questions and get legal advice from a qualified person. Saying you did not know something was illegal or violated your contract is not a legal defense.

Agreements

A company may require you to sign a confidentiality agreement and noncompete agreement. Both of these agreements are to help keep information secret from other companies with similar products.

A ***confidentiality agreement*** is a contract that states you cannot share any information about the company or its products with any other company. This protects your employer from developing a game and having the employees leak information to the press or other game companies. A leak might destroy the competitive advantage for the game and make it hard to make a profit.

A ***noncompete agreement*** is a contract that states you cannot create work that competes with the company while you are employed by it and for a certain period of time after you leave the company. Most noncompete agreements in the game industry are for six months or one year. The company makes a financial investment when they hire you, not only in your salary, but in the potential money it may earn from products on which you work. A noncompete agreement prevents you from taking what you know about the company and its current products and going to a competing company.

Copyrights

The owner of a creative work will want to protect the work from being copied. The United States and most other countries have ***copyright laws*** to protect the owner of a creative work. Under US copyright laws, as soon as a creative work is in **tangible** form, it is automatically copyrighted.

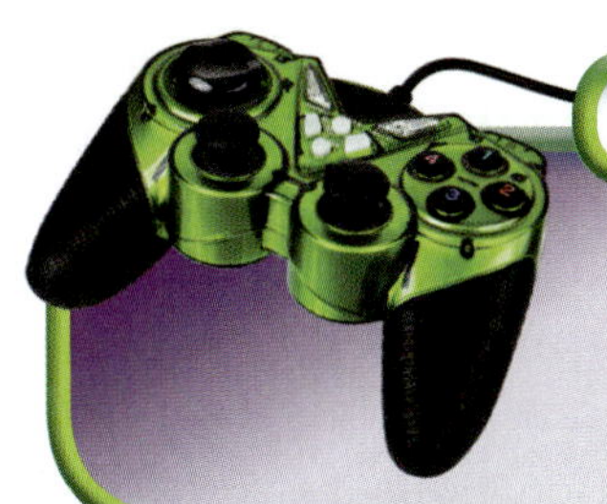

CHEAT CODE: TANGIBLE

Tangible means capable of being perceived. In this sense, a creative work is tangible as soon as it can be seen or heard.

Misusing or making unauthorized copies of a copyrighted work is called ***copyright infringement.*** In the United States, copyright infringement carries a heavy penalty. For example, any motion picture you rent or purchase carries a warning similar to the one shown in **Figure 10-12.** Violators can end up in prison or be fined. Some people found this out the hard way when downloading music. Downloading a copyrighted song without permission is an infringement on the copyright of the creative work (music), regardless of whether or not money exchanged hands. Many people were found guilty of copyright infringement and were ordered to pay a penalty of between $750 and $30,000 per download. Some ended up having to pay millions of dollars in fines and penalties.

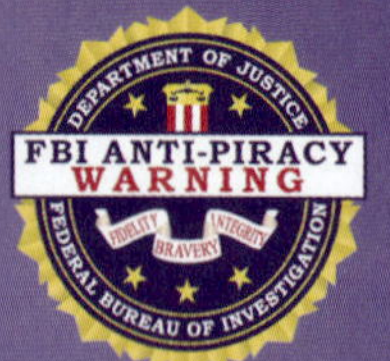

Goodheart-Willcox Publisher

Figure 10-12. This is the antipiracy warning from the Federal Bureau of Investigation (FBI).

Copyright laws are both statutory and case. ***Statutory laws*** have been passed by the legislature. Written into the law is a formal definition of how the law is to be interpreted. ***Case laws*** are enacted when the first lawsuit to deal with the problem has determined the outcome. That case is then cited in other lawsuits as an example of previous judgment (called precedence). Case law is very important because the legislature cannot enact all of the laws needed as society and technology change.

There are some legal ways to copy and use creative works without getting permission from the owner. These concepts include Creative Commons licenses, fair use/fair dealing doctrine, and public domain. A copyright holder may assign a ***Creative Commons license*** to the work so it can be used for free with or without restrictions, as shown in **Figure 10-13.** Often, a Creative Commons license may require citing authorship and may prohibit derivative works.

The ***fair use/fair dealings doctrine*** also allows a creative work to be used without permission, but under very strict guidelines. The fair use/fair dealings doctrine allows someone to reprint or display a copyrighted work without permission for the purpose of describing or reviewing the creative work. That means a student can write a paper about *Halo 3* and include a picture of the game box and the characters. Students, critics, and bloggers often use the fair use/fair dealings doctrine when reproducing pictures or other content. Newspapers and other media also use this doctrine as a tool to report the facts. This doctrine does *not*, however, allow reproducing any copyrighted work outside of the context of describing or reviewing the work nor does it allow claiming the copyrighted work as your own.

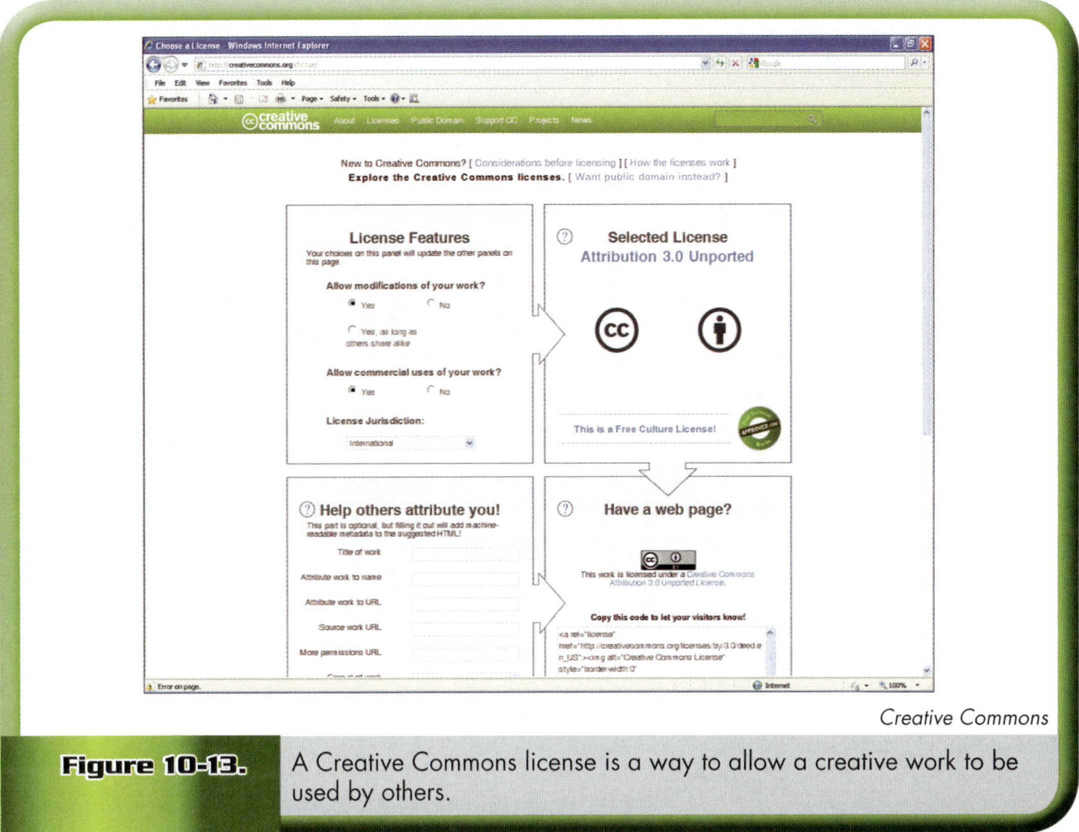

Creative Commons

Figure 10-13. A Creative Commons license is a way to allow a creative work to be used by others.

When a creative work has been around for a long time, it is placed in the public domain. ***Public domain*** applies to any work for which the copyright term has expired. It means any and all copyrights on the work have been removed. When the copyright expires, there is no more legal protection preventing duplication and these works are free to use. The concept of public domain assumes that the creative work holds little or no value after a long time. The law establishes different time periods for different types of intellectual property to hold copyright. For example, in the United States the term for work published since 1978 is the life of the creator plus 70 years.

Antipiracy Measures

Piracy is theft. In addition to work being protected under the law, an artist or game designer may want to protect work by making it hard to copy. A game company may use a ***software key code*** to unlock the game software and allow only one installation. After the game is installed once, it cannot be installed again. To protect works like digital art, tactics such as digital watermarks are used. A ***digital watermark*** is something that makes the image unusable as final artwork, but allows somebody to review the art for potential use, as shown in **Figure 10-14.** To use the artwork, you must contact the artist or company offering the artwork to obtain a final version without the watermark.

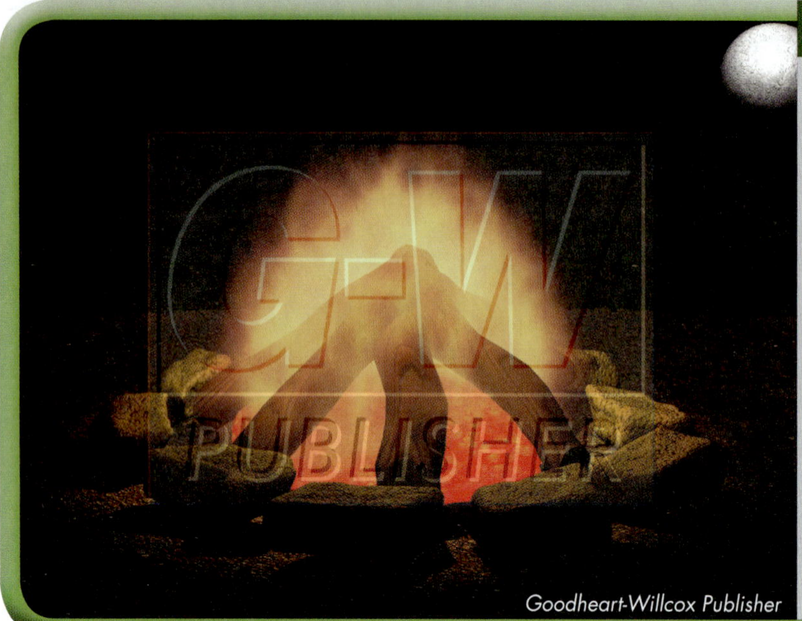

Goodheart-Willcox Publisher

Figure 10-14. A digital watermark allows artwork to be evaluated before purchase. The watermarked image can even be used as a placeholder before the purchase is completed.

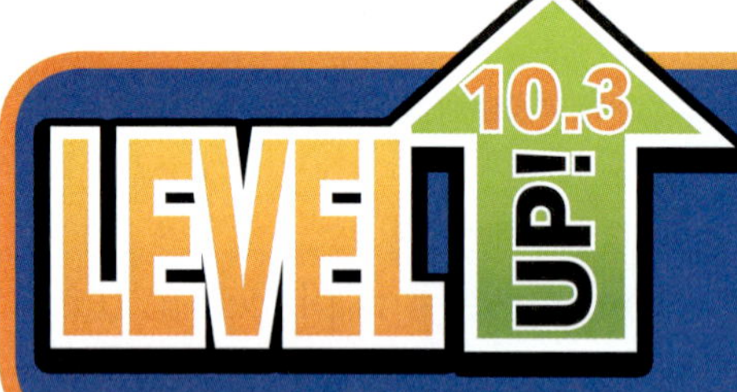

Select five games. Identify what copyright notices and antipiracy measures are used on each game.

Chapter Summary

- Many artists who work on a design team; roles include: art director, lead artist, concept artist, texture artist, environment artist, three-dimensional modeling artist, video director, asset manager, and animator.
- The key elements of three-dimensional modeling include meshes, mesh smoothing, NURBS, lighting composition, and material composition.
- Raster images record the location and color of each picture element (pixel) of the image while vector images store image data as a mathematical definition, not pixel-by-pixel data; raster images lose clarity when enlarged and reduced while vector images do not; the file size of a raster image can be very large, since each pixel must be recorded as data, so the file must be compressed; vector images must be rasterized to be displayed on a standard computer monitor.
- The most critical legal standing is ownership—if you create something, you own it unless you have a contract with a company that gives them ownership rights to work you produce; ownership is protected by copyright and steps can be taken digitally to prohibit illegal reproduction of copyrighted work.

Check Your Video Game IQ

Now that you have finished this chapter, see what you know about video game design by taking the chapter posttest.

www.m.g-wlearning.com

www.g-wlearning.com

Review Your Knowledge

On a separate sheet of paper or in a word processing document, match the following terms with the definition that fits best.

A. art director	F. tessellation
B. point light	G. Creative Commons license
C. lead artist	H. geodesic sphere
D. spotlight	I. public domain
E. concept artist	J. UV sphere

1. A light source that illuminates in all directions, like a common household lightbulb.
2. Manages the details of a single project and makes sure all art is designed correctly.
3. The breaking up of the overall texture image so a part of the image can be applied to each individual polygon in the model.
4. Sphere constructed of regular polygons such as triangles, pentagons, and octagons.

5. A creative work that has been around for a long time; applies to any work for which the copyright term has expired.
6. The highest-ranking artist; person who sets the vision for the game art and makes sure it is what is needed for the theme and story.
7. A light source that projects light rays in a cone shape.
8. An artist strong in creating new characters and objects that have never existed before.
9. A designation made by a copyright holder to their work so it can be used for free with or without restrictions.
10. Sphere constructed of rectangular and triangular polygons.

On a separate sheet of paper or in a word processing document, answer each of the following questions.

11. Describe the authority structure of the design teams in the game industry.
12. Explain the difference between concept art and model sheets.
13. Describe the duties of the lead artist.
14. How many polygons are used to create a cube?
15. What two attributes of a 3D model would a game artist monitor when smoothing?
16. In video game design, what is the benefit of using a NURBS sphere instead of a geodesic sphere?
17. List at least three material components where a map may be assigned.
18. How is the surface geometry altered using a bump map?
19. Which basic type of image must have interpolation applied to create new pixels when the image is enlarged?
20. At what point does an original work have a copyright?

Apply Your STEM Knowledge

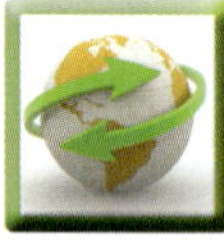

Social Studies

1. The Internet has increased the opportunity for copyright infringement. Many websites offer free viewing of movies and downloading of games and software. Research the topic of *video game piracy*. Prepare a PowerPoint presentation that explains how many games are pirated, lists landmark legal cases against pirate distributors, and identifies the cost of piracy to the video game industry. Form an opinion about whether or not those who downloaded pirated games would have purchased the legitimate game if the pirated version was not available. Explain why or why not.

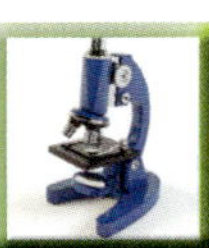

Science

2. Three-dimensional modeling of objects requires the simulation of many types of surfaces. Each surface has different properties to explain how light reacts to the material. Some of the most difficult materials to simulate are glass and transparent liquids. Light refracts, or bends, as it travels through these materials. Research light refraction and create a PowerPoint presentation of seven to ten slides to explain your findings.

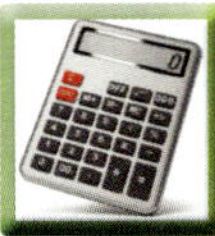

Mathematics

3. Suppose a 3D modeling program requires 0.1 MB of memory to store the information and location of a single polygon in a mesh. Using spreadsheet or word-processing software, create the table below. Complete the table by calculating the amount of memory used for the models and polycount.

Model	Polycount	Memory (in MB)
Teapot	2000	200
Alien	16,000	
Building		12
Weapon	916	
Spaceship		1 GB

Language Arts

4. Research five common software products used to create 3D models. Write a paper to summarize the features, options, advantages, and disadvantages of using each product. Include your opinion of the best product. Support your opinion with facts.

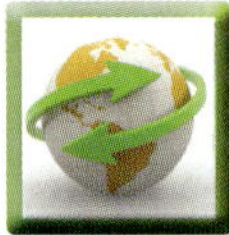

Social Studies

5. Consider collaborating with artists in three different countries. Select three countries of your choice. Research each country, its language and customs, and its typical workweek. Create a PowerPoint presentation that describes what accommodations you would need to make when collaborating with each artist.

Working in Teams

Working with the team assigned by your instructor, assign roles for each member as part of a game art team. Brainstorm at least three assets for a 3D game. Then, determine what responsibility each team member would have in developing each asset.

Gamer Portfolio

You have collected documents that show your skills and talents. However, some skills and talents are not shown effectively using only documents. Do you have a special talent in an area such as art, music, or design? Have you taken part in volunteer activities? Create a video to showcase your talents and activities. For example, create a video that shows your completed artist works. If you are a musician, create a video with segments from your performances. If you have taken part in a volunteer or service activity, create a video that tells viewers about it. Be sure you have permission from people to include them in your video.

1. Place the video file in an appropriate subfolder for your e-portfolio.
2. Print a few screen shots from the video. Create a document that describes the video. State that the video will be made available on request or provide a link to it online. Place the information in the container for your print portfolio.

G-W Learning Mobile Site

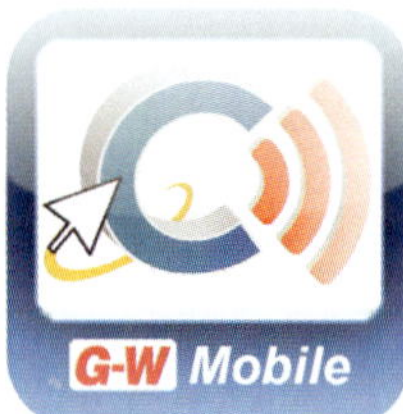

Visit the G-W Learning mobile site to complete the chapter pretest and posttest and to practice vocabulary using e-flash cards. If you do not have a smartphone, visit the G-W Learning companion website to access these features.

G-W Learning mobile site: www.m.g-wlearning.com

G-W Learning companion website: www.g-wlearning.com

Common Core

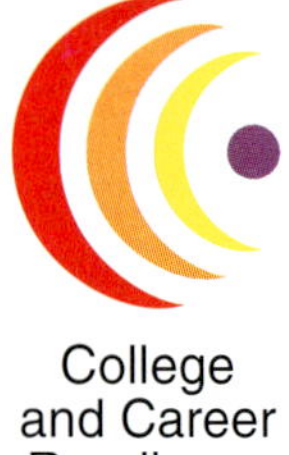
College and Career Readiness

CTE Career Ready Practices. You may have been taught to treat others how *you* would like to be treated. This is often referred to as *the golden rule.* Productively working with others who have a background different from yours may require that you learn to treat others as *they* wish to be treated. Conduct research on the Internet about cultural differences related to personal space, time, gestures and body language, and relationship toward authority figures. Create a T-chart that shows the difference on the left and ways you would adapt your interactions to account for that difference.

Reading. Many argue that piracy has cost the gaming industry millions of dollars in lost sales revenue. What do you think? Research piracy from the early days of video games to the present day. Based on your research, what do you believe? Write a paper on your opinion on this issue. Be sure to include trustworthy sources in your explanations and reasoning.
Writing. Conduct a short research project to answer the question, "How do I keep the file size small in a 3D model while maintaining image quality?" Using information from multiple sources, write a report on your response to this question.

Event Prep: Community Service Project

Many Career and Technical Student Organizations (CTSOs) competitions offer events that include a community service project. This project is usually carried out by the entire CTSO chapter and will take several months to complete. There will be two parts of the event: written and oral. The chapter will designate several members to represent the team at the competitive event. To prepare for the community service event:

1. Read the guidelines provided by your organization. Make certain that you ask any questions about points you do not understand. It is important you follow each specific item as it is outlined in the competition rules.
2. As a team, select a theme for your chapter's community service project.
3. Decide which roles are needed for the team. There may be one person who is the captain, one person who is the secretary, and other roles that will be necessary to create the plan. Ask your instructor for guidance in assigning roles to team members.
4. Identify your target audience, which may include business, school, and community groups.
5. List the benefits of and opportunities for supporting a community service project.
6. This project will probably span the school year. During regular chapter meetings, create a draft of the report based on direction from the CTSO. Write and refine drafts until the final report is finished.

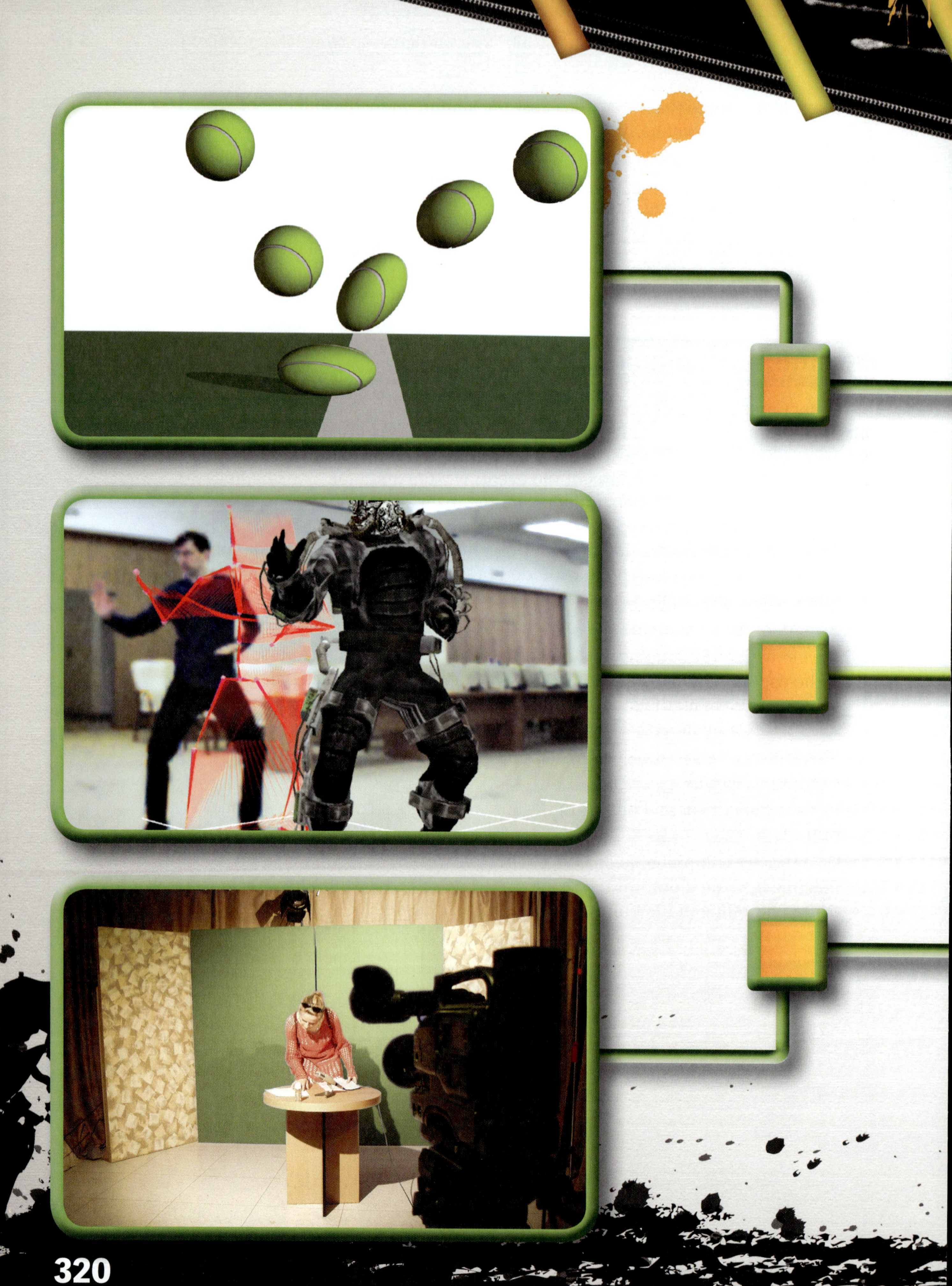

Chapter 11
Animation Composition

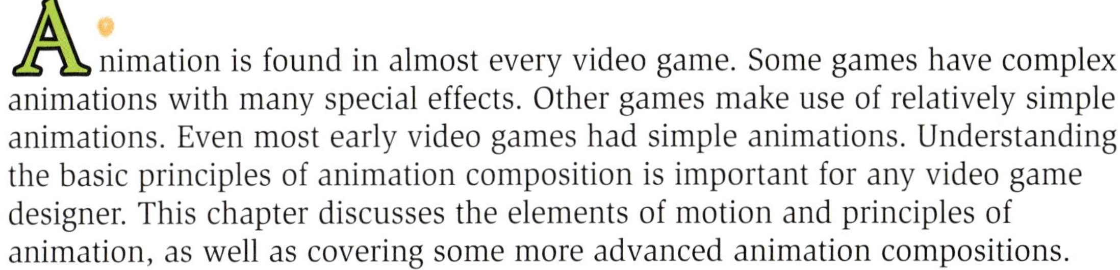

Animation is found in almost every video game. Some games have complex animations with many special effects. Other games make use of relatively simple animations. Even most early video games had simple animations. Understanding the basic principles of animation composition is important for any video game designer. This chapter discusses the elements of motion and principles of animation, as well as covering some more advanced animation compositions.

Check Your Video Game IQ

Before you begin this chapter, see what you already know about video game design by taking the chapter pretest.

www.m.g-wlearning.com

www.g-wlearning.com

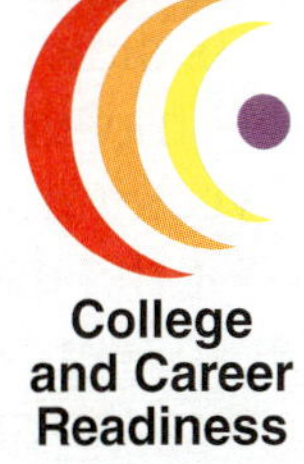

College and Career Readiness

Reading Prep. Recall all of the things you already know about animation. As you read, think of how the new information presented in the text matches or challenges your prior understanding of the topic. Think of direct connections you can make between the old knowledge and the new material.

Objectives

After completing this chapter, you will be able to:

- Outline the six basic elements of motion.
- List the 12 principles of animation as documented by Frank Thomas and Ollie Johnson in their 1981 book *Disney Animation: The Illusion of Life.*
- Define animation and differentiate between static and active animation.
- Describe the specialized aspects to creating animations with a computer.
- Demonstrate an understanding of sound synchronization.
- Identify sources of game art movement other than animation.

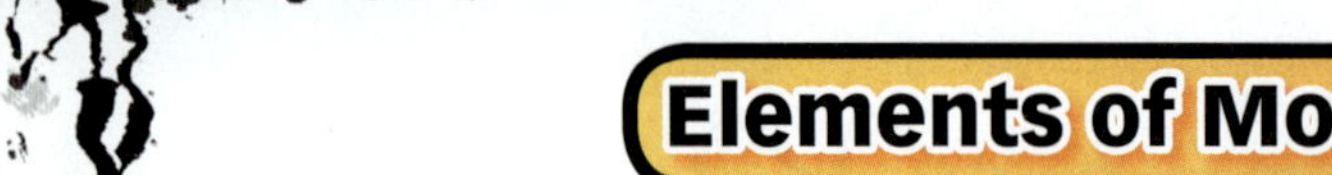

Elements of Motion

At the core of interactivity in a video game is motion. ***Motion*** is the change of position of an object over time. The player avatar and other game objects move or change to create the challenges and goals of the game. The game artist forms the objects and creates a visual world in which game events can exist. To make these realistic, the artist must apply certain elements to make the movement of these objects realistic. To fully explore how motion is put into a video game, an understanding of six basic elements of motion is needed. The six elements, which are explained in the following sections, are:

- persistence;
- perception;
- translation;
- rotation;
- articulation; and
- morphing.

Persistence

The first element of motion is persistence. ***Persistence*** in its simplest definition is, to continue to exist. Physicists have formulas to explain persistence and what type of motion is occurring. Some of the more common examples are acceleration, velocity, displacement, and vector.

Acceleration is the rate at which an object is speeding up or slowing down. *Velocity* is the speed an object is traveling. *Displacement* describes how much something has moved. These are all bundled together with vectors. *Vectors* are the direction of forces. In a video game the objects, backgrounds, and characters can all have motion. Each object will have attributes that define how it can move and what forces act on it.

Acceleration is a positive vector when a car is speeding up, as shown in **Figure 11-1.** Acceleration is a negative vector when a car is slowing down. The velocity vector determines the direction the car is traveling. In a video game, "vector up" might be moving forward, while "vector down" is moving backward. The velocity in both cases is the same, but the direction is different. Displacement vectors are also directional. A car may have driven a displacement vector of North or South and traveled the same distance for each trip.

Perception

Perception is the observation of something, such as motion. Motion is perceived as movement **relative** to a frame of reference. A person observes how things are moving relative to his or her position and motion. Without a frame of reference, motion is not perceived.

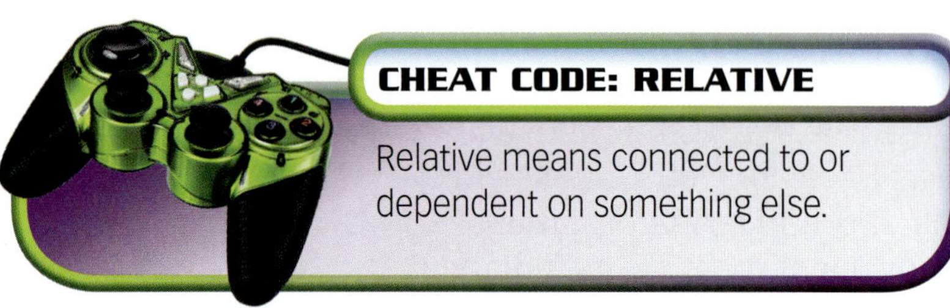

CHEAT CODE: RELATIVE

Relative means connected to or dependent on something else.

For example, if you are traveling in a car and look at a book on the seat next to you,

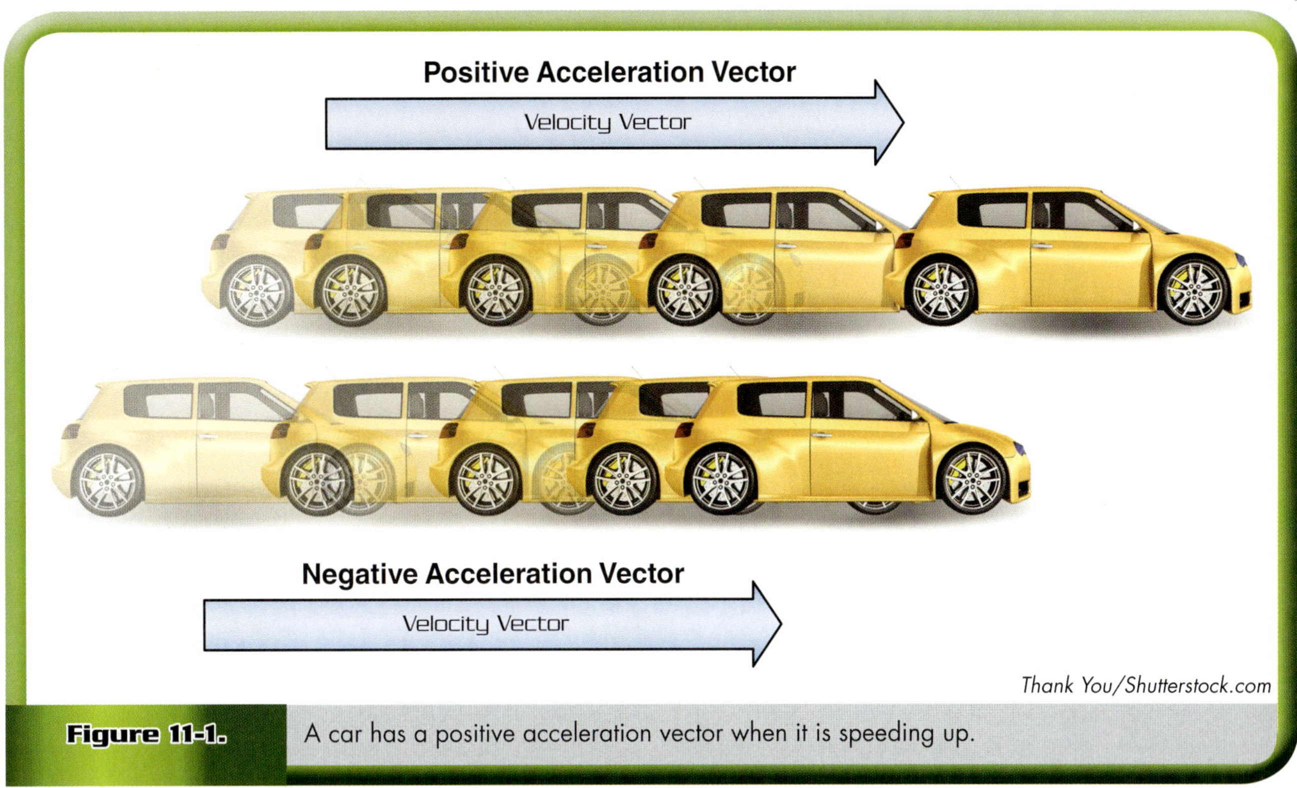

Figure 11-1. A car has a positive acceleration vector when it is speeding up.

the perception is that the book is not moving. This is because you are seeing it relative to your own frame of reference. You, the car, and the book are traveling at the same speed. If you held up the book, a person on the side of the road would see the book moving even though the book is not moving from your perspective.

In video games, perception is determined by the camera. In a side-scrolling 2D game, the camera is looking at objects from the side. Motion is perceived as left, right, up, and down. In a top-down 2D game, the camera location is above the game looking down. In this view, motion is perceived as North, South, East, and West. In a first-person shooter (FPS) game, the entire game map moves with each step of the player character. Motion is perceived as all objects moving while the player remains still. The player's view remains centered on the screen.

Translation

The most basic of all movement types is translation motion. ***Translation*** is the movement from one point to another. This is simple right-left, up-down, and in-out movement. If a ball is located in the Cartesian coordinate system at the coordinate (0,0,0) and it is translated to coordinate (5,0,0), the ball has moved five units from the origin on the X axis. This is shown in **Figure 11-2.**

Translation is very important in video game design. Each object on the screen is plotted using the coordinate system. A collision occurs when two objects have the same coordinates. Game designers must create collision detection for all of the interactive objects in the scene.

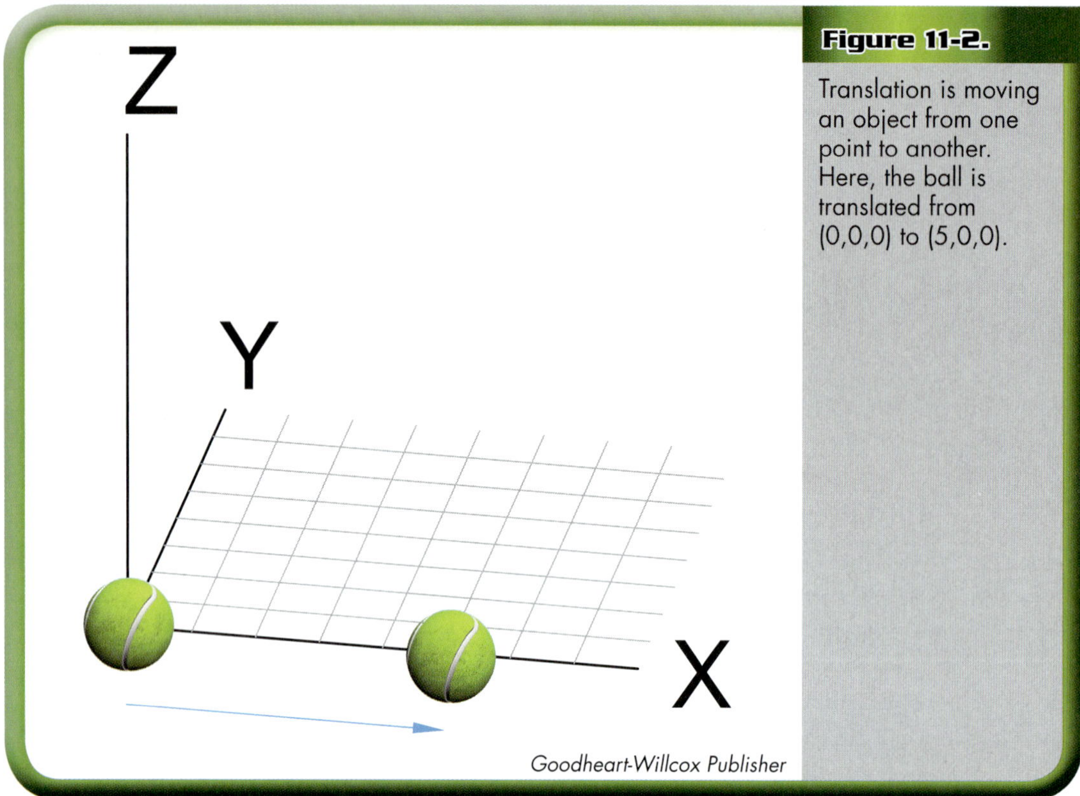

Figure 11-2. Translation is moving an object from one point to another. Here, the ball is translated from (0,0,0) to (5,0,0).

Rotation

Rotation is circular movement about a central point. In video games, rotation occurs around the X axis, Y axis or Z axis of the object.

A good example of rotation can be seen in the movement of an airplane. In a right-hand turn, the right wing rotates down and the left wing rotates up, as shown in **Figure 11-3.** This rotation is about the long central axis of the plane, which can be thought of as the X axis. To make the airplane go up or down, the pilot controls the pitch. When taking off, the airplane nose is rotated up and the tail is rotated down. This rotation is about an axis running from wingtip to wingtip, which can be thought of as the Y axis. The yaw controls for the pilot come from the rudder input. When the airplane turns to the left with the rudder input, the nose rotates to the left and the tail rotates to the right. This rotation is about a vertical axis, which can be thought of as the Z axis.

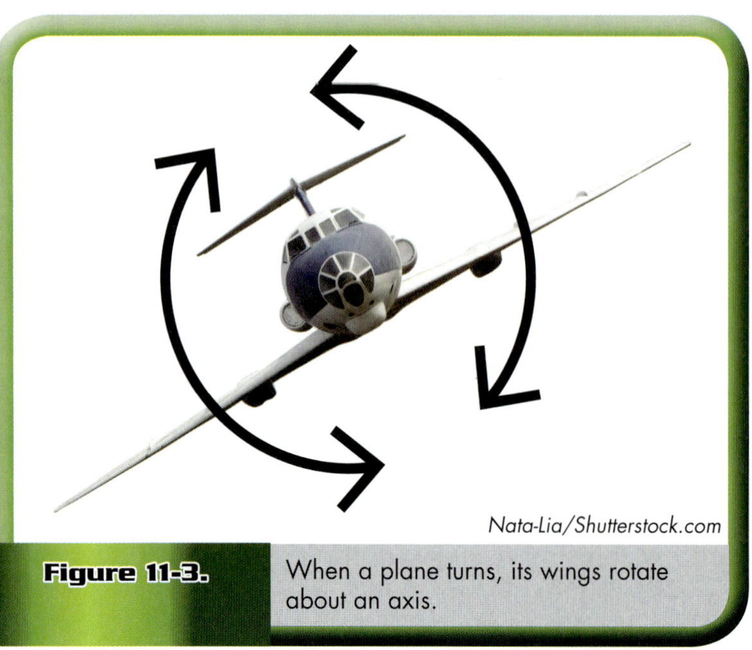

Figure 11-3. When a plane turns, its wings rotate about an axis.

Articulation

Articulation is the bending and positioning of movable parts, such as arms and legs in synchronization with the translation of a walking character. The legs articulate in a stepping motion as the character is translated to a new position. If the legs are articulated without translating the character, the active animation would look as if the character is running in place.

Articulation is plotted by mapping a point on an object and following it through the motion path, or animation arc. An ***animation arc*** is the path an articulated feature follows through the animation. This is shown in **Figure 11-4.** Video game designers need to be aware of the animation arc. How many games have you played where a character's arm or leg moves through another object when it is articulated? This is an error and reflects poorly on the game.

In video game design, an artist often must duplicate the articulation of real objects or humans. A 3D modeling animator might use a motion-capture system to record the actual articulation movements of a person. Motion capture is discussed later in this chapter.

Morphing

Morphing is a change in the physical shape of an object. Objects can be squashed, stretched, exploded, joined, and more. Each time the size or shape of the object changes, a morph occurs. Objects that collide impart energy to each other when they hit. This energy causes waves or deformations. Additionally, objects can change state. Water can boil into a gas and metal can be melted into a liquid.

The law of *conservation of energy* states that energy cannot be created or destroyed, but can change state. *Kinetic energy* is the energy of movement. The kinetic energy of two items colliding cannot be destroyed. Rather it is transformed into heat, sound, and stored energy. Stored energy is *potential energy.* Potential energy can exist as gravitational, elastic, chemical, electrical, or magnetic energy, as described in **Figure 11-5.**

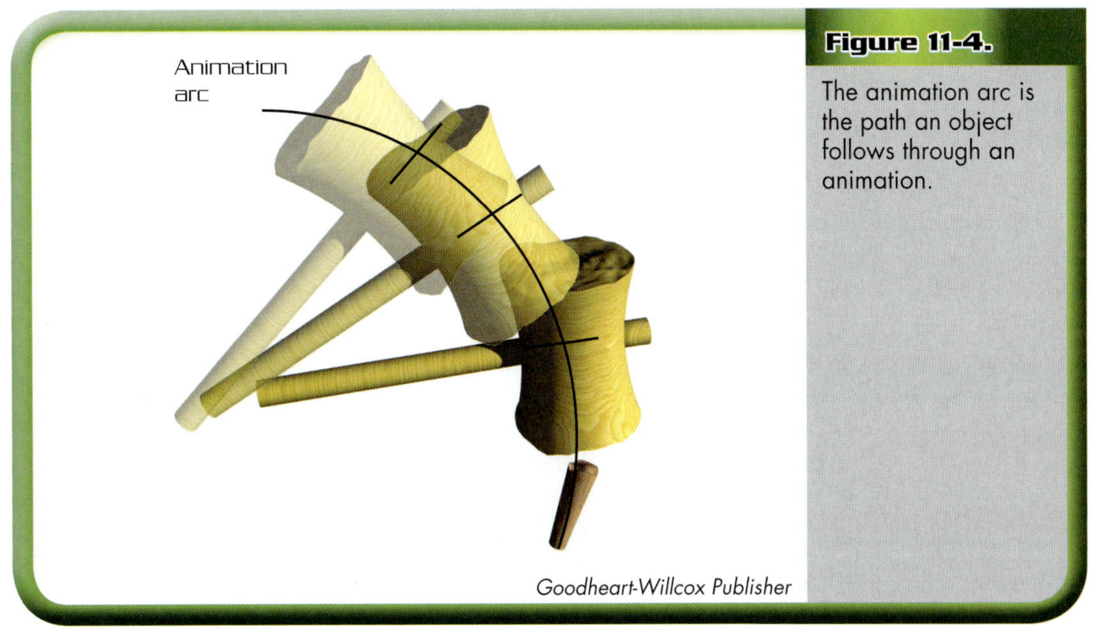

Goodheart-Willcox Publisher

Figure 11-4.

The animation arc is the path an object follows through an animation.

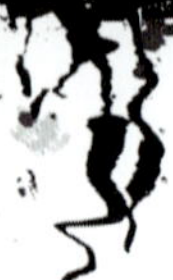

Type of Potential Energy	Example
Gravitational	Falling object, planetary rotation
Elastic	Stretched rubber band, spring
Chemical	Stick of dynamite, lead-acid battery
Electrical	Lightning, capacitor
Magnetic	Earth's poles, refrigerator magnets

Figure 11-5. Potential energy can be in several different forms.

Goodheart-Willcox Publisher

If you hold a rock above the ground, the rock has potential energy relative to the ground. The potential energy of the rock is formed by the force of gravity pulling the rock toward the ground. When you let the rock fall, the potential energy is transformed into kinetic energy as it moves toward the ground. When the rock hits, the kinetic energy of the rock transforms into sound and vibration. It is also likely that the rock and the ground have morphed in the collision. The rock may break and the ground may have an impact crater.

In video game design, an artist must understand morphing and create objects and systems that change shape. A classic example of morphing that can be seen in many video games is water. Dropping a pebble in a pond creates motion ripples as the energy moves through the water. The waves crash against a shoreline. The water system must morph as it moves energy through the water.

An important consideration in game art is to follow conservation of **matter** in a morph. *Conservation of matter* means that all mass content must be the same before and after an interaction. If a rock is broken up, the sum of the pieces will have the same mass as the whole rock. When morphing a game object, the mass must appear to remain constant. Take the example of a car crash. The car will morph as the parts wrinkle and break, but the mass of the car and its pieces should appear to be the same.

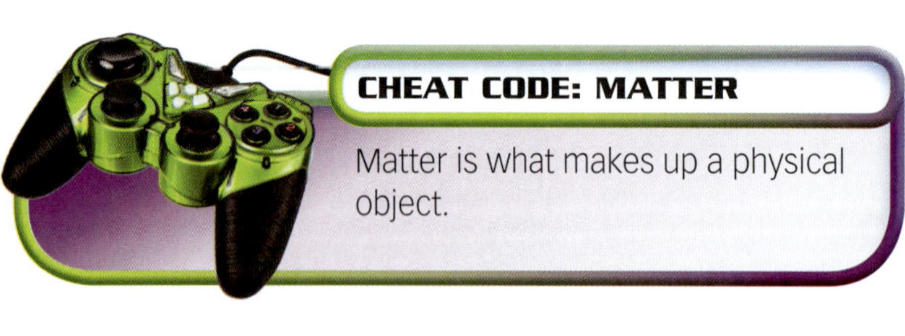

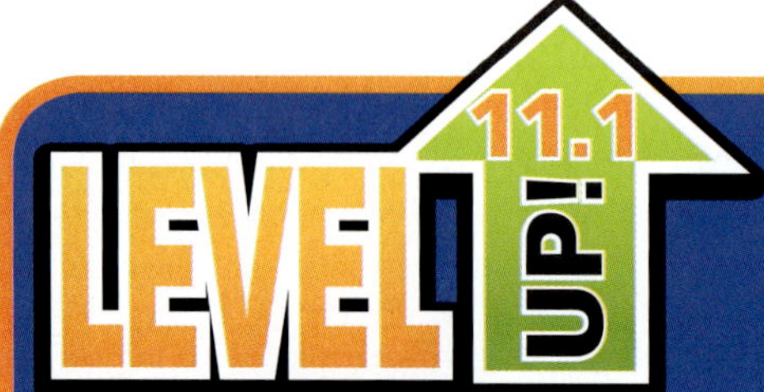

Play at least two different types of games. Compare and contrast how the elements of motion are applied in each game.

Principles of Animation

With an understanding of how motion exists in the real world, a designer can create art and motion for the game world. The key components to simulating motion in a game are animation, actor physics, and game physics. *Actor physics* uses a mathematical model to control the articulation of a character or object. *Game physics* uses a mathematical model to control the general motion of objects in the virtual world.

Animating is the process of creating the illusion of movement in a drawing, rendering, or inanimate object. An animation is the end result. Frank Thomas and Ollie Johnson documented the 12 principles of animation in their 1981 book *Disney Animation: The Illusion of Life.* Thomas and Johnson were two of Walt Disney Studio's legendary Nine Old Men. The Nine Old Men were the core group of animators who started working for Disney between 1927 through 1935. The book, shown in **Figure 11-6,** contains a huge collection of animations and has become known as the "bible of animation." It details the physics involved in simulating real life through animation. The 12 principles of animation are:

- squash and stretch;
- anticipation;
- staging;
- straight-ahead and pose-to-pose action;
- follow-through and overlapping action;
- slow in and slow out;
- arcs;
- secondary action;
- timing;
- exaggeration;
- solid drawing; and
- appeal.

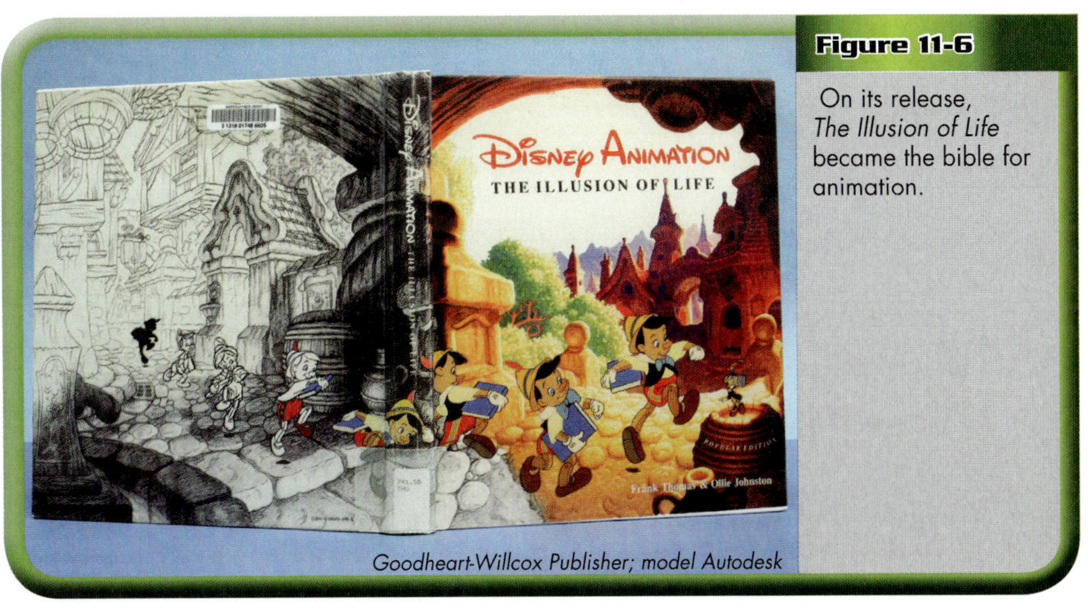

Goodheart-Willcox Publisher; model Autodesk

Figure 11-6

On its release, *The Illusion of Life* became the bible for animation.

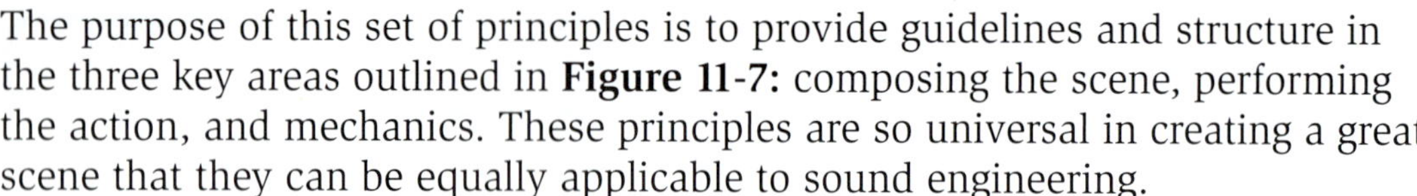

The purpose of this set of principles is to provide guidelines and structure in the three key areas outlined in **Figure 11-7:** composing the scene, performing the action, and mechanics. These principles are so universal in creating a great scene that they can be equally applicable to sound engineering.

Composing the Scene

Constructing the scene is creating the basic objects needed in the scene. The principles of animation that apply to this stage are appeal, staging, timing, and exaggeration.

Appeal

Before beginning to animate a scene, it is important to review the concepts of character development and storytelling. Appeal is the emotional connection between the character, the scene, and the audience. In the case of a character, the design and animation should match the character's personality. A shy and timid character should have slow movements, slack posture, and withdrawn body language. Conversely, a boss character should have bold and flamboyant movements and exaggerated body language.

The characters should have attributes that viewers can relate to and like, even for enemy characters. Use symbolism and color to convey meaning and set the mood. Posture, movements, and actions must be consistent with the archetype of the character. Finally, the character should have unity on its own and unity with the action and scene. The traits that make the character interesting should fit with the role and abilities needed in the story.

Staging

Animation is not just about moving an object, it is also how that object is seen. In a game, there are many ordinary objects and some important objects. ***Staging*** allows the artist to draw attention to the area or objects of greatest importance. Techniques such as hiding or revealing the item of central interest and visual causal chains help add to the suspense and draw interest into the scene. A visual causal chain is simply one consisting of elements that can be seen.

Composing the Scene	Performing the Action	Mechanics
Appeal	Anticipation	Solid Drawing
Staging	Squash and Stretch	Straight-Ahead and Pose-to-Pose Action
Timing	Arcs	
Exaggeration	Follow-Through and Overlapping Action	
	Secondary Action	
	Slow In and Slow Out	

Figure 11-7. The three key areas of animation are: composing the scene, performing the action, and mechanics. This table shows the area in which each of the 12 principles of animation fits.

Goodheart-Willcox Publisher

Staging includes setting the scene and positioning characters inside the scene. Light and shadow can be used to help draw attention to details. A book on a table in a dark room will not attract attention. Putting the book on the same table under a desk lamp highlights its importance. Movement of an object will also attract attention. Animating branches moving in the distance or smoke from a fire gives visual clues to the important area of the scene.

In character animation, staging should include the perspective that best displays the item. This can be demonstrated through **silhouetting,** as shown in **Figure 11-8.** When a character carries an object inside his or her silhouette frame, little attention is drawn to the object. This communicates that object is unimportant. An object positioned outside of the silhouette frame attracts attention and indicates importance. Next time you see a television commercial or a game show, pay attention to how the model holds the product. It will almost always be outside of the model's silhouette.

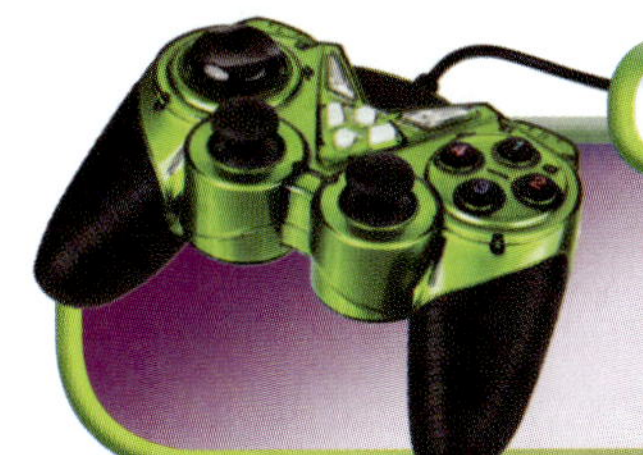

CHEAT CODE: SILHOUETTING

Silhouetting is creating a shadow image that shows only the outline of the object.

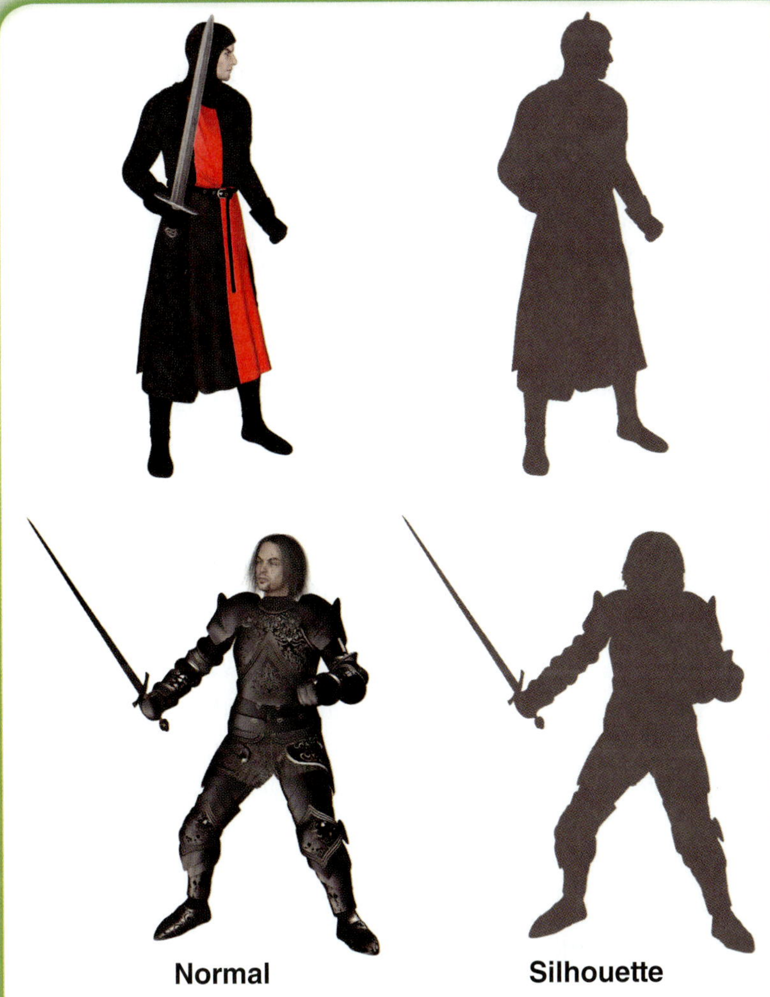

Figure 11-8.

An object carried within the silhouette of a character has less emphasis than one carried outside of the silhouette.

Normal **Silhouette**

Goodheart-Willcox Publisher; images: Algol/Shutterstock.com

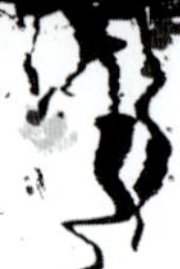

Timing

Timing is how long a given action lasts. When simulating an action, the action should match either real-world physics or the physics the player expects to see in the game world. That means that a falling hammer should take as long to fall as it does in the real world. Animation timing falls in two categories: physical timing and theatrical timing.

Physical timing matches the time for animated events with real world events. *Theatrical timing* is slowing down, rewinding, and speeding up sections of an animation for an emotional effect. Using a slow-motion section of animation to show the hammer smashing the character's hand instead of the nail is an example of theatrical timing. This helps show detail and creates an emotional connection with the audience to feel the pain felt by the character. In another example of theatrical timing, many video games have a "kill cam" to replay the game events that show how the player's character died.

Timing can also involve the use of *moving holds.* A character should never be static for a long time. Instead, some slight movement should be animated. In the real world, even when somebody is standing still, there is usually some movement. He or she might sigh, wipe his or her forehead, scratch an itch, or blink. People and animals are almost never completely motionless.

Exaggeration

Exaggeration is amplifying some aspect of the action beyond what is normal. Artistic license is taken to divert from reality. An item can be made larger, brighter, or noisier to provide higher contrast or interest in the object. If the hammer hits the character's thumb instead of the nail, the thumb can be made bright red, super-sized, and pulsing to show the pain. This exaggeration draws attention to the main action of the scene.

In video game design, it is common to exaggerate items. The motion of a strong character's kick or height the character can jump is exaggerated to demonstrate super strength. Objects are drawn larger for emphasis, like the coins or tokens the player needs to collect. Often, things like health rewards, ammo, or weapons are exaggerated with a glowing **aura** so the player can find them easily. The story will usually determine which items need additional focus and emphasis.

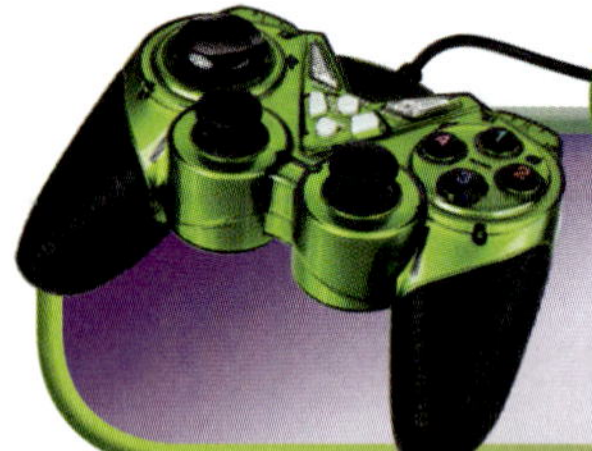

CHEAT CODE: AURA

An aura is an energy field around an object or character that serves to highlight it.

Performing the Action

Performing the action is animating the objects to achieve the objective. The principles of animation that apply to this stage are anticipation, squash and stretch, arcs, follow-through and overlapping action, secondary action, and slow in and slow out.

Anticipation

Anticipation is an event to announce a major action. In the real world, many events have anticipation. Think about a sneeze. Before you sneeze, you inhale quickly, tip your head back, and raise your hand or arm to cover your nose. Everyone who sees this move knows exactly what is about to occur.

Creating anticipation prepares the audience for the main action to follow. It provides an audio or visual hint that an action is about to happen. Get ready to duck, the enemy's weapon is glowing red and about to discharge a photon pulse in your direction, as shown in **Figure 11-9.** An NPC team member yells "incoming!" Do you know what is going to happen next? Maybe not exactly, but you have a good idea that you need to move your character to cover.

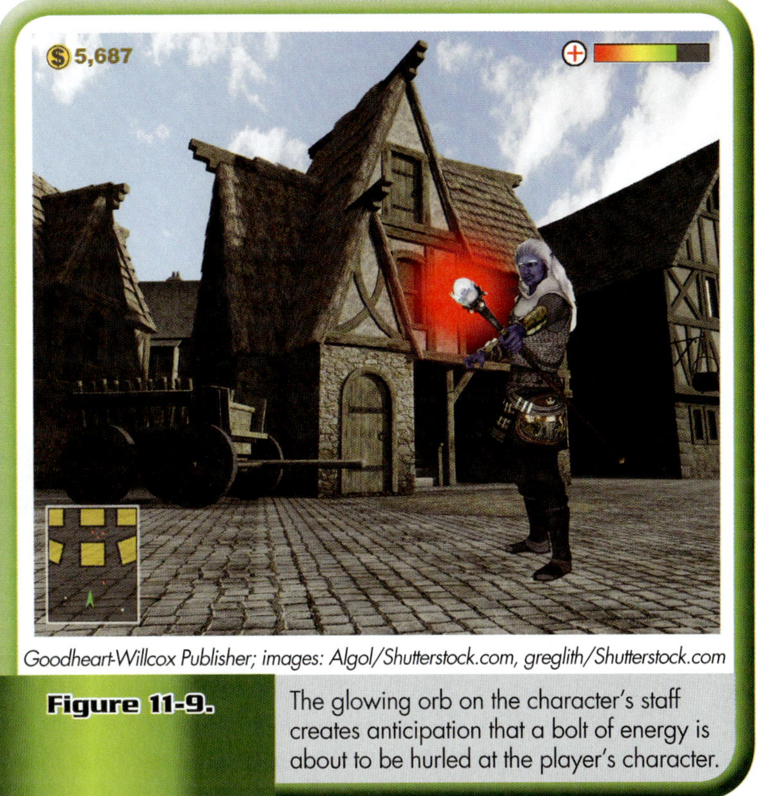

Goodheart-Willcox Publisher; images: Algol/Shutterstock.com, greglith/Shutterstock.com

Figure 11-9. The glowing orb on the character's staff creates anticipation that a bolt of energy is about to be hurled at the player's character.

Squash and Stretch

Squash is a flattening of an object. ***Stretch*** is an extension of an object. Squash and stretch deal with morphing motion. Originally conceived to exaggerate the natural morphing motion for comedic effect, squash and stretch are now practiced in all forms of animation. In general, squash and stretch give a sense of weight and flexibility to an object. The volume of the object remains the same, but the shape changes due to the forces creating movement.

A key concept in realistic use of squash and stretch is to keep the same structural dimensions and volume. Look at the bicep muscle in your arm while moving your forearm up and down. Notice how the muscle moves. As you extend your arm, the muscle is stretched from end to end. As you bend your arm closed, the muscle is squashed from end to end. However, the structure of the arm does not change. The bones are rigid and keep the length of the arm constant.

Squash and stretch must be applied to nonridged objects like muscles, clay, or a rubber ball. In the case of a rubber ball, the entire object can be squashed and stretched, as shown in **Figure 11-10.** The key is to maintain volume. If the height of the ball is squashed, then the width will have to be stretched. A balloon can be used as an aid when learning to animate squash and stretch. Squash and stretch the balloon to see how the shape morphs while holding the same volume of air.

Squash and stretch can also be applied to body articulation. A person performing a jump will squash by bending the knees and swinging the arms down. The person will then stretch by throwing the arms up and extending the legs. When the person lands, the body is again squashed to absorb the impact.

Arcs

Movements in nature rarely occur in straight lines or at sharp angles. When you walk around a corner, you move in an arc even though the hallway is constructed at a right angle. When a dog appears to run in a straight line, the path is not truly straight. The dog's body moves from side to side as well as up and down as it runs. Therefore, if a character is animated to move in

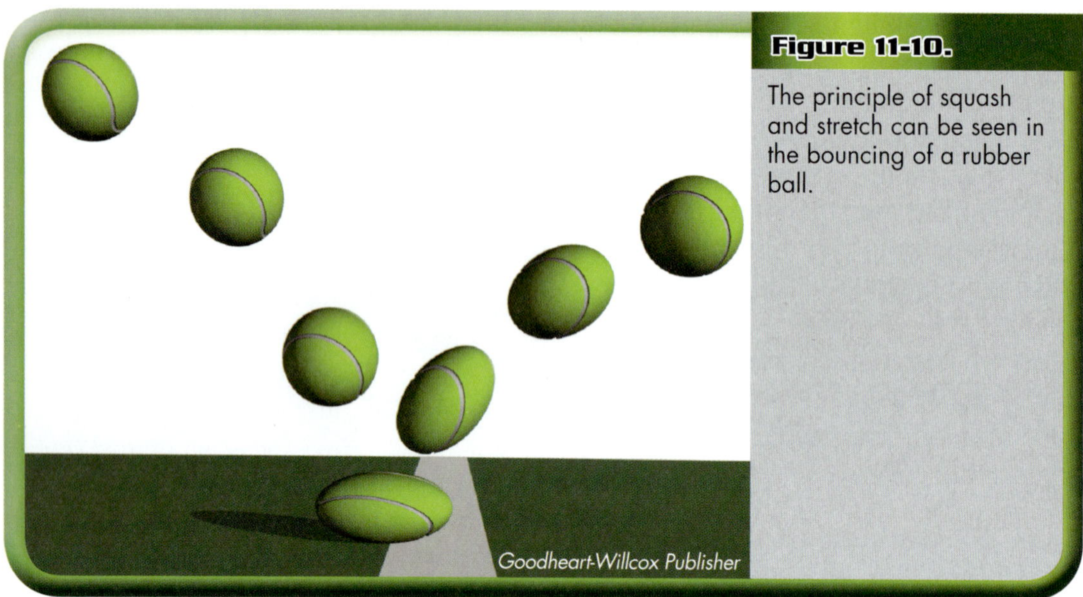

Figure 11-10.

The principle of squash and stretch can be seen in the bouncing of a rubber ball.

Goodheart-Willcox Publisher

a straight line, the result will look unnatural. Mechanical items may move in straight lines, such as a window opening or closing, but natural objects, such as characters and trees, move in arcs.

As discussed earlier in the chapter, arcs define the natural movement of an articulated rotating joint. When you throw a ball, the ball does not move in a straight line. As you rotate your arm to throw the ball, the ball moves in an arc while it is in your hand. Also, once you release the ball, the ball curves toward the ground as gravity pulls it downward.

Follow-Through and Overlapping Action

The principle of follow-through and overlapping come at the end of an animated action. ***Follow-through*** is a continuation of movement beyond the main event. When a baseball player swings a bat, the bat does not stop moving when it hits the ball. The **momentum** of the bat causes follow-through. The movement of the bat continues to *follow* the motion *through* the entire swing. In another example, when a character quickly turns his or her head, hair, jewelry, and other items the character is wearing briefly continue moving after the head stops. Animations should incorporate the concept of follow-through for realistic movement.

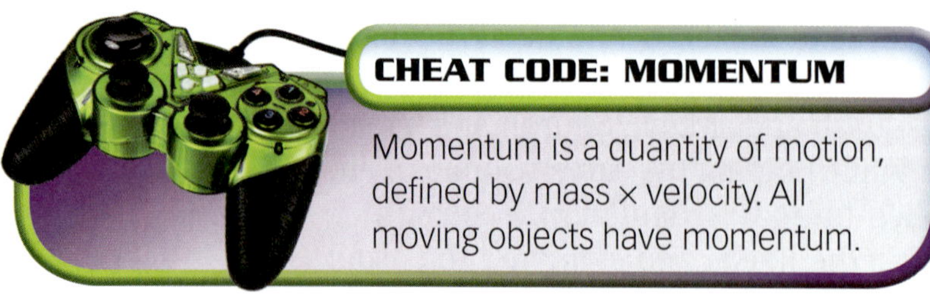

CHEAT CODE: MOMENTUM

Momentum is a quantity of motion, defined by mass × velocity. All moving objects have momentum.

Overlapping describes more than one motion occurring at the same time. It is unusual to have one motion completed before the next motion starts. Think about raising a glass to take a drink of water. As you raise the glass, your lips begin to open and your head tips down before your arm completely raises the glass to your lips. Now, try it the opposite way. Move the glass completely to your lips before tipping your head down, and wait until your head is fully tipped down before opening your lips. This feels unnatural. If you watch somebody performing this activity, it looks unnatural, too.

Complex and articulated systems of motion have many parts moving at different speeds, in different arcs, and in different directions. Each component of the character or system must be allowed to continue independent movement from the main body.

Secondary Action

A ***secondary action,*** or complementary action, is motion caused by the dominant or primary action. Many secondary actions are part of the overlapping actions system, but are not required to be part of that system. The addition of secondary action is when things really start to come together for the animated movement.

Imagine a baseball player swinging at the ball. The primary action of swinging the bat is animated following the principles of anticipation, squash and stretch, arcs, and follow-through and overlapping action. But, what about the details outside of that motion? The player's uniform wrinkles, his hat spins, his teeth clench, dirt in the batter's box is moved around, and if the player makes contact, the ball travels away from the bat. Each of these secondary actions helps complement the primary action. If the player does not hit the ball, then the ball ends up in the catcher's mitt, which causes a whole different set of secondary actions to occur.

Animations of animals often involve secondary actions of the tail, fur, tongue, and ears. Many animations of a dog, for example, have the tongue hanging outside of the mouth to add a comical secondary action of a wet, flopping tongue, as shown in **Figure 11-11.** The tongue bounces along in response to the primary action of the dog, whether running, turning its head, or barking.

Slow In and Slow Out

Slow in describes how motion begins gradually, not at once. ***Slow out*** describes how motion ends gradually, not at once. In physics, this principle is known as **inertia.** Due to inertia, objects take time to start moving and to stop moving. From a stop, a car does not instantly move at 65 miles per hour, even if the driver presses the accelerator pedal to the floor. The car slowly gains speed. When stopping, the car does not instantly reach a speed of zero. Even with hard braking, the car will gradually come to a stop.

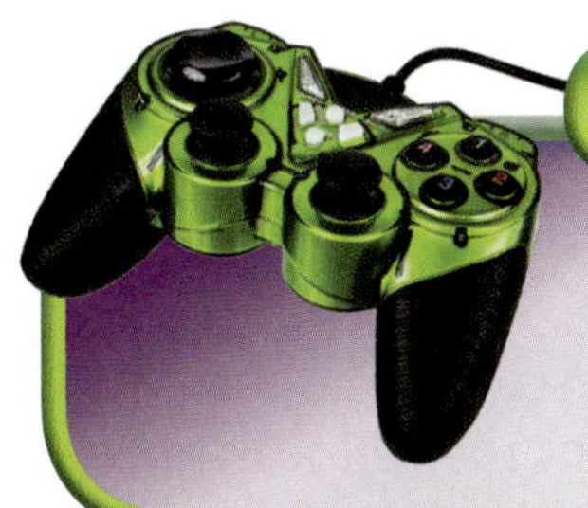

CHEAT CODE: INERTIA

Inertia is a resistance to a change in motion. This means that an object that is stopped wants to stay stopped. An object in motion wants to stay in motion.

In an animation, increasing or decreasing the number of frames over which a motion occurs adjusts the slow in and slow out. If the motion occurs over a greater number of frames, the slow in or slow out is increased. If the motion occurs over a fewer number of frames, the slow in or slow out is reduced.

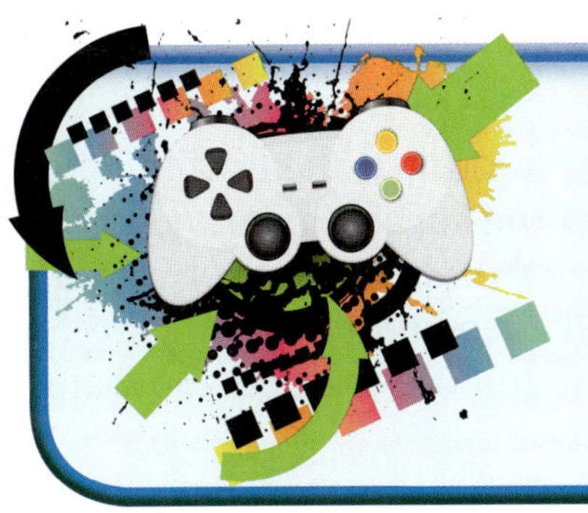

Ethical Gamer

It is unethical to present information as your own when it is not and doing so can be illegal. Do not use free artwork from the Internet and call it your own. In addition to being unethical and possibly illegal, doing so may be a reason for dismissal from your job.

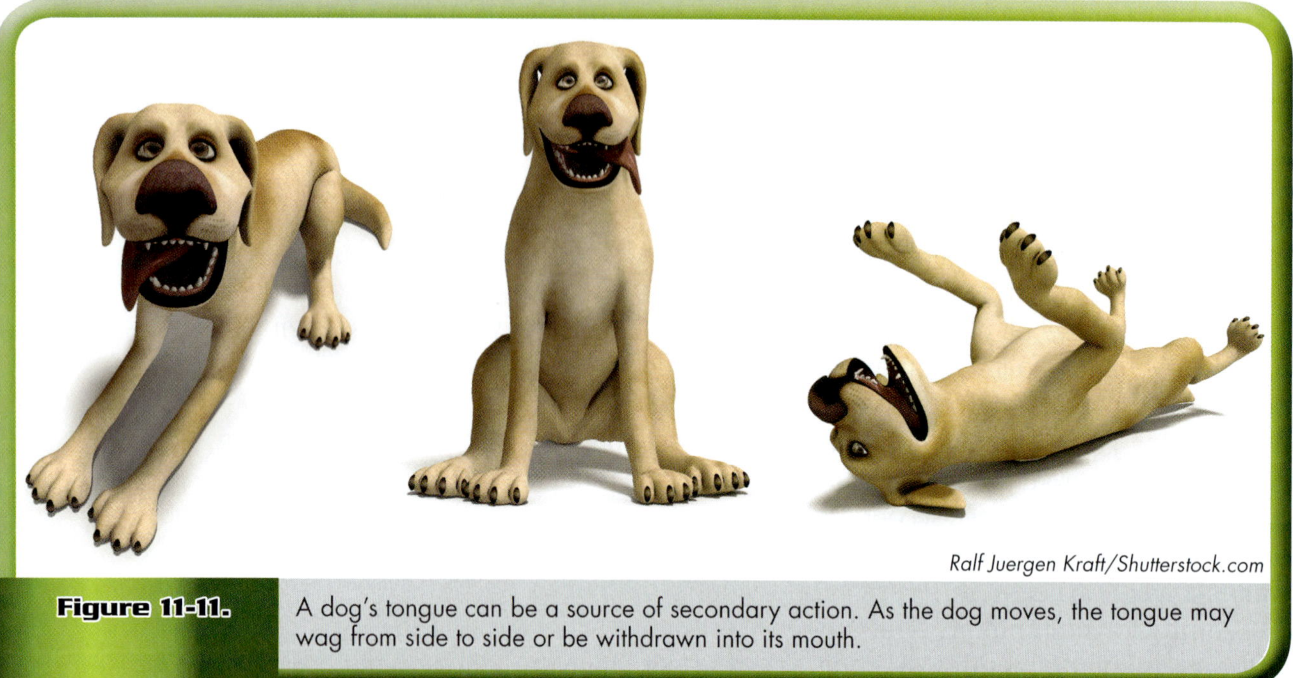

Ralf Juergen Kraft/Shutterstock.com

Figure 11-11. A dog's tongue can be a source of secondary action. As the dog moves, the tongue may wag from side to side or be withdrawn into its mouth.

Mechanics

Mechanics are the technical aspects of creating the objects and animation. Solid drawing together with straight-ahead and pose-to-pose action are the animation principles that apply to this stage.

Solid Drawing

Solid drawing describes the technical skill with which an animation is composed to represent the fullness of characters and objects occupying space. Characters and objects should not be drawn so they appear flat or wooden. Rather, they should have a fullness of presence in the animation. To achieve this, the mechanics of the elements of art, principles of design, anatomy, and three-dimensional space must be applied to the animation.

Most animations are not hand drawn anymore, so the artist needs the technical skill to produce 2D and 3D digital images. In addition to understanding the theory of solid drawing, a video game artist needs to properly use technology such as photo-editing software, 3D modeling software, and motion-capture devices. The amount of technical skill required depends on the type of animation being created and the technology being used.

Straight-Ahead and Pose-to-Pose Action

Straight-ahead action refers to creating motion starting at the beginning of a scene and continuing in sequence until the end of the scene. ***Pose-to-pose action*** refers to planning the motion for a scene based on key points at which certain motion must happen. A storyboard is usually used to identify the key points. Both methods have advantages, but the pose-to-pose method allows for more planning and control.

Pose-to-pose action is the basis of computer animation. The key points are called keyframes, and the animation process is called keyframe animation. Keyframe animation is discussed later in this chapter.

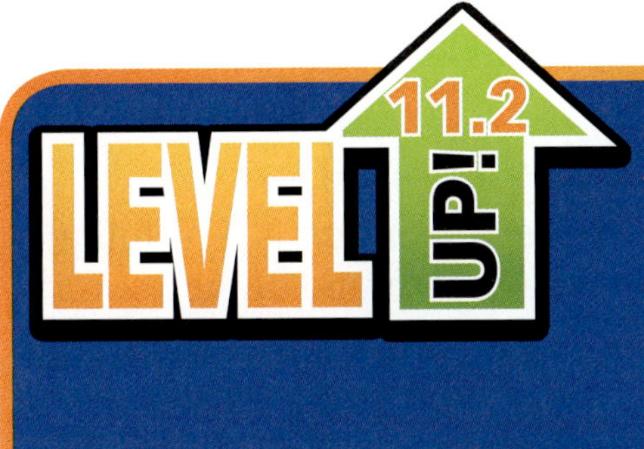

Consider two of your favorite games that feature characters in the gameplay. Select an animated character action from each game. How are the 12 principles of animation applied to the character actions? Could the animator have improved the animation by differently applying the principles?

Creating an Animation

Anybody can create a simple animation with a pencil and a notebook. A *flip-book animation* is created by drawing a picture on the edge of each page in a notebook with a slight difference between each picture. When the pages are fanned, the brain interprets the differences between the pictures as motion. At the most basic level, all animations are a series of still images played in sequence to create the illusion of motion, as shown in **Figure 11-12.**

Each still image in an animation is called a ***frame.*** The speed at which frames are played is called the ***frame rate.*** The frame rate is controlled by the playback device. Motion pictures are played at a frame rate of 24 frames per second (fps). Computers typically have a frame rate of 30 fps.

An object can be animated as a **static** animation or active animation. The difference between the two types of animation is whether translation or articulation is used. A ***static animation*** is translation without articulation.

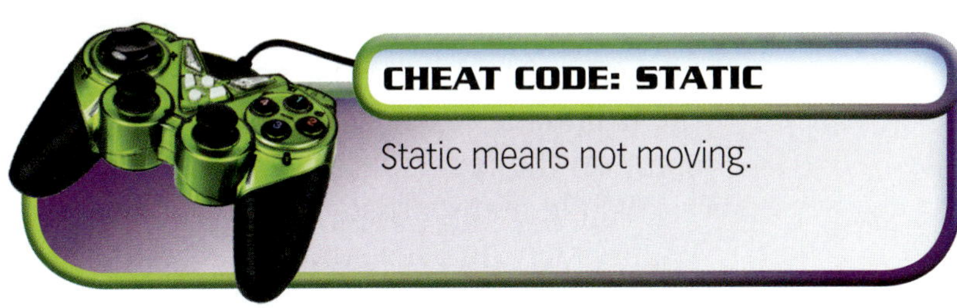

CHEAT CODE: STATIC

Static means not moving.

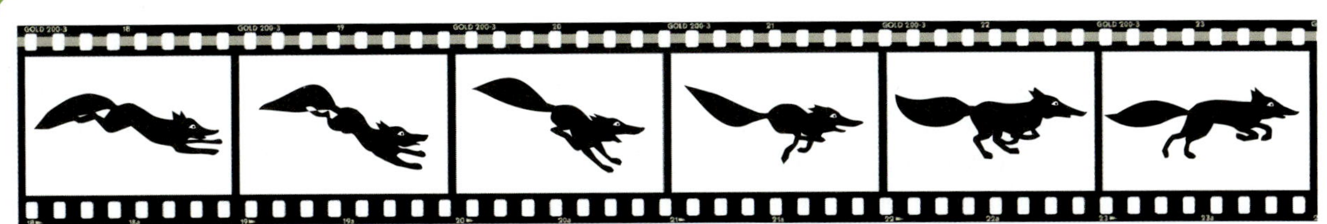

Goodheart-Willcox Publisher; images: abeadev/Shutterstock.com, pegasusa/Shutterstock.com

Figure 11-12. An animation is a series of still images, each with small differences, played in sequence.

This type of animation requires only one character pose. For example, an airplane flying across the sky requires only a single pose of the craft. The animation of the airplane is static because it requires only translation to move across the sky. An ***active animation*** is the combination of translation and articulation. A human character walking across the screen requires translation to move the character and articulation to move the arms and legs.

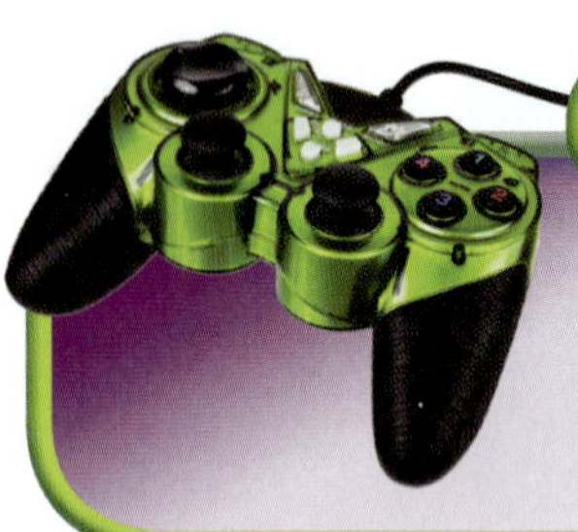

CHEAT CODE: CEL

The term *cel* refers to cellulose acetate, which is a transparent plastic on which the animation frames are drawn.

Cel Animation

Cel animation is a technique where each frame of the animation is drawn by hand on a **cel** and photographed. The individual photographs are quickly played back in sequence to display the animation. A single frame of animation may contain multiple cels, such as static background, moving background, main characters, and so on, as shown in **Figure 11-13.** Cel animation is the type of animation most people associate with animated films and cartoons.

To create a cel animation, the lead artist identifies certain points where key actions must take place. These frames are called the keyframes, and they are drawn by the lead artist. A ***keyframe*** is any frame on which a specific action must take place. For example, the specific action may be a window must be completely open. The frame on which the window must be completely open is the keyframe for that action. Even a short animation may have hundreds of keyframes. A feature-length animation will have thousands of keyframes.

After the lead artist creates the keyframes, the assistant artists draw each frame or cel between the keyframes. The frames between keyframes are known as *tweens.* These artists are known as *tweeners,* and the process is known as *tweening.* The lead artist and the tweeners create the ink lines of the images on the front side of the cel. Colorists follow the lead artist and tweeners and paint color on the reverse side of the cel.

While many artists and studios have produced cel animations, the works of Walt Disney and his studio are perhaps the most famous. Today, hand-drawn cel animations are rarely created because of the time and expense to do so.

Keyframe Computer Animation

Keyframe animation is an approximation of traditional cel animation using a computer. The artist identifies the keyframes and the computer draws the tweens. While cel animation is also keyframe animation, and vice versa, most computer animation software uses the term keyframe animation. Creating a computer-generated (CG) keyframe animation requires much less time over creating a hand-drawn cel animation.

The basic theory for creating a CG keyframe animation using software such as Flash, Blender, 3ds Max, or Maya is similar to that of a cel animation. The designer specifies keyframes and defines the action to be completed on those frames. The tweens are created by the computer when the animation is rendered.

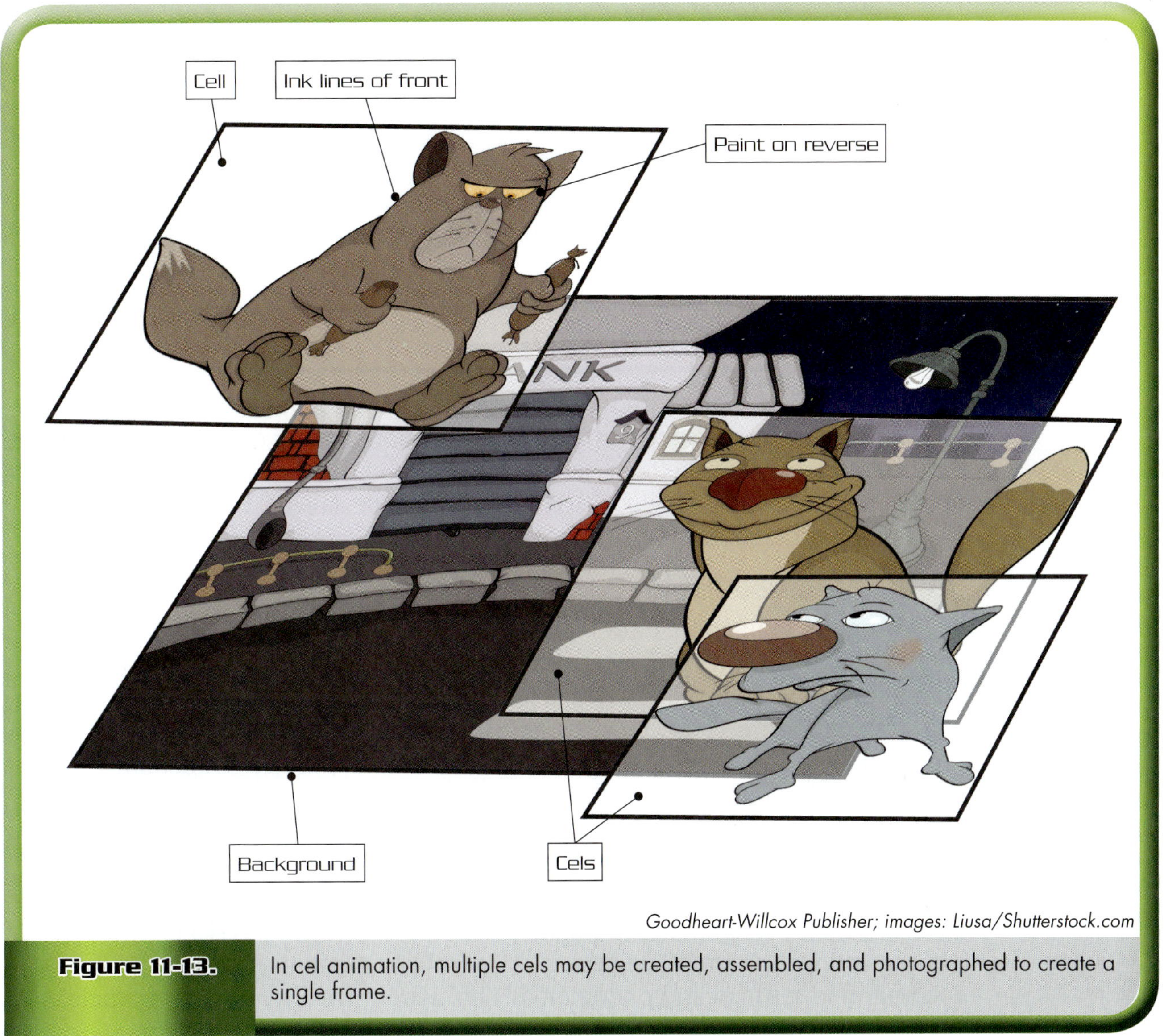

Goodheart-Willcox Publisher; images: Liusa/Shutterstock.com

Figure 11-13. In cel animation, multiple cels may be created, assembled, and photographed to create a single frame.

For example, a simple animation is required to show a square moving from left to right. The keyframes of the animation are the starting frame (square left) and the ending frame (square right). If this animation is one second in length and to be played back on a computer, there should be 30 frames in the animation. On frame 1, the designer positions the square on the left. On frame 30, the designer positions the square on the right. The designer does nothing on the rest of the frames (2 through 29). When the animation is rendered, the computer calculates how the square should appear on frames 2 through 29.

Stop-Motion Animation

Creating an animation of physical objects typically involves capturing a single frame, slightly adjusting the objects, and capturing another single frame, repeating this over and over until the animation is completed. This process is called ***stop-motion animation***. Each frame of the animation is a picture of the motion in progress. By quickly playing the frames in order, the illusion of motion is created.

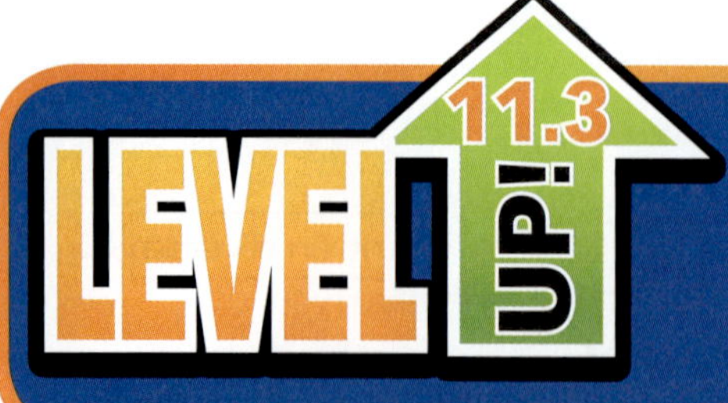

Review a simple animation in a game or a single element in a more complex animation. See if you can determine what actions were defined on keyframes, such as foot down, foot up and forward, and foot down.

Specialized Animation

The previous section discussed the basics of CG keyframe animation. There are many specialized aspects to creating animations with a computer. Depending on the software, special effects such as motion blur, lens flare, and combustion, to name a few, can be applied. Two examples of specialized animation—particle animation and motion capture—are discussed in the next sections.

Particle Animation

Computer animation allows for many other means of creating images for each frame. One of the most interesting and useful of these techniques is particle animation. A particle animation is used for many effects that are difficult to draw, as shown in **Figure 11-14.** Sparks, rain, snow, flowing water, falling leaves, and other small objects that move are best created with a particle animation.

Particles in a particle animation are generated from an emitter. When rendered, the particle animation is captured one frame at a time, just like any other animation. The *emitter* is an object in a 3D modeling program that has settings for the particles it generates. Settings include rate of generation, size, color, disbursement, and lifetime. The table in **Figure 11-15** shows typical settings for a particle system. Generally, depending on the software, each particle setting can be animated. Throughout the lifetime of a particle,

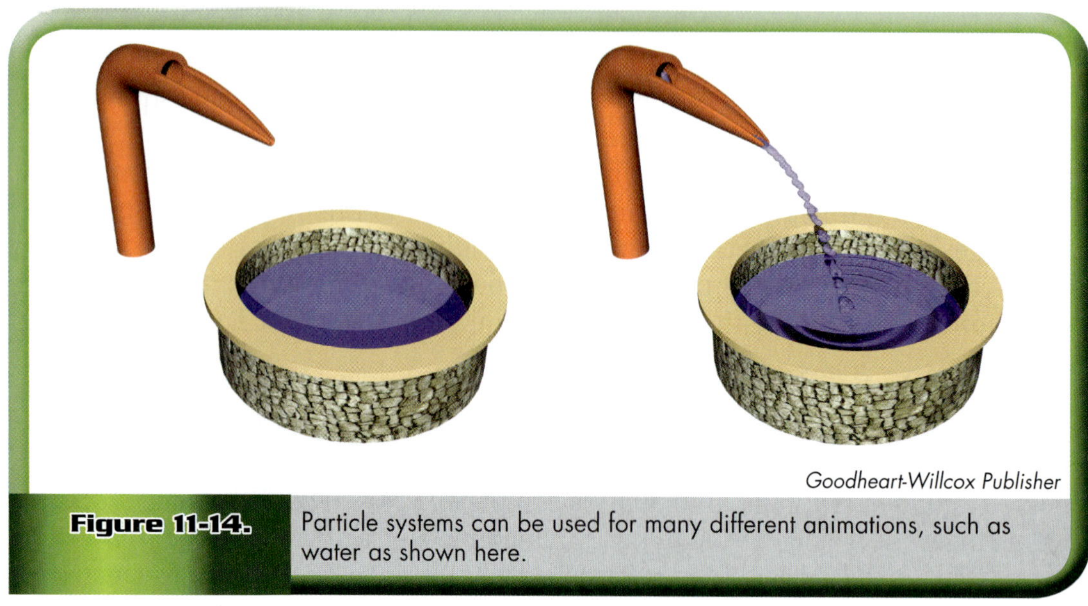

Goodheart-Willcox Publisher

Figure 11-14. Particle systems can be used for many different animations, such as water as shown here.

Particle Settings	Description
Initial Position	How far from the emitter the particles will be created
Initial Speed	How fast particles travel when created
Initial Vector	What direction particles travel when created
Initial Size	How big particles are when created
Initial Color	What color particles are when created
Initial Opacity	How transparent particles are when created
Shape	What shape the particles are when created
Lifetime	How long each particle will be displayed

Figure 11-15. These are typical settings for a particle system. Depending on the software, there may be different settings or the settings may have different names.

Goodheart-Willcox Publisher

it is controlled by whatever environmental physics have been assigned to it. Environmental physics simulate gravity and wind. These settings control how the particle interacts with the virtual environment.

For example, to create sparks, the particles might be set as orange, a size of two, a random initial vector, and a rate of four per second. The spark may have a lifetime of about one second. The color and opacity of the particles may be animated from an initial **opaque** red particle to semitransparent gray to simulate a transition from glowing particle to smoke. In terms of particle systems, sparks are larger particles. Something like smoke will have much smaller particles, longer lifetime, and be disbursed over a larger area to make it realistic.

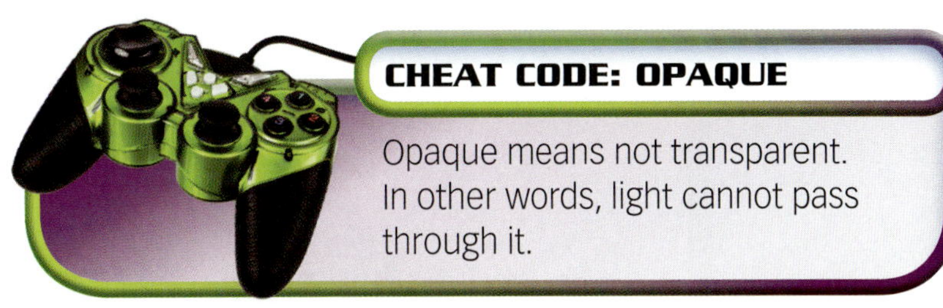

Some modeling programs have emitter settings specifically to simulate liquids, as shown in **Figure 11-14.** However, liquid can be simulated using basic particles as well. For example, the emitter can be placed at the top of a fountain. Gravity can be set to pull the particles down toward a basin, where they can pool together. As the basin fills with particles, some spill over the edge. Or, to prevent spillover, set the lifetime of the particles so they are removed before the basin fills up. To make the water appear realistic and not just a single stream of water that follows the same path, vary the rate, direction, and lifespan of the particles. In most software, varying settings is not totally random. Generally, a setting contains a randomizing constraint, such as ±20 percent. This allows for a 40 percent (–20 percent to + 20 percent) variance for all particles emitted.

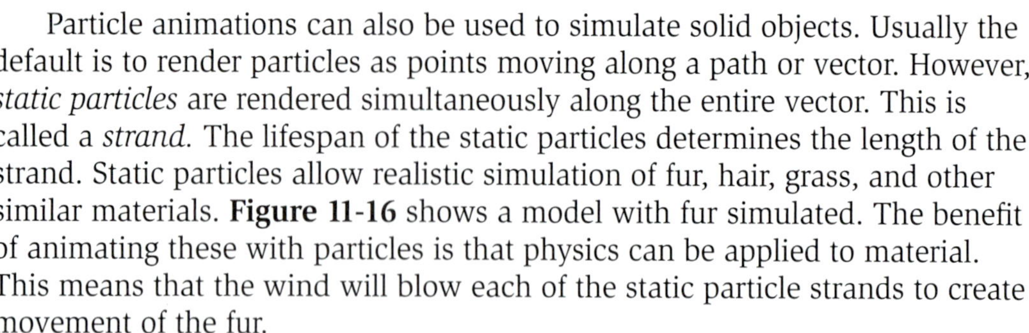

Particle animations can also be used to simulate solid objects. Usually the default is to render particles as points moving along a path or vector. However, *static particles* are rendered simultaneously along the entire vector. This is called a *strand*. The lifespan of the static particles determines the length of the strand. Static particles allow realistic simulation of fur, hair, grass, and other similar materials. **Figure 11-16** shows a model with fur simulated. The benefit of animating these with particles is that physics can be applied to material. This means that the wind will blow each of the static particle strands to create movement of the fur.

Inverse Kinematics

Kinematics is the science of motion. In terms of 3D modeling, kinematics refers to how the movement of an object either controls or is controlled by the movement of another object. There are two basic types of kinematics in 3D modeling software: forward and reverse. *Forward kinematics* is a parent object

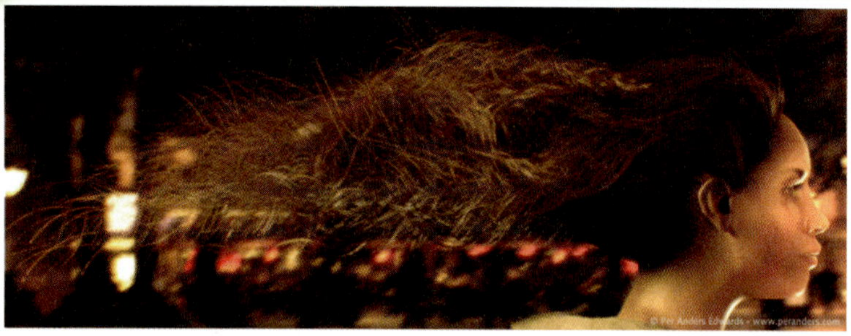

A

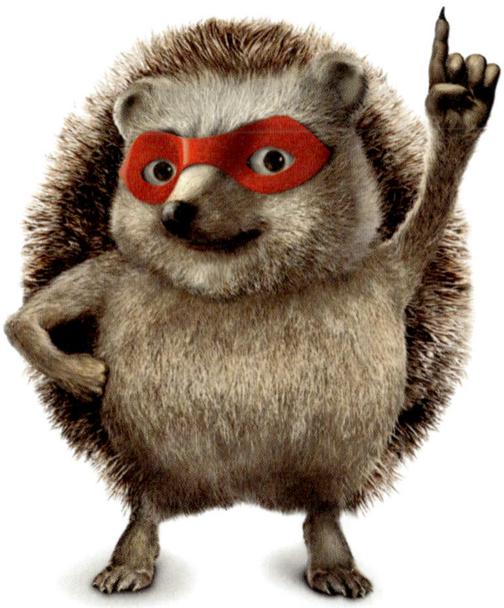

B

MAXON/Per-Anders Edwards (www.peranders.com) and S. Scatola (www.boxy.co.uk)

Figure 11-16. Particle systems can be used to simulate hair (A), fur (B), and other similar materials.

controlling the motion of a child object, but the child object does not control the motion of the parent. ***Inverse kinematics*** is a parent object controlling the motion of a child object *and* the child object controlling the motion of the parent. Inverse kinematics is the principle behind bones and rigging systems in 3D modeling software.

Bones and rigging systems are modeling tools used to animate characters. **Figure 11-17** shows a 3D model and the bones system attached to it. The designer can move any of the bones objects and the model will move appropriately. Since bones systems use inverse kinematics, the designer can move a finger and the arm will move if needed. Or, if the arm is moved, the hand and fingers **inherit** the motion from the arm. Setting up a bones system is a time-consuming process. If the design requirements do not include a fully rigged model with inverse kinematics, then do not create a model with bones.

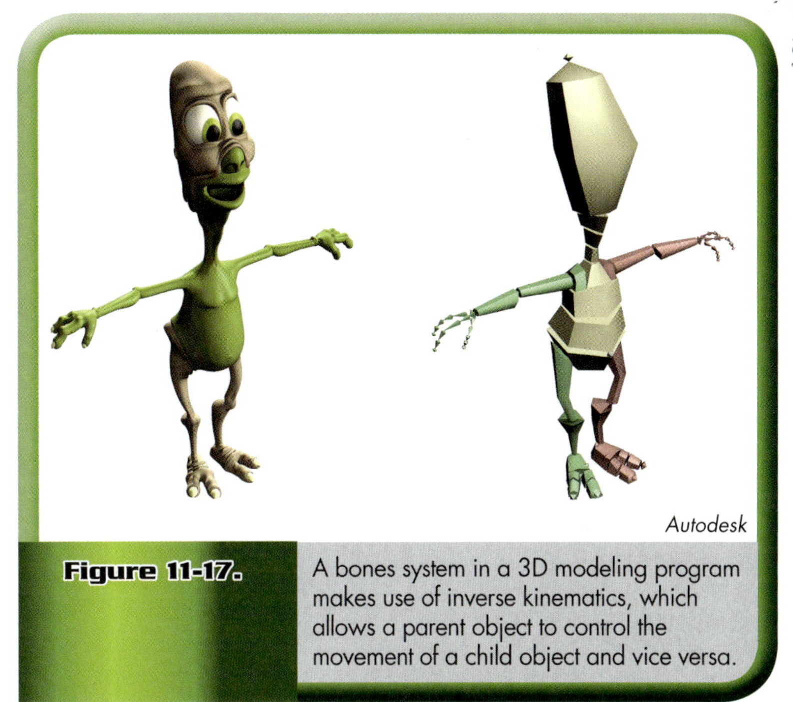

Autodesk

Figure 11-17. A bones system in a 3D modeling program makes use of inverse kinematics, which allows a parent object to control the movement of a child object and vice versa.

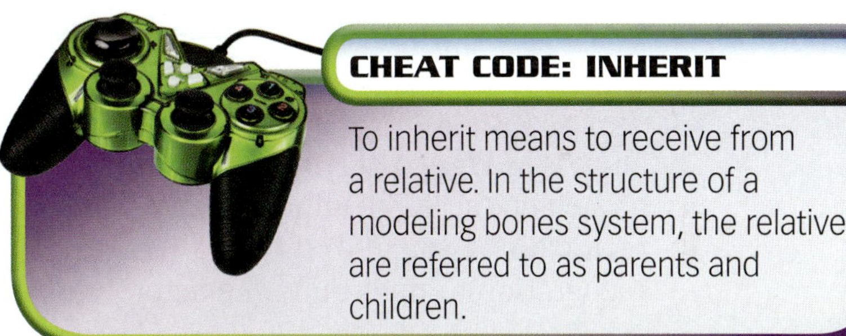

CHEAT CODE: INHERIT

To inherit means to receive from a relative. In the structure of a modeling bones system, the relatives are referred to as parents and children.

Motion Capture

Advances in technology have brought motion capture to animation and video game design. ***Motion capture (mocap)*** is a technology that records the movement of an actor and assigns that movement to a virtual character, as shown in **Figure 11-18.** Two basic types of mocap are sensor based and markerless.

Sensor-based mocap involves placing markers on the actor's body to track body movement. The markers are optical or radio frequency sensors placed at critical points on the actor's body. Sensors on the hands, arms, feet, legs, belly, and head would be used to record the movement of each part of the body. After recording the movement of the sensors, the animator can modify the motion capture data by editing the sensor position for each individual frame of the animation. Next, the animator assigns each sensor data point to a part of the rigging or bones system for the character model.

You may have the Kinect system for the Xbox 360 or the Move system for the PS3. Each of these technologies uses motion capture to animate the player avatar in the game. This technology is markerless mocap. *Markerless mocap* does not require a sensor marker worn by the actor. This is the type of mocap

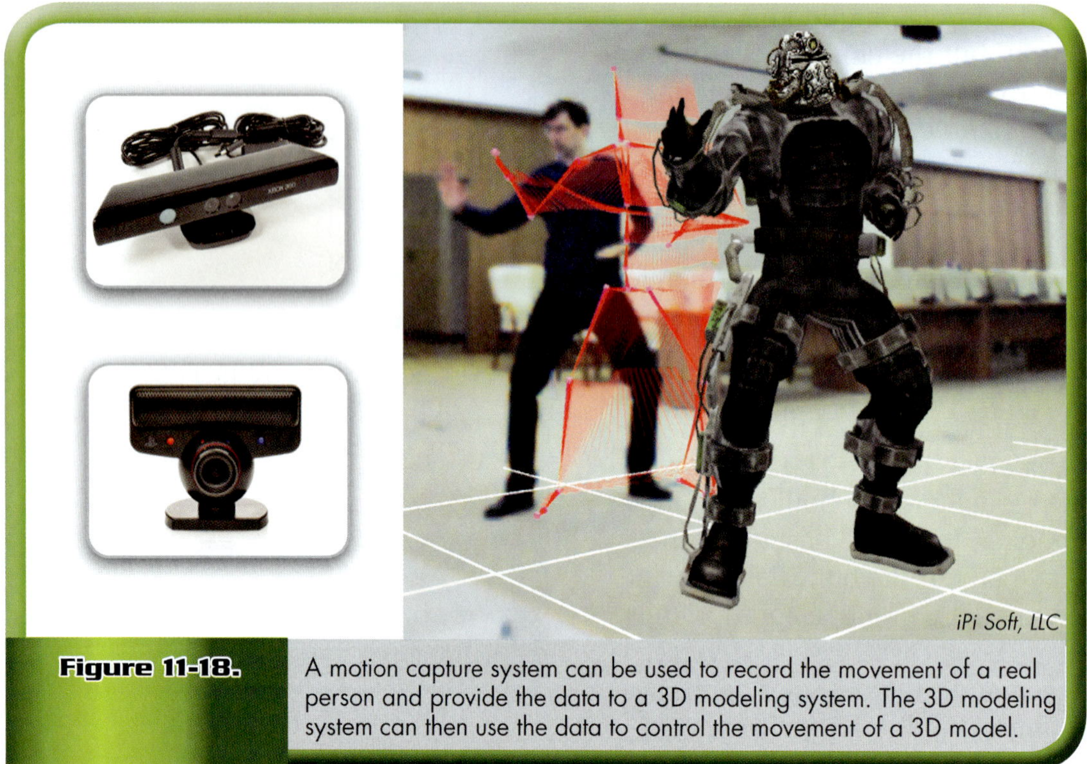

Figure 11-18. A motion capture system can be used to record the movement of a real person and provide the data to a 3D modeling system. The 3D modeling system can then use the data to control the movement of a 3D model.

shown in **Figure 11-18.** In addition to translating movement of the player into game action, this technology can be used to create motion data for animating characters. Instead of tracking sensors on the actor, the technology uses spatial recognition to determine the actor's movements.

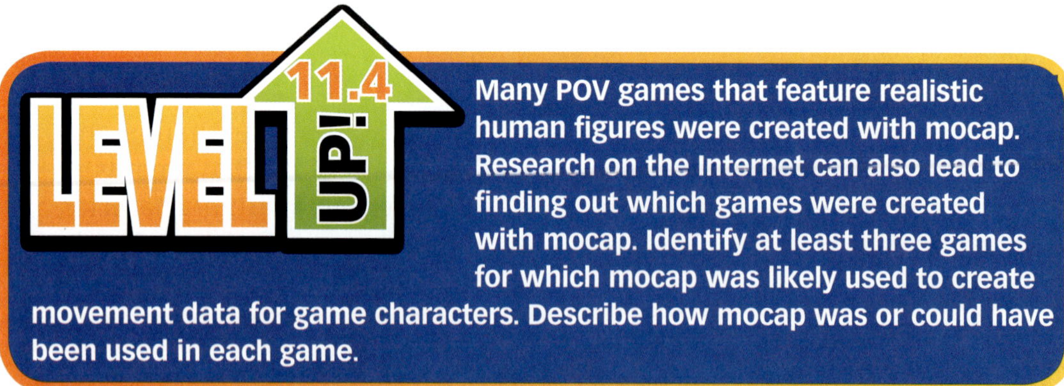

Synchronization

Sound is recorded and edited before models are animated. Animation of the models must be synchronized to the recorded sounds. ***Sound synchronization*** is matching the timing of visual action to the corresponding sounds. If you have ever seen a television show or movie where the actor's lips do not seem to match the words being spoken, you have seen an example of where the sound synchronization was not correct.

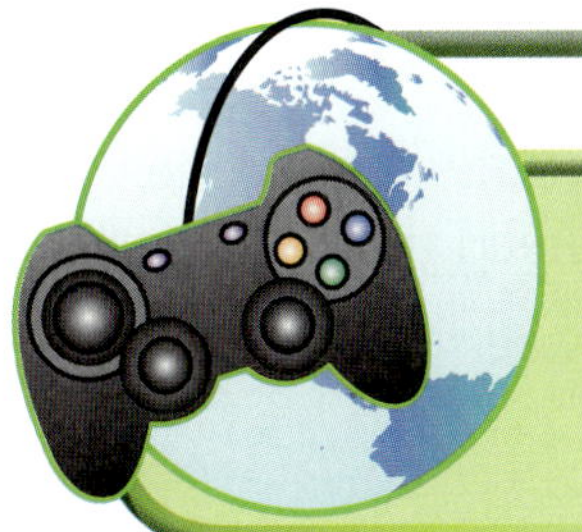

Green Gamer

Take empty ink or toner cartridges to a local office supply and see if they will refill them. Recycling printer ink cartridges instead of buying new ones is a way to save money and help the environment.

Sound synchronization must occur with both voice and background sounds. Synchronization is very important for a scene. If there is even a slight delay, the player will likely notice the misalignment of the sound file. There are two basic areas where sound synchronization must be addressed:

- character synchronization
- effects synchronization

Character Synchronization

There are many examples of where sound and character movement must be synchronized. The most obvious synchronization of sound and character movement is matching voice to lip movement, called *lip syncing*. The animation of the character's lips must match the words the character is speaking, as shown in **Figure 11-19.** Playing a video game that has poor lip syncing is frustrating and causes a loss of immersion.

A character's other movements also need to match the sounds in the game. When a character walks, the sounds of the footsteps need to match when the feet touch the ground in the animation. For machinery like a car, the sound of the wheels chirping around a corner, squealing during a burnout, or screeching to a stop all have to match the movement of the car. The animator often must make many adjustments to the animation before it is in sync with the corresponding sound.

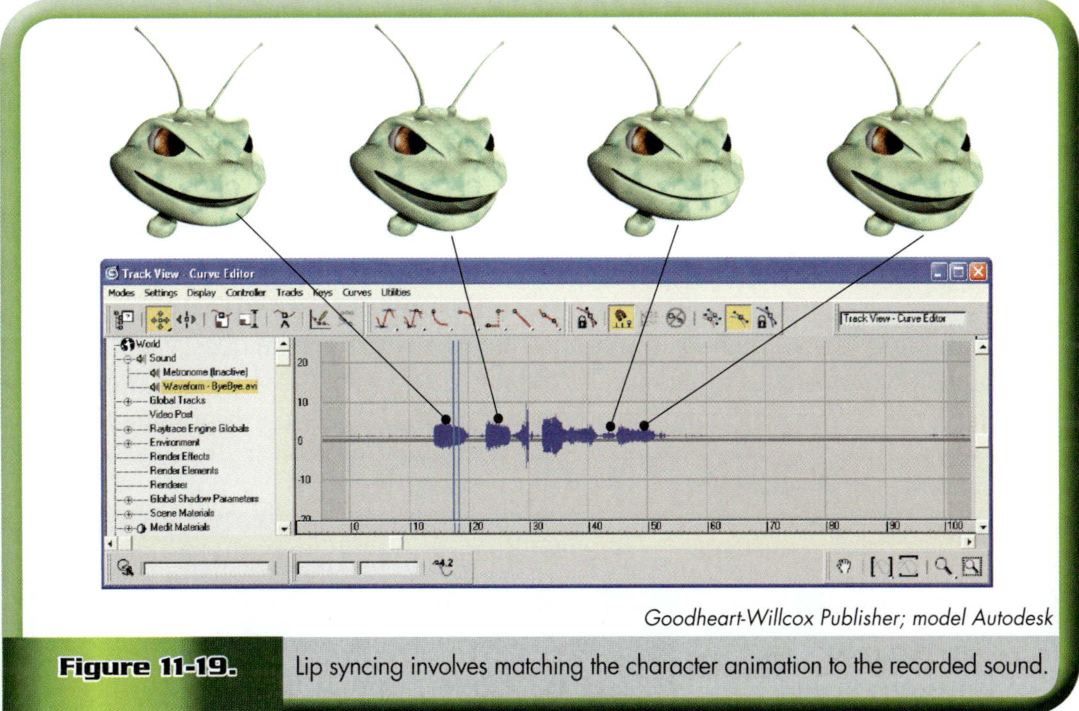

Goodheart-Willcox Publisher; model Autodesk

Figure 11-19. Lip syncing involves matching the character animation to the recorded sound.

Effects Synchronization

In many cases, special effects are the most dynamic portions of a scene. Effects such as an explosion involve multiple parts that all need to be properly synchronized to the sound. An explosion has four stages:

- ignition
- concussion
- debris
- fade

Other effects such as water waves, fires, and so on, have similar patterns that must be synchronized to match the action of the animation.

The ignition stage is the first part of the explosion. This is where the spark creates the initial sound. This is the primary sound of the explosion. A *primary sound* is the sound of the actual interaction. *Secondary sounds* are caused from the first interaction. A primary sound might be a yell and a secondary sound would be the echo the yell produced. In the case of an explosion, the primary sound is the loud boom. The animation of the explosion must be synchronized so the fireball starts to appear when the boom occurs.

The next stage of an explosion is concussion. Concussion is the energy of the explosion reaching the observer. In reality, a pressure wave is created and pushes through the air. Sound is distorted in the pressure wave and sounds like a rumble and whoosh as the concussion passes. In an explosion, this may occur as the fireball reaches its maximum size, but this will vary. If this is the case, the animation of the maximum fireball must be synchronized to match the concussive sound.

The next stage of an explosion is debris falling and burning. In an animation of an explosion, the shards of glass, wood, and metal colliding with the ground and other objects must be synchronized with the sounds of impact. Each piece of debris might have a different sound as it collides with other objects. Additionally, the same type of debris, such as wood, may collide with different objects of metal, wood, stone, or other material. Different sounds should be recorded for each interaction.

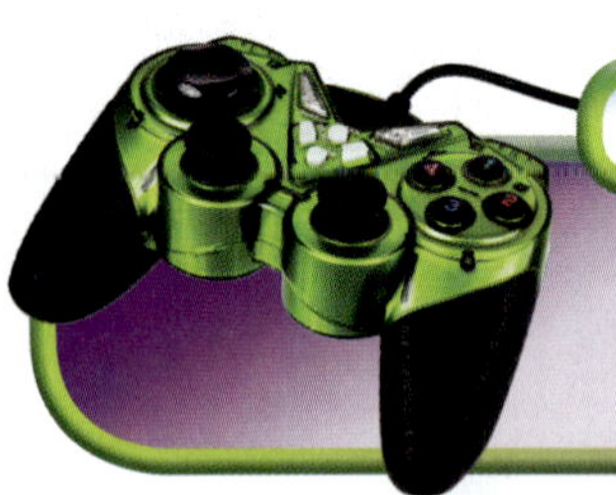

CHEAT CODE: DISSIPATING

Dissipating means breaking up or scattering.

The final stage of an explosion is fade. Fade is the energy of the explosion **dissipating.** Sound engineers use the Doppler effect to simulate the sound traveling away from the explosion. The Doppler effect states that as the sound moves toward the observer, it gets higher in pitch, volume, and frequency. Then, as the sound moves away from the observer, it gets lower in pitch, volume, and frequency. As animated effects of the explosion move away from the player's viewpoint, they must be synchronized to the corresponding sounds.

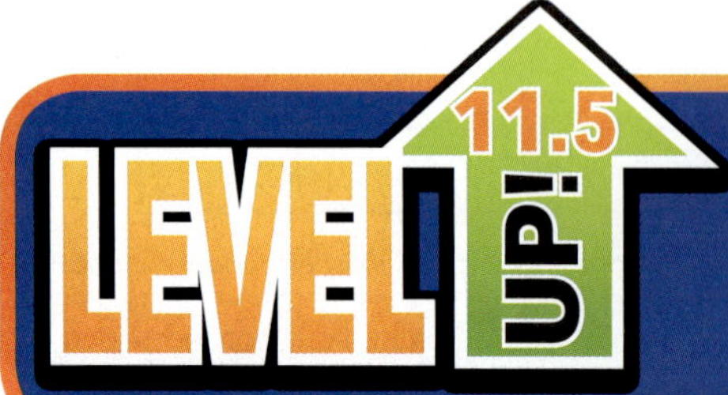

Play at least three video games that include speech and lip syncing. Compare how successful each game is in synchronizing the animation to the speech.

Video and Effects

Not all game art movement is manufactured through animation. In many cases digital video is used as a cut scene in the game or simulation. A cut scene, as you may recall from Chapter 2, is a movie-like segment between levels, scenes, or major actions in a video game that does not require player interaction. Often, a cut scene is used to occupy the player while the game loads a new portion of the programming. Additionally, the cut scene may be part of the pause-and-relax structure of the game.

In most cases, video is used to tell part of the story not included in the gameplay. A video cut scene at the end of the level may have the king presenting the hero with treasure or being knighted. These activities would be difficult to produce in gameplay as the player may leave the scene or otherwise act unexpectedly.

Effects or special effects are visual or mechanical additions. Visual effects change the appearance. In first person perspective, a red color overlay of the game world would be a visual effect of the player being injured. Visual effects may also be integrated into cut scenes or other videos using chroma keying. ***Chroma keying*** involves removing a specified color, usually chroma green or blue, from a photograph or video. A chroma screen, or *green screen,* is a typical way of removing the background from a video. An actor is filmed in front of a chroma screen, as shown in **Figure 11-20.** After the video footage is recorded, the chroma screen is removed from the footage. Only the actor and any items not colored in green remain in the video footage. An animated background can then be composited, or layered, with the footage of the actor and items to create the final video.

A scene for a racing game might have video footage of a real car interior and an actor with the windows of the car painted chroma green. The actor pretends to drive the car as he or she follows the script. To take it a step farther, the actor may be wearing a sensor for use in a mocap application. The chroma green windows are

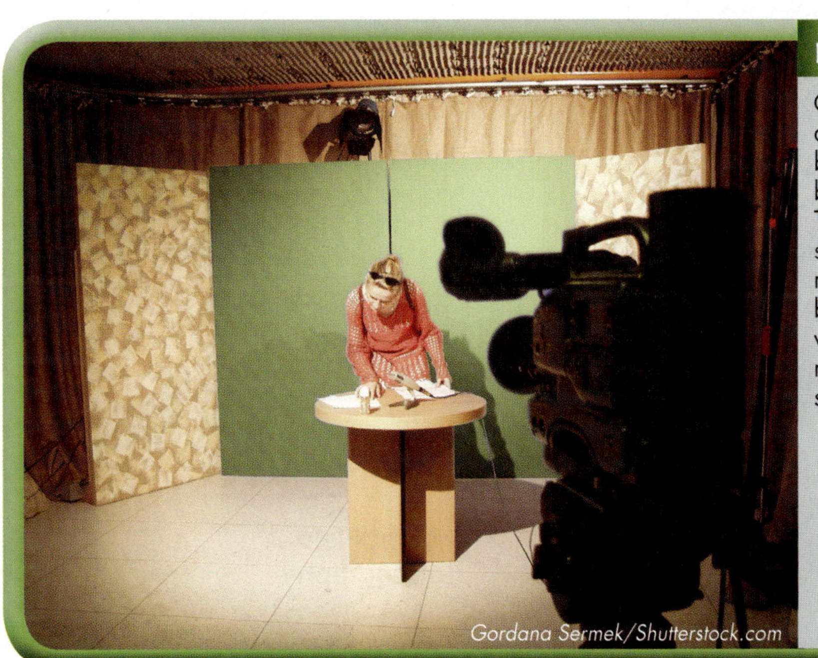
Gordana Sermek/Shutterstock.com

Figure 11-20. Chroma keying allows a different background to be added later. The chroma color seen here will be replaced with a new background and it will appear as if the model is actually standing in front of it.

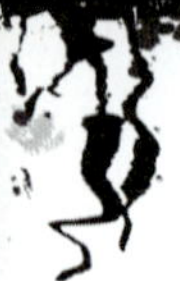

later replaced in post production with animated views of passing cars and buildings. The mocap data are translated into movements for the character model of the driver. The scene looks realistic as the actor drives, the window scenes change to match the environment in the video game. This may add to immersion because the interior of the car is not an artistic representation, rather it is an actual car.

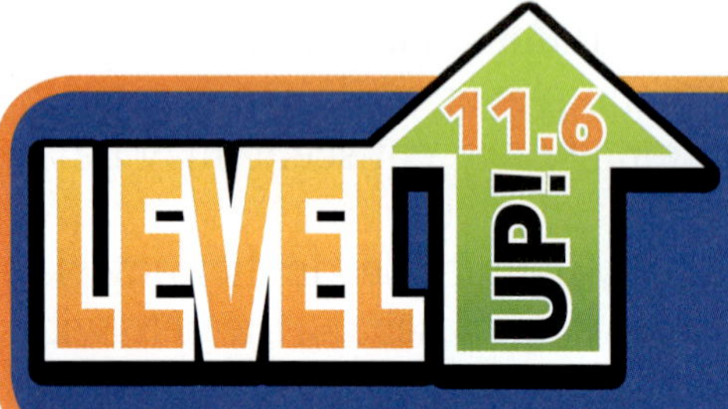

Think about games that you have played in which real actors appear in the game. Try to identify what else besides the actor is real and what is a digital creation.

CASE STUDY

Light Field Photography

Photography has typically been a 2D technology. In recent years, 3D photography using stereoscopic lenses (two lenses) has been available on high-end cameras and smartphones. Enter the next generation of photography: light field capturing.

Light field capturing involves capturing and storing the entire light field, including the vector of each point of light, as shown below. In the click of the camera's shutter, the scene is completely captured and mapped. So what is the big deal about light field capturing? With the entire light field recorded, the photographer can change the perspective of the image just like moving the camera in a 3D video game. This technology also allows the viewer to click on different objects and refocus the image. Consumers can currently access this technology thanks to innovations like the Lytro camera.

The technology used in light field capturing holds the possibilities of capturing live action in completely new ways. Video and animation may be viewable from whatever angle the viewer desires. Users can zoom in on the action in crisp detail.

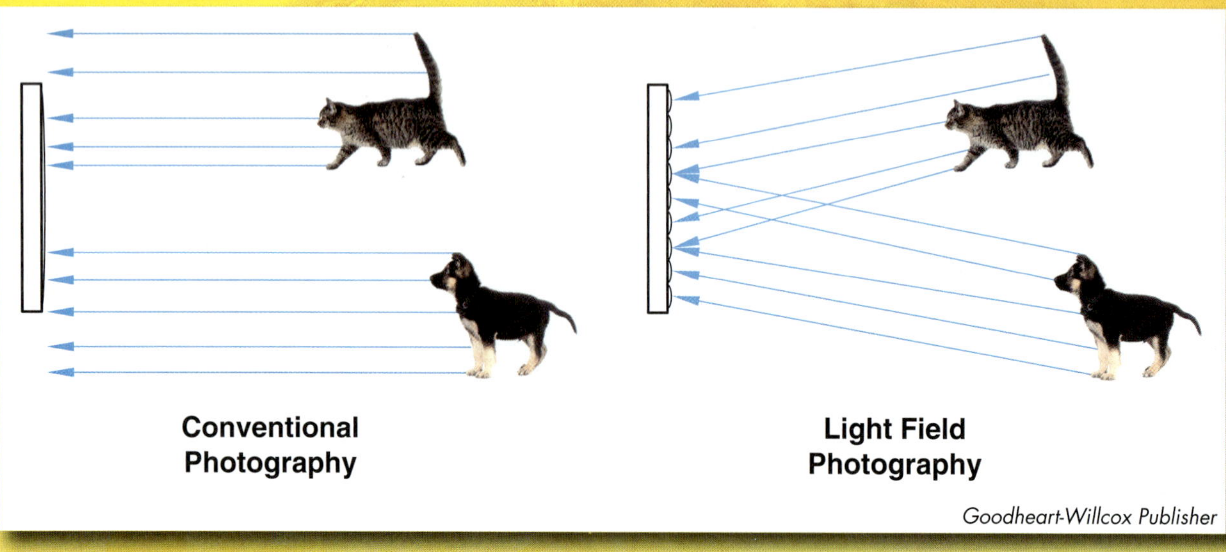

Goodheart-Willcox Publisher

Chapter Summary

- The six basic elements of motion are: persistence, perception, translation, rotation, articulation, and morphing.
- The principles of animation as documented by Frank Thomas and Ollie Johnson are squash and stretch; anticipation; staging; straight-ahead and pose-to-pose action; follow-through and overlapping action; slow in and slow out; arcs; secondary action; timing; exaggeration; solid drawing; and appeal.
- Animations are a series of still images played in sequence to create the illusion of motion; static animation is translation without articulation while active animation is the combination of translation and articulation.
- There are many specialized aspects to creating animations with a computer, including: special effects such as motion blur, lens flare, and combustion and specialized animation such as particle animation and motion capture.
- Sound synchronization is matching the timing of visual action to the corresponding sounds and must be addressed for both character synchronization and effects synchronization.
- Not all game art movement is manufactured through animation—video is used to tell part of the story not included in the gameplay and effects or special effects are used for visual or mechanical additions.

Check Your Video Game IQ

Now that you have finished this chapter, see what you know about video game design by taking the chapter posttest.

www.m.g-wlearning.com

www.g-wlearning.com

Review Your Knowledge

On a separate sheet of paper or in a word processing document, match the following terms with the definition that fits best.

A. static animation
B. squash
C. translation
D. inverse kinematics
E. motion capture
F. active animation
G. stretch
H. rotation
I. keyframe animation
J. articulation

1. The bending and positioning of movable parts.
2. Translation without articulation.
3. Term used by most animation software to describe an approximation of traditional cel animation using a computer.
4. Flattening of an object.
5. Circular movement about a central point.

6. Movement from one point to another.
7. An extension of an object.
8. A parent object controlling the motion of a child object and the child object controlling the motion of the parent.
9. The combination of translation and articulation.
10. A technology that records the movement of an actor and assigns that movement to a virtual character.

On a separate sheet of paper or in a word processing document, answer each of the following questions.

11. List the six elements of motion.
12. Describe how an object traveling 200 mile per hour could have no motion from your frame of reference.
13. How is collision detection established in a game?
14. Which element of motion involves the movement of energy?
15. List the 12 principles of animation.
16. Describe how silhouetting helps demonstrate staging.
17. Why are moving holds important in game design?
18. Which principle of animation allows for morphing of nonridged objects that are compressed?
19. Would stop-motion animation be considered straight ahead or pose-to-pose animation? Explain your answer.
20. What are the two basic areas of sound synchronization?

Apply Your STEM Knowledge

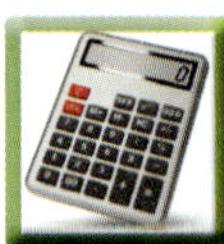

Mathematics

1. Using spreadsheet or word-processing software, complete the table. Calculate the frame rate, frames, and time for each animation. The number of frames must round up to the next whole number.

Animation	Frame Rate (frames per second)	Frames needed (rounded up always)	Approximate Time Length (Seconds)
Cat jumping	24	20	0.8
Hero swinging a sword	24	15	
Villain spin kicking	24		0.7
Bomb exploding		36	1.2
Volcano erupting	30		3.8

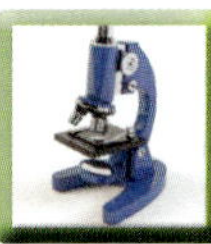

Science

2. Research how the bicep and tricep muscles in the human arm work together. Write a one-page paper to explain how this muscle pair works and how the animation principle of squash and stretch is applied when the forearm moves.

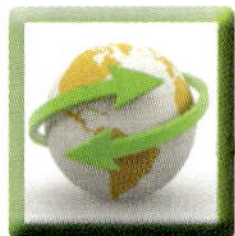

Social Studies

3. The human face can communicate using expressions. These expressions are natural or exaggerated movements. Working with classmates, examine how each person shows laughter, unhappiness, fear, and surprise. Make notes or sketches. Work with at least three other classmates. Then, examine yourself in a mirror as you make the same expressions.

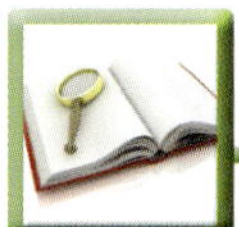

Language Arts

4. Research the newest technology used in motion capture. Form an opinion on which type of technology could be used to build an inexpensive mocap studio for your school. Write a one-page paper to explain how new technology is changing motion capture animation. Conclude your paper with a recommendation on which mocap system you would want to see implemented at your school.

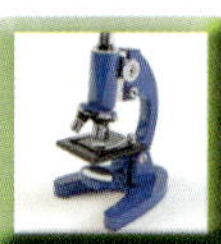

Science

5. Springs are common in mechanical-articulation systems. Research the three major types of springs: compression, tension, and torsion. Create a PowerPoint presentation to picture and explain each type of spring. Include examples of how each spring would be animated and demonstrate the direction of force.

Working in Teams

In teams, research one of the following motions as it occurs in nature: human sneeze, cat jump, human kicking a ball, human swinging a golf club, horse running. Break down the action using the set of principles of animation for performing the action. Create a PowerPoint presentation, complete with a title slide and slides with pictures for each stage of the natural action. Label each action slide with the corresponding principle of animation.

Gamer Portfolio

As part of a job interview, you may be asked about your travel or other experiences with people from other cultures. Companies are interested in this information for good reasons. Many companies serve customers from a variety of geographic locations and cultures. Some companies have offices or factories in more than one area or country. As an employee, you may need to work with people from other cultures. Your job may involve travel to company locations in other areas or countries. Employees that speak more than one language and have traveled, studied, or worked in other areas can be valuable assets. These employees can help the company understand the needs and wants of its customers. They may also be better able to communicate and get along with coworkers.

1. Identify travel or other experiences you have had that helped you learn about another culture.
2. Write a paragraph that describes the experience. Tell how the information you learned might help you better understand customers or coworkers from this culture.
3. Save the document file in your e-portfolio. Place a printed copy in the container for your print portfolio.

G-W Learning Mobile Site

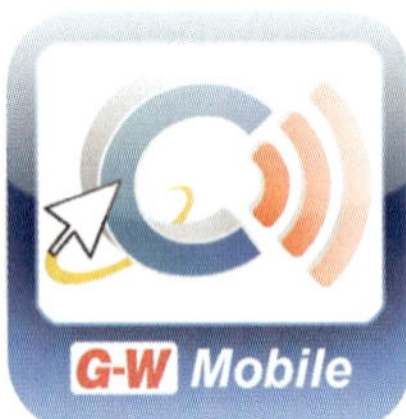

Visit the G-W Learning mobile site to complete the chapter pretest and posttest and to practice vocabulary using e-flash cards. If you do not have a smartphone, visit the G-W Learning companion website to access these features.

G-W Learning mobile site: www.m.g-wlearning.com

G-W Learning companion website: www.g-wlearning.com

Common Core

College and Career Readiness

CTE Career Ready Practices. Create a one-act play for two persons that depicts a positive interaction between two students or coworkers. Be sure to include notes to the actors about body language and facial expressions. Do the same to illustrate a negative interaction on the same topic. What is the essential difference between the two plays/interactions? How does the way you say something influence whether it will be received negatively or positively?

Writing. Research the history of cel animation. Where did the concept of cel animation originate? Write an informative report, consisting of several paragraphs to describe your findings.

Speaking and Listening. Perform an Internet search on straight-ahead action versus pose-to-pose action. Look for opinions for and against each type of animation. After reading a few expert opinions on this topic, use this information to form your own opinion. Discuss your findings and reasoning with the class. As you listen to your classmates' opinions on this topic, evaluate your own position. How does their reasoning contribute to your understanding of the two types of action? Does your opinion change or is it strengthened?

Event Prep: Proper Attire

Some Career and Technical Student Organizations (CTSOs) require appropriate business attire from all entrants and those attending the competition. This requirement is in keeping with the mission of CTSOs: to prepare students for professional careers in business. To be certain that the attire you have chosen for the competition is in accordance with event requirements:

1. Visit the organization's website and look for the most current dress code.
2. The dress code requirements are very detailed and gender specific. Some CTSOs may require a chapter blazer to be worn during the competition.
3. Do a dress rehearsal when practicing for your event. Are you comfortable in the clothes you have chosen? Do you present a professional appearance?
4. Be sure the clothes you wear are clean and pressed. You do not want to undermine your appearance or event performance with wrinkled clothes that may distract judges.
5. Make sure your hair is neat and worn in a conservative style. If you are a male, you should be clean shaven. Again, you do not want anything about your appearance detracting from your performance.
6. As far in advance of the event as is possible, share your clothing choice with your organization's advisor to make sure you are appropriately dressed.

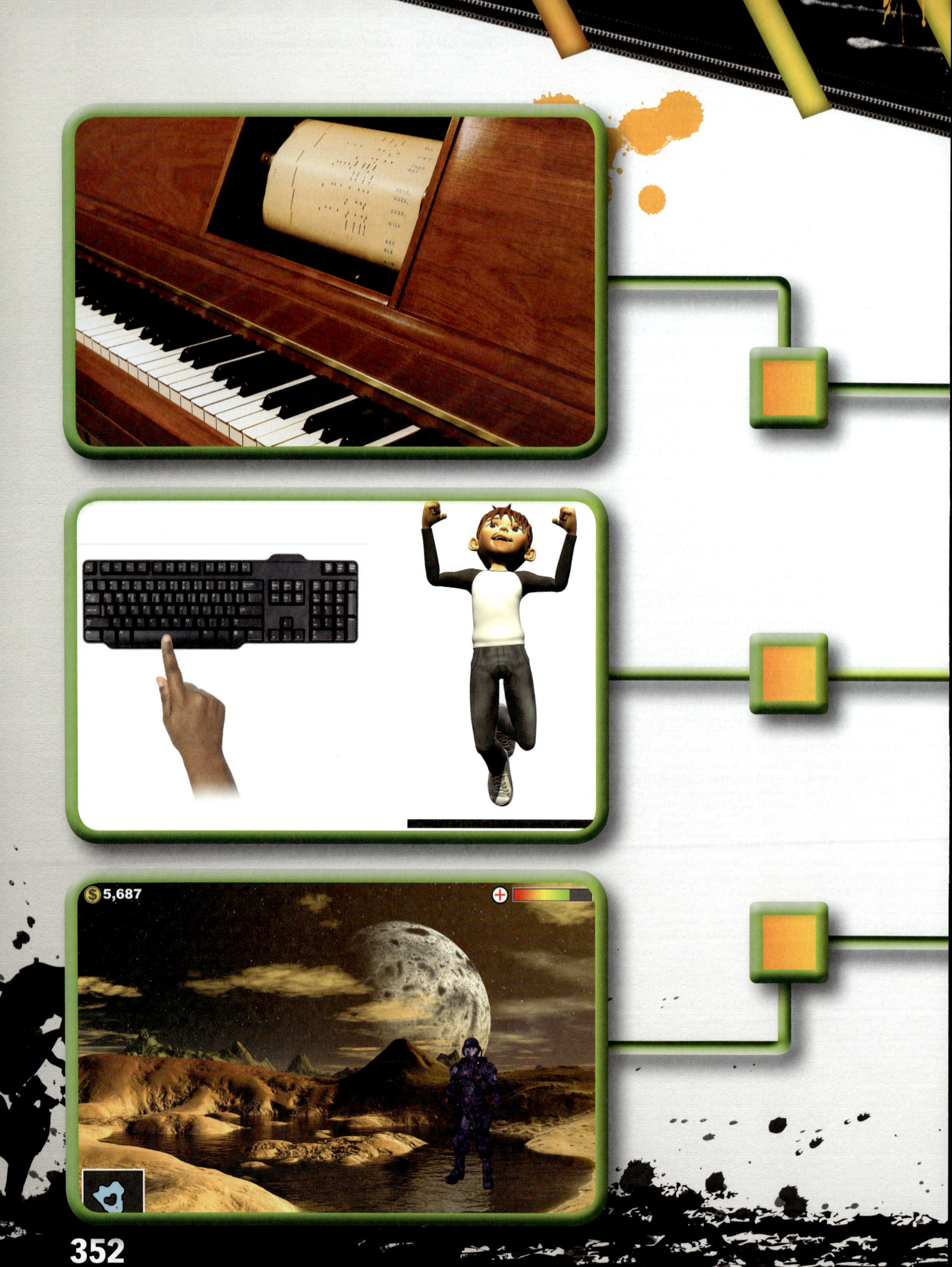
5,687

Chapter 12
Programming Composition

Game programming interprets the rules of the game and provides instructions to the computer to provide the player with a working, interactive program. The programming also enforces the rules. This chapter provides the basics of computer programming through an explanation of the common structure of computer programs and programming languages. It also demonstrates techniques for maintaining order in programming code through naming conventions and commenting. Discussions of syntax, data types, and logic operators used in coding a program and development of skills in iteration for object oriented computer languages are also presented.

Check Your Video Game IQ

Before you begin this chapter, see what you already know about video game design by taking the chapter pretest.

www.m.g-wlearning.com

www.g-wlearning.com

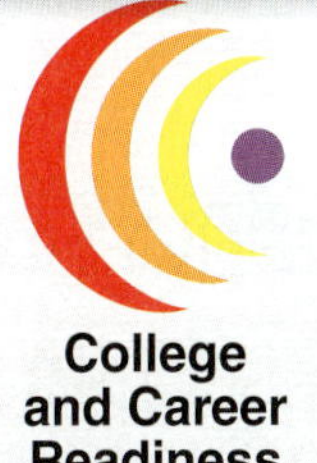

Reading Prep. Before reading, observe the objectives for this chapter. As you read, focus on how the chapter is structured. Does this structure make points clear, convincing, and engaging?

Objectives

After completing this chapter, you will be able to:

- Describe the types of computer languages and their components.
- Outline the ways in which data is used by computer programs.
- List the operators used in logic statements.
- Define computer algorithm and list the components of an algorithm.
- Describe the basics of collision theory.
- Summarize the ways in which physics applies to video games.

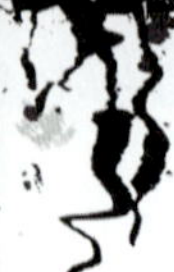

Languages

Computers do not "speak" the same language as people. This makes some people afraid of computer programming. It is much like the fear of traveling to a country like China when you do not speak Chinese. In fact, until you learn a computer language, it can seem like a foreign language. Just as many languages are spoken throughout the world, there are many different computer languages.

Machine Language

Machine language, or machine code, is the instruction set that is interpreted by the computer's central processing unit (CPU). It is a binary language. A binary language or code represents instructions as one of two values, such as on or off. In machine code, on is represented by a 1 and off is represented by a 0. These on and off settings are seen as the rows of 1s and 0s in the binary code.

An early form of a binary language was found in the programming for a player piano or music box. The program (the song) was cut into a sheet of paper or metal, as shown in **Figure 12-1.** Each hole on the sheet represented "on," and a note would be played. Where there was no hole, no note would be played.

Early computers used the same technology of punched paper as a means of inputting binary instructions into the computer. Sometimes the punched paper was a tape and sometimes it was in the form of punch cards, as shown in **Figure 12-2.** Each binary on/off control represented one **bit** of information. So each bit is either a single 1 or a single 0. In computers today, electrical signals are used to represent on and off.

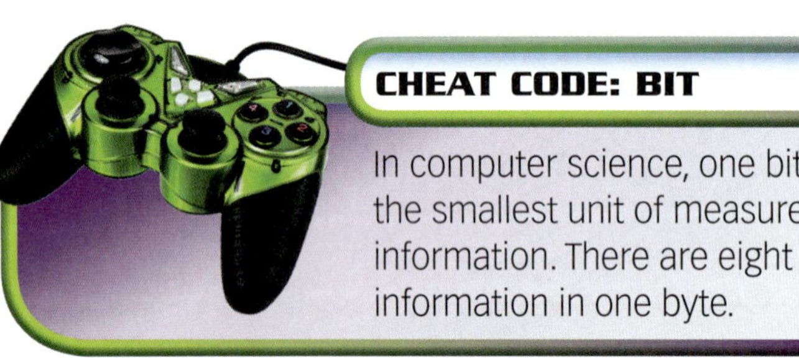

CHEAT CODE: BIT

In computer science, one bit is the smallest unit of measure of information. There are eight bits of information in one byte.

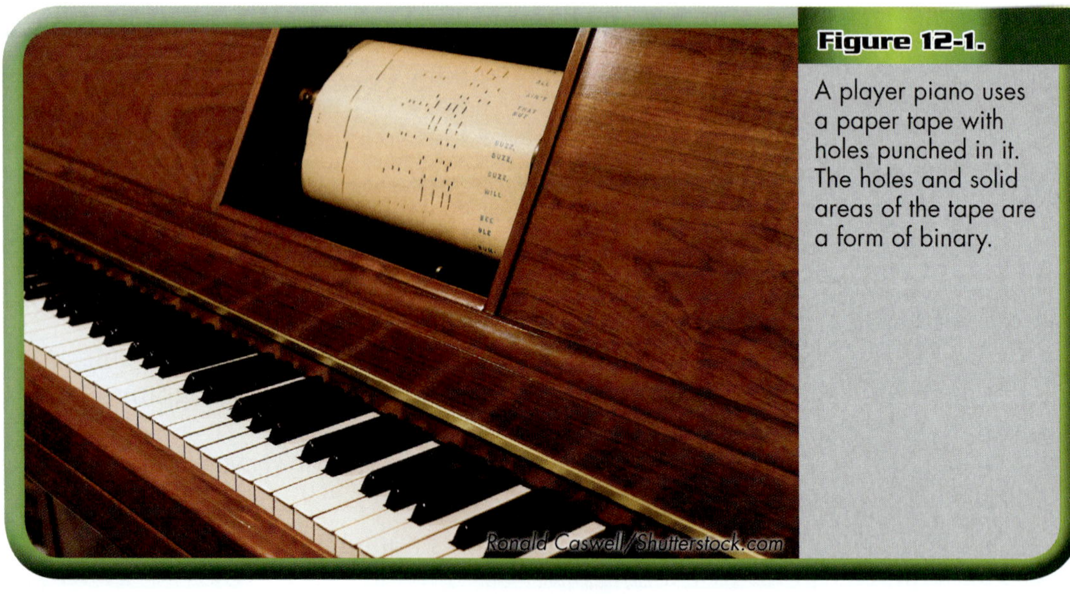

Figure 12-1.

A player piano uses a paper tape with holes punched in it. The holes and solid areas of the tape are a form of binary.

Ronald Caswell/Shutterstock.com

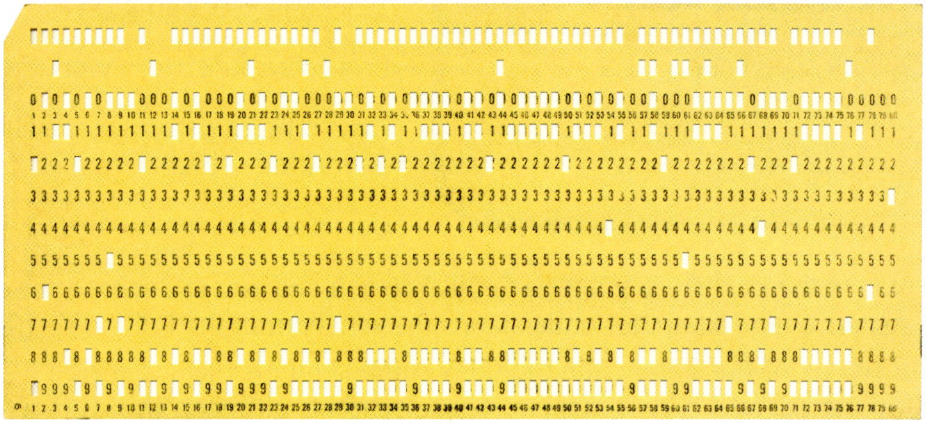

Claudio Divizia/Shutterstock.com

Figure 12-2. Early computer programming was done using punch cards. The combination of holes and lack of holes created the instructions for the computer.

Machine language or code is rarely used by a computer programmer. It is a *low-level computer language,* which is abstract and does not contain words and symbols similar to everyday spoken and written languages. With a low-level language, the programmer interprets human language into machine language. However, machine language is very efficient to use by the computer.

Programming Language

Most computer programmers use high-level computer languages to code instructions for the computer. A *high-level computer language* contains words and symbols that are similar to those found in everyday spoken and written language. The words and symbols are not exactly English, but close enough to a natural language that programmers can easily understand them.

Computer languages like BASIC, Java, Python, Ruby, C, C++, and C# are high-level computer languages. High-level languages are easier to program than machine code, but must be compiled to be used by a computer. A ***compiler*** translates, or compiles, the program into machine code.

Syntax

The programming words and symbols and their arrangement is called ***syntax.*** Your language arts teachers have been teaching you proper English syntax for years. Most high-level programming languages use syntax that reads like a regular sentence. A line of programming code contains some words that act like nouns, others that act like verbs, and some numbers and adjectives to help make it all work. Read this line of Ruby code.

```
5.times { print "Hello World!" }
```

This is a command. Just like in language arts class, the word *you* is often omitted from a command. When your mom says, "Wash the dishes!" she is omitting the word *you.* For programmers, the word *you* refers only to the computer, and it takes commands well without having to call it by name.

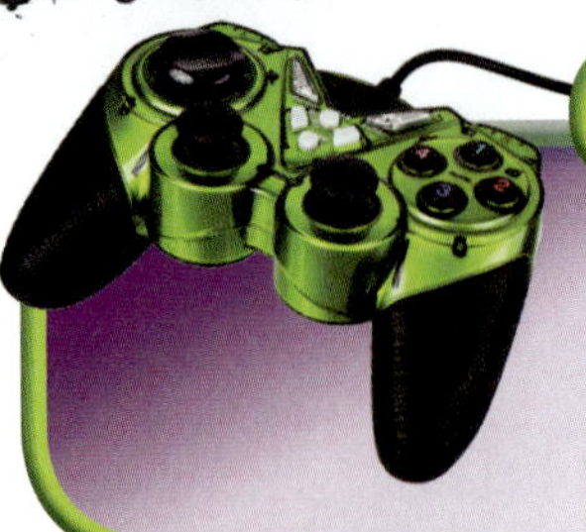

CHEAT CODE: RUBY

Ruby is one of many computer programming languages. It is a general purpose, object-oriented language.

Reading the **Ruby** command as a sentence states:

Five times print "Hello World!"

Converting this broken English to a working sentence makes it:

Computer, print "Hello World!" five times.

The syntax of the English language is familiar to you and you understand the syntax of this sentence. The computer understands the syntax from the Ruby code better.

The syntax of the Ruby code includes some symbols like a period, quotation marks, and curly brackets. These symbols all mean things in a computer program. Additionally, lowercase and capital letters in front of words often have special meaning. In English, punctuation symbols are part of language syntax. An exclamation point has different meaning than a question mark. Capital letters also have special meaning in English language syntax. Capital letters denote proper nouns or the start of a sentence. Syntax for computer languages use symbols such as punctuation and capital letters just as is done with the syntax for the English language.

Syntax for computer languages creates objects the same way the English language uses nouns. Definition subroutines are called objects. ***Objects*** are defined by their attributes and properties.

Attributes are characteristics associated with an object. A baseball would have the color attribute white. An attribute makes an object unique from others of the same type. Properties define the size, shape, movement, and use of an object. The properties of a baseball would be a 2.875-inch diameter sphere, five percent friction decrease, a weight of 5.25 ounces, the maximum speed of 100, and so on, as shown in **Figure 12-3.**

Actions are how an object reacts to input or interacts with other objects. The actions of a ball would be to bounce against walls, accelerate when thrown, arc toward gravity, move left when the left arrow button is pressed, and so on. Attributes and properties are written in the object subroutine and allow the computer to draw the correct object and determine how that object is affected by the game environment.

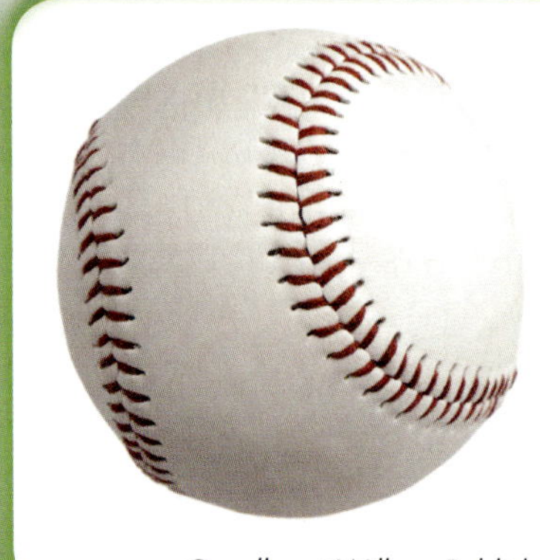

Attributes

Color: white
Size: 2.875-inch diameter
Friction decrease: five percent
Weight: 5.25 ounces
Maximum speed: 100

Goodheart-Willcox Publisher; image: Alex Staroseltsev/Shutterstock.com

Figure 12-3. The attributes for an object must be programmed in a video game.

Other subroutines are called methods. ***Methods*** are the actions or verbs used in syntax. A **JUMP** method will execute instructions contained in the **JUMP** subroutine. The instructions would tell you how to bend your knees and quickly snap them straight so your feet leave the ground.

Some symbols are used as operational syntax. Most of the mathematical symbols, such as +, –, <, >, and parentheses, work just as they do in math class. These symbols will add, subtract, and compare values. In a line of computer code these symbols can also work like words.

```
Fruit = apples + bananas + grapes
```

In this example, the words and operational syntax form a sentence. This sentence is also a formula to find the total number of fruit. Each word is also a variable.

Choice of Language

Several popular programming languages and web page–creation languages are shown in **Figure 12-4.** Some programming languages use fewer words, more symbols, or have more built-in methods. The choice of language used when programming has more to do with a programmer's likes and dislikes

Language	Description
ASP	Server-side scripting language. Used to create HTML pages under Windows servers.
C	Non-object oriented programming that offers much freedom in creating programs.
C++	A variation of C that includes objects, a library, and templates.
C#	Similar to C++, but generally found to be easier to use.
HTML	Hypertext markup language. Not truly a programming language. Used to create web pages and similar features.
Java	Designed as a portable replacement for C++. Used for web services and mobile-device apps.
LISP	List processing. Originally designed for artificial intelligence and still in use in some applications.
Perl	Scripting interpreted language used mostly by network administrators. Generally considered hard to use.
PHP	Designed to be used with HTML. Not truly a programming language.
Python	Interpreted language. Generally considered easy to use and very powerful.
Ruby	Interpreted language. Generally considered simple and easy to use for scripts.
XML	Extensible markup language. Similar to HTML. Not truly a programming language.

Figure 12-4. These are some common programming languages.

Goodheart-Willcox Publisher

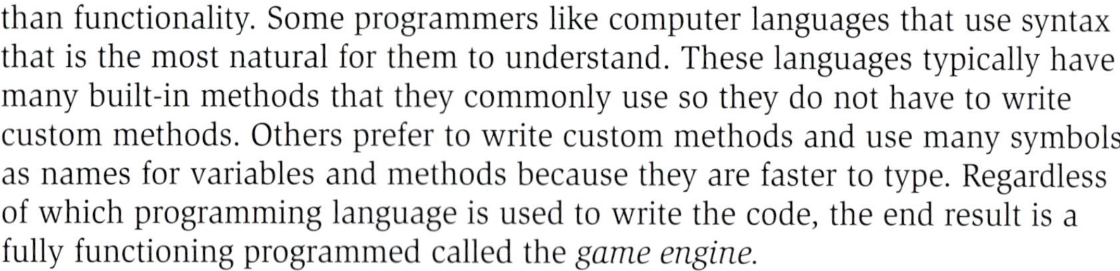

than functionality. Some programmers like computer languages that use syntax that is the most natural for them to understand. These languages typically have many built-in methods that they commonly use so they do not have to write custom methods. Others prefer to write custom methods and use many symbols as names for variables and methods because they are faster to type. Regardless of which programming language is used to write the code, the end result is a fully functioning programmed called the *game engine.*

Some languages are designed for financial calculations and have many built-in methods like **SUM**, **AVERAGE**, **DEVIATION**, and more. Other languages are designed for physics and have methods for **VELOCITY**, **ACCELERATION**, **TANGENT**, and more. A programming language takes a very long time to create, so it is usually written to a specific audience of users. The memory and speed of computers has greatly increased the ability of computer languages to hold more methods and calculate them quickly. This allows for a language to grow and include more specialty components. This makes the language more appealing to more people because they can write more types of programs easily with the same language.

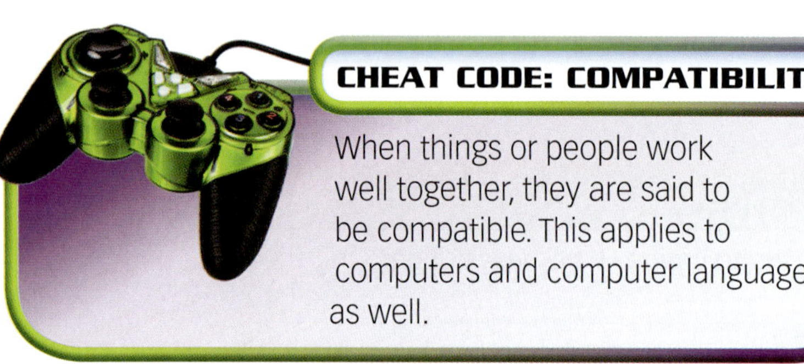

CHEAT CODE: COMPATIBILITY

When things or people work well together, they are said to be compatible. This applies to computers and computer languages as well.

Other issues with the choice of computer language have to do with **compatibility**. A language may not compile properly for a specific type of computer. A computer that could run BASIC language well might not be able to compile C++ or Java. Fortunately, most computers today have the ability to compile in many different formats. Modern game engines and design software also have the ability to save in different language formats so the game can play on multiple devices. Consequently, the compatibility issues are quickly going away as programs come out that translate one computer language to another quickly and accurately. Today, an efficient game engine may allow the design team to make the game once and compile it to work on many different platforms.

Pseudo Code

No matter the computer language used, logic statements are usually written before code is written. Logic statements are covered later in this chapter. Writing logic statements is not actual computer code, but is a form of pseudo code. ***Pseudo code*** is similar to, but not actual computer code. An example of pseudo code is a basic **IF...THEN** logic statement:

IF the player moves the joystick forward
THEN the player character will jump

Logic statements are covered in detail later in this chapter.

Pseudo code helps by breaking down the interactions into the logical steps that will be converted into the final code statements of a specific computer language. Using the framework of the pseudo code, many programmers can work on the same project at the same time by converting segments of pseudo code into computer language.

CASE STUDY

XNA

Microsoft provides XNA software as free solution for those looking to design games for the PC, Xbox 360, or Windows phone. XNA is not a programming language, it is a set of tools in a managed runtime environment and uses the C# (C sharp) programming language. It allows a game developer to obtain the software development kit (SDK) for all the devices that run on Microsoft operating system.

Games developed with XNA can be released through the App Hub for purchase by Xbox Live users. A developer must pay a $99 fee for premium membership to be able to sell games through the App Hub. Schools and other educational institutions can receive premium membership for free. Even with a free membership, there is still a cost associated with selling on the App Hub. You receive a 70 percent of the sale price of the game, but Microsoft keeps 30 percent (price in Xbox Live points). This is, in part, to cover the costs of providing the distribution portal.

Microsoft offers a large amount of support with the Beginner Developer Learning Center and the MSDN forum. There are also many YouTube videos that can be very helpful when getting started using XNA.

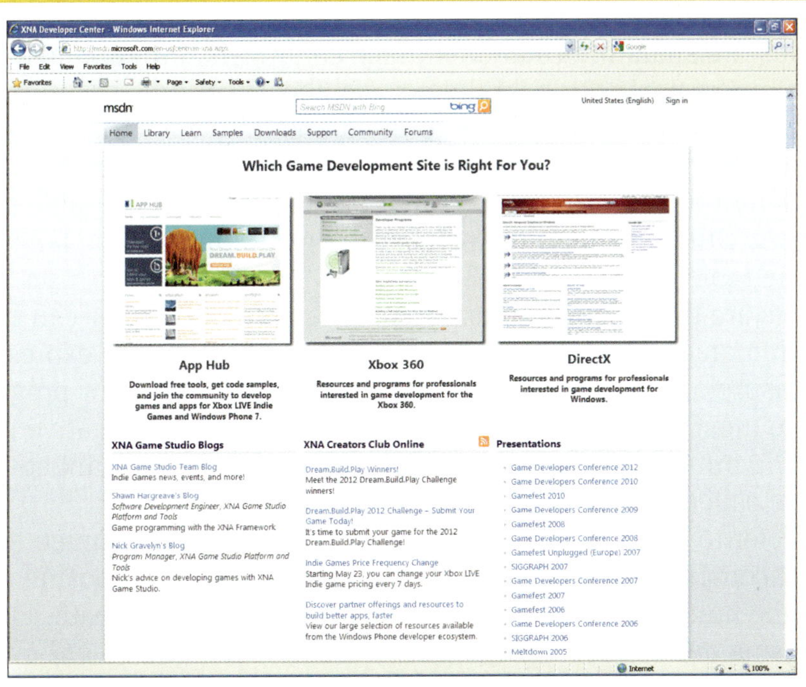

Microsoft

Another benefit of pseudo code is that is can be used as the structure for many different computer languages. Separate programs may need to be created for different platforms. The choice of computer language used for each platform may be different. With pseudo code, a team could create the program in Java while another team creates the program in Python. A programmer that can write and understand pseudo code then only needs to learn the syntax of a specific computer language to program in many different languages.

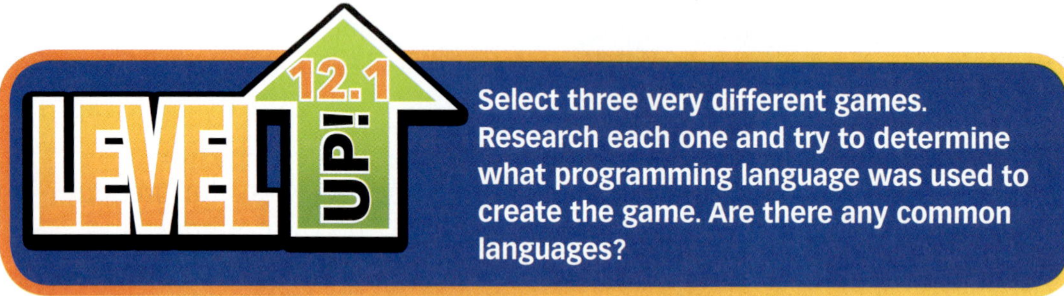

Select three very different games. Research each one and try to determine what programming language was used to create the game. Are there any common languages?

Storing Data

Computer programs work with information, or data. The data may come from user input or from stored locations within the program. Data are what the computer program operates to produce an end result. In order to operate on the data, the data need to be somehow stored within the program.

Variable

Variables are small information-storage containers. Programmers give these storage containers names to help them remember what type of information is inside the container. An easy way to think about how a variable works is to think about a cell in a spreadsheet. The cell has a name, like A1. Inside cell A1, different data types can be stored, as illustrated in the table shown in **Figure 12-5A.** Other common data types for most programming languages are shown in the table in **Figure 12-5B.**

Numbers are the most common type of variable. A number can be expressed in many different ways. In real life, numbers can be expressed as money, measurements, amounts, totals, decimals and more. For programming, numbers are most often integers. ***Integers*** are positive and negative real whole numbers. The numbers 1, –6, 23, and 5000 are all integers. Numbers with decimals are called floats.

Floats refer to the floating decimal point that must be accounted for in any decimal computation. The computer has to remember the position of the decimal in the number calculation as well as doing the actual math. Floats can be expressed using decimal notation (1. 0234, –36.7, 15.15, and so on) or scientific notation ($10 \times e^{-16}$, $3.14 \times e^{2}$, and so on). Scientific notation does not record the nonsignificant digits of a number. As a decimal number extends past the decimal point the value of those digits become less and less significant. Even extremely exact measurements do not require more than a few digits after the decimal point. Scientific notation includes the significant digits and then tells where to place the decimal. Nonsignificant digits would be replaced with zero.

Fruit	Apples	Bananas	Grapes			
= Apples + Bananas + Grapes	5	2	3			

A

Name	Data	Range	Description	Example
integer	Whole Number	–2,147,483,648 and 2,147,483,647	Number values up to 4 bytes	X = 543210987
short	Whole Number	–32768 and 32767	Number values up to 2 bytes	X = –12345
long	Whole Number	A very large amount	Number values up to 8 bytes	X = 1234567890111213
string	Character	Any size text amount	Holds text only shown in "quotation". Numbers entered into a string variable are text and not numbers. Meaning those will not be able to be used to calculate.	X = "hello world" X = "4" X = "anything"
Boolean	True/False	On or off state only	Used to check if something is true/active/enabled or not	X = true
single	Decimal Number	Short decimal values	Number with decimal value up to 4 bytes. Single precision floating point	X = 3.14159
double	Decimal Number	Long decimal values	Number with decimal value up to 8 bytes. Double precision floating point	X = 12345.1234567890

B

Figure 12-5. A—Basic data types include numbers, strings, and formulas. B—Common data types for programming languages include whole numbers, decimal numbers, characters, and Boolean operators.

Goodheart-Willcox Publisher

Variables can also store text. Text stored in a variable is called a string. A ***string*** is a series of letters, numbers, or punctuation. The computer will not try to interpret a string. It will only remember the order of the characters of a string. A string is most often identified with quotation marks or quotes. "Hello World", "8746 Main Street", "Applesauce!" or anything else set in quotes would be a string. Strings are often used as labels in spreadsheets and databases or as dialog in a video game.

Variables can contain formulas. In the world of mathematics, variables are common. In the expression:

$$Y = mX + B$$

all of the values have been replaced with variables. The variable Y stores a formula. Inside this formula, the variables m, X, and B can have a value that changes.

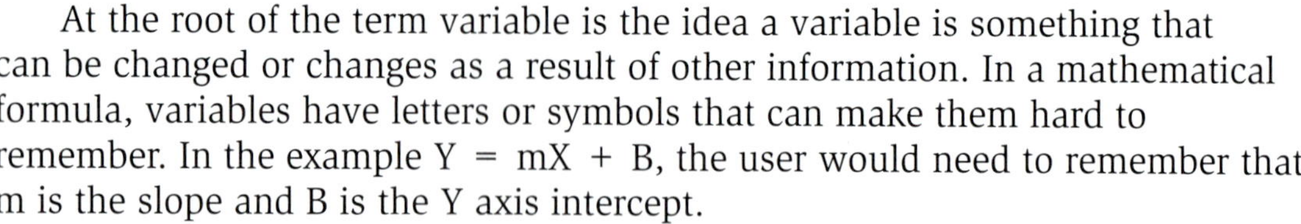

At the root of the term variable is the idea a variable is something that can be changed or changes as a result of other information. In a mathematical formula, variables have letters or symbols that can make them hard to remember. In the example Y = mX + B, the user would need to remember that m is the slope and B is the Y axis intercept.

In programming, a variable name is not limited to letters and old Greek symbols. Variable names should describe the information stored. These are more like nicknames for the information inside. A variable with the name strGreeting might store the string, "Good morning, how are you today?" A program may contain over 1000 variables. It is therefore important to give each variable a name that is unique and helps describe the contents.

Variables can also contain symbols. Using a symbol to represent a variable is common with mathematics and programming. A symbol can be representational or abstract. A representational symbol might be something like this → or ← (produce by keying --> or <--) to represent direction or vector.

Vector is a physics term that means direction. An avatar in the game moves at a speed of 10. The vector of right, left, up, down, and so on determines what direction the avatar is moving. Other symbols are abstract such as the pi symbol (π) or dollar sign ($). These symbols have meaning only because they are assigned meaning in a program. A $ in formula in an Excel spreadsheet, for example, is used to lock an absolute cell reference and has nothing to do with currency.

Notice how a variable can change an action with the example shown in **Figure 12-6.** Variables here will control the amount or direction of a property that can be changed. In the statement "Jump 10 feet," 10 is a variable.

Persistence means that something continues to exist after the event that caused it has ended. If you have your picture taken with a flash and see spots, you have persistence of vision from the flash. Likewise, you do not have to memorize the definition of each word you use each time you use it. You use the same words every day to mean the same thing. This is not true of a computer. A computer does not remember a definition from one program to another. For a computer, the name of a function, subroutine, variable, and so on, must be **declared.** Therefore, use names that make sense. Use common syntax you already know to easily understand the language you are using.

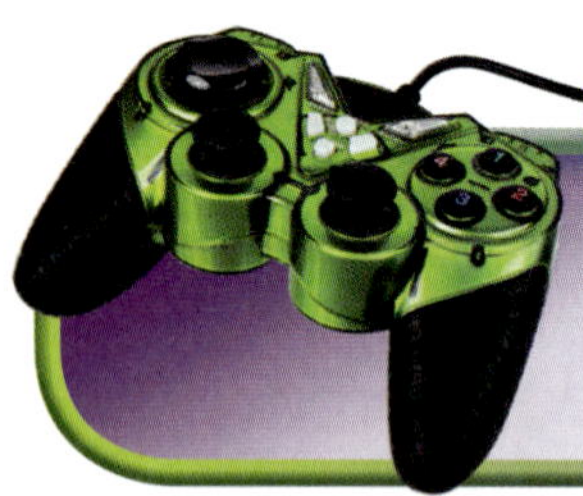

CHEAT CODE: DECLARED

Declared means that the item is given a name and a function in the program you are writing.

Statement	Variable	Variable Type
Jump 5 feet	5	Number
Jump left	Left	Vector
Jump left 5 feet	Left, 5	Vector, Number

Figure 12-6. Variables can be used to change an action. Changing the value of the variable changes the result of the action.

Goodheart-Willcox Publisher

A ***global*** subroutine or variable works everywhere in the program that you are writing. Global subroutines can be declared by a programmer if the subroutine needs to work inside the current module and also in another module. If you define a global subroutine for level 1 of the game, it can be recalled in level 2. In this way, global subroutines have persistence between modules.

A ***local*** subroutine or variable does not have persistence outside of the module in which it was declared. If you use a local subroutine on level 1 of the game, the computer will "forget" what it means in level 2. This allows you to use an object called Ball in different levels and have that ball be unique on each level. An example in your class might be using the name Joe for a student in your computer class. Using just the first name of Joe as a local variable works well in the module of your computer class because there is only one student declared with the name Joe. However, Joe does not work well as a global declaration because there are many students with the name Joe at school. A global declaration for the same student might best be done using the first and last name, like Joe Phillips, so he can be identified throughout the school.

Array

Arrays are a common **data structure** to store and manipulate data. An ***array*** is a look-up table where the table cells hold variable data, like that shown in **Figure 12-7.** The program can access the array and find the value or string contained in an array cell.

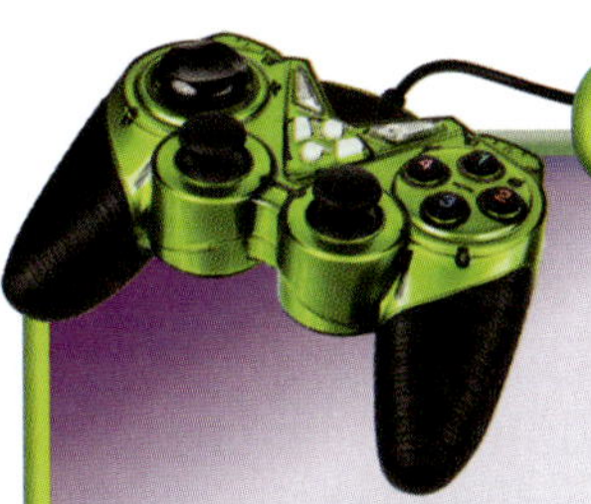

CHEAT CODE: DATA STRUCTURE

A data structure is a way of storing and organizing data. The data can be held in a simple counter, array, or other type of structure. The idea is to use the structure that will most efficiently store and retrieve data for a particular application.

In the array in **Figure 12-7,** the cells contain different data types. To find a value in an array, plot the X and Y locations to identify a cell. In the example for Array_1, the value of X1,Y1 is 24. Also in this array, cell X2,Y3 stores the current value for the experience points, or XP. An array allows values to be easily accessed, recalled, and calculated. An array is also a great way of storing dialogue strings. The possible statements for a character can be inserted into an array and later recalled using a programming statement.

Array_1	X1	X2	X3	X4
Y1	24	56	4	0
Y2	Error	Win	Loss	Tie
Y3	HP( )	XP ( )	MP ( )	Gold ( )

Figure 12-7. Arrays are look-up tables used to store and manipulate data.

Goodheart-Willcox Publisher

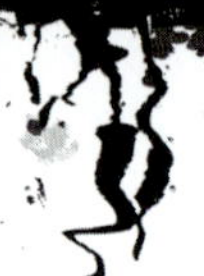

Class versus Instance

In addition to being declared as either local or global, variables and subroutines can be a class or instance. A ***class variable*** is an umbrella device that contains a nonspecific type of item and on which operations can be performed. Suppose you need to program the opening of doors in a video game. Most doors open and close the same, so it makes sense to create a class called door. A door.open method could then be used to call the programming needed to open the door. A door.close method would call the programming needed to close the door.

However, all doors in the game may not be exactly the same. An ***instance variable*** describes a single type of item. In the case of the door example, an instance variable may be oak@door. The instance has a specific attribute to describe it. The attribute oak attached to the class door makes an oak door different from all other doors. The oak door would have a different texture, knocking sound sample associated with it, and hinge creak sample associated with it than an iron door would. While each instance would be different, they would still be classified under the class of door. Each would use the same class methods door.open and door.close to control functions of opening and closing. For example, oak@door.open would call the programming to display the animation of an oak door opening.

In other cases, a program may require more than one instance of the same object. In the case of an oak door, the program might require one oak door at the entrance and a different one at the exit. Both would need to work independent of each other so one could be opened without the other being opened at the same time. If each object requires different programming attached to it, then additional instances of the object would have to be declared. Separate instances of the doors would have to be created such as entrance_oak@door and exit_oak@door.

Modules

There is a way for the computer to recall subroutines and variables from one module to another. ***Modules*** are separate units of programming that perform one function and contain all of the information needed to execute that function. A subroutine or variable can be classified as global or local to a module.

For computer programming, each module is written to control a different system. Computers can operate many system modules in parallel, or at the same time. If a program has to do things in series, it has to do things one after the other. Planning parallel and series modules is very similar to the planning needed to manage a game construction project. Gantt charts can be used to plan how jobs by different team members can be done at the same time. That is parallel operation using workflow modules. The entire construction process is a series of milestone achievements. Each part of the design has to be completed before the next part can be added to the game. All of the work modules, from art, sound, character, and story, are assembled into a single production to create a finished game. A module system helps keep everything organized for a workflow project as well as for a computer programming project.

To create a module within a game, it is important to plan all of the parts of the operation using a flowchart or other organizational tool. ***Flowcharts*** have different text box shapes and connectors to add visual detail to a decision process, as shown in **Figure 12-8.** A flowchart begins with a start/terminal

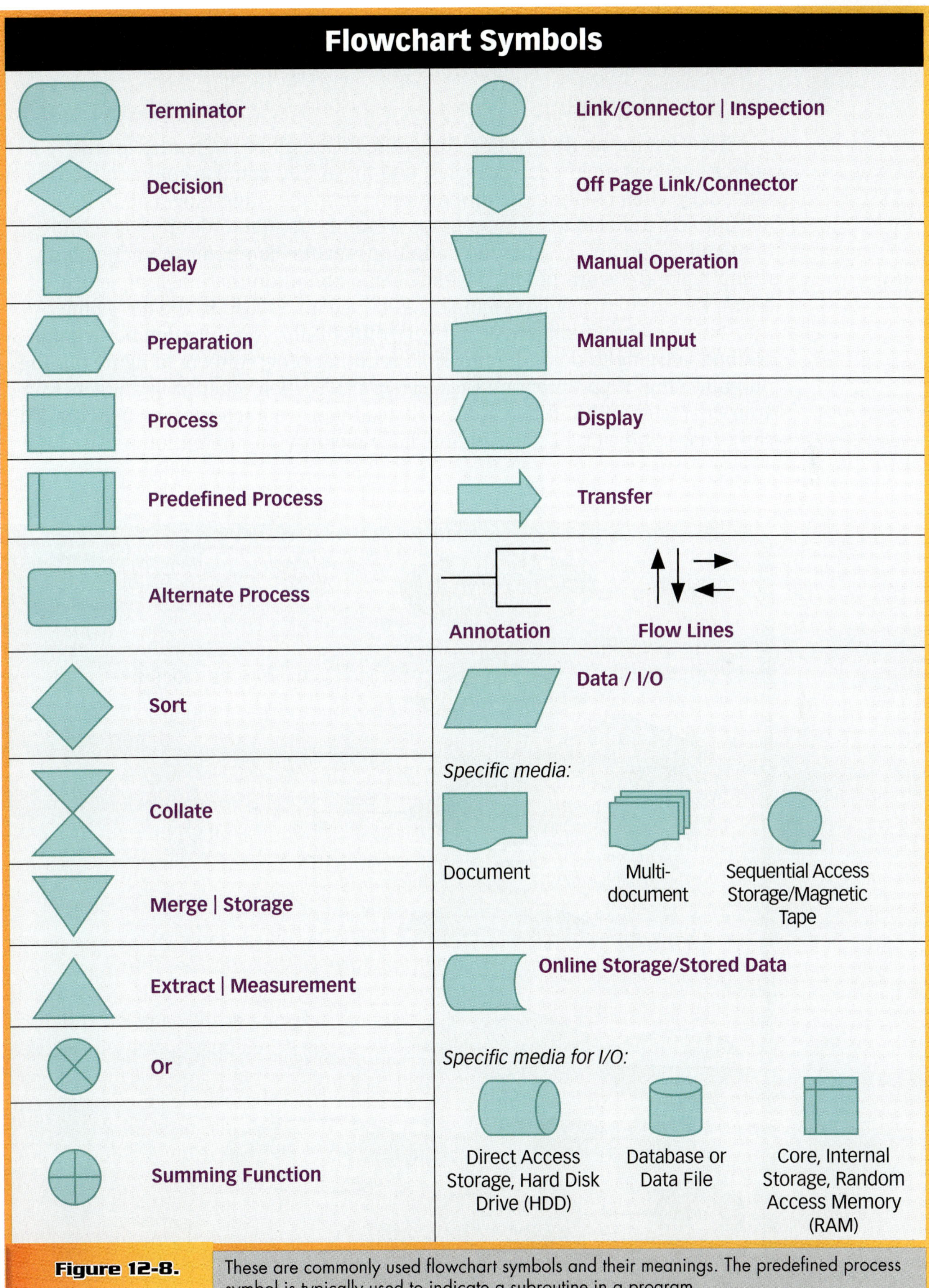

Figure 12-8. These are commonly used flowchart symbols and their meanings. The predefined process symbol is typically used to indicate a subroutine in a program.

Goodheart-Willcox Publisher

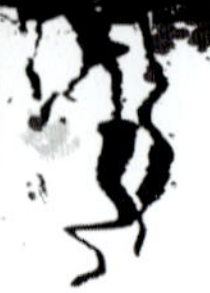

shape and the name of the problem. At an endpoint of a flowchart would be an end/terminal shape and a solution to the problem, as illustrated in **Figure 12-9.** A flowchart works well to map out a process, system, and module.

Naming Convention

Here comes the tricky part! You get to create all of the names for the objects, actions, methods, variables, and more. You can use common words like **JUMP** when creating the programming to make something leap in the air, but you can also make up a crazy word like **APPLE** to do the same thing. Remember, you are creating the definitions for the computer to understand. If you make the word **APPLE** have the same definition that most of us use for **JUMP**, the computer will remember **APPLE** means to leap in the air. Doing this "junk" programming makes it very difficult for you to remember what a method is trying to do and impossible for other programmers to figure out the programming. If you program **Character APPLE 5**, then other programmers think your character will find five apples. Instead your character jumps five feet. This can cause confusion because people have memory and definition persistence.

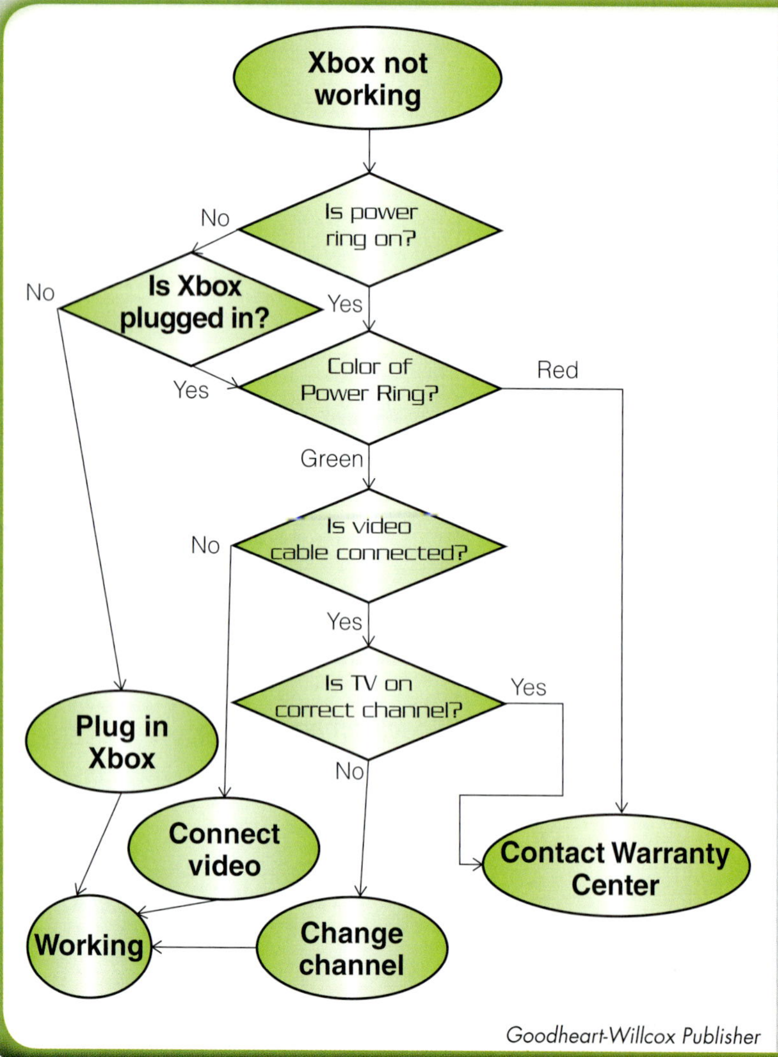

Xbox not working
Is power ring on?
No
Is Xbox plugged in?
No
Yes
Color of Power Ring?
Yes
Red
Green
Is video cable connected?
No
Yes
Is TV on correct channel?
Yes
No
Plug in Xbox
Connect video
Contact Warranty Center
Working
Change channel

Goodheart-Willcox Publisher

Figure 12-9. A flowchart can be used to break down a process into simple, clearly-defined steps, as in this example for resolving the issue of a broken Xbox 360.

Objects should also be named to add information about the use and type. Programmers should avoid just numbering things. It is very difficult to debug a program with 60 objects called Object 1, Object 2, Object 3...Object 60. It is much easier to debug if you have descriptive names such as objCat_Red, objCat_Yellow, objDog_Black,...objWall_Brick. This keeps you from having to read the properties of each object to find out which one is the black dog.

A common naming convention is called *Hungarian notation* after Charles Simony, who worked at Xerox Palo Alto Research Center in the 1970s. With this type of notation, the name of a variable starts with lowercase letters that indicate what type of variable it is. Notice the examples in the previous paragraph. The variable objCat_Red indicates it is a variable for an object. Other common abbreviations that can be used in Hungarian notation are shown in **Figure 12-10.** Hungarian notation is still used, but not as widely as it used to be. Some programmers feel it is no longer needed because computer languages have evolved to the point where elements of a program are obvious.

Abbreviation	Type of Variable
str	String
obj	Object
ch	Character
b	Boolean
db	Double
i	Integer
fn	Function

Figure 12-10. These are some common Hungarian notation abbreviations that are used as prefixes to variable names.

Goodheart-Willcox Publisher

Comments

Comments are used to identify and explain what the computer code is supposed to do. Comments are only for programmers and are *not* read by the computer. Placing the comment 'makes the player jump' before the programming for a **JUMP** subroutine allows you or anyone else reading the code to see what the block of code should do. It is not uncommon to have a comment before each line of code. Comments are *very* important and should always be included, even in programs only you will see. In team projects, comments are critical as they help team members add to your work or debug your mistakes.

Green Gamer

Paper manufacturers are always looking for renewable resources and new ideas to produce environmentally friendly paper products. One ecofriendly paper is made from by-products of sugarcane with no wood involved in its production. Sugarcane products actually biodegrade faster than wood products, and sugarcane paper is cleaner to make than wood-based paper. When purchasing video games, look for companies that use sugarcane paper in the packaging materials.

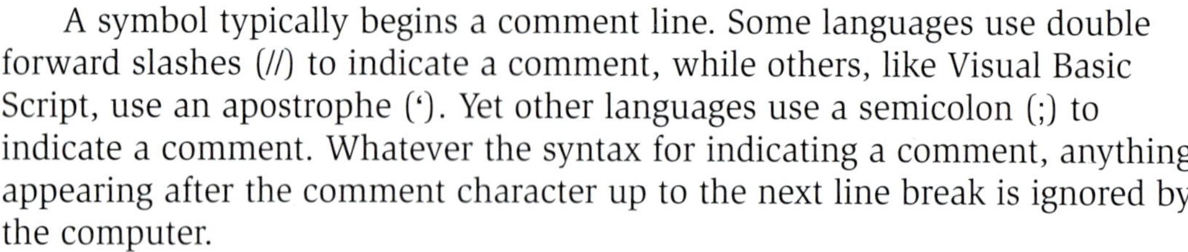

A symbol typically begins a comment line. Some languages use double forward slashes (//) to indicate a comment, while others, like Visual Basic Script, use an apostrophe ('). Yet other languages use a semicolon (;) to indicate a comment. Whatever the syntax for indicating a comment, anything appearing after the comment character up to the next line break is ignored by the computer.

In the example below, the Visual Basic Script is commented for a block of code used to calculate the score.

```
'************Adding Score Variable and Formula
Dim Score
Sub AddScore(points)
    iSCORE = iSCORE + iPOINTS
    ScoreText.Text = FormatNumber(Score,0,–1,0,–1)
End Sub
'************Adding Score Ends Here
```

The asterisks have no significance to the syntax of the language. They are placed there simply to draw attention to the comment, since the apostrophe can easily be overlooked.

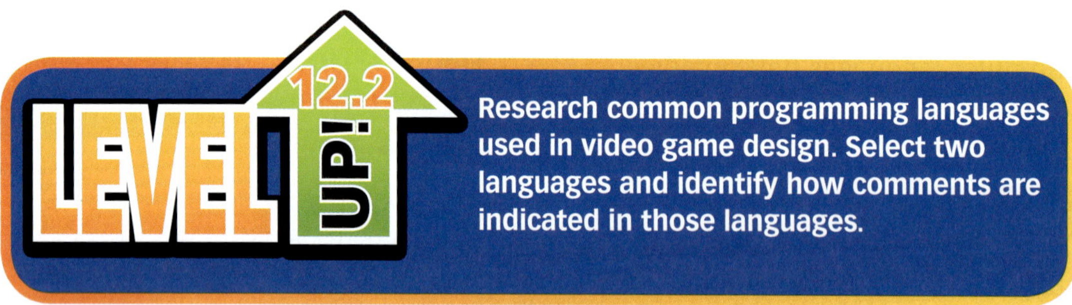

Operators

As discussed earlier, logic statements are one of the most common statements in pseudo code. A ***logic statement*** consists of a possible condition and subsequent actions. Logic statements are sentences using these seven common operators: **IF**, **THEN**, **AND**, **OR**, **NOT**, **NOR**, **ELSE**. In computer programming, an ***operator*** provides a logical qualification to a condition. For easy coding, most high-level languages use these same operators, either by word or symbol.

An ***event*** is a change in a computer program. The player character jumping is an event. An event is typically stated with an **IF**...**THEN** logic statement. **IF** is the condition and **THEN** is the action. The game rules may state that when the player presses the space bar the character player jumps, as shown in **Figure 12-11.** This translates to an **IF**...**THEN** logic statement in pseudo code as follows.

IF the player presses the space bar
THEN the player character will jump

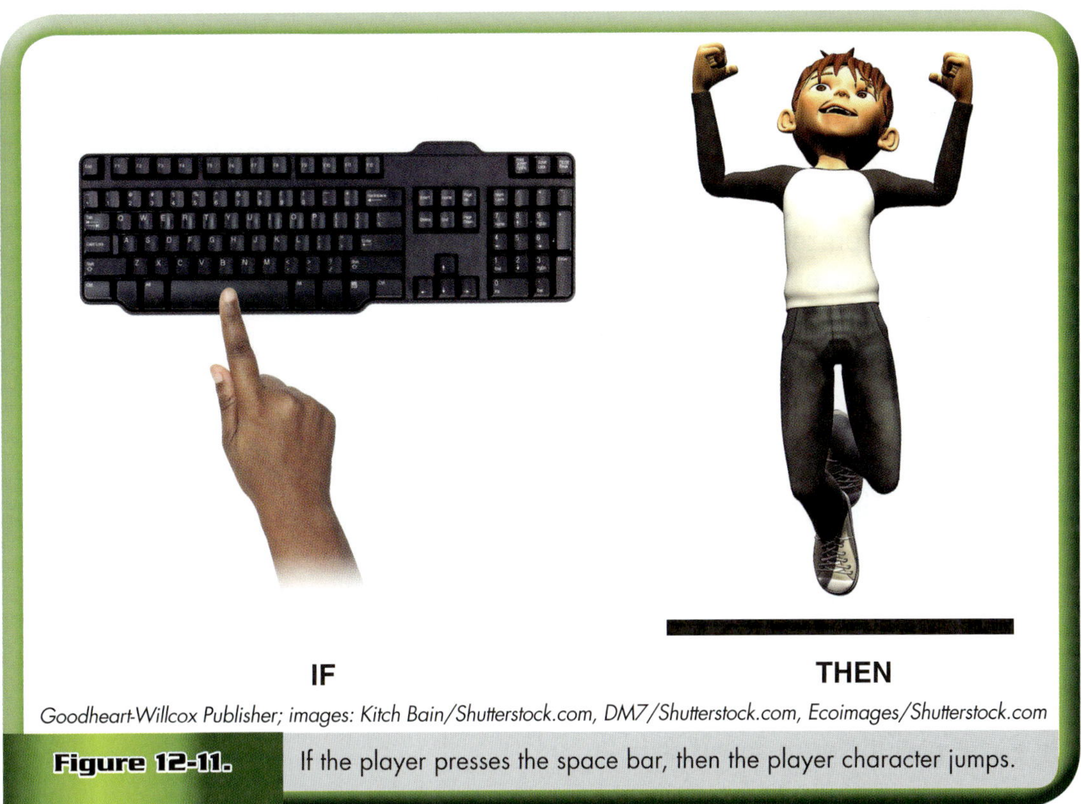

Goodheart-Willcox Publisher; images: Kitch Bain/Shutterstock.com, DM7/Shutterstock.com, Ecoimages/Shutterstock.com

Figure 12-11. If the player presses the space bar, then the player character jumps.

The actual computer language can be written to interpret the pseudo code so the computer can understand. In the example below, the curly brackets {} represent **THEN** and contain the actions that will be completed when the **IF** statement is true.

```
IF keypress (space)
    {
          player1 (Jump)
    }
```

Notice how each line in the above example is indented. ***Intercalating*** is the process of indenting all lines that are part of a block of one code. Programmers intercalate to make the program easier for a person to read. It separates the program into chunks the same way a book is separated by paragraphs.

AND Operator

The **AND** operator is used to join items together, just as it does in English. It can be used in either the condition or action side of the logic statement. In the example below, the **AND** operator is used to make sure the jump does not occur when the player character is in the air or otherwise not touching the floor.

```
IF the player presses the space bar
    AND the player character is touching the floor
THEN the player character will jump
    AND play a spring sound sample
```

AND is also used to join actions in the **THEN** statement. In this event, the jump animation will be activated *and* a sound will play at the same time.

OR Operator

The **OR** operator allows more than one condition to activate the actions of an event. It is used only in the condition side of the logic statement. In the example below, the player can press either the space bar or the [Enter] key to make the player character jump.

IF the player presses the space bar
  OR the player presses the enter key
THEN the player character will jump
  AND play a spring sound sample

ELSE Operator

The **ELSE** operator activates a set of actions only when the condition statement is false. When used, it is part of the action side of the logic statement.

IF the player presses the space bar
  AND the player character is touching the floor
THEN the player character will jump
  AND play a spring sound sample
ELSE play the error sound sample

Suppose the player character is falling off of a cliff when the player presses the space bar. The player character is not touching the floor. In other words, the **IF** statement is false. So, the program does not activate the jump action or play the spring sound sample. Instead, the **ELSE** action is activated and the error sound sample is played.

NOT and NOR Operators

The **NOT** operator, sometimes called the **NOR** operator, excludes a condition or action. In the example below, the **NOT** operator is used to exclude the blue tile as part of the floor. Additional programming allows a jump from a blue tile to activate a super jump.

IF the player presses the space bar
  AND the player character is touching the floor
  NOT a blue tile
THEN the player character will jump
  AND play a spring sound sample

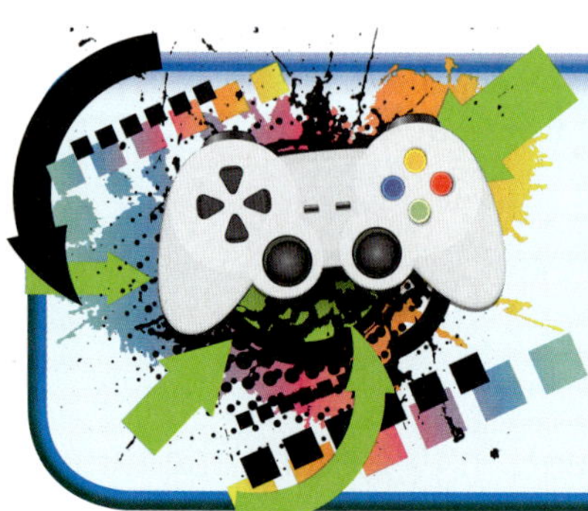

Ethical Gamer

Ethics is a set of rules that define what is wrong and right. Ethics helps people make good decisions in both their personal and professional lives. Ethics is also very important when interacting with other players in online games.

IF the player presses the space bar
  AND the player character is touching a blue tile
THEN the player character will super jump
  AND change the avatar to the blue flame animation

Suppose the player character is standing on the floor, but not touching a blue tile, when the player presses the space bar. The program will activate the first **THEN** statement (shown at the bottom of the previous page) because the first **IF** statement is true. The second **THEN** statement (shown above) is not activated because the player character is not touching a blue tile. In other words, the second **IF** statement is false

Now, suppose the player character is moved so it is touching a blue tile and the player presses the space bar. The first **THEN** statement is not activated because the **NOT** operator specifies that the player character cannot be touching a blue tile, which it is. So, the first **IF** statement is false. Instead, the second **THEN** statement is activated because the second **IF** statement is true. The player character performs a super jump and the avatar is changed to the blue flame animation.

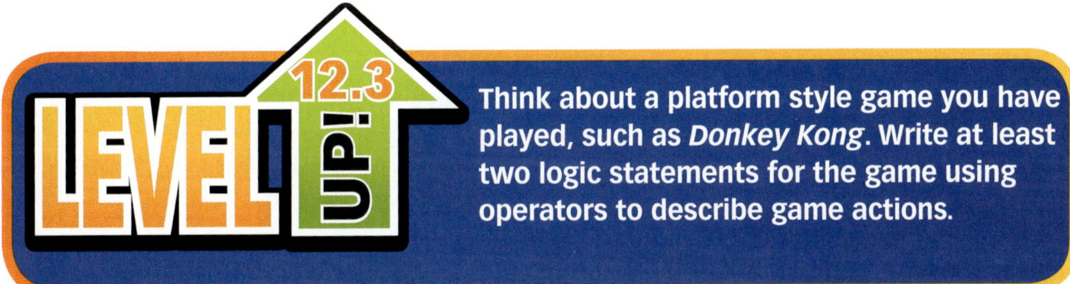

Think about a platform style game you have played, such as *Donkey Kong*. Write at least two logic statements for the game using operators to describe game actions.

Algorithm

An ***algorithm*** is a computer script that performs the steps needed to solve a problem. An algorithm is considered to be *elegant* if it is the simplest, smallest, and most efficient computer code to perform all needed functions. To form an algorithm requires three components: structure, sequence, and iteration.

The first component of an algorithm is structure. ***Structure*** is the syntax and logic form of the programming language. Structure goes beyond pseudo code to include the actual words and symbols organized to make the computer perform as desired.

The second component of an algorithm is sequence. ***Sequence*** is the predetermined order or steps the computer program will follow. Just as outlined in the flowchart, such as the one shown in **Figure 12-9**, the sequence gives order to the instructions needed to get from start to finish.

The third component of an algorithm is iteration. In computer programming, an iteration is a single run through a programming loop. The iteration component controls how long and how often the algorithm will be active.

To better understand what an algorithm is and how these three components combine to create an algorithm, a real-world example of an algorithm might help. Look at the algorithm needed to wash your hair shown in **Figure 12-12.** The algorithm shown to wash hair demonstrates all three components of an algorithm.

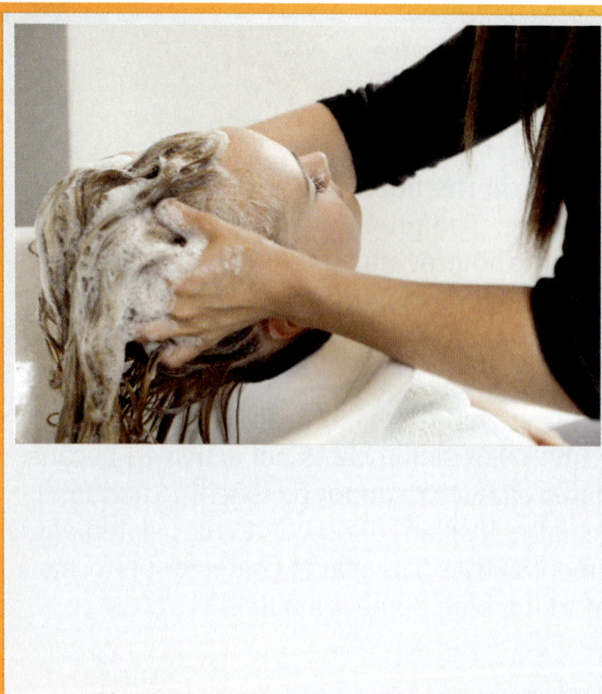

Directions: Wet hair, apply shampoo to hair, lather, rinse, and repeat. After shampooing, apply conditioner to hair, lather, and rinse.

Computer program to wash hair:

```
DECLARE variables—objHair,
objShampoo, objConditioner
DEFINE method subroutines—WET,
APPLY, LATHER, RINSE
Predefined methods—LOOP

WET (objHair)
APPLY (objShampoo, objHair)
LATHER (objShampoo)
RINSE (objHair)
LOOP (1)
APPLY (objConditioner, objHair)
LATHER (objConditioner)
RINSE (objHair)
```

Figure 12-12. This is an algorithm for washing your hair.

Goodheart-Willcox Publisher; image: Tyler Olsen/Shutterstock.com

The structure of the computer program is the declaring of variables, defining methods, and the syntax of how the variables are called by the methods. The sequence is the order required to get the hair shampooed and then conditioned. The steps must be followed in order to get the hair washed. You cannot do the steps out of order or the process will not work. Finally, iteration is demonstrated by the loop command. The instructions required that it be washed twice and conditioned once. The loop was set to 1, which means that the steps above the **LOOP** command will repeat one additional time. There was no **LOOP** command for the set of instructions for the conditioner steps. Without a **LOOP** command, those steps will not repeat and the algorithm ends.

Loops

Programming often requires a loop command. There are four different loop commands common to most languages. These include **LOOP**, **FOR**, **DO WHILE**, and **DO UNTIL**.

The **LOOP** command allows the subroutine to be active for a specific number of iterations. To program a sound effect to repeat three times (play four times), a program would include **LOOP (3)** code. This specifies that the activity will be performed, cycle only three times, and then stop until activated again.

The **FOR** command allows the subroutine to be active for a specific number of times. To program an avatar to have limited super speed when it collides with a speed fruit object, a programmer would include **FOR (90)** code.

The loop will be repeated 90 times. If the program operates at 30 **steps** per second, then the super speed would last for three seconds.

The **DO WHILE** command allows the subroutine to be active only when another condition is active. To program calculating a bonus when using super speed, a **DO WHILE** command would be appropriate. A programmer might write code to have points double when using super speed.

CHEAT CODE: STEPS

When programming, steps refers to how many iterations occur per second. If the steps are set to 20, then the computer will check for interactions every 1/20th of a second. The higher the steps setting, the smoother the game will run. If the steps setting is too high, however, the program will lag as it tries to test each conditional statement in a fraction of a second.

```
DO WHILE (Animation = SuperSpeed)
Bonus = (Points * 2)
```

Note that an asterisk (*) is used for the multiplication symbol. When the super speed animation is over, the bonus stops being calculated.

The **DO UNTIL** command allows the subroutine to be active until another specific interaction takes place. If a programmer wanted to have the avatar in super-size animation until it collided with a minion, then the code might look similar to:

```
DO UNTIL (minion_class, collision)
Animation = Super_Size
```

Different loop commands allow programmers to have limits to special conditions within the program. When the loop ends, the condition would need to be reactivated to start over.

Recursion

Computer logic and use of variables is very similar to mathematics but not an exact match. One of the best examples of this is recursion. Recursion calls a function inside of another function. Take the recursive statement:

```
X = X + 1
```

If you use mathematics to solve for X by subtracting X from each side of the equation, the result is $0 = 1$, which makes no sense. However, recursion can occur in computer programming. It even makes perfect sense.

Look at this snippet of code from the earlier example for calculating score:

```
Sub AddScore(points)
    iSCORE = iSCORE + iPOINTS
```

The variable iSCORE is used as the answer and part of the question. It makes perfect sense that the game score is the sum of current score and new points from a game interaction. This is a recursive statement.

The difference between the mathematical example of $X = X + 1$ and the computer programming example iSCORE = iSCORE + iPOINTS is iteration. The **LOOP** command is not included, so the computer only iterates the action one

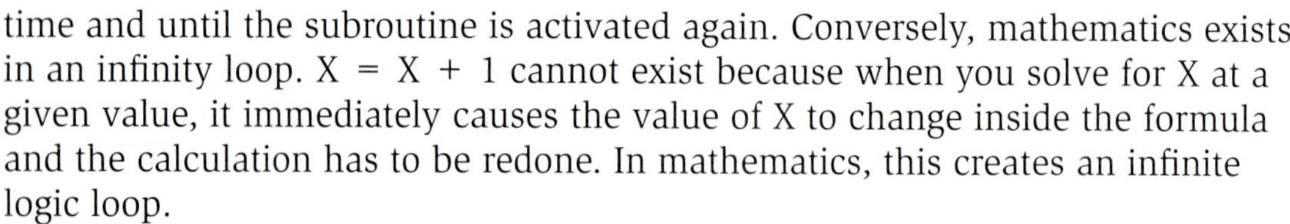

time and until the subroutine is activated again. Conversely, mathematics exists in an infinity loop. X = X + 1 cannot exist because when you solve for X at a given value, it immediately causes the value of X to change inside the formula and the calculation has to be redone. In mathematics, this creates an infinite logic loop.

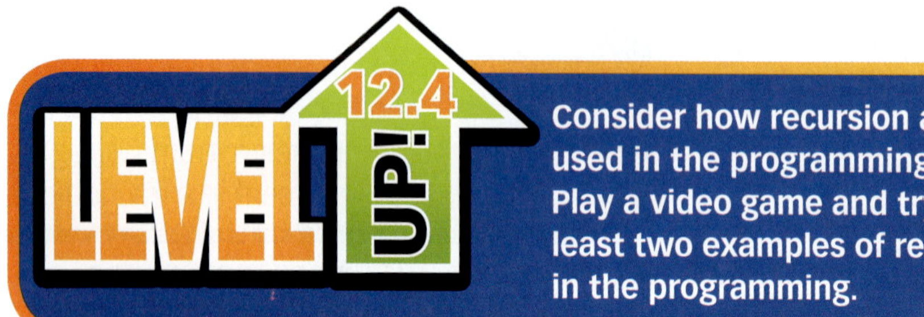

Consider how recursion and loops can be used in the programming for a video game. Play a video game and try to identify at least two examples of recursion and loops in the programming.

Collision Theory

The most common interaction in game programming is a collision. A ***collision*** occurs when one game object touches another game object. A difficult concept for many new game programmers to grasp is that an object that *looks* like a wall does not *act* like a wall unless programmed to do so. Without proper programming, a player character could walk through a wall during gameplay. The computer is displaying images of the objects in pixels and, unless told so, it has no idea if those pixels are supposed to be solid like a wall.

Collision theory for game programming has been borrowed from its meaning in science. In science, collision theory explains how collisions of particle cause reactions. In game programming, collision theory explains how object collisions cause reactions. The key to collision theory in science or game programming is **interactivity.** Physical laws dictate interactivity of one chemical element with another, while game rules dictate interactivity of one object with another object.

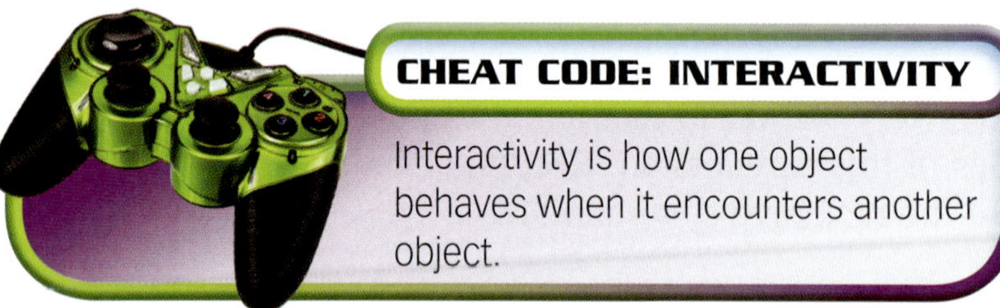

CHEAT CODE: INTERACTIVITY

Interactivity is how one object behaves when it encounters another object.

Players and programmers expect in-game objects to behave like real-world objects. When a dart collides with a balloon, then the balloon should pop. When programming with the concept of collision theory, object properties have to be set to mimic real world objects. If the player character steps on a game object of water, the object must have properties that will present the illusion of water. The player character should sink in the water or be able to float and swim. These settings are part of the physics settings for the game engine. If the player character does not sink in the water, as shown in **Figure 12-13,** then the interaction with the water object does not follow what the player expects. When the player character can walk through a wall, fall through a floor, or is not damaged by an obstacle, the player sees this as a glitch. Every possible interaction in a video game must be properly programmed using collision theory.

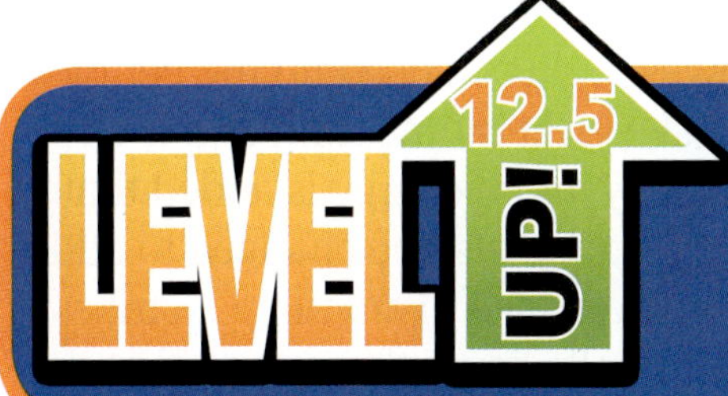

Play one of your favorite video games. Make a list of at least ten interactions within the game. Identify the collision theory for each interaction.

Physics

Physics is the field of science involving the study of matter and motion. In a video game, real-world physics has to be simulated using programming. In the real world, forces like gravity affect the movement of all objects. When you throw a ball on the ground, it bounces over and over, but each time it does not go as high, as shown in **Figure 12-14.** The force of gravity pushes the ball back down. Also, friction from the air and ground causes the ball to slow down as it travels and with each bounce.

Momentum

A cornerstone of physics is momentum, which can be thought of as the energy of movement. In the real world, momentum is calculated:

mass × velocity = momentum

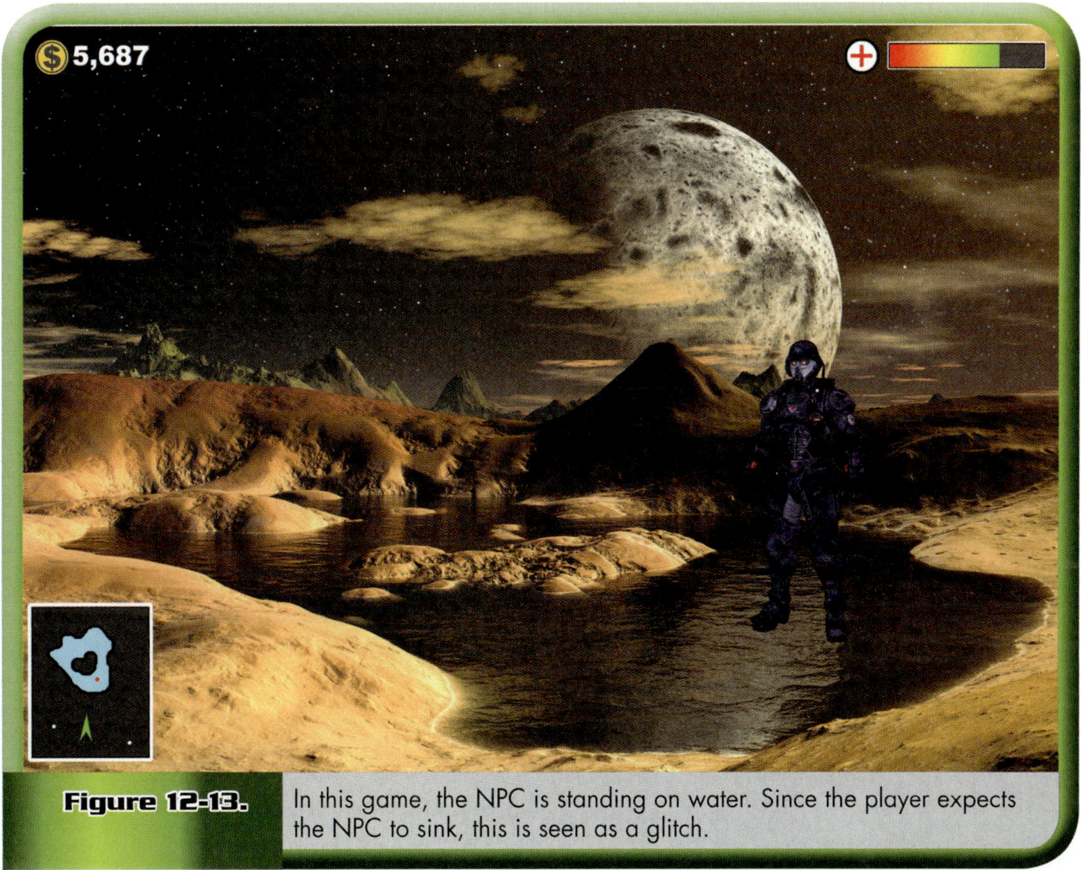

Figure 12-13. In this game, the NPC is standing on water. Since the player expects the NPC to sink, this is seen as a glitch.

Goodheart-Willcox Publisher; images: greglith/Shutterstock.com, diversepixel/Shutterstock.com

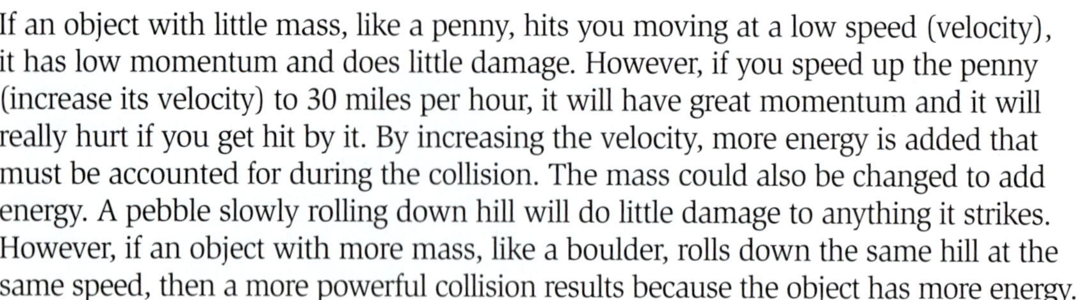

If an object with little mass, like a penny, hits you moving at a low speed (velocity), it has low momentum and does little damage. However, if you speed up the penny (increase its velocity) to 30 miles per hour, it will have great momentum and it will really hurt if you get hit by it. By increasing the velocity, more energy is added that must be accounted for during the collision. The mass could also be changed to add energy. A pebble slowly rolling down hill will do little damage to anything it strikes. However, if an object with more mass, like a boulder, rolls down the same hill at the same speed, then a more powerful collision results because the object has more energy.

Inertia

To create movement, a force must be applied to change the velocity. The law of inertia states that a body at rest will stay at rest unless an unbalanced force is applied. Applied to a car, the law of inertia means the car will stay stopped unless some force is applied to make it move again. For example, the driver uses the engine to make the car move from a stop.

The law of inertia also states that a body at motion will stay in motion unless an unbalanced force is applied. Looking again at the car, if it is moving it will stay in motion until the driver applies the brakes, the friction between the tires and road stops the car, or the driver hits something. This is because the moving car has inertia, just as the stopped car has inertia.

Conservation of Matter and Energy

Another concept of physics deals with the conservation of matter and energy. In a closed system, like a game world or simulation, all energy and mass will remain constant. Conservation of matter means that all of the matter (the "stuff") existing before the collision must exist after the collision or be converted to energy. Conservation of energy means that no energy can be created or destroyed, only changed in form (electrical energy into heat energy, for example). Only when matter is converted to energy, like wood burning in a fire, will the total amount of matter be different from the starting point.

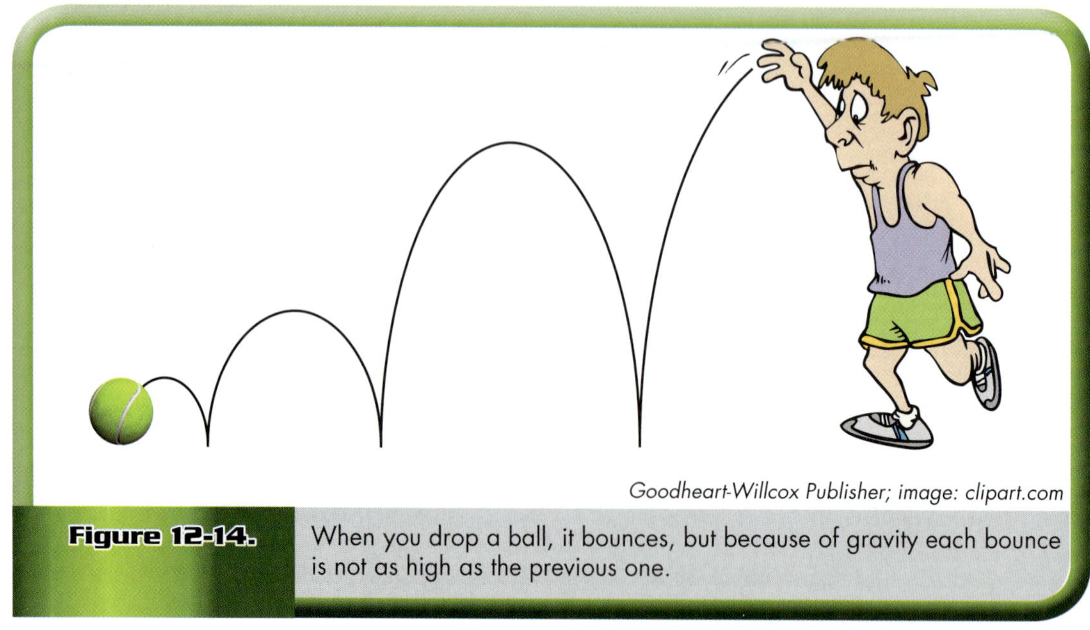

Goodheart-Willcox Publisher; image: clipart.com

Figure 12-14. When you drop a ball, it bounces, but because of gravity each bounce is not as high as the previous one.

So, if you were to weigh two large meteors before they collide, collect all the shattered pieces after the collision, and weigh all of the pieces, the two measured values should be the same, as shown in **Figure 12-15.** However, note that weight and mass are not the same thing. The mass of an object is the same everywhere in space, while weight of an object is based on gravity.

Gravity

Gravity is the force associated with large masses (like planets) that pulls or pushes everything toward the center of the mass. Gravity varies from planet to planet. The gravity on Jupiter is much stronger than on Earth, while the gravity on Mercury is much less. On Earth, when an object is dropped, its downward acceleration due to gravity is 9.81 meters per second per second (9.81 m/s^2).

Acceleration is the rate of change in velocity, or speed, with respect to time and can be positive or negative. For example, if you jump at an acceleration of 9.81 m/s^2 for one second, you would have traveled 9.81 meters or about 32 feet (9.81 m/s^2 for one second equals 9.81 $m/1^2$ or 9.81 m). That is more than a three-story building! Of course, you cannot generate that much upward acceleration without help from a trampoline or other spring.

The ground you are standing on is currently exerting a force equal to the force of gravity acting on your body. When the ground is not holding you up, you fall. This is clearly demonstrated when you step off of the end of a diving board into a swimming pool. You fall into the water, and you do so at an acceleration of 9.81 m/s^2. Additionally, you sink into the water until the buoyancy force on your body is equal to the downward force on your body from gravity. At that point, you stop sinking.

On a jump, once your legs stop providing upward acceleration, you begin to slow down, or *decelerate,* as the acceleration due to gravity counteracts the

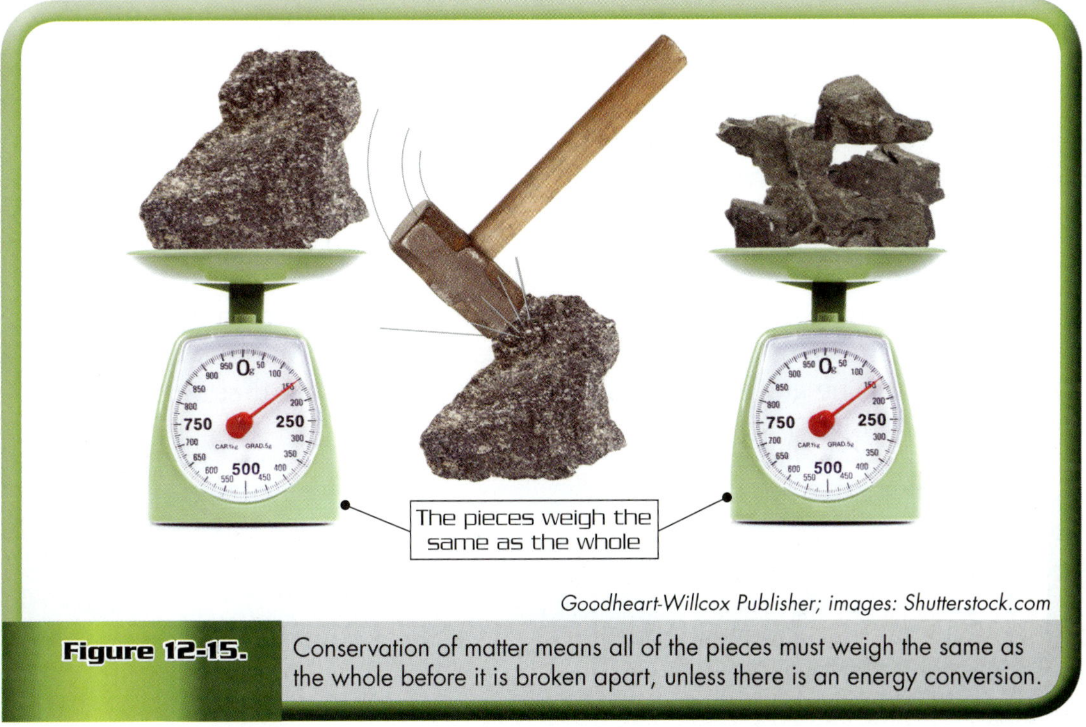

Goodheart-Willcox Publisher; images: Shutterstock.com

Figure 12-15. Conservation of matter means all of the pieces must weigh the same as the whole before it is broken apart, unless there is an energy conversion.

acceleration due to your leg muscles. The instant your feet leave the ground, your muscles are no longer providing acceleration, and you start slowing down. You decelerate until your speed, or velocity, reaches zero.

When your speed reaches zero, you will start to fall as gravity pulls you toward Earth. During your fall back to Earth, you have a negative speed in relation to your starting point. Gravity pulls you back to Earth in the same amount of time it took you to reach the top of your jump. It is important to note that in the real world, the speed is positive as you move up from Earth and negative as you move down. In most video games, the speed to move toward the top of the screen is negative and the speed to move toward the bottom of the screen is positive because –Y is up and +Y is down.

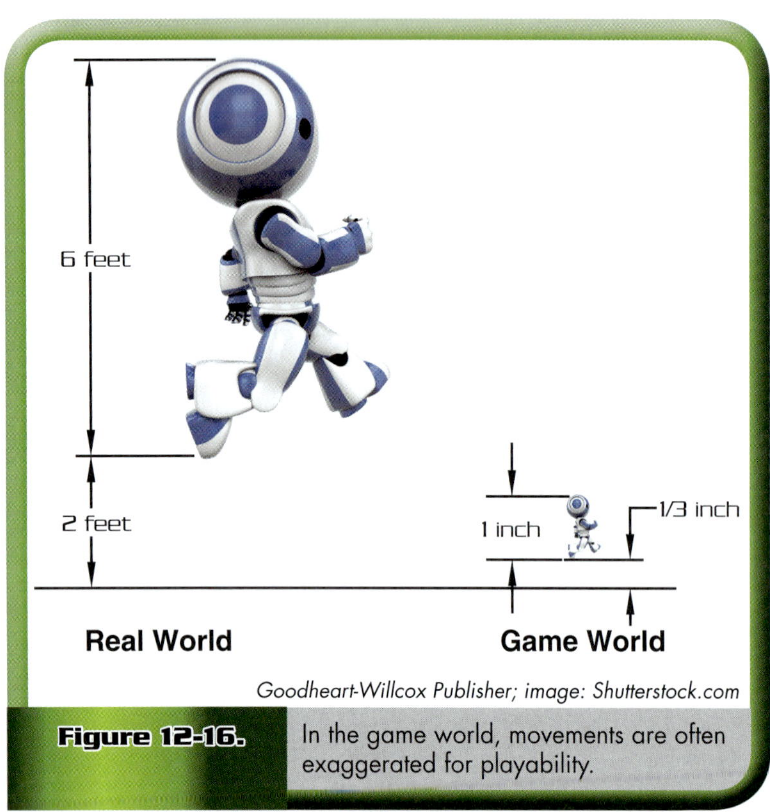

Goodheart-Willcox Publisher; image: Shutterstock.com

Figure 12-16. In the game world, movements are often exaggerated for playability.

In the virtual world, gravity needs to be programmed to provide the same function as Earth's gravity, although the force and acceleration may not be the same. Usually, game designers give the player the ability to jump very high in comparison to real-world physics. In platform games, for example, designers have to give the player a large leaping ability to clear obstacles. Because of the screen size, the player character may be displayed one inch tall, for example. In this case, a leap of two feet high in the real world would only be 1/3 of an inch, as shown in **Figure 12-16.** That is only slightly greater than the height of the capital letter in this sentence. In a video game, that small of a jump would not be noticed. Additionally, the obstacles would need to be very small in order for the player character to jump over them.

In a *Mario* platform game, the obstacles are almost the same size as Mario himself. Mario must have the ability to jump more than his own height to get on the next platform or over an obstacle. That is because Mario is jumping in "Mario world." The gravity in a game world can differ from that on Earth.

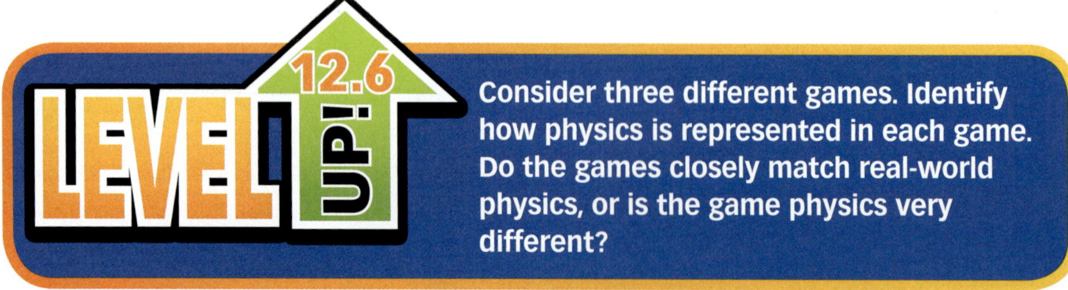

Consider three different games. Identify how physics is represented in each game. Do the games closely match real-world physics, or is the game physics very different?

Chapter Summary

- Programmers use either machine language or programming language; syntax is the programming words and symbols and their arrangement.
- Computer programs work with data, which may come from user input or from stored locations within the program; data are what the computer program operates on to produce an end result.
- The operators used in logic statements are **IF**, **THEN**, **AND**, **OR**, **NOT**, **NOR**, and **ELSE**.
- An algorithm is a computer script that performs the steps needed to solve a problem; components of an algorithm are structure, sequence, and iteration.
- The basics of collision theory is the **IF**...**THEN** statement.
- Physics is the field of science involving the study of matter and motion; in a video game, real-world physics (such as momentum, inertia, and gravity) has to be simulated using programming.

Check Your Video Game IQ

Now that you have finished this chapter, see what you know about video game design by taking the chapter posttest.

www.m.g-wlearning.com
www.g-wlearning.com

Review Your Knowledge

On a separate sheet of paper or in a word processing document, match the following terms with the definition that fits best.

A. class variable	F. instance variable
B. global	G. local
C. string	H. float
D. object	I. attribute
E. action	J. method

1. The actions or verbs used in syntax.
2. An umbrella device that contains a nonspecific type of item and on which operations can be performed.
3. Characteristics associated with an object.
4. A subroutine or variable that works everywhere in the program.
5. The decimal point that must be accounted for in any decimal computation.
6. A series of letters, numbers, or punctuation.
7. A subroutine or variable that does not have persistence outside of the module in which it was declared.
8. Definition subroutines that are defined by their attributes and properties.

9. A single type of item.
10. How an object reacts to input or interacts with other objects.

On a separate sheet of paper or in a word processing document, answer each of the following questions.

11. Which computer language is used by the CPU?
12. What defines programming objects?
13. Which type of variable would be used to store “Good Morning”?
14. Compare and contrast global variables and local variables.
15. How is parallel operation different from series operation?
16. Write an **IF...THEN** logic statement in pseudo code for when the player presses the up arrow key that the player character will climb a ladder.
17. Which logic operator is used to join two actions so they will occur at the same time?
18. List the three requirements to construct an algorithm.
19. Compare and contrast the **LOOP** command with the **FOR** command.
20. Give the formula for real-world momentum.

Apply Your STEM Knowledge

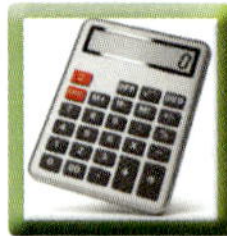

Mathematics

1. Calculate the number of bits in the following file sizes. There are eight bits in one byte.

File Size	Bits
14.7 kilobytes	
58 bytes	
11.37 megabytes	
14 gigabytes	
1.76 terabytes	

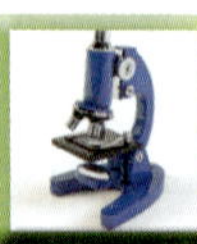

Science

2. Gravity is based on the mass of the body, such as the mass of the planet. Research the planets in the solar system and determine what the acceleration due to gravity is on each planet.

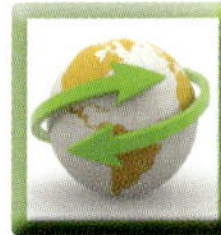

Social Studies

3. Games like *Angry Birds* and *Dirt Bike* that use physics as a primary feature of the gameplay are very popular. Research current games that use physics as a primary feature of the gameplay. Create a 25-slide PowerPoint presentation to list five of the most popular physics gameplay games. Add slides to show screen shots of the physics used in each game. List the sales data for each game and try to find demographic data about the users. Describe why you think each game is entertaining to so many people.

Language Arts

4. Research the newest technology used to create game physics in popular games. Write a one-page paper to explain how new technology is improving the realism of game physics.

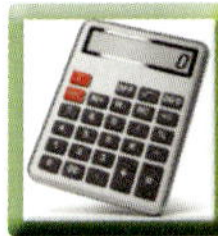

Mathematics

5. Using spreadsheet or word processing software, create the table shown below. Then, complete the table.

Momentum	Mass	Velocity
27 pound feet/second		3 feet/second
50.75 ounce inch/second	14.5 ounces	
	2.8 pounds	4.7 feet/second
	2.7 tons	12.05 miles/second
43.95 ounce feet/second		11.74 feet/second

Working in Teams

Work with the team as assigned by your teacher. Your team has been chosen to work on an educational game about the human body. The human body functions using a module system. Each system, such as the circulatory, respiration, digestive, and muscular systems, has a set of controls to monitor and regulate the system. As a team, research the system you have been assigned. Create a flowchart for each biological module.

Gamer Portfolio

Your portfolio should not only showcase your academic accomplishments, but the technical skills you have. Working in the video game design industry requires a high level of technical aptitude. Do you have any software or hardware certifications? Technical skills are very important. Interviewers will want to know what talents and skills you have.

1. Write a paper that describes the technical skills you have acquired. Describe the skill, your level of competence, and any other information that will showcase your skill level.
2. Save the document file in your e-portfolio folder. Create a subfolder named Skills. Save each a document for each skill with the file names Skills01, Skills02, and so on.
3. Place a printed copy in your container for your print portfolio.

G-W Learning Mobile Site

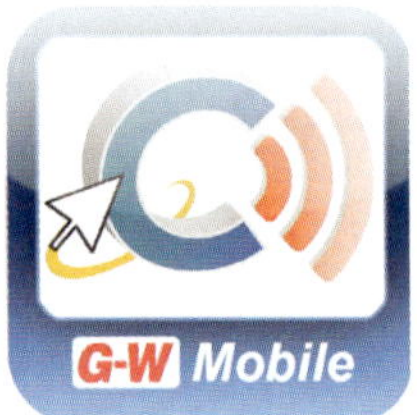

Visit the G-W Learning mobile site to complete the chapter pretest and posttest and to practice vocabulary using e-flash cards. If you do not have a smartphone, visit the G-W Learning companion website to access these features.

G-W Learning mobile site: www.m.g-wlearning.com
G-W Learning companion website: www.g-wlearning.com

Common Core

College and Career Readiness

CTE Career Ready Practices. The ability to read and interpret information is an important workplace skill. Presume you work for a video game design studio. Your interpersonal skills—your ability to listen, speak, and empathize—are a great asset in working with outside contractors. Lilly is an artist working as a freelancer for your studio. She has a question about the appearance of a character she is designing. Select three attributes of a character and describe them in detail to Lilly.

Reading. Research information on the ratings of the most popular computer programming language. What is the highest rated programming language? Do all sources rate the languages the same? What factors are used to determine "the best" programming language? Do different sources use different criteria and choose different programs as best? Write a report in which you analyze the strengths and weakness of the top programming languages, using information from your research and this text. Present your findings to the class.

Speaking and Listening. Research the features of some of the common high-level programming languages. Compile information about the aspects of each language that, in your opinion, makes it easy to use. Look for information about the use of words, symbols, or built-in methods versus custom methods.

Use this information, along with what you may already know about a programming language, to create a list of the features of an ideal programming language. Using various elements (visual displays, written handouts, technological displays), present your ideal high-level language to the class. Explain why you chose the features you did.

Event Prep: Day of the Event

No matter what competitive events you will participate in for a Career and Technical Student Organization (CTSO), you will have to be well organized and prepared. Of course, you will have studied the content exhaustively before the event, but you also have to prepare by making sure all the tools you need for the event or to travel to the event are taken care of. Finalizing all the details well in advance of an event will decrease stress and leave you free to concentrate on the event itself. To prepare for a competition:

1. Pack appropriate clothing, which includes proper shoes and undergarments.
2. Prepare all technological resources, including anything that you might need to prepare or compete. Double check to make sure that any presentation material that is saved electronically is on media compatible with the machines at the event.
3. If the event calls for visuals, make sure you have them prepared in advance, packed, and ready to take with you.
4. Bring registration materials, including a valid form of identification.
5. Bring study materials, including the flash cards and other materials you have used to study for the event. If note cards are acceptable when making a presentation, make sure your notes are complete and easy to read. Have a back up set in case of an emergency.
6. At least two weeks before you go to the competition, create a checklist of what you need for the event. Include every detail down to a pencil or pen. Then use this checklist before you go into the presentation so that you do not forget anything.

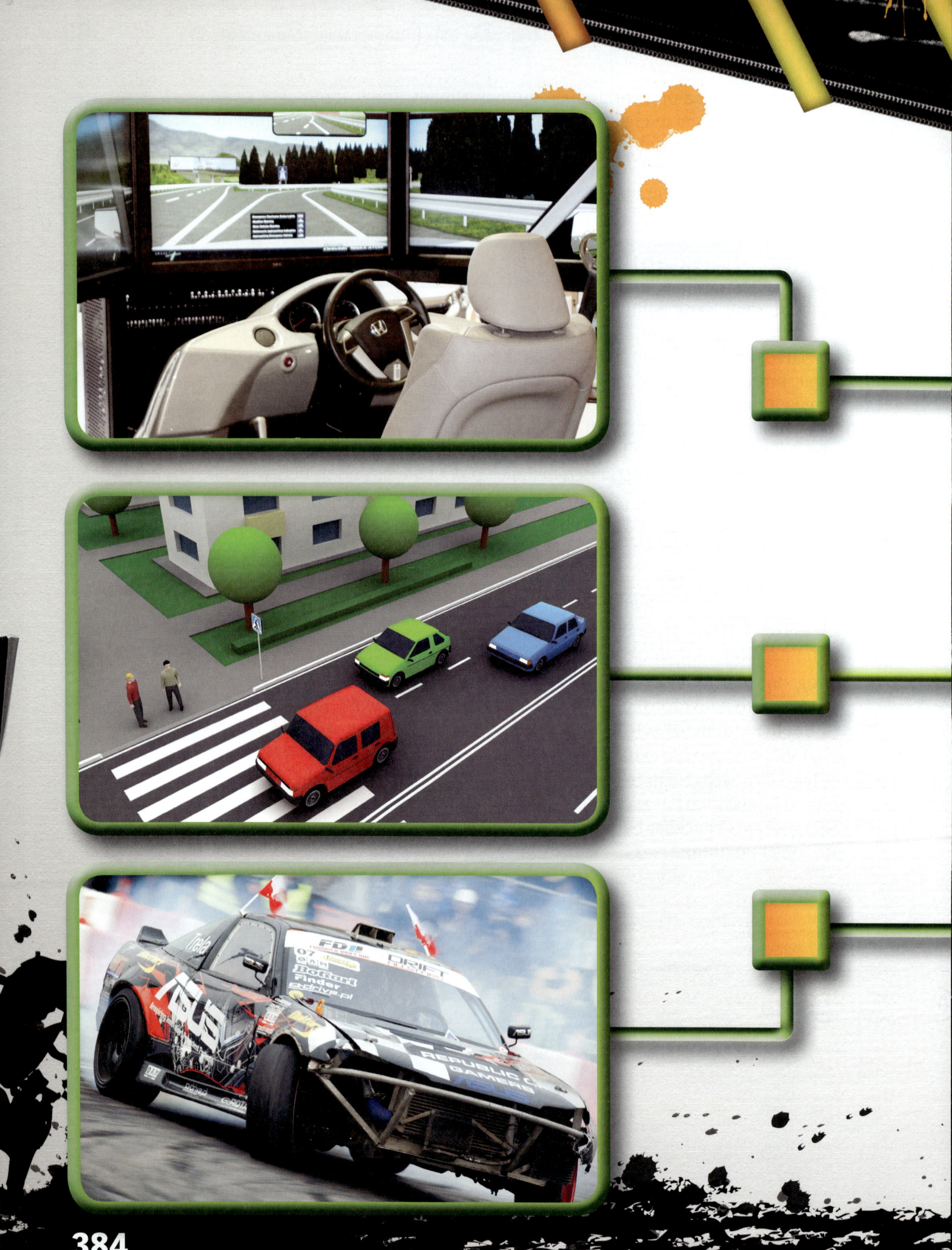
Bottari
Finder

Chapter 13
Simulation Composition

Game designers often find employment in the field of digital simulation. Both game design and simulation design involve digital art, programming, and world creation. Simulations are undertaken for crime scenes, car accidents, and similar events to determine how the real-world event might have occurred. In other cases, a simulation is created to test a scenario that has not happened. A flight or driving simulation allows for the user to test the controls and systems of devices without needing to build or crash a vehicle. This chapter will highlight the means of creating a simulation and how to repurpose your skills as a game designer for simulation design.

Check Your Video Game IQ

Before you begin this chapter, see what you already know about video game design by taking the chapter pretest.

www.m.g-wlearning.com

www.g-wlearning.com

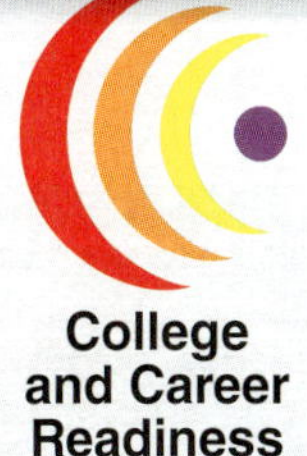

College and Career Readiness

Reading Prep. In preparation for this chapter, research the various uses of simulations. As you are reading the chapter, keep in mind the information you learn from your research.

Objectives

After completing this chapter, you will be able to:

- Compare and contrast simulations and video games.
- Describe the components of a simulation.
- Identify the classifications of simulations.
- Outline how the purposes of a simulation determine what to include in a simulation.
- Summarize applied event modeling.
- Define the iterative design process.
- Consider the importance of understanding the application framework.

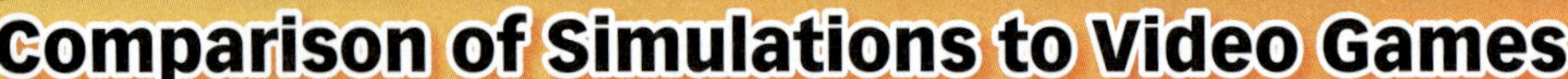

Comparison of Simulations to Video Games

A virtual ***simulation*** attempts to replicate a real-world situation, as shown in **Figure 13-1.** The purpose of a simulation is to find an answer to a real-world problem. To do this, many observations and data recordings must take place. Each of the variables that could alter the situation, called ***parameters,*** must be taken into consideration for the simulation to perform correctly. If the simulation is of flying a paper airplane, the parameters would be wind vector, wind speed, throwing angle, throwing speed, wing shape, and so on. The parameters of a simulation are very specific and may be numerous.

A video game may have only a few parameters. The game has only the parameters needed to create a playable entertainment object. The same object in a simulation must include all parameters that may influence the object in real life. In the case of a paper airplane, parameters for different paper and materials used, plane design, aerodynamics, weight, balance, altitude, humidity, and many more could be needed for a true simulation.

A simulation may have less detailed graphics than a video game. While a 3D perspective is normal for a simulation, the graphics and textures are typically of much lower quality than a similar object in a game. There are four reasons for the reduced quality graphics:

- focus is on function, not appearance
- reduce computer resources needed for graphic processing
- better representation of data
- reduced cost of developing graphics

The objective of a simulation is to produce a situation or event. The focus is on how things work and not how things look. Few textured graphics are used. Most objects will have solid surface colors applied. The colors provide contrast between objects, but may not be visually appealing or even appropriate in terms of realism. An example of this is shown in **Figure 13-2.**

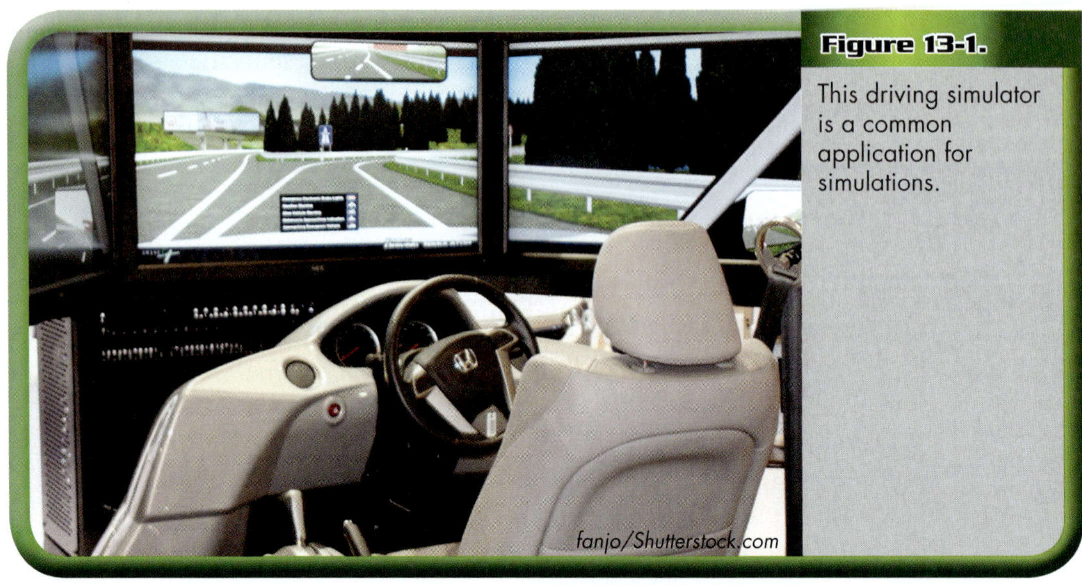

Figure 13-1. This driving simulator is a common application for simulations.

fanjo/Shutterstock.com

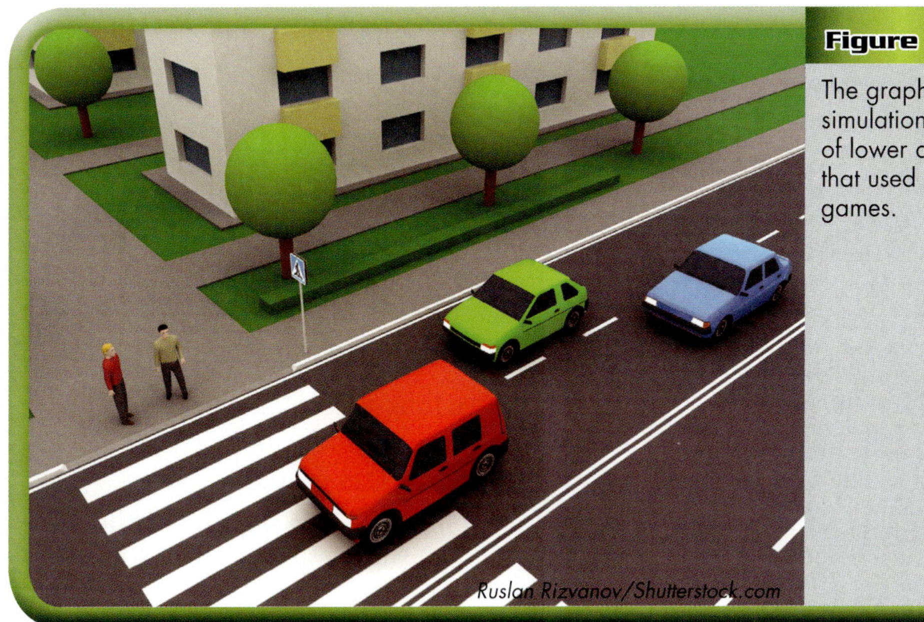

Figure 13-2.

The graphics in a simulation are often of lower quality than that used in video games.

Using lower-resolution graphics allows more computer power to be dedicated to processing parameters. A simulation will have hundreds or thousands of parameters to track. Most of the processing power of the computer must be reserved for computing these variables. Adding a high quality texture to the object may substantially slow the movement and processing for the simulation.

Many simulations contain wireframe or semitransparent objects. These see-through objects allow more information and interaction to be seen. Additionally, the simulation may use colors to represent levels of heat or stress on areas of the object. For example, red may be used to show a hot spot or point of high stress, as shown in **Figure 13-3.** Dark blue may be used to show areas of normal temperature or low stress. These visual data will help the viewer interpret data better than a detailed texture that realistically shows the object.

Using lower-quality graphics is also a way to reduce the cost of the simulation. Money is required to have an artist create and wrap a texture onto an object. If a textured graphic adds little or no value to the simulation, then it is just a waste of time and money to create. The money that would have been spent to create a detailed graphic is better spent on accurately modeling the data in the simulation.

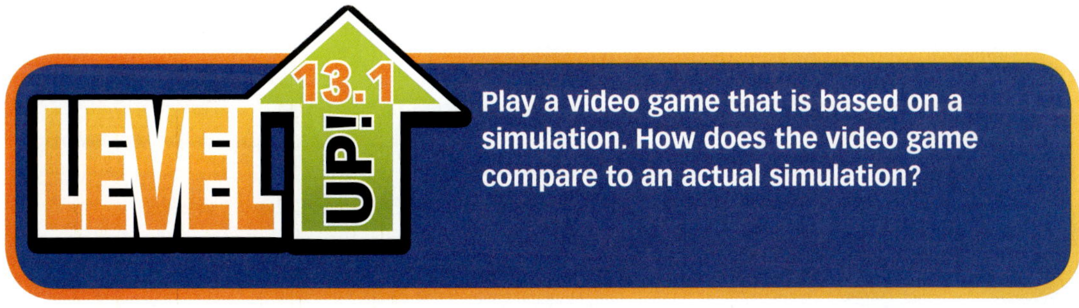

Play a video game that is based on a simulation. How does the video game compare to an actual simulation?

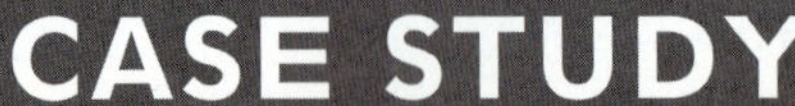

Crowd Funding

A great way to get attention and funding for a new game project is through crowd funding. Crowd funding is a new way for people to get startup capital for their creative projects or companies. It is usually done through the Internet on a website like KickStarter.com or Indiegogo.com, as shown below. Everyday people like yourself and high-powered investors alike can log on to a crowd funding website and pledge an amount of money to invest in a project. The idea behind crowd funding is that finding many investors to contribute small amounts of money is easier than finding one or two investors to contribute large amounts of money.

Crowd funding is a form of equity financing. It became legal under the JOBS Act signed by President Obama on April 5, 2012. Investors in these projects should take the time to read about the project before making a pledge. With a pledge, an investor will receive some sort of perk or benefits from the company.

Many very exciting video game concepts can be found on a crowd funding website. Sometimes these ideas generate a lot of interest. This interest can catch the attention of a major game studio or publisher. A startup company with great game ideas that generate a lot of interest might be something a big company will invest in, hire, or purchase.

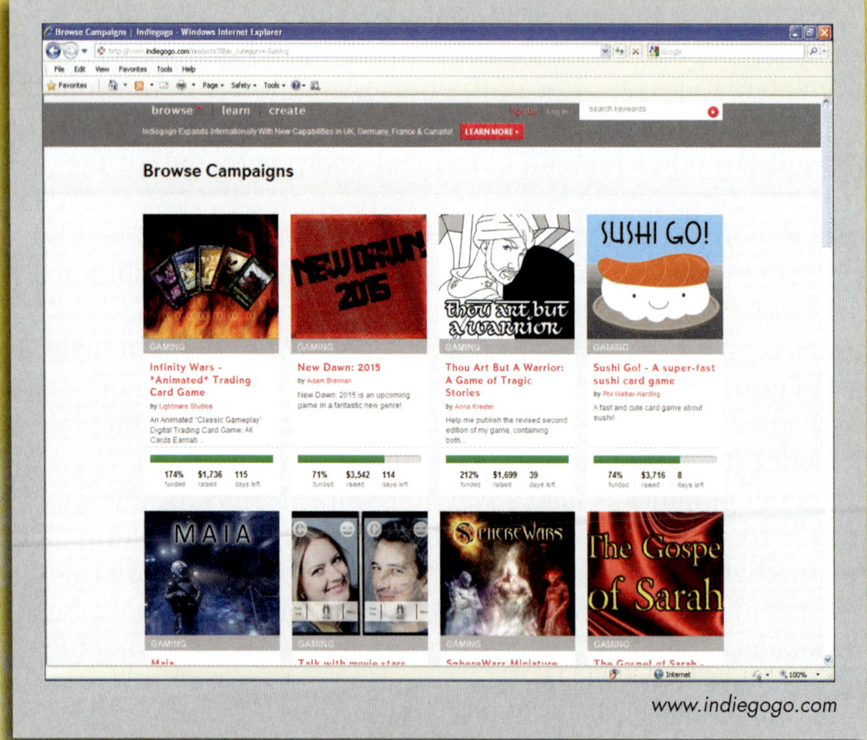

www.indiegogo.com

Green Gamer

Video game equipment is considered electronic waste. Electronic waste should be properly disposed of, not just placed in the trash, due to components that may be toxic. Video game equipment can also be donated to charities for refurbishing.

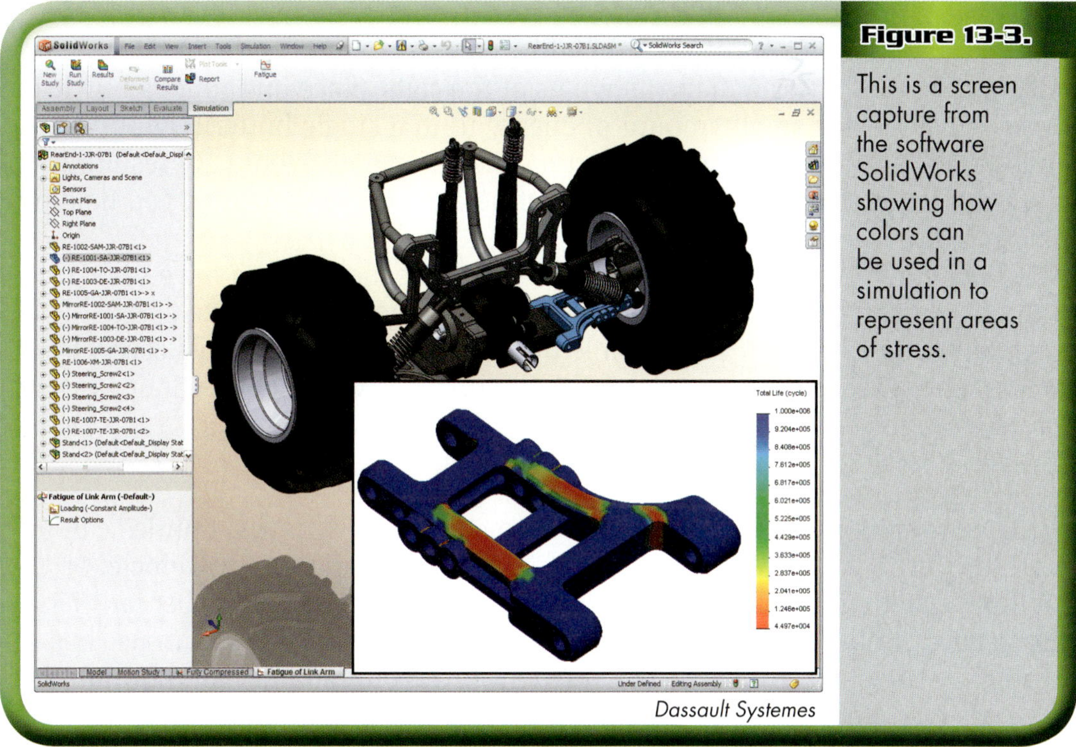

Dassault Systemes

Figure 13-3. This is a screen capture from the software SolidWorks showing how colors can be used in a simulation to represent areas of stress.

Simulation Components

Creating a simulation requires a workflow very similar to that of a video game. In addition, creating a simulation requires special attention to the system, entities, and events.

System

The system for a simulation is like a virtual **ecosystem.** The ***system*** controls all of the parameters and constraints to make the simulation work. Behind all of the images and objects that can be seen by the user are very complex mathematical equations used by the program to control every part of the simulation. The system also records data for analysis.

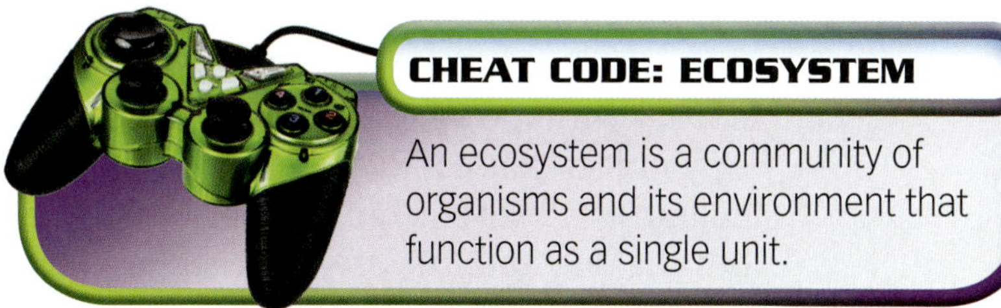

CHEAT CODE: ECOSYSTEM

An ecosystem is a community of organisms and its environment that function as a single unit.

For example, a scientific simulation on global warming may test what happens if ocean temperature rises over time. The simulation system would record the changes to parameters. Scientists could replay the simulation to determine the effect of temperature rise on different land masses and ice sheets. A complex knowledge of the Earth and the ocean currents needs to be translated into a simulation system to get accurate results. So far, global weather has proven difficult to model due to the number of possible influences, or parameters, of the system. Leaving out just one parameter could result in an inaccurate simulation of the real world. This effect has been called the butterfly effect.

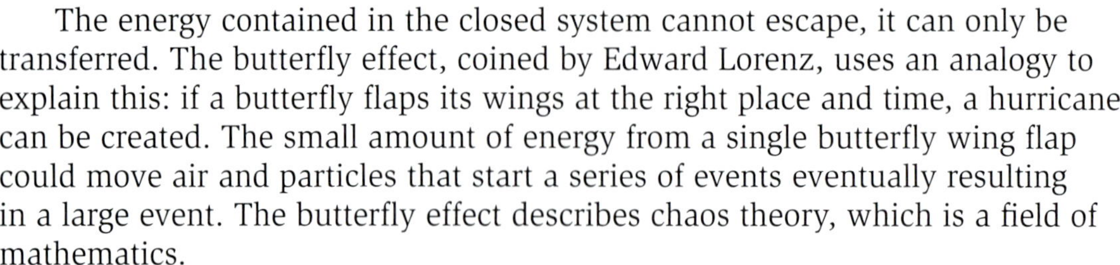

The energy contained in the closed system cannot escape, it can only be transferred. The butterfly effect, coined by Edward Lorenz, uses an analogy to explain this: if a butterfly flaps its wings at the right place and time, a hurricane can be created. The small amount of energy from a single butterfly wing flap could move air and particles that start a series of events eventually resulting in a large event. The butterfly effect describes chaos theory, which is a field of mathematics.

Chaos theory is why the simulations for hurricane tracking have several different forecast models. Each simulation uses different parameters and constraints to best match the possible track of a hurricane. In most cases, a forecast simulation can come close, but the uncertainty of many parameters still leaves room for the butterfly effect.

Entities

The "thinking" components of a system are called ***entities.*** Entities can be anything in the system, such as a person, insect, bacteria, robot, vehicle, or anything else that can be given artificial intelligence (AI). Remember, artificial intelligence is not real thought. It is a series of algorithms a programmer has created for the entity to react to interaction. If the programmer did not think of a possible interaction and program a reaction to it, then the entity will ignore that interaction. Most AI involves use of perception, navigation, and motivation.

Perception

The perception component of AI is the ways in which the entity obtains information from its environment. A human has perception through the five senses of seeing, hearing, touching, tasting, and smelling. Other entities, such as robots, might have perception components for magnetism, electro sensory, pressure sensory, or something else.

Video game designers will likely focus on the sense of sight for an entity. A line of sight can be easily programmed. By creating a cone shape and placing it level with the eyes of a character, the basic cone of vision can be simulated. Any object that collides with the cone would be programmed as visible to the character. Refer to **Figure 13-4.** In that example, the cat is visible to the entity, but the dog and tree are not visible. The cone of vision would move with the direction of the entity's eyes.

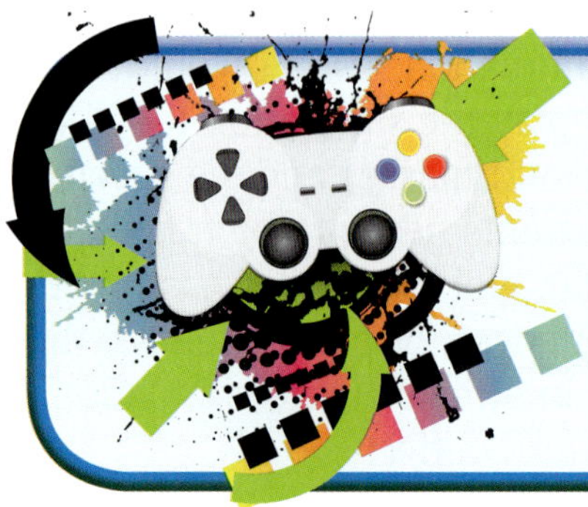

Ethical Gamer

Distorting information for your own gain is an unethical practice. Honesty, accuracy, and truthfulness should guide all reviews of games. Do not take credit for ideas that belong to someone else; always credit your sources.

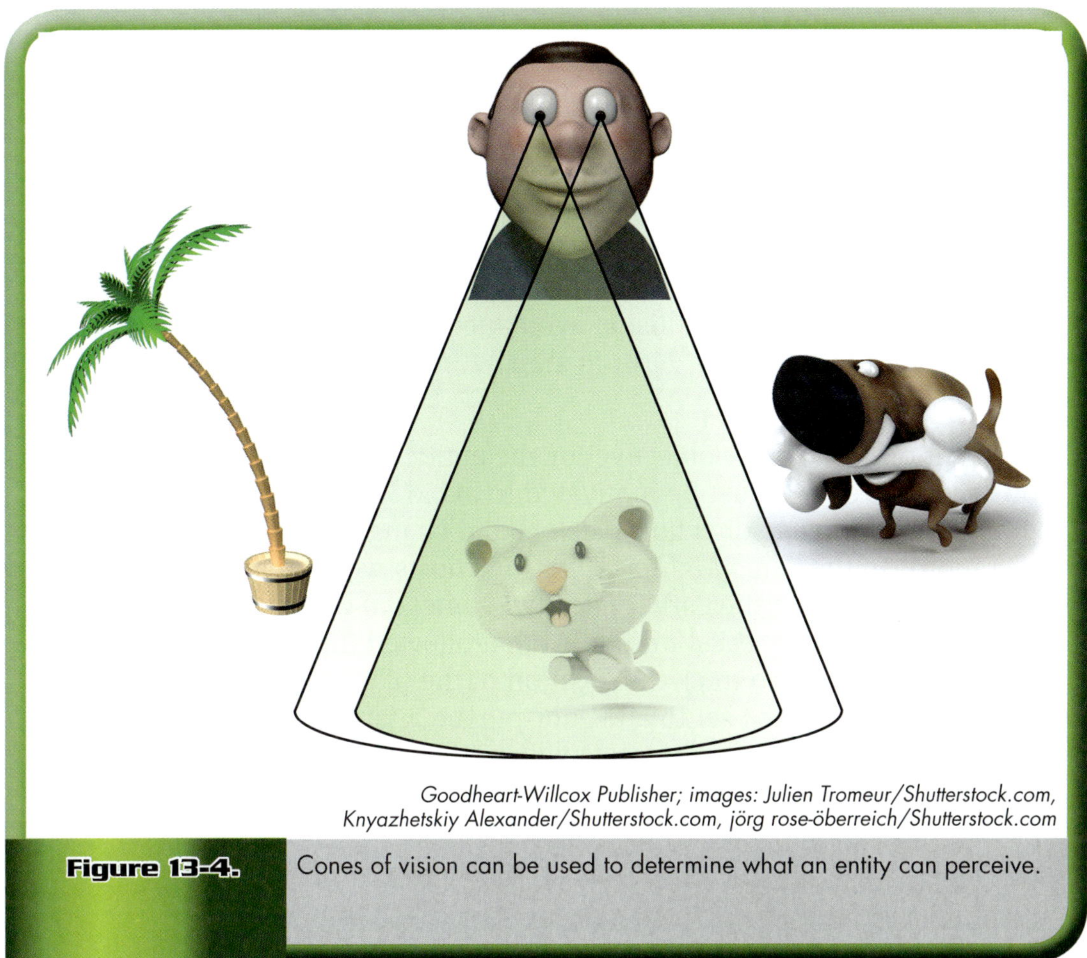

Goodheart-Willcox Publisher; images: Julien Tromeur/Shutterstock.com, Knyazhetskiy Alexander/Shutterstock.com, jörg rose-öberreich/Shutterstock.com

Figure 13-4. Cones of vision can be used to determine what an entity can perceive.

The sense of hearing can be accomplished in a similar fashion. A cone of hearing can be created for each ear and a sound radius for another object. Each time the dog barks, for example, the sound radius appears. If the sound radius collides with the cone of hearing, then the entity would perceive the sound. A smell or touch sensory model can be created for an entity using a similar process.

These visual interpretations of other senses can accurately show a programmer when an entity can perceive other entities or objects. When complete, the programmer need only set the objects such as the cone of vision to be fully transparent. For beginner and intermediate programmers, it works very well and is easy to debug. This simple visual model for other senses can be replaced with more complex mathematical models. The complexity of the sensory model depends on how closely the sense must simulate the real world.

An advanced means of simulating sound perception can be achieved using a particle system. The particles could bounce off of surfaces such as walls the same way sound would travel. The particle system could even produce an echo if reflected back to the entity. This same particle system could produce more than one particle of sound to simulate different sound frequencies and volume. It could have some particles that bounce off of objects and others that pass through them based on density settings. This would reproduce the faint sounds heard through a window or door.

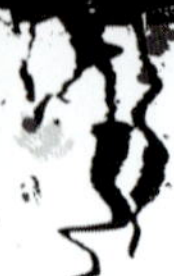

Navigation

Navigation is the ability of an entity to move about, avoid obstacles, and reach a goal. A human has legs. When a human sees a wall, he or she would move toward an open space to keep walking. A programmer could allow an entity to find its way through a complex maze by having the entity look ahead and move toward an opening in the maze when the forward path is blocked by a wall. This is shown in **Figure 13-5.** When the entity reaches a dead end, it could be programmed to turn around. These types of commands allow simple entity navigation known as collision avoidance. With ***collision avoidance,*** the entity tries not to hit items or have to stop.

Motivation

Motivation is a goal or objective for the entity. When the entity perceives an obstacle, the entity must be motivated to avoid it. The entity would have programming to change direction (vector) and change speed (velocity and acceleration). In the game *Ms. Pac-Man,* the ghosts were programmed to pursue the player character. In the earlier *Pac-Man* game, the ghosts followed a static path. The ghosts in *Ms. Pac-Man* had AI that allowed them to alter their paths and change directions to track the location of the player character.

An entity can also be set to attack or pursue a target. In a scientific simulation of how an antibody reacts with certain bacteria, an antibody entity would be programmed to pursue and attack bacteria. The programmer would

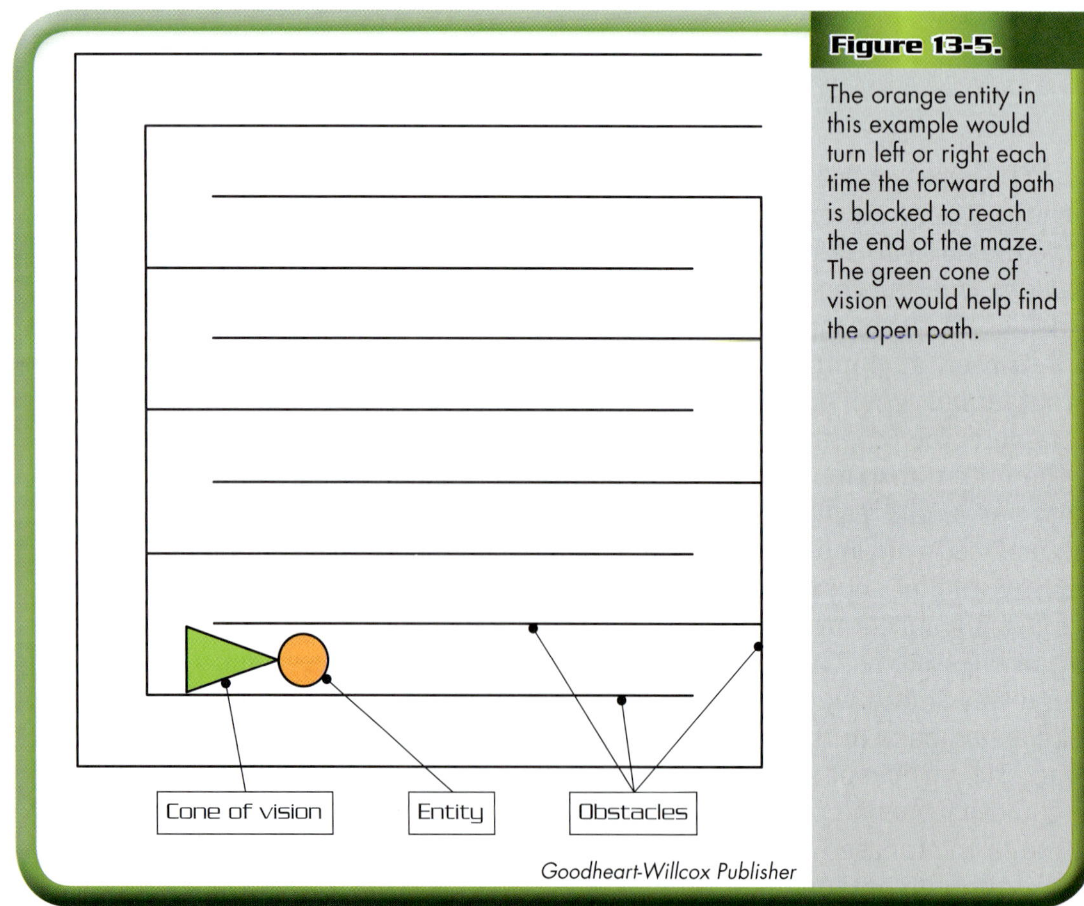

Goodheart-Willcox Publisher

Figure 13-5. The orange entity in this example would turn left or right each time the forward path is blocked to reach the end of the maze. The green cone of vision would help find the open path.

have to program the antibody to accelerate to catch the bacteria and set the vector to pursue in the direction of the bacteria.

In a complex simulation, an algorithm for motivation needs to include **weighted** priority for targets. This type of algorithm would assign a weighting value for each type of enemy or goal and compute the distance to target along with strength and other factors. In this way, an entity would be able to choose the best option if two or more enemies or goals are perceived. The total weighting and programming for AI can be very complex.

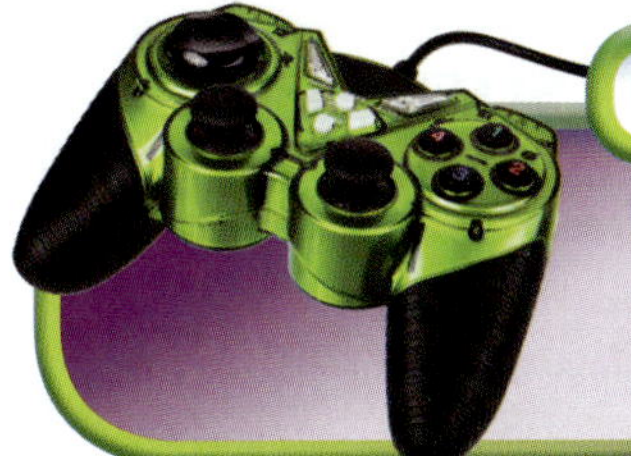

CHEAT CODE: WEIGHTED

Weighted means an increased or decreased statistical likelihood is assigned.

In cases such as flocks and swarms, AI might be programmed to stay close to other similar entities. A school of fish would be programmed to match the velocity and vector of the fish closest to itself. A general dynamic of the swarm would be to move as a mass and not individuals. A central control object is programmed as the center of the swarm. That control object moves the entire swarm as a particle system. Many animation programs such as Maya, 3ds Max, Rhinoceros, or Panda 3D include a behavioral animation setting in the particle system. This movement can be imported into the simulation for quick construction.

Events

An event is an occurrence that may change the state of the system. The state of a system is the collection of parameter values and the results that describe the system at a given time, such as when the system is first set up. An event is anything that causes the parameter values or results to change.

For example, in the simulation of a vehicle's engine, the engine might be running smoothly at 3,000 revolutions per minute (RPM). An event for this simulation might be changing the parameters to simulate rain or high humidity. This event may change the performance of the engine system. The new state of the system may be running smoothly at 2,800 RPM. The data change from the rain event suggest that rain causes a reduction in performance of the engine by 200 RPM. There are six basic states of a simulation, as described in **Figure 13-6.**

Simulation Model	Description
Static	The state of the system remains constant.
Dynamic	The state of the system changes.
Deterministic	No random variables in parameters.
Stochastic	Uses random variables in parameters.
Continuous	Allows continuous state changes over time.
Discrete	Allows only state changes at points where events occur.

Figure 13-6. When constructing an event model, it is important to choose the best type of simulation model.

Goodheart-Willcox Publisher

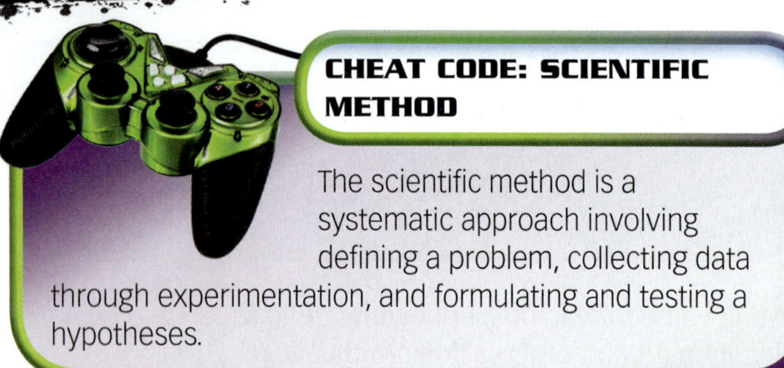

CHEAT CODE: SCIENTIFIC METHOD

The scientific method is a systematic approach involving defining a problem, collecting data through experimentation, and formulating and testing a hypotheses.

In event modeling, the **scientific method** will yield the most valuable and accurate data. For that reason, a discrete-event simulation is the most popular event model. The ***discrete-event simulation*** tests a system by changing variable parameters at instantaneous points. This method best isolates the results of an event to a system, as summarized in **Figure 13-7.** By changing only a single variable during the simulation, the discrete-event simulation produces results that can confirm or deny the effects of that change. Many experiments can be quickly completed to test single variables on a system using a discrete-event simulation.

Discrete-event simulations are the ultimate "what if" testing platform. By changing a single variable, each event can be retested many times to evaluate the impact of changing each parameter. In human development, this type of learning is called heuristics. ***Heuristics*** is the process of making predictions based on past events, or learning by trial and error. A discrete-event simulation allows for many errors to be safely and quickly tested.

However, a discrete-event simulation is not always the best choice for event modeling. Many systems are actually the combination of partly discrete and partly continuous systems. A continuous system, like an airplane in flight, has many variable parameters that change. Throughout the flight of an airplane, temperature, altitude, wind vector, wind speeds, clouds, and coverage are a few variables that continuously change. When an event is modeled to simulate a severe weather

Scientific Method	Function	Event Modeling Example
Purpose	State the problem.	Engine power decreases in bad weather.
Research	Find out information on the topic.	Engine requires fuel and air mixture for combustion; weather conditions change ability of fuel to mix in air.
Hypothesis	Predict the outcome of a problem.	Engine performance will decrease when humidity increases.
Experiment	Procedures to test hypothesis.	Construct engine simulation to test humidity parameters.
Analysis	Record the results of the experiment.	Engine RPM decreased by 200 RPM at 100% humidity.
Conclusion	Compare hypothesis to data results.	Results confirm that engine performance is decreased as humidity increases.

Figure 13-7. The six elements of the scientific method are outlined in this table.

Goodheart-Willcox Publisher

condition, there are many variables changing at once. The pilot has to react to many different changes and situations that are part of the storm. Many parameters of the flying airplane system will be changing over a short period of time.

Dynamic and continuous event modeling typically involve a human operator that is interacting with the system. In many of these simulations, the human operator attempts to correct dynamic and continuous events to keep the system in a static state. In the example of flying an airplane, the storm event occurs and the pilot tries to keep the airplane in a static, level-flight state. Even with all of the buzzers sounding, lights blinking, lightning flashing, and more, the human operator uses skill to maintain a static state for the system.

The use of a human-in-the-loop simulation helps develop learning and skill for the user. A ***human-in-the-loop (HITL) simulation*** refers to any simulation that has a real human user as part of the event model. A very complex set of parameters and rules need to be constructed for any HITL event modeling. This reveals one of the great truths of simulations: a complex simulation is very complex to construct. Any simulation that attempts to anticipate the reactions of a human is a very complex simulation.

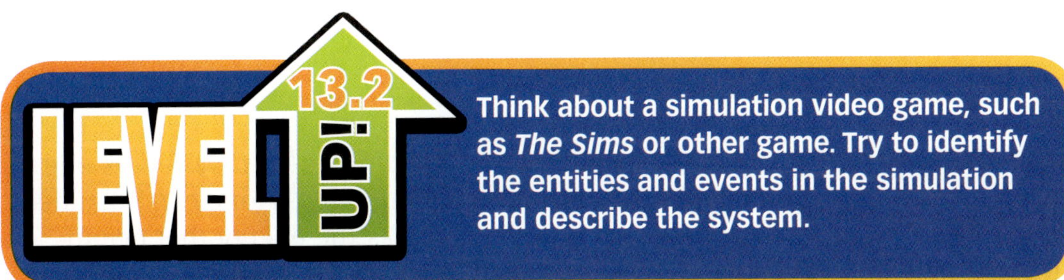

Simulation Classification

Simulations come in many forms. A ***physical simulation*** contains devices that are substitutes for real devices. A physical simulation takes the place of a real object or system. The physical simulation might be something like a driving simulator. Instead of using a real car, a driving simulator is used to train new drivers. This allows a safer environment and the ability to adjust for skill level. Physical simulations may use computers, but they are different from computer simulations. A ***computer simulation*** uses a computer to imitate a physical system. To do that, a virtual system, entities, and events must be created. There are three categories of simulations that are created to imitate different types of systems: automated, interactive, and reconstruction.

Automated

An ***automated simulation*** requires no input once the simulation has started. The parameters are set at the beginning of the simulation and all interactions within the simulation are automated. This type of simulation relies heavily on artificial intelligence. Each entity must be properly programmed to act, learn, and grow. The system is controlled by parameters and constraints. Constraints restrict parameters of the system. A single run of the simulation is an event. The event details the variable parameters and constraints being tested. After the event, the results are analyzed to see how the system performed with those settings. Several applications of automated simulations are listed in **Figure 13-8.**

Simulation	Description
Urban Planning	People using roads and utilities.
Transportation	Managing moving cars, planes, subways, vessels, and other vehicles.
Computer Networks	User data flowing within the network system.
Communication Systems	Integration of different communication systems.
Disaster Response	Allocation of emergency services to a disaster.
Financial Markets	Money and price changes in stock market and other financial markets.
Economics	Money supply and velocity changes due to government policy.
Manufacturing	Material flow through manufacturing based on changes to employees and equipment.
Weather	Storms, changes in temperature, and other variables as a prediction model.

Figure 13-8. These are some typical examples of where automated simulations may be used.

Goodheart-Willcox Publisher

An automated system is typically a closed system. A *closed system* is one in which all material and energy of the system are contained. None can be added or deleted. However, items can change form, such as the energy that occurs during an explosion. Complex rules govern how a closed-system simulation manages resources to sustain a population like an ecosystem. For simple systems, three components are required for sustainability:

- regulating (climate, floods, nutrient balance)
- provisioning (food, medicine, minerals)
- supporting (nutrient cycling, photosynthesis, soil formation)

Special knowledge of each component of a closed system may be required to correctly complete an automated simulation. Many automated simulations examine the use of resources. These simulations look at how a system might work more efficiently by using less time, money, labor, or other resource.

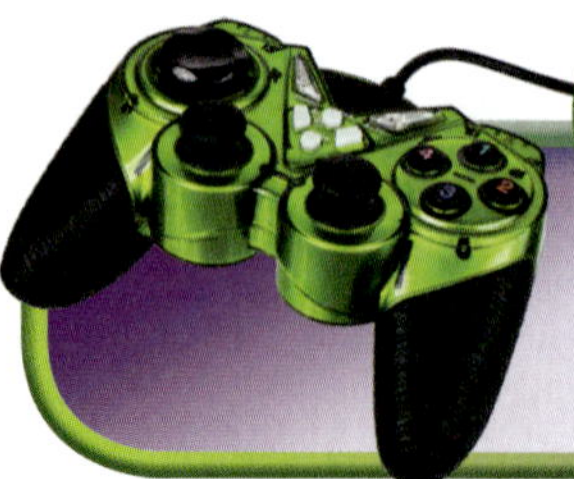

CHEAT CODE: QUEUING

Queuing is lining up or waiting in line. A queue is a line of people, vehicles, or other things waiting.

Another important observation in many automated simulations is **queuing** time. At a business, customers queue for service. Traffic queues as it waits at a red light, stop sign, or interstate on-ramp. Data queues as it waits in memory to enter processing components. By tracking where and how long a system queues it can be determined how resources should be allocated to reduce wait times. Tracking queuing time also identifies bottlenecks where objects or entities slow down or pile up. This is an important factor for traffic and manufacturing modeling. A traffic lane might be widened or an assembly line slowed to make sure bottlenecks do not cause a system failure at peak times.

Interactive

An ***interactive simulation*** allows a user to actively control some part of the system. This type of simulation is the most similar to a video game. Typically, the user is an entity of the simulation, such as the pilot in a flight simulator. Instead of programming an entity with artificial intelligence, the user provides human intelligence to the simulation system. Interactive simulations are mostly used to train humans to better perform tasks. The simulation imitates many different real world conditions. The user can practice how to best perform under those conditions.

For example, pilots using a **vestibular** flight simulator, such as the one shown in **Figure 13-9,** might practice flying in high winds or storms, during engine failure, over dangerous terrain, or other situations. The simulator uses actuators to tip, tilt, pitch, roll, and yaw the entire simulation vehicle. This motion produces similar sensations as the actual vehicle on the human user. The pilot has many attempts at solving the problems presented during the simulation. Additionally, the pilot cannot be hurt or damage a real aircraft.

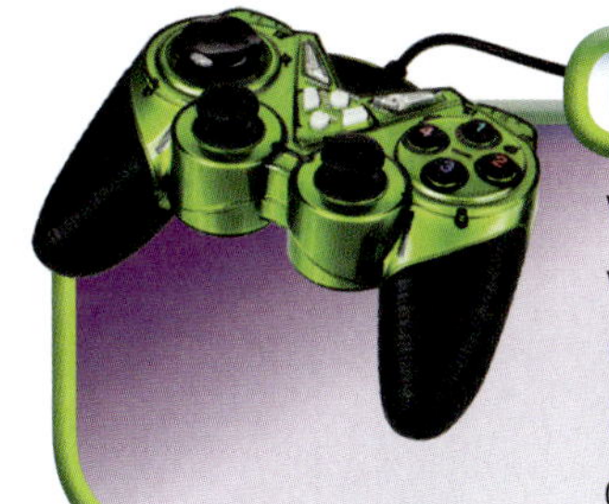

CHEAT CODE: VESTIBULAR

Vestibular means acting like a vestibule. One meaning of a vestibule is a cavity. So, a vestibular simulator is like a cavity in which the user sits or stands.

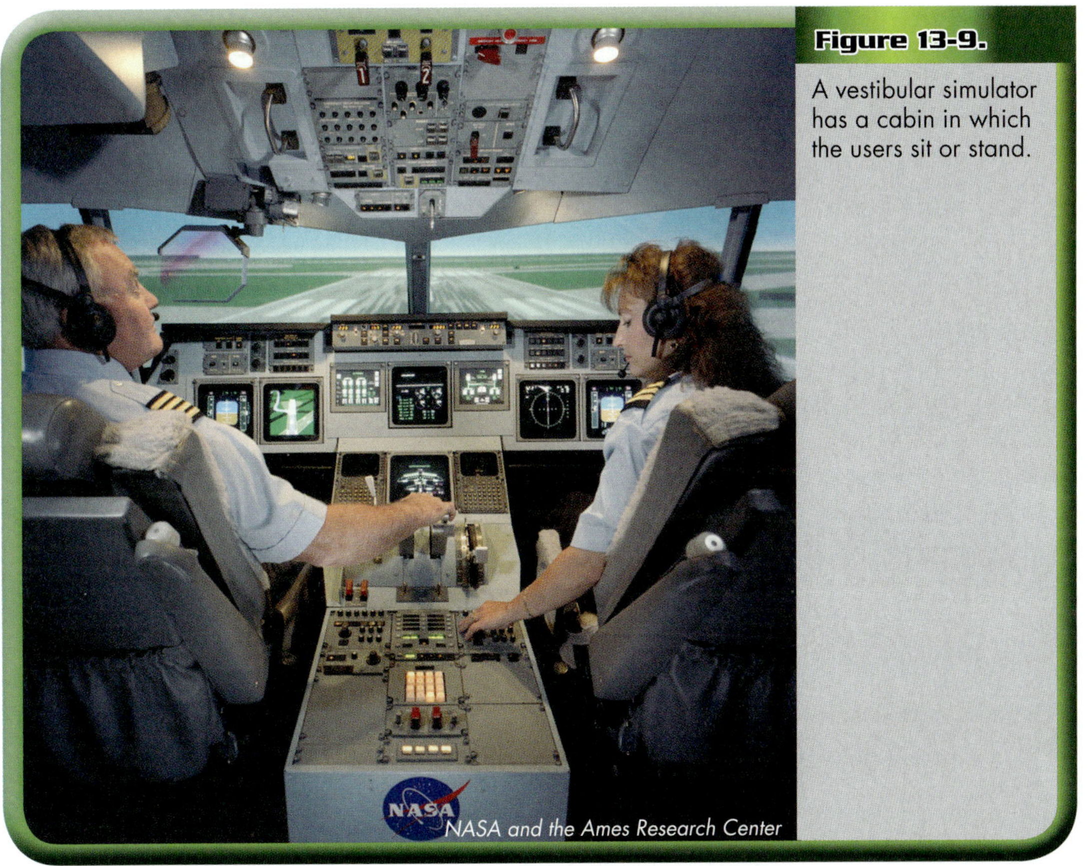

Figure 13-9. A vestibular simulator has a cabin in which the users sit or stand.

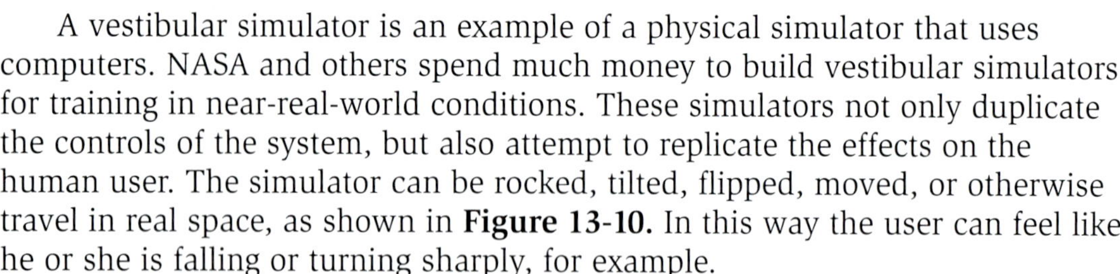

A vestibular simulator is an example of a physical simulator that uses computers. NASA and others spend much money to build vestibular simulators for training in near-real-world conditions. These simulators not only duplicate the controls of the system, but also attempt to replicate the effects on the human user. The simulator can be rocked, tilted, flipped, moved, or otherwise travel in real space, as shown in **Figure 13-10.** In this way the user can feel like he or she is falling or turning sharply, for example.

An interactive simulator can also be used as an entertaining ride at theme parks, fairs, and carnivals. Even Chuck E. Cheese has a ride simulator for a roller coaster that rocks and turns to allow the user to see, hear, and feel the motion of a real roller coaster. Some of these theme park rides may be simple and relatively inexpensive, while others may be very large and expensive. NASA created a shuttle simulator for tourists who visit the Kennedy Space Center. This simulator holds a large audience that can safely experience movement and vibration similar to what would have been felt by an astronaut on the space shuttle.

NASA and the Ames Research Center

Figure 13-10. Vestibular simulators are typically capable of moving in several directions.

A user can participate in an interactive simulation in ways other than with moving vestibular simulation. The most popular method involves virtual reality. In ***virtual reality,*** the user's body motions are read by the user interface and displayed in the game or simulation world. The user's body movements become movements of their entity in the virtual world. Some virtual reality systems require a capture suit. A ***capture suit*** is worn by the user and contains sensors to read movements. The capture suit will record movement much like the Kinect for Xbox 360, Move for PS3, or a sensor marker for 3D animation. Additionally, some capture suits can provide feedback. Pressure, vibration, or even mild electric shock can be used to simulate painful interactions in the virtual world. These touch and feel components are classified as **haptic** feedback.

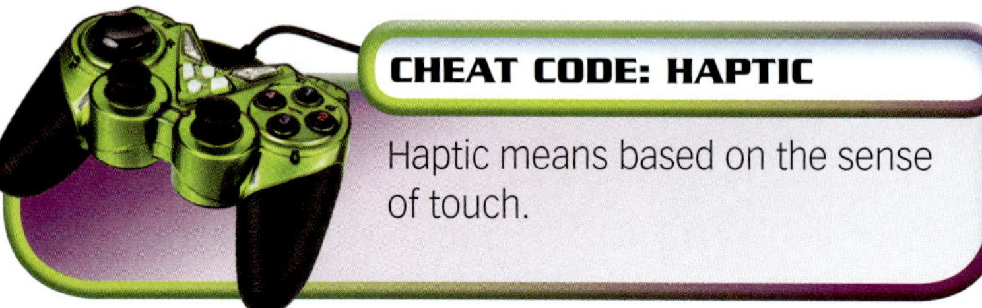

CHEAT CODE: HAPTIC

Haptic means based on the sense of touch.

Reconstructive

Reconstructive simulations attempt to duplicate a situation by reverse engineering the end result. Crime scene investigation, building collapses, and car crashes are just a few examples of where a reconstructive simulation may be used. Many companies are also creating reconstructive simulations to build factories and manufacturing plants to see how workers will be able to function best.

For a crime scene investigation, creating the simulation would begin with information from the crime scene. The scene is built in reverse, starting from where the event ended. By working backward from the end, the simulation attempts to find the answer of how the crime happened. To complete the simulation, an entire 3D scene has to be built in correct proportions. The people involved must be created as 3D models that match the height, weight, mobility, and other features of the real participants. Weapons and projectiles must be created as 3D models with the same performance standards as the originals from the scene. Vehicles and other moving object also have to be created as 3D models and inserted to match the criteria of the scene. When everything has been modeled to match the scene, the physics need to be analyzed to determine the starting point, starting time, velocity, and orientation of all entities in the scene. Specialists in reconstruction will assist to help define the parameters of each object. When all of the parameters are correctly set, a reconstruction simulation will rewind the scene in an attempt to find out how the event started.

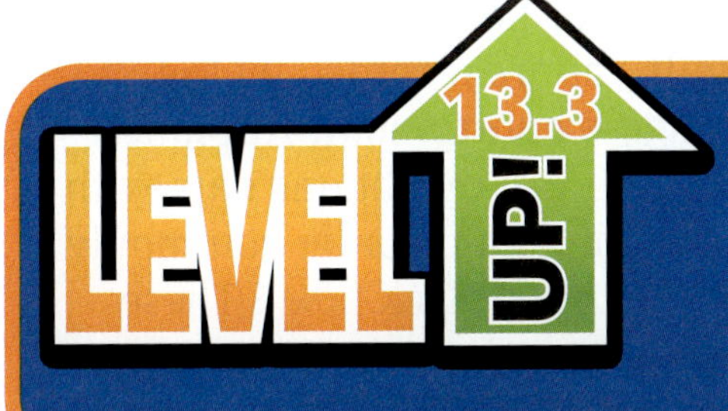

There are several video games that are based on real-world events, such as many military games. Identify a video game that is based on a simulation of a real-world event and try to determine which type of simulation system it most closely matches.

Simulation Purpose

It might be unrealistic to create a simulation that incorporates all parameters possible in the real world. For reasons of time, expense, and simplicity the simulation should be limited to the most important or useful parameter sets. Creating a simulation is very time consuming and expensive. Just as in video game design, there is a budget and deadline for most simulation projects. The designers have to focus on the most important aspects first, and then build in less meaningful interactions as time and budget permit.

Determining what to include and assigning priorities really comes down to the purpose of the simulation. If a race car simulator is supposed to help train a driver, then this purpose dictates which parameters are most important. Car physics, road surface, wind, rain, tire traction, temperature, and interface design might be the most important items for the purpose of training a driver. Other real world parameters might be ignored. Items such as audience, trees, position of the sun, bugs that hit the windshield, and many more parameters of the real world system are not included in the simulation.

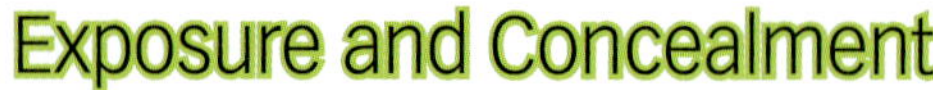

Exposure and Concealment

The purpose also determines how information from the simulation is displayed or reported. This part of the process balances exposure and concealment. Exposure describes the simulation data that are part of the user interface. Concealment describes the simulation data that is collected but is not part of the user interface.

Most often, exposure is done through a visual display or feedback to a physical component. These data are sensed through sight, sound, haptic touch, or in some cases even smell and taste. While smell and taste are more difficult to output as part of the user experience, introducing smoke or a burning smell could be an important part of a physical simulation. For example, a simulator for training a bomb-sniffing dog would need to have data feedback that includes smell.

Not all data need to be part of the user interface. A race car uses a tachometer to show the driver the strain on the motor in RPMs. A family car often does not have a tachometer to allow room for a larger speedometer. Since it is unlikely that the family car will strain the motor in everyday use, the tachometer does not serve a high enough purpose to be included. In comparison, the race car is allowed to travel at any speed and has no purpose for a speedometer. Without a purpose for having a speedometer, it is not included in the race car user interface.

That does not mean the data are not important or not collected and stored. Most of the data from the operation of the family car are recorded by the **engine control unit**. Airplanes also record operations data with a flight data recorder commonly called the "black box." These computers contain important information that is not displayed or exposed to the user. These data are part of the concealment structure.

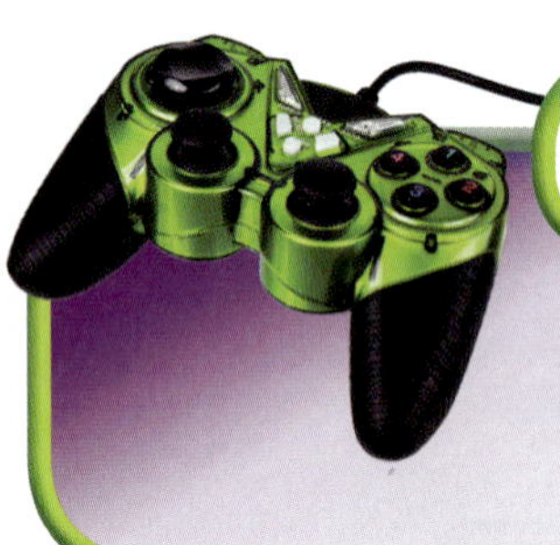

CHEAT CODE: ENGINE CONTROL UNIT

The engine control unit (ECU) is the computer found in production vehicles that controls many of the functions of the vehicle.

Significance

The purpose of the simulation determines how learning from the simulation is obtained. Primarily, the simulation must have significance to an observer or a participant. Significance relates to quality of learning. A flight simulation has significance to the pilot learning how to handle the airplane during an extreme event. It also has significance to the engineers evaluating any data concealed from the user. Both pilots and engineers receive significant learning from the flight simulation.

In a flight simulator, the pilot receives significant learning in the form of inductive logic. ***Inductive logic*** is critical thinking and learning from inside the system. The pilot makes decisions inside the system of an airplane in flight. The learning is induced by the system itself.

In a flight simulator, the engineers receive significant learning in the form of iconic logic. ***Iconic logic*** is critical thinking and learning from outside of the system. The engineers make decisions on airplane design outside of the system of the airplane in flight. They apply the results of the simulation to knowledge of material tolerances, stress points, and other areas of design. The engineers also bring other knowledge from outside the system to the simulation results.

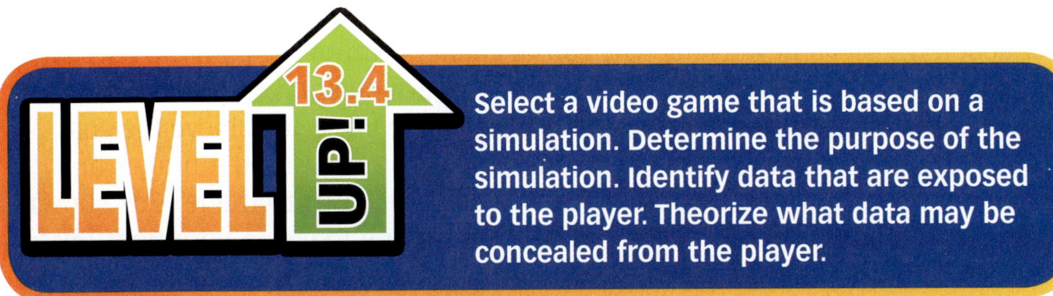

Select a video game that is based on a simulation. Determine the purpose of the simulation. Identify data that are exposed to the player. Theorize what data may be concealed from the player.

Applied Event Modeling

Applied event modeling describes how a human-in-the-loop (HITL) simulation is constructed. Applied event modeling borrows from video game design to achieve learning by the user. The major difference between applied event modeling and video game design is the user experience. In video game design, the resulting user experience is entertainment. In an HITL simulation, the user experience is learning. Constructing an HITL simulation starts with the same basic requirements for constructing a game: goal (victory condition), environment, and rules.

In video game design, the victory condition might be to defeat a boss. In an HITL simulation, the goal might be to learn how to fly a plane. In a racing game, the victory condition is finishing in first place. In a driving simulation, the goal might be handling the car without crashing during an engine failure or tire blowout. The goal is determined by what the user needs to learn from an event or series of events.

Both video games and simulations have rules. In a video game, the rules determine what the player is and is not allowed to do. In a simulation, the rules are the parameters of each component and entity in the system. The rules for a simulation also create the system in the same way rules for a video game create the core mechanics.

The system established by the rules is used to create the environment. A video game has an environment that enables play. An HITL simulation also requires an environment, but with a different purpose. The environment in an HITL simulation is one that enables learning during the operation of the system. This stage of simulation design is often referred to as map making.

Map Making

In ***map making,*** the simulation system is rendered in realistic form. A simulation map incorporates the goal and allows the user to interact with the system. The user must make choices to discover the best path to the goal. Just as in video game design, varying the obstacles and increasing options allows the user to discover multiple sequences that lead to the goal. In simulations, the obstacles are the events being tested. The user must discover patterns within the system and interpret information from the system to overcome the obstacle and achieve the goal.

Event Exploration

In a simulation system, the user is undertaking event exploration. In ***event exploration,*** the user interacts with an event and tries to return the system back to a static state. Each event and user action becomes part of the causal chain where a user action triggers a new event. The causal chain is part of the path the user takes to achieve the goal. The causal chain is also the learning part of the simulation. By applying heuristics, the user learns what steps can be taken to achieve the goal.

For example, a race car driver might learn that pounding the brakes and turning sharply right will cause the rear of the car to drift to the left, as shown in **Figure 13-11.** The driver learns that this technique makes a very tight left turn even though the steering wheel is turned to the right.

Use Case

The causal chain for an entity creates a use case. A ***use case*** details the path an entity takes in the simulation, such as that shown in **Figure 13-12.** It is an analysis of how the simulation was used and navigated. At each event during the simulation, the user made a decision and took action. Those actions caused other events to trigger. Each decision point is a node on the path taken to reach the goal. The use case can be analyzed to discover what caused a certain decision and how that altered all other events in the causal chain.

The analysis of a use case is similar to the analysis of game metrics. Game metrics, like those discussed in Chapter 5, typically track several thousand elements to determine patterns of behavior. Both simulation use cases and game metrics can help in designing the next iteration of the program and system.

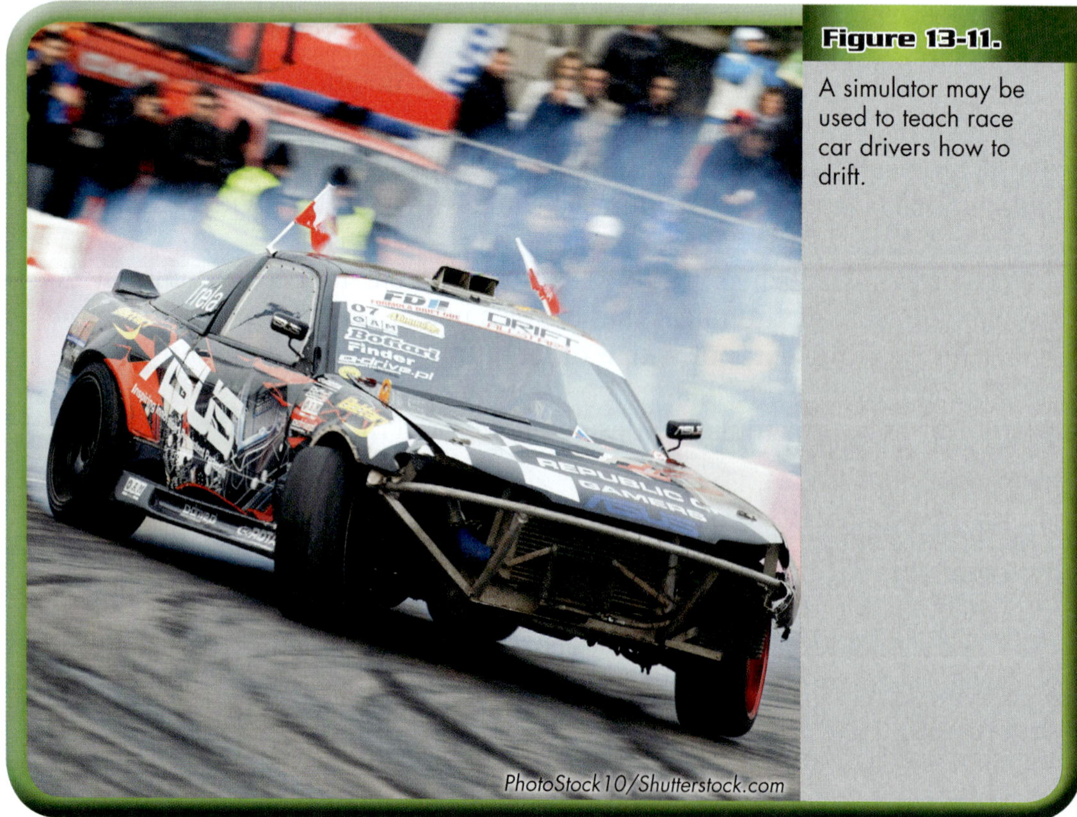

PhotoStock10/Shutterstock.com

Figure 13-11. A simulator may be used to teach race car drivers how to drift.

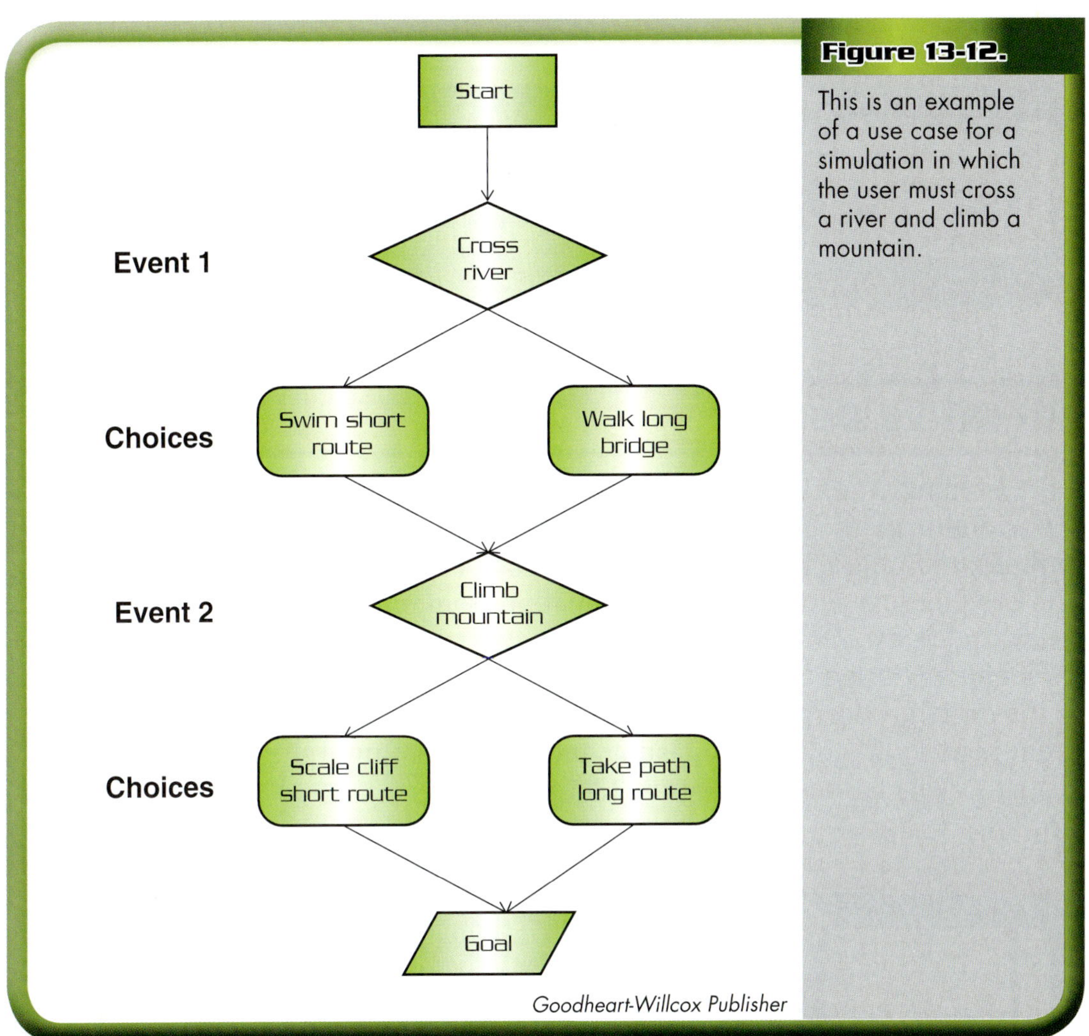

Figure 13-12. This is an example of a use case for a simulation in which the user must cross a river and climb a mountain.

Incentives

The system in a simulation may offer incentives. ***Incentives*** are ways of encouraging a specific action or path. In basketball, there is an incentive to try a longer shot because of the three-point line. A basket made behind the three-point line has the incentive of one extra point if it is made. Penalties are also part of the incentive model. The user has an incentive *not* to do certain actions that would incur a penalty.

Designers of HITL simulations use incentives when trying to train a user to follow a specific path. This path may have already been determined as the best or safest path for achieving the goal. A flight simulator to train pilots flying into a dangerous airport surrounded by mountains may include a preflight plan to look for specific landmarks to properly align the plane.

Regeneration

The greatest learning component of a simulation is regeneration. ***Regeneration*** is where the system is reset to its original state. All of the entities are regenerated at their original locations and all parameters are reset to their original values. This repeatability allows for learning using heuristics. In this way, an HITL simulation allows the user to repeat the same simulation over and over again, thereby, enabling trial-and-error learning.

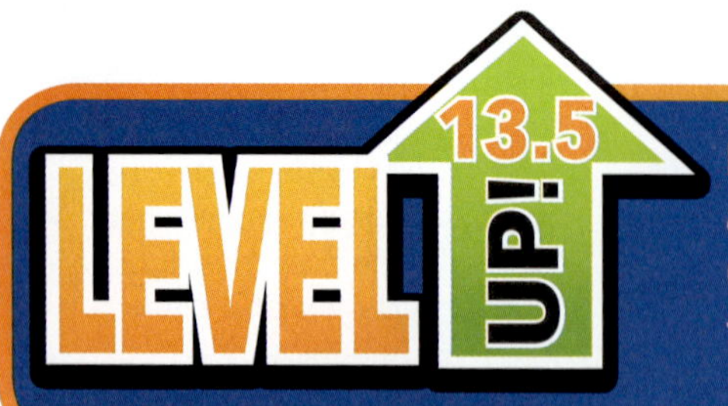

Play one video game based on a simulation and one that is not based on a simulation. Compare and contrast the event modeling for each game.

Iterative Design

The iterative design process works well for simulation design and follows the scientific method, as outlined in **Figure 13-13.** With the ***iterative design process,*** the program will improve with each run through the design cycle. The design cycle allows for the information from one experiment to be used to refine and retest another attempt.

Iterative design also involves prototyping. *Prototyping* is an iterative step in the design process that tests the system to discover errors. A prototype of an event model will go through testing and refinement until the system functions properly. This is shown in **Figure 13-14.**

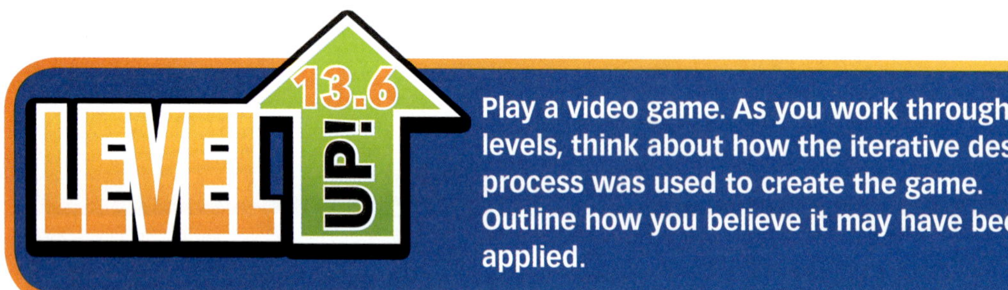

Scientific Method	Iterative Design Process
Purpose of the simulation.	Identify the problem.
Research system and entity components.	Discover what is needed in the system.
Hypothesize most probable event model.	Predict reaction of system to event changes.
Build experimental simulation.	Build or refine simulation system.
Analyze simulation data.	Analyze results of simulation.
Form conclusion.	Confirm or deny hypothesis.
Recommend changes for retest.	Suggest refinements to system and retest.

Figure 13-13. This table compares the scientific method with the iterative design process.

Goodheart-Willcox Publisher

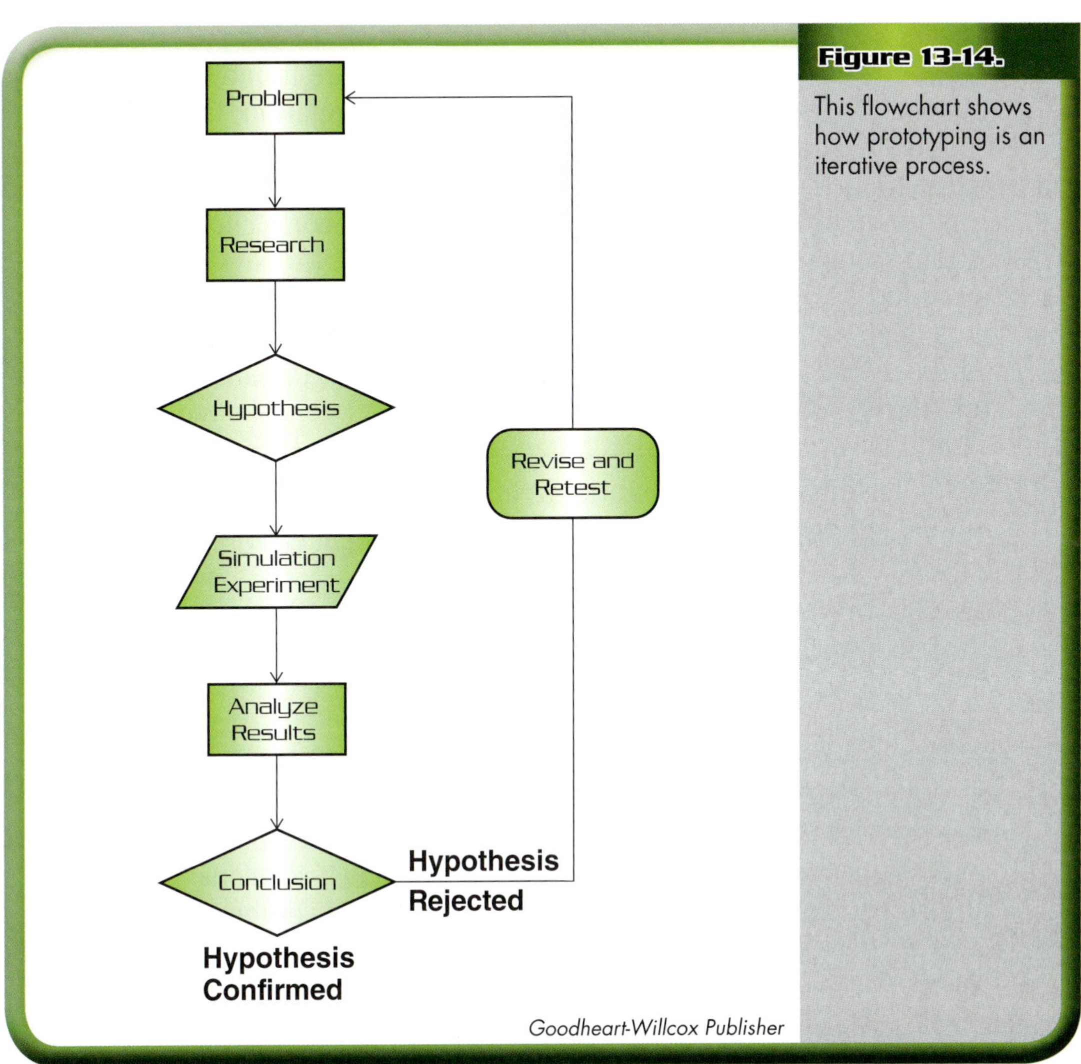

Figure 13-14. This flowchart shows how prototyping is an iterative process.

Application Framework

Before programming a simulation, the problem must be identified and a causal chain and storyboard constructed to understand the choices for the entities. The next step is to decide what design platform will be used to create the simulation. The platform can be custom code, specialized software, or a game engine. The choice depends on the time and customization needed for the project. Many game engines have the power to construct automated and interactive simulations. Since much game design software is easy to use and program, many simulations are constructed using game design software. If a more precise simulation is required or the game design software does not offer features required for the simulation, then custom software may have to be used.

When starting simulation programming, the first requirement is to understand the application framework. The ***application framework*** is the structure of the software. If using an existing game engine, then the game engine contains the framework to which custom programming is added. The simulation programmer cannot change or alter the framework, only modify or

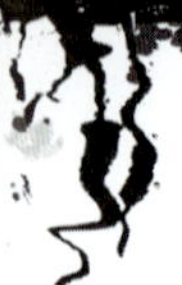

extend it. An *extensible framework* allows programmers to add custom classes and subroutines that extend the use of the basic software framework.

To choose the best application framework for a simulation, list what the program must accomplish. Compare this list to the functions the software framework supports. When the list matches an existing framework, use it. If the list does not match the functions of the software framework, choose another or build custom software.

In order to list what the program must accomplish, the system-shall commands need to be written. A ***system-shall command*** is a rule to guide the design of the application framework. The system-shall commands layout what the simulation system requires, the extensible changes, and the requirements for the user. Below is a list of basic system-shall commands that helps determine the scope of design.

<001> The system shall support application development for Windows, Mac, and Linux.
<002> The system shall support complex real world physics.
<003> The system shall support 3D graphic display and stereo sound.
<004> The system shall support creation of worlds.
<005> The system shall support creation of entities.
<006> The system shall support input from complex interface controls.
<007> The system shall support output to a vestibular simulator.
<008> The system shall enable the user interactivity with events and entities.
<009> The system shall enable the programmer to add animations.
<010> The system shall enable the programmer to modify environmental conditions.

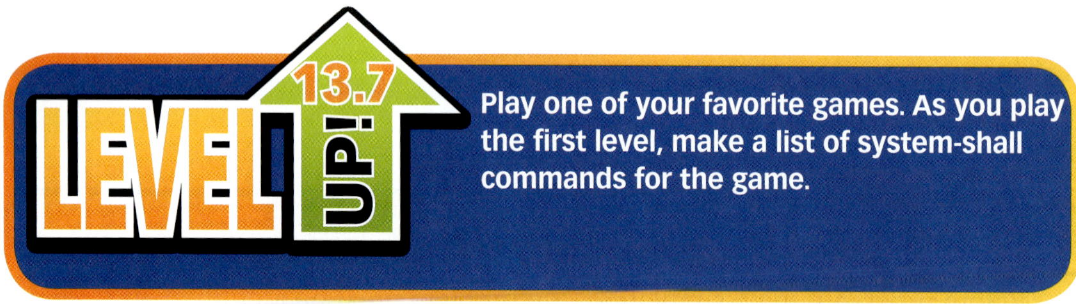

Play one of your favorite games. As you play the first level, make a list of system-shall commands for the game.

Chapter Summary

- The parameters of a simulation are very specific and may be numerous while a video game may have only a few parameters, additionally, a simulation may have less detailed graphics than a video game.
- Creating a simulation requires special attention to the simulation components: system, entities, and events.
- The two main forms of simulations are physical simulations and computer simulations; there are three categories of simulations that are created to imitate different types of systems—automated, interactive, and reconstruction.
- The purpose of a simulation determines what to include in the simulation, how to assign priorities, how information from the simulation is displayed or reported, and how learning from the simulation is obtained.
- Applied event modeling describes how a human-in-the-loop (HITL) simulation is constructed; it borrows from video game design to achieve learning by the user.
- With the iterative design process, the design cycle allows for the information from one experiment to be used to refine and retest another attempt.
- When starting simulation programming, the first requirement is to understand the application framework; the application framework is the structure of the software.

Check Your Video Game IQ

Now that you have finished this chapter, see what you know about video game design by taking the chapter posttest.

www.m.g-wlearning.com

www.g-wlearning.com

Review Your Knowledge

On a separate sheet of paper or in a word processing document, match the following terms with the definition that fits best.

A. collision avoidance
B. vestibular simulator
C. inductive logic
D. regeneration
E. reconstructive simulation
F. discrete-event simulation
G. heuristics
H. iconic logic
I. physical simulation
J. interactive simulation

1. Simple entity navigation in which the entity tries not to hit items or have to stop.
2. Allows a user to actively control some part of the system.

3. Simulator like a cavity in which the user sits or stands.
4. Contains devices that are substitutes for real devices; takes the place of a real object or system.
5. Critical thinking and learning from inside the system.
6. Tests a system by changing variable parameters at instantaneous points; this method best isolates the results of an event to a system.
7. Resetting the system to its original state.
8. Critical thinking and learning from outside of the system.
9. An attempt to duplicate a situation by reverse engineering the end result.
10. The process of making predictions based on past events, or learning by trial and error.

On a separate sheet of paper or in a word processing document, answer each of the following questions.

11. List three areas of game design that are similar to simulation design.
12. List four reasons why graphics in simulations are typically of lower quality than those in a video game.
13. How can collision avoidance be used in navigation for an entity?
14. Why is a particle system used to program a swarm of bees?
15. List the steps of the scientific method.
16. Which classification of simulator uses a device that is a substitute for a real-world object?
17. Which type of simulation is most similar to a video game and why?
18. What is the purpose of reconstructive simulations?
19. How does a use case relate to event exploration?
20. How do rewards or penalties influence a use case?

Apply Your STEM Knowledge

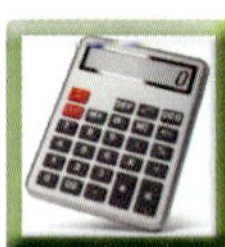

Mathematics

1. A traffic flow simulation was able to predict a backup at an intersection during morning rush hour traffic. It compiled the following minute and second data on cars waiting at the intersection. Determine the average stopped waiting time for each direction for the two-hour period of rush hour.

Time of Day	Northbound cars	Southbound cars	Eastbound cars	Westbound cars
7:00	2:16	1:40	1:38	1:15
7:15	3:25	3:02	1:27	1:11
7:30	2:27	2:45	2:02	1:40
7:45	3:45	2:35	2:11	1:58
8:00	3:17	3:10	0:45	2:12
8:15	3:21	3:16	1:10	1:36
8:30	3:39	3:22	1:17	1:21
8:45	2:48	2:25	1:48	1:16
Average Time				

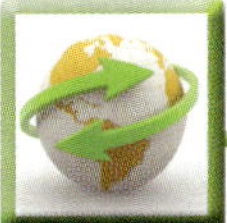

Social Studies

2. Humans learn many cause-and-effect hazards through heuristics. Think about the last time you got hurt. List the activity that was the cause of the injury. Detail what took place during the activity that led to the injury. State what you could have done differently to avoid injury in the future.

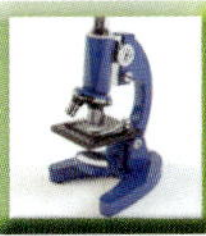

Science

3. Many animals have more senses than humans. Research how some underwater animals have adapted extrasensory perception, such as electromagnetism and pressure-sensing organs. Select an animal and create a 20- to 30-slide PowerPoint presentation describing the animal, its extrasensory organs, the functions of each organ, and how it provides a benefit to the animal. Imagine a sensory model and how to recreate these senses in a simulation.

Language Arts

4. Many animals travel in flocks, herds, schools, or swarms. Research why animals travel in these formations. Write a one-page paper to describe the motivation of the group to stay in tight formation and the benefit it provides to the individuals and the group.

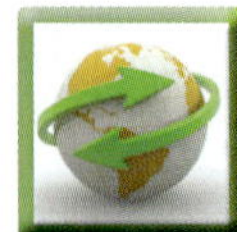

Social Studies

5. The end result of many critical events in history may have been significantly different if only one small item had changed. The result would be an alternate history than the one we know today. Research the decisions and events that lead to the sinking of the RMS *Titanic.* Create a PowerPoint presentation to describe five or more parameters that can be tested in a simulation for this event.

Working in Teams

Your team has been asked to figure out how a corn plant could be made to grow on the International Space Station. Review the scientific method example in this chapter. Create a PowerPoint presentation with title slide, purpose, research summary, and hypothesis slides to explain how the microgravity of space and lighting conditions might affect growth. On the last slide, propose an experimental virtual simulation model and list the parameters that should be monitored and controls needed to perform a simulated experiment.

Gamer Portfolio

Employers and colleges review candidates for various positions. For example, the ability to communicate effectively, get along with customers or coworkers, and solve problems are important skills for many jobs. These types of skills are often called *soft skills.* Make an effort to learn about and develop the soft skills you will need in the video game design field. Document these skills in your portfolio.

1. Research on the Internet to find articles about soft skills and their value in helping employees succeed.
2. Make a list of the soft skills that you possess. Select three of these soft skills, and write a paragraph about each one that describes your abilities in this area. Give examples that illustrate your skills.
3. Save the document file in your e-portfolio. Place a printed copy in your print portfolio.

G-W Learning Mobile Site

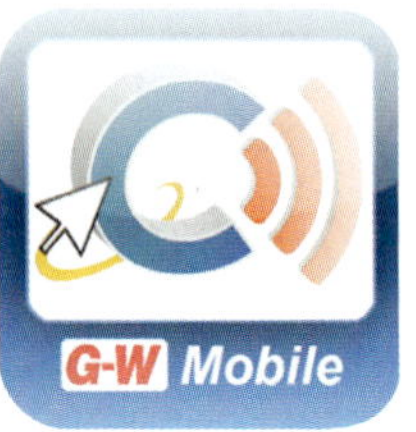

Visit the G-W Learning mobile site to complete the chapter pretest and posttest and to practice vocabulary using e-flash cards. If you do not have a smartphone, visit the G-W Learning companion website to access these features.

G-W Learning mobile site: www.m.g-wlearning.com

G-W Learning companion website: www.g-wlearning.com

Common Core

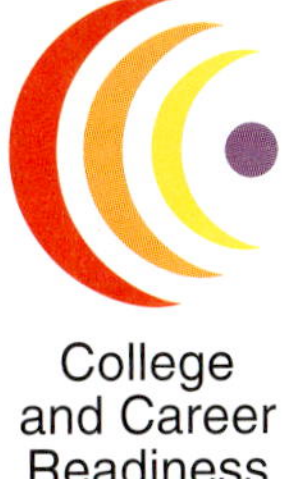
College and Career Readiness

CTE Career Ready Practices. Use Internet or print catalogs of computer equipment and CAD systems to design and equip the workspace for your home-based game design studio. Locate equipment that will enhance your productivity. List prices of all items necessary to fully equip your office from two different vendors—include technology and manual design tools. Create a digital spreadsheet to compare the cost data for the equipment from the two vendors. Which vendor offers the best quality products for prices that meet your budget?

Reading. Using independent research and the information contained in the text, write a report in which you compare and contrast simulations and video games. In what situations would you choose to use one versus the other? How does the purpose of the activity dictate which should be used? How are the costs balanced with the needs? Cite specific evidence from the text and your research to support your understanding of this topic.

Writing. Using the Internet, research the advice that experts have for designers of simulations. Make sure to look at, among other sources, newspaper and magazine articles, scholarly reports, and public addresses from prominent simulation designers. Write a final research report in which you cite the sources that you used and the strengths and weaknesses of each. Be sure to consider the background and point of view of the sources that you find, as well as any bias that the author may bring to the topic.

Event Prep: Day of the Event

You have practiced all year for this competition, and now you are ready. Whether it is for an objective test, written test, report, or presentation, you have done your homework and are ready to shine. To prepare for the day of the event:

1. Be sure to get plenty of sleep the night before the event so that you are rested and ready to go.
2. Use your event checklist before you go into the presentation so that you do not forget any of your materials that are needed for the event.
3. Arrive early at the room where the competition will take place. If you are late and the door is closed, you will be disqualified.
4. If you are making a presentation before a panel of judges, practice what you are going to say when you are called on. State your name, your school, and any other information that has been requested. Be confident, smile, and make eye contact with the judges.
5. When the event is finished, thank the judges for their time.

Glossary

A

acceleration: Rate at which an object is speeding up or slowing down. (11)

action: How an object reacts to input or interacts with other objects. (12)

action context clue: Move or ability a character has. (2)

action-fail: Disallowing an action. (4)

action-fulfill: Allowing an action. (4)

active animation: Combination of translation and articulation. (11)

actor physics: Uses a mathematical model to control the articulation of a character or object. (11)

actual sound: Sound made by a real object, animal, or person. (8)

additive method: Starts with no color, or black, and colors are added to create the final color. (9)

aesthetic value: Qualities of an object that provide decorative appeal. (2)

agent of change: Main game element that changes the outcome of the game. (6)

aha moment: Point where a player has a realization of what to do or the solution to a problem. (7)

algorithm: Computer script that performs the steps needed to solve a problem. (12)

allies: Other players, either NPCs or human players, who agree to join forces to achieve victory over a common enemy or reach a common goal. (6)

alpha version: When most of the game is assembled. (1)

ambient color: Dark areas where the light source cannot provide direct illumination. (9)

ambient sound: Sound in the background of a scene that seems to be coming from the scene. (5)

animation arc: Path an articulated feature follows through the animation. (11)

animator: Team member strong in rendering objects in motion; requires great technology skills to use animation software for 2D or 3D animation rendering. (10)

antagonist: Main adversary or opponent to the protagonist. (2)

anticipation: Event to announce a major action. (11)

application framework: Structure of the software. (13)

archetype: Universal character that is easily identifiable by any culture. (2)

art bible: Contains a drawing or mock-up for every asset that needs to be created for the game. (1)

art director: Team member who sets the vision for the game art and makes sure it is what is needed for the theme and story. (10)

art movement: Particular dominant style or technique. (9)

articles of incorporation: Charter that is a legal document outlining how a business will be organized and managed. (1)

articulation: Bending and positioning of movable parts. (11)

artificial intelligence (AI): Computer science and engineering to make machines think and behave on their own. (5)

asset: Any element in a game, such as characters, objects, backgrounds, sounds, and visual elements. (1)

asset manager: Team member who keeps track of all art assets being produced and makes sure each asset is designed to specifications, catalogued, and properly stored. (10)

asymmetrical balance: Use of similar objects to create balance, or the use of color and light balance instead of object balance; also called *informal balance.* (9)

asymmetry: A work, such as an artistic composition, in which the elements are not at all balanced. (9)

atomic challenge: Smallest component of the action.

attribute: Characteristic associated with an object. (12)

audience: Group of typical players the game is targeted to attract. (4)

audience appeal: Measure of how attracted an audience is to something. (4)

aura: Energy field around an object or character that serves to highlight it. (11)

automated simulation: Requires no input once the simulation has started. (13)

avatar: Image used to represent the player in the game. (2)

B

background music: Artificial ambient sound. (5)

backlight: Used to add a sense of depth to the scene by illuminating the back of the primary object. (10)

back-office tasks: Administrative activities and tasks such as keeping score and tracking the health level of the player character. (5)

Bayeux tapestry: Famous embroidered cloth nearly 230 feet long that records the battle of Hastings in which the Normans successfully invaded England in 1066. (9)

beta testers: Loyal customers and players who play trial versions before the game is available to the general public. (1)

beta version: More polished iteration of the alpha version. (1)

big boss: Most powerful enemy in the game. (2)

bit rate: Number of bits of data transferred per second; refers to the number of bits of information recorded for every unit of time, such as bits per second (bit/s). (8)

boom mount: Places the microphone at the end of a long overhead pole so the microphone can be placed above the source being recorded. (8)

boon: Benefit or favor granted in response to a request. (6)

boss: Second-most powerful antagonist in the game. (2)

bot: In video games, a program that controls the movement and actions of a game character; short for robot. (5)

brainstorming: Recording as many ideas as possible without sorting, editing, or eliminating any of the ideas. (3)

branching story: Story that has several paths that branch from decision points. (3)

bug level: See *bug type.* (1)

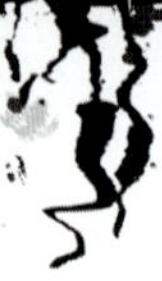

bug report: Document that lists an error, its location in the game, how the error occurs, and how important the error is. (1)

bug type: Importance level of an error; also called *bug level.* (1)

bump map: Texture assigned to the bump property of a material. (10)

button combination: Two or more buttons must be pressed at the same time to activate a game command. (4)

byte: Unit of measure of storage capacity of computer data or information; one byte equals eight bits of information. (10)

C

camaraderie: Spirit of friendship between two or more people, who may or may not be friends. (9)

camera: Provides the perspective of the game that is shown to the player on the screen. (5)

canned sound: A prerecorded, standard or stock sound that can be used in various applications; comes from the physical metal containers that were used to store tape recordings. (8)

capture suit: Worn by the user and contains sensors to read movements. (13)

case laws: Enacted when the first lawsuit to deal with a problem has determined the outcome; that case is then cited in other lawsuits as an example of previous judgment (called precedence). (10)

causal chain: Relates to a series of cause-and-effect events that form an ordered sequence. (6)

causality: Relationship in which one event results in or is caused by another event. (6)

cel: Refers to cellulose acetate, which is a transparent plastic on which animation frames are drawn. (11)

cel animation: Technique where each frame of the animation is drawn by hand on a cel and photographed. (11)

central premise: Basic idea or situation of the story. (2)

challenge escalation: When a player performs new tasks that are more difficult than in the previous challenge. (5)

challenge retracement: When a player performs similar tasks from the previous challenge or challenges. (5)

channel: Means of game distribution, such as disc, online, as an app, or as a coin-operated cabinet. (1)

channel of distribution: Chain of stops a product makes from the publisher to the final user. (1)

character: Motivated participant in the game; also the makeup of talents, skills, abilities, and physical attributes needed to achieve the victory condition. (2)

character-design document: Document that contains all of the information needed to fully define the characters, from descriptions and attributes of each character to model sheets showing the character's appearance. (3)

character profile: Question-and-answer document, like an interview or matchmaking questionnaire. (2)

cheat code: Command embedded in the game and used during game development so a part of the game can be properly tested without having to play the entire game. (4)

checkpoint: Point on the gameplay timeline to which the player will be returned if the player character runs out of health or life. (4)

chiaroscuro: Describes how value is used to create the illusion of depth, shape, and shadow. (9)

chorus: Similar to reverb except it adds a delay to the sound to simulate more than one sound source. (8)

chroma keying: Removing a specified color, usually chroma green or blue, from a photograph or video. (11)

circular logic: Solution keeps changing the statement, which, in turn, changes the solution. (7)

class variable: Umbrella device that contains a nonspecific type of item and on which operations can be performed. (12)

climax: Most dramatic part of a story; the turning point in a story. (3)

clock rate: See *clock speed.* (4)

clock speed: Speed at which the computer central processing unit (CPU) processes instructions; also called *clock rate.* (4)

closed system: All material and energy of the system are contained. (13)

closure: Sense of conclusion to a game and its story. (4)

collision: Occurs when one game object touches another game object. (12)

collision avoidance: Entity tries not to hit items or stop. (13)

color model: Mixing base colors to create a spectrum of colors. (9)

color palette: Standard set of colors used throughout the game. (10)

combined arms: Combat strategy that uses dissimilar assets to complement each other in specialized units. (6)

comment: Used within the code itself to identify and explain what a line or piece of code is supposed to do. (12)

compatible: When things or people work well together. (12)

competition model: How the player will interact with the game to complete it. (5)

competitive NPC: Any non-player game character who is attempting to stop the player from completing an objective. (2)

compiler: Translates, or compiles, the program into machine code. (12)

complexity: State of something being intricate or complicated. (6)

composing: Creating music. (8)

composite sound: Several sound assets mixed to render a single sound. (8)

computer simulation: Uses a computer to imitate a physical system. (13)

concept art: Series of simple sketches that show what a character or other major game asset might look like; typically the first iteration of the visual appearance of a character, background, or other element of the game. (2, 10)

concept artist: Team member strong in creating new characters and objects that have never existed before. (10)

confidentiality agreement: Contract that states one cannot share any information about the company or its products with any other company. (10)

conflict strategy model: Requires players to engage each other in conflict or battle. (6)

congruous characters: In-game characters who look like they belong and fit the mood and theme of the game. (2)

conservation of matter: All mass content must be the same before and after an interaction. (11)

context clue: Piece of information evaluated within the surrounding environment. (2)

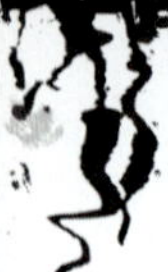

contrast: Variation of color and brightness to make objects stand out from each other. (9)

cookie-cutter design: Repeating design. (5)

cooperative NPC: In-game character who helps the player complete the game objectives. (2)

copyright: Indication of legal ownership of creative work. (1)

copyright infringement: Misusing or making unauthorized copies of a copyrighted work. (10)

copyright laws: Protect the owner of a creative work; under US copyright laws, as soon as a creative work is in tangible form, it is automatically copyrighted. (10)

core mechanics: Computer programming used to enforce the rules. (1)

core values: Moral, ethical, and cultural rules that a person (or character) applies to his or her life. (2)

corporation: Legal entity that limits the personal liabilities of its owners while being able to engage in activities such as entering into contracts, making money, and buying property. (1)

covert clue: Clue that is hidden or hard to read. (6)

Creative Commons license: Work can be used for free with or without restrictions; may require citing authorship and may prohibit derivative works. (10)

critical path method (CPM): All tasks are first prioritized. The next step is to find dependencies for each task. Tasks are then scheduled in the most efficient progression. The tasks are then analyzed to find how the project can be fast-tracked. (1)

crunch time: End of a project when time begins to run short and decisive action is required. (1)

cue: Trigger for an action, such as playing a sound sample. (8)

cultural influences: Characteristics unique to a geographic region or the people of that region. (9)

cultural values: Rules that a character applies as part of its ancestral heritage, religion, and family. (2)

cut scene: Short video presentation usually placed between levels or at checkpoints within a level. (2)

D

data mining: Process of discovering patterns from a set of raw statistical information. (6)

data structure: Way of storing and organizing data. (12)

database: Organized system of storing information that allows for searching and retrieval of the data. (8)

decelerate: Slow down. (12)

declared: Item is given a name and a function in the program being written. (12)

demographics: Measureable characteristics of a person or group. (4)

derivative work: Anything based on, or derived, from any part of the original. (10)

design documents: Documents that contain all of the decisions used to make the game. (1)

design team: Group of very creative people who bring the idea of a video game into a playable version. (1)

developer: Game-design studio that is responsible for creating all of the art, sounds, programming, and design elements of the video game. (1)

dexterity: Readiness and skill in a physical activity, especially one involving use of the hands. (4)

dialect: Variance in language found in a specific region or social group. (2)

dialogue: Conversation between characters. (8)

dice: Cubes with numbered sides commonly used to randomize gameplay. (10)

differentiate: To show a difference. (8)

diffuse color: Main color or value of an object. (9)

digital artwork: Created using a computer. (9)

digital watermark: Mark that makes the image unusable as final artwork, but allows somebody to review the art for potential use. (10)

digitized: Converted to digital form. (8)

direct marketing: Publisher sells the game to the user. (1)

discrete-event simulation: Tests a system by changing variable parameters at instantaneous points. (13)

displacement: How much something has moved. (11)

dissection puzzle: Take a geometric shape that has been cut into a certain number of pieces and reassemble the shape. (7)

dissimilar assets: In-game objects that have unique characteristics. (6)

dissipating: Breaking up or scattering. (11)

distribution: How a game is sent to the customer. (1)

diversion: Strategy that involves drawing the attention of the opponent to one location so an attack can be made in a different location. (6)

drain: Occurs when a player has something taken away. (6)

dramatic action of the story: How the character reacts when faced with immediate conflicts or obstacles. (3)

dramatic arc of the story: Rising action, a climax, and falling action. (3)

dramatic tension: Feeling of anxiety or anticipation related to the story being told. (3)

E

easter egg: Hidden message or special feature. (6)

economy of force: Requires that minimal essential resources be allocated to secondary efforts. (6)

ecosystem: Community of organisms and their environment that function as a single unit. (13)

editor: Computer program that allows the designer to prototype the gameplay. (7)

elegant: Describes an algorithm that is the simplest, smallest, and most efficient computer code to perform the needed function. (12)

elements of art: Individual features needed to compose artwork. (9)

embossed: When an image is raised above the background. (10)

emitter: Object in a 3D modeling program that has settings for the particles it generates. (11)

emphasis: When a designer draws attention to an object. (9)

engine control unit (ECU): Computer found in production vehicles that controls many of the functions of the vehicle. (13)

entities: "Thinking" components of a system. (13)

environment artist: Team member who creates scenes for the game world; strong in use of color and landscape drawing. (10)

environmental illustration: Illustration that shows the details of the virtual world in the game. (3)

ergonomics: Study of how the body works and how humans interact with tools and environments. (4)

escalate: Increase intensity. (5)

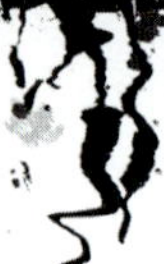

ethical values: Rules that a character uses to decide if something is right or wrong. (2)

event: Change in a computer program. (12)

event exploration: User interacts with an event and tries to return the system back to a static state. (13)

exaggeration: Amplifying some aspect of the action beyond what is normal. (11)

exclusive right: Allows the creative work to be used or reproduced only by the person or company who owns the contract, or to whomever they give permission to do so. (10)

explicit challenge: Task that the player is specifically instructed to complete. (5)

exposition: Introduction of the primary conflict of a story. (3)

expression sketch: Sketch that shows a set of body positions and facial expressions for each emotion needed. (2)

expressive context clue: Appears in the body language of the character. (2)

extensible framework: Allows programmers to add to custom classes and subroutines that extend the use of the basic software framework. (13)

extrinsic skills: Essential to complete a task. (5)

F

factory: Nonmaneuverable game asset with some strategic value. (6)

fair use/fair dealings doctrine: Allows a creative work to be used without permission, but under very strict guidelines; allows someone to reprint or display a copyrighted work without permission for the purpose of describing or reviewing the creative work. (10)

falling action: Events that lead to the resolution of the basic conflict of a story; the level of dramatic tension begins to decrease as the conflicts are sorted out. (3)

fast track: To analyze a project's tasks to find which can be done in parallel, or at the same time. (1)

field recording: Made by a sound engineer using a microphone and recording device outside of the studio. (8)

file-naming convention: Standardized way of naming an asset. (8)

file size: Amount of storage space required for the file; measured in bytes, megabytes, or gigabytes. (10)

fill light: Used to eliminate unwanted shadows or dark areas in the scene; also called *flood light*. (10)

filter effect: Alters the base image based on parameter definitions or settings for the filter. (9)

firewall: Computer program or physical device that prevents users or information from entering a computer network. (5)

first playable level: First iteration of the game's first level that can be played and tested. (1)

first-person perspective: Positions the camera as the player's eyes. (5)

five essential questions: Questions that form the foundation of the concept for the game. (1)

five Ps of video game publishing: Pitch; preproduction; production; post production; patch and return distribution. (1)

flat character: Character who does not develop or change throughout a story. (3)

flip-book animation: Created by drawing a picture on the edge of each page in a notebook with a slight difference between each picture. (11)

float: Floating decimal point that must be accounted for in any decimal computation. (12)

flood light: See *fill light*. (10)

flow: In video games, state of immersion in the task or activity being undertaken. (7)

flowchart: Chart with different text box shapes and connectors to add visual detail to a decision process. (12)

focus group: Small group of target audience members play the game and are asked questions about the game and how to make it better. (4)

foldback event: Resolution point within the game that the player must go through to move the story forward. (3)

foldback story: Story that allows the player to make decisions, but all paths lead, or fold, back to the same end point. (3)

follow-through: Continuation of movement beyond the main event. (11)

form: Assembly of 2D shapes to represent a third dimension; measureable dimensions of length, width, and depth. (9)

forward kinematics: Parent object controls the motion of a child object, but the child object does not control the motion of the parent object. (11)

frame: Each still image in an animation. (11)

frame rate: Speed at which frames are played. (11)

functional rules: Control how each part works. (7)

functionality test: Using audience members to provide valuable information about the physical skills needed for a specific game challenge. (4)

functionality testing: Process of evaluating if everything works the way it should. (1)

G

gain: Occurs when a player receives something like a resource, skill, or knowledge. (6)

game: Activity that has three parts: game environment, rules, and a victory condition. (1)

game designer: Person who works for the developer whose main tasks are to create the structure of the game and dream up great interactions within the game; generically, almost everyone who works on a design team. (1)

game economy: Determines which resources are available, in what amount, and at what cost. (6)

game environment: Game environment is an area specifically designed to enable gameplay. (1)

game flow: Design of levels, processes, and gameplay integration that a player should follow. (6)

game layout chart: Chart that displays an overhead view of game. (3)

game physics: Uses a mathematical model to control the general motion of objects in the virtual world. (11)

gameplay: What the player does and how he or she interacts with the game while playing it. (1)

gameplay-attributed character: In-game character who only needs the realistic physical features required to complete the game objectives. (2)

game-select avatars: Avatars that are provided by the game designers and cannot be changed. (2)

game-treatment document: Document that explains the vision of the game in greater detail than the high-concept document. (1)

gamut: Total spectrum of colors a given model can create. (9)

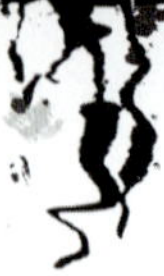

Gantt chart: Chart that displays the project broken down into tasks and subtasks, length of time assigned to each task, and tasks that must be performed before other tasks are identified. (1)

genre: Major category of video game gameplay. (1)

geodesic sphere: Constructed of regular polygons such as triangles, pentagons, and octagons. (10)

geometric shapes: Regular figures, like a square, circle, triangle, octagon, or trapezoid. (9)

global: Subroutine or variable that occurs throughout the program being written. (12)

gold master: Disc containing the perfected final game that is used as the original from which all other copies will be made. (1)

Goldberg, Rube: See *Rube Goldberg*. (7)

governing game design document (GGDD): Design documents that contain all of the concept elaboration information and are more detailed than the pitch documents. (1)

graphical user interface (GUI): Buttons, icons, and other graphics that are needed to work the game interface; how the user will send and receive information with the computer. (1, 3)

green screen: Chroma screen. (11)

guardian: Protector of an area, object, or objective. (2)

H

hack: Programming created to alter the original functions of the game or hardware. (5)

hacking: Means of cheating by creating hacks that change the gameplay to give a player an advantage. (5)

handicap: In gaming, an advantage provided to a low-level character or a disadvantage provided to a high-level character so all players are similarly matched. (2)

haptic: Based on the sense of touch. (13)

hard skills: Technical abilities a person possesses. (1)

harmony: Use of similar elements; helps hold the image or scene together. (9)

heads-up display (HUD): Means of displaying information to the player during gameplay. (3)

helper: Any character who gives vital information to the hero when the hero is trying to make moral and ethical decisions, is undergoing internal changes, or needs direction on the quest. (2)

herald: Character who brings news to the hero or narrates the story. (2)

hero: Main character in the story, represents good. (2)

heuristics: Process of making predictions based on past events, or learning by trial and error. (13)

hierarchy: Structure in which one person has authority and decision-making power over others. (10)

high-concept document: One-page overview of the basic idea for your game. (1)

high-level computer language: Contains words and symbols that are similar to those found in everyday spoken and written language. (12)

histogram: Bar graph that uses rectangles of different heights to show the variation in data. (6)

horizontal symmetry: Right side is a mirror image of the left side. (9)

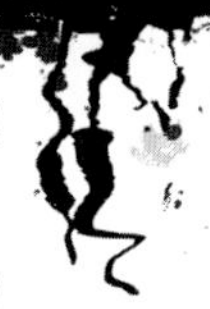

hub-and-spoke level design: Level design that allows the player to start in the center, complete a mission, and return to the center to choose another mission. (3)

human-computer interface (HCI): Connection and communication between the player and the game system. (4)

human-in-the-loop (HITL) simulation: Any simulation that has a real human user as part of the event model. (13)

Hungarian notation: Name of a variable starts with lowercase letters that indicate what type of variable it is. (12)

I

iconic logic: Critical thinking and learning from outside of the system. (13)

imbalance: State of being out of proportion. (5)

immersion: Level to which the player feels he or she is actually experiencing the events of the game, or how well the player connects to the game world. (4)

implicit challenge: Task that the player interprets and discovers on his or her own. (5)

implied line: Path the viewer's eye takes to connect the two endpoints of the line when it is not continuous. (9)

incentives: Ways of encouraging a specific action or path. (13)

incongruous character: Characters who seem out of place or different than the rest of the game mood and theme. (2)

indie: Term to describe a company that is small and considered to be independent or outside of the traditional gaming business. (1)

induction puzzle: Requires deductive reasoning from a limited amount of information about the opponents with no information about the player. (7)

inductive logic: Critical thinking and learning from inside the system. (13)

inertia: Resistance to a change in motion. (11)

inflection: Vocal tones of spoken words. (2)

inherit: Receive from a relative; in the structure of a modeling bones system, the relatives are referred to as parents and children. (11)

input: Instruction from the player sent to the computer. (4)

input-interaction model: Includes the player controls and the programming needed to interpret the button presses or other commands. (4)

inspiration: Suggests or influences an idea or motivates a particular thought. (7)

instance variable: Describes a single type of item. (12)

intangible feature: Attribute that is part of the emotional or inner character. (2)

integer: Positive and negative real whole number. (12)

interactive simulation: Allows a user to actively control some part of the system. (13)

interactive story: Game in which the player performs the actions of the story. (3)

interactivity: How one object behaves when it encounters another object. (12)

intercalating: Process of indenting all lines that are part of a block of one code. (12)

interpolation: Process of creating a new pixel; an approximation of combining the colors of the original pixels surrounding it. (10)

intrinsic skill: Skill essential to complete a task. (5)

intuitive controller: Needs little explanation on how to use it in the game. (4)

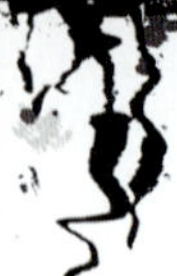

inverse kinematics: Parent object controls the motion of a child object *and* the child object controls the motion of the parent. (11)

isosurfacing: Uses the light and dark regions of the texture map to create raised and lowered areas on the model, like a bump map; unlike a bump map, isosurfacing actually alters the mesh. (10)

iteration: Different version. (1)

iterative design process: Program improves with each run through the design cycle. (13)

J

jailbreak: Altering a smartphone's operating system to allow greater control over the device. (1)

just barely fail: Allows the player to believe that his or her next attempt may be the one that provides victory. (5)

K

key light: Provides the primary illumination. (10)

key mechanics of strategy: Resource management (strategic management), dissimilar assets (arms race), maneuvers (risk/reward), pacing (speed and recovery), economy (gains and drains). (6)

keyframe animation: Approximation of traditional cel animation using a computer (cel animation is also keyframe animation, and vice versa). (11)

keyframe: Any frame on which a specific action must take place. (11)

kinematics: Science of motion; in terms of 3D modeling, kinematics refers to how the movement of an object either controls or is controlled by the movement of another object. (11)

kinetic energy: Energy of movement. (11)

L

lagging: Falling behind or happening later than intended. (8)

lateral thinking: Describes the process of thinking along a line to find the solution. (7)

law of conservation of energy: Energy cannot be created or destroyed, but can change state. (11)

lead artist: Team member who manages the details of a single project and makes sure all art is designed correctly. (10)

leave-behind document: Document that stays with the publisher after you have made your presentation as a reminder of your proposal. (1)

level up: Character increases in game status by one level and acquires more abilities. (2)

limited liability company (LLC): Hybrids of a corporation and a partnership; also called *limited liability partnership (LLP)*. (1)

limited liability partnership (LLP): See *limited liability company (LLC)*. (1)

limited partnership: Partnership in which at least one of the partners is just an investor and does not participate in the running of the company. (1)

linear level design: Level that has a single starting point and follows a single path to a single end point. (3)

linear structure: Story that follows a single path from beginning to end. (3)

linguistic puzzle: Uses words or sounds related to language. (7)

lip syncing: Synchronization of sound and character movement; matching voice to lip movement. (11)

local: Subroutine or variable that does not have persistence outside of the module in which it was declared. (12)

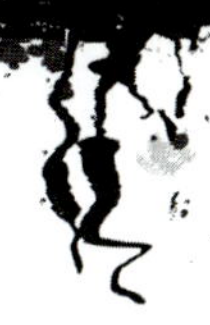

local area network (LAN) party: Players connect to a single local computer network to play with or against each other. (5)

logic maze: Simple maze with some additional rule to increase the difficulty. (7)

logic puzzle: Player applies reasoning to determine the correct answer. (7)

logic statement: Consists of a possible condition and subsequent actions; using these seven common operators: **IF**, **THEN**, **AND**, **OR**, **NOT**, **NOR**, **ELSE.** (12)

logic-grid puzzle: Player is given certain clues to the solution, which the player then organizes into a grid to determine the solution. (7)

looping: Sound or animation restarts at the end of playing. (8)

lossless compression algorithm: Compresses the image and keeps perfect clarity when uncompressed; the file size may be larger than the same image compressed with the lossy compression algorithm; also called *losslessly compression algorithm*. (10)

lossy compression algorithm: Compresses the image, but does not keep perfect image clarity. (10)

low-level computer language: Abstract and does not contain words and symbols similar to everyday spoken and written languages. (12)

M

machine language: Instruction set that is interpreted by the computer's central processing unit (CPU); also called *machine code*. (12)

magic circle: How the rules and game environment create structured play. (1)

main character: In-game character around which the entire game revolves. (2)

maneuvering: Positioning resources at their most needed or beneficial location. (6)

map making: Simulation system is rendered in realistic form. (13)

mapping: Process of determining how a material is positioned on an object. (10)

markerless mocap: Does not require a sensor marker worn by the actor. (11)

massively multiplayer online game (MMO): Game with thousands of real people playing at the same time; each person uses his or her own avatar and interacts with other players as the game is played online. (2)

material: Image stretched over the model to make it look as if it is made of wood, plastic, skin, or any other material. (10)

matter: What makes up a physical object. (11)

mechanical puzzle: Solved by physically linking, unlinking, or maneuvering pieces. (7)

mechanics: Technical aspects of creating the objects and animation. (11)

Medieval: Refers to the Middle Ages, the historical time period from about 400 AD to about 1400 AD. (9)

mental acuity: Measure of focus, memory, and concentration. (4)

mentor: Character who teaches moral lessons and skills to the hero and directs the hero on the quest. (2)

mesh: Combination of four or more polygons connected to make one piece. (10)

metapuzzle: Single, large puzzle made up of smaller puzzles. (7)

methodology: General rules or principles on how a character does things. (2)

methods: Actions or verbs used in syntax. (12)

metrics: Measureable parameters that can be analyzed for performance and behavior. (6)

microphone: Device that detects sounds,

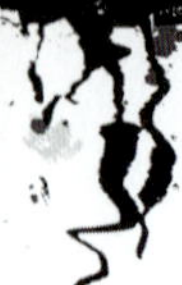

converts it to an electrical signal, and transmits the signal to an output. (8)

milestone: Critical point of achievement. (1)

minions: Minor characters, like soldiers; can come in several ranks, strengths, and abilities. (2)

mission: In a video game, a large assignment the protagonist must complete in order to reach the end of the game. (3)

mixing: Process of combining two or more recorded sounds into a single sound. (8)

mockup: Physical representation of the character or game element. (2)

mod: Alteration of the gameplay of an existing game, typically done by players, not the game studio; short for modification. (5)

modding: Act of creating a mod. (5)

model sheet: Sketch of different poses and viewing angles for a single character. (2)

modules: Separate units of programming that perform one function and contain all of the information needed to execute that function. (12)

momentum: Quantity of motion, defined by mass times velocity. (11)

mono: Having a single audio channel; short for monophonic. (8)

monochromatic: Only one hue is used in the image. (9)

mood: Emotional feeling of the setting. (3)

moral: Lesson to be learned. (3)

moral values: Rules that a character uses to decide if something is good or evil. (2)

morphing: Change in the physical shape of an object. (11)

motion: Change in position of an object over time. (11)

motion capture (mocap): Technology that records the movement of an actor and assigns that movement to a virtual character. (11)

mount: Device used to hold and place a microphone. (8)

movement sketch: Sketch of a few frames of animation to show what movement for the character looks like. (2)

moving holds: Characters should never be static for a long time; instead, some slight movement should be animated. (11)

multiplayer dialogue: In-game speech between human players. (5)

multiuser domain (MUD) bot: Often used to perform trivial tasks while the player is doing other things. (5)

muscle memory: When a physical task has been repeated enough that the task can be completed without conscious effort. (4)

musical instrument digital interface (MIDI): Used to connect musical instruments to a computer using a cable connection. (8)

N

narration: Any spoken details or commentary on the game. (5)

Nash equilibrium: Occurs in a game when all players know the strategies of the others and no single player can gain when only his or her strategy is changed; named after American mathematician John Nash. (7)

navigation map: Small map in the corner of the game frame that displays relative locations of obstacles, enemies, and objectives. (4)

negative space: Area or volume around or between primary objects. (9)

nested victories: Smaller victories that lead to the ultimate victory condition. (6)

network design: Level design that allows the player to move freely without restriction from any room to any other room in the game; also called *sandbox level design*. (3)

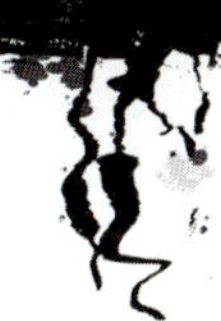

neutral NPC: Non-player game characters who are not motivated by what the player is doing. (2)

noncompete agreement: Contract that states you cannot create work that competes with the company while you are employed by it and for a certain period of time after you leave the company. (10)

nonlinear structure: Story that has more than one path from the beginning to the end, and there may be more than one possible ending. (3)

non-player character (NPC): Any game character controlled by the game instead of by the player. (2)

nontrivial task: Task with purpose, like finding a potion to defeat an enemy. (3)

NPC dialogue: Occurs when a non-player character speaks directly to the player. (5)

NURBS: Model is based on a mathematical calculation that creates a curve or surface from specified control points; stands for non-uniform rational basis spline. (10)

O

object: In programming, a definition subroutine; defined by attributes and properties. (12)

one bit: Smallest unit of measure of information in computer science; one byte is eight bits. (12)

opacity: Quality of being see-through; the higher the opacity, the less see-through a material is. (10)

opaque: Not transparent. (11)

optical texture: Variation in what is seen. (9)

optimizing: Formatting audio so it sounds best from a playback device. (8)

organic shapes: Irregular shapes. (9)

other player character (OPC): In-game character controlled by another human player. (2)

output: Information that the computer sends to the player. (4)

output-interaction model: The portion of the user interface that performs the action-fulfill commands and provides feedback to the player. (4)

over budget: When more money is spent than was allowed for the project. (1)

overlapping: More than one motion occurring at the same time. (11)

overt clue: Clue that is easy to find and understand. (6)

P

pacing: Rate at which a player must make decisions. (6)

parallel-branching level design: Level design that allows the player to start and make choices as to which room to enter to get to the end point. (3)

parameters: Variables that could alter the situation. (13)

partial-conversion mod: Mod that only adds content to the game. (5)

partnership: Agreement between two or more people to open a business together. (1)

parts: Pieces of a puzzle that are manipulated in the game. (7)

patch: Software installation program that fixes known bugs or damaged programming. (1)

pattern recognition: Occurs when a player can observe repeating actions or conditions and use that to predict future game movements and events. (6)

pause-and-relax activity: Gives the player a chance to recover from the stress of a major challenge. (5)

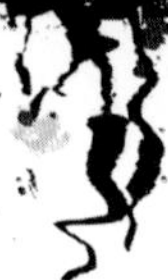

perception: Observation or sensing of something. (11)

perk: Attribute locked at the beginning of the game, but unlocked as the game progresses. (2)

persistence: To continue to exist. (11)

perspective: Point of view from which the game action is viewed. (5)

physical simulation: Contains devices that are substitutes for real devices; takes the place of a real object or system. (13)

physical timing: Matching the time for animated events with real-world events. (11)

physics: Science field involving the study of matter and motion. (12)

physiology: Physical shape, characteristics, and traits of a character. (2)

piracy: Illegal copying or distribution of copyrighted material such as a video game; a form of theft. (1)

pitch document: Document used to sell a game idea to a video game publisher or the decision makers at a game studio. (1)

pixel shading: Use of lighter and darker colors, or changes in value, to create light and shadow. (9)

placeholder: Substitute for the asset that is being created. (8)

platform: Device on which a game will be played. (1)

playability attribute: Helps the player recognize each puzzle piece and maneuver it into place. (7)

playability testing: Testing to check if the level difficulty is appropriate for a human player, make sure the story flows, and verify that objectives can be achieved. (1)

player character (PC): In-game character who is controlled by the player. (2)

player-centric design: Understanding the player and centering the game design on what the player wants and needs. (4)

player-designed avatar: Avatar created by the player. (2)

player-select avatars: Player can choose from a set of avatars; selection has no impact on the gameplay, but reflects the player's mood or personality. (2)

plot: Plan or map for a story. (3)

plug-in: Software that enhances another program by extending its capabilities. (8)

point light: Light source that illuminates in all directions, like a common household lightbulb. (10)

polycount: Number of 2D faces (polys) used to create the 3D mesh model. (10)

pop screen: Placed in front of a microphone to diffuse air pressure created by a voice. (8)

porting: Converting a game from one platform to another. (1)

pose-to-pose action: Refers to planning the motion for a scene based on key points at which certain motion must happen. (11)

positive space: Area or volume occupied by primary objects. (9)

post production: Testing, tuning, and distribution. (1)

potential energy: Stored energy. (11)

predevelopment tool: Document or other item used before the project is approved for design. (3)

preloading: Sound sample is loaded into a computer memory before it plays. (8)

preproduction: Concept elaboration and prototyping. (1)

presentation: How art will be viewed or experienced. (9)

primary sound: Sound of an actual interaction. (11)

primitives: Regular shapes and objects that are used to assemble more complex shapes or objects; standard building blocks used to create other objects. (9, 10)

principles of design: Govern how to effectively combine the elements of art to compose a pleasing work of art. (9)

production: Stage at which specialists such as artist, programmers, sound engineers, and other team members build all of the parts for a game and put them together to create a fully functioning game. (1)

project evaluation and review technique (PERT) diagram: Diagram that maps milestones for a project and the estimated completion time for each milestone. (1)

proof of concept: Main function of a prototype; shows that the concept can work. (1)

proportion: Size of an object in relation to other objects around it. (9)

protagonist: Main character of a story. (2)

prototype: Very basic version of the game to test that the concept can be constructed. (1)

prototyping: Iterative step in the design process that tests the system to discover errors. (13)

provisional approval: Approval has been given to start the project, but only to a point before additional approval must be obtained to finish the project. (1)

proximity: How closely objects are arranged. (9)

pseudo code: Similar to, but not actual computer code. (12)

public domain: Applies to any work for which the copyright term has expired. (10)

puzzle: Mental challenges whereby a player must find a solution to a problem. (7)

puzzle design specifications document: Document that is a smaller version of the governing game design document (GGDD). (7)

Q

quality-assurance (QA) team: Team that does functionality testing and playability testing continuously to find and report all the errors in a game. (1)

queuing: Lining up or waiting in line. (13)

R

radial symmetry: Equal in length from a center point. (9)

raster images: Record the location and color of each picture element (pixel) of the image; made up of "dots." (10)

rasterize: Existing image is converted into a raster image. (10)

ready to market (RTM): When all testing and tuning are complete, the game is finalized. (1)

recon: Ability to spy on an opponent; short for reconnaissance. (6)

reconstructive simulation: Attempt to duplicate a situation by reverse engineering the end result. (13)

recording device: Piece of equipment that takes electronic signals from a microphone and stores them on media. (8)

recursion: When a method calls itself as part of the solution. (7)

recursive puzzle: Contains the solution as part of the puzzle; also called *self-reference puzzle.* (7)

Red Book standard: Refers to specifications for the physical properties of compact discs and for the digital audio on the discs. (8)

red herring: Task that takes a player in the wrong direction. (5)

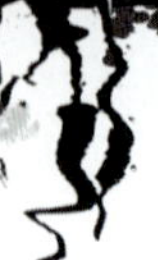

regeneration: System is reset to its original state. (13)

relative: Connected to or dependent on something else. (11)

rendering: Applying colors and textures to create a final image. (2)

repetitive-motion injury: Injury that occurs as a result of doing the same motion over and over. (4)

reseller marketing: Publisher allows someone else to sell its game. (1)

resolution: When the conflict of a story is over. (3)

resolution strategy model: Requires players to negotiate a diplomatic solution. (6)

resource management: Using limited resources effectively to achieve a goal. (6)

retail marketing: Boxed game is shipped from a manufacturing point and travels through several other points before reaching the customer. (1)

reverb: Echo effect that makes sound full by simulating the reflecting of sound waves off of walls and objects. (8)

riddle: Linguistic puzzle solved with wit and skill. (7)

rising action: Events that create the basic internal conflict of a story; tension builds to the climax. (3)

room: In video game design, a scene in a level. (3)

rotation: Circular movement about a central point. (5, 11)

round character: Character who develops and changes throughout a story. (3)

Rube Goldberg: Synonym for overly complicated; Goldberg was an American cartoonist who became famous for his drawings of machines that were overly complex or over-engineered to perform very basic tasks. (7)

Ruby: General purpose, object-oriented language. (12)

rule of thirds: Guideline that states an image should be divided into three sections horizontally and three sections vertically to create nine areas. (9)

rules: State how a game is to be played, what is allowed, and what is not allowed. (1)

S

sample: Small segment of recorded sound. (8)

sampler: Device that records a sound and plays it back at different pitches. (8)

sampling: Taking a small group from an audience and asking them questions on their likes and dislikes. (4)

sampling frequency: How many times per second the sound data are recorded. (8)

sandbox level design: Level design that allows a player to move freely without restriction from any room to any other room in the game; also called *network design*. (3)

Sanskrit: Classical language of India. (2)

sawtooth-challenge design: Allows for challenges to increase and then decrease in difficulty. (5)

scientific method: Systematic approach involving defining a problem, collecting data through experimentation, and formulating and testing a hypothesis. (13)

scope: Area of a game map displayed by the camera. (5)

secondary action: Complementary action; motion caused by the dominant or primary action. (11)

secondary sounds: Caused from the first interaction. (11)

second-person perspective: Uses the eyes of the opponent as the camera position. (5)

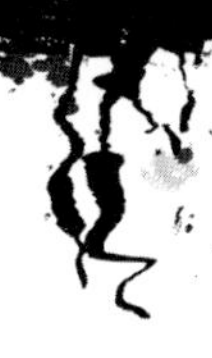

self-enlightenment: Learning and understanding problems and flaws within yourself. (2)

self-leveling: Provides additional help for less-skilled players that can be ignored or turned off by more-skilled players. (7)

self-reference puzzle: See *recursive puzzle.* (7)

semiotics: Science dealing with the meaning and relationship of symbols and features. (2)

sensor-based mocap: Placing markers on an actor's body to track body movement. (11)

sequence: Predetermined order or steps a computer program will follow. (12)

setting: Time and place of the action in a story. (3)

shadow: Villain or enemy of the hero; motivates the hero to do good. (2)

shell menus: Menus used for starting the game or for actions outside of gameplay, such as making screen and sound settings. (4)

shell screen: Nonmenu item displayed outside of gameplay, such as the title frame, credits, and cut scenes. (4)

shock mount: Suspends the microphone on rubber or springs so any vibration from the main mount will not interfere with the recording. (8)

shock wave: Pulse of energy moving through a medium as the result of a shock, explosion, earthquake, and so on. (7)

sidekick: Companion character who is subordinate to the player character. (2)

silhouetting: Creating a shadow image that shows only the outline of an object. (11)

similar sound: Sound that imitates the sound from something else. (8)

simulation: Attempts to replicate a real-world situation. (13)

situational enlightenment: Learning and understanding the cause of a problem that affects others. (2)

situational puzzle: Player must find the solution to a riddle by looking at the puzzle from a different and often obscure angle; also called *lateral-thinking puzzle.* (7)

slow in: Motion begins gradually. (11)

slow out: Motion ends gradually. (11)

smoothing: Takes a sharp edge between faces and applies a radius to create a rounded transition. (10)

soft skills: Personal qualities and behaviors, such as punctuality, teamwork, and attitude. (1)

software key code: Code used to unlock game software; allows only one installation. (10)

sole proprietorship: When a single person opens a business. (1)

solid drawing: Technical skill with which an animation is composed to represent the fullness of characters and objects occupying space. (11)

sound context: Description of what and where an action is occurring. (8)

sound effects: Active sounds or audio game assets used as content or artistic enhancements within gameplay and usually played in response to action in the game; also called *sound FX.* (5, 8)

sound engineer: Team member responsible for sound production. (8)

sound engineering: Art and science of creating, editing, mixing, and synchronizing sounds. (8)

sound FX: See *sound effects.* (5,8)

sound library: Collection of completed sound samples that are available for use. (8)

sound meter: Measures the level, or volume, of sound in decibels. (8)

sound rendering: Process of using sound to communicate feelings, effects, and acoustic reality in a virtual world. (8)

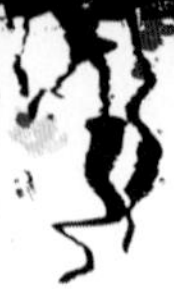

sound synchronization: Matching the timing of visual action to the corresponding sounds. (11)

spatial: Having or occupying space. (9)

specular color: Highlights, or shiny spots, on an object. (9)

spotlight: Projects light rays in a cone shape. (10)

squash: To flatten. (11)

staging: Allows the artist to draw attention to the area or objects of greatest importance. (11)

static: Not moving. (11)

static animation: Translation without articulation. (11)

static particles: Rendered simultaneously along the entire vector. (11)

statutory laws: Passed by legislature. (10)

steps: In programming, refers to how many iterations occur per second. (12)

stereotyped character: In-game character that performs a standard game role, but has very general characteristics that provide some variation among the same type of characters in a game. (3)

stock character: In-game character that has standard traits and performs a standard role. (3)

stock dividend: Amount of money paid to the owners of the company stock as their portion of the profits made by the company. (1)

stockholder: Person or company who has purchased stock in a corporation. (1)

stop-motion animation: Capturing a single animation frame, slightly adjusting the objects, and capturing another single frame; repeated over and over until the animation is completed. (11)

story-based character: In-game character who conveys some portion of the game story. (2)

storyboard: Series of panels that contain sketches of the game action and a description of the actions in that room. (3)

straight-ahead action: Creating motion starting at the beginning of a scene and continuing in sequence until the end of the scene. (11)

strand: Static particles are rendered simultaneously along the entire vector. (11)

strategy: Plan for defense and offense. (6)

stretch: To extend. (11)

string: Series of letters, numbers, or punctuation. (12)

structure: Syntax and logic form of the programming language. (12)

sub missions: Series of activities that make up a mission and are themselves made up of atomic challenges. (3)

subordinate: Below, beneath, or lower. (2)

subroutine: Group of code within the main game program that controls a segment of the overall program function. (1)

subtractive method: Starts with all color, or white, and colors are removed to create the final color. (9)

sunlight: Light source that provides constant illumination in one direction; the light rays are parallel, like natural sunlight. (10)

survey: Questionnaire given to a group of people with the purpose of collecting data from that group. (4)

sustainable community: Community that has or can obtain the resources needed to keep meeting the needs and wants of its citizens. (6)

swarm: Collection of characters that move, act, and behave as a single entity. (2)

symmetrical balance: When the right and left sides, top and bottom, or all sides are equal; also called *formal balance*. (9)

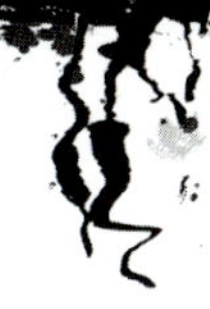

syntax: How words are arranged into phrases and sentences; also, programming words and symbols and their arrangement. (2, 12)

synthesizer: Creates artificial sounds from pure tones. (8)

system: Controls all of the parameters and constraints to make a simulation work. (13)

system-shall command: Rule to guide the design of the application framework. (13)

T

tactic: Method of achieving a strategy. (6)

tactile texture: Irregular surface that can be physically felt, like sandpaper. (9)

tangible: Capable of being perceived. (10)

tangible feature: Quality of a character that can be seen or demonstrated. (2)

target market: Who the game is intended to appeal to most. (1)

technical bible: Binder filled with all of the programming structure for a game. (1)

tell: Signal, gesture, movement, pattern, or other effect that hints to what an opponent is doing. (6)

tessellation: Breaking up the overall texture image so a part of the image can be applied to each individual polygon in the model. (10)

texture: Flat image that is wrapped around the avatar model like skin. (2)

texture artist: Team member who creates 2D art using digital or traditional art media; strong in creating artwork that embodies all of the basic elements of art. (10)

texture fill: Image that is wrapped around an object. (9)

texture map: Picture or pattern assigned to an element of the material definition. (10)

theatrical timing: Slowing down, rewinding, and speeding up sections of an animation for an emotional effect. (11)

thematic element: Each object that contributes to or conveys a theme. (3)

themes: Subcategories of gameplay within a genre. (1)

third-person perspective: Positions the camera as a spectator that is looking at the player character. (5)

Three Laws of Robotics: A robot may not injure a human being or, through inaction, allow a human being to come to harm; a robot must obey the orders given to it by human beings, except where such orders would conflict with the first law; and a robot must protect its own existence as long as such protection does not conflict with the first or second law. (5)

three-dimensional modeling artist: Team member who creates game objects in 3D; strong in the use of 3D modeling software such as 3ds Max, Maya, Blender, or Rhinoceros. (10)

timeout: When a game resets after a period of player inactivity. (4)

timing: How long a given action lasts. (11)

title: Each video game in a publisher's library. (1)

total-conversion mod: Mod that results in an entirely new game. (5)

toy: Item that does not have all three components of a game and is, therefore, not a game. (1)

translation: Movement from one point to another, especially when the camera moves on the game map. (5, 11)

transport puzzle: Requires the player to move pieces within the confined space of the game board. (7)

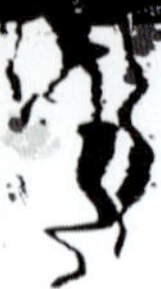

triangle lighting: Traditional way to illuminate a scene; consists of three lights: key light, fill light or flood light, and backlight. (10)

trickster: Character who tries to distract the hero from the objective. (2)

trigger pull: Button press. (4)

triple-A game: Game that generates a large portion of a game studio's sales. (1)

trivial task: Task that has no point or purpose and does not move a game story forward. (3)

Trompe l'oeil: Translates to "fool the eye"; perspective, depth, and shadow are used to create ultra-realistic scenes. (9)

tuning: When a game is polished to perfection. (1)

tweeners: Assistant artists who draw each frame or cel between keyframes. (11)

tweening: Process of drawing each frame or cel between keyframes. (11)

tweens: Frames between keyframes. (11)

typical player profile: Document that outlines the common characteristics of the group that is most likely to play the game. (4)

U

unique selling point (USP): What makes your game different or unique from other games; also called *unique selling proposition*. (1)

unique selling proposition (USP): See *unique selling point*. (1)

unit: Any maneuverable game asset. (6)

unity: Appears as a single piece and not an assembly of different parts. (9)

upgrade: Choice a player makes to obtain better equipment, weapons, magic, abilities, and so on. (2)

use case: Details the path an entity takes in a simulation. (13)

UV sphere: Constructed of rectangular and triangular polygons. (10)

V

value: Use of light and dark to add highlight, shading, or shadows. (9)

vanishing point: Point at which parallel lines meet. (9)

variable: Small information-storage containers. (12)

variety: Purposeful absence of harmony to create visual or contextual interest; also called *alternation*. (9)

vector image: Stores image data as a mathematical definition, not pixel-by-pixel data. (10)

vector: Direction of force. (11, 12)

velocity: Speed of an object. (11)

vertex shading: Moving the points on an object to resize it such that the object appears smaller in the distance. (9)

vestibular: Acting like a vestibule. (13)

vicarious immersion: Designer imagining himself or herself in place of the player to experience the gameplay. (4)

vicariously: When a player lives through the in-game character, he or she imagines the experiences of the character as if they were happening directly to the player. (2)

victory condition: What it takes to win a game. (1)

video director: Team member who creates the cinematic cut scenes between levels or records video for use in promotional materials. (10)

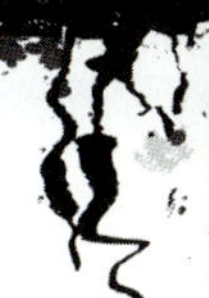

video game publisher: Company that oversees the entire process of bringing a video game to the retail market. (1)

virtual reality: A user's body motions are read by a user interface and displayed in a game or simulation world. (13)

visual perspective: Proportional scaling of objects as they move toward a vanishing point. (9)

voice actor: Person hired to be the voice of a game character. (8)

W

weighted: Increased or decreased statistical likelihood. (13)

windscreen: Foam or furry cover over a microphone that reduces wind noise detected by it. (8)

word puzzle: Constructed of written or spoken words. (7)

workflow identifier: Item or information that helps keep a work moving forward. (8)

work-for-hire contract: States what someone is expected to produce, the starting and ending dates of the work, and what he or she will be paid; also states the company owns the work he or she produces and whether he or she may use the work in any way. (10)

world-design document: Document that lists the items needed to create game worlds. (3)

Z

zoom: Increases or decreases the magnification of the view; does not move or rotate the camera. (5)

Index

A

B

C

D

E

F

G

H

I

J

K

L

M

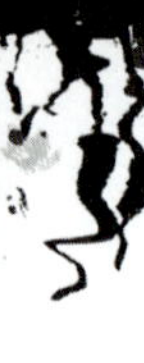

N

O

P

Q

R

S

T

U

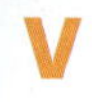

V

W

X

Z